D0211911

EX LIBRIS

SOUTH ORANGE
PUBLIC LIBRARY

Encyclopedia of Archaeology

History and Discoveries

Encyclopedia of Archaeology

History and Discoveries

Volume III, N–Z

Edited by Tim Murray

A B C ⊜ C L I O
Santa Barbara, California • Denver, Colorado • Oxford, England

REF
930.1
ENC
V.3 N-Z

Copyright © 2001 by Tim Murray

All rights reserved. No part of this publication may be reproduced, stored in a
retrieval system, or transmitted, in any form or by any means, electronic, mechanical,
photocopying, recording, or otherwise, except for the inclusion of brief quotations in
a review, without prior permission in writing from the publishers.

Library of Congress Catalog Card Number

Encyclopedia of archaeology : History and discoveries / edited by Tim Murray.
    p. cm.
Includes bibliographical references.
    ISBN 1-57607-198-7 (hardcover : alk. paper) — ISBN 1-57607-577-X (e-book)
    1. Archaeology—History—Encyclopedias. 2. Archaeologists—Biography—Encyclopedias.
3. Antiquities—Encyclopedias. 4. Historic sites—Encyclopedias. 5. Excavations (Archaeology)—
Encyclopedias. I. Murray, Tim, 1955–
    CC100.E54 2001
    930.1—dc21   20011002617

07 06 05 04 03 02 01   10 9 8 7 6 5 4 3 2 1

ABC-CLIO, Inc.
130 Cremona Drive, P.O. Box 1911
Santa Barbara, California 93116–1911

This book is printed on acid-free paper ∞.
Manufactured in the United States of America

Advisory Board

K.-C. CHANG
Harvard University

DOUGLAS R. GIVENS
Peabody Museum, Harvard University

LEO KLEJN
European University, St. Petersburg

COLIN RENFREW
University of Cambridge

ALAIN SCHNAPP
Université de Paris 1 Pantheon-Sorbonne

BRUCE G. TRIGGER
McGill University

Contents

History and Discoveries

Encyclopedia of Archaeology

History and Discoveries

N

National Geographic Society

Founded in Washington, D.C., in 1888 with the object of fostering the development and dissemination of geographic knowledge, the National Geographic Society has made a significant contribution to archaeology through its publications and its Committee of Research and Exploration. Between 1912 and 1915 the society funded the work of Hiram Bingham at MACHU PICCHU, and between 1938 and 1946 it supported eight expeditions by Matthew Stirling that culminated with his excavation of the OLMEC site of LA VENTA. Other highlights have been the work it supported at CHICHÉN ITZÁ, the exploration of PUEBLO BONITO by Neil Judd beginning in 1921, and the excavation of the Hellenistic site of Aphrodisias in TURKEY by Kenan Erim.

Notwithstanding its strong support of the archaeology of more recent periods, the society has made its greatest impact in the field of paleoanthropology. The most famous recipients of society funding since 1959 were LOUIS LEAKEY and MARY LEAKEY and, through Louis Leakey's influence, the primatologists Jane Goodall and Diane Fossey.

National Geographic magazine and other society publications have also played an important role in reporting archaeological research to the public. As the society rightly acknowledges, the act of disseminating geographic knowledge has the capacity to make some archaeologists internationally famous. However, the magazine's greatest impact on archaeology may well derive from the ways in which its staff writers and artists have sought to communicate the sense of archaeological research to nonspecialist audiences.

Tim Murray

See also Maya Civilization

References

Bryan, C. D. B. 1997. *The National Geographic Society: 100 Years of Adventure and Discovery.* 2d ed. New York: Abrams.

National Museum of Slovenia

The National Museum of Slovenia (Narodni Muzej Slovenije) was founded in Ljubljana as the Krainisch Ständisches Museum by provincial orders of the Austrian province of Carniola in 1821. The museum's name was changed to Krainisches Landesmuseum after confirmation by the Austrian Emperor Franz I in 1826, and its collections were opened to the public in 1831. After 1882 the name was changed to Krainisches Landesmuseum Rudolphinum (after the Austrian Archduke Rudolph, the heir to the throne). The museum was transferred to a new building in 1888, the most expensive building ever built for any cultural institution in the province of Carniola. After World War I and the formation of the kingdom of Serbs, Croats, and Slovenes (known as the kingdom of Yugoslavia after 1929), the museum was officially renamed Narodni Muzej (National Museum) in 1921. The museum has been called by its present name, Narodni Muzej Slovenije (National Museum of Slovenia) since 1997.

The museum was to be the central cultural and scientific institution in the province of Carniola, so it therefore embraced several functions: museum, exhibition place, research center, public library, gallery, public archive. It was meant to cover all the major fields representative of the province of Carniola: natural history,

history, ethnography, art, crafts, etc. The encyclopedic nature of the museum is well reflected in the first museum guide published in 1836: minerals (6,064 pieces), birds (405 species), herbs (6,002 specimens), insects (1,476 butterflies and 1,200 beetles), local wood (108 specimens), local grapes (45 species), mammals (56 species), coins (over 8,000), craft pieces (357), antiques (324), paintings (17), and graphics (2,392 items). An ethnographic collection of objects of North American native peoples was even included. These first collections were almost exclusively donated.

Further developments in the twentieth century lead to a separation of the ethnographic, artistic, and natural history collections and archives into newly established institutions: the Ethnographic Museum of Slovenia was established in 1923, the National Gallery in 1933, the Natural History Museum in 1944, and the Central Archive of the Republic of Slovenia in 1946. Currently, the National Museum of Slovenia comprises three departments—archaeology, history and applied arts, and conservation and restoration—and two cabinets—numismatic and graphic. The museum was also equipped with a library from the very beginning, and together with the Lycaeum Library (which was transformed in 1850 into the Provincial Study Library, in 1919 into the State Study Library, and in 1945 into the National and University Library), the museum library is one of the oldest and the most important public and scientific libraries in SLOVENIA. It contains more than 150,000 volumes, including numerous rare items from the sixteenth and seventeenth centuries.

Scientific and research issues and publications were initially governed by two societies. The first, the Verein des Krainischen Landes-Museum (Society of Provincial Museum of Carniola) was founded in 1839, later became the Musealverein für Krain (Museum Society of Carniola), was transformed into Muzejsko Društvo za Slovenijo (Museum Society of Slovenia) in 1919, and then became the Zgodovinsko Društvo za Slovenijo (Historical Society of Slovenia). The second society, the Historisches Verein für Krain (Historical Society of Carni-

ola), was founded in 1843 and merged with the Museum Society in 1885. This was almost exclusively devoted to the study of natural history while the Historical Society dealt mainly with the study of local history.

The first guidebook was published in 1836 (Hohenwart 1836), the second was published after the museum moved to its new building (Deschmann, 1888), and guides to the cultural history and natural history collections were published in 1931 and 1933. Regular publications began with the bulletins of the Historical and Museum Societies (*Mittheilungen des historischen Vereins für Krain* 1–23 [1846–1868]; *Mittheilungen des Museal-Vereins für Krain* 1–20 [1866, 1889–1907]; *Izvestja Muzejskega društva za Kranjsko* 1–19 [1891–1909], and *Glasnik Muzejskega društva za Slovenijo* 1–26 [1919–1945]). Other early periodicals included the journals *Argo* (1–10, 1892–1903), *Carniola* (1–2, 1908–1909), and *Carniola* new series (1–9, 1910–1919). Today the museum regularly publishes two journals—*Situla* (since 1955) and *Argo* new series (since 1962); two series of monographs—*Arheolo-ki katalogi* (1955–1969) and *Katalogi in monografije / Dissertationes et monographiae* (since 1970); monographs on important archaeological sites and monuments in Slovenia; and since 1994, a new series, *Viri—gradivo za materialno kulturo Slovencev* [Sources for the Material Culture of Slovenes].

Natural history dominated the museum's work in its first decades, and archaeology only gained in importance from the mid-1870s onward under the directorship of Carl Deschmann (1852–1888). In 1875, Deschmann began large-scale excavations of prehistoric pile-dwelling sites in the LJUBLJANSKO BARJE. These attracted great interest in archaeological and anthropological circles in Europe and provided a rich collection for display. The prehistoric collection was further enriched in the late 1870s when Deschmann extended his fieldwork to late prehistoric and Roman sites and created an exemplary collection of local prehistoric antiquities. Using his political influence as a former member of the parliament in Vienna, he successfully lobbied for the new museum building in which the new prehistoric collection had pride of place and was accompanied by a modern and systematic guide. In his last fifteen years as curator, Deschmann (a naturalist by profession) succeeded in applying high standards of systematization and research to prehistoric archaeology, extending its goals far beyond the antiquarianism and ethnocentrism practiced by many scholars, as well as by the Carniola Historical Society. With his fieldwork, archaeological studies, and organizational skills, he developed the museum to an exemplary level among all of the museums in the Austro-Hungarian Empire.

Subsequent curators broke with the natural history tradition. Alfons Müllner (1888–1903) reorganized the archaeological collection according to typological principles and consequently irreparably demolished the original grave-and-hoard contexts of the finds. He also published an important catalog of finds in 1900, which was considered to be the model publication for typological studies of artifacts in Austria. Müllner also significantly contributed to the development of the Roman collection in the museum. His successor, Walter Schmid (1905–1909), applied a different, historical approach to archaeology. One of Schmid's principal objectives was study of prehistoric and Roman settlement in the southeastern alpine area. He intensively excavated a number of archaeological sites, developing new standards for excavation and new agendas for archaeological studies in Slovenia.

In 1909, the provincial government failed to confirm Schmid's directorship, and the museum and archaeology in general in Carniola were left without a professional archaeologist for nearly two decades. Museum directors and curators were either historians or ethnographers and were very much involved in the cultural and political life of the last years of the Austro-Hungarian Empire and, after 1919, with the newly constituted national and political entity of Slovenes within the kingdom of the Serbs, Croats, and Slovenes. RAJKO LOZAR, an archaeologist, ethnographer, and art historian who worked in the museum as an assistant curator and librarian (1928–1940) provides a good example. During his period as curator (1929–1940), the museum gradually lost its central role in archaeological research in Slovenia. Although Lozar contributed some important archaeological studies, such as those on the history of Slovenian archaeology and early Slavonic pottery, much of his effort was devoted to other scientific, cultural, and political issues, and in 1940, he became director of the Ethnographic Museum of Slovenia. Schmid (at the Graz Museum from 1919) and Balduin Saria, professor of ancient history at the University of Ljubljana, were responsible for the major archaeological works and studies during the period between the two world wars.

The first years after World War II were marked by considerable structural changes in Slovene archaeology. New and national institutions were established in the late 1940s to plan the development of archaeology. The Department of Archaeology at the University of Ljubljana became the major archaeological educational institution, and the Institute of Archaeology at the Slovene Academy of Arts and Sciences became the major research institution for archaeology. The National Museum became the central museum institution in the newly created Republic of Slovenia.

One of the major problems for Slovenian archaeology in the late 1940s was the lack of well-trained, professional personnel. Almost all the prewar archaeologists had emigrated, and a new generation of archaeologists was needed. The role of reestablishing an archaeological service at the National Museum was given to JOŽEF KASTELIC, who was its director between 1945 and 1969. The only active professional archaeologist among the archaeologists of the pre-1945 period who had stayed in Slovenia, he reorganized the museum into a number of specialized departments and pioneered archaeological research work at important sites such as the Slavonic cemetery at Bled and the early–Iron Age barrows at STICNA. Kastelic also played an important part in establishing a regional museum network in Slovenia in the 1950s. He initiated the new series of *Situla, Argo,* and *Arheološki katalogi.* Under his directorship, the National Museum became a central national institution and gradually reached a highly respected level in the international networks.

STANE GABROVEC, head of the Archaeological Department at the National Museum (1948–1988) and an eminent prehistorian, began to research late–Bronze and Iron Age sites in Slovenia in the late 1940s. He also initiated a large-scale program, documenting numbers of Slovenian sites excavated during the Austro-Hungarian period and deposited in foreign museums. In less than two decades, Gabrovec succeeded in developing the chronology and cultural-history synthesis of the Bronze and Iron Ages of Slovenia and neighboring lands, and the prehistoric collection, once again, became the pride of the museum.

Developments after 1950s reflect a gradual rise in the complexity of the museum. Its rich archaeological collections were divided into prehistoric, Roman, and early mediaeval units, with each unit having specialized curators. Peter Petru, director of the National Museum from 1970 to 1983, continued and completed the organizational structure of the museum and also contributed much to the development of Roman archaeology in the museum. In the last decades of the twentieth century, the numismatic cabinet developed into one of the major regional reference centers for Celtic and Roman coinage.

Predrag Novakovic

References

Deschmann, K. 1888. *Führer durch das Krainische Landes-Museum Rudolphinum in Laibach.* Ljubljana.

Gabrovec, S. 1971. "Sto petdeset let arheologije v Narodnem muzeju." *Argo* 10: 35–48.

Petru, P. 1971. "Misli ob stopetdesetletnici Narodnega muzeja." *Argo* 10: 3–34.

Nautical Archaeology

The term *nautical archaeology,* as in the archaeology of ships, comes from the Greek word for ship (naos) and is used in preference to the terms marine or underwater archaeology.

Beginnings

Interest in ships of earlier times began at least as far back as the classical period when Jason's famed Argo was supposedly preserved and displayed at a sanctuary of Poseidon in what is now Greece near the Isthmus of Corinth. Then, as today with the *U.S.S. Constitution* ("Old Ironsides") in Boston and other historic vessels, there was the philosophical question of how much wood could be replaced before the ship would no longer be considered to be its original self. Also in the classical period, an old-fashioned vessel said to be similar to the one that had carried Theseus to Crete to slay the Minotaur was sailed annually from Athens to Delos for a religious festival. In the sixth century A.D., Procopius of Caesarea recorded a description of the ship of Aeneas, founder of Rome, that was said to be on display in a specially built shed on the bank of the Tiber River in the middle of the city. A fresco of a naval procession dating from around the middle of the second millennium B.C. that was uncovered on the Aegean island of Thera shows, according to some scholars, the practice of depicting or replicating watercraft from the still more distant past.

The conservation and replication of old ships are still elements of nautical archaeology, but the actual surveying for and excavation of ships of prior ages may have begun in the Renaissance. Traditional reports of two ancient vessels in Lake Nemi, seventeen miles southeast of Rome, led to salvage attempts by the architect Leon Battista Alberti in 1446. After having the wrecks examined by breath-holding Genoese divers, Alberti tried to raise and tow one of the hulks ashore with hooks lowered from a raft of barrels. Although the attempt was unsuccessful, he did recover a statue from one wreck. His failed salvage effort was followed in 1535 by more-detailed observations and measurements made by Francesco Demarchi, who dived in perhaps the earliest recorded diving suit to take samples of the ship's wood while wearing a wooden helmet outfitted with a small crystal viewing plate.

Nineteenth Century

Three centuries later, in 1827, the engineer Annesio Fusconi, working from an eight-seat diving bell, raised artifacts from the Lake Nemi wrecks that eventually were acquired by the Vatican Museum. However, Fusconi, too, failed to raise either of the hulls.

Early inventors of diving equipment in England soon became involved in nautical archaeology. In 1836, John Deane and William Edwards found the remains of Henry VIII's warship *Mary Rose*, which sunk in 1545 off Portsmouth, England. During the next four years, they salvaged numerous artifacts, including a variety of armaments and some wooden hull remnants, many of which they recorded in exquisite watercolors.

Not all early nautical archaeology required diving. Remains of an earlier battleship, Henry V's *Grace Dieu*, which had been launched in 1419, were reported in the mud of the Hamble River in Harold J. Osborne White's *1859 Hampshire and Isle of Wight Directory* but were not properly identified before the twentieth century. After an amateur's crude excavation of the site in the 1870s, perhaps with explosives, the Hampshire Field Club in the last year of the nineteenth century removed some of the ship's timbers to a museum in Winchester, England, where they were displayed as being from a "Danish galley."

Other European discoveries followed that of the *Grace Dieu*. In 1864, part of a Roman hull of the second or third century A.D. was salvaged from the harbor in Marseille and fancifully named "Caesar's galley." Other parts of the hull, raised in the 1950s, showed its planks to be fastened edge-to-edge by mortise-and-tenon joints in the shell-first kind of construction now known to have been in fashion in the Mediterranean from at least the fourteenth century B.C. until around the eleventh century A.D. Most modern wooden hulls are built in the frame-first manner, in which planks are simply nailed to a pre-erected framework of keel, stem, sternpost, and frames (ribs).

A different tradition of shell-first hull construction existed in Northern Europe, and a great deal of research was conducted there in the nineteenth century. Instead of being joined edge to edge, the planks of these hulls overlapped one another like shingles, and in this case were fastened together by long metal nails driven through them from the outside and clenched over inside, coining the term *clinker built*.

The clinker-built hull of a great open war vessel from the second half of the fourth century A.D., deposited as an offering to the gods in a bog at Nydam in Schleswig, GERMANY, was, in 1864, the first ancient ship excavated by an archaeologist. Less than two decades later, in 1880, a clinker-built, ninth-century ship found at Gokstad became the first of a number of Viking ships recovered from royal burials in Norway, where the clay soil remarkably preserves wood and iron. A replica of this ship crossed the Atlantic in 1893, an early example of experimental archaeology.

Far away in Africa, hot desert sands preserved hull timbers equally well. Five funerary boats from about 1,850 B.C., intentionally buried near the pyramid of Sesostris III at Dashur, were discovered in 1894 by the French archaeologist Jacques De Morgan. The planks of the ten-meter hulls were held together by mortise-and-tenon joints. Two of the hulls are now in the Cairo Museum, one is in the Field Museum in Chicago, and one is in the Carnegie Museum in Pittsburgh; one is missing, perhaps reburied at Dashur.

1900–1960

The first half of the twentieth century saw a dramatic increase in salvage by helmet divers. Although a Roman wreck found in 1900 by Greek sponge divers off the Aegean island of Antikythera gained notoriety mainly because of spectacular discoveries of bronze and marble Greek statues, and a unique astronomical instrument, a few planks were raised that showed mortise-and-tenon joinery. Concentration on statuary and pottery rather than hulls continued in the salvage of artifacts by Greek and Turkish sponge divers from another Roman wreck, at Mahdia off the coast of Tunisia, in the six years following its discovery in 1907. Although fragments of wood were raised in 1928 by the Greek sponge divers who salvaged famed bronze statues of Zeus or Poseidon and a jockey and horse off Cape Artemision, they were never properly studied. Nor were the fragments of wood netted by a fisherman three years earlier along with the bronze statue of a nude youth in the Bay of Marathon in the Aegean.

Detailed records of a hull of the Roman period had already been made at this early date, but not by divers. A ship built in the third century A.D. in northern Europe, but with Mediterranean-style mortise-and-tenon joints, was found underground during the construction of a new county hall in London in 1910. Horses dragged the carefully cradled hull to the London Museum where it has remained.

The final chapter in the story of Lake Nemi also involved dry-land archaeology. Two gigantic and once lavish "pleasure barges" from the time of the first-century emperor Caligula were finally exposed in the early 1930s after Benito Mussolini had the lake level lowered twenty meters by pumping its water into another lake over a four-year period. Both vessels were burned during World War II, but records show that their hull planks were mortise-and-tenon joined and then sheathed with lead over fabric. Because the hulls lay in a freshwater lake, without the marine borers that consume wood in most seas of the world, the lead must have served as a kind of caulking. The fresh water also preserved the wooden parts of the barges' huge anchors, providing firsthand evidence for the use of the lead anchor stocks that are so frequently found in the Mediterranean, often with lead collars that prevented the anchors' wooden arms from spreading out from their shanks.

Draining of the harbor at Kalmar in southeastern Sweden in the 1930s revealed more than a dozen wrecks, including a well-preserved clinker-built vessel of the thirteenth century. In North America, while the Lake Nemi barges were being studied and the Kalmar harbor was being drained, the diver L. F. Haggland buoyed to the surface of Lake Champlain in New York State Benedict Arnold's flagship *Royal Savage,* which had been sunk by the British in 1776 during the American War of Independence, by tying empty metal drums to the ship's hull and filling them with air on the lake bed. The following year, in 1935, Haggland returned for the better-preserved gondola *Philadelphia,* which had been lost in the same battle and is now displayed in the SMITHSONIAN INSTITUTION in Washington, D.C.

Unfortunately, in the first half of the twentieth century clam-shell drags were sometimes lowered from the surface to dig violently into shipwrecks in an indiscriminate search for artifacts. Such was the case in the 1930s with several of the ships scuttled in the York River, Virginia, by General Cornwallis shortly before the decisive battle of Yorktown that ended the American War of Independence in 1781. Such, too, was the case in 1950 with a Roman wreck at Albenga, Italy, where the steel claws were guided by an observer in an underwater chamber who telephoned directions to operators on the surface.

Nor were divers needed in continuing work in northern Europe in the early 1900s. In 1904, a magnificent and beautifully preserved Viking ship of the early ninth century was excavated in a female burial mound at Oseberg, Norway, only thirty kilometers from Gokstad. In England, surveyors of the partly clinker-built hulk in the Hamble River concluded in 1933 that it was the *Grace Dieu,* an identification corroborated by tree-ring dating of the timbers that had been taken to the Winchester Museum at the end of the nineteenth century. Also in England, in 1939, the impression of a clinker-built ship was found in a royal burial mound, probably of a Saxon king, at SUTTON HOO in Suffolk; gold coins among the fabulous treasures in the burial date the grave to the seventh century A.D. And in 1946, the discovery of the first of three Bronze Age, plank-built boats of around 1500 B.C., in the Humber estuary at North Ferriby in Yorkshire, began a lifetime of work for the amateur archaeologist E. V. Wright, who demonstrated how the boats' planks were sewn (or laced) together with branches of yew.

In Egypt, in 1954, archaeologists discovered a 4,500-year-old dismantled boat in a stone pit next to the great pyramid of Cheops at Giza. After spending years fitting together over a thousand pieces of wood, Ahmed Youssef Moustafa of the Egyptian Department of Antiquities had reconstructed for display at the pyramid a river craft, nearly forty-four meters long, built of massive cedar planks that were not fastened together by mortise-and-tenon joints but were laced together, like the planks of the Ferriby boats, except with ropes instead of yew branches. Lacking a keel and mast and with only a dozen paddles, the boat was probably designed to be towed from the bank of the Nile.

Perfection of a self-contained underwater breathing apparatus (scuba) by Jacques-Yves Cousteau and Emile Gagnan in FRANCE in the 1940s revolutionized the study of ancient and historic shipwrecks by providing divers with the mobility they needed for the careful excavation of delicate ships' hulls. A number of pioneering efforts conducted in the 1950s along the coasts of France and Italy introduced the regular use of airlifts (suction pipes) for removing overburden, air-filled lifting balloons for raising heavy objects to the surface, underwater photography, and even underwater television. In 1958, to aid in photographic mapping, Gianni Roghi, working with Nino Lamboglia, laid a tape grid over a Roman wreck at Spargi, a small island north of Sardinia; the tape was replaced in 1959 by rigid pipes.

Mistakes were unavoidably made along the way. Because careful archaeological plans were not kept, the site at Grand Congloué near Marseilles in France was thought to be that of a single Roman wreck whereas it is now recognized that it is instead one Roman wreck lying atop another of earlier date. Philippe Taillez, after his exemplary excavation of a Roman wreck near Le Titan in the same region, bemoaned the fact that diving archaeologists were not part of such excavations. Nevertheless, the nondiving archaeologists, especially Lamboglia in Italy and Fernand Benoit in France, who received finds and assessed information from the professional and amateur divers under their direction, began to pay close attention to the construction techniques of ancient ships. It became accepted that Roman ships were generally edge-joined with mortise-and-tenon joints and that hulls frequently were sheathed in lead.

Salvage mistakes were also made in North America. In 1956, the historian Edwin C. Bearss and colleagues, using a simple magnetic compass to detect a mass of iron, located the American Civil War ironclad *Cairo* in the Yazoo River, Mississippi, where it had lain in perfect condition since becoming, in 1862, the first vessel ever sunk by an electrically detonated mine. Beautifully preserved artifacts and what is left of the hull, which was mostly destroyed by misguided salvage methods in 1965 and a lack of

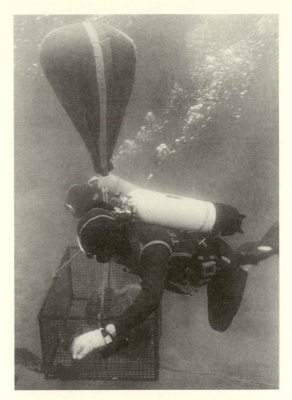

Archaeologists explore an ancient shipwreck in the Mediterranean, June 1969. (Hulton Getty)

prompt conservation, are displayed in the Vicksburg National Military Park.

Other wrecks, like those in the York River, were found by dragging. The Swedish engineer Anders Franzén, knowing that the Baltic Sea does not support ship worms, dragged the bottom of Stockholm's harbor from 1953 until 1956 in a successful search for what he rightly guessed would be a perfectly preserved warship, the *Vasa,* which sank on its maiden voyage in 1627.

1960s

After 1960, the field of nautical archaeology expanded rapidly in a number of new directions. "Whitewater archaeology" began in Minnesota and CANADA when amateur divers found goods lost by fur traders who had unsuccessfully tried to shoot rapids in their canoes. These finds led to a long-term survey for other such goods by Robert C. Wheeler of the Minnesota Historical Society and Walter A. Kenyon of the Royal Ontario Museum.

In 1961, the *Vasa* came to light for the first time since its loss more than three centuries earlier. Following the ship's discovery in 1956, Swedish navy helmet divers spent three years digging tunnels under the ship and then passing through them huge steel cables that were attached to lifting pontoons on the surface. In a series of slow and deliberate moves, the pontoons were partially filled with water, the cables tightened, the pontoons pumped dry, and the *Vasa* brought ever closer to shore and the surface.

In Denmark, Ole Crumlin-Pedersen and Olaf Olesen had a coffer dam built in 1962 around five Viking ships sunk around A.D. 1000 to block part of the Roskilde Fjord. After water was pumped from the coffers, excavators could uncover and disassemble the ships by working from scaffolding placed over the mud. Peter Marsden used the same method to study a Roman ship found in 1962 in the Thames in London. In the same year, a fourteenth-century cog, or trading ship, was discovered during dredging operations in the harbor at Bremen, Germany.

Building on the experience of French and Italian pioneers, divers in 1960, working on a Bronze Age shipwreck twenty-seven meters deep near Cape Gelidonya, TURKEY, carried to completion for the first time the excavation of an ancient shipwreck on the seabed. It was also the first time that an excavation was directed by a diving archaeologist. Almost none of the hull had been preserved, but brushwood dunnage under part of a ton of metal cargo explained an ambiguous passage in Homer's *Odyssey*. The ship's large stone anchor, of Syro-Palestinian or Cypriot type, was found during a return to the site in 1994.

The Cape Gelidonya wreck had been discovered by Turkish sponge divers who guided the amateur archaeologist Peter Throckmorton to it, and it was excavated by a UNIVERSITY OF PENNSYLVANIA MUSEUM team. Throughout the remainder of the 1960s, the Pennsylvania group introduced new techniques of underwater survey and excavation while excavating two Byzantine shipwrecks off the coast of Turkey, also found by Throckmorton through interviews with Turkish sponge divers, off Yasslada near Bodrum.

The new techniques included using plane tables, metal grids with photo towers, and stereophotography to map sites; a submersible decompression chamber; the use of pure oxygen for routine decompression; an air-filled clear-plastic hemisphere that acted both as an on-site underwater telephone booth and as a refuge for divers in distress; and, as an underwater command center, a specially built two-person submersible, the *Asherah,* which was also used for taking underwater stereophotographs. Core samplers, metal detectors, and the normal array of lifting balloons and airlifts also came into play. From the resultant detailed site plans, Frederick van Doorninck was able to reconstruct the ships' hulls accurately on paper, providing information from which J. Richard Steffy could build a series of research models.

The middle 1960s saw continuing work in ITALY. The amateur archaeologist Enrico Scandurra discovered and mapped a fifteenth-century Venetian galley that was part of a fleet moved over the mountains to Lake Garda, a feat requiring not only oars and sails but winches and as many as 2,000 oxen. The German Gerhard Kapitän and an Englishman, A. J. Parker, explored many wrecks around Sicily, including one at Marzamemi that carried the stone elements of a Byzantine church.

The 1967 discovery of an immense Roman amphora carrier at Madrague de Giens near Toulon in southern France led to a textbook excavation under the direction of Patrice Pomey and André Tchernia. The following year, Sidney Wignall and Colin Martin found in Blasket Sound, Ireland, the first of three Spanish Armada wrecks that would be studied by Martin, who worked at the Institute of Maritime Archaeology at the University of St. Andrews in Scotland.

In the 1960s, conservation was given an increasingly important role in ship excavation. Iron, for example, eventually corrodes and disappears in seawater, usually after becoming encrusted with a seabed concretion of calcium carbonate. Accurate casts of the original iron objects can be made by pouring plaster or, far better, liquid epoxy into the natural molds formed when the iron disappears and the calcium carbonate concretion remains.

At the end of the 1960s, Michael and Susan Katzev from the University of Pennsylvania Museum team located and excavated a fourth-century classical Greek ship off Kyrenia, CYPRUS. They advanced the field of nautical archaeology by raising and preserving, for the first time in the Mediterranean, the ship's hull, its planks fastened with pegged mortise-and-tenon joints. The hull was then reassembled for display and study by Richard Steffy, a task that lasted into the early 1970s.

Waterlogged wood, unless properly treated, will shrink and warp out of recognition when exposed to air. The Kyrenia ship was conserved with polyethylene glycol, as had been the restored Viking ships from Roskilde Fjord, the *Vasa* in Sweden, and three colonial bateaux raised at the beginning of the decade from Lake George, New York.

Survey techniques also improved. Many shipwrecks in the Mediterranean were initially spotted by local sponge divers, but in 1967, sonar and underwater television were used successfully for the first time to locate an ancient wreck, later examined from the submersible *Asherah,* eighty-five meters deep off the coast of Turkey. In England, Alexander McKee, working with Harold Edgerton's subbottom sonar, relocated the *Mary Rose,* its position having been lost after the nineteenth-century salvage of some of its cannons. Magnetometers, which detect iron, proved equally successful in searches for more modern ships, which, even if built of wood, often carried large iron objects such as cannons and anchors. Unfortunately, scuba equipment and better search techniques also caused an increase in underwater treasure hunting and the looting of wrecks in the 1960s, especially in the waters around FLORIDA AND THE CARIBBEAN islands.

1970s

In the 1970s, surveys and excavations of high quality were conducted around the globe, starting in 1970 in England with the discovery and excavation of a clinker-built boat of around A.D. 950 at Graveney in Kent. Beginning in 1972, archaeologists from the Western Australian Museum, led by Jeremy Greene, not only excavated, published, and restored Dutch East Indiamen from their own waters, notably the *Vergulde Draeck* lost in 1656 and the *Batavia* in 1629, but traveled farther afield to study wrecks from Kenya to Thailand. Another Dutch East Indiaman, the *Amsterdam*, sunk deeply in sand in 1749 just off Hastings, England, was examined and sampled by Peter Marsden after its 1969 discovery—on those few days each year when it was revealed by exceptionally low tides.

The *San Esteban,* one of three ships driven aground on Padre Island, Texas, by a storm in 1554, was, between 1972 and 1976, the first Spanish treasure ship excavated archaeologically. One ship had already been destroyed by dredging operations in the 1940s, and another had been partly exploited by treasure hunters in 1967 before the Texas Antiquities Committee was formed to take on the job of excavating, under Carl Clausen, and conserving, under Donny Hamilton, what remained. These events led to a state law of protection for historic shipwrecks.

Veterans of the University of Pennsylvania team founded the Institute of Nautical Archaeology (INA) in 1972 and began projects on four continents. Excavation of a cargo of pottery lost around 1600 B.C. near Sheytan Deresi in Turkey was followed by the excavation of a ship sunk in the natural harbor of Serçe Limanl on the southwestern Turkish coast around A.D. 1025. The latter ship produced the largest collection of medieval Islamic glass in the world and is the earliest known example of a seagoing hull built in the frame-first manner. Elsewhere in the Mediterranean, INA, with the assistance of Sub Sea Oil Services of Milan, conducted the first excavation using saturation diving of a Hellenistic wreck off the island of Lipari north of Sicily.

In North America, under the direction of David Switzer, INA undertook the excavation of two ships, one American and the other British, sunk during the War of Independence. The American privateer *Defence* was excavated in Penobscot Bay, Maine, by Switzer in a joint project begun in 1975 with the Maine Maritime Academy and the Maine State Museum. An INA investigation in 1976 of a British ship scuttled by General Cornwallis at Yorktown led to the proposal that such ships should be excavated within coffer dams in which the murky water of the York River could be clarified by industrial filters, an idea Norman Scott had earlier suggested for other sites with zero visibility.

Elsewhere in the United States, the famed "cheesebox on a raft," the Civil War ironclad *Monitor,* the first gunboat with a revolving turret, was located in 1973 seventy meters deep about seventeen miles off Cape Hatteras, North Carolina, by a Duke University team using sonar. Two years later, the archaeologists Gordon Watts, John Broadwater, and others visited the *Monitor* in the Harbor Branch Foundation's *Johnson-Sea-Link I,* a submersible from which they could be launched into open water to swim around and examine the site.

The 1968–1969 dryland excavation of the steamboat *Bertrand,* sunk in 1865 twenty-five miles north of Omaha, Nebraska, in the Missouri River (which had since changed course), was supervised by U.S. National Park Service archaeologists. The project yielded not only a well-preserved hull but nearly 2 million artifacts, including bottles with their paper labels intact.

In Canada, the amateur archaeologist Daniel A. Nelson, after searching with side-scanning sonar in an area narrowed by archival research to thirty-two square miles, in 1973 located two warships sunk during the War of 1812, the *Hamilton* and the *Scourge,* ninety meters deep in Lake Champlain. Inspected and recorded from a research submarine and by a remotely operated vehicle (ROV), the ships proved to be almost perfectly preserved with upright masts, figureheads in place, and skeletons of the crew on the decks.

Pioneering work on ships in the Far East was conducted both on land and under water in the 1970s. At the port city of Quanzhou, CHINA, a thirty-four-meter ship of the thirteenth century A.D. was discovered and excavated in 1973, and a fourteenth-century wreck with an immense collection of Chinese ceramics was excavated by the Korean navy after the ship was discovered near Shinan, Korea, by a fisherman in 1975. Both ships offered the surprise of V-shaped hulls from a time when scholars assumed that all Chinese ships were flat-bottomed.

In Mombasa, Kenya, Robin Piercy of INA began, in 1977, the first full-scale shipwreck excavation in East Africa on the remains of the

Santo Antonio de Tanna, a Portuguese ship built at Goa and sunk in 1696 while trying to help relieve a siege of the Portuguese fort, Fort Jesus, by Omani Arabs. During the same period, Colin Martin continued excavating two Spanish ships—*El Gran Grifón* and *La Trinidad Valencera*—that had fled north around Scotland and Ireland following the defeat of the Spanish Armada in 1588.

1980s

A number of projects in the 1980s proved that wrecks could be found and at least partly recovered from any depth and at any temperature. In the first year of the decade, using sonar, a team led by Joe MacInnis discovered the well-preserved *Breadalbane* under two meters of surface ice at a depth of a hundred meters in Canada's Northwest Passage. The British bark had been sunk by ice in 1853 while on a rescue mission for the ill-fated Franklin expedition of 1846. MacInnis's team was able to explore the site in a one-person submersible, the *WASP,* lowered through a hole in the ice.

In 1985, a French-American team, searching an area of the North Atlantic 350 miles southeast of Newfoundland and 150 miles square, was able to locate and examine, at a depth of 4,000 meters, the "unsinkable" *Titanic,* a ship sunk by an iceberg on its maiden voyage in 1912 with a loss of 1,522 lives. Preliminary images of the wreck were seen via television from ROV, and in 1986, Robert Ballard of the Woods Hole Oceanographic Institute visually inspected the site from the submarine *Alvin.* After the discovery, amid some controversy, artifacts were raised from the ship by a French group for display.

Equally impressive was the discovery in 1987 of the SS *Central American,* lost 200 miles off Charleston, South Carolina, in 1857 in water a mile and a half deep. The Columbus-America Discovery Group, admittedly after the gold bullion the ship was known to be carrying, surveyed 1,400 square miles of ocean floor with sonar to locate the vessel and then retrieved much of the cargo and other artifacts with advanced robots. In the muddy York River, John Broadwater of the Virginia Department of Conservation and Historic Resources showed that archaeologists could work with excellent visibility by building a coffer dam around another of Cornwallis's scuttled ships and filtering the water inside.

These spectacular tours de force did not mean that controlled excavations at lesser depths did not continue. In Red Bay, Labrador, Robert Grenier of Parks Canada directed the excavation, between 1980 and 1984, of the sixteenth-century Basque whaler *San Juan* and several small boats, including one of the ship's whaleboats, probably the oldest and best specimen of an early boat used to hunt whales. To the south, Kevin Crisman and Arthur Cohen created a specialty of studying ships sunk during the War of 1812 in Lake Ontario and in Lake Champlain for the Champlain Maritime Society and the Vermont Division for Historic Preservation.

Anders Franzén returned to nautical archaeology in 1980 with the discovery of another well-preserved seventeenth-century Swedish warship, the Kronan. The *Mary Rose,* carefully excavated under the direction of Margaret Rule since 1979, was finally raised in 1982 but must undergo decades of chemical conservation before the remains of the hull are fully restored for public viewing. In the meantime, a stunning array of artifacts, including rare examples of English longbows, have already been conserved and are on display in Portsmouth, England; many have also been shown around the world in a traveling exhibit.

The most careful underwater excavation in the Caribbean was begun in 1982 when Donald H. Keith of the Institute of Nautical Archaeology undertook the excavation and conservation of what was then the oldest wreck known in the New World, presumably a Spanish vessel of the early fifteenth century, at Molasses Reef in the Turks and Caicos Islands. Keith explored other fifteenth-century wrecks in the Caribbean for INA before forming his own group, Ships of Discovery, which has established a museum for the Molasses Reef wreck on Grand Turk Island.

Also in 1982, Mensun Bound of MARE at Oxford University excavated a probable Etruscan wreck of around 600 B.C. at Giglio, an island off the southwestern coast of Tuscany in central Italy. In Turkey, the Institute of Nautical Archaeology, in a project that continued from 1983 into the 1990s, surveyed and excavated a fourteenth-century B.C. wreck that has produced fifteen tons of raw goods. These include the oldest known tin ingots, glass ingots, a wooden writing tablet, ebony logs, a fragmentary seagoing hull, ten tons of copper ingots, a unique gold scarab that once belonged to Egypt's Queen Nefertiti, and pottery, seals, jewelry, and stone objects from half a dozen ancient civilizations. Twenty-four stone anchors were carried in the fifteen-meter hull made of fir planks fastened with pegged mortise-and-tenon joints. Lying between forty-four and sixty-one meters deep off Uluburun, near Ka in Turkey, it is the deepest site yet excavated by scuba divers.

Israeli archaeologists and divers had long been finding and mapping artifacts from the Bronze Age onward in the Mediterranean, including the bronze ram of a Hellenistic warship off Atlit on the coast of ISRAEL. A severe drought in 1985 lowered the level of the Sea of Galilee sufficiently to expose a fishing boat from the time of Christ. It was removed for conservation and study in early 1986 by Shelley Wachsmann.

In Egypt, a covered pit next to the great pyramid of Cheops was opened to reveal a second dismantled boat. And in 1987, the Abandoned Shipwreck Act, which was signed into law in the United States, removed historic shipwrecks in states' waters from the jurisdiction of admiralty salvage law.

1990s

By the last decade of the twentieth century, nautical archaeology had become a respected subdiscipline of archaeology, and there were graduate programs devoted to training future specialists at St. Andrews University in Scotland; Texas A&M University, with which INA affiliated in 1976; East Carolina University in North Carolina, studying not only local wrecks but wrecks in Bermuda; Haifa University in Israel; the University of Copenhagen; and Bilkent University in Ankara, Turkey. Courses in nautical archaeology were also being offered from Australia to Oxford to the University of Texas.

Proceedings of conferences and journals devoted to the field have become commonplace.

Laws to protect ancient and historic wrecks have been passed by an increasing number of states and nations, and an increasing number of state and national programs have been developed around the globe.

Splendid museums of nautical archaeology attract an increasing number of visitors. Noteworthy are those devoted to single ships (such as the *Vasa,* the *Mary Rose,* the Bremen cog, and the Molasses Reef Wreck) or groups of ships (for instance, in the Roskilde Museum in Denmark, the Bodrum Museum of Underwater Archaeology in Turkey, the Viking Ship Museum in Oslo, and the National Maritime Museum in Greenwich, England).

Results of fieldwork in progress were eagerly awaited from projects such as the Greek excavations of a Bronze Age wreck at Iria and an unexpectedly large fifth-century B.C. amphora carrier in the Northern Sporades in the Aegean Sea. There was also ongoing work on dozens of vessels revealed through land reclamation in the Netherlands, the excavation of early dynastic Egyptian boats found by the University of Pennsylvania in the sands at ABYDOS, the conservation with sugar rather than polyethylene glycol of an early Spanish hull excavated in Cuba, and surveys conducted by INA from the Red Sea to the Persian Gulf to the Black Sea and by the Western Australian Museum throughout the Far East.

George Bass

References

Bass, G. F. 1970. 2d ed. *Archaeology under Water.* Harmondsworth, UK, and Baltimore: Penguin.

Bass, G. F., ed. 1972. *A History of Seafaring Based on Underwater Archaeology.* London and New York: Thames and Hudson and Walker.

————. 1988. *Ships and Shipwrecks of the Americas.* London and New York: Thames and Hudson.

Muckelroy, K., ed. 1980. *Archeology under Water: An Atlas of the World's Submerged Sites.* New York and London: McGraw Hill.

Throckmorton, P., ed. 1987. *The Sea Remembers: Shipwrecks and Archaeology.* London and New York: Mitchell Beazley International and Weidenfeld and Nicolson.

Journals and Proceedings of Conferences

Archaeonautica. 1977– . Paris: Centre National de la Recherche Scientifique.

Bulletin of the Australian Institute for Maritime Archaeology. 1977– .

Institute of Nautical Archaeology (INA) Newsletter. 1973–1991. College Station, TX.

Institute of Nautical Archaeology (INA) Quarterly. 1991– . College Station, TX.

International Journal of Nautical Archaeology. 1972– . London: Academic Press.

Tropis. 1985– . Piraeus: Hellenic Institute for the Preservation of Nautical Tradition.

Underwater Archaeology Proceedings from the Society for Historical Archaeology Conference (1987–) in the U.S. Pleasant Hill, CA.

Naville, Henri Edouard (1844–1926)

Born in Geneva, SWITZERLAND, and educated at the University of Geneva; King's College, London; and the universities of Bonn, Paris, and Berlin, Henri Edward Naville was a biblical scholar and philologist who studied under the great Egyptologist KARL RICHARD LEPSIUS. Naville first visited Egypt in 1865 and copied the Horus texts at Edfu, a site in Upper Egypt. He later worked on the Solar texts and published four volumes of the Book of the Dead. The decipherment of these ancient texts and inscriptions enabled a chronology and history of ancient Egypt to be devised.

Naville was the first archaeologist to be employed by the EGYPTIAN EXPLORATION SOCIETY (at that time the Egypt Exploration Fund), and he excavated at Tell el-Makhuta in 1883 and the Wadi Tumilat in 1885–1886, the western end of which was identified as the biblical land of Goshen. Between 1886 and 1889, Naville excavated at Bubastis on the southeastern Nile Delta and brought back many artifacts from there to the BRITISH MUSEUM, including a huge granite head of the pharaoh Amenemhat III. He then excavated another ten sites in the Nile Delta, including Herakleopolis, Mendes, and Tell Mukdam.

From 1893 to 1896, Naville worked in Upper Egypt finishing the excavation of Hatshepsut's mortuary temple at Deir el-Bahari begun by AUGUSTE MARIETTE, and his field assistants there included DAVID HOGARTH and HOWARD CARTER. In 1903, Naville returned to excavate the temple's mounds, discovering tombs and the temple of King Menthuhotep II from the eleventh dynasty. Naville was the successor of earlier archaeologists such as HEINRICH SCHLIEMANN, Mariette, and Gaston Maspero, who were interested in architectural ruins and large monuments, not in the smaller details or the kind of painstaking work of the younger generation of archaeologists in Egypt such as SIR WILLIAM MATTHEW FLINDERS PETRIE. Naville's last excavation was at ABYDOS in 1909, where he cleared the Osireion, which had been discovered by Petrie in 1902.

Naville was awarded many honors and distinctions from most European countries including his own, Switzerland, and he published many articles, reviews, and books on his work in Egypt.

Tim Murray

See also Champollion, Jean-François; Egypt, Dynastic; French Archaeology in Egypt and the Middle East

References

Drower, M. S. 1995. *Flinders Petrie: A Life in Archaeology*. 2d ed. Madison: University of Wisconsin Press.

Nelson, Nels (1875–1964)

Nels Nelson was a pioneering American archaeologist who was a great advocate and developer of new approaches to stratigraphic excavation. Taught by the great New World archaeologists MAX UHLE and Alfred Kroeber, Nelson learned his craft excavating shell mounds on the California coast and participating in the excavation of Paleolithic cave sites in France and Spain. He undertook stratigraphic excavations in the southwestern United States after 1914, especially at San Cristobal Pueblo.

Tim Murray

See also United States of America, Prehistoric Archaeology

References

Fitting, James E. 1973. *The Development of North American Archaeology*. University Park: Penn State University Press.

Willey, Gordon R., and Jeremy A. Sabloff. 1993. *A History of American Archaeology*. 3d ed. London: Thames and Hudson.

Netherlands

According to Dutch archaeological lore, archaeology became a scientific endeavor in the early years of the twentieth century when a young zoology graduate, ALBERT EGGES VAN GIFFEN, studied faunal remains unearthed during a study of *terpen* as indicators of prehistoric economies. *Terpen* ("terps") are artificial mounds on the coastal wetlands of the Netherlands on which Iron Age and early medieval villages were built, and after the area was diked after A.D. 1000, they were exploited as sources of manure.

At the time, the only archaeological institution in the country was the State Museum of Antiquities in Leiden where the traditionalist Jan Hendrik Holwerda dominated Dutch archaeology. Inevitably, he and Van Giffen became enemies, and after some years of struggle, Holwerda and his museum faded away to be superseded by Van Giffen and the archaeological institute he had founded at the University of Groningen in the north of the country, right in the middle of terp-land. Because of Van Giffen, Dutch archaeology won international status, especially because of its meticulous excavation techniques, use of auxiliary sciences (botany, zoology, geology), and settlement excavations. Later, Van Giffen's students ran archaeological institutes at every university in the country as well as staffing the State Archaeological Service. Today, almost all archaeological research in the Netherlands is directly or indirectly related to Van Giffen's exploits.

In the late 1990s, that was still the majority view of the modernization of Dutch archaeology (e.g., Slofstra 1994), because when Van Giffen's students became dominant in the late 1940s and early 1950s, their view of the discipline's history became the founding myth of Dutch archaeology. However, the myth is mainly a repeat of Van Giffen's arguments that he used in his attempt to bypass Holwerda between 1910 and 1915—a construct used in the battle for academic positions. Van Giffen and his students have retired or died now, so perhaps it is time to sketch a different picture.

Historians distinguish three periods of nation building in the Netherlands: the sixteenth and

Archaeological Sites in the Netherlands

seventeenth centuries, before and during insurrection against and independence from the Hapsburg Empire; 1813–1830, after the French Revolution and occupation; and 1945–1960, after World War II and the German occupation. There was a general economic and cultural stagnation between 1835 and 1900 after which the economy took off during the period of political neutrality between Germany, France, and Great Britain (1900–1930). The economic slump and German occupation were followed by Anglo-American dominance and restoration (1930–1965); growth and consolidation (1965–1980); economic stagnation again (1980–1990); and very slow recovery after 1990. The country had about 2 million inhabitants in 1775, 4 million by

1879, 8 million in 1931, and over 15 million in 1994.

At the universities, the number of students started to increase rapidly in the 1950s with growing participation of middle-class groups after 1960. At first, that swell generated new academic jobs and ever more participation, but after 1970–1975, academic job opportunities tended to decrease, resulting in misemployment first and later substantial underemployment of later university trainees. The number of archaeological jobs closely followed suit, as did the number of academic and nonacademic archaeological institutes. Presently, heritage and rescue archaeology fare much better than academic archaeology in this respect.

An Institutional History

The State Museum of Antiquities in Leiden (Rijksmuseum van Oudheden, hereafter RMO) was the first public archaeological institution in the Netherlands, and its foundation in 1818 marked a shift from traditional to positivist thinking about the past. The museum has been and is active as a collector of antiquities from the Old World and in fieldwork in the Netherlands and abroad. The first director of the RMO, Caspar J. C. Reuvens, was also appointed professor of archaeology at Leiden State University in 1818, but that appointment was not a recognition of the subject in the Netherlands. "[Archaeology is] not so much a distinct, useful science, as it is a pleasant pastime . . . when not useless, then not really necessary" as one obituary of Reuven put it after his untimely death in 1835 (Byvanck-Quaries van Ufford 1984).

By and large, that was the dominant attitude toward archaeology in the Netherlands until well into the twentieth century. Accordingly, the chair was left vacant until A. E. J. Holwerda (1845–1923) was appointed to the chair of Archaeology, Ancient History, and Greek Antiquities. Later, Holwerda also became director of the RMO (1903–1919), and from there, he revived contact with the university. In 1907, Holwerda founded the *Oudheidkundige Mededelingen van het Rijksmuseum van Oudheden* as an outlet for the publications of the museum's investigations, but even then, there was no continuity, and Hol-

werda's successor at the university was an ancient historian who had no use for archaeology except as an illustrator of early events. In 1922, Alexander Byvanck, who had studied with Holwerda, succeeded to this chair. Byvanck pushed the appointment of assistants whose major interests were in classical archaeology, and that subject rapidly became well entrenched at Leiden University. In 1921, archaeology had been legally acknowledged as a separate discipline, and only then could a degree in archaeology be obtained.

Meanwhile, at the University of Utrecht, two classical philologists had been lecturing on archaeology. One of them, G. van Hoom, also lectured at Groningen from 1919 onward, thus paving the way for a chair of classical archaeology at that university in 1951. C. W. Vollgraff, the other Utrecht philologist, excavated the acropolis of Argos from 1903 until 1930 in a joint project with the French Archaeological School at Athens. He also participated in excavations of the Roman core of the city of Utrecht led by Van Giffen between 1934 and 1938. One of Vollgraff's students, H. G. Beyen, became the first professor of classical archaeology at the University of Groningen.

When Leiden University was reopened in 1945 after its forced closure by the Germans in 1941, a separate chair of classical archaeology was finally established, and it was held by Byvanck until 1954. There were good and varied relations with the chair of art history (which is still named Art History and Archaeology) at the same university, and contact with the material products of the ancient world was maintained through yearly student excursions to the Mediterranean's monumental sites. Only when H. A. A. P. Geertman was appointed in 1979 did interest in fieldwork reemerge.

At the University of Groningen, Van Giffen founded the Biological Archaeological Institute (hereafter BAI) in 1920. He also became an active consultant of local antiquarian committees and exercised great influence in the archaeological field in the northern Netherlands. Van Giffen was appointed professor of prehistory and Germanic archaeology in 1939, and in the 1950s he convinced the Groningen physicist and

Nobel Laureate H. de Vries to set up a carbon–14 laboratory at that university, to be partially paid for by the BAI. The first readings were taken in 1952.

Van Giffen became professor of archaeology at the University of the City of Amsterdam in 1940, and there he successfully set up the Institute of Pre- and Proto-history in 1951. The University of Amsterdam's chair of (classical) archaeology was established in 1928, and its first incumbent, G. A. S. Snijder, founded the Allard Pierson Museum of Archaeology in 1934 to display the classical antiquities collections of Lunsingh Scheurleer and Allard Pierson. Snijder had good relations with Germany and also with top Nazis in Holland during the German occupation. Appointed director of the Dutch branch of a Nazi foundation in 1943, he was convicted and dismissed after the war and moved to Germany.

Van Giffen's main contribution concerned the institutionalization of archaeological research in the country. In the years before World War II, several so-called recognized local institutions had started to dig for archaeological artifacts for local museums, and this practice was regarded as a threat to the archaeological record by the more responsible people in the RMO at Leiden, the BAI at Groningen, and the civil service in the Hague. In 1939, F. C. Bursch and W. C. Braat, keepers at the RMO, recommended curbing this unwanted development by centrally organizing excavations, administration, registration, and preservation of finds and sites.

The government accordingly set up a state committee, which came into office in 1940; Van Giffen, Byvanck, and Van Wijngaarden, director of the RMO, were on the board. The RMO was recognized as both the central national museum and excavator while the BAI was nominated to be the academic and national excavator; regional museums and others were supposed to cooperate with these major institutions on a voluntary basis. A small bureau was installed at the RMO to act as the executive branch of the committee, and it was headed by Bursch, who held firm Nazi convictions and was oriented toward Germany in scientific matters. Bursch wanted a field survey to set up an archaeological monuments list, after a German model developed in Bonn, but

he could not control the National Archaeological Service and most people simply ignored him because of his political views.

After the war, it was clear that the impoverished country could not support several archaeological institutes, and Van Giffen considered his peripherally situated BAI particularly vulnerable. With strong support from the Monument Council and the new Government of Reconstruction, he worked to establish a centralized archaeological service to avoid a proliferation of archaeological institutes all over the country. The Archaeological State Service (Rijksdienst voor Oudheidkundig Bodemonderzoek, hereafter ROB) was finally established in 1947 at Amersfoort, a city between Leiden (RMO) and Groningen (BAI). Many of the service's intended aims have never been fulfilled; it is neither the only excavator nor an archaeological educator. In fact, since 1961, excavation licenses have been issued by the Monument Council, and academic archaeological training has continued and expanded at the various universities.

Between 1945 and 1947, few archaeologists were interested in preservation, not even Van Giffen, and excavation was apparently considered the single most important task of the professional archaeologist. The Provisional Monuments Act (drawn up by the government in 1946 to protect historical and archaeological monuments) took the Dutch archaeological world by surprise. A Provisional Monuments Council incorporated the existing Archaeological State Committee and its bureau without notice. In 1961, this Provisional Act was replaced by a comprehensive Monuments Act in which archaeological interests were considerably expanded and registration of the archaeological heritage of the Netherlands became the responsibility of the ROB. To that end, ROB archaeologists were appointed in every Dutch province: they check development plans, are consulted by local authorities, and initiate rescue excavations if necessary.

As a result of the Monuments Act and the activities of the ROB, it dawned on local authorities that modernization and reconstruction in inner cities is fairly destructive of medieval remains above and in the soil. In several old cities, archaeologists have been appointed to manage that heritage and to take care of at least the excavation, if not the preservation of ancient structures.

Early in the 1980s when job opportunities in archaeology were no longer rapidly expanding, several small bureaus were set up by unemployed young archaeologists who offered specialist expertise, mainly in fieldwork-related tasks: drawing, pollen analysis, bone determination, computer-aided analysis, reconnaissance, and survey. The most successful bureau is the Regional Archeologisch Archiverings Project (Regional Archaeological Filing Project, hereafter RAAP), which is loosely affiliated with the Amsterdam Prehistoric Institute, and the RAAP has achieved a powerful position as a commercial archaeological surveying bureau in the Netherlands and in central Europe. More than any other, this agency has become the center of technical innovation in archaeology, and many graduates aspire to a position within its ranks.

In the nineteenth century and well into the twentieth, Dutch archaeologists were trained in classical philology, and many were active in the classical countries of southern Europe as well as in the Netherlands. It was only after the legal recognition of archaeology as a discipline in its own right in 1921, and the consequent establishment of permanent chairs in the subject, that students were explicitly trained in archaeology. Initially, this training was after the student had earned a bachelor's degree in classical arts, geography, geology, or ethnography, but after 1986, archaeology became a full undergraduate and postgraduate university training program.

As in other countries, prehistoric and classical archaeology have gradually separated in the Netherlands. Until 1930, all archaeology was aligned with ancient history (as at Leiden University) or art history (as at Amsterdam), and a training in classics was considered essential. Then an ecological bias came to be associated with prehistoric research, as conducted mainly at the BAI in Groningen, and historical archaeology became more text/art oriented in Amsterdam, Leiden, and Utrecht.

After World War II, the trend was reinforced by the founding of prehistoric archaeological institutes at Amsterdam and Leiden, which were led by students of Van Giffen who were more inclined toward fieldwork and ecological analysis than their historical colleagues. Like Bursch and Van Giffen, W. J. Glasbergen (Van Giffen's successor at the Amsterdam Institute of Pre- and Proto-history from 1956 to 1979) attempted to make his institute *the* scientific branch of Dutch archaeology, mainly through a rapid expansion of its staff. The differences between the institutions were mutually elaborated and emphasized until 1980 when the threat of a reduction of funds and institutes made cooperation, at least in education, imperative. Today, all universities have joint basic training programs for undergraduates studying classical and prehistoric archaeology, but although a steady rapprochement is perceptible, it is not appreciated by everyone (e.g., Slofstra 1994; also Hodges 1990).

Several provincial and/or regional museums were founded in the Netherlands in the nineteenth century, generally in the wake of the establishment of local scientific salons, historical associations, or antiquarian societies. As was the case elsewhere in Europe, the nation building and nationalism of the bourgeoisie occurred hand in hand with ancestor veneration. Many of these museums are depositories of important and specialized collections. For instance, the Provincial Museum of Drenthe at Assen has an impressive set of peat corpses and bog sacrifices from the Iron Age. The top prehistoric, peri-Roman, and medieval objects, however, are in the RMO, which is the national repository for Dutch archaeology. The RMO also contains important collections of Egyptian, classical Greek, and Roman artifacts.

Attempts to regularly publish research reports have been made by the RMO. Reuvens cooperated with a well-known antiquarian in editing the journal *Antiquiteiten* (1819–1826), which had almost the same formula the English-language journal ANTIQUITY has today. Also between 1842 and 1846, and from 1855 to 1859, *Mededeelingen* were issued. A. E. J. Holwerda finally succeeded where his predecessors had failed, and from 1907 onward, the *Oudheidkundige Mededelingen van het Rijksmuseum van Oudheden* has appeared yearly. This publication is primarily filled with reports on research or acquisitions by the museum, and articles range from Dutch prehistoric excavations to discussions on Coptic grammar. Van Giffen's BAI also began issuing an archaeological journal, *Palaeohistoria,* in 1953. It contains research reports on activities by the staff of that institute, both in the Netherlands and abroad—for example, in the Middle East and INDONESIA.

An important backbone of classical archaeology has been the Vereeniging tot Bevordering der Kennis van de Antieke Beschaving (Society for the Furtherance of Knowledge of Antique Civilization). From 1925 onward, the *Bulletin* of this society (presently called *Bulletin Antieke Beschaving,* or *BABesch*) has appeared yearly and is the major journal of Mediterranean archaeology in the Netherlands. There are more archaeological journals with a Dutch background, the larger ones being *Berichten ROB* (which reports on the research by the ROB), *Helinivm* (which caters to Dutch and Belgian audiences, mainly prehistory), *Iranica Antiqua, Persica, Anatolica,* and *Bibliotheca Orientalis* (concerned with Middle Eastern philology and archaeology), and *Tijdschrift voor Mediterrane Archeologie* (archaeology in the Mediterranean). Of the others, *Analecta Praehistorica Leidensia* (which appears irregularly) and *Archaeological Dialogues* (which has a theoretical orientation) should be mentioned.

Major Collections and the Archaeological Record

The major archaeological collection of the Netherlands is in the RMO. The origin of this collection lies in the first systematic display of antiquities in the Netherlands, begun in the early years of the sixteenth century, when the Baron of Wassenaar looted the Roman fortress of Brittenburg, which had emerged at the ancient mouth of the Rhine owing to natural excavations by the North Sea. In a contemporary chronicle, the Wassenaar lineage was said to have descended from the fortress's Roman lord (Aurelius 1517), and almost two centuries later, that attribution was echoed and extended (Pars 1697). To further substantiate his claims, the baron also bought Roman artifacts from other places. The Wassenaar collection remained in the family's Duivenvoorde Castle in Voor-

schoten (south of Leiden) and was enlarged over later centuries. Part of it is still there, but another part is now in the ROM in Leiden.

The antecedents of Batavian (the native Germanic dialect) were eagerly sought after the sixteenth and seventeenth centuries. The years of insurrection against the Hapsburg's centralism and taxation resulted in the foundation of the Republic of the United Provinces of the Netherlands, and territorial claims were bolstered by reference to a mythical past. Reconstructions of Batavian society were published or painted, and the collection of antiquities kept pace with the political situation, tacitly forgoing local, native remains for objects from classical civilization that exemplified humanist and Renaissance ideas. One example among many stems from the early-seventeenth-century Antwerp painter Peter Paul Rubens who assembled classical statuary, which, after a detour to the collection of the Duke of Buckingham in London, was obtained by the Rotterdam brewer Reiner van der Wolff in 1660; today, part of the collection is in the RMO. In 1647, the Nehalennia sanctuary—the temple of a Romanized local goddess near the mouth of the river Scheidt—was exposed by the sea, and several altars were found on the beach. Ultimately, they ended up in the RMO.

Dutch collectors were also active in classical countries: a set of antique statues ultimately attributable to a Venice collector was bought by the Council of Holland in 1660, and early in the following century, an important collection of 150 classical *marmora* was bought by Gerard van Papenbroek at auction and bequeathed to Leiden University in 1743. This "cabinet of antiquities" was put on display in a specially constructed pavilion in that university's Botanical Gardens, probably the first public exhibition of antiquities in the United Provinces. The Papenbroek collection is remarkable for its relatively complete documentation, and it, too, is now in the RMO. In the same period, another important collection was begun when the Duke of Thoms, a Dutch diplomat in Italy, published an extensive catalog of his large collection of gems and coins in 1740. This collection was purchased by the Prince of Orange in 1751, who passed it on to his heirs. Looted by the French in 1795 and later repatriated to the Netherlands, it constitutes the core of the collection of the newly founded Royal Numismatic Cabinet in the Hague.

There have been more private and public collections of classical artifacts, and most of them have found their way to the RMO or to local museums. Some of the Dutch merchant dynasties amassed extensive private collections of ancient and contemporary art, which are still kept in their city palaces. Occasionally, such collections are put into public trust, most notably the collections of Allard Pierson and Lunsingh Scheurleer, which have been handed over to the archaeological museum of the University of Amsterdam (now the Allard Pierson Museum), and the important Van Beuningen collection of medieval pottery, which has been donated to the Van Beuningen Museum in Rotterdam.

A few examples of the forgery and fraud that have existed throughout the history of archaeology in the Netherlands are in order. For instance, the reason for the collection of the sixteenth-century finds from the Brittenburg fortress was to construct a Roman pedigree for an aristocratic lineage, a fraudulent enterprise. In the 1840s, Janssen of the RMO excavated a "Neolithic" pit village near Hilversum, and it took a century for the finds to be recognized for what they were, nineteenth-century forgeries, perhaps by one of Janssen's laborers. Famous among prehistoric fraud is Holwerda's misidentification of late Bronze Age tree coffins as the wall blocks of wooden "dome graves," based on a supposed analogy with Mycenaean *tholoi* (chamber tombs).

Several World War II finds that were later identified as probable forgeries by a Nazi bureau active in the Netherlands include "the Viking treasure" of Winsum (Elzinga 1975; Maarleveld and Pieper 1983). In the 1970s, news media ran stories about "the Vermaning hoax"—the Drenthe museum at Assen had for years been buying Paleolithic tools from the amateur archaeologist Tjerk Vermaning that were later recognized as forged. It was rumored that Vermaning was acting in good faith and that a conspiracy against official archaeology was behind the affair.

In the Netherlands—as elsewhere—interest in the archaeological record has never been very extensive. As Johan Picardt wrote (1660): "In the investigation of these antiquities of our home country, I do not find our compatriots very curious. They used to heed foreign, and external, more than indigenous histories. Yet I cannot understand or perceive that there are rarities or particularities in external histories, which we would not have, too, within our own country." Indeed, both the general public and the government have been rather unconcerned. Only megalith graves have been protected since 1734, as a result of a provincial law to prevent their destruction during the construction of roads and dikes, and grave barrows, Celtic fields (late Bronze Age–early Iron Age field systems), and other early sites have been destroyed in agricultural reallotment schemes. The legacy of the Middle Ages—such as city houses and in places whole city quarters, sixteenth- and seventeenth-century city defenses, and even old windmills and dikes—have only recently been or are still threatened by city construction. Only the Monuments Act of 1961 provides a means to preserve selected parts of the archaeological record.

A Gallery of Dutch Archaeologists

Dutch names are mentioned in few of the overviews of archaeological history (for example, Hodder 1991; Trigger 1989), a reflection of the importance that Dutch archaeology has been accorded by the world. Nevertheless, from this local archaeology some names can be proposed as worthy of international stature, if only because of their impact, long after their death, on Dutch archaeology. Of particular importance are Caspar Reuvens, Jan Hendrik Holwerda, Albert Egges van Giffen, and Hendrik Beyen, but some lesser figures have played important roles as well.

Casper J. C. Reuvens (1793–1835) studied law and defended his dissertation at the University of Paris in 1813. A professor of classical art at the (now closed) college of Harderwijk, in 1818 he became the first director of the RMO and also the first professor of archaeology at Leiden University. His first excavations (1826–1834) were at Arentsburg near Voorburg on an estate bought by the government especially for the purpose of archaeological investigation. It was here that the Forum Hadriani of the Peutinger Map was thought to be situated, mainly because of the discovery of Roman remains in preceding centuries.

Although a literary man, Reuvens had a keen eye for technical detail, and he meticulously recorded his field observations—plans with different scales, carefully measured cross sections of walls, full leveling, and even perspective drawings of important aspects. Soil samples from his excavations were analyzed by chemists; cremations were analyzed by physicians. In other words, he was interested in the archaeological context, not solely or even mainly in objects, and he achieved a very high standard of fieldwork. Reuvens also worked on Iron Age field systems and had planned to excavate a megalith grave. His early death at the age of forty-two prevented that research, and it also prevented the foundation of a tradition of high quality fieldwork. Posthumously, the first archaeological map of the Netherlands was produced, based on his notes.

Willem Pleyte (1836–1903) was keeper and later director of the RMO. Educated as an Egyptologist, he had to teach himself Dutch archaeology, but he did so so thoroughly that he wrote the first synthesis of Dutch antiquities (Pleyte 1877–1903). His previous vocation is visible in that work, for one of the chapters is preceded by a frontispiece showing a pharaonic Egyptian for no obvious reason, and all the wonderful places in it were lithographed by Pleyte himself "after the original objects or photographs." He interfered with the "conservation" practices of local authorities to such an extent that some denied further cooperation. For example, in his day, most megalithic graves were threatened by restorations, which were no doubt well meant. Covering mounds were removed, as they were considered to be dunes; tumbled and leaning stones were set upright; and capstones were straightened by the local authorities. Pleyte argued against such practices, and local authorities became considerably annoyed with him. Fortunately, there was also international opposition to such restorations, and at the 1874 Prehistoric Congress in Stockholm, it was specifi-

cally recommended that "the ruins of the megalith graves in Drenthe remain ruins and in that state be protected." Soon afterward, the restorations ceased.

Jan Hendrik Holwerda (1873–1951) became a keeper at the RMO in 1904 and its director in 1919 when he succeeded his father, A. E. J. Holwerda. One of the son's major accomplishments in the museum was a reorganization of the collections and documentation. He modernized exhibitions by putting reconstructions and models on display with original artifacts, and he wrote the accompanying guidebooks and appointed instructors to show visitors around. Holwerda wrote for a wider public than his contemporaries, and several of his books became quite popular, so much so that one can credit him with putting prehistory into Dutch schoolbooks. One major work was his *Oudheidkundige Kaart van Nederland* (1924; Archaeological Map of the Netherlands), which was followed by *Nederland's vroegste geschiedenis* (1925; Netherlands' Earliest History), the first attempt to systematize and present this knowledge to a wider public. In 1939, he retired from the Leiden Museum. His writings show that he believed that the archaeologists' task was to describe people rather than draw up the typo-chronology of a certain class of artifacts.

In 1908, Holwerda joined the German archaeologist Carl Schuchardt, who was excavating the Roman castellum (fortified settlement) at Haltern, Germany, to be trained in the modern German field technique of wide area digging and the systematic registration of soil discolorations as vestiges of ancient timber structures. Holwerda was the first in Dutch archaeology to emphasize the necessity of large-scale settlement research, and with his early assistant (1912–1917) and later enemy Van Giffen, Holwerda turned Dutch archaeology into a field science. His first large-scale excavations were at the Arentsburg site (1910–1912), the same site Reuvens had excavated almost a century before him. Holwerda's excavations were well below contemporary German standards, for he dug in narrow trenches, presumably to save time and money, and he conducted excavations all over the country, some bad by any standard and some good even by modern standards. However, given his aim of extensive excavation and the unaffordable amounts of (manual) labor required for that purpose, he could not have done better. Holwerda's technical possibilities were not up to his theoretical insights. He never dug for curiosity's sake or contingency alone; he always started off with a research question and set the feasibility of an excavation against the possibilities and the results to be obtained.

Holwerda had a lively interest in theoretical matters, he was much aware of developments in field techniques, he was a progressive museum director with a keen eye for the lay public, and importantly, he was never late in publishing his results. On the other hand, his obstinacy and his unwillingness to mend earlier opinions gradually isolated him from his contemporaries. His scientific inheritor, A. E. Remouchamps, died before he was able to write his thesis.

Albert Egges van Giffen (1884–1973) was a man of strong and lasting likes and dislikes. He had university training in botany and zoology and while still a graduate student (1908–1910), he was appointed to look after artifacts and bones being unearthed in ever-increasing quantities from terps. Some responsible people were becoming uneasy about the loss of old artifacts. Van Giffen did what he could, and in 1910 he was invited to join the RMO in Leiden because of his knowledge of terps. The museum recognized its responsibilities, but it lacked trained personnel—only Holwerda was considered a trained excavator, and he had other jobs to do. Van Giffen learned modern excavation techniques from Holwerda while taking part in the Arentsburg excavations as a volunteer.

Van Giffen took his degree at the University of Groningen and went to Leiden in 1912 where he was soon in conflict with Holwerda, accusing him of sloppiness because field drawings had to be "adapted" before publication. Holwerda in turn accused Van Giffen of withholding geological information. Van Giffen took this quarrel as far as the home secretary, and reports were written. In consequence, according to his biographer H. T. Waterbolk, Van Giffen had to abandon his hopes of ever becoming the director of the state museum. Fifty years later, at the end of his career, Van Giffen would still refer to his lost succession as the major disappointment of his life. Instead, a job in the Zoological Department at the University of Groningen was found for him, but he soon succeeded in founding an institute of his own, the BAI. When Holwerda retired in 1938, Van Giffen's application to become the director of the RMO was turned down by the Department of Culture. Instead, Van Giffen became professor in prehistory and Germanic archaeology at Groningen and a professor of archaeology at the University of Amsterdam.

After World War II, he sought to centralize archaeological investigation into a single state service, and of course, that service was to be under his control and established in Groningen: "Above all the formation of the new service meant at long last a certain reparation for the wrong done to him as a young man in Leiden" (Sarfatij 1972, 77). He succeeded in the establishment of such a service (the ROB), but he did not succeed in the full centralization of everything archaeological in the Netherlands. From 1950 onward, Van Giffen became quite prickly toward deviating opinions. He left the ROB in 1950 after many quarrels, and in 1954, he retired from his professorships.

As lecturer and author Van Giffen was not exciting, yet in the field and in informal situations he could be interesting. He had many students, most notable among them his successor at Groningen, H. T. Waterbolk (1924); his successor at the University of Amsterdam, W. Glasbergen (1923–1979); and P. J. R. Modderman (1919) at Leiden University. Other students trained by him included P. V. van Stein Callenfels and W. J. A. Willems of the Archaeological Service of the Netherlands Indies. As an excavator, Van Giffen was brilliant, but he was not particularly good as a reporter, and the results of his most important excavation of the Ezinge terp have never been published—however, he is not alone in this respect.

The civil servant E. A. Kuipers is a curious figure in Dutch archaeology. Engaged in monument preservation on behalf of the government in the same years that Van Giffen and Holwerda were active, Kuipers was in the Department of the Interior when Van Giffen and Holwerda had their clashes (1914–1920). Kuipers subsequently went to the Department of Education and Science where Van Giffen's succession to Holwerda was thwarted. After World War II, Kuipers was director of archaeology and nature preservation until 1952, the period when decisions concerning the foundation and scope of Van Giffen's ROB were made. It is difficult to gauge Kuipers's influence, for in the years 1939–1949, J. K. van der Haagen was head of his department, and the latter is generally credited with the decisive measures that led to the foundation of the State Service for Archaeological Investigations. With regard to van der Haagen, Kuipers said: "He wanted to centralize archaeological management, and to this end he drew up a whole series of legislations . . . Leiden [was to be] the hub" (Sarfatij 1972).

Carl W. Vollgraff (1876–1968) studied classical arts at the University of Brussels in Belgium and defended his thesis there in 1901. He was soon appointed private lecturer in Greek and Roman mythology at the University of Utrecht and started excavations in Greece that continued until 1930. He was appointed professor at Utrecht University in 1917 and may be considered "the father" of Dutch classical archaeology. Among his students, H. G. Beyen, C. H. E. Haspels, and G. A. S. Snijder need to be mentioned. They, in turn, tutored most of the presently active classical archaeologists. Vollgraff also participated in Van Giffen's excavations of the Roman core of the city of Utrecht (1934–1938), and the results were published jointly. Vollgraff retired in 1948.

Until the 1970s, there was no real tradition of fieldwork in Dutch classical archaeology. In the years before the prehistoric institutes were established, before archaeology became differentiated into historic and prehistoric branches, students from classical arts departments were sometimes interested in classical (or Egyptian, or Mesopotamian, or biblical, or Indonesian) archaeology. One of them, A. W. Byvanck (1884–1970), started out as an art historian of Greek antiquity, and for a time he was keeper at the Museum Meermanno-Westrianum in the Hague. After he ascended to the chair of archaeology and ancient history in Leiden in 1922, he also studied Roman and Byzantine art. Gradually, Byvanck extended his interest toward local archaeology as well, and he was well acquainted with Van Giffen, whom he met in the State Committee for Archaeology. In 1941, Byvanck published a popular synthesis of Dutch archaeology. After the war, when Leiden University was reopened, a chair of archaeology was established separate from that of ancient history and Byvanck was appointed to it.

Hendrik G. Beyen (1901–1965) is a well-known Dutch classical archaeologist. From an artistic family, he studied ancient art with Vollgraff in Utrecht and wrote a dissertation on mural art in POMPEII and HERCULANEUM (1928). He became the first professor of classical archaeology at Groningen University (1951), with the support of Van Giffen. In 1954, Beyen transferred to Leiden (succeeding Byvanck) but retired in 1964. His short scientific life was devoted to art history, specifically in the realm of classical mural painting, and he was the first to describe the successive styles of Roman wall painting in Pompeii. After Beyen's retirement, his work was continued by his students W. J. Th. Peters and F. L. Bastet. Architectural studies by members of the Dutch School in Rome (Th. Heres, E. Moormann) and by H. Geertman at Leiden may ultimately be credited to Beyen's leadership. Organizationally, Beyen and the RMO director A. Klasens succeeded in the establishment of an Institute of Prehistory at Leiden University in 1962; the institute was directed by P. J. R. Modderman, one of Van Giffen's students.

As far as can be ascertained, Van Giffen and his Groningen successor H. T. Waterbolk, Byvanck, and Beyen at Leiden; the RMO's director Klasens and his predecessor Van Wijngaarden; W. Glazema (Van Giffen's successor at the ROB) and W. A. van Es (managing director of the ROB in the 1960s and 1970s) were all on reasonably good terms. However, after the establishment of the ROB along lines inconsistent with Van Giffen's ideas, and especially after the appointment of Glasbergen to the Amsterdam Institute of Pre- and Proto-history (1956–1979), tensions between prehistorians and art historical archaeologists increased. The former considered themselves to be the "real" scientific archaeologists while the art historical archaeologists regarded the prehistorians as newcomers who threatened funds and opportunities. The foundation of ARCHON, a government subsidizing agency (one of the suboffices of the Netherlands Organization for the Advancement of Pure Scientific Research), in 1981 was a major step toward easing these tensions. Classical, prehistoric, and other archaeologists met on commissions where research proposals were judged, and this work fostered a mutual understanding. The economic slump of 1980s set ceilings on university budgets, and this fact also resulted in closer cooperation as the various groups shared the burdens of student training.

A History of Dutch
Archaeological Discussion

Most archaeologists are rather provincial in outlook, with little knowledge of problems elsewhere, and it is possible that nowhere has the universal ideology of positivism been achieved. Dutch archaeology is no exception, and historic-humanitarian ("culture historical") rather than scientific leanings have been dominant. In the Netherlands, the study of the relation of material culture to society has involved a study of the relation of the Dutch archaeological record with previous Dutch cultures, and those Dutch archaeologists who worked elsewhere (Middle or Far East, Mediterranean) have related to their particular problems elsewhere in the same way. This situation held true until at least the 1970s.

In addition to the general provincialism of Dutch archaeology, there is the scientific influence of politically dominant neighbors. Thus, when France was dominant during much of the nineteenth century, references to French archaeology were frequent, and texts were written in French. With Germany in the political ascendancy, references (if any to non-Dutch texts) were to German writings, German congresses and training programs were attended, German ideas were copied, dedications were to German scholars, and texts were sometimes published in the German language. After World War II, when England and then the United States dominated the political scene, former German references were gradually replaced by English ones, and the general orientation, especially in prehistoric texts, became Anglo-Saxon and there was an almost complete ignorance of other—for example, French, Italian, or Russian—developments.

In Dutch classical archaeology, with its art history orientation, the same trend is present although slightly attenuated. The number of English references surpassed that of German texts only in 1980, and in prehistoric archaeology that index changed around 1970. Perhaps the languages in which the Dutch research is reported is even more eloquent. Before World War II, more than 90 percent of articles were in Dutch; during the war, only Dutch texts were offered; after the war, the percentage dropped from 60 percent in the 1950s to 15 percent in the 1990s, and in the same years, German texts decreased from 25 percent to 5 percent, and English texts rose from 10 percent to over 60 percent.

Whenever ideas of non-Anglo-Saxon scholars are discussed in the Netherlands, they have been introduced through English translations, even though the study of at least two foreign languages is compulsory in the universities. Thus, Italian archaeologist Bianchi-Bandinelli's ideas are understood by only a handful of classical archaeologists, and French archaeologist ANDRÉ LEROI-GOURHAN and philosophers Foucault, Derrida, and Bourdieu only became known to prehistoric archaeologists when they were translated into English. The Russian archaeologist Leo Klejn is referenced only for his *Current Anthropology* contributions. Postmodernism is understood in its U.S./U.K. variant, with Ian Hodder and Michael Shanks as major leaders; Marxist (and other nondominant) archaeology are referenced rarely, if at all.

In Dutch mainstream prehistoric archaeology after the 1960s, the old (Childean) normative paradigm of archaeological culture as a recurrent set of archaeological traits was gradually replaced by a more anthropologically informed model of a systematically networked set of organizing subsystems of archaeological attributes (Bloemers and Van Dorp 1991; Slofstra 1994). A further development is visible in the Amsterdam Kempen Pioneer project, which began in the 1980s from an evolutionary and systems theoretical systems background but has evolved toward a historical anthropological framework. In other quarters, a history of science stance is evident. One of the research goals of the Leiden Pioneer project is the critical examination and analysis of the archaeological image of the Paleolithic period. Likewise, classical (now called Mediterranean) archaeology at Groningen is more fieldwork and less philological in its orientation, as are smaller, individual research undertakings at the major institutes throughout the country.

Archaeologists of provincial Rome are a possible exception, for their work has been less provincial than their name suggests. Early students (Reuvens, Holwerda) were well aware that the Netherlands was only a corner of the Roman Empire and that developments in that area should be related to more central regions. Of late, several studies connect the Roman colonization of the Low Countries to wider concerns of Roman home politics. For instance, Johan Bloemers, Willems, and Nico Roymans work on the interaction of the native population with the foreign occupation, has been informed by the world systems, dependency, and frontier theory ideas of Friedman, Galtung, and Wallerstein. The latter's work belongs to the post-1970 period and should be seen in that light (e.g., Brandt and Slofstra 1983; Roymans 1990).

There are some isolated examples of attempts at a larger problematic. Holwerda (1910, 1925) challenged the evolutionism of his day as well as "the typological method" along lines similar to those Hans Eggers was to develop later (Eggers 1958). He was ignored, and there were no arguments. A few years later, when immigration as a cause for the appearance of a new type of pot in medieval Frisia was questioned by a historian, Dutch archaeologists, including Van Giffen and Holwerda, closed ranks, thus stifling a potentially informative discussion (Heidinga and Verhoeven 1992). In classical archaeology, Snijder (1934) did notable work on the origins of artistry. In Middle Eastern studies, H. J. Franken opened up a new approach to pottery research by employing artisan potters on his staff as a critique of traditional typology development.

Apart from these abstract and almost ignored problems, the theoretical discussion of Dutch archaeological practice has been mainly concerned with observational theories (Hodder 1994). Reuvens sought better observation by the introduction of geodetic methods in the registration and description of field monuments. Holwerda introduced Schuchardt's ideas on soil traces and attempted to come to grips with settlement-sized archaeological sites, but his technical means were insufficient. Van Giffen transported plant anatomical methods of sectioning to archaeological fieldwork and invented the so-called quadrant method in order to obtain better insights into the structure of three-dimensional archaeological objects like barrows and even terps. The discussion about Holwerda's ill-fated dome barrows redirected the interpretation of traces of tree coffins in burial mounds. With the gradual rise to dominance of Van Giffen, theoretical interests shifted toward typochronology and ecological context, with vague but frequent references to cultural developments elsewhere, which were introduced by migrations and diffusion of traits.

The project of Beyen and his successors involving the meticulous analysis of Roman wall painting resulted in a typochronological scheme that contributed to the foundation and operation of a radiocarbon laboratory at the University of Groningen. Modderman's pioneering large-scale settlement excavations utilizing massive mechanical soil removal solved some of Holwerda's observational problems, but did not eventuate in the questioning of cultural historical assumptions. Similarly, excavations in the delta peat district—first by Modderman, then by Glasbergen, and later by Modderman's pupil Louwe Kooijmans—were aimed at sidestepping the effects of postdepositional erosion of archaeological vestiges common to regular, dry sites. Waterbolk's version of Van Giffen's culture area diagram (a kind of *longue durée*, Braudel's long-time scale, history of an area of a few square miles; Van Giffen 1947) originated as a method to wed time to change in the artifactual repertory. It remained in vogue in Dutch archaeology for many years, even with different epistemological props. In these larger ventures, ever more diverse phenomena were incorporated (ecology, locational analysis, historical traditions), and discussion thus moved on to more abstract levels.

In the 1970s, several young archaeologists produced less narrow texts: Bloemers and Willems and their work on Romanization have already been mentioned; Sander Van der Leeuw did comparative work on pottery production (Van der Leeuw and Pritchard 1984); and Jan Slofstra (1994) and Van de Velde argued for a social archaeology, the former with an evolutionist/functionalist emphasis (e.g., Brandt and Slofstra 1983), the latter being more structuralist (e.g., Van de Velde 1979). Later, two task groups ("pioneer programs") were set up, one to work on political developments in the Iron Age, Roman, and early medieval periods as a historical anthropological exercise, the other to attempt to integrate earth sciences with anthropological notions of the Paleolithic period of northern Europe.

No matter whether there were written records or not, archaeology has probably always been understood as ancient history in the Netherlands. Views regarding the means to write that history have varied as have the understandings of how such a history should read. A kings-and-battles approach is not feasible, as was clear even to Reuvens; however, a bourgeois emphasis on "high culture" (art, literature) has hampered Dutch archaeological discussion. A more general approach has recently been gaining ground. The means to read ancient history through archaeology have also varied considerably, with emphasis swinging repeatedly from objects toward context and back, and from observation to inferences—the increasing efficiency of soil removal (in the early years by crofters, in the twentieth century by vast numbers of unemployed people and later by mechanical equipment and technicians), which resulted in an ever-larger scale of field operations, has been utilized primarily by the empirically minded.

Finally, a word or two should be said about present archaeological practice in the Nether-lands. Theorizing (or general critical discussion) began when it became clear that there was no simple one-to-one correspondence between Dutch archaeological data and Dutch archaeological history—as was still assumed tacitly or openly in the major field projects of the 1970s and 1980s. Probably, it was a matter of reflexivity emerging from repression: the implications of fieldwork had been authoritatively taught to be straightforward ("This is no archaeology," a comment by an archaeologist working on DAVID L. CLARKE's *Analytical Archaeology,* may be considered typical for much of Dutch archaeology until recently). In its turn, the self-perceived peripheral nature of Dutch archaeology can be invoked. Archaeology was considered either a handmaiden of ancient history, a collector of objects for art history, or a consumer of the advances in ecological research, in each of which the numbers of scholars were many times larger than all the archaeologists combined.

In other words, the referent groups, or the intellectual debates to which Dutch archaeologists used to refer to, were external to the discipline. The archaeologists were not in a position to contribute substantially to the core debates nor were they in a position to establish a general discussion of their own. Only when the number of archaeologists had crossed a quantitative threshold (Van der Leeuw 1994), could internal discussion become effective: first, through the full implementation of a complete archaeological training program in 1986; second, when in archaeological academia distinction could be obtained by the additional deployment of a perceptibly different outlook; and third, through the fierce competition for junior jobs when too many students to be employed archaeologically took their degrees in the period after 1975. The discussion has been channeled through a yearly congress on theoretical archaeology and communicated to a wider audience through a semiannual journal, *Archaeological Dialogues,* which was first issued in 1994.

Some Other Dutch Archaeological Enterprises

Apart from provincial Roman, classical, and prehistoric archaeologists, there were others interested in other periods and other regions: Mesopotamia, Egypt, and, of course, the Dutch colonies in Southeast Asia and the Caribbean. Many of these scholars continued philological pursuits and were hardly interested in field archaeology, but several philologists have been and are active in excavation and survey programs.

In the Dutch East Indies (present-day Indonesia), an early pioneer was EUGENE DUBOIS (1858–1940), a physician and paleontologist who discovered the remains of *Homo erectus* (Pithecanthropus) on Java in 1891. Although work on these protohumans continues (by C. ter Haar, G. H. R. von Koenigswald, H. R. van Heekeren, and G.-J. Bartstra), the main interest of colonial archaeologists has been in the monumental remains of the classical Hindu period, most of them on Java (the Borobudur complex, the temples at Prambanan, etc.). These scholars came up with remarkably modern ideas on restoration as early as the 1910s and 1920s (especially N. J. Krom and Th. Van Erp; Bernet Kempers 1978). Some members of the Colonial Antiquities Service were sent to the Netherlands to be trained by Van Giffen (notably W. J. A. Willems and P. V. van Stein Callenfels), and they almost inevitably returned with prehistoric interests: for example, megaliths and the Hoabinh shell heaps. The Dutch did not set up a training program for prospective indigenous archaeologists.

After World War II and after Indonesian independence in 1949, the Archaeological Service of the Indonesian Republic was run by a Dutch planter and amateur archaeologist, H. R. van Heekeren, and he was succeeded by his Indonesian assistant and trainee, R. P. Soejono. Dutch interest in the archaeology of Indonesia has never been great. Bartstra of the University of Groningen has taken over the Paleolithic interests of Van Heekeren and has been cooperating with Soejono on the Pleistocene hominids in the archipelago since the 1970s.

In the Caribbean, the ethnologist J. P. B. de Josselin de Jong worked on Amerindian prehistory and did some small excavations on the islands of Aruba and Curaçao. Since the 1970s, was a more regular interest in the past of these Dutch colonies (including Surinam) on the part of archaeologists from Leiden University—

E. Boerstra, A. H. Versteeg, C. Hofman, M. Hoogiand, each having had appropriate field training by Modderman.

Of the Dutch archaeologists who have been active in the Middle East, the best known is perhaps HENRI FRANKFORT (1897–1954), an international figure who was born in Amsterdam. He worked with SIR WILLIAM MATTHEW FLINDERS PETRIE at the British School in Athens and with J. H. Breasted at the Chicago ORIENTAL INSTITUTE, where he organized the multidisciplinary Diyala project in Iraq while simultaneously holding a professorship of Middle Eastern archaeology at the University of Amsterdam (1932–1939). Later, Frankfort went to the Warburg Institute in London to become professor of the history of preclassical antiquity at London University.

Another well-known name in Mesopotamian archaeology is M. N. van Loon, who also worked in the Chicago Oriental Institute before he was appointed professor in Amsterdam (1972–1987). Excavations at Tell Hammam in Syria are continued by D. J. W. Meijer, who presently works at Leiden. H. J. Franken, a theologian turned archaeologist, worked in Palestine at Deir Alla (where work is now carried on by G. van der Kooij). Franken also collaborated with KATHLEEN KENYON at Jericho and Jerusalem and contributed to both the recording and the interpretation of tell stratigraphy and pottery studies by employing artisan potters in his institute. The Groningen BAI has also conducted investigations in this region (H. T. Waterbolk at Bouqras in Syria), as has the RMO (P. M. M. G. Akkermans at Tell Sabi Abyad in Syria; H. Schneider in Egypt).

Conclusions

This account has made it clear that Dutch archaeology is not primarily the development of Van Giffen's ideas but, rather, that he was part of an important phase of an ongoing tradition. From the very beginning of academic archaeology, even from the first recorded excavation in the Netherlands (Titia Brongersma and Ludolf Smids at the Borger megalith grave in 1685), auxiliary sciences have systematically been called on to aid in or back up interpretation.

Modern theorizing did not start with Van Giffen either, for several of his established predecessors (notably Reuvens and Holwerda) had been concerned with and active in discussions of field methodology. Indeed, Van Giffen's empiricism overran the more abstract problem of evolutionism and Holwerda's "typological method." It was not until the 1970s that any such discussion was attempted again, and by then, the size of the archaeological community had grown and the audience had finally become sufficient to sustain discussion on more theoretical levels. This all amounts to the description of a healthy archaeological field in the Netherlands, especially since the split between prehistoric and historic archaeology seems to have been replaced by deeper concerns.

Pieter van de Velde

References

Addink-Samplonius, M., ed. 1983. *Urnen delve—het opgravingsbedrijf artistiek bekeken.* Dieren.

Aurelius, C. 1517. *Die chronycke van Hollandt, Zeelandt ende Vrieslandt.* Leiden. Commonly known as *Divisie-Chronycke.*

Bakker, J. A. 1979. *The TRB West Group.* Amsterdam: Albert Egges van Giffen Instituut voor Prae- en Protohistorie.

Bernet Kempers, August J. 1978. *Herstel in eigen waarde—monumentenzorg in Indonesië.* Zutphen: Walburg Pers.

Bloemers, Johan H. F., and T. van Dorp 1991. *Pre-& protohistorie van de Lage Landen.* Netherlands, De Haan: Open Universiteit.

Boersma, Johannes S., et al. 1976. *Festoen.* Groningen: H. D. Tjeenk Willink; Bussum: Fibula-Van Dishoeck.

Bogaers, J. E., W. Glasbergen, P. Glazema, and H. T. Waterbolk, eds. 1959. *Honderd eeuwen Nederland.* Special issue, *Antiquity and Survival* 11, no. 5–6.

Brandt, Roel, and Jan Slofstra, eds. 1983. *Roman and Native in the Low Countries.* Oxford, England: BAR International 184.

Brongers, A. 1989. "Giffen, A. E. van" and "Holwerda, J. H." In *Biografisch woordenboek van Nederland.* Ed. J. Charite. Gravenhage: Nijhoff.

Brunsting, H. 1992. *Oudheden met een verleden.* Privately printed.

Byvanck, Alexander W. 1941. *De voorgeschiedenis van Nederland.* Leiden.

Byvanck-Quaries van Ufford, L. 1984. "De arche-

ologie aan de Leidse Universiteit (van eind 19e tot midden 20e eeuw)." In *Een universiteit herleeft,* 125–139. Ed. W. Otterspeer. Leiden.

Daniel, G. 1981. *A Short History of Archaeology.* London: Thames and Hudson.

Eggers, Hans J. 1958. *Einführung in die Vorgeschichte.* Munich: R. Piper.

Elzinga, G. J. 1975. "Rondom de 'Vikingschat van Winsum.'" *De Vrije Fries* 55: 82–122.

Halbertsma, H. 1992. *Van Sneek naar Amersfoort: Hherinneringen van een oudheidkundige.* Utrecht: Matrijs.

Heidinga, H. A., and A. A. A. Verhoeven. 1992. "Handel en wandel in de vroege middeleeuwen." In *Rotterdam Papers VII,* 1–6. Ed. A. Carmiggelt. Rotterdam.

Hodder, Ian 1994. "The Dutch Experience Experienced from Britain." *Archaeological Dialogues* 1, no. 1: 36–38.

Hodder, Ian, ed. 1991. *Archaeological Theory in Europe: The Last Three Decades.* London: Routledge.

Hodges, R. 1990. "Glyn Daniel: The Great Divide and the British Contribution to Italian Archaeology." *Accordia Research Papers* 1: 83–94.

Holwerda, Jan Hendrick. 1910. *De ontwikkeling der Praehistorisch-Romeinsche Archaeologie.* Leiden.

———. 1925. *Nederland's vroegste geschiedenis.* 2d. ed. Amsterdam: S. L. van Looy.

Hoogland, M. 1993. "The Setting." In *In Search of the Native Population of Pre-Columbian Saba,* 5–25. Ed. C. L. Hofman. Leiden: Rijksuniversiteit te Leiden.

Louwe Kooijmans, L. P. 1976. *Archaeologie in Nederland: Het hoe en waarom van opgraven.* Hilversum.

Maarleveld, Th. J., and E. P. Pieper 1983. "Merkwaardige prehistorische beenfragmenten, nogmaals bekeken." *Oudheidkundige Mededelingen* 64: 229–243.

Meijer, D. J. W. 1986. "De archeologie van West-Azie." In *Driehonderd jaar Oosterse Talen in Amsterdam,* 74–80. Ed. J. de Roos, A. Schippers, and J. W. Wesselius. Amsterdam.

Pars, A. 1697. *Catti aborigines Batavorum, dat is: De Katten, De Voorouders der Batavieren.* Leiden.

Picardt, Johan. 1660. *Korte beschryvinge van eenige vergetene en verborgene antiquiteten.* Groningen.

Pleyte, W. 1877–1903. *Nederlandsche Oudheden van de vroegste tijden tot Karel den Groote.* 3 vols. Leiden.

Renfrew, C. 1980. "The Great Tradition versus the Great Divide: Archaeology as Anthropology?" *American Journal of Archaeology* 84: 287–298.

Reuvens, C. J. C. 1818: *De laudibus archaeologiae.* Leiden.

Roymans, Nico. 1990. *Tribal Societies in Northern Gaul.* Amsterdam: University of Amsterdam.

Sarfatij, H. 1972. "Conversations about the Pre- and Protohistory of the State Service for Archaeological Investigations, Amersfoort." *Berichten ROB* 22: 73–79.

Slofstra, Jan. 1994. "Recent Developments in Dutch Archaeology." *Archaeological Dialogues* 1, no. 1: 9–33.

Snijder, G. A. S. 1934. "Das Wesen der kretischen Kunst: Versuch einer Deutung." *Jahrbuch des Deutschen Archäologische Instituts* 317–338.

Trigger, B. G. 1989. *A History of Archaeological Thought.* Cambridge: Cambridge University Press.

Van der Leeuw, Sander E. 1994. "Whispers from the Context of Real Life: Towards Pluriformity in Archaeology." *Archaeological Dialogues* 1, no. 2: 133–164.

Van der Leeuw, Sander E., and Alison C. Pritchard, eds. 1984. *The Many Dimensions of Pottery.* Amsterdam: Universiteit van Amsterdam.

Van der Velde, P. 1979. *On Bandkeramik Social Structure.* Leiden.

Van der Woud, A. 1990. *De Bataafse hut: Verschuivingen in het beeld van de geschiedenis (1750–1850).* Amsterdam: Meulenhoff.

Van Es, W. A. 1972. "The Origin and Development of the State Service for Archaeological Investigations in the Netherlands." *Berichten ROB* 22: 17–71.

Van Es, W. A., et al. 1973. *Archeologie en historie.* Bussum: Brunsting festschrift.

Van Gelder, H. E., P. Glazema, G. A. Bontekoe, H. Halbertsma, and W. Glasbergen, eds. 1947. *Een kwart eeuw oudheidkundig bodemonderzoek in Nederland.* Meppel: Boon. A. E. Van Giffen festschrift.

Van Giffen, Albert E. 1925. *De hunebedden in Nederland.* 3 vols. Utrecht.

———. 1930. *Die Bauart der Einzelgräber: Beitrag our Kenntnis der älteren individuellen Grabhügelstrukturen in den Niederlanden.* 2 vols. Leipzig: C. Kabitzsch.

———. 1947. *Oudheidkundige perspectieven: In het bijzonder ten aanzien van de vaderlandsche prae- en protohistorie.* Groningen/Batavia.

Waterbolk, H. T. 1973. "A. E. van Giffen, 1884–1973." *Palaeohistoria* 15: 7–34. Obituary; includes curriculum vitae and full bibliography.

———. 1977. "Albert Egges van Giffen, 1884–1973." In *Jaarboek van de Maatschappij der Nederlandse Letterkunde te Leiden 1975–1976,* 123–153.

Westendorp, N. 1815. "Verhandeling." In *Letter: En oudheidkundige verhandelingen van de Hollandsche Maatschappij der Wetenschappen te Haarlem,* vol. 1.

Willems, W. J. H. 1986. *Romans and Batavians: A Regional Study in the Dutch Eastern River Area.* Amsterdam.

Zadoks-Josephus Jitta, A. N. 1938. *Antieke cultuur in beeld.* Antwerpen: De Sikkel.

New Zealand: Historical Archaeology

Culture contact, extractive industry, and urban domesticity are themes that dominate the archaeological history of New Zealand since 1769 when European exploration brought New Zealand into the historic era. Originating in the 1920s, public and academic interest in the field of historical archaeology in New Zealand has grown dramatically since the mid-1970s.

Archaeological interest in the prehistoric Maori occupants of the country developed within a few decades of the founding of the first European settlement in 1792, but it was almost 120 years before attention turned to the post-contact period. The earliest work focused on sites from the mid-nineteenth-century wars between the Maori and the colonists, the most important being Elsdon Best's description of European redoubts, stockades, and blockhouses in the Wellington district (Best 1921) and his analysis of the manner in which Maori *pa* (earthwork fortifications) adapted to the introduction of muskets and artillery bombardment (Best 1927). These and other early works (*see* Smith 1990) concentrated on the description of surface features and reconstruction from historical sources rather than excavation. These works were also driven by the enthusiasm of individual scholars rather than by an institutionally based concern for the sites or the material culture of the historic period. Once the attention of those scholars turned elsewhere, historical archaeology in New Zealand became dormant.

The first excavation of a historic period site took place in 1959 at Orongo Bay, Gisborne, and was of a nineteenth-century Maori occupation overlying prehistoric deposits (Green and Pullar 1960). This project was followed by investigation of the British army's mid-nineteenth-century Paremata Barracks just north of Wellington (Davis 1963), but most excavations during the 1960s were on Maori sites (Smith 1991). Many of these were investigated as part of projects led by archaeologists Les Groube in the Bay of Islands and Peter Coutts in Fiordland. These projects were concerned with documenting and explaining the processes of change in early historic Maori culture brought about by contact with Europeans. However a substantial number of the Maori sites were excavated by Trevor Hosking as part of the Tongariro Power Project, the first major development project in New Zealand to involve archaeological mitigation work. The high proportion of historic sites encountered during this project was one of the factors that lead the New Zealand Archaeological Association in 1966 to modify its national site recording scheme to include historic as well as prehistoric sites. With the major emphasis of this period on indigenous responses to culture contact, sites of immigrant cultures received minimal attention. Excavations were restricted to two examples of agricultural features and an armed constabulary redoubt while other research included the first recording of sites connected with the gold-mining industry.

During the early 1970s, attention began turning to the sites and material culture of the European colonists, and there were investigations of mission stations, whaling stations, early farmhouses, and sites of the forestry industry. However, the most significant developments took place in the second half of the 1970s when there was dramatic growth in the number of both excavations and publications in historical archaeology. One stimulus was the Historic Places Act of 1975, which gave protection to all archaeological sites 100 years or more in age. This act provided the means by which developers could be made to pay for site investigations and required the government-funded Historic Places Trust to take greater cognizance of historic sites than it had previously.

Two landmark projects in the development of New Zealand historical archaeology also be-

gan at this time. In 1977, archaeologist Nigel Prickett commenced a program of survey and excavation of fortifications associated with the Taranaki wars of the 1860s and 1870s (Prickett 1981). This was the first substantial attempt to excavate a coherent set of European sites and to describe and analyze the resulting material, and it also set out to place the Taranaki evidence within the broader contexts of imperial expansion and developments in the technology of warfare.

In the same year, archaeologist Neville Ritchie began the archaeological component of the Clutha Valley Development Project. Continuing for ten years, this project contributed the first detailed survey of one of New Zealand's major historic gold-mining areas as well as excavations at some twenty-five historic period sites and a smaller number of prehistoric ones. These investigations focused on the archaeological remains of Chinese gold miners in the area and produced detailed descriptions of their living sites, material culture, and diet, which permitted assessment of the conservatism and adaptations of this discrete ethnic group (Ritchie 1986). This project is by far the largest yet undertaken in New Zealand, involving almost 20 percent of all the historic period sites excavated up to 1990 and just over 20 percent of all the publications on historical archaeology (Ritchie 1990).

With those two projects came an increasing institutional involvement in historical archaeology. Prickett conducted most of his research from the Taranaki Museum while Ritchie was employed by the Historic Places Trust and funded by the Ministry of Works and Development. Both men developed their research into doctoral dissertations, at Auckland and Otago universities respectively, and some of their excavations were used as field training schools for students from those institutions. However, apparent resistance from the academic community delayed the introduction of formal university courses in historical archaeology until the late 1980s.

The first half of the 1980s was the single most productive period so far in New Zealand historical archaeology, in large part because of the continuing activity of the Clutha Valley Development Project. Although there was some diversification into excavations of industrial sites and agricultural sites, and some for the cultural tourism industry, the major areas of growth were in the analysis of site content and site recording. Thorough descriptions of excavated assemblages, along with detailed analyses of fauna, various artifact classes, and site features make up almost a third of the published literature in the period (Smith 1990).

An even greater proportion of the literature reports on surveys of the distribution, form, and features of historic period sites in specific areas. These surveys are overwhelmingly dominated by gold-mining sites, reflecting in part the significance of this extractive industry in New Zealand's economic and social life, from the alluvial gold rushes of the 1860s to the decline of hard-rock mining in the early decades of the twentieth century. However, this interest also reflects the growth of public archaeology. Funding of historical archaeology by government agencies had its origins in the late 1960s, but it was another decade before it became a routine component of government activities. By the early 1980s, nearly 70 percent of all site surveys were being undertaken by or for two government departments, the Forest Service and the Department of Lands and Survey. The main interest of those two departments concerned the management of their own lands, which included a considerable proportion of New Zealand's main gold-mining areas.

There was a significant change in focus toward urban historical archaeology in the second half of the 1980s. Prior to 1986, there had been only four excavations on historic period sites in urban areas, but over the next four years more than half of all excavations were on urban sites, largely within the city of Auckland during a period of extensive urban redevelopment. Most of the excavations were funded by developers and undertaken by the Regional Archaeology Unit, which was established by Susan Bulmer of the Historic Places Trust and after public service restructuring in 1987 became part of the Department of Conservation. These excavations were focused on sites from the period between 1840, when the city was founded, and 1865, when the colony's capital was shifted to Wellington. Excavated sites included major public buildings such as the original Parliament buildings and the first courthouse and jail, hotels, and early industrial sites as well as the cottages and houses of early residents (Macready 1991). Artifactual remains from these sites have derived predominantly from residential refuse and provide insight into early urban domestic life.

A decline in urban redevelopment by the end of the 1980s and the rising price of gold have seen the emphasis in fieldwork shift again from the urban sector to the mining industry. However, with the introduction of university courses in historical archaeology by Ian Smith at Otago and Rod Clough at Auckland, greater continuity has been maintained in research into the broader themes of culture contact, extractive industry, and urban domesticity.

Ian Smith

References

Best, E. 1921. "Old Redoubts, Blockhouses, and Stockades of the Wellington District." *Transactions of the New Zealand Institute* 53: 14–28.

———. 1927. *The Pa Maori.* Dominion Museum Bulletin no. 6. New Zealand.

Davis, S. 1963. "A Note on the Excavation of the Barracks at Paremata." In *The Paremata Barracks,* pp. 25–29. Ed. R. I. M. Burnett. New Zealand: Historic Places Trust Bulletin no. 4.

Green, R. C., and W. A. Pullar. 1960. "Excavations at Orongo Bay, Gisborne." *Journal of the Polynesian Society* 69, no. 4: 332–353.

Macready, S. 1991. "A Review of Urban Historical Archaeology in Auckland to 1990." *Australian Journal of Historical Archaeology* 9: 14–20.

Prickett, N. 1981. "The Archaeology of a Military Frontier: Taranaki, New Zealand, 1860–1881." Ph.D. dissertation, University of Auckland.

Ritchie, N. A. 1986. "Archaeology and History of the Chinese in Southern New Zealand during the Nineteenth Century." Ph.D. dissertation, University of Otago.

———. 1990. "The Clutha Valley Archaeological Project 1977–1987: A Summary Report." *Archaeology in New Zealand* 33, no. 1: 4–20.

Smith, I. W. G. 1990. "Historical Archaeology in New Zealand: A Review and Bibliography." *New Zealand Journal of Archaeology* 12: 85–119.

———. 1991. "The Development of Historical Archaeology in New Zealand, 1921–1990." *Australian Journal of Historical Archaeology* 9: 6–13.

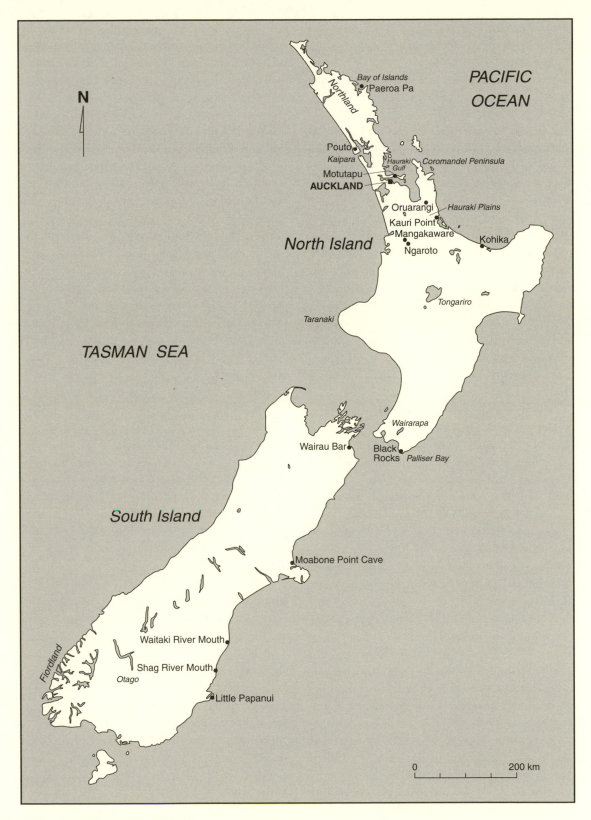

N

PACIFIC
OCEAN

Bay of Islands
Paeroa Pa

Northland

Pouto
Kaipara
Hauraki
Gulf
Coromandel Peninsula
Motutapu
AUCKLAND

Oruarangi
Hauraki Plains
Kauri Point
Mangakaware
Kohika
North Island
Ngaroto

Tongariro

Taranaki

TASMAN SEA

Wairarapa

Wairau Bar
Black
Rocks
Palliser Bay

South Island

Moabone Point Cave

Waitaki River Mouth

Shag River Mouth
Fiordland
Otago
Little Papanui

0   200 km

Archaeological Sites in New Zealand

New Zealand: Prehistoric Archaeology
Early Problems: 1769–1950
Natural History: 1769–1892

Initial research into the presence of the Maori in New Zealand was carried out by historians, philosophers, and scientists who studied aboriginal peoples as an aspect of natural history. In 1770, English explorer Captain James Cook and English botanist Joseph Banks noted similarities between the New Zealand Maori and the inhabitants of other South Seas Islands and concluded that both had a common origin to the west (Beaglehole 1962). By the time of his third voyage in 1777, Cook was able to discuss the distinctive features of Maori material culture (fortified villages, carved canoes, weapons, and ornaments) and the dissimilarities between Maori and eastern Polynesian cultures, such as the absence of the monumental stone *marae* (temples comprising a rectangular enclosure with a stone platform) he had seen in Tahiti (Reed and Reed 1969).

The presence of the giant ratite *Dinornithiformes,* or moa, in New Zealand was demonstrated by Richard Owen on the eve of the signing of the Treaty of Waitangi (Owen 1839), and knowledge that the extinct moa occurred in human habitation sites followed shortly after. Scientific demonstration of the association of moa and human remains came from the work of the German-trained geologist Julius von Haast (1872), though other scientists such as Walter Mantell and James Hector were also active at the same time.

Through the works of English geologist SIR CHARLES LYELL (1869), Haast was influenced by John Lubbock's (1865) division of human cultural development into the Paleolithic period, characterized by crudely chipped stone artifacts and extinct mammals such as the mastodon, and the more recent Neolithic period, containing polished stone implements. Haast assumed that the moa remains from human encampments in the South Island were of Pleistocene age and that the moas had been finally exterminated by a Paleolithic race who used only chipped stone implements. He initially identified this race with the Australian Aborigines but later accepted that its members were of Polynesian origin. He denied that these moa hunters were the ancestors of the Neolithic Maori, as the latter manufactured polished stone implements and used nephrite (greenstone), indicating that they had reached a higher state of civilization.

Haast's views were challenged by Alexander McKay, whom Haast had employed to excavate Moabone Point Cave near Christchurch, New Zealand. McKay (1874) noted that moa bones and polished stone adzes occurred together and argued that this was proof that the moa hunters had a technology similar to that of the Maori. He concluded that whether or not the Maori had been responsible for the extinction of the moas depended on how old the sites were as well as on the date of first arrival of the Maori. Basing his estimate on the length of time required to produce the Maori population present in 1769, McKay suggested the Maori had probably been in New Zealand for about 1,350 years and furthermore that their first impact on the country was the extermination of the moa.

Traditional History: 1892–1950

The POLYNESIAN SOCIETY was created in New Zealand in 1892, and its formation marked a split between the humanities and the natural sciences following the reorganization of science into specialized disciplines. Most of the research at the end of the nineteenth century and in the first half of the twentieth was carried out by a small number of professionals in museums or else was done on a part-time basis by interested individuals working for private firms or in public service. Although the Polynesian colonization of the Pacific archipelago was diffusionist by necessity, the study of Maori origins retained other aspects of the older natural history approach. In particular, changes in culture were invariably interpreted as the result of racial replacement. Innovative peoples were seen as emanating from a center as waves that left isolated peoples on the margins as the embodiment of these primordial events.

The idea that the existing Maori were the product of a mixture of darker Melanesians and a lighter race goes back to French explorer Julien-Marie Crozet's observations of 1772

(Ling Roth 1891) and to naturalist J. R. Forster on Cook's second voyage (Sorrenson 1979). Sir George Grey's collections of Maori traditions contained references to the presence of an aboriginal people, thought to be represented by the contemporary Chatham Islanders, who were displaced by a later migration from "Hawaiki," the original homeland of the Maori. Not all contemporary writers, however, accepted the idea that Maori oral legends could provide a reliable historical account (see Travers 1871).

The discovery of human artifacts with the extinct moa added credence to the idea of a pre-Maori population, and a sort of scientific seal of approval was given by the scholar S. Percy Scott (1893) who made an osteological comparison of Maori and (Chatham Island) Moriori craniums. He concluded that the existing Maori race was the result of a mixture of Melanesian and Polynesian types with the Melanesian or Papuan characteristics being greatest in the north of the North Island and least on the South Island.

The various threads of evidence bearing on these questions—Maori traditions, physical anthropology and archaeology, and a chronology provided by genealogical dating—were brought together in works of Percy Smith (1921) and Elsdon Best (1915) published in the *Journal of the Polynesian Society*. Smith created an elaborate migration scenario that began with the discovery of an uninhabited New Zealand by Polynesian chief Kupe I in A.D. 925 and the arrival of its first inhabitants a generation later. Subsequent voyages by chiefs Toi and Kupe II culminated in the arrival of "the great fleet" consisting of Tainui, Arawa, Takitimu, and Mataatua canoes in 1350. Smith and Best identified the first inhabitants as Maruiwi or Moriori, a dark-skinned people of mixed Melanesian and Polynesian ancestry who were expelled to the Chatham Islands by the later Polynesian immigrants. Both authors thought that their ultimate Polynesian origins were Vedic or Aryan.

It is fashionable to dismiss the assembling of Maori traditions into a comprehensive historical account as the product of inept Pakeha (a New Zealander of European origin) scholarship (Sorrenson 1979), but it was the Maori scholar Te Rangi Hiroa (Sir Peter Buck) who added to their popularity in works such as *Vikings of the Sunrise* (1938) and *The Coming of the Maori* (1949). Buck made use of both the culture-area and the age-area theories to organize his data. In his accounts, Buck's Polynesians came from Asia via Micronesia, and it was from the latter that they settled the central Polynesian area of Samoa and the Society Islands, known in traditions as Hawaii. From this center, new developments appeared and spread to more distant areas, and as a result of overpopulation, marginal POLYNESIA, including New Zealand, was settled from this hub.

Buck accepted the traditional accounts of earlier and later waves of migration but substituted an economic advantage, the possession of domestic animals and crops, for Smith's racial one. Mimicking World War I terminology, Buck described the second wave of Polynesian migration as the main body of "the Polynesian expeditionary force," arguing that the food plants and domestic animals were first developed and tested in the Society Islands and then carried to other parts of Polynesia. It was these domesticates, including the sweet potato, brought from South America by a Polynesian "unknown hero," that allowed the full flower of Polynesian society to bloom. In the *Coming of the Maori*, Buck used Smith's and Best's chronology of settlement, linking the earliest immigrants with the moa hunters. The final settlement period was the time of the great fleet migration (A.D. 1350) when the *kumara* ("sweet potato") and other food plants were successfully transferred from Polynesia to New Zealand.

The weakest link in Smith's and Best's scheme of racial replacement was the lack of any ethnological or archaeological evidence in its favor. This lack was explored by Henry Skinner, who received his ethnological training at Cambridge University from anthropologist Alfred C. Haddon. Skinner quickly revised his initial conclusion that the differences between a northern cultural area, where Maori art was curvilinear, and a southern cultural area, defined by more rectilinear art forms, might be explained by waves of immigrants, the first being from the west Pacific and a later wave from central and eastern Polynesia (Skinner 1921). Subsequently, Skinner maintained the Polynesian identity of all the prehistoric inhabitants of New Zealand. In 1924, Skinner drew attention to the presence of tanged adzes in New Zealand, the Chatham Islands, and Polynesia and also in those areas of Southeast Asia where Austronesian languages are spoken. In so doing, he substantiated his conclusions of the previous year (Skinner 1923) that the closest relationship of the Moriori culture (Chatham Islands) and the southern culture of the Maori was with eastern Polynesia.

Skinner's insights were confirmed by ethnographer Edwin G. Burrows's (1938) differentiation of Polynesia into a western cultural block (Samoa, Tonga, and neighboring islands) and eastern Polynesia, which joined the Society Islands with Hawaii, the Marquesas Islands, Easter Island, and New Zealand. Skinner employed the untrained but enthusiastic David Teviotdale as his archaeological collaborator, and Teviotdale's collections of tanged adzes, fishhooks, bone and stone ornaments, and greenstone artifacts clearly demonstrated the association of Maori artifacts with moas at sites such as Waitaki, Shag River, and Little Papanui (Teviotdale 1932).

Culture-Historical Studies: 1950–1965

The excavation of thirty-six human burials at Wairau Bar, near Blenheim on the South Island, between 1939 and 1952 represents the introduction of culture-historical archaeology to New Zealand. Accompanying the human remains were grave goods, including parts of moa skeletons, moa egg "waterbottles," tanged adzes, fishhooks, and necklaces of whale ivory "reels" and imitation whale teeth. The site also incorporated housing, areas for stone working, and cooking and midden dumping areas.

ROGER DUFF (1950) reformulated the ideas of Haast, Smith, Buck, and Skinner to argue that New Zealand's prehistory could be divided into an early, or moa hunter, period of Maori culture, and a later period of Maori culture. Duff defined Maori culture in terms of the observations of Cook and the earliest ethnographers. He was, however, unable to accurately date the Wairau Bar burials or to demonstrate the chronological and stratigraphical relationships between his two culture periods. Consequently, Duff made use of the presence of tanged adzes and the age-area concepts of centers of innovation and marginal survival to argue that Wairau Bar dated from the earliest period of Hawaiki dispersals. Second, he used Smith's chronology of the discovery of New Zealand in A.D. 950 and the arrival of the domestic plants kumara, taro, yams, and gourds with the great fleet in A.D. 1350 to both date and explain the development of the later Maori culture.

In 1955, Duff was able to announce a C-14 date of A.D. 1150 for Wairau Bar (Duff 1956). His predictions regarding the nature of the early period of eastern Polynesian culture were confirmed by Kenneth Emory and Yoshihiko Sinoto of Hawaii's Bishop Museum, who in 1964 discovered human burials at Maupiti in the Society Islands, which were associated with whale tooth pendants, fish lure shanks, and tanged adzes, items almost identical to those recovered in New Zealand.

Ideas of adaptation to the temperate New Zealand environment continued to run alongside ideas of migrations and racial or economic replacement as explanations for the development of the distinctive Maori material culture. Cook thought that the Maori houses reflected the cool New Zealand environment while Skinner (1924) explained divergences between Maori and eastern Polynesian art and culture as a response to the move from the tropics. Buck (1949) similarly maintained that local developments were responsible for the most distinctive Maori cultural items, including warm houses, clothing, and kumara storage pits. The use of large canoes and carved houses was stimulated by the availability of large trees while fortified pa, warfare, and curvilinear art forms were a response to the tribal rivalry and competition that took place after the arrival of the great fleet. Finally, Duff (1947) explained the terraced pa, the tangless rounded 2B adze, and greenstone ornaments, which he used to define his Maori period in terms of population growth and the innovative use of local materials.

The arrival of JACK GOLSON at Auckland Uni-

Terraced volcanic cone, Mt. Wellington, Auckland (Department of Anthropology, University of Auckland)

versity in 1954 marked a shift from individual-to university-based research following the expansion of tertiary education in New Zealand. Such expansions occurred first between 1950 and 1960 and again during the early 1970s. Golson worked in three ways to create a firm institutional and intellectual base for the discipline of archaeology in New Zealand. First, through the establishment of the New Zealand Archaeological Association, Golson reincorporated archaeology into the natural sciences (Golson 1956). Second, he (1959) used VERE GORDON CHILDE's concept of archaeological cultures to redefine Duff's periods into an archaic phase of New Zealand eastern Polynesian culture followed by the classic Maori phase of New Zealand eastern Polynesian culture. Third, Golson embarked on a program of field recording and excavation to test both the validity of these two phases and the explanations for their differences. He sought to drive a clear division between the traditional explanations for cultural change put forward by Percy Smith and later by Roger Duff (racial replacement, economic replacement, and the great fleet) and archaeological explanations by restating them as a choice between diffusion, on the one hand, and local adaptation, on the other (Golson 1960, 1965).

The initial results of Golson's program were promising. First, after 1960, conferences of the New Zealand Archaeological Association (NZAA) were included as part of the New Zealand Science Congress and, in 1967, the NZAA became a member society of the Royal Society of New Zealand. Second, the NZAA site-recording scheme, set up with ROGER C. GREEN, has proved to be an essential tool for research and heritage management more than thirty-five years. Third, a major blow against the traditional accounts of the past was struck with the publication of Andrew Sharp's *Ancient Voyagers in the Pacific* in 1956. Sharp produced considerable evidence to argue that the settlement of Polynesia was the result of accidental voyages by isolated canoes rather than by any planned and systematic process of colonization as the great fleet traditions demanded. Golson did not directly attack the use of Maori traditions but separated the two theories of colonization as distinctive sources of knowledge of the past. In so doing, he successfully portrayed archaeology as the more reliable and scientific of the two. Finally, Golson and associated workers were able to define the content and characteristics of the archaic phase on the North Island of New Zealand through excavations on the Coromandel Peninsula and Motutapu Island.

Other aspects of Golson's program were less successful. The contribution of the natural sciences to the problem of chronology has been mixed, and the utility of using tree rings, tephrachronology, pollen analysis, and obsidian DATING has yet to fully be proved. Even C-14 dating, which elsewhere has largely replaced artifact assemblages as a way of defining the space and time correlates of archaeological phenomena, has had limited usefulness in New Zealand (Shawcross 1969).

The precise definition of the classic Maori phase, the most recent period of New Zealand prehistory, has continued to be problematic. Owing to changes in Maori artifact curation (preservation of stone tools by the Maori) and site layout, the majority of late period archaeological sites in New Zealand (fortified pa, agricultural complexes of storage pits and terraces, and SHELL MIDDENS) contain few if any artifacts. Consequently, Golson, like his predecessors, had to rely on museum collections and ethnographic descriptions of Maori life to fill the role usually taken by artifact assemblages in the definition of cultures. His espousal of the processes of adaptation as a dynamic explanation for the differences between Maori culture and cultures elsewhere in Polynesia, and for the changes in Maori material culture over time, was at odds with his division of the New Zealand past into two distinct and static phases. Finally, Golson's excavation of a late period ring-ditch pa at Kauri Point also proved to be inconclusive and revealed a complex construction sequence that did not fit well within the archaic/classic framework.

The archaeology of New Zealand's South Island better suited the requirements of the culture-historical approach than did that of the North Island. On the South Island, which lies beyond the climatic limits of tropical Polynesian food crops, there are multiple early sites defined in terms of a distinctive archaic artifact assemblage (tanged adzes, harpoon points, ornaments, and one-piece fishhooks), and they often have cooking and refuse dumping areas that contain moa remains. Following the demise of the moa, the hunting and foraging economy of the South Island was reorganized to concentrate on shellfish, fish, and sea birds. Finally, archaeo-

logical and ethnographic evidence document the intrusion of classic culture from the North Island in terms of people, ideas, and artifacts—plain adzes, composite fishhooks, nephrite ornaments, bone flutes, toggles, and defended sites—(Anderson 1982). The South Island evidence points to the agricultural North Island for the origin of classic Maori culture, and this clear indication (of diffusion) made the difficulty of archaeologically defining the classic phase on the North Island even greater.

Using evidence for the presence of agriculture on the earliest North Island archaic sites, Golson and English archaeologist Peter Gathercole (1962) argued against Duff's and Buck's idea that the change from moa hunter to Maori was also an economic transformation from hunting to agriculture. Golson, however, despite his rejection of Duff's great fleet hypothesis in favor of local development as the preferred explanation for culture change in New Zealand, still set himself the task of archaeologically documenting the moa hunter to the Maori sequence. This task was all the more remarkable because (in one guise or another) this sequence was formulated prior to the advent of culture-historical archaeology in New Zealand. Duff borrowed the conception from Buck's *The Coming of the Maori* (1949), which was first published in 1925 but has antecedents in the works of Elsdon Best and Percy Smith and even back to the eighteenth century (Sorrenson 1979, 13).

Dissatisfaction with the division of New Zealand archaeology into the archaic and classic phases led to a number of reformulations. Drawing together the ideas of Richard Beardsley et al. (1956) on community patterning, paleobotanist Doug Yen's (1961) sequence for the introduction of *kumara* to the cool New Zealand environment and paleo-geographer K. B. Cumberland's (1962) scenario of recent climatic deterioration enabled Green (1963) to subdivide the archaic and classic into early, middle, and late phases.

Green's six phases, which extended into the postcontact era, attempted to document an independent evolutionary progression for New Zealand. This effort followed ROBERT J. BRAIDWOOD in advancing through stages from dis-

Pa defended by a ditch and bank system, Kauri Point, Katikati (Department of Anthropology, University of Auckland)

persed hunter-forager (moa hunting) camps and low populations through to nuclear-centered pa with a large population supported by agriculture based on the storage of seed *kumara*. After his work encountered some criticism, Green (1974) largely abandoned his finer subdivisions of the archaic and classic but retained the explanatory scenario of an adaptation to deteriorating environmental circumstances, now humanly induced, as the motive behind the shift to systematic agriculture.

Arguing that the extent of economic and cultural change during the prehistoric period had been overestimated, Leslie Groube (1964, 1967, 1969) launched an ambitious attack on the findings of Duff, Golson, and Green. Groube argued that the definition of Duff's Maori period and that of Golson's classic phase were compromised by the use of nineteenth-century ethnographic accounts, which masked the extent of change that closely followed the arrival of the Europeans. Noting that the least change had occurred on the South Island, the area with the greatest climatic contrast with island Polynesia, Groube suggested that the later Maori culture was little different than that introduced by the initial Polynesian settlers. The changes in adze forms and ornaments, on which the definition of the archaic and classic largely depended, were the result of stylistic rather than functional changes. He also argued that distinctive greenstone *hei-tiki* (small ornaments with a humanlike form), carved storage houses, and decorated meeting houses reflected post-European alterations in wealth, trading opportunities, and the availability of iron carving tools. Using KWANG-CHI CHANG's (1958) division of settlements into households and communities to test Green's model of evolution, Groube concluded that there was little evidence for a change from simple to complex settlements in New Zealand.

The attack on the archaeological credibility of Golson's archaic and classic phases was effective, and it, together with the realization that the majority of North Island archaeological sites contained few if any portable artifacts that would enable the employment of the culture-historic method (Golson 1965; Terrell 1965), pushed New Zealand archaeologists to examine the archaeological record to see if other phenomena might do the job. Golson (1957), but most particularly Green (1963), advocated the use of nonartifactual evidence to establish the space and time coordinates of sites and prehistoric social entities. In quick succession, flaked stone artifacts (Shawcross 1964b), storage pits (Parker 1962; Shawcross 1964a), and shell middens (Davidson 1967) were tested and found to be poor indicators of either chronological periods or regional styles.

Additional attention was given to archaeological sites where artifacts might be better preserved, in particular swamp sites—such as Ngaroto (Shawcross 1968), Kauri Point (Shawcross (1976), Mangakaware (Bellwood 1978), and Kohika (Irwin 1975)—or artificial pa constructed out of shell in low-lying areas such as Oruarangi on the Hauraki Plains (Shawcross and Terrell 1966). The artifacts from these sites have contributed to the knowledge of artifact and carving styles, and they have proved to have an antiquity that has undercut many of Groube's prescriptions for the classic phase. However, the specialized and rare nature of these sites has precluded the extension of these findings to other areas (Furey 1996).

Much attention has also been given to purifying the ethnographic and archaeological record of European influences in order to define a pristine classic Maori culture, an approach criticized by Stuart Bedford (1996). Artifact collections and observations made by the earliest visitors to New Zealand have been studied in detail (Salmond 1991; Shawcross 1970a), and some research has concentrated on archaeological sites known to have been occupied at the time of first contact such as Paeroa pa, which was mapped by Marion du Fresne in 1772 and destroyed by his men after du Fresne's death. In almost every case, either the historically documented phase could not be identified or else it had been destroyed by subsequent occupation (Groube 1965).

Studies of Process: 1965–1999

Because of the short time depth of New Zealand prehistory, culture-historical archaeology in New Zealand has always included some study of the processes of change. After 1965, the lack of success in defining culture periods culminated in an explicit shift to the study of processes.

Regional and Thematic Studies

The appointment of English archaeologist Charles Higham and other archaeological staff members at Otago University in the 1960s initiated a fruitful period of regional studies. These began with Australian archaeologist Peter Coutt's study of contact between Europeans and Maori in the Foveaux Straits region (Coutts 1969).

The Wairarapa Research Programme, initiated by Foss Leach and Helen Leach in 1969, marked a further stage in the development of a regional approach as a viable alternative to the definition of cultural periods (Leach 1976). This program, carried out at Palliser Bay in the Wairarapa, a marginal area for Maori agriculture on the northern side of Cook Strait, brought together studies of site distribution, settlement types, agriculture, house forms, shell midden content, stone artifacts, and traditional history (Leach and Leach 1979). It provided a model for similar regional studies that have been carried out for the Chatham Islands (Sutton 1982), Auckland (Davidson 1978; Irwin 1985), Northland (Sutton 1990), the Hauraki Plains (Phillips 2000), and the South Island (Anderson 1998). Such regional studies have not always escaped presenting their evidence within the culture-historical framework (see Prickett 1982), but for the most part, they have documented increases or decreases in the magnitude of human populations or changes in the complexity of regional, economic, or social organization for which the division of New Zealand prehistory into archaic or classic periods is largely irrelevant.

A number of studies, however, have continued to rely on adaptational or environmental explanations. Doug Sutton and Yvonne Marshall's (1980) use of convergent adaptation to explain similarities between the Chatham Island Moriori, southern South Island Maori, and other southern foragers such as the Tasmanians is an example (see Anderson 1981). In a more recent study of the emergence of a northern Maori chiefdom, Sutton (1990) modified this stance by also considering sociopolitical and ideological factors. On the other hand, Atholl Anderson (1991) has returned to modeling the initial colonization of New Zealand in terms of the arrival of a small and highly mobile population that was stimulated by the rich environment to live more by hunting than by swidden agriculture, which involved effort in field preparation through cutting down and burning trees.

A major investigation of the various traits used by Duff, Golson, and Green to define their culture periods—e.g., material culture (including fishing gear, ornaments, adzes, and other stone artifacts), subsistence and technology, house and settlement forms, burials, warfare and pa design, and art styles—led New Zealand archaeologist Janet Davidson (1984) to conclude that changes in these traits took place at different times and in different places in response to quite different stimuli. Arguing that classic Maori culture could not have had a single point of origin, Davidson stressed that the polarization of New Zealand prehistory into the archaic and classic periods created insuperable difficulties for the explanation of the changes she had documented.

Thematic and regional projects in historical archaeology have been well documented by Ian Smith. Apart from Groube's (1965) study of proto-historic settlement patterns in the Bay of Islands, major projects have included the excavation of sites affected by the central North Island Tongariro power scheme carried out by Hoskins, a study of culture contact sites in Fiordland (Coutts 1969), Prickett's study of historic sites of the Taranaki wars (between Maori and the Crown), Neville Ritchie's explorations of the Otago goldfields affected by the Clutha dam development project, and, finally, a program on sites affected by urban development in the Auckland region led by Bulmer and others (see I. Smith 1990).

The last two projects were initiated under the Historic Places Amendment Act of 1975, a monument to the work of Green that gave the New Zealand Historic Places Trust control of the destruction of archaeological sites. Since 1975, the number of archaeologists employed by public and private agencies has matched the combined total of archaeologists in the universities and museums (about eighteen). Salvage archaeological projects have resulted in new surveys of remote or forested areas and the de-

tailed archaeological investigation of the layout of fortified, residential, agricultural, and colonial industrial sites (Clough 1990).

Economic and Ecological Archaeology

In an innovative series of studies of North Island shell middens, Wilfred Shawcross combined GRAHAME CLARK's economic approach with that of the Californian school of midden analysis (Heizer and Cook 1956). Using the interrelationships among site size, population, and the energy content of shell middens, Shawcross's work ranged from a study of the length of time a small group might have occupied a site (Shawcross 1967b) to the potential of harbor shellfish resources to support a human population (Shawcross 1967a) to the carrying capacity of both the North and South Islands based on seaboard productivity (Shawcross 1970b) and, finally, to the use of shell middens to construct a thermodynamic model that would allow a comparison of an early and late period midden in terms of work and efficiency (Shawcross 1972).

Detailed investigations of midden content and shellfish gathering practices have also been carried out by Reg Nichol (1988) and Atholl Anderson (1973). Anderson's study of prehistoric shellfish gathering behavior at Black Rocks, Palliser Bay, represents an early and probably independent use of ecological niche and optimal foraging models in New Zealand archaeology. Since 1978, Anderson has pursued the interaction of the prehistoric human population and moas in New Zealand. The results of this taphonomic and chronological study are correlated with the ecology of the moa and the distribution and contents of early archaeological sites to show the rapid extinction of the moa through hunting between 900 and 400 B.P. (Anderson 1989; Anderson, Allingham, and Smith 1996). Anderson and Smith (1996) argue that the early period of base settlements (villages), supported by localities rich in moas and seals, was a short-lived phenomenon and an unsustainable colonizing strategy. Villages reemerged on the southern part of the South Island in the later part of its prehistory as the result of an intrusion of peoples from the North Island who were equipped with a more highly organized exploitation strategy based upon stored foods and exchanges, including the payment of tribute to chiefs.

Chronological and Demographic Studies

In research on fortified pa, Groube (1964, 1970) plotted the regional distribution of chronological types based on their evolution from large, open-terraced pa to small pa that were heavily defended by multiple ditches, banks, and palisade posts. Initially, Groube explained this change in social terms as reflecting the breakdown of large tribal entities (and chieftainships?) into small, highly competitive descent groups. Chronology, demography, and resource stress were also included as factors. Groube argued that it would take 200 years or more for the population of a small group of colonists arriving in A.D. 1000 to reach about 25,000. After that, however, even moderate growth would take the population up to 100,000 by A.D. 1700. The thousands of fortified pa sites that dot the North Island landscape were the outcome of increasing competition for good-quality agricultural land within the zone of favorable climate. This was a form of resource stress through overpopulation that only had major effects during the final 200 years of New Zealand's prehistory.

It was many years before the information on pa distribution and chronology would allow the testing of Groube's hypotheses. Matt Schmidt (1996), using Anderson's (1991) suggestions for chronometrical reliability, derived 72 robust dates from a series of 221 radiocarbon dates from ninety-six pa. These dates suggested, first, that pa sites appeared rather suddenly at about A.D. 1500 and, second, that Groube's different classes of pa were spatially and chronologically coterminous. These conclusions repeated those of Geoffrey Irwin's (1985) study of spatial and hierarchical relationships of the pa of Kaipara Harbor and elsewhere. Irwin found that there was evidence that the settlement system (of Pouto) went through a stress threshold during the late prehistoric period that resulted in a spate of pa building. Multiple small pa and a few massive ones indicative of a higher order of organization suggested that the pa building was a response to both internal division and external threat.

Anderson (1991), in an extensive review of the time of initial settlement of New Zealand based on radiocarbon dates, found little evidence for settlement earlier than A.D. 1200. He added that the possibility of a planned immigration by some hundreds of people could not be ruled out. Sutton (1987, 1994), by contrast, used indications of fire disturbance in New Zealand pollen cores to claim that initial settlement was substantially earlier than A.D. 800. Part of Sutton's argument for an early date of colonization is based on life expectancy data and the implications of fertility and diet for population growth (Brewis, Malloy, and Sutton 1990).

Questions regarding the chronology of settlement and population growth in prehistoric New Zealand directly concern the time available for cultural processes. At present, the short chronology supports the idea of multiple settlement episodes and rapid and possibly intrusive changes in population, technology, and settlement patterns. The longer chronology supports arguments for the internal development of Pacific societies through evolutionary processes that led to the development of chiefly societies as a result of population increase, resource stress, agricultural intensification, or competition (Kirch and Green 1987).

Groube (1970) allied his model of population growth and resource stress with David Simmons's attempt (Simmons 1976) to reinstate the status of Maori canoe traditions by shifting their location to voyages around and between the islands of New Zealand (see Orbell 1985). Linking the distribution of the highly defended "ring ditch" pa with the historic movements of the "Awa" peoples enabled Groube to claim that the exile and forced migration of this group followed a standard Polynesian response to overpopulation. Computer simulations (Levison, Ward, Webb 1973), experimental voyages (Finney 1977), and increased knowledge of Pacific archaeology and Polynesian sailing techniques (Irwin 1992) have led to a reassessment of Andrew Sharp's pessimistic views. His model has now been replaced by the possibility of planned voyages, multiple episodes of discovery and colonization, and continuous interaction among the different islands of the Pacific. Matisoo-Smith and others (Matisoo-Smith et al. 1998) have presented an innovative attempt to examine these questions using mitochondrial DNA from rats that were fellow travelers on these voyages. Two results of these studies and the experimental voyages are a reinvigoration of Maori traditions linking canoe stories and genealogies with those of other Pacific communities (O'Regan 1987) and a renewal of the connection between Maori traditions and archaeology that has been severed since the 1960s.

There has been a renaissance in Maori cultural life stimulated in part by the "Te Maori" exhibition at the Metropolitan Museum of Art in New York, in 1985, the legal recognition given to the Treaty of Waitangi in 1986, and the granting of powers to the Waitangi Tribunal to examine Maori grievances against the Crown going back to the signing of the treaty in 1840. In the hearings of this tribunal, land, *whakapapa* ("genealogy"), and traditions have become central issues in the definition of Maori rights and being. Archaeologists have appeared for the plaintiffs and the Crown, and archaeological and traditional evidence has been reexamined in Maori claims for resource control, including the control of archaeological resources and their interpretation (Waitangi Tribunal 1988). Anderson, through his explorations of southern Maori ethnohistory and archaeology (Anderson 1998; Anderson, Allingham, Smith 1996), has made a significant contribution in this regard.

The Maori renaissance, the application of new archaeological techniques, a greater measure of protection for archaeological sites, plus a renewed optimism that the problems of New Zealand archaeology can be solved, either in the field or the laboratory, have led to a renewal of the discipline since 1980. If New Zealand archaeologists have bypassed rather than answered the questions posed by Cook in 1777, there has been in the meantime a great deal of testing and refinement of the terms of the questions and the exploration of diverse archaeological pathways toward their solution. Furthermore, there is now an environment where Pacific peoples, and

the Maori in particular, continue a dialogue with archaeologists about the relevance of these questions in this third millennium of discovery.

Harry Allen

See also New Zealand: Historical Archaeology
References
Anderson, A. 1973. "Archaeology and Behaviour: Prehistoric Subsistence Behaviour at Black Rocks Peninsula, Palliser Bay." M.A. thesis, Department of Anthropology, University of Otago.
———. 1981. "The Value of High Latitude Models in South Pacific Archaeology." *New Zealand Journal of Archaeology* 3: 143–160.
———. 1982. "North and Central Otago." In *The First Thousand Years: Regional Perspectives in New Zealand Archaeology,* 112–128. Ed. N. Prickett. Palmerston North, New Zealand: Dunmore Press.
———. 1989. *Prodigious Birds: Moas and Moa-hunting in Prehistoric New Zealand.* Cambridge: Cambridge University Press.
———. 1991. "The Chronology of Colonization in New Zealand." *Antiquity* 65: 767–795.
———. 1998. *The Welcome of Strangers: An Ethnohistory of the Southern Maori, A.D. 1650–1850.* Dunedin, New Zealand: University of Otago Press.
Anderson, A., and I. Smith. 1996. "Shag River Mouth as an Early Maori Village." In *Shag River Mouth: The Archaeology of an Early Southern Maori Village,* 276–291. Ed. A. Anderson, M. Allingham, and I Smith. Canberra: ANH Publications, RSPAS, Australian National University.
Anderson, A., B. Allingham, and I. Smith, eds. 1996. *Shag River Mouth: The Archaeology of an Early Southern Maori Village.* Canberra: ANH Publications, RSPAS, Australian National University.
Beaglehole, J. C., ed. 1962. *The Endeavour Journal of Joseph Banks 1768–1771.* Sydney: Trustees of the Public Library of New South Wales in association with Angus and Robertson.
Beardsley, R. K., P. Holder, A. D. Krieger, B. J. Meggers, J. B. Rinaldo, and P. Kutsche. 1956. "Functional and Evolutionary Implications of Community Patterning." *American Antiquity* 22: 133–158. Memoir 11.
Bedford, S. 1996. "Post-Contact Maori: The Ignored Component in New Zealand Archaeology." *Journal of the Polynesian Society* 105: 411–439.

Bellwood, P. 1978. *Archaeological Research at Lake Mangakaware, Waikato, 1968–70.* Monograph no. 9. New Zealand: New Zealand Archaeological Association.

Best, E. 1915. "Maori and Maruiwi." *Transactions of the New Zealand Institute* 48: 435–447.

Brewis, A., M. Molloy, and D. Sutton. 1990. "Modelling the Prehistoric Maori Population." *American Journal of Physical Anthropology* 81: 343–356.

Buck, P. H. [Te Rangi Hiroa] 1938. *Vikings of the Sunrise.* New York: Frederick A. Stokes.

———. 1949. *The Coming of the Maori.* Wellington: Whitcombe and Tombs. First published 1925.

Burrows, E. G. 1938. "Western Polynesia: A Study in Cultural Differentiation." *Etnologiska Studier* 7: 1–192.

Chang, K. C. 1958. "Study of the Neolithic Social Grouping: Examples from the New World." *American Anthropologist* 60: 298–334.

Clough, R. 1990. "Documents and Digs." *New Zealand Journal of Archaeology* 12: 157–185.

Coutts, P. 1969. "Merger or Takeover? A Survey of the Effects of Contact between Europeans and Maori in the Foveaux Straits Region." *Journal of the Polynesian Society* 78: 495–516.

Cumberland, K. B. 1962. "Climatic Change or Cultural Interference? New Zealand in Moahunter Times." In *Land and Livelihood: Geographical Essays in Honour of George Jobberns,* 88–142. Ed. M. McCaskill. Christchurch: Geographical Society.

Davidson, J. 1967. "Midden Analysis and the Economic Approach in New Zealand Archaeology." *Records of the Auckland Institute and Museum* 6: 203–228.

———. 1978. "Auckland Prehistory: A Review." *Records of the Auckland Institute and Museum* 15: 1–14.

———. 1984. *The Prehistory of New Zealand.* Auckland: Longman Paul.

Duff, R. 1947. "The Evolution of Native Culture in New Zealand: Moa Hunters, Morioris, Maoris." *Mankind* 3: 281–291, 313–322.

———. 1950. *The Moa Hunter Period of Maori Culture.* Wellington: Department of Internal Affairs.

———. 1956. "The Evolution of Polynesian Culture in New Zealand." *New Zealand Science Review* 14: 147–151.

Emory, K. P., and Y. Sinoto. 1964. "Eastern Polynesian Burials at Maupiti (Society Islands)." *Journal of the Polynesian Society* 73: 143–160.

Finney, B. 1977. "Voyaging Canoes and the Settlement of Polynesia." *Science* 196: 1277–1285.

Furey, L. 1996. *Oruarangi: The Archaeology and Material Culture of a Hauraki Pa.* Bulletin of the Auckland Institute and Museum no. 17. Auckland, New Zealand: Auckland Museum.

Golson, J. 1956. "New Zealand Archaeological Association, First Annual Conference." *Journal of the Polynesian Society* 65: 77–81.

———. 1957. "Field Archaeology in New Zealand." *Journal of the Polynesian Society* 66: 64–109.

———. 1959. "Culture Change in Prehistoric New Zealand." In *Anthropology in the South Seas,* 29–74. Ed. J. D. Freeman and W. R. Geddes. New Plymouth: Thomas Avery.

———. 1960. "Archaeology, Tradition, and Myth in New Zealand Prehistory." *Journal of the Polynesian Society* 69: 380–402.

———. 1965. "Some Considerations of the Role of Theory in New Zealand Archaeology." *New Zealand Archaeological Association Newsletter* 8: 79–92.

Golson, J., and P. Gathercole. 1962. "The Last Decade in New Zealand Archaeology." *Antiquity* 36: 168–174, 271–278.

Green, R. C. 1963. *A Review of the Prehistoric Sequence of the Auckland Province.* Monograph no. 2. Auckland: Auckland Archaeological Society and New Zealand Archaeological Association.

———. 1974. "Adaptation and Change in Maori Culture." In *Ecology and Biogeography in New Zealand,* 1–44. Ed. G. Kuschel. The Hague: W. Junk.

Groube, L. M. 1964. "Settlement Pattern in Prehistoric New Zealand." M.A. thesis, University of Auckland.

———. 1965. "Excavations on Paeroa Village, Bay of Islands." *Historic Places Trust Newsletter* 9: 5–7.

———. 1967. "Models in Prehistory: A Consideration of the New Zealand Evidence." *Archaeology and Physical Anthropology in Oceania* 2: 1–27.

———. 1969. "From Archaic to Classic Maori." *Auckland Student Geographer* 6: 1–11.

———. 1970. "The Origin and Development of Earthwork Fortifications in the Pacific." In *Studies in Oceanic Culture History,* 1:133–164. Ed. R. Green and M. Kelly. Pacific Anthropological Records 11. Honolulu: Bishop Museum, Department of Anthropology.

Haast, J. 1872. "Moas and Moa Hunters." *Transactions of the New Zealand Institute* 4: 66–107.

Heizer, R., and S. Cook. 1956. "Some Aspects of

the Quantitative Approach in Archaeology."
Southwestern Journal of Anthropology 12:
229–248.

Irwin, G. 1975. "The Kohika Site, Bay of Plenty."
Historical Review 23: 101–104.

———. 1985. *Land, Pa, and Polity*. Monograph no.
15. New Zealand: New Zealand Archaeological
Association.

———. 1992. *The Prehistoric Exploration and Colonisation of the Pacific*. Cambridge: Cambridge University Press.

Kirch, P., and R. Green. 1987. "History, Phylogeny, and Evolution in Polynesia." *Current
Anthropology* 28: 431–456.

Leach, B. F. 1976. "Prehistoric Communities in
Palliser Bay." Ph.D. thesis, University of Otago,
Dunedin.

Leach, B. F., and H. M. Leach, eds. 1979. *Prehistoric Man in Palliser Bay*. Bulletin no. 21. Auckland: National Museum of New Zealand.

Levison, M., R. Ward, and J. Webb. 1973. *The
Settlement of Polynesia: A Computer Simulation*.
Canberra: Australian National University Press.

Ling Roth, H., tr. 1891. *Crozet's Voyage to Tasmania,
New Zealand, the Ladrone Islands, and the Philippines in the Years 1771–1772*. London: Truslove
and Shirley.

Lubbock, J. 1865. *Prehistoric Times*. London.

Lyell, C. 1869. *Principles of Geology*. 10th ed., rev.
London: John Murray.

McKay, A. 1874. "On the Identity of the Moa
Hunters with the Present Maori Race." *Transactions of the New Zealand Institute* 7: 98–105.

Matisoo-Smith, L., R. M. Roberts, G. J. Irwin,
J. S. Allen, D. Penny, and D. M. Lambert.
1998. "Patterns of Prehistoric Mobility in Polynesia Indicated by mtDNA from the Pacific
Rat." *Proceedings of the National Academy of Science*
95: 15145–15150.

Nichol, R. 1988. "Tipping the Feather against a
Scale: Archaeozoology from the Tail of the
Fish." Ph.D. dissertation, Department of
Anthropology, University of Auckland.

O'Regan, T. 1987. "Te Kupenga o Nga Tupuna." In
From the Beginning: The Archaeology of the Maori,
21–26. Ed. J. Wilson. Auckland: Penguin.

Orbell, M. 1985. *Hawaiki: A New Approach to Maori
Traditions*. Publication no. 35. Christchurch:
University of Canterbury.

Owen, R. 1839. "On the Bone of an Unknown
Struthious Bird from New Zealand." *Proceedings
of the Zoological Society of London* 7: 169–171.

Parker, R. H. 1962. "Aspect and Phase on Skip-
pers' Ridge (Opito) and Kumara-Kaiamo
(Urenui)." *New Zealand Archaeological Association
Newsletter* 5: 222–232.

Phillips, C. 2000. *Waihou Journeys: The Archaeology of
Four Hundred Years of Maori Settlement*. Auckland,
New Zealand: University of Auckland Press.

Prickett, N., ed. 1982. *The First Thousand Years: Re-
gional Perspectives in New Zealand Archaeology*.
Palmerston North, New Zealand: Dunmore
Press.

Reed, A. H., and A. W. Reed, eds. 1969. *Captain
Cook in New Zealand*. 2d ed. Wellington: A. H.
and A. W. Reed.

Salmond, A. 1991. *Two Worlds: First Meetings between
Maori and Europeans 1642–1772*. Auckland:
Viking.

Schmidt, M. 1996. "The Commencement of Pa
Construction in New Zealand." *Journal of the
Polynesian Society* 105: 441–460.

Scott, J. 1893. "Contributions to the Osteology of
the Aborigines of New Zealand and the
Chatham Islands." *Transactions of the New Zealand
Institute* 26: 1–64.

Sharp, A. 1956. *Ancient Voyagers in the Pacific*.
Wellington: Polynesian Society.

Shawcross, F. W. 1964a. "Archaeological Investigations at Ongari Point, Katikati, Bay of Plenty."
New Zealand Archaeological Association Newsletter
7: 79–97.

———. 1964b. "Stone Flake Industries in New Zealand." *Journal of the Polynesian Society* 73: 7–25.

———. 1967a. "An Evaluation of the Theoretical
Capacity of a New Zealand Harbour to Carry a
Human Population." *Tane* 13: 3–11.

———. 1967b. "An Investigation of Prehistoric
Diet and Economy on a Coastal Site at Galatea
Bay, New Zealand." *Proceedings at the Prehistoric
Society* 33: 107–131.

———. 1968. "The Ngaroto Site." *New Zealand
Archaeological Association Newsletter* 11: 2–29.

———. 1969. "Archaeology with a Short, Isolated
Time-Scale: New Zealand." *World Archaeology* 1:
184–199.

———. 1970a. "The Cambridge University Col-
lection of Maori Artefacts Made on Captain
Cook's First Voyage." *Journal of the Polynesian
Society* 79: 305–348.

———. 1970b. "Ethnographic Economics and the
Study of Population in Prehistoric New
Zealand: Viewed through Archaeology." *Mankind*
7: 279–291.

———. 1972. "Energy and Ecology: Thermodynamic Models in Archaeology." In *Models in Ar-*

chaeology, 577–622. Ed. D. L. Clarke. London: Methuen.

———. 1976. "Kauri Point Swamp: The Ethnographic Interpretation of a Prehistoric Site." In *Problems in Economic and Social Archaeology,* 277–305. Ed. G. de G. Sieveking, I. H. Longworth, and K. E. Wilson. London: Duckworth.

Shawcross, F. W., and J. Terrell. 1966. "Paterangi and Oruarangi Swamp Pas." *Journal of the Polynesian Society* 75: 404–429.

Simmons, D. 1976. *The Great New Zealand Myth: A Study of the Discovery and Origin Traditions of the Maori.* Wellington: Reed.

Skinner, H. D. 1921. "Culture Areas in New Zealand." *Journal of the Polynesian Society* 30: 71–78.

———. 1923. "The Morioris of the Chatham Islands." *Memoirs of the Bernice P. Bishop Museum* 9 (1).

———. 1924. "The Origins and Relationships of Maori Material Culture and Decorative Art." *Journal of the Polynesian Society* 33: 229–243.

Smith, I. 1990. "Historical Archaeology in New Zealand: A Review and Bibliography." *New Zealand Journal of Archaeology* 12: 85–119.

Smith, S. P. 1921. *Hawaiki: The Original Home of the Maoris.* 4th ed. Auckland: Whitcombe and Tombs.

Sorrenson, M. P. K. 1979. *Maori Origins and Migrations.* Auckland, New Zealand: Auckland University Press.

Sutton, D. 1982. "Chatham Islands." In *The First Thousand Years: Regional Perspectives in New Zealand Archaeology,* 160–178. Ed. N. Prickett. Palmerston North, New Zealand: Dunmore Press.

———. 1987. "A Paradigmatic Shift in Polynesian Prehistory: Implications for New Zealand." *New Zealand Journal of Archaeology* 9: 135–155.

———. 1990. "Organisation and Ontology: The Origins of the Northern Maori Chiefdom, New Zealand." *Man* 25: 667–692.

Sutton, D., ed. 1994. *The Origins of the First New Zealanders.* Auckland, New Zealand: Auckland University Press.

Sutton, D., and Y. Marshall. 1980. "Coastal Hunting in the Subantarctic Zone." *New Zealand Journal of Archaeology* 2: 25–49.

Terrell, J. 1965. "Limitations on Archaeology in New Zealand." *New Zealand Archaeological Association Newsletter* 8: 125–130.

Teviotdale, D. 1932. "The Material Culture of the Moa-Hunters of Murihiku." *Journal of the Polynesian Society* 41: 81–120.

Travers, W. T. L. 1871. "Notes upon the Historical Value of the 'Traditions of the New Zealan-

ders,' as collected by Sir George Grey, K.C.B., late Governor-in Chief of New Zealand." *Transactions of the New Zealand Institute* 4: 51–62.

Waitangi Tribunal. 1988. *Report of the Waitangi Tribunal on the Muriwhenua Fishing Claim (Wai–22).* Waitangi Tribunal Reports no. 2. Wellington: Government Printing Office.

Yen, D. E. 1961. "The Adaptation of Kumara by the New Zealand Maori." *Journal of the Polynesian Society* 70: 338–348.

Nicaragua

See Costa Rica and Nicaragua

Nilsson, Sven (1787–1883)

The son of a farmer who was taught to read and write by his father, Sven Nilsson enrolled at Lund University in SWEDEN in 1806 with the intention of becoming a priest. He finished a degree in theology but then studied philology, natural history, and philosophy. In 1812, Nilsson was offered a position at Lund's natural history cabinet (or premuseum collection) as well as an associate professorship in natural history.

Through his work of classifying donations to the cabinet Nilsson became interested in fossil remains and research. He was elected to the Royal Swedish Academy of Sciences in 1812 and drew up plans for the academy's transformation into the Swedish Museum of Natural History, where he was eventually a curator.

While he was working in the museum, Nilsson continued to study zoology, geology, and anatomy and finished a medical degree in 1818. In 1832, he returned to the University of Lund as a professor of zoology, and the natural history museum at Lund became the center for Swedish zoology. In Nilsson's view, all natural-scientific research rested ultimately on careful comparisons, which made collecting decisive for the development of the sciences. He became a central figure in nineteenth-century Swedish zoology through his forty-year career as a university teacher and through the popularization of his scientific interests via lectures and publications. He was also one of the pioneers of the embryonic discipline of quaternary geology, linking geology, zoology, and archaeology to create a picture of the environment and living conditions in Sweden over long periods of time—the beginning of late-quaternary research.

Although Nilsson had collected archaeological artifacts since the 1820s and had participated in archaeological excavations as early as 1819, it was not until later in his career that he began to devote much of his time to archaeology, when he endeavored to translate a natural-science approach into a complex model of cultural development that could be measured empirically through technological change. Nilsson was the first to use comparative ethnography to elucidate cultural history—and thus he exercised great influence on the development of modern anthropology, particularly on American anthropologist LEWIS H. MORGAN and English ethnographer E. B. TYLOR. OSCAR MONTELIUS, who was critical of Nilsson in other contexts, believed that his cultural-evolutionary scheme and his comparative method had elevated antiquarian research into a science.

Nilsson began to lose prestige within the archaeological establishment mainly because his attempts to determine the origin of the Swedish Bronze Age led to chronological misjudgments. But his contributions were considerable: he provided a picture of prehistory that was more complex than any other; he clarified how flint tools were made, both through the use of experiments as well as through ethnographical and ethnological analogies; and he helped confirm and develop the THREE-AGE SYSTEM. Perhaps most significant of all, however, was the fact that he showed how Stone Age societies had probably lived and demonstrated that the three-age system applied to Sweden as well as to DENMARK.

Johan Hegardt

See also Hildebrand, Bror E.; Hildebrand, Hans; Thomsen, Christian J.; Worsaae, Jens Jacob

References

For references, see *Encyclopedia of Archaeology: The Great Archaeologists, Vol. 1* ed. Tim Murray (Santa Barbara, CA: ABC-CLIO, 1999), pp. 77–78.

Nimrud

Also known as Kalhu, Nimrud was an Assyrian city on the banks of the Tigris River quite close to NINEVEH. Made famous as a result of its exca-

Phoenician bronze bowl from Nimrud (Image Select)

vation, initially by AUSTEN HENRY LAYARD beginning in 1845 and later by SIR MAX MALLOWAN in 1954, Nimrud suffered fluctuating fortunes during its history. First established in the late second millennium B.C., the city was designated an imperial Assyrian city around 883 B.C. but shortly afterward lost that status to Khorsabad.

But there had been time enough to produce the palaces, major sculptures (such as the winged bulls), and hundreds of cuneiform texts that were so enthusiastically excavated by Layard. The public exhibition of the results of his excavations in England after 1849 created a high level of public interest, which can in part be explained by the lure of spectacular objects. By the same token, Layard was quite aware of the powerful attraction of archaeological "proofs" of stories from the Old Testament (even though he managed to confuse Nimrud with the biblical Nineveh). In 1954, the site was systematically reexcavated in a somewhat less bravura manner by Mallowan, who had signal successes of his own, particularly in the recovery of the famous Nimrud ivories.

Tim Murray

See also Mesopotamia

References

Layard, Austen Henry. 1849. *Nineveh and Its Remains.* London.

Mallowan, Max. 1978. *The Nimrud Ivories.* London: British Museum Publications.

Nineveh

Nineveh, the great capital of the Assyrians on the river Tigris, became prominent around 700 B.C. during the reign of Sennacherib, who moved his capital there. Notwithstanding its great size and the magnificence of its architecture, Nineveh was sacked by the Medes and the Babylonians in 612 B.C.

First excavated by PAUL EMILE BOTTA in 1842, the site is most famously associated with SIR AUSTEN HENRY LAYARD, who began excavating at Sennacherib's Palace in 1846. Layard was fortunate in his assistant Hormuzd Rassam, and the latter developed into an excavator of skill and vigor and took over the excavations after Layard's return to England in 1851. Between 1846 and 1851, during two major expeditions, spectacular examples of Neo-Assyrian art such as winged bulls and stone wall relief carvings were recovered and sent back to the BRITISH MUSEUM—which was the major sponsor of the work. Rassam later excavated the famous relief carvings of the royal lion hunt, which also grace that museum.

Of equal importance to the architecture and art works were the numerous cuneiform tablets that made up the Assyrian royal archives in the seventh century B.C., which have since been deciphered. Given the significance of the site, it is hardly surprising that it has attracted constant attention, including the valuable and technically excellent excavations undertaken by SIR MAX MALLOWAN in 1931 and 1932 and the postwar work of Iraqi archaeologists such as Manhal Jabr and the short tenure of the University of California, Berkeley, team under the direction of David Stronach (1987–1990).

Tim Murray

See also Mesopotamia
References
Russell, J. M. 1998. *The Final Sack of Nineveh: The Discovery, Documentation, and Destruction of King Sennacherib's Throne Room at Nineveh, Iraq.* New Haven: Yale University Press.

Excavating a low-relief carving of the fish god, Dagon; drawing from Austen H. Layard, Discoveries in the Ruins of Nineveh and Babylon; with Travels in Armenia, Kurdistan, and the Desert *(London, 1853) (Ann Ronan Picture Library)*

Novgorod

Novgorod is an urban medieval site that served as the capital of northwestern RUSSIA from the twelfth to fifteenth centuries A.D. Located on the northern shore of Lake Ilmen in northwest Russia, Novgorod occupied a strategic position with access to the Volga and Dnieper Rivers and the Baltic Sea; therefore, it connected Russia, western Europe, Byzantium, and the Muslim East (Yanin et al. 1992). The territory of Novgorod, an early state, spread as far as the White Sea to the north and the Ural Mountains to the east, and the city served as the largest center of international and domestic trade in medieval Russia (Yanin 1990).

Archaeologists such as Elena Rybina and Valentin Yanin have conducted research at the site, adding to the 21,000 square meters excavated so far, which still represents less than 1 percent of the total area (Ostman 1997). The waterlogged conditions at the site contributed to the complete preservation of many organic remains such as wood, bone, leather, and birchbark, as well as houses, streets, and medieval topography. Archaeologists have been able to analyze individual households, including the homes of artists, craftspeople, nobles, and slaves (Rybina 2001).

A most interesting feature of medieval Novgorod was the existence of thousands of documents scratched onto birchbark pages (*beresty*), of which almost 1,000 have been recovered. These deal with a wide range of subjects and include peasant complaints, financial records, school exercises, notes on literature, and love letters. Other preserved objects include tools, weapons, musical instruments, toys, jewelry, clothes, and craft materials.

Thalia Gray

See also Medieval Europe

References

Birnbaum, H. 1996. *Novgorod in Focus.* Columbus, OH: Slavica Publishers.

Ostman, R. 1997. "'Our Land Is Great and Rich, But There Is No Order in It': Reevaluating the Process of State Formation in Russia." *Archaeological News* 22: 73–91.

Rybina, E. 2000. "Novgorod." Pp. 239–241 in *Medieval Archaeology, An Encyclopedia.* Ed. P. J. Crabtree. New York: Garland Publishing.

Yanin, V. L. 1990. "The Archaeology of Novgorod." *Scientific American* 262, 2: 84–91.

Yanin, V. L. et al. 1992. *The Archaeology of Novgorod, Russia.* Society for Medieval Archaeology, Monograph Series 13. Lincoln.

Novo Mesto

A late prehistoric settlement and complex of burial sites in Dolenjska (lower Carniola) in SLOVENIA, Novo Mesto is characterized by a number of cemeteries dated from the whole first millennium B.C. The settlement is located on the Marof and was probably occupied from the late–Bronze Age to Roman times. The first excavations of the cemeteries began at the end of the nineteenth century (by the Naturhistorisches Museum, Vienna, and the National Museum, Ljubljana). However, more intensive research was initiated by the Dolenjski Muzej (lower Carniola museum) in Novo Mesto from 1967 onward.

The Novo Mesto cemeteries date to three main periods: late–Bronze Age (ninth–eighth centuries B.C.), early–Iron Age (eighth–fourth

A medieval church in Novgorod, Russia (Image Select)

centuries B.C.), and the late–Iron Age to the Roman period (third century B.C.–second century A.D). From the first period, the sites of Mestne njive, Kapiteljska njiva, and Brsljin contain some 400 urned cremation graves and were part of the Ljubljana Urnfield group. Grave goods consisted mostly of dress ornaments (fibulae, bracelets, pins) and ceramic vessels. Only a few graves contained weapons (axes, spearheads), razors, necklaces, knives, or glass beads.

The early–Iron Age sites of Kapiteljske njive and Kandija are made up of some twenty earthen barrows. The burial rite was inhumation (from few to seventy graves per barrow). Some rich princely graves of this period were recorded containing body armor, tripod, various helmet types, weapons, and decorated bronze vessels together with numerous warrior graves and graves with standard personal ornaments and ceramic vessels. In the early–Iron Age period, Novo Mesto was one of the most important centers of the Dolenjska (lower Carniola) group of the Hallstatt culture.

The late–Iron Age sites of Kapiteljske njive, Kandija, and Beletov vrt are characterized by cremation burials in flat cemeteries. Graves contain mostly middle and late LA TÈNE artifact types (swords with scabbards, shields, knives, belt pieces, fibulae, necklaces, bracelets, and pottery) and early Roman provincial objects.

Peter Turk

References

Knez T. 1986. *Novo mesto I (Halstatski grobovi / Hallstatt Graves)*. Carniola Archaeologica no. 1.

———. 1992. *Novo mesto II (Keltsko-rimsko grobisce Beletov vrt / Celtic-Roman Cemetery at Beletov vrt)*. Carniola Archaeologica no. 2.

———. 1993. *Novo mesto III (Kapiteljska njiva— knezja gomila/Kapiteljska njiva—Princely Barrow)*. Carniola Archaeologica no. 3.

Nubia

Nubia is the name that has been given in modern times to a region that was known to ancient Egyptians and their neighbors as Kush (or Cush) and to Greeks and Romans as Aethiopia. Today, it comprises the most southerly part of Egypt and the adjoining northern part of the Republic of Sudan. Historically, however, the region has usually been both culturally and politically autonomous, neither wholly Egyptian nor wholly Sudanese. Its peoples speak languages of the African eastern Sudanic family and exhibit both racial and cultural characteristics that connect them with peoples further to the south in Africa as well as with their Egyptian neighbors. Nubia was the seat of the ancient Empire of Kush and later of medieval Christian kingdoms that successfully resisted the incursion of Islamic Egypt for a thousand years.

The northern boundary of Nubia since time immemorial has been at the First Cataract of the Nile, just upriver from the town of Aswan in Egypt. The peoples to the south of that point have always been and remain ethnically and linguistically different from the Egyptians. The southern limit of Nubia is more difficult to specify, for it has varied at different times in history. However, in the usage of archaeologists and culture historians, the term is generally synonymous with ancient Kush and Aethiopia; it designates that portion of the Nile Valley, upriver from Egypt, that was strongly affected by cultural and political currents from Egypt and the Mediterranean world. In that sense, the historic southern limit of Nubia should be placed somewhere to the south of modern Khartoum at the confluence of the Blue and White Nile Rivers.

The Nubian environment resembles that of Egypt in that the fertile Nile Valley is flanked, for most of its length, by totally lifeless deserts. Instead of a broad and continuous floodplain, however, the valley in Nubia contains only limited and disconnected patches of alluvium while elsewhere, bare granite or sandstone outcrops come right to the water's edge. In most of the region, moreover, the Nile did not annually overflow its banks, and irrigation required the use of man-made lifting devices. The agricultural potential was, as a result, very much less than that of Egypt, and the population was proportionately smaller. The prosperity of ancient and medieval Nubian civilizations did not depend on agricultural fertility, as in the case of Egypt, but on the country's position astride one of the world's oldest and richest trade routes. Before the development of trans-Saharan caravan trade in the first century A.D., the Nile Valley represented the only secure corridor across the Sahara through which gold, ivory, slaves, and other coveted goods from the African interior could reach the Mediterranean Basin.

A Resume of Cultural History

The late Palaeolithic and early Neolithic cultures of Nubia conformed to a general pattern that has been observed all over the eastern Sahara. Although pottery made its appearance surprisingly early, other aspects of Neolithic cultural development lagged far behind contemporary developments in the Near East. As the Sahara gradually became drier and wild animal and bird life retreated to the Nile corridor, the abundance of aquatic and game resources seems to have actually retarded any heavy reliance on agriculture until near the end of the Neolithic period; similarly, the warm climate retarded the development of permanent housing. It was only during the time of "the copper age," more or less contemporary with the beginnings of dynastic civilization in Egypt, that advanced Neolithic cultures made their appearance in Nubia.

The distinctive late Neolithic cultures of Nubia were first discovered as a result of excavations near Aswan in 1907. Because the finds corresponded to nothing previously known from Egypt, they were designated by the discoverer simply as the A-, B-, and C-Groups. The B-Group is no longer generally accepted as a distinct cultural horizon, but the categories of A-Group and C-Group remain in use down to the present day. Both cultures are known very largely from cemetery sites, and they are distinguished from each other partly by grave types and partly by their distinctive pottery wares. The graves of both horizons contain an abundance of Egyptian-made goods, including wheel-made pottery, copper implements and weapons, and faience ornaments, while the Nubian-made goods are mostly handmade pottery and objects of stone.

On the basis of imported Egyptian goods, the A-Group has been dated to a time corresponding to the late Egyptian Predynastic period and the First Dynasty (ca. 3600–3000 B.C.) while the C-Group coincides with the subsequent Egyptian dynasties down to the beginning of the New Kingdom (ca. 3000–1580 B.C.). Although there is evidence of a powerful but short-lived chiefdom during the time of the A-Group, the graves from both periods generally give evidence of an egalitarian society without marked distinctions of rank and without centralized political institutions. Subsistence depended primarily on cereal agriculture, although cattle raising also played an important role, especially in the C-Group. Settlements in both periods seem to have been small encampments of tents or of grass structures with rather irregular mud-brick houses appearing only late in the C-Group period. Nothing that can be interpreted as a religious structure has been identified from either period.

The Egyptian pharaohs traded regularly with Nubia from at least the Sixth Dynasty (ca. 2400 B.C.) onward, and there were intermittent raiding expeditions as well. During the Middle Kingdom (ca. 2000–1800 B.C.), the Egyptians took temporary possession of the northern part of the country and built a chain of enormous fortresses in order to protect their trade route to the south. However, this incursion had almost no effect on the indigenous C-Group culture, which did not begin to show evidence of Egyptianization until after the time when the Egyptian garrisons were withdrawn.

Remains of the A-Group and C-Group cultures have been found only in the northerly parts of the country, the region traditionally called Lower Nubia. Further to the south, a somewhat similar culture made its appearance at Kerma, near the Third Cataract of the Nile, around 2500 B.C. The earliest Kerma graves and pottery types were generally similar to those of the contemporary C-Group further north although distinguished by a few unique pottery types and by details of burial practice. But while the C-Group culture remained little changed for over a thousand years, Kerma rapidly developed into a powerful and autocratic chiefdom, which at times treated on equal terms with the Egyptian pharaohs. The culture reached its apogee in the time of the Egyptian Second Intermediate Period (ca. 1800–1580 B.C.), when the site of Kerma comprised an enormous sprawling townsite with houses, granaries, and workshops of mud brick as well as massive brick temples and a series of monumental royal tombs, some of which contained literally hundreds of sacrificial human burials.

Kerma was evidently the main depot for the shipment of Nubian goods to Egypt, and the power of its chiefs depended on the control of that trade. Finds within the townsite indicate that there was a resident colony of Egyptian artisans, shipping agents, and ambassadors, but the place was always independent of Egyptian political control. When the pharaohs withdrew their garrisons from the Lower Nubian forts, in the Second Intermediate Period, the Kerma rulers themselves took possession of the installations. Kamose, the last pharaoh of the Egyptian Seventeenth Dynasty, complained that he sat between an Asiatic (the Hyksos ruler in the north) and an African (the Kerma chieftain), each in possession of a slice of the Nile.

Some time shortly after 1580 B.C., the cultural and political autonomy of Nubia came to an abrupt end. Pharaoh Ahmose not only reoccupied the fortresses of Lower Nubia but extended Egyptian dominion upriver as far as the Fourth Cataract of the Nile. For the next five centuries, Nubia was to be an Egyptian colony administered by a viceroy called the King's Son of Kush. The Kerma chiefdom as well as the independent C-Group polities of Lower Nubia were promptly extinguished, and authority passed entirely into the hands of Egyptian overlords. The fortresses of the Middle Kingdom were repaired and enlarged, and new towns and temples were built at strategic points. Napata, at the upstream limit of Egyptian control, was established as the administrative capital for the whole region, and an enormous temple was built to the god Amon there. This deity, known to Nubians as Amani, was to remain the principal state god of Nubia, as he was also in Egypt, for centuries to come.

Under the colonial regime the Nubian population was acculturated to Egyptian standards of dress, religion, and burial, and most vestiges of the indigenous cultural traditions disappeared. In later years, particularly in the Nineteenth and Twentieth Dynasties (ca. 1340–1085 B.C.), Nubian dignitaries were increasingly co-opted into the colonial administration itself, and the ethnic Egyptian population substantially declined.

Around 1000 B.C., beset by internal political troubles, the Egyptians withdrew as colonial masters from Nubia, but they left behind a typical postcolonial population that continued to follow Egyptian cultural practices and to worship Amon and other Egyptian gods. Political circumstances are obscure for about 200 years, after which time there arose a new indigenous monarchy based at Napata, evidently in alliance with the priests of Amon there. Perhaps a century afterward, one of the new Nubian rulers, a certain Kashta, took possession of Upper Egypt and was recognized as pharaoh there. His successor, Piye, conquered the whole of Egypt in 751 B.C. and became the first ruler of the Twenty-fifth Dynasty, known to historians as the Ethiopian Dynasty. The Nubian pharaohs ruled both Egypt and Nubia from a capital in Lower Egypt, but after death their bodies were returned to their homeland for burial in the great royal cemeteries at Napata. Piye adopted the Egyptian practice of building the royal tomb in the form of decorated, underground chambers surmounted by a pyramid, and this custom continued to be followed by all his successors until the final end of the dynasty a thousand years later.

Nubian rule in Egypt lasted just under a century and was terminated by a series of Assyrian invasions. Within their own country, however, the erstwhile pharaohs continued to maintain a pharaonic-style state and civilization for almost a millennium longer. Their domain was now officially called the Empire of Kush. The rulers kept up the worship of the Egyptian gods, built additional temples as well as pyramids, and for several centuries wrote their royal annals in hieroglyphic characters.

In time, the center of gravity in the Empire of Kush shifted to the south. A new royal capital was established at Meroe, some 300 miles upriver from the old capital of Napata. There a huge new temple of Amon and a walled palace complex were constructed, and all of the later rulers of Kush chose to build their pyramids there. The subsequent, later phase of Kushite civilization is usually referred to as Meroitic, after the new royal capital. Eventually, a new alphabetic form of writing, also called Meroitic, was developed. Unfortunately, it remains largely undeciphered at the present time.

The Alexandrian and Roman conquests of Egypt ushered in a new era of flourishing trade with the Mediterranean world, as is attested by the wealth of Greco-Roman goods found in the later Kushite royal tombs. A newly important commodity in the export trade was cotton, which was highly prized by the Greek and Roman settlers in Egypt but had not yet been introduced as a crop in the north. It was at this time, too, that Aethiopia and Meroe became known to Greek and Roman scholars through the writings of Herodotus, Strabo, Pliny, and other classical authors. Graffiti of many Greek and Roman visitors have been found in the temple ruins at Meroe and neighboring settlements.

In the earlier years of the Kushite Empire, the northern part of the country had become very much a political and economic backwater and seems in fact to have been largely depopulated. Then, in the last century B.C. and the first two centuries A.D., there was a virtual land rush of repopulation, possibly brought about by the introduction of the saqia (ox-driven waterwheel) for irrigation. The repopulated north soon became especially prosperous because of its advantageous position for trading with Roman Egypt, and at the same time, the south was being weakened by nomadic incursions and by the development of Red Sea maritime trade as an alternative to the Nile route. By the fourth century A.D., the Kushite temples in the south were dilapidated, and the last of the royal pyramids were small and unimpressive affairs of brick, while the northern region was near the peak of its prosperity.

The final demise of the Empire of Kush seems to have occurred early in the fourth century A.D., though both the date and the circumstances are obscure. Much of the territory of Meroe in the central Sudan was overrun by migrating seminomadic peoples from the west, and the region seems to have lapsed for a time into a state of tribal anarchy. In the region of Lower Nubia, however, a powerful local kingdom arose from the ashes of Kushite sovereignty, and it continued to maintain a flourishing trade with Byzantine Egypt. When its archaeological remains were first discovered in 1907, they were designated as the X-Group because they corresponded to no historically known entity in Egypt. Although the term is still sometimes used in archaeological literature, especially as a designation for pottery and grave types, the political entity and the cultural period are now more commonly referred to as the Ballana kingdom and culture after the locality near the Egyptian-Sudanese border where the rulers were buried. The Ballana monarchs continued to employ some of the iconography of the Kushite pharaohs and kept up the worship of the Egyptian and Kushite gods, but the art of Meroitic writing entirely disappeared. The Ballana culture, which endured into the sixth century A.D., represents the last surviving manifestation of ancient Egyptian civilization, long after its disappearance in Egypt itself.

In the middle of the sixth century, Christian missionaries appeared in Nubia, and within half a century they had succeeded in converting the whole country to the faith that by now had been long established both in Egypt to the north and in Abyssinia to the south. The missionaries encountered, and converted, three Nubian kingdoms: Nobadia (their name for the Ballana kingdom) in the north, Makouria in the region between the Third and Fourth Cataracts, and

A section of the seventy-four frescoes depicting Christian scenes that were found in Nubia near the temples of Abu Simbel (Hulton Getty)

Alodia (afterward known to Arabs as Alwa) in the region around the confluence of the Blue and White Nile Rivers. Sometime in the eighth century, the kingdoms of Nobadia and Makouria were merged under a single ruler with a capital city at Dongola. Alodia, however, always remained independent, with its capital at Soba near modern Khartoum.

In 642 A.D., Arab armies conquered Egypt and immediately attempted an invasion of Nubia as well. However, both this attempt and another incursion ten years later were successfully resisted, and the invaders then negotiated a treaty, called the Baqt, that left the Nubian kingdoms independent of Arab and Islamic control throughout the Middle Ages. As a result, Nubia remained Christian until near the end of the fifteenth century. The Nubians, like their coreligionists in Egypt and Syria, allied themselves with the Monophysite sect of Christianity, which meant that their church was under the

Coptic patriarch of Alexandria rather than under the patriarch of Constantinople. However, the Nubians always used Greek rather than Coptic as their liturgical language.

Protected by the Baqt treaty, the medieval Nubians enjoyed once again a prosperous trade with Egypt throughout the Middle Ages. Relations were especially close with the Egyptian Fatimid Caliphate (969–1171), which was often on bad terms with other Islamic powers and depended heavily on the support of Nubian troops. In these circumstances of prolonged peace and prosperity, Nubian civilization flourished once again as it had in Kushite times, and there were major developments in architecture and art as well as in several crafts. As in earlier times, the most outstanding achievements were in the religious sphere, but iconography now always emphasized a heavenly rather than an earthly king. No royal monuments of any kind have been found from the entire medieval period, and the names of only a few of the kings are known, mainly from Arabic records. Nevertheless, the indigenous language (now usually called Old Nubian) was once again written, this time in a modified Greek alphabet. It was used mainly for administrative and commercial correspondence while religious documents were usually in Greek. There was also widespread literacy in Arabic as a result of the extensive trade with Egypt.

When the warlike Mamluks seized control in Egypt in 1250, they repudiated the Baqt treaty and began an intermittent series of military incursions into Nubia. At the same time, the monarchy at Dongola was weakened by dynastic quarrels, and local magnates began increasingly to assert their authority. The final blow to Nubia's medieval civilization came from the massive Arab nomad migrations, some from Egypt and some directly from the Arabian peninsula, that overran the central Sudan in the fourteenth to sixteenth centuries. Many of the newcomers settled along the Nile and intermarried with the Nubian population; at the same time, they destroyed the older kingdoms and divided their territory up into a series of petty warring principalities after the fashion of Arab tribes.

Lower Nubia was largely spared from these ravages because of its total lack of pastoral resources, and a splinter Christian kingdom called Dotawo survived there until near the end of the fifteenth century. However, contact with the church in Egypt had been lost by this time, and Nubian Christianity gradually died out because of a lack of a trained priesthood. When the Ottoman Turks, who had conquered Egypt in 1517, added Lower Nubia to their dominions half a century later, they found no surviving trace either of the Dotawo kingdom or of an established church.

The centuries that followed were a time of political anarchy and economic and cultural impoverishment. Ottoman rule in the north was wholly extractive and corrupt while further to the south, warlike tribes and principalities formed a series of endlessly shifting coalitions. Meanwhile, the development of European maritime trade with the African coasts had almost wholly supplanted the Nile trade route. The written Nubian language and all the great architectural and artistic achievements of the medieval period were lost, and the mass of Nubians reverted to a purely subsistence economy and a condition of life hardly different from that of the Neolithic period. Many people clung to remnants of their older Christian faith, but there was no established religion until, in the seventeenth century, Islamic teachers from North and West Africa came as missionaries and established religious schools, mainly in the area around present-day Khartoum. In the prevailing cultural and ideological vacuum of the times, the new religion spread rapidly, laying the foundations for the basically Islamic civilization of northern Sudan today.

The Arab migrations set in motion a process of linguistic displacement as the indigenous Nubian languages gave way to Arabic. The process began in central Sudan, and from there has been spreading gradually northward down to the present day. As a result, the Nubian languages now survive only in Egyptian Nubia and the most northerly part of the Sudan. Today, the term *Nubia* is applied, in an ethnic and linguistic sense, only to the region where Nubian is still spoken, although archaeologists and culture historians continue to employ it in its older and broader sense.

Early Archaeology in Nubia

Because of its historical connection with Egypt, Nubia has always been regarded by Egyptologists as part of "their" rightful domain. However, chaotic political conditions prevented any actual exploration in the country until the early nineteenth century when Nubia was once again annexed as an Egyptian colony. The Swiss explorer J. L. Burckhardt made the first full traverse of the country by any European in 1813, noting along the way a number of ruined Egyptian temples, including the huge rock-cut colossi of ABU SIMBEL. He was followed over the next three decades by several other explorer observers who left descriptions and sometimes woodcut illustrations of the major Nubian antiquities. Systematic and scientific investigation began, however, with the monumental work of KARL RICHARD LEPSIUS, who between 1842 and 1845 copied all of the then-visible hieroglyphic inscriptions and reliefs on all of the ancient monuments both in Egypt and in Nubia as far south as the ruins of Meroe. His resulting five-volume *Denkmäler aus Ägypten und Äthiopien* (1849) remains today as the sole authoritative source for a great many monuments that have since been destroyed.

In the later nineteenth century, political conditions were again disturbed as a result of the Mahdist rebellion in the Sudan, and field investigation did not resume until after the Anglo-Egyptian reconquest in 1898. The highly publicized military campaign in the Sudan aroused a great deal of interest not only among the general public but among archaeologists, and within a decade of the reconquest, no fewer than nine expeditions took the field in the Egyptian and Sudanese portions of Nubia. In the years immediately following the reconquest, Wallis Budge of the BRITISH MUSEUM carried out a series of rather desultory excavations at several places in northern Sudan while James Breasted and a team from the University of Chicago's ORIENTAL INSTITUTE made photographic records of all the major temples and inscriptions in Nubia. A little later an expedition from the Vienna Academy of Sciences began work in the area just upstream from Aswan, and two expeditions, one from Oxford University and one from the UNIVERSITY OF PENNSYLVANIA MUSEUM, worked on sites in the Egyptian-Sudanese border area. Far to the south, a Liverpool University expedition began to excavate the royal palace compound at the city of Meroe, and an expedition privately financed by Sir Henry Wellcome, a pharmaceutical manufacturer, worked at Gebel Moya south of Khartoum. The architect Somers Clarke, also with private financing, undertook to record all of the medieval Christian remains of both Egypt and Nubia.

Although all the early expeditions, except that of Wellcome, were led by Egyptologists, it is noteworthy that they did not confine themselves to only the archaeological remains of the pharaonic periods. Several of them dug at sites of the Kushite period, and the Oxford and Pennsylvania groups, as well as Somers Clarke, also made major contributions to the study of medieval Nubian remains. There thus arose very early the idea that Nubian archaeology should be a unified study, embracing the whole history of the country, rather than being strictly divided between the Egyptologist and the medievalist, as was the case in Egypt. On the other hand, all of the early expeditions, except that of the Pennsylvania Museum, paid primary attention to monumental architectural remains, mainly of the pharaonic and Kushite periods, although several also did some excavation in cemeteries. There was a conspicuous neglect of townsites, which mostly appeared to be of medieval or later date and which, in any case, were not expected to yield attractive and intact objects for display.

The single most important turning point in the development of Nubian archaeology came about through an act of destruction. The Egyptian irrigation authorities had built a small dam on the Nile just above Aswan at the turn of the century, and in 1907, it was decided to enlarge it so as to create a lake almost 100 miles long. The region to be inundated included a substantial part of Lower Nubia and a number of its important temples as well an unknown, but presumably large, number of other sites. In advance of the destruction, the Egyptian Survey Department sponsored what was, in fact, the world's first archaeological salvage program. It was called the Archaeological Survey of Nubia, although its mandate called for the excavation as well as the discovery and recording of all important sites.

The survey was active in the field for four seasons from 1907 to 1911. It was directed in the first season by GEORGE A. REISNER and in the subsequent years by C. M. Firth. By its own reckoning, the team excavated 151 cemeteries and over 8,000 individual graves, of all periods from the predynastic to the late medieval. However, only about half a dozen sites other than cemeteries were investigated and only one with any thoroughness. Townsites were mostly bypassed because they appeared to be of recent date and the excavators believed that the later phases of Nubian history were adequately documented by historical records. Temples were also bypassed because, since the Aswan Reservoir was to be emptied every summer, the buildings would still be available for study during the summer months. However, a considerable amount of architectural consolidation was undertaken to protect the buildings from the effects of wave action and currents.

The major contribution of the Archaeological Survey of Nubia was the discovery of a whole series of previously unsuspected Nubian cultures that had no Egyptian counterparts. Because they were historically unrecorded, Reisner simply gave them letter designations: A-Group, B-Group, C-Group, and X-Group. The first three were believed to represent a developmental sequence, spanning a period from about 3400 to 1600 B.C., and the X-Group was a unique Nubian culture corresponding to the time of Byzantine rule in Egypt, ca. 350–600 A.D. These designations, except for B-Group, still remain in regular use among archaeologists working in Nubia.

Having developed the basic chronological framework for the understanding of early Nubian history, Reisner's interest in the country was thoroughly aroused. In 1913 he asked for and received, on behalf of Harvard University and the Boston Museum of Fine Arts, a concession to excavate the great early Nubian necropolis at Kerma. When this work was completed in 1915, the Harvard-Boston expedition was granted a series of other concessions that eventually embraced all of the Kushite royal monuments at both Napata and Meroe as well as the great Middle Kingdom Egyptian fortresses in the area of the Second Cataract. These excavations occupied the Harvard-Boston expedition over a period of twenty years and formed by far the largest body of coordinated archaeological activity carried out in Nubia up to that time. The results provided the backbone for all later studies of the Kushite period.

In 1928, plans were made to heighten the dam at Aswan, an operation that would flood an additional 120 miles of the Nile Valley upriver as far as the Sudanese border. In advance of this destruction, a second archaeological survey was set in motion under the direction of WALTER B. EMERY. It was in the field from 1929 to 1934 and excavated a total of 76 cemeteries and about 2,400 individual graves. Once again, as in the first archaeological survey, the emphasis was almost wholly on mortuary remains, although the Emery team did excavate one Kushite townsite and one ancient Egyptian fortress. The major discovery of the second survey was the great X-Group of royal tombs at Ballana and Qustul near the Sudanese border, which showed for the first time that Lower Nubia after the fall of Kush had evolved a powerful chiefdom of its own.

Concurrently with this second survey, a number of distinguished Egyptologists and epigraphers were commissioned to draw up architectural plans and to copy all the inscriptions and reliefs in the temples that would be inundated by the newly enlarged reservoir. At the same time, a German expedition led by Georg Steindorff excavated a series of A-Group, C-Group, and pharaonic cemeteries in Egyptian Nubia while the Italian scholar Ugo Monneret de Villard undertook, at his own expense, a complete survey of all medieval Christian monuments from Aswan to Khartoum. Later in the 1930s, British expeditions from the EGYPT EXPLORATION SOCIETY and Oxford University worked at several pharaonic and Kushite townsites and temple sites in northern Sudan.

Virtually all of the archaeological expeditions to Nubia before World War II were led by Egyptologists, and their work exhibits the typical characteristics of Egyptological archaeology. There was heavy emphasis on the excavation of monumental structures—fortresses, temples, and palaces—from the pharaonic and Kushite periods and also on the excavation of graves from all periods that would yield objects for museum display. Typically, an expedition worked at the same site for four or five seasons in succession, with a small team of European supervisory personnel and a very large native labor force. The quality of architectural recording and mapping was generally very high, since this work was done by trained specialists, but excavation controls were likely to be lax and written documentation poor. A few scholars like Somers Clarke, F. Ll. Griffith, and Monneret de Villard took a special interest in the numerous ruined churches of Nubia, but in other respects the medieval period was neglected. The numerous and well-preserved Christian Nubian townsites were considered too recent to be of interest, and cemeteries were wholly avoided once it was discovered that Christian Nubian graves contained no objects.

World War II brought an end to all archaeological work in Nubia for more than a decade, but when work by European expeditions resumed in the middle 1950s, British, French, Italian, and German expeditions all began excavating some of the pharaonic and Kushite monumental sites that had been bypassed earlier. At the same time, Sudan's Government Antiquities Service made its first entry into the field and immediately enlarged the scope of Nubian archaeology by investigating both prehistoric (Paleolithic and Neolithic) remains and medieval townsites.

The High-Dam Campaign and After

At the end of the 1950s, the Egyptian government announced plans to build a new and much higher dam at Aswan, one that would back up the Nile waters for more than 100 miles into the territory of the Sudan and complete the final destruction of what had once been Lower Nubia. The new reservoir would not be emptied in the summer, as its predecessor was, and the sixteen major temples in Egyptian and Sudanese Nubia would therefore have to be either physically removed to higher ground or surrendered permanently to the lake's waters. Both the

Egyptian government and the newly independent Sudanese government (independent of Anglo-Egyptian rule since 1956) chose the former alternative, and the International Campaign to Save the Monuments of Nubia was launched, with great fanfare, in 1960. The United Nations Educational, Scientific, and Cultural Organization (UNESCO), with headquarters in Paris, agreed to provide overall coordination and to serve as a fund-collecting agency for the campaign, and throughout the next decade it generated a steady flow of publicity that served to focus world attention on the archaeology and culture history of Nubia.

Throughout the 1960s, the tremendous engineering feats of temple removal and reconstruction engaged the world's attention, particularly in the case of the great rock-cut temple of Abu Simbel. It and most of the other Egyptian temples were taken apart and reassembled on higher ground along the lake shore, close to their original sites. The four temples of Sudanese Nubia were removed to the national capital at Khartoum, several hundred miles to the south of the lake area.

Although much less publicized, the Campaign to Save the Monuments of Nubia had also a purely archaeological component, which was and remains the largest coordinated body of archaeological work undertaken anywhere in the world. Between 1959 and 1970, when the new lake reached its full contour, no fewer than sixty expeditions, representing twenty-three different countries, took part in the effort to excavate the sites of Lower Nubia before their final destruction. The high-dam campaign, as it came to be known, in effect broke the monopoly of Egyptologists on the study of Nubian archaeology, for the new expeditions included a large number of European and American prehistorians as well as classicists, Africanists, and many other kinds of specialists. The newcomers brought new and often more-advanced excavation methods to the Nubian field as well as a new and more global cultural perspective.

The salvage campaigns were organized somewhat differently in Egypt and in the Sudan. In Egypt, the territory to be flooded was divided into parcels of more or less equal size, and these were awarded as excavation concessions to various foreign expeditions with the understanding that each expedition would dig whatever was encountered within its territory. This requirement was not always followed in practice, with the result that a number of important sites were destroyed with little or no investigation. The Egyptian Antiquities Service (now the Antiquities Organization) took one concession for itself but otherwise maintained no overall coordination of the work of other groups.

Although the area to be flooded in the Sudan was considerably smaller than that in Egypt, the archaeological challenge was substantially greater since this area had not been previously flooded as had much of Egyptian Nubia. The Sudan Antiquities Service (now the Directorate-General of Antiquities and National Museums) adopted a practice of giving each foreign expedition an individually negotiated concession including just those remains in which the archaeologists were particularly interested and for which they had the resources to carry out the job effectively. Under this procedure, only about one-third of the territory of Sudanese Nubia was awarded to foreign expeditions while the remainder was surveyed and excavated by a team from the Antiquities Service itself. The technical and supervisory personnel of the Antiquities Service team were actually provided by UNESCO, and the group's operation has come to be known as "the UNESCO archaeological survey of Sudanese Nubia." The team was headed for the first seven years by William Y. Adams and for three subsequent years by Anthony J. Mills.

The UNESCO-Sudanese team maintained a coordination and documentation center in the town of Wad Halfa, where a complete file was kept continually up to date of all the sites being recorded and excavated by all the expeditions. The team was thus able to arrange its own field priorities in such a way as to supplement rather than to duplicate the work of the foreign expeditions, concentrating especially on medieval sites and on very early sites that were of little interest to most other archaeologists at the time. It was hoped that the various separate parts of the Nubian campaign in the Sudan would, in the end, add up to something like a comprehensive,

overall picture of Nubian cultural history with no significant gaps. The single most-outstanding achievement of the UNESCO-Sudanese team was to develop a cultural chronology for the thousand-year Christian Nubian period, including developmental typologies of pottery, house architecture, and church architecture.

Since Nubia in 1960 had already been the scene of extensive archaeological activity for half a century, it was inevitable that the high-dam campaign, for all its concentration of effort, should enlarge rather than drastically revise the previously known record. There was, however, one spectacular and wholly unexpected discovery: the buried cathedral at Faras with its well-preserved program of wall decoration. It was already well known, from the numerous standing church ruins in Nubia, that these buildings had once been elaborately decorated, but the ravages of time and Muslim vandalism had left only scraps of the paintings in most cases. The Faras Cathedral, however, had been sanded up and abandoned before the end of the Christian period, and thus a great many of its paintings were preserved intact. This find and the subsequent discovery of three other buried churches made it clear that medieval Nubia had developed its own elaborate and distinctive artistic tradition, different from that of Coptic Egypt. Medieval Nubian mural art has since become a major field of art history study.

Many of the archaeologists who took part in the high-dam campaign continued to work in Nubia in subsequent years, mainly in the areas upstream from the flooded northern portion of country. Particularly important have been the Swiss excavations at Kerma, a site first investigated by the Harvard-Boston expedition in 1913–1915. Although the earlier archaeologists concentrated on the great royal and noble tombs, the Swiss over a dozen years methodically uncovered an enormous townsite with a very long history, including numerous shrines, granaries, workshops, and palaces. Their work has revealed that the indigenous Nubian civilization before the area was overrun by the pharaohs had reached a much higher level of complexity and centralization than was previously thought.

Equally important has been the continuing excavation at Qasr Ibrim in Egyptian Nubia, a fortified townsite originally situated so high above the Nile that the impounded lake waters have not quite reached it. Excavations conducted by a British expedition since 1963 have revealed that the place was a major political, administrative, and religious center in every successive Nubian civilization, from pharaonic times to the early nineteenth century. The elevated situation at Qasr Ibrim has resulted in the total preservation of organic materials, and the site has yielded literally thousands of inscribed documents in nine languages, from hieroglyphic to Turkish. Collectively, and in some cases individually, these have substantially revised the interpretation of many episodes and periods in Nubian history.

Also important have been a number of expeditions working on Paleolithic and Neolithic remains, not only in the Nile Valley but in the adjoining Eastern Desert and the Red Sea Hills. As a result of this work, it is now apparent that Neolithic cultures in the Sudan were much more diversified than was previously thought. There are, in addition, European and American expeditions working at the pharaonic and Kushite temples of Napata, at the townsites of Meroe and Naqa, at the old Christian Nubian capital cities of Dongola and Soba, and on medieval remains in the Third Cataract area. About a dozen major expeditions are working annually in the Sudan at the present time, only a minority of which are now led by Egyptologists. Although present-day techniques of excavation control and recording are vastly improved over those of earlier times, expeditions generally continue the older tradition of working for extended periods—often an indefinite number of years—at a single site. Their aim continues to be basically historical rather than problem focused: to recover everything possible about the history of a site rather than to address specific historical or theoretical questions.

In the broadest sense, the major achievement of the high-dam campaign and subsequent excavations has been the development of a new paradigm, or perspective, of Nubian cultural history. To a large extent, this is owing to the entry of anthropologists and prehistorians into what had previously been regarded as a field of Egyptology. Where earlier scholars since the time of Reisner had tended to see the successive phases of Nubian cultural development as evidence of the arrival of new peoples, or new foreign influences, the new perspective emphasizes the continuity of Nubian cultural development from beginning to end. This view is now generally accepted by the Nubian people themselves as well as by most of the scholars who study them. It provides the theoretical backbone for the newly developed discipline of Nubiology, which, unlike Egyptology, embraces all phases of Nubian history from the Stone Age to the present.

Thanks to its destruction by the successive Aswan dams and the attendant salvage campaigns, Lower Nubia is probably the most thoroughly investigated archaeological zone in the world. There was literally not a square yard of its territory, for a distance of over 300 miles, that was not at least examined from the surface at some time prior to its inundation. Although many sites were eventually destroyed without adequate excavation, the number that went wholly undiscovered was almost certainly very small. The amount of archaeology done in the three salvage campaigns is probably greater than would have been undertaken for several centuries had it not been for the coming inundation.

William Y. Adams

See also Africa, Sahara; Egypt: Dynastic; Egypt: Predynastic

References

Adams, W. Y. 1984. *Nubia: Corridor to Africa*. 2d ed. London: Allen Lane.

Emery, W. B. 1965. *Egypt in Nubia*. London: Hutchinson.

Save-Soderbergh, T. 1987. *Temples and Tombs of Ancient Nubia*. London: Thames and Hudson.

Shinnie, P. L. 1967. *Meroe*. New York: Frederick A. Praeger.

Trigger, B. G. 1976. *Nubia under the Pharaohs*. London: Thames and Hudson.

Vantini, G. 1985. *Cristianesimo nella Nubia antica*. Verona: Museum Combonianum.

Wendorf, F., ed. 1968. *The Prehistory of Nubia*. Dallas: Southern Methodist University Press.

Nyerup, Rasmus (1759–1829)

During the early-nineteenth century, Copenhagen was the administrative and intellectual center of the joint kingdom of DENMARK and Norway, and, as in the rest of Europe, there was growing concern about the destruction of ancient monuments and archaeological sites. A royal collection of artifacts, or a Kunstkammer, was located in Christianborg, but it was unordered and overflowing with material. SWEDEN had already passed legislation for the protection of its monuments and artifacts, and groups in Denmark and Norway became interested in similar legislation.

Professor Rasmus Nyerup researched these issues and traveled throughout Europe to find the best solutions. In 1801, he visited the Museum of French Monuments in Paris, which had been set up under the new republic, and was most impressed. In 1806, he published the results of his research and recommendations: *Survey of the National Monuments of Antiquity Such as May Be Displayed in a Future National Museum,* the last volume of which outlined his ideas as to how prehistoric material and later remains from Denmark and Norway should be exhibited in a museum similar to the one in Paris.

The defeat of the Danish by the English in 1801 and 1807 stimulated national enthusiasm for past greatness now perceived to be circumscribed by contemporary politics, and by 1806, Nyerup was beginning to receive the first contributions of archaeological material for a future national museum. In 1807, the first legislation for the protection of monuments and archaeological finds was enacted, and it provided for the setting up of a commission to advise on the foundation of a state museum. Nyerup became secretary and member of this commission.

By 1816, the job had become too big for him, and a young numismatist, with a deep interest in antiquity, the right connections, and a talent for classification, CHRISTIAN JURGENSEN THOMSEN, replaced him as secretary. Although it was Thomsen who gradually brought the Danish national collection into working order, which involved developing a whole new system of classification, it was Nyerup's survey that helped Thomsen formulate the system. And it was Nyerup's passion for, and knowledge of, antiquities that helped found the Danish National Museum, whose collections and scholars greatly contributed to the elucidation of prehistory, not only in Scandinavia, but also in Europe as a whole.

Tim Murray

References

Klindt-Jensen, O. 1975. *A History of Scandinavian Archaeology.* London: Thames and Hudson.

O

Obermaier Grad, Hugo (1877–1946)

Hugo Obermaier Grad was born into a traditional and cultured family fond of humanist studies and collecting. Between 1886 and 1895, Obermaier's training alternated between the study of the classics (Greek and Latin) and reading the work of the archaeologist HEINRICH SCHLIEMANN, which, combined with familiarity with Roman Bavarian antiquities, awoke his interest in archaeology. He then studied philosophy and theology and was ordained as a Catholic priest in 1900.

At the University of Vienna, Obermaier studied geology with A. Penck, anatomy and anthropology with C. Toldt, and prehistoric archaeology with M. Hörnes. In 1904, he obtained his Ph.D. Between 1904 and 1906, he completed his training in Paris where he was in contact with the great French prehistorians Lapparent, Gaudry, MARCELLIN BOULE, EMILE CARTAILHAC, Commont, and Capitan and studied French Paleolithic sites, museums, and private collections. It was here and at this time that he began to work with the French prehistorian and priest HENRI BREUIL. Indeed, Obermaier and Breuil shared the secretariat position in sessions of the Congrès International d'Anthropologie de Monaco in 1905.

In 1909, Obermaier visited SPAIN for the first time, and he subsequently spent summers participating in the excavations and study of the art of important Cantabrian Paleolithic sites in the caves of Castillo (1910–1914, with Breuil and H. Alcalde del Río), at ALTAMIRA (1925 on), and in La Pasiega as well as in the Pileta Cave, Málaga, among other sites.

From 1909 to 1911, Obermaier taught a course on the Primitive History of Man at the University of Vienna without giving up his cooperative work with French researchers. In 1911, he went to Paris to work with Boule and Breuil, who were directors of the Institut de Paléontologie Humaine founded by Prince Albert I of Monaco in 1910.

In view of the great importance of his research in Spain, the Real Academia de la Historia (Royal Academy of History) made Obermaier an honorary member in Munich in 1913. His connection with the Institut de Paléontologie was interrupted by the outbreak of World War I, but the Junta para la Ampliación de Estudios e Investigaciones Científicas (Board for the Expansion of Study and Scientific Research) offered him the post of assistant lecturer in the Museo de Ciencias Naturales (Museum of Natural Sciences) in Madrid while the Duke of Alba took him into his household as chaplain. From then until 1938, Obermaier worked in Spain and became a Spanish citizen in 1924. In 1922, at the request of the Philosophy and Arts Faculty of the Universidad Central (Central University) in Madrid, the chair of Primitive History of Man was created for him, and he was head of the section of the Museo Antropológico in Madrid until 1936.

In 1926, he was admitted to the Royal Academy of History, and he was made an honorary doctor by the universities of Friburg, Oporto, and Lisbon as well as the Skandinaviska Släkt Tudie Samfundet (Germanitas Genealogiae Gothica). He belonged to the Academy of Sciences of Bavaria and the Pontificia of the Nuovi Lincei of Rome. He was a member of the DEUTSCHES ARCHÄOLOGISCHES INSTITUT (German

Archaeological Institute) and a honorary member of the Prussian Academy of Sciences (both in Berlin), a honorary member of the Anthropological Society of Vienna, and a honorary fellow of the Royal Irish Academy.

In 1927, Obermaier founded, and directed until 1936, the monthly magazine *Investigación y Progreso* sponsored by the Center for Germano-Spanish Cultural Exchange, which published short papers on all fields of knowledge and research, mostly by German authors. Absent from Spain at the outbreak of the Civil War, he never resumed his academic career or residence there again. He was in Italy for a short time and then, in 1937, became a lecturer in prehistory at the Catholic University of Friburg in Germany, where he died.

Obermaier made important contributions to knowledge of Iberian prehistory in Europe, and to the development of the discipline of prehistory in Spain, through his teaching activity at the University of Madrid and through his research, which was primarily published in German and French. This research was concerned with Quaternary geology, the European Paleolithic period, Paleolithic rock art, and rock art during the postglacial period, both on the Iberian Peninsula and in Africa. He was responsible for the fundamental study of megalithic burial grounds, such as the dolmen of Matarrubilla (Seville) and the passage grave of Soto (Huelva).

Obermaier's first work of synthesis, *Der Mensch der Vorzeit* (1931), was translated into Russian a year later. The books *El hombre fósil* (1916) and *El hombre prehistórico y los orígenes de la humanidad* (1932) have been fundamental references for the study of the Paleolithic period in Spain for several decades.

In Spain, Obermaier's solid empirical training helped "to definitely overcome the distrust and prejudice which existed in academic circles with regard to Prehistory" (Peiro Martin and Pasamar Alzuria 1989–1990, 24). The introduction of Obermaier into these circles was additionally facilitated by his position as a Catholic author and by the sponsorship of the Duke of Alba. His most original contribution was his attempt to convert prehistory into paleoethnology by using ethnographic parallels. He was close to the historical-cultural school, but he did not consider it adequate for the study of the origins of human cultures (Obermaier 1926, 19). His paleoethnology was based on the community of ideas among peoples with the same degree of maturity, "how ever distant they were placed in space and in time" (Pairo Martin and Pasamar Alzuria 1989–1990, 27), and archaeological data. Some of the most important Spanish archaeologists were his pupils.

Isabel Martínez Navarrete

References

Ballesteros y Beretta, Antonio. 1926. "Discurso de contestación." In *Discursos leídos ante la Real Academia de la Historia en la recepción de Don Hugo Obermaier el 2 de Mayo de 1926*, 103–117. Madrid: Imprenta Caro Raggio.

Bandi, H. G., and Maringer, J. 1953. "Das Werk Professor Dr. Hugo Obermaiers 1877–1946." *Eiszeitalter und Gegenmart* 3: 136–143.

Breuil, H. 1950. "Hugo Obermaier (1877–1946)." *Revue Archéologique,* 6th ser., 35: 105–119.

Garcia Bellido, Antonio. 1947. *Hugo Obermaier.* Madrid: Imprenta y Editorial Maestre.

"Noticias." 1935. *Sociedad Española de Antropología, Etnografía y Prehistoria, Actas y Memorias* 14: 311–312.

Obermaier, H. 1926. "La vida de nuestros antepasados cuaternarios en Europa." In *Discursos leídos ante la Real Academia de la Historia en la recepción de Don Hugo Obermaier el 2 de Mayo de 1926,* 7–101. Ed. A. Ballesteros y Beretta. Madrid: Imprenta Caro Raggio.

Peiro Martin, Ignacio, and Gonzalo Pasamar Alzuria. 1989–1990. "El nacimiento en España de la Arqueología y la Prehistoria (Academicismo y profesionalización, 1856–1936)." *Kalathos* 9–10: 9–30.

Perez de Barradas, José. 1948. "Hugo Obermaier Grad." *Trabajos del Instituto "Bernardino de Sahagún" de Antropología y Etnología* 6: 9–14.

Okladnikov, Aleksei Pavlovich (1908–)

The son of a village schoolteacher, Aleksei Pavlovich Okladnikov was born in Siberia and developed an interest in the history, traditions, and folklore of that region. Okladnikov finished school in 1925 and entered the teacher-training institute in Irkutsk, majoring in history. Irktutsk was a center for Siberian studies, and Okladnikov became actively involved in archaeological-ethnographic and ethnological circles. A visit to the Lake Baikal area to survey archaeological sites and collect ethnographic material resulted in his first paper on the Neolithic period and set the direction of his future career. In 1928 he became chief of the ethnographic section of the Irkutsk Local Lore Museum, where he studied the collections and made many archaeological survey trips throughout Siberia, discovering the famous Fofanovo burial ground with its elaborate tombs from the Neolithic period and the Bronze Age.

During the 1930s, a number of hydroelectric projects resulted in a large archaeological surveys of the Angara and Lena Rivers and the Lake Baikal area, and there were many excavations of Neolithic and Bronze Age sites. Okladnikov participated in this work and was instrumental in writing the cultural history of the region from 5000 B.C. In 1934, he enrolled for further study at the State Academy in Leningrad under P. P. Yefimenko, the head of Paleolithic studies in the Soviet Union. In 1935, Okladnikov joined the Nizhne-Amur expedition, which provided evidence for the history of that western region of Siberia from early Neolithic times to the sixteenth century A.D.

From 1936 to 1940, Okladnikov researched the archaeology of the Angara River valley and discovered the famous Paleolithic site of Buret', a complex of houses built from mammoth and rhinoceros bones, with reindeer antler roofs, containing stone and bone implements and decorative effigies carved from mammoth tusks. Together with the Mal'ta site, Buret' represented the earliest stage of the Upper Neolithic period in eastern Siberia, dating from 2300 to 2100 B.C. In 1938 Okladnikov submitted his M.A. thesis on this research and later published it as *The Neolithic and Bronze Age in the Lake Baikal Area* (1955), in which he used ethnography and folklore in the interpretation of archaeological sources.

In 1938, Okladnikov took up the post of senior researcher at the Institute of the History of Material Culture at the Academy of Sciences and went to central Asia to study the Stone Age in Uzbekistan. He discovered a number of Paleolithic sites, including the famous cave site of Teshik-Tash in Tadjikistan, a multilevel Mousterian site containing the burial remains of a Neanderthal boy. This skeleton was the first Neanderthal burial to be found east of Palestine, and in 1950 Okladnikov received the Stalin Award for its discovery and excavation.

Okladnikov began to explore the archaeology and history of Yakutia—an immense and little understood part of Siberia—in 1940. Despite World War II and a lack of funds, he led a six-year expedition and amassed a huge body of data and artifacts, pushing back the known history of Yakutia by thousands of years and elucidating the ancient settlement patterns of Siberia, the origin of the Yakuts, and their relation to Turkic and Mongolian peoples. This was the basis of his Ph.D. thesis, which he completed in 1947, and his most famous book, *Yakutia before Its Incorporation into the Russian State* [History of Yakutia], the first volume of which was published in 1949 and published in English in 1970.

In 1946, Okladnikov took another expedition to the Okhotsk and Bering seacoast in eastern Siberia, and from 1947 to 1952, he traveled to central Asia to excavate Stone Age sites such as Djebel cave in Turkmenistan and Khodjaken cave in Uzbekistan. In 1949, he traveled to Mongolia for the first time and discovered Paleolithic sites near Uland Ude and Kharakhorin (Moiltyn-Am). From 1952 to 1962, Okladnikov was head of the Paleolithic and Neolithic section of the Leningrad branch of the Institute of Archaeology. During this time, he published extensively in scientific journals and continued to lead expeditions to Siberia and Central Asia.

He began studying the Russian Far East in 1953 and led expeditions there between 1953 and 1958, which resulted in his book *The Soviet Far East in Antiquity: An Archaeological and Historical Study of the Maritime Region of the USSR,* which was published in English in 1965. In 1961, Okladnikov became director of the humanities research department in Novosibirsk at the newly opened Siberian Branch of the USSR Academy of Sciences.

In 1964, he was elected member of the Academy of Sciences of the USSR, and in 1966, he

The landscape of the Olduvai Gorge (Gallo Images/Corbis)

became first director of the Institute of History, Philology, and Philosophy in Novosibirsk. During the 1960s and 1970s, Okladnikov edited and authored the *History of Siberia,* for which he received the USSR's State Award in 1973. He returned to work in Soviet Mongolia and put forward a general scheme of the evolution of the Paleolithic period there. He also studied petroglyphs, discovering and examining thousands of them and publishing his interpretations. He supervised over forty doctoral dissertations, and his students now work in positions in archaeology across the whole of RUSSIA. He was awarded the Gold Medal of the Hero of Labor in 1978, on his seventieth birthday.

Ruslan S. Vasilevsky

References

For references, see *Encyclopedia of Archaeology: The Great Archaeologists, Vol. 2,* ed. Tim Murray (Santa Barbara, CA: ABC-CLIO, 1999), pp. 579–580.

Olduvai Gorge

Located near the Serengeti Plain in northern Tanzania, Olduvai Gorge is an erosional feature connected to the Rift Valley of Africa. Discovered as a fossil locality by the Germans before World War I (notably by Wilhelm Kattwinkel [1866–1935] and Hans Reck [1886–1937]), Olduvai Gorge was taken up as a research area by LOUIS B. LEAKEY when Reck revisited the area with him between 1931 and 1932. Leakey and his wife, MARY LEAKEY, conducted regular fieldwork in the gorge over the next thirty years, but it was not until 1959 (with Mary Leakey's discovery of the cranium of what Louis Leakey named *Zinjanthropus boisei*) that the spectacular discoveries which are synonymous with the place were made.

In many ways, Olduvai Gorge is an ideal fossil locality with a geological history spanning the last 2 million years and fossil-bearing sediments sandwiched by datable volcanic tuffs that have so far yielded australopithecines and early forms of the genus *Homo* (*Homo habilis* and *Homo erectus*). Notwithstanding its importance as a fossil locality, the sediments at Olduvai also contain a vitally important cross-sequence of early hominid stone technology. It is the type site of the Oldawan industry, the oldest yet dis-

Skulls discovered in Olduvai Gorge (Gamma)

covered, and archaeologists have been able to trace the development of that industry through three phases (A, B, and C) on the site, and there is clear evidence of the replacement of these industries by the Acheulean around 1.4 million years ago.

Work continued in the Olduvai Gorge after the death of Louis Leakey and the retirement of Mary Leakey from a leadership role at the site. Apart from being one of the world's most significant localities for hominid fossils, it is also one of the most important training grounds for the current leaders in paleoanthropology and Pleistocene archaeology.

Tim Murray

See also Africa, East, Prehistory; Laetoli
References
Leakey, L. S. B., et al. 1965–1996. *Olduvai Gorge.* Cambridge: Cambridge University Press.
Sept, J. M. 1997. *Investigating Olduvai: Archaeology of Human Origins.* Interactive CD. Bloomington: Indiana University Press.

Olmec Civilization

The Olmec civilization is often called the "mother culture" of MESOAMERICA. The first complex society of the area, the Olmecs developed and formalized many of the great hallmarks of Mesoamerican civilization.

The term *Olmec* means "people of the land of rubber." The name was applied by the AZTECS to the people living on the southern edge of the Gulf of Mexico—a low-lying, hot, and humid region where rubber trees are native. When archaeological sites with colossal heads carved in basalt were discovered in the area, archaeologists

thought that they were relatively recent in date. A few scholars, however, argued for a greater antiquity. With the advent of more refined DATING techniques such as radiocarbon dating, the debate was settled: the florescence of Olmec culture dated from about 1200 to 400 B.C.

Many of the most famous Olmec sites are in the steamy lowlands along the southern coast of the Gulf of Mexico, which is where the colossal heads were first found. This area has been called by many scholars the "Olmec heartland," and sites such as San Lorenzo and LA VENTA are two of the best-known and most excavated of all Olmec sites. Olmec San Lorenzo flourished between about 1200 and 900 B.C. The main part of the site was a huge, partly human-built earth mound some 1,200 meters long by 800 meters wide, on top of which were constructed ceremonial mounds, ritual pools, and a stone drainage system. The huge stone heads and other sculptures (carved from boulders dragged from about 60 kilometers away as the crow flies) were originally set in groups atop the large mound. Some were found to have been intentionally buried in large trenches; recently some heads have been discovered where they were apparently stored for recarving. About 900 B.C. many of the stone monuments at San Lorenzo were defaced (it was presumably at this time that some were buried in trenches), and the site was largely abandoned.

La Venta's florescence followed the decline of San Lorenzo and is dated from about 900 to 400 B.C. By that time the Olmecs had become master craftspeople in another medium, jade, which then became the most prized commodity throughout subsequent Mesoamerican cultures. La Venta suffered a fate similar to that of San Lorenzo: around 400 B.C. some of its monuments were smashed or defaced, and the site was abandoned.

The Olmec heartland was not the only place where the Olmec peoples flourished. Their presence in the highlands of central MEXICO is also attested at dozens of sites. Major highland Olmec sites included Chalcatzingo (ca. 1000–500 B.C.), just south of Mexico City, and another with the tongue-twister name of Teopantecuanitlan (ca. 900–600 B.C.). These and many other Olmec sites were strategically located to control important resources and trade and communication routes. The large numbers and sheer volume of imported objects in many such sites clearly offer evidence of the Olmecs' ability to command resources from a wide area.

There are still many unanswered questions regarding the Olmecs. For example, was their widespread presence and influence based on political control, economic power, or the spread of an Olmec religion? All three possibilities have been proposed, but as yet there are no clear answers.

The Olmecs were wonderful artists and produced the first great art style of Mesoamerica. Their stone carvings great and small, their beautifully made and decorated ceramics, and their surviving paintings all are indicative of a mature and self-confident civilization. Many of their images are portraits of their gods, and major advances have been made in recent years in "deciphering" the Olmec pantheon. But other pieces are more personal, from the 20-ton portrait heads of their rulers to the smaller jade masks and other objects that have often been found in large numbers in caches.

What can be called classic Olmec civilization declined around 400 B.C., but the Olmec people survived. One of their achievements in later times was the development of a writing system. Traces indicating the first steps toward developing a script can be seen in monuments from La Venta, but evidence indicates that a full-fledged writing system was not used until near the time of Christ. This script, called epi-Olmec, has been brilliantly deciphered by two American scholars, John Justeson and Terrence Kaufman.

Peter Mathews

See also Maya Civilization
References
Coe, Michael D., and Richard A. Diehl. 1980. *In the Land of the Olmec.* Austin: University of Texas Press.

Olorgesailie

Although this Acheulean site south of Nairobi, in Kenya, was first discovered by LOUIS LEAKEY and MARY LEAKEY, it is most famously associated with the work of GLYN ISAAC, who excavated there in the 1960s and early 1970s. The site originally aroused considerable interest because of the extensive record of hand-axe manufacture noted by Isaac and because he argued that he had identified clear evidence of butchery there. One part of the site also exhibited a large number of gelada baboon remains near a concentration of hand-axes, which gave rise to some speculation about whether these animals had been killed by hominids. Isaac's original interpretations of Olorgesaillie have been challenged on the basis that the sites are found in sandy stream channels, which at least makes it possible that the accumulations of stones and bones were not the direct result of hominid action.

Tim Murray

See also Africa, East, Prehistory
References
Isaac, Glyn, with Barbara Isaac. 1977. *Olorgesailie: Archaeological Studies of a Middle Pleistocene Lake Basin in Kenya.* Chicago: University of Chicago Press.

Oriental Institute of Chicago

Founded in 1919 by the U.S. Egyptologist James Henry Breasted, with support from John F. Rockefeller, the Oriental Institute was the expression of a strong interest at the University of Chicago in the archaeology, history, and linguistics of the ancient Near East. Rockefeller's generosity continued into the 1930s when the institute took possession of a purpose-built museum and an office and laboratory complex. But Breasted envisioned a greater role for the institute than simply being a repository of ancient artifacts; he believed it should also physically document the significant part played by Near Eastern civilizations in the evolution of western culture. Since its inception the Oriental Institute has been heavily involved in fieldwork throughout the Near East, and its staff members have been particularly active in the study of the ancient languages of the region, especially Assyrian and SUMERIAN. In this regard, they have created dictionaries and advanced the systematic study of ancient texts through epigraphy (most notably in Egypt).

Tim Murray

See also Albright, William F.; Egypt, Dynastic; Egypt, Predynastic; Iran; Israel; Jordan; Mesopotamia; Syro-Palestinian and Biblical Archaeology

Ozette Village

The Ozette Village is a Northwest North American coastal SHELL MIDDEN site on the Olympic Peninsula of Washington State. It was occupied for at least 2,000 years until the early-twentieth century, and a portion of the site was preserved intact by a catastrophic mudslide in protohistoric times.

The coastal shell middens of the Olympic Peninsula were first excavated in the early-twentieth century. Radiocarbon dates place the sites within the last 3,000 years. Like many of the coastal sites, Ozette is a shell midden, located at the top of Cape Alava, the westernmost tip of the continuous United States. The village was a multiseason and winter-use food processing site. The primary food resource was whale.

Although the site, composed of several locations between the mainland and the nearby offshore islands, may have been occupied for 2,000 years, a portion was covered in a catastrophic mudslide around 1500 A.D. A mudslide capped the site with a six- to ten-foot layer of clay, rendering a unique opportunity to study the native village on the Olympic Peninsula Pacific coast. Many food-processing remains were recovered at Ozette. Ozette is unique in the preservation resulting from the mudslide. Not only did the clay mud cover occur before contact with Europeans, but it also created a water-soaked environment for the contents of the houses it covered. The wet condition preserved materials such as fiber and wood, which would normally deteriorate very rapidly.

Scientists have been fascinated with the Northwest Coast cultures because of their elaborate development of a mostly sea animal—based subsistence that included hunting whales, sea lions, seals, and sea otters. As a result of the mudslide, Ozette provides a complete material record of village daily and seasonal life. Over 85 percent of the artifacts from Ozette were made of perishable materials that have not survived at other sites such as wood, plant fiber, and structural components.

Ozette was first test-excavated in 1967 by Richard D. Daugherty. Ozette was one of the five Makah Indian tribe villages on the Peninsula, located between a low ridge and a narrow beach facing the Bodeltah Islands. The Makah call themselves "people of the seagulls and rocks." The area is rich in bird, fish, and mammal life. The Islands protect the shore and waters for canoeing and are part of the village site. Ozette has mainly sea mammal remains, including sea lions, harbor seals, and sea otters. Whale remains are the most abundant of all; over 75 percent of recovered faunal remains are from a few species of whale. The rich variety of sea life brought whales near the shore, where they were hunted from canoes by the Makah. Other abundant food and material resources included ducks, geese, shorebirds, and shellfish.

In the winter of 1947, Daugherty surveyed Ozette as part of an archaeological survey of the entire Pacific coast of Washington. Ethnographic studies were conducted in 1948 and 1949. In 1955 Stallard and Denman conducted a small test excavation at Ozette. In the summers of 1966 and 1967 Daugherty, Roald Fryxell, and Carl Gustafson tested all areas of the site; the earliest radiocarbon dates they received were 2010 +/- 190 years ago. In 1967 Area B, a recent longhouse area, was excavated on the sea bank edge. Normally perishable materials such as fiber matting, cordage, basketry, wooden wedges, and boxes were found in the test excavations. In 1970, storms uncovered more perishable artifacts on the bank edge. At that time, the Makah Tribal Council asked Daughtery to return and salvage the materials. From that point on, excavations were continued year-round until 1981. After initial testing, a singular excavation project was conducted for over ten years, in cooperation with with the Makah Indian Nation.

The sheer volume of well-preserved fragile artifacts from the site is overwhelming. A special processing and exhibit center was constructed just for Ozette materials. The location required many helicopter trips to the exhibit center with artifacts. Researchers traveled in by foot on a four-mile forest trail. A special system was developed using pressurized water to wash away the sterile clay layer. Delicate wooden artifacts were preserved in Carbo wax 1500 and water. Many artifacts were processed on-site and at the nearby Neah Bay. The Makah Indian Nation, including elders and youths, was heavily involved with the excavation. In 1979 the Makah Cultural Research Center opened to the public.

Danielle Greene

See also United States of America, Prehistoric Archaeology

References

Samuels, Stephan R., ed. 1991. *Ozette Archaeological Project Research Reports, Volume 1: House Structure and Floor Midden.* Seattle: Department of Anthropology, Washington State University, Pullman, and National Park Service, Pacific Northwest Regional Office.

Sturtevant, William C., vol. ed. 1990. *Handbook of North American Indians: Northwest Coast, Volume 7.* Washington, DC: Smithsonian Institution.

Thomas, David Hurst. 1989. *Archaeology.* Fort Worth: Holt, Rinehart and Winston.

P

Palenque

Palenque is a classic Maya site and kingdom in the southern state of Chiapas in MEXICO. Its florescence was during the late classic period, ca. A.D. 600–800, and after its decline and abandonment it became enveloped by dense forest until it was rediscovered in the late-eighteenth century. During the nineteenth century, the beauty of its architecture and art made the site famous, and during the twentieth century, excavations and mapping at the site have revealed an extensive city. The discovery in 1952 of a royal tomb beneath the Temple of the Inscriptions at Palenque was one of the greatest Maya archaeological finds.

Palenque's early history was not particularly stellar. A king list extending back to the early fifth century exists at the site, and some early remains have been found dating from Palenque's early years. Nevertheless, most of Palenque's archaeological remains excavated thus far date to the period after A.D. 600.

Shortly before and after that date, Palenque was devastated by a series of defeats in war. It appears that the capital itself was invaded, and a series of royal deaths around this time indicates that the kingdom was rocked to its foundations. The new king to emerge from this period of upheaval was a man called Hanab'-Pakal. He came to the throne in A.D. 615, at the age of twelve, and proceeded to guide his kingdom to a period of stability and power. By the time he died in 683, Palenque was one of the greatest kingdoms in the Maya area.

Hanab'-Pakal achieved that stability by consolidating the eastern frontier of his kingdom with military victories over his old enemies while a probable kinsman of his simultaneously extended the kingdom to the west. With his kingdom stabilized, Hanab'-Pakal turned his attention to his capital city and embarked on a major building program. Much of the palace at Palenque was his work, and he also began work on his most famous monument, the Temple of the Inscriptions. This temple pyramid, which contains the tomb of Hanab'-Pakal, has an interior stairway (filled in and covered in antiquity) leading to the temple above. Hanab'-Pakal was buried in a beautifully carved stone sarcophagus upon his death at the age of eighty.

Hanab'-Pakal was succeeded by his oldest son, Kan-Balam II, who extended his father's building program, building most notably the famous "Group of the Cross," an arrangement of three temples that are widely considered to be among the most elegant of all Maya buildings.

Palenque's fortunes waxed and waned over the following decades, but by A.D. 800, the site was in decline. Late construction at Palenque consisted of such work as poorly built walls subdividing the elegant chambers of the palace—a sad conclusion to Palenque's great architectural tradition.

In addition to its beautiful architecture (which features the widest corbeled vaults in the Maya area), Palenque is famous for its elegant art. Many of the temples have beautiful scenes in modeled stucco adorning their outer facades. Stone carving at Palenque was mostly done using flat panels of finely grained limestone rather than the upright, free-standing stelae that typify other sites. These panels were carved and then set on walls in the interior of buildings, so for the most part they have been

A pyramid in the ruins of Palenque (Gamma)

beautifully preserved. The Tablet of the Cross, for example, is one of the masterpieces of Maya sculptural art. The central scene shows an episode from the Maya creation epic and is flanked by King Kan-Balam II portrayed on his accession day. The hieroglyphic text that accompanies the scene tells about the Maya creation before presenting a list of the kings of Palenque.

Peter Mathews

See also Mesoamerica
References
Schele, L., and P. Mathews. 1998. *The Lode of Kings.* New York: Scribners.

Paleolithic Archaeology

Paleolithic archaeology was born in the decades between 1840 and 1860 by the interweaving of a number of intellectual threads that gave meaning to the material relics of the distant past. These included the antiquarian tradition (literally, an interest in artifacts manufactured in the past), a long-standing idea of progress and development as a general human characteristic, the establishment of human antiquity, and the idea of evolution (i.e., descent with modification).

The Discovery of the Archaeological Record
Individuals in many societies have, throughout history, expressed an interest in the human past and its visible antiquities, but much of this was philosophical speculation removed from the study of the remains themselves. It was the European Renaissance that provided the foundations for a material study of the past. The classical writers discussed the ancestors of the northern Europeans, which led some renaissance scholars to speculate on the origin of European antiquities (Daniel 1975, 17). Some sixteenth-century scholars were able to travel to GREECE and ITALY and see classical antiquities for themselves. During this time, however, the focus was on art and architecture, on visible standing monuments rather than on buried remains.

Interest in the classical world also stimulated an interest in the standing monuments of Europe—the henges, hill forts, and ancient churches—particularly by scholars who could not afford the cost of travel to Mediterranean Europe (Daniel 1975, 22). A romantic, barbarian past was created, bound up with an interest in natural history as taught by the great Swedish botanist Carolus Linnaeus.

By the late eighteenth century, antiquarian interest had extended to the excavation of Roman and pre-Roman remains, but as the Danish scholar RASMUS NYERUP bemoaned, the past seemed to be wrapped in a thick fog and was a period for which no measure of time was available (Daniel 1975, 38). Some indication of the problem can be gauged from JOHN FRERE's 1797 account of flint artifacts buried with bones of extinct animals. He illustrated two pieces, now recognized as hand-axes, and commented that they came from "a very remote period indeed; even beyond that of the present world" (cited in Grayson 1983, 57). However, while Frere appeared to argue for the existence of people who lived in a world not yet in its modern form (Grayson 1983, 59), it is likely that his notions of past times were simply those of the book of Genesis (Sackett 2000). The artifacts he had found had belonged to people who had lost the art of metalworking during the time before the biblical great flood and they, like the animals whose bones lay with their artifacts, had succumbed to the deluge.

Frere, like his contemporaries, faced the problem of imagining a history unrelated to that described in the records of the classical writers (Sackett 2000). Celtic-speaking Gauls, as described in the texts, might populate Europe, but if other societies had existed in the past, it was hard to imagine what they might have been like or when they might have existed. Frere lacked a method for recognizing that similar types of artifacts and monuments cluster in time and space and that a culture history could be constructed from this information. It took sixty years for such methods to be developed and the significance of his finds to be recognized.

The method that Frere lacked was developed by CHRISTIAN THOMSEN, curator of the Danish National Museum. Thomsen sorted artifacts according to the material from which they were made. Although this was not a new technique (the historian Vedel-Simonsen had already proposed such a method [Daniel 1975, 40]), under Thomsen the technique won wide acceptance. Not only could artifacts be separated by raw materials, but the groups of artifacts that resulted suggested to another Danish archaeologist, SVEN NILSSON, that an age of stone was followed by an age of bronze and then by an age of iron (Daniel 1975, 42). Nilsson found functional analogues for antiquities in the objects used by modern-day peoples outside Europe (Daniel 1975, 48).

The eighteenth-century Enlightenment ideal of universal human progress seemed to have a material representation, one that the archaeologist JENS JACOB WORSAAE was able to establish in stratigraphic excavations using the recently established laws of superimposition. Materials changed through time but so did artifact form and decoration. Nilsson and Worsaae applied the methods of Linnaeus to artifacts and thereby developed the forerunner to the typological method as well as seriation (Daniel 1975, 47). Worsaae's Copenhagen museum guide of 1836 was probably the most important archaeological work produced in the first half of the nineteenth century since it laid down the principles of a prehistoric archaeology (Daniel 1975, 45).

One of the reasons why Frere's discovery of 1797 caused so little comment was that scholars had been attempting to identify humans contemporary with the biblical flood for many years (Schnapp and Kristiansen 1999). The evidence for human antiquity existed, but the concepts and methods needed to make sense of it were not in place until midway through the nineteenth century. First, it was critical that artifacts be recognized for what they were: the product of human modification of natural materials. Human remains were also potentially important, but compared to artifacts, such remains are rare in the archaeological record. Although differentiating artifacts from natural objects continued to be a problem in some cases, artifacts were recognized as such by the end of the eighteenth century, at least partly as a result of European worldwide colonization and parallels between modern "primitive" peoples and prehistoric Europeans (Trigger 1989, 52).

Second, stratigraphy and the law of superimposition were essential concepts if a method were to be developed that could be used to order events that had occurred in the past. This method was also in place by the end of the eighteenth century. However, the ordering of levels on their own provided only localized sequences, and the third method to be developed linked strata identified in different places according to their fossil content. English geologist William Smith assigned relative ages to rocks based on their fossil contents in 1816 and argued for orderly deposition over a long period of time, but the great French anatomist, Georges Cuvier, who collected and described fossil animals at the end of the eighteenth century, had laid the basis for the approach (Schnapp and Kristiansen 1999).

The fourth method was based on the recognition that geological deposits in Europe contained both the remains of extinct animals and artifacts of human manufacture. Cuvier recognized the former based on his discoveries in the Paris basin, and he proposed that the earth had passed through a series of stages in which every successive landscape and plant and animal community was replaced by another, each one coming closer to the modern world (Sackett 2000). Each stage was separated by a geological catastrophe with people present only in the most recent period—the Holocene (from 10,000 years ago). This scheme was the one into which evidence for human antiquity was fitted during the first half of the nineteenth century. Cuvier estimated that the last catastrophe, which separated the Pleistocene from the Holocene, was dated some 5,000–6,000 years ago. At the hands of British geologists—first Jameson, then Parkinson, and finally Buckland—this final catastrophe quickly became associated with the biblical flood (Grayson 1983, 59). Thus, in Great Britain, more so than in Continental Europe, the lack of human remains until the Holocene period took on theological as well as geological significance (Grayson 1983, 98).

Opposition to the catastrophist theories of Cuvier and Buckland can be found in the work of James Hutton, who published the forerunner of a uniformitarian theory in 1785 (Daniel 1975, 37). However, the development of an effective alternative to catastrophism is associated with CHARLES LYELL, who argued during the early nineteenth century that the processes responsible for the formation of the geological record operated in a uniform way and at a uniform rate (Daniel 1975, 38). Catastrophes were unnecessary to explain the history of the world, for the conditions existing in the past were essentially the same as those that existed in modern times. Therefore, the deposits that WILLIAM BUCKLAND attributed to the flood were the result of geological processes operating over a long period of time, and the extinction of animals whose bones appeared in these deposits must also have occurred in the remote past (Grayson 1983, 82).

However, Lyell did not accept a great antiquity for humanity. Like the catastrophists, he supported a notion that humans are unique in the world and appeared late in its history (Sackett 2000). In fact, by removing the link between deposits containing the remains of extinct animals on the one hand and the biblical concept of the flood on the other, Lyell removed the need to discover human remains dating from the period after Adam and Eve had been expelled into the world but before the deluge (Grayson 1983, 70). The remains of extinct animals now suggested a much older age for the premodern world than had been previously imagined. If humans appeared only in the modern world, their remains should not appear in ancient deposits, and those few instances that appeared to contradict this position were dismissed as the result of a fluvial mixing of deposits—a particular problem in limestone caves (Grayson 1983, 71).

Geological deposits with the remains of extinct animals occur in three forms in Europe: caves, rock shelters, and gravel terraces (Sackett 2000). Of the three, caves (i.e., large cavities in limestone bedrock) were the most often investigated in the first half of the nineteenth century. These frequently contained substantial deposits of animal bones but only limited artifacts. More substantial artifact deposits awaited archaeological research on the rock overhangs in the limestone cliffs running along the valley edges, but such investigations did not begin in earnest until the second half of the nineteenth century. Gravel terraces were formed from water-laid sediments and contained a stratigraphic record of artifacts and animal bones, but this record was not as substantial as that found in caves (Sackett 2000).

A series of investigations in the late eighteenth and early nineteenth centuries reported the association of human remains or artifacts with the remains of extinct animals, but in each case doubts were cast on the stratigraphic integrity of the finds since they derived from limestone caves known to be affected by water movement. Thus, after French archaeologist Torunal discovered human bones associated with the bones of extinct animals at Grotte de Bize (a cave in southwest France) his colleague Serres claimed that both sets of bones were in the same state of preservation, but a committee led by Cuvier that evaluated the finds dismissed the suggestion. Belgian archaeologist PHILIPPE SCHMERLING, excavating a number of caves near Liege in Belgium, uncovered human remains as well as many artifacts associated with rhinoceros and mammoth bones, but reports of these finds were not taken seriously by contemporary scholars (Daniel 1975, 33–35; Sackett 2000).

At KENT'S CAVERN in southern England, excavated by amateur archaeologist John MacEnery between 1825 and 1829, artifacts were discovered associated with rhinoceros remains beneath a stalagmite floor. At first MacEnery concluded that the associations were real, thereby demonstrating human antiquity, but after discussions with Buckland he became convinced that they were the result of postdepositional admixture (Grayson 1983, 75–76). Buckland himself sought an explanation for human remains from Goats' Hole Cave in Paviland (England) that would enable him to associate both the human remains and the artifacts he found with the Roman-British period (Daniel 1975, 37; Grayson 1983, 67).

The Establishment of High Human Antiquity

Although the number of discoveries of artifacts associated with bones of extinct animals contin-ued to mount, the demonstration of high human antiquity required that the stratigraphic integrity of deposits be accepted. This first occurred at two locations: in the Somme gravel terraces in northern France and at BRIXHAM CAVE in England. From 1837 onward, inspired by the earlier studies of French archaeologist Picard, JACQUES BOUCHER DE PERTHES collected artifacts and the bones of extinct animals from the Somme River gravels. He published his findings in *Antiquités celtiques et antédiluviennes* in 1847, describing the stratigraphic position and integrity of his discoveries (Daniel 1975, 58; Grayson 1983, 119). However, intertwined with his stratigraphic observations were a range of speculative assertions that did little to further the acceptance of his views by his contemporaries. He assigned symbolic significance to many of the artifacts he discovered and interpreted them all according to a catastrophist theory that would have been more at home in the late eighteenth century than in the 1840s (Grayson 1983, 126; Sackett 2000).

In 1858, a grant was given to amateur geologist WILLIAM PENGELLY to excavate the newly discovered cave at Brixham in search of paleontological samples. The project was supervised by a group of eminent British geologists: JOSEPH PRESTWICH, Lyell, HUGH FALCONER, Richard Owen, and R. Godwin-Austen. Excavations revealed the bones of extinct animals, but unexpectedly, thirty-six artifacts were also recovered beneath a stalagmitic layer three to eight inches thick. Their discovery sparked a variety of explanations, but these were quickly unified as the result of a visit by Falconer to the sites of Boucher de Perthes in 1858. Impressed by what he saw at the Somme excavations, Falconer encouraged Lyell, Prestwich, and Godwin-Austin, together with the antiquarian Henry Flower and SIR JOHN EVANS, to also visit the sites of Boucher de Perthes. As a result of these visits, Prestwich and Evans were able to photograph a hand-axe *in situ*, associated with the bones of extinct animals at ST. ACHEUL in northern France (Daniel 1975, 58; Grayson 1983, 172–176; Sackett 2000).

In 1859, Prestwich read a paper to the Royal Society recalling Frere's work at Hoxne and describing how Pengelly's work at Brixham and the discoveries of Boucher de Perthes in the Somme had convinced him of high human antiquity. Evans read a similar paper to the SOCIETY OF ANTIQUARIES OF LONDON (Daniel 1975, 58). A number of French scholars supported the British proposals. ÉDOUARD LARTET, for instance, almost immediately thereafter published the results of a study of cut marks on the bones of extinct animals that suggested the presence of humans in the remote past. The speed of his publication suggested that he had accepted high human antiquity sometime before the 1859 consensus (Sackett 2000).

The year 1859 also marked the publication of Charles Darwin's *Origin of Species,* but the two events were not connected. Darwin's theory of evolution to explain human ancestry was owing to Thomas Henry Huxley, who had published *Man's Place in Nature* in 1863 (Daniel 1975, 65), and Darwin's theory dealt with descent with modification, that is, successive generations of a species over time change in form, character, and behavior. The establishment of high human antiquity demonstrated that humans, like other animal species, had a long history on earth, which inevitably led to questions about the nature of human evolution.

The intellectual climate had changed considerably before 1859 as a result of debates between supporters of monogenesis and polygenesis. Those who supported a theory of monogenesis suggested that all humans belonged to a single species, and this was the prevailing view during the late eighteenth and early nineteenth centuries. However, after the 1840s, scholars who believed in multiple human species, or polygenesis, were able to use archaeological discoveries made in Egypt to argue that different human races were in existence as early as 2500 B.C. If a pre-1859 biblical chronology was accepted for the antiquity of humanity, there remained insufficient time for human racial differences to occur. Morton was able to use this evidence in support of the case of polygenesis (Grayson 1983, 158). In attempting to refute this position, monogenesists like Pickard were forced to abandon the biblical chronology to provide sufficient time for the development of racial differences. Therefore, well before 1859, many scholars were convinced that the Bible was inadequate as a source for determining human antiquity.

Early Years of the Discipline: 1860–1880

Three challenges dominated archaeological research following the acceptance of high human antiquity: establishing the validity of the THREE-AGE SYSTEM; explaining progress in terms of economic, social, and political factors; and relating patterns of technological change in the archaeological record to human evolution.

French archaeologists proposed two ages of stone, the *période de la pierre taillée* (flaked-stone tools) and the *période de la pierre polie* (polished-stone tools), and these periods were adopted by Sir John Lubbock (LORD AVEBURY) in his book *Pre-historic Times* (1865). He applied the term Paleolithic to the period when artifacts were deposited with the remains of mammoths, cave bears, and rhinoceros, and the term Neolithic was applied to the period when polished stone artifacts were made. Such technological changes could be demonstrated through stratigraphic excavation and showed a pattern of increasing complexity through time—thus illustrating the universality of human progress.

By the 1860s, the twofold division had been increased to four based on the excavations of Lartet and HENRY CHRISTY in the Dordogne region of southern FRANCE (Lartet and Christy 1865–1875), where Lartet provided stratigraphic evidence for their existence based on associated animal remains. The cave period of the aurochs, or bison, was preceded by the reindeer period, the woolly mammoth and rhinoceros period, and finally the cave-bear period. To these Garrigou added earlier periods based on the presence of warm climate fauna. Finds from the Somme River gravel terraces associated with such fauna suggested that the people there lived mainly in open sites. The great bear and mammoth periods were characterized by both rock-shelter and open-site deposits (Daniel 1975, 100).

In his use of paleontological categories as a basis for organizing archaeological materials, Lartet was well ahead of his time (Daniel 1975, 101). Indeed, the book by Lartet and Christy (1865–1875) on their Dordogne research reads like an ambitious attempt at paleoethnology (Sackett 2000). However, it was not a direction that was followed for very long, and French archaeologist GABRIEL DE MORTILLET reformulated Lartet's scheme, substituting archaeological names for the paleontological descriptions.

The hippopotamus age became the Chellean, later renamed the Abbevillian. Much of the great bear and mammoth age was classified as Mousterian, named after the site of LE MOUSTIER in central France. De Mortillet identified the mammoth period with the site of Aurignac and called it Aurignacian. The reindeer age was divided into two, the earliest ultimately named the Solutrian after the site of SOLUTRÉ in eastern France, and the later named after LA MADELEINE in central France (Daniel 1975, 103). However, even though site names had replaced the names of animals as labels, the scheme still owed much to paleontology. Each stage was thought of as an epoch, a vaguely defined temporal phase, rather than as an artifact complex (Sackett 1991). It was easy, therefore, to relate a unilinear succession of technological change to a unilinear theory of human evolution (Trigger 1989, 95–97).

The idea that all human groups passed through the same stages of cultural development, albeit not at the same time nor at the same rate, provided the rationale for using more-primitive living human groups to model the lifestyles of prehistoric groups with similar technologies. This analogy also provided an answer to the problem of explaining progress in terms of economic, social, and political factors. Huxley (1863) suggested that the Australian Aborigines could be used to flesh out reconstructions of the Neanderthals and their Middle Paleolithic tool kits (Trigger 1989, 113) while Lubbock (1865) applied descriptions of the Eskimo lifestyle to paint a picture of long-extinct Upper Paleolithic communities (Trigger 1989, 115).

By the 1880s, the Enlightenment ideal of universal human progress had been replaced by the idea that differences between cultural groups had deep-seated biological origins. As nationalism was encouraged, so was the search for the biological roots of those national characteristics, and racial factors replaced environmental ones as explanations for the different

historical trajectories of different cultural groups (Trigger 1989, 111). Darwinian evolution seemed to equate with these ideas and helped to lay the foundations for a form of cultural evolutionism in which natural selection was invoked to explain both the differences between cultures and the biological capacity for culture. Thus, the sequence of stone artifact technologies described by Paleolithic archaeologists seemingly provided the tangible evidence needed to document the evolution of modern human societies (Sackett 1991).

Artifacts as Cultural Markers

Toward the end of the nineteenth century, a growing European nationalism fostered an interest in the history and archaeology of particular ethnic groups and focused attention on the archaeology of more recent time periods. By now, archaeologists had documented far more variation in material culture assemblages than could be accommodated comfortably within a unilinear evolutionary framework. In seeking to explain this variation, a resemblance was noted between the patterning of archaeological assemblages and differences in the material cultures of living peoples, with the diffusion of ideas contributing to the creation of distinct culture areas (Robertshaw 1990; Sackett 1981; Trigger 1989, 122).

Those observations laid the foundations for an explanatory model that was to dominate Neolithic, Bronze, and Iron Age archaeological research for much of the twentieth century. The model's development can be traced through the work of OSCAR MONTELIUS on typology and seriation (Trigger 1989, 158), GUSTAF KOSSINNA on material remains used to track the history of ethnic groups (Trigger 1989, 163), and the late-nineteenth-century German ethnologists who established the association between material remains and ethnic groups, but it is perhaps best exemplified by the work of English archaeologist VERE GORDON CHILDE (Childe 1925).

Childe sought to identify recurring sets of material remains whose spatial and temporal boundaries could be used to define the boundaries between prehistoric cultures. Those prehistoric cultures were considered analogous to ethnological cultures (e.g., Childe 1925, 1929). Therefore, change and variation in the material record could be explained in terms of the diffusion of ideas, the migrations of peoples, and/or the adaptation of a particular ethnic group to a particular set of environmental and social circumstances (e.g., Childe 1928, 1936). Artifact analysis thus consisted of the sorting of assemblages into formal types and the tracking of the spatial and temporal distribution of recurring sets of types in order to identify a prehistoric culture. Functional inferences could be made about those recurring morphologies, providing information about the adjustments that different societies made to prevailing environmental conditions (Trigger 1989, 172).

These ideas were not immediately transferred to studies of the Paleolithic record, partly because students of the Paleolithic period maintained an interest in the evolution of human behavior and partly because the existing database did not lend itself easily to the task of identifying particular ethnic groups. For many portions of the record, little change and variation were noted in either stone technology or the types of artifact forms produced. Instead, Paleolithic archaeologists were more interested in documenting a sequence of technological changes that could be related back to the fossil record, thus providing tangible evidence for the evolution of modern human behavioral capacities.

However, the schemes proposed at the end of the nineteenth century to replace de Mortillet's scheme reflected a growing awareness of the inadequacy of a single unilineal scheme for all of the Paleolithic record (Daniel 1975, 124). If it was a universal scheme, the archaeological evidence from outside France should show the same sequence of epochs, but continued archaeological investigations revealed an increasing regional diversity. Clearly, units of classification were needed that dealt with geographic as well as with temporal differences.

HENRI BREUIL's paper of 1912 foreshadowed the breakup of the epoch system. In that paper, Breuil introduced a complex subdivision of the Upper Paleolithic, with three divisions of the Aurignacian and Solutrean followed by six divisions of the Magdalenian (Daniel 1975, 232).

He thought the Upper Paleolithic was distinct from the Middle and Lower Paleolithic and a product of a diverse set of modern human races, all from outside Europe. Although the French Aurignacian might appear as a lineal succession of assemblages, it did not represent a unilineal evolutionary sequence (Sackett 1991).

Breuil conducted research outside France, particularly in eastern Europe but also in the Near East and China, and became convinced that regional variation in the types of artifacts found in the archaeological record was the result of the coexistence of contemporary groups (Daniel 1975, 240). Demonstrating that core, flake, and blade assemblages did not always follow in a neat temporal sequence, he was able to argue, for example, that overlap between Acheulean hand-axe and pebble-tool technologies meant the coexistence of different cultural traditions (e.g., Breuil 1939). This and other studies laid the foundation for the so-called parallel phyla model, which dominated European research for the next two to three decades (Movius 1953; Trigger 1989, 155).

Given the time span of the Paleolithic record, it is not surprising that parallel phyla came to be viewed not just as the coexistence of major cultural traditions but as the material record of different biological groups (races) or different types of human ancestors (i.e., different species). DENIS PEYRONY (1933, 1936), for instance, developed a rigid scheme for the French Upper Paleolithic with Aurignacian and Perigordian assemblages manufactured by distinct races of *Homo sapiens* (Sackett 1991).

The old idea of epochs, which was still apparent in the textbooks of the 1920s, gave way to parallel phyla in the textbooks of the 1930s as can be seen by comparing Miles Burkitt's 1921 *Prehistory* with his 1933 *The Old Stone Age* (Daniel 1975, 244). Childe's *The Dawn of European Civilisation* was published in 1925, and that work can be credited with much of the impetus for a change in the concept of culture.

Also of significance was the broadening of the Paleolithic database, particularly the discovery of Paleolithic records outside Europe (Daniel 1975, 9). The French had been involved in archaeology in North Africa at an early stage, and in the first half of the twentieth century, knowledge of North African prehistory was extended by the work of Sandford and Arkell (1929, 1933, 1939) in the Nile Valley, GERTRUDE CATON-THOMPSON (1934) at Kharga Oasis in Egypt, and CHARLES MCBURNEY and R. W. Hey (1955) in Cyrenaica in what is now eastern Libya.

Initial work in the Near East was carried out by Godefroy Zumoffen between 1897 and 1900, and he was followed by Henry Neuville (1934, 1951) and Francis Turville-Petre (1932). However, the most significant excavations were by Neuville, Stékelis, and DOROTHY GARROD (Garrod and Bate 1937) at Skhul, el-Wad, and et-Tabun in Israel.

In 1926, LOUIS S. LEAKEY began research in the Rift Valley of Africa for sites. In his *Stone Age Cultures of Kenya Colony* (1931) Leakey used European terminology to describe the African industries. Astley John Hilary Goodwin and Clarence Van Riet Lowe (1929) developed the first lasting African terminology based on their assessment of archaeological materials on the terraces of the Vaal River valley. They introduced the classic tripartite sequence of early, middle, and late Stone Age, which was applied widely in Africa during the 1930s and 1940s (Fagan 1981). However, Europe, not Africa, was seen as the source for new ideas. The Sahara acted as a significant barrier preventing movement from south to north and allowing only "higher" cultures to move north to south (Deacon 1990).

Parallel Phyla after World War II

Explanation for change according to the parallel phyla scheme was found in diffusion and migration, sometimes leading to quite dramatic explanations for supposed major changes in the artifact record. A species difference, for instance, was proposed to account for the change from the Mousterian to the initial Upper Paleolithic by both Burkitt in 1933 and Leakey in 1934 (Isaac 1972b).

After World War II, the French archaeologist FRANÇOIS BORDES and his colleague Maurice Bourgon developed a new approach to the description, analysis, and interpretation of Lower and Middle Paleolithic artifact assemblages. This approach, which was to become enormously influential (Bordes 1950; Bordes and Bourgon 1951), separated the description of an artifact assemblage from the description of the artifacts it contained and distinguished the description of artifact forms from the description of the techniques involved in their production. The Bordes approach thus removed the circularity inherent in the work of Breuil and Peyrony, who had relied on certain diagnostic artifact types (type fossils) to simultaneously describe the content of an assemblage and assign it a position in an evolutionary scheme (Sackett 1981). Although developed initially to describe French Lower and Middle Paleolithic assemblages, Bordes's approach soon became the accepted method for characterizing assemblages from other parts of Europe as well as those from North Africa, the Middle East, and Asia.

Bordes used a common set of attributes to describe sixty-three different tool types that were recurring features of Middle Paleolithic assemblages. These attributes included the location of the retouched edges on the tool blank, the type of retouch applied to those edges, the number of retouched edges, and their shapes (Bordes 1961a, 1961b). The great majority of artifacts recovered from Lower and Middle Paleolithic sites could be classified using this typological scheme.

There are several reasons for the rapid and widespread acceptance of Bordes's methodology. First, the classificatory scheme on which it was based proved applicable to Lower and Middle Paleolithic artifact assemblages from many different contexts in many different regions. Second, artifact assemblages were not characterized solely on the basis of a few, apparently diagnostic, tool types. Third, the methodology facilitated comparisons between assemblages. Not only were they described using the same set of tool types, but Bordes introduced a simple statistical method for describing the composition of artifact assemblages that showed how the percentage frequency of each tool type found in an assemblage altered in response to changes in the percentage frequencies. Fourth, because it provided a way of examining spatial and temporal variation in the co-occurrence of artifact types, Bordes's method broadened the range of interpretative possibilities. Finally, the conclusion that variation in contemporaneous artifact assemblages reflected the existence of established cultural traditions brought Paleolithic archaeology closer to the explanatory frameworks being applied under the influence of Childe.

Functional Approaches

At the same time that Bordes was discussing cultural traditions, other archaeologists were exploring the possibility that recurring assemblage types might represent seasonal or functional differences in activities undertaken at different sites (e.g., Binford and Binford 1966; Clark 1959; Freeman 1966; McBurney 1950; Oakley 1952, 18). Of these, LEWIS BINFORD's study became the best known because of a lively debate between Binford and Bordes (e.g., Binford 1973; Bordes 1973; Bordes and de Sonneville-Bordes 1970), a debate that arose from fundamentally different views about the type of behavioral information preserved in the archaeological record.

Bordes argued that variation in material remains reflected ethnic or cultural groupings. Binford argued that differences in the activities undertaken in different parts of the landscape, at different times of the year, were such pervasive features of hunter-gatherer societies that they must have been major influences on the composition of past material culture assemblages. At the heart of the debate lay the problem of disentangling the effects of functional and stylistic differences on the composition of artifact assemblages and of deciding which artifact attributes were stylistic or functional in origin.

Although the debate between Bordes and Binford dominated the literature for a time, there were archaeologists working on other time periods who were keen to explore the interpretative implications of new data being generated, not only by an expanding archaeological record but also by the incorporation of new techniques. For example, in a discussion of the implications of new dating techniques for the interpretation of the archaeological data, GLYN ISAAC (1972a) noted that there are orders of magnitude of difference in the geographic and temporal distribu-

tions of Lower and Middle Paleolithic assemblages when compared with those recovered from the Upper Paleolithic record.

Isaac suggested that these differences could relate to the evolution of specific behavioral capacities and that different explanations for the existence of patterned variation in artifact assemblages might be sought for different portions of the record. For example, he postulated that while Upper Paleolithic artifacts may have served as cultural markers, this could not be considered an appropriate explanation for the similarities and differences exhibited, for example, by Acheulean artifact assemblages, simply on the basis of the spatial and temporal scale of the documented pattern of variation. This observation, coupled with the long-standing suggestion that the Upper Paleolithic record marked the establishment of modern human populations and a unique set of behavioral traits (e.g., Burkitt 1955, 143–161; McBurney 1950), was reinforced by studies of many different components of that record (e.g., Binford 1973; Mellars 1989).

From the 1960s to the Present

In the last four decades of the twentieth century, another shift occurred in the way Paleolithic archaeologists ascribed meaning to the succession of stone technologies first documented in the late nineteenth century. Even during the 1950s, a number of archaeologists working with the earliest Paleolithic record had expressed dissatisfaction with the multiple phyla concept (Isaac 1972b), opting instead for an explanation that involved relating assemblage differences to different activities between sites (e.g., Clark 1950, 1959; Howell and Clark 1963; Kleindienst 1961). Following this lead, archaeologists once again became interested in the comparative method as a means for learning about human evolutionary history.

During the late nineteenth century, evolutionists like Darwin, Huxley, and Haeckel had begun to ask questions about the kind of ancestor that had given rise to humans. In trying to answer the question, they attempted to identify the closest living relatives to humans and drew up a list of human-versus-ape characteristics.

Common characteristics could then be attributed to the last common ancestor and evolutionary scenarios developed to identify the critical changes that had led to the development of modern humans. Darwin, for instance, argued that movement to the ground, bipedal locomotion, which freed the hands, and natural selection resulting from an adaptive system involving tool use, social cooperation, and warfare were all critical components leading to the development of modern humans. Paleolithic archaeologists were faced with the challenge of finding supporting evidence for such scenarios.

During the 1940s, the new evolutionary synthesis had finally done away with goal-directed change by integrating natural selection and migration with mutation and chance. Washburn (1951a, 1951b) integrated this new evolutionary theory into physical anthropology, shifting the emphasis from descriptive anatomy to the analysis of adaptation. In one of the first studies to come from the new physical anthropology, Bartholomew and Joseph B. Birdsell (1953) proposed that the loss of the estrus cycle and continuing mutual sexual attraction among humans demonstrated that the long surviving family was central to human society. These two men suggested that early hominid groups formed stable family groups providing parental care to dependent young. Following physical anthropologist RAYMOND DART's (1949) suggestion that Australopithecines were dependent on tools for hunting and butchering animals, they proposed that sexual dimorphism was associated with competition among males for females and that aggressive hunting behavior was derived from this dimorphism (Zihlman 1997).

Studies like that of Bartholomew and Birdsell, together with work by Dart, suggested a feedback between large brains, bipedalism, and tool use. Although it is now known that Dart's interpretation of the Makapansgat faunal assemblage (literally, the animal bones that were excavated at the site) was in error (Brain 1981), his work, together with that of other scholars, set out a methodology for extracting behavioral information from the material debris left in archaeological sites. In the years since 1960, archaeologists have used evolutionary theory to generate different scenarios that can be tested against the Paleolithic record. The best-known example of this research is Isaac's food-sharing hypothesis.

Isaac noted two major differences between apes and humans: humans may feed as they forage as apes do, but apes do not regularly postpone food consumption until they have returned to their home base; also, humans actively share food as they acquire it (Isaac 1978). Based on these observations, Isaac hypothesised that the HAS and KBS sites at Koobi Fora (East Africa, Kenya) were formed by hominids carrying stones and bones to a site. These differences in turn suggested the existence of provisioning, the existence of home bases, and the sexual division of labor early in human prehistory.

Beginning in the 1940s, African archaeologists also changed the way they excavated sites. The first excavation of a "living floor" by Louis Leakey and MARY LEAKEY occurred at OLORGESAILIE in 1943 (Fagan 1981), and it was followed by similar excavations at Isimila by F. Clark Howell (Howell, Cole, and Kleindienst 1962) and Kalambo Falls by J. DESMOND CLARK (Clark 1969, 1974).

At Isimila, Howell emphasized artifact variation within one stratigraphic horizon, thereby challenging the concept of progressive typological and morphological development through time (Gowlett 1990). Interest in defining living floors spread from Africa to Eurasia (Isaac 1972b), and a series of excavations in Europe and the Middle East were conducted at a range of sites: for example, Torralba-Ambrona (Howell 1966), Latamne (Clark 1966), Vértesszöllös (Kretzoi and Vértes 1965), 'Ubeidiya (Stekelis 1966), and Terra Amata (de Lumley 1969). In the Dordogne region in France, Hallam L. Movius (1974) selected Abri Pataud for excavation and adopted a strategy that would allow for the exposure of horizontal surfaces of contemporary occupation.

Conclusion

Among the more recent Paleolithic studies, some seek to provide a more detailed investigation of the patterns of similarity and difference which characterize each division of the record and the exploration of different behavioral interpretations for the patterns exhibited by each of those divisions. Thus, the division of the record that was devised by the late-nineteenth-century and early-twentieth-century archaeologists, which was based on changes in stone technology, is now being used to document, at least in a broad sense, the evolution of specific behavioral capacities (e.g., Mithen 1996). Current research is aimed at providing more detailed accounts of the ways in which artifacts were made in different time periods (e.g., Böeda 1988), of the factors that contributed to the recurring artifact forms being produced (e.g., Dibble 1987), and to variations in the composition of contemporaneous artifact assemblages as a basis for identifying the behavioral information encapsulated by that particular stone technology (e.g., Jones 1994). Yet despite the methodological innovations, the greatly extended chronology, and the greatly expanded geographic scope of Paleolithic archaeology, there are many aspects of the subject that would be familiar to its late-nineteenth- and early-twentieth-century practitioners. As always, the challenge for Paleolithic archaeologists is to reconstruct the behavior of our ancestors in their own terms.

Simon Holdaway and Nicola Stern

References

Bartholomew, G. A., and J. B. Birdsell. 1953. "Ecology of the Protohominids." *American Anthropologist* 55: 481–498.

Binford, L. R. 1973. "Interassemblage Variability: The Mousterian and the 'Functional' Argument." In *The Explanation of Culture Change,* 227–254. Ed. C. Renfrew. London: Duckworth.

Binford, L. R., and S. R. Binford. 1966. "A Preliminary Analysis of Functional Variability in the Mousterian of Levallois Facies." *American Anthropologist* 68: 238–295.

Böeda, E. 1988. "Le Concept levallois et évaluation de son champ d'application." In *L'Homme de Néandertal,* vol. 4, *La Technique,* 13–26. Ed. M. Otte. Liege: Études et Recherches Archéologiques de l'Université de Liège.

Bordes, F. 1950. "Principes d'une méthode d'étude des techniques de débitage et de la typologie du Paléolithique ancien et moyen." *L'Anthropologie* 54: 19–34.

———. 1961a. "Mousterian Cultures in France." *Science* 134: 803–810.

———. 1961b. *Typologie du paléolithique ancien et moyen.* Publications de l'Institut de Préhistoire de Bordeaux, mémoire 1. Bordeaux: Delmas.

———. 1973. "On the Chronology and Contemporaneity of Different Palaeolithic Cultures in France." In *The Explanation of Culture Change,* 217–226. Ed. C. Renfrew. London: Duckworth.

Bordes, F., and M. Bourgon. 1951. "Le Complexe moustérien: Moustérien, levalloisien et tayacien." *L'Anthropologie* 55: 1–23.

Bordes, F., and D. de Sonneville-Bordes. 1970. "The Significance of Variability in Palaeolithic Assemblages." *World Archaeology* 2: 61–73.

Boucher de Perthes, J. 1847. *Antiquités celtiques antédiluviennes: Mémoire sur l'industrie primitive et les arts à leur origine.* Vol. 1. Paris: Treuttel and Wurtz.

Brain, C. K. 1981. *The Hunters or the Hunted: An Introduction to African Cave Taphonomy.* Chicago: University of Chicago Press.

Breuil, H. 1912. "Les sub-divisions du Paléolithique Supérieur." *Congrés International d'Anthropologie.*

———. 1939. "The Pleistocene Succession in the Somme Valley." *Proceedings of the Prehistoric Society* 5: 33–38.

Burkitt, M. C. 1921. *Prehistory: A Study of Early Cultures in Europe and the Mediterranean Basin.* Cambridge: Cambridge University Press.

———. 1933. *The Old Stone Age.* New York: Macmillan; Cambridge: Cambridge University Press.

———. 1955. *The Old Stone Age: A Study of Palaeolithic Times.* 3d ed. London: Bowes and Bowes.

Caton-Thompson, G. 1934. "Recent Discoveries in Kharga Oasis, Egypt." In *Proceedings of the First Congress of Prehistoric and Protohistoric Sciences,* 74. London: Oxford University Press.

Childe, V. G. 1925. *The Dawn of European Civilisation.* London: Kegan Paul.

———. 1928. *The Most Ancient East: The Oriental Prelude to European Prehistory.* London: Kegan Paul.

———. 1929. *The Danube in Prehistory.* Oxford: Oxford University Press.

———. 1936. *Man Makes Himself.* London: Watts.

Clark, J. Desmond. 1950. *The Stone Age Cultures of Northern Rhodesia.* Claremont, Cape: South African Archaeological Society.

———. 1959. "Further Excavations at Broken

Hill, Northern Rhodesia." *Journal of the Royal Anthropological Institute* 89: 201–232.

———. 1966. "Acheulian Occupation Sites in the Middle East and Africa: A Study in Cultural Variability." In *Recent Studies in Paleoanthropology*, 202–229. Ed. J. D. Clark and F. C. Howell. American Anthropologist Special Publication, vol.68.

———. 1969. *Kalambo Falls Prehistoric Site*. Vol. 1, *The Geology, Palaeoecology, and Detailed Stratigraphy of the Excavations*. Cambridge: Cambridge University Press.

———. 1974. *Kalambo Falls Prehistoric Site*. Vol. 2, *The Late Prehistoric Remains*. Cambridge: Cambridge University Press.

Daniel, G. 1975. *A Hundred and Fifty Years of Archaeology*. London: Duckworth.

Dart, R. 1949. "The Predatory Implemental Technique of *Australopithecus*." *American Journal of Physical Anthropology* new ser. 7: 1–38.

Deacon, J. 1990. "Weaving the Fabric of Stone Age Research in Southern Africa". In *A History of African Archaeology*, 39–58. Ed. P. Robertshaw. London: James Curry.

Dibble, H. L. 1987. "The Interpretation of Middle Paleolithic Scraper Morphology." *American Antiquity* 52: 109–117.

Fagan, B. M. 1981. "Two Hundred and Four Years of African Archaeology." In *Towards a History of Archaeology*, 42–51. Ed. G. Daniel. London: Thames and Hudson.

Freeman, L. 1966. "The Nature of Mousterian Facies in Cantabrian Spain." *American Anthropologist* 68: 230–237.

Garrod, D., and D. M. A. Bate. 1937. *The Stone Age of Mount Carmel: Excavations at the Wady el-Mughara*. Vol. 1. Oxford: Clarendon Press.

Goodwin, Astley John Hilary, and Clarence Van Riet Lowe. 1929. "The Stone Age Cultures of South Africa." *Annals of the South African Museum* 27: 1–289.

Gowlett, J. A. J. 1990. "Archaeological Studies of Human Origins and Early Prehistory in Africa." In *A History of African Archaeology*, 13–38. Ed. P. Robertshaw. London: James Curry.

Grayson, D. K. 1983. *The Establishment of Human Antiquity*. New York: Academic Press.

Howell, F. C. 1966. "Observations on the Earlier Phases of the European Lower Palaeolithic." *American Anthropologist* 68, no. 2: 88–201.

Howell, F. C., and J. D. Clark. 1963. "Acheulian Hunter-Gatherers of Sub-Saharan Africa." In *African Ecology and Human Evolution*. Ed. F. C. Howell and Boulière. Chicago: Aldine.

Howell, F. C., G. H. Cole, and M. R. Kleindienst. 1962. "Isimila, an Acheulean Occupation Site in the Iringa Highlands, Southern Highlands Province, Tanganyika." In *Actes du Ive Congrès Panafricain de Préhistoire*. Ed. G. Mortelmans and J. Nenquin. Tervuren.

Huxley, T. H. 1863. *Man's Place in Nature and Other Anthropological Essays*. New York: Appleton and Company.

Isaac, G. 1972a. "Chronology and the Tempo of Cultural Change during the Pleistocene." In *Calibration of Hominoid Evolution*, 381–430. Ed. W. W. Bishop and J. A. Miller. Edinburgh: Academic Press.

———. 1972b. "Early Phases of Human Behaviour: Models in Lower Palaeolithic Archaeology." In *Models in Archaeology*, 167–199. Ed. D. L. Clarke. London: Metheun.

———. 1978. "Food-sharing Behavior of Proto Hominids." *Scientific American* 238, no. 4: 90–108.

Jones, P. R. 1994. "Results of Experimental Work in Relation to the Stone Industries of Olduvai Gorge." In *Olduvai Gorge*, vol. 5, *Excavations in Beds III, IV, and the Masek Beds, 1968–1971*, 254–298. Ed. M. D. Leakey and D. A. Roe. Cambridge: Cambridge University Press.

Kleindienst, M. 1961. "Variability within the Late Acheulian Assemblage in Eastern Africa." *South African Archaeological Bulletin* 16: 35–52.

Kretzoi, M., and L. Vértes. 1965. "Upper Biharian (Inter Mindel) Pebble Industry Occupation Site in Western Hungary." *Current Anthropology* 6: 74–87.

Lartet, E., and H. Christy. 1865–1875. *Reliquiae Aquitanicae: Being Contributions to the Archaeology and Palaeontology of Perigord and the Adjoining Provinces of Southern France*. London and Edinburgh: T. Rupert Jones.

Leakey, L. S. B. 1931. *The Stone Age Cultures of Kenya Colony*. London: Cambridge University Press.

———. 1934 *Adam's Ancestors*. London: Methuen.

Lubbock, J. 1865. *Pre-historic Times, as Illustrated by Ancient Remains and the Manners and Customs of Modern Savages*. London: Williams and Norgate.

Lumley, H. de. 1969. "A Paleolithic Camp at Nice." *Scientific American* 220, no. 5: 42–50.

McBurney, C. B. M. 1950. "The Geographical Study of the Older Palaeolithic Stages in Europe." *Proceedings of the Prehistoric Society* 16: 163–183.

McBurney, C. B. M., and R. W. Hey. 1955. *Prehistory and Pleistocene Geology in Cyrenaican Libya*. Cambridge: Cambridge University Press.

Mellars, P. A. 1989. "Major Issues in the Emergence of Modern Humans." *Current Anthropology* 30: 349–385.

Mithen, S. 1996. *The Prehistory of the Mind: A Search for the Origins of Art, Religion, and Science*. London: Thames and Hudson.

Mortillet, G. de. 1873. "Classification des diverses périodes de l'age de la Pierre." In *Comptes Rendus de la VIe Congrès Internationale d'Anthropologie et d'Archéologie Préhistorique, Brussels (1872)*, 432–456.

Movius, H. L. 1953. "Old World Prehistory: Paleolithic." In *Anthropology Today: An Encyclopedic Inventory*, 163–192. Ed. A. L. Kroeber. Chicago: University of Chicago Press.

———. 1974. "The Abri Pataud Program of the French Upper Palaeolithic in Retrospect." In *Archaeological Researches in Retrospect*. Ed. G. R. Willey. Cambridge: Winthrop.

Neuville, R. 1934. "La préhistoire de Palestine." *Revue Biblique* 43: 237–259.

———. 1951. *Le Paléolithique et le Mésolithique du Désert de Judée*. Archives de l'Institut de Paléontologie Humaine no. 24. Paris: Masson et Cie.

Oakley, K. P. 1952. "Swanscombe Man." *Proceedings of the Geologists' Association* 63: 271–300.

Peyrony, D. 1933. "Les industries 'aurignaciennes' dans le bassin de la Vézère." *Bulletin de la Société Préhistorique Française* 32: 418–443.

———. 1936. "Le Périgordien et l'Aurignacien: Nouvelles observations." *Bulletin de la Société Préhistorique Française* 33: 616–619.

Robertshaw, P. 1990. "The Development of Archaeology in East Africa." In *A History of African Archaeology*, 78–94. Ed. P. Robertshaw. London: James Curry.

Sackett, J. R. 1981. "From de Mortillet to Bordes: A Century of French Paleolithic Research." In *Towards a History of Archaeology*, 85–99. Ed. G. Daniel. London: Thames and Hudson.

———. 1991. "Straight Archaeology French Style: The Phylogenetic Paradigm in Historic Perspective." In *Perspectives on the Past: Theoretical Biases in Mediterranean Hunter-Gatherer Research*, 109–139. Ed. G. A. Clark. Philadelphia: University of Pennsylvania Press.

———. 2000. "Human Antiquity and the Old Stone Age: The Nineteenth Century Background to Paleoanthropology." *Evolutionary Anthropology* 9: 37–49.

Sandford, K. S., and A. J. Arkell. 1929. *Palaeolithic Man and the Nile-Faiyum Divide*. Chicago: Oriental Institute.

———. 1933. *Palaeolithic Man and the Nile Valley in Nubia and Upper Egypt*. Chicago: Oriental Institute.

———. 1939. *Palaeolithic Man and the Nile Valley in Lower Egypt*. Chicago: Oriental Institute.

Schnapp, A., and K. Kristiansen. 1999. "Discovering the Past." In *Companion Encyclopedia of Archaeology*, 1:3–47. Ed. G. Barker. London: Routledge.

Stekelis, M. 1966. *Archaeological Excavations at 'Ubeidiya 1960–1963*. Jerusalem: Israel Academy of Sciences and Humanities.

Trigger, B. G. 1989. *A History of Archaeological Thought*. Cambridge: Cambridge University Press.

Turville-Petre, F. 1932. "Excavations in the Mughuret el-Kebara." *Journal of the Royal Anthropological Institute* 62: 271–276.

Washburn, S. L. 1951a. "The Analysis of Primate Evolution with Particular Reference to the Origin of Man." *Cold Spring Harbor Symposium on Quantitative Biology* 15: 67–77.

———. 1951b. "The New Physical Anthropology." *Transactions of the New York Academy of Science* 13, no. 2: 298–304.

Zihlman, A. 1997. "The Paleolithic Glass Ceiling." In *Women in Human Evolution*, 91–113. Ed. L. D. Hager. London: Routledge.

Palestine

See Israel; Syro-Palestinian and Biblical Archaeology

Palynology in Archaeological Research

Archaeological palynology is the study of ancient pollen that is preserved in a few particular archaeological deposits or in natural deposits that can be related to archaeological events by DATING. The on-site study of pollen from archaeological deposits can show what the vegetation around the site was like or what plant materials were deposited there. The off-site study of pollen from natural deposits such as lake sediments can show what the effects of human activity were on the surrounding landscape at various times.

Beginnings: Landscape Change, Dating, and Archaeology

The first application of pollen analysis was to explore vegetation history in the 1920s, first in SWEDEN by the geologist Lennart von Post (Erdtman 1967). The new science spread rapidly throughout northern and central Europe (including Russia) so that by 1927 more than 150 papers had been published (Erdtman 1927). In Great Britain, following Gunnar Erdtman (1924), A. J. H. GODWIN and M. E. Godwin (1933; H. Godwin 1940) began a long tradition of pollen analysis with archaeological connections. As pollen analysis developed in Europe (Faegri 1981), a significant development was the division of pollen diagrams into zones representing time phases with characteristic pollen records, first in DENMARK (Jessen 1935) and then somewhat similar schemes in other places such as Britain (Godwin 1940). These zonations provided the basis for the initial use of pollen analysis, as they provided a means of dating suitable sediments that was used for the next twenty years until the advent of radiocarbon dating. Erdtman listed the publications on palynology in the journal *Geologiska Foreningens I Stockholm Forhandlingar* each year from 1927 to 1955, thus providing thorough coverage of the early literature.

The Effects of Human Settlements on Past Landscapes

Early research worked out vegetation history, mostly that of woodlands, from the study mainly of tree and shrub pollen. This developed into study of the influences of climate and human activity on past vegetation (Bertsch 1928). Refinements in technique led to the identification of more types of pollen, particularly those of herbs, many of which (such as weeds) are important indicators of past human activity (Firbas 1934); for example, cereal pollen indicates farming (Firbas 1937). These refinements permitted the interpretation of certain features seen in pollen diagrams from natural deposits as the faint traces of the activities of the first farmers in the Neolithic period in Denmark (Iversen 1941) and in Norway (Faegri 1944).

One such feature is the elm decline, which is a noticeable and widespread reduction in elm pollen at a particular point in many pollen diagrams that is used to divide the Atlantic pollen zone from the succeeding subboreal one. There has been much discussion over the years whether the elm decline was caused by human activity, climatic change, or other factors.

Many pollen diagrams also show changes just above (after) the decline horizon, and Iversen (1941) elegantly showed that these probably represent prehistoric episodes of woodland clearance, farming, and abandonment, which he termed *Landnam*. The pattern of landscape change as a result of human activity has since been studied and dated in detail up to the present.

Recent archaeological palynology in central Europe has concentrated on particular aspects of archaeology, such as the detailed history of vegetation change as a result of human activity near a particular settlement area, such as H.-J. Beug's (1992) study in northern Germany, covering the period from the Neolithic period to the Middle Ages, in which the cereals wheat, barley, oats, rye, and millet are distinguished. Other work has concentrated upon a particular culture, such as A. J. Kalis's (1988) work on the early Neolithic *Linearbandkeramik,* also in Germany.

Another development of archaeological palynology since the 1960s has been its extension to drier regions with fewer suitable deposits, such as the lands bordering the Mediterranean. Here the effects of human occupation are expressed rather differently when compared with human occupation effects further north. Beug (1962) worked on sites in Croatia while S. Bottema and H. Woldring (1990) have summarized results from the eastern Mediterranean region, K.-E. Behre (1990) those from the Near East, and A. C. Stevenson (1985) those from the western Mediterranean. In these areas, woodland disturbance swiftly led to its replacement by evergreen woods and then by scrub. Some typical crops such as *Olea* ("olive") and *Vitis* ("vine") are also recorded.

In North America, archaeological aspects of pollen analysis from natural sites have also been a minor interest compared with quaternary vegetation change as a whole. The effects of human activity have often been slighter than in Europe, and therefore harder to detect and to separate from other factors such as climate. E. T. Burden, J. H. McAndrews, and G. Norris (1986) succeeded in showing the vegetation changes caused first by Native Americans and then by European settlers (characterized by the presence of *Plantago lanceolata,* an alien in North America), in Ontario, CANADA.

Other parts of the world have been less intensively studied. In Central America, D. J. Rue (1987) has conducted archaeologically oriented palynology, and others have done so elsewhere; for example, R. L. Clark (1983) in Australia, N. Fuji (1990) in JAPAN, and Y. V. Kuzmin (1992) in eastern RUSSIA. Although there are many other pollen results from different parts of the world, only few of them have sufficient detail with regard to data and chronology to be very useful for archaeological research.

Pollen Analyses of Wet Archaeological Deposits

K. Bertsch (1926) pioneered on-site archaeological applications of pollen analysis in Germany, and H. Harri (1929) did so in SWITZERLAND on waterlogged lake shore settlements. This kind of work has been done by a few other researchers, such as W. Beijerinck (1931), who carried out on-site studies of settlement mounds *(terpen)* in the NETHERLANDS that included pollen analyses.

Many of the later developments have been made by researchers concentrating on one particular aspect of archaeological palynology in a particular region. Where archaeological deposits were wet enough for good pollen preservation, pollen analysis could be done on the occupation deposits themselves, as in the case of occupation mounds in northern Germany (Korber-Grohne 1967).

Further work has been done on lakeshore settlements around the Alps, which provide wet sediments closely linked with the occupation of the sites. At Seeberg-Burgaschisee-Sud, one pollen diagram was obtained from a sediment profile going through the archaeological occupation layer itself, and others were obtained from profiles through natural deposits at in-creasing distances from the settlement, thus tracing the decreasing effects of occupation at increasing distances from the site itself (Welten 1967). This site also provided rare evidence of leafy branches having been brought to the site for fodder, evidence obtained from pollen records of plants that are in flower when the leaves are fully developed such as *Tilia* (lime), *Acer* (maple), and *Hedera* (ivy).

Wet archaeological sediments have also been studied from deposits from wells (Dauber, Fietz, and Lang 1955; Firbas 1930), ditches, etc., at otherwise dry archaeological sites. Coprolites (fecal remains), mostly from dogs, have been analyzed in Europe (Paap 1976) along with a number of other archaeological materials (Greig 1982), including human feces (Knights, Dickson, Dickson, and Breeze 1983).

Waterlogged archaeological deposits in which pollen is preserved often also contain other remains such as the seeds of plants, remains of insects, and eggs of parasitic worms. The study of a range of biological remains from a particular deposit can provide complementary results on past environments, for example the research on Lindow Man, a prehistoric bog body found in Cheshire, in England (Stead, Bourke, and Brothwell 1986).

Pollen Analyses of Dry Archaeological Deposits

Certain soil conditions can preserve pollen. Acid soils, for example, inhibit the processes of decay. Some archaeological features such as burial mounds or structures built from turf sod have buried ancient soil surfaces together with the preserved pollen content. Such soil pollen has been extensively studied in Britain by G. W. Dimbleby (1962) and in the Netherlands by H. T. Waterbolk (1950) and by A. J. Havinga (1963).

Cave sediments have been studied by M. van Campo and ANDRÉ LEROI-GOURHAN (1956) as well as a number of other workers in France. Some archaeological objects may themselves contain pollen and even contribute to its preservation by the presence of metal corrosion products, for example, the remains of honey or mead in a bronze container found in southern Germany and studied by U. Korber-Grohne (1985).

In the United States, archaeological pollen analysis has involved much work on coprolites, often preserved in dry conditions in arid environments. Some work began in the 1960s, such as that by E. O. Callen and T. W. M. Cameron (1960), P. S. Martin and F. W. Sharrock (1964), and J. Schoenwetter (1962). Human fecal material from latrine pits has also been studied (Reinhard, Mrozowski, and Orloski 1986). The results yield much information about the diets of the people concerned, both Native American and European.

Syntheses of Results

As sufficient results have accumulated in particular regions, they have been synthesized into regional accounts of landscape change including archaeological considerations, as, for example, those covering central and northern Europe (Firbas 1949–1952), the British Isles (Godwin 1956), and the Netherlands (van Zeist 1967). Further work has resulted in highly detailed regional studies, for example, in northern Germany and southern Scandinavia (Muller-Wille, Dorfler, Meier, and Kroll 1988), southern Germany (Kuster 1988), POLAND (Ralska-Jasiewiczowa 1977), and a summary of Europe (Behre 1988). Useful collected works have been published on subjects such as human impact in pollen results (Behre, ed. 1986), and on archaeological palynology (Dimbleby 1985; Renault-Misovsky, Bui-Thui-Mai, and Giraud 1985).

James Greig

See also United States of America, Prehistoric Archaeology

References

Behre, K.-E. 1988. "The Role of Man in European Vegetation History." In *Vegetation History.* Ed. B. Huntley and T. Webb III. Dordrecht: Kluwer.

———. 1990. "Some Reflections on Anthropogenic Indicators and the Record of Prehistoric Occupation Phases in Pollen Diagrams from the Near East." In *Man's Role in the Shaping of the Eastern Mediterranean Landscape.* Ed. S. Bottema, G. EntjeNieborg, and W. van Zeist. Rotterdam: Balkema.

Behre, K.-E., ed. 1986. *Anthropogenic Indicators in Pollen Diagrams.* Rotterdam: Balkema.

Beijerinck, W. 1931. *De subfossile plantenresten in de terpen van Friesland en Groningen.* 3. Overige macro-en microresten, Wageningen, 64 pp.

Bertsch, K. 1926. "Die Pflanzenreste aus der Kulturschichte der neolithischen Siedlung Riedsachen bei Schussenried." *Schriften der Verein fur Geschichte des Bodensees und seiner Umgebung* 54.

———. 1928. "Klima, Pflanzendecke, und Besiedlung Mitteleuropas in vor-und fruhgeschichtlicher Zeit nach de Ergebnissen der pollenanalytischen Forschung." *Bericht der romisch-germanischen Kommission* 18.

Beug, H.-J. 1962. "Uber die ersten anthropogenen Vegetationsveranderungen in Suddalmatien an Hand eines neuen Pollendiagramms von 'Malo Jezero' auf Mlhet." *Veroffentlichungen des geobotanischen Instituts ETH Rubel (Zurich)* 37: 9–15.

———. 1992. "Vegetationsgeschichtliche Untersuchungen uber die Besiedlung im unteren Eichsfeld, Landkreis Gottingen, vom fruhen Neolithikum bis zum Mittelalter." *Neue Ausgrabungen und Forschungen I Niedersachsen* 20: 261–339.

Bottema, S., and H. Woldring. 1990. "Anthropogenic Indicators in the Pollen Record of the Eastern Mediterranean." In *Man's Role in the Shaping of the East Mediterranean Landscape,* 231–264. Ed. S. Bottema, G. Entjes-Nieborg, and W. van Zeist. Rotterdam: Balkema.

Burden, E. T., J. H. McAndrews, and G. Norris. 1986. "Palynology of Indian and European Forest Clearance and Farming in Lake Sediment Cores from Awanda Provincial Park, Ontario." *Canadian Journal of Earth Sciences* 23: 43–51.

Callen, E. O., and T. W. M. Cameron. 1960. "A Prehistoric Diet Revealed in Coprolites." *New Scientist* 8, no. 190: 35–40.

Campo, M. van, and A. Leroi-Gourhan. 1956. "Note préliminaire à l'étude des pollen fossiles de différents niveaux de grottes d'Arcy-sur-Cure." *Bulletin du Museum,* 2d. ser., 28: 326–330.

Clark, R. L. 1983. "Pollen and Charcoal Evidence for the Effects of Aboriginal Burning on the Vegetation of Australia." *Archaeology in Oceania* 18: 32–37.

Dauber, A., A. Fietz, and K. Lang. 1955. "Romische Brunnen in Pforzheim." *Beitrage zur naturkundlichen Forschung im Sudwestdeutschand* 14: 43–56.

Dimbleby, G. W. 1955. "Pollen Analysis as an Aid to the Dating of Prehistoric Monuments." *Proceedings of the Prehistoric Society* 20: 231–236.

————. 1962. "The Development of British Heathlands and Their Soils." *Oxford Forestry Memoirs* 23.

————. 1985. *The Palynology of Archaeological Sites.* London: Academic Press.

Erdtman, G. 1924. "Studies in the Micropalaeontology of Post-Glacial Deposits in Northern Scotland and the Scotch Isles." *Journal of the Linnean Society B* 46: 449–504.

————. 1927. "Literature on Pollen Statistics Published before 1927." *Geologiska Foreningens I Stockholm Forhandlingar* 49: 196–211.

————. 1967. "Glimpses of Palynology 1916–1966." *Review of Palaeobotany and Palynology* 1: 23–29.

Faegri, K. 1944. "On the Introduction of Agriculture to Western Norway." *Geologiska Foreningens I Stockholm Forhandlingar* 66: 449–462.

————. 1981. "Some Pages of the History of Pollen Analysis." *Striae* 14: 42–47.

Firbas, F. 1930. "Eine Flora aus dem Brunnenschlamm des Romerkastells Zugmantel." *Saalburg Jahrbuch* 7: 75–78.

————. 1934. "Uber die Bestimmung der Walddichte und der Vegetation waldloser Gebiete mit Hilfe der Pollenanalyse." *Planta* 22: 109–145.

————. 1937. "Der pollenanalytische Nachweis des Getreidebaus." *Zeitschrift fur Botanik* 31: 447–478.

————. 1949–1952. *Spat-und nacheiszeitliche Waldgeschichte Mitteleuropas.* Parts 1 and 2. Jena: Fischer.

Fuji, N. 1990. "Impacted Community of Palaeovegetation around the Middle Neolithic Mawaki Site, Noto Peninsular, Japan." *INQUA Newsletter* 3: 40–43.

Godwin, H. 1940. "Pollen Analysis and Forest History of England and Wales." *New Phytologist* 39, no. 4: 370–400.

————. 1956. *History of the British Flora.* Cambridge: Cambridge University Press.

Godwin, H., and M. E. Godwin. 1933. "British Maglemose Harpoon Sites." *Antiquity* 7: 36–49.

Greig, J. 1982. "The Interpretation of Pollen Spectra from Urban Archaeological Deposits." In *Environmental Archaeology in the Urban Context,* 47–65. Ed. A. R. Hall and H. K. Kenward. Council for British Archaeology Research Report no. 42.

Harri, H. 1929. "Blutenstaubuntersuchung bei der bronzezeitlichen Siedlung 'Sumpf' bei Zug." *Zuger Neujahrsblatt.*

Havinga, A. J. 1963. "A Palynological Investigation of Soil Profiles Developed in Cover Sand." *Mededelingen van de Landbouw-hogeschool te Wageningen, Nederland* 63: 1–92.

Hevley, R. H. 1964. "Pollen Analysis of Quaternary Archaeological and Lacustrine Sediments from the Colorado Plateau." Ph.D. dissertation, University of Arizona, Tucson.

Iversen, J. 1941. "Landnam I Danmarks Stenalder" [Land Occupation in Denmark's Stone Age]. *Danmarks geologiske Underogelse, 2 Rakke,* 66. Reprinted in 1964.

————. 1973. "The Development of Denmark's Nature since the Last Glacial." *Danmarks geologiske Undersogelse,* Række 5, no. 7c.

Jessen, K. 1935. "Archaeological Dating in the History of North Jutland's Vegetation." *Acta Archaeologica* 5: 185–214.

Kalis, A. J. 1988. "Zur Umwelt des Fruhneolithischen Menschen: Ein Beitrag der Pollenanalyse." In *Der prahistorische Mensch und seine Umwelt,* 125–137. Ed. H.-J. Kuster. *Forschungen und Berichte zur Vor- und Fruhgeschichte in Baden-Wurttemberg* 31.

Knights, B. A., C. A. Dickson, J. H. Dickson, and D. J. Breeze. 1983. "Evidence Concerning the Roman Military Diet at Bearsden, Scotland, in the Second Century A.D." *Journal of Archaeological Science* 10: 139–152.

Korber-Grohne, U. 1967. *Geobotanische Untersuchungen auf der Feddersen Wierde.* Wiesbaden: Steiner.

————. 1985. "Die biologischen Reste aus dem hallstattzeitlichedn Furstengrab von Hochdorf, Gemeinde Eberdingen (Kreis Ludwigsburg)." *Forschungen und Berichte zur Vor-und Fruhgeschichte in Baden-Wurttemberg* 19: 87–164.

Kuster, H.-J. 1988. *Vom Werden einer Kulturlandschaft: Vegetationsgeschichtliche Studien am Auerberg (Sudbayern).* Weinheim: Acta Humaniora.

Kuzmin, Y. V. 1992. "Human Impact on Landscapes in the Past (the Far East USSR)." In *Abstracts, Eighth International Palynological Congress, Aix-en-Provence,* 81.

Martin, P. S., and F. W. Sharrock. 1964. "Pollen Analysis of Prehistoric Human Faeces: A New Approach to Ethnobotany." *American Antiquity* 30: 168–180.

Moe, D., K. Kihno, and R. Pirrus. 1992. "Anthropogenic Disturbance of Vegetation in Estonia through the Holocene Based on Some Selected Pollen Diagrams: A Preliminary Survey." *PACT* 37: 79–95.

Muller-Wille, M., W. Dorfler, D. Meier, and H. Kroll. 1988. "The Transformation of Rural Society, Economy, and Landscape during the First Millennium A.D.: Archaeological and Palaeobotanical Contributions from North Germany and South Scandinavia." *Geografiska Annaler* 70B: 53–68.

Papp, N. 1976. "Preliminary Results of the Investigation of Prehistoric Faeces from West Friesland (Prov. Noord-Holland)." *Berichte van de Rijkdienst voor het Oudheidkundig Bodemonderzoek* 25: 127–132.

Ralska-Jasiewiczowa, M. 1977. "Impact of Prehistoric Man on Natural Vegetation Recorded in Pollen Diagrams from Different Regions of Poland." *Folia Quaternaria* 49: 75–91.

Reinhard, K., S. A. Mrozowski, and K. A. Orloski. 1986. "Privies, Pollen, Parasites, and Seeds: A Biological Nexus in Historical Archaeology." *MASCA Journal* 4, no. 1: 31–36.

Renault-Misovsky, J., Bui-Thui-Mai, and M. Giraud. 1985. *Palynologie Archeologique.* Paris: CNRS.

Rue, D. J. 1987. "Early Agriculture and Early Postclassic Maya Occupation in Western Honduras." *Nature* 326: 285–286.

Schoenwetter, J. 1962. "Pollen Analysis of Eighteen Archaeological Sites in Arizona and New Mexico." In P. S. Martin et al., Chapters in the Prehistory of Eastern Arizona, *Fieldiana: Anthropology* 53: 168–209.

Stead, I. M., J. B. Bourke, and D. Brothwell, eds. 1986. *Lindow Man, the Body in the Bog.* London: British Museum.

Stevenson, A. C. 1985. "Studies in the Vegetation History of Southwest Spain, Part II: Palynolotical Investigations at Laguna de las Madres, SW Spain." *Journal of Biogeography* 12: 293–314.

Waterbolk, H. T. 1950. "Palynological Investigations of Burial Mounds." *Congres International des Sciences Prehistoriques et Protohistoriques Zurich* 130–133.

Welten, M. 1967. "Bemerken zur Palaobotanischen Untersuchung von vorgeschichtlichen Feuchtbodenwohnplatzen und Erganzungen zur pollenanalytischen Untersuchung von Burgaschisee-Sud." *Acta Bernensia* 2: 9–20.

Zeist, W. van. 1967. "Archaeology and Palynology in the Netherlands." *Review of Palaeobotany and Palynology* 4: 45–65.

Panama

Before World War I Panamanian archaeology was known largely through grave goods collected by dilettantes in Panama's western isthmus. Museum studies focused on the Chiriquí culture (now known as Gran Chiriquí) (Haberland 1984). Paleolithic stone tools from a Caribbean valley (along the Río Obispo) and shard scatters in Darién forests (Cana) were soon forgotten. A 1915 exhibition of pottery from Coclé included polychrome vessels that were rare in Chiriquí tombs, and in their designs German archaeologist MAX UHLE (1924) saw Maya influences. Soon after, freelance writer Alpheus Hyatt Verrill drove disorderly trenches through the El Caño site, mistakenly believing that a volcanic eruption had destroyed a temple there. The sculpted and unsculpted monoliths of the site in fact belonged to a ceremonial center, which has been largely overlooked by professional archaeologists. In the early 1930s Harvard University sent archaeologists Henry Roberts and Samuel K. Lothrop to Sitio Conte; they excavated 59 graves in which mostly adult males were buried with large quantities of pottery and personal ornaments, including more than 1,000 metal objects. In 1940 J. Alden Mason excavated a further 41 graves.

Lothrop derived Panama's second archaeological culture—Coclé—from Sitio Conte's mortuary arts and believed it spanned a period of 190 years before the Spanish conquest (A.D. 1330–1520). He assumed that Sitio Conte's hinterland was the Coclé culture's epicenter, from which its influences emanated to neighboring regions. He thought that most pottery and jewelry was made locally and that a few objects were imports from COLOMBIA and ECUADOR. Influenced by the Spanish chronicler Fernández de Oviedo, he proposed that the richest graves belonged to hereditary chiefs and nobles and the more modest ones to commoners and slaves.

In 1927 Swedish archaeologist Sigvald Linné traveled by boat with Baron Nordenskiöld to the Pearl Islands, the Darién, and the Caribbean coast east of the Calovébora River. Although his mandate was to search for contacts with "higher" cultures and for evidence of transisthmian migrations, Linné intuitively laid the foun-

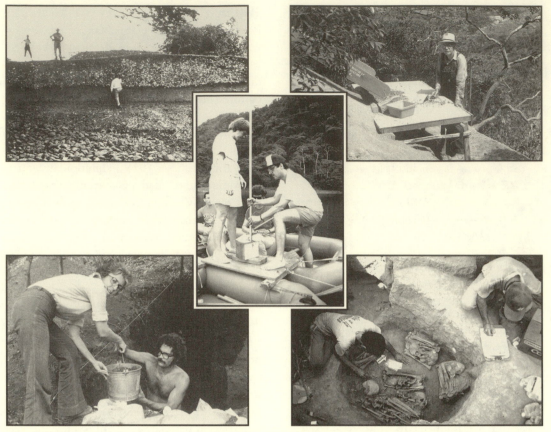

Top left: Gordon Willey (foreground) and Charles R. McGimsey III (on bank) at the Cerro Girón (AG-2) site, Coclé Province, 1952; top right: Junius Bird sieving materials at Cueva de los Ladrones, Coclé Province, 1974; center: Dolores Piperno and Paulo De Oliveira take sediment samples from the Laguna de San Carlos, Coclé Province, 1997; bottom left: Anthony Ranere and Olga Linares excavating at the preceramic Cerro Mangote site, Coclé Province, 1979; bottom right: Luís Alberto Sánchez and Adrián Badilla (right) excavate a shaft tomb with multiple secondary burials at Cerro Juan Díaz, Los Santos Province, 1992. (Richard Cooke)

dations for Panamanian pottery sequences. He noted that painted shards associated with rectangular houses in the area were most similar to Verrill's finds from Coclé and that round houses contained a different pottery style (now known to be more recent). Precisely identified mollusk remains provided insights about food procurement and trade. But neither Lothrop's team nor Linné sieved for other faunal or plant materials.

Soon after World War II Matthew Stirling and GORDON WILLEY surveyed the coastal plains of Coclé and the Azuero Peninsula and excavated at cemeteries and dwelling sites. Willey and John Ladd applied pottery seriation to stratified middens and identified painted pottery styles antecedent to and later than Sitio Conte's mortuary sample; a large cemetery at El Hatillo (heavily looted in the 1960s) definitely postdated most

Sitio Conte graves. Stirling's brief helicopter and canoe surveys revealed cave burials and dwelling sites in the Caribbean, at Utivé, in the Coclé highlands, on the Panama Bay islands, and at Barriles in highland Chiriquí, where stone statues of double human figures and massive metates (stone slabs used to grind vegetable material) were evidence for a looted ceremonial center.

In a continental context the most significant postwar research concerned older coastal sites associated with fossil Holocene landforms. In 1954 American archaeologists Gordon Willey and Charles McGimsey identified a simple red-painted and incised pottery style (Monagrillo) among Parita Bay shell middens. McGimsey trenched a preceramic shell deposit (Cerro Mangote) and associated its unifacially flaked and ground stone tools and primary and secondary burials with Panama's first radiocarbon date (4860 ± 110 B.C.). Later a date of 2090 ± 70 B.C. was obtained on charcoal from the Monagrillo type-site (He-5). Willey and McGimsey inferred that preceramic and ceramic populations were preagricultural hunter-fisher-gatherers with a littoral focus. Their macroscopic analysis of sediments and the distribution of shell species through time spawned an accurate model of coastal progradation and habitat use.

The amateur Isthmian Archaeology Society became active in the 1950s, and some of its members wrote careful reports. At Playa Venado hundreds of graves were excavated, some under Lothrop's guidance. A few contained gold jewelry, whose social and temporal contexts were usually not revealed. Lothrop's contention that some skeletons were mutilated and sacrificed requires verification by modern bio-anthropology. In 1998 Luís Sánchez compared Playa Venado pottery in U.S. museums to samples excavated in the 1990s at Cerro Juan Díaz and confirmed that most of Playa Venado's polychrome pottery corresponds stylistically to the Cubitá (A.D. 500–750) and Conte (A.D. 700–850) styles of the Gran Coclé semiotic tradition. Shell and bone jewelry and burial practices have close parallels at Cerro Juan Díaz for the same time period. Contact among littoral populations around Panama Bay appears to have been strong from about A.D. 500 to 850, when *Spondylus* shell was an important exchange commodity.

In the 1960s archaeologists' opinions about external connections were influenced by JAMES FORD's formative paradigm, which argued for constant contact among American *littoral* populations (Ford 1969). One result of this mode of thought was the Interrelationships of New World Cultures project, whose Panama Pacific branch was directed by McGimsey, accompanied by the Panamanian Olga Linares. In 1961 sixty sites along the Chiriquí coast and islands were recorded, twelve of which were tested. In the late 1950s and early 1960s Wolfgang Haberland studied Chiriquí mortuary sites and described their pottery. Linares established three ceramic phases for the Gulf of Chiriquí, from about A.D. 300 to 1520. The following year researchers from the program tested sites in the

Gulf of Montijo and the Darién, including deep shellmounds at Mariato.

The "New Archaeology" convinced Linares that research in the Neotropics should be more than Fordian seriation based on arbitrary stratigraphy. She designed a multidisciplinary program for testing hypotheses concerning the origins, dispersal, and economies of the past and present Native Americans of Panama and COSTA RICA. Archaeological sediments were sieved, excavations followed natural stratigraphy, and features were cleared. Systematic surveys used subsurface testing. Linares chose three regions with contrasting ecologies—the Aguacate Peninsula on the Caribbean coast, the environs of the 3,400-meter-high Barú volcano, and the central Chiriquí coast. Anthony J. Ranere's simultaneous discovery of preceramic deposits (dated to 4600–350 B.C.) at four Pacific-side foothill rock shelters showed that not all small-scale preagricultural peoples in tropical America were coastal. He proposed the "Tropical Forest Archaic" as an alternative to Willey's "Northwestern South American Littoral Tradition," which then included Cerro Mangote and Monagrillo (He-5) (Linares and Ranere 1980; Ranere 1975; Willey 1971).

Linares hypothesized that maize-based agriculture developed originally in the Pacific foothills and spread to the Pacific highlands, coast, and islands in the first millennium B.C. (Linares 1977a). Her own surveys—and Catherine Shelton's later survey in the Chiriquí Viejo and Chiriquí Rivers—indicated that highland farming villages coalesced into two territories dominated in the lower chiefdom by Barriles and in the upper one by Sitio Pittí. Volcanic ash atop house features at Sitio Pittí from A.D. 300 indicated that an eruption caused the abandonment of settlements in the upper chiefdom but occupation continued around Barriles (Linares, Sheets, and Rosenthal 1975). Excavations at Cerro Brujo on the Caribbean coast revealed two occupations. Pottery modes in the thin basal level were similar to those manufactured on the Pacific slopes between about A.D. 400 and 600. Linares therefore surmised that highland peoples migrated to the western Caribbean coast at this time; subsequently, settlement patterns, material culture, and subsistence economy on both watersheds diverged, although constant exchange favored cross-cordilleran social contacts. Caribbean populations grew little maize, lived in impermanent hamlets, and exploited coastal resources and forest-edge mammals. Pacific populations, by contrast, congregated in larger and more permanent villages, were more stratified socially, and depended more heavily on maize.

In the late 1960s the military government appointed Panamanian anthropologist Reina Torres de Araúz to run the National Heritage Department of the government. In that position she constrained amateur archaeology, built a new anthropology museum, and set up research and conservation programs. Constitutional reforms in 1972 improved legislation for site protection, and Panamanian Gladys de Brizuela and London University graduate Richard Cooke were contracted to direct salvage excavations. Panamanian university teams carried out systematic surveys and test excavations east of the Panama Canal and discovered new pottery types. Their work confirmed the existence of a Gran Darién material culture that diverged from that of Gran Coclé after about A.D. 700 (Cooke 1998). The Gran Darién culture sequence, however, remains very poorly dated. From 1979 to 1981 extensive excavations were conducted by Cooke and Beatriz Rovira in the Old Quarter of the "new" (post–A.D. 1673) Panama City; in the 1990s the Panama Viejo Patronage excavated at "old" Panama City (Panamá la Vieja), where Rovira's research team has uncovered pre-Columbian remains under the sixteenth-century colonial occupation.

Some research in the 1960s and 1970s continued the regional culture-history tradition established in former decades. From 1967 to 1970 French archaeologist Alain Ichon surveyed the Tonosí Valley on the Azuero Peninsula. He used stratified (but arbitrarily divided) midden and mortuary samples to establish a four-phase ceramic sequence, which highlighted many similarities and some differences between that area and Parita Bay. He also discovered ritual-cum-defensive hilltop sites. Cooke's 1969–1971 survey and test excavations in western Coclé refined the ceramic sequence proposed by

Lothrop, Willey, and Ladd. He argued that the Gran Coclé culture was not the product of diffusion from an epicenter but rather the consequence of continual interaction among culturally related polities dispersed across central Panama (Cooke 1984, 1985). Ichon gave greater explanatory weight to extraisthmian impacts and established that metallurgy had appeared in Panama coevally with the Tonosí polychrome style (A.D. 200–500). Linares (1977b) reanalyzed Sitio Conte art and proposed that Gran Coclé chiefs won power through personal prowess in war and politics, rather than through inherited status. Drolet conducted a systematic survey along the Costa Arriba de Colón and found evidence for specialized stone-tool manufacture at Ronsuao.

Linares's western Panama project benefited from the expertise of paleobotanists C. Earle Smith and Walton Galinat and zooarchaeologists Donald K. Grayson, Elizabeth Wing, and Richard White. One keystone paper argued that Cerro Brujo's Caribbean residents hunted in forest gardens (Linares 1976). Another compared Caribbean and Pacific fishing strategies (Wing 1980). At Sitio Sierra (from 1971 to 1975) Cooke recovered copious data on hunting and fishing around Parita Bay from about A.D. 200 to the conquest and initiated a Neotropical vertebrate skeleton collection (Cooke 1992; Cooke and Ranere 1999). Robert Bird's study of Sitio Sierra maize macroremains complemented Galinat's evaluation of highland Chiriquí cobs and kernels (Bird 1980, 1984; Galinat 1980). Clearly, by A.D. 1–500, four- to twelve-rowed dent and flour corns were being consumed intensively in Pacific-side settlements in Panama.

In the 1970s and 1980s new models were proposed for the lifeways and interrelations of small-scale societies that lacked fine pottery, statuary, and goldwork. JUNIUS B. BIRD searched for late-glacial (Paleo-Indian) sites around man-made Lake Madden, where amateurs earlier collected a Clovis-like whole fluted point and a fishtail–like broken fluted point. Bird did not find Paleo-Indian materials *in situ*, although simultaneous surface collections recovered additional fluted points. In 1974 Bird and Cooke failed to locate Paleo-Indian materials at the

Cueva de los Ladrones (Coclé), but they did discover preceramic deposits with a unifacial stone industry (5000–2000 B.C.) lying over other deposits with Monagrillo ceramics (2500–1000 B.C.). The year before, Anthony Ranere recorded a similar sequence and materials at the Aguadulce Shelter. These discoveries of inland sites around Parita Bay rekindled interest in coastal Monagrillo and Cerro Mangote, where, in 1975 and 1979, Ranere and Linares executed careful tests by a coring survey of the Parita Bay littoral. They verified and refined Willey's coastal progradation sequence, improved radiocarbon dating, and, aided by Patricia Hansell's study of shellfish exploitation, vastly improved the database relevant to subsistence economy.

Linares and Ranere began this project believing that Parita Bay preceramic and early-ceramic peoples were not farmers. But for her 1975 master's thesis, Dolores Piperno found maize phytoliths at the Aguadulce Shelter associated with Monagrillo potsherds. That maize was also cultivated in *preceramic* times was apparent from pollen and phytolith analyses of column samples obtained in 1981 at Cueva de los Ladrones. The hypothesis that Pacific Panamanian populations adopted farming and cultivated domesticated maize and root crops long before the development of sedentary, nucleated villages with stone statuary, clay vessels, and metal jewelry was fortified by Piperno's analysis of archaeological sediments from the Cueva de los Vampiros, the Los Santanas rock shelter, and, more recently, the Aguadulce Shelter, which she retested with Ranere in 1998. Also in 1998, Piperno and Irene Holst discovered starch grains from maize, yuca, sweet potatoes, squashes, and arrowroot embedded in late-preceramic and early-ceramic (5000–1000 B.C.) grinding stones. Lynette Norr, who has undertaken a detailed study of stable carbon and nitrogen isotopes in Panamanian pre-Columbian skeletons, has confirmed the heavy consumption of maize and coastal resources at Parita Bay sites, including Sitio Sierra, La Mula–Sarigua, Cerro Juan Díaz, and Cerro Mangote. Discrepancies between bone-collagen radiocarbon dates and the stratigraphic position of Cerro Mangote's burials, however, await clarification. Norr is currently reassessing the Zapotal site, discovered by Willey, in order to determine whether it was a fishing camp or a more permanent (agricultural) settlement.

Until the 1980s site surveying in Panama relied on intuition, geography, and visibility. From 1981 to 1986 researchers in the Proyecto Santa María used randomly selected, 0.5-kilometer-wide linear transects and purposive foot surveys to sample a 184,000-square-kilometer watershed in central Panama. Small tests were excavated in stratified rock shelters (Cooke and Ranere 1999). An early-preceramic component (8000–5000 B.C.) was added to the Gran Coclé sequence, and evidence was found for late-glacial occupation, both at the Corona rock shelter and in cores extracted from Lake La Yeguada, where pollen, phytolith, and charcoal distributions alluded to human-induced burning and clearance of late-glacial-stage *Quercus-Ilex* montane forests after about 9000 B.C. In 1988 Ranere discovered new Paleo-Indian locations at Lake Madden and La Mula–Sarigua, where Clovis-like tools were manufactured from outcropping agate (Ranere and Cooke 1991, 1996). A 1998 lakeshore survey of Lake La Yeguada by Georges Pearson (1999) supported the sediment record for early human activity by locating several quarry sites with bifacially worked chalcedony tools, including one fluted point.

The collation of paleoecological and archaeological data vouched for the continuous occupation of the Santa María drainage after about 9000 B.C., the initiation of plant cultivation during the early Holocene (8000–2500 B.C., when the climate became wetter and warmer), and the nucleation of farming populations in colluvial bottomlands at the end of the first millennium B.C. In 1988 Hansell recorded a 50- to 80-hectare village at La Mula–Sarigua, where specialized grinding and cutting stone tools were associated with a new polychrome pottery style (La Mula). This pottery has recently been well dated at the Cerro Juan Díaz site to between 250 B.C. and A.D. 200.

The Proyecto Santa María also demonstrated that early-ceramic and preceramic populations were dispersed across the watershed and not re-

Panama

Legend (left column)

Sitio Pittí	Sites investigated before or during the Second World War
Cerro Brujo, Casita de Piedra	Sites investigated between 1945 and 1960
Mariato	Sites investigated by the French mission to Azuero (1967–1970)
	Sites investigated in the 1960s' and '70s
Sitio Pittí	Sites investigated by the Linares-Ranere 'western Panama' project (1969–1972)
Los Santanas	Sites investigated by the 'Santa María Project' (1981–86)

'New' Panamá	Sites with colonial period remains
Ronsuao	Site investigated by Drolet in the late '70s
Natá	Site investigated in the 1990s

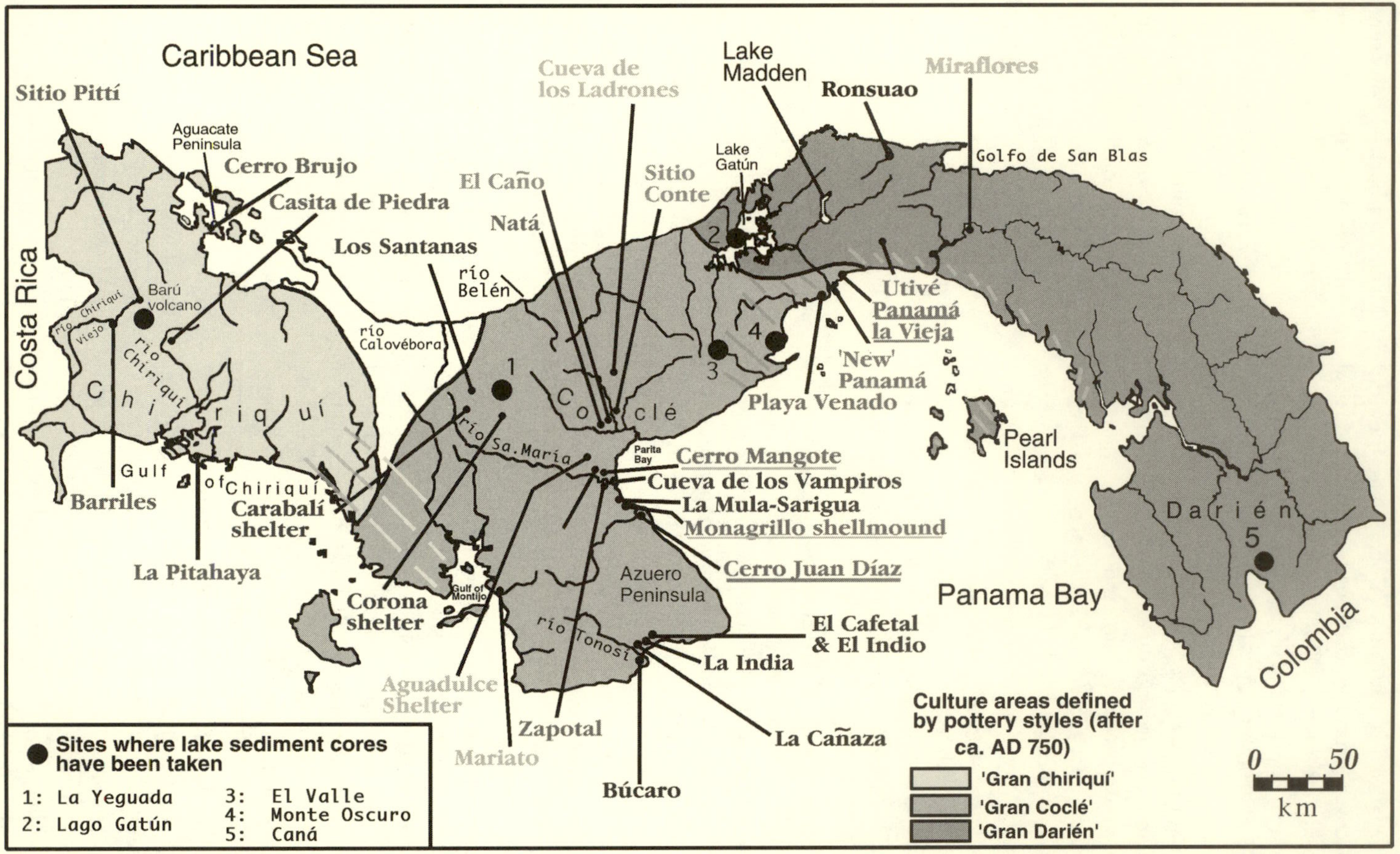

Culture areas defined by pottery styles (after ca. AD 750)
- 'Gran Chiriquí'
- 'Gran Coclé'
- 'Gran Darién'

Sites where lake sediment cores have been taken
1: La Yeguada
2: Lago Gatún
3: El Valle
4: Monte Oscuro
5: Caná

Map labels

Caribbean Sea

Costa Rica

Aguacate Peninsula
Barú volcano
río Chiriquí Viejo
río Chiriquí
Gulf of Chiriquí
Chiriquí

Sitio Pittí
Cerro Brujo
Casita de Piedra
Carabalí shelter
La Pitahaya
Barriles

Los Santanas
río Calovébora
río Belén
El Caño
Natá
Corona shelter

Cueva de los Ladrones
Sitio Conte
Coclé
río Sta. María
Aguadulce Shelter
Gulf of Montijo

Lake Madden
Lake Gatún
Ronsuao
Utivé
Panamá la Vieja
'New' Panamá
Playa Venado

Golfo de San Blas

Miraflores

Pearl Islands

Panama Bay

Cerro Mangote
Cueva de los Vampiros
La Mula-Sarigua
Monagrillo shellmound
Parita Bay
Cerro Juan Díaz
Azuero Peninsula
El Cafetal & El Indio
La India
Tonosí
río Tonosí
Zapotal
La Cañaza
Búcaro
Mariato

Darién
5

Colombia

0   50
km

stricted to lowland habitats. At La Yeguada slashing and burning of the seasonally dry forests peaked around 5000 B.C. Piperno's phytolith analysis of cores from Lake Gatún, whose pollen distributions were studied in the 1960s by Alexandra Bartlett and Elso Barghoorn, suggested that farming populations in the central Caribbean opened forest clearings between 3000 and 2000 B.C. Her hypothesis is supported by John Griggs's 1990–1999 surveys in the very humid Coclé del Norte and Belén basins. Griggs identified second-millennium-B.C. activities with Monagrillo-style pottery in stratified rock shelters and open sites. He also demonstrated that later ceramic-using populations were most closely related to populations located on the opposite side of the mountain chain, thus adding credence to the importance of transcordilleran social contact for maintaining material cultural homogeneity. Sediment cores taken in the 1990s from the Cana swamp in eastern Darién indicated that pre-Columbian farmers were practicing slash-and-burn agriculture in this now-forested area by 2000 B.C. Both there and at La Yeguada, forests reoccupied disturbed landscapes at about the time the Spanish invaded Panama. In 1997 Laurel Breece found archaeological evidence for native populations living around the early colonial town of Natá in Coclé Province.

In sum, archaeology currently suggests that strong local and regional integrative processes characterized intercommunity relations in pre-Columbian Panama for millennia. They included continual exchange, fluctuating alliances, and small-scale migrations in response to ecological and/or political pressures. External contacts and perhaps some population movement are evident in new technologies imported from outside the isthmus, such as metallurgy and, probably, pottery, as well as the presence of certain plant cultigens (e.g., maize and yuca). In the 1960s and 1970s geographer Carl Sauer and anthropologist Mary Helms popularized the hypotheses that fine arts and crafts (especially those using cast gold) were imported from Colombia and that Panamanian elites made long-distance journeys in order to obtain scarce objects and esoteric knowledge. Archaeology

suggests, however, that the closest contacts were among neighbors. People in Panamanian political territories located near coasts and productive colluvial soils were apparently quite self-sufficient in terms of daily commodities but less so in terms of sumptuary or symbolic ones. Ongoing excavations at Cerro Juan Díaz have demonstrated that some valuable items, such as shells for personal ornaments, were imported—but from no more than 100 kilometers away.

Archaeology also lends support to human population genetics and historical linguistics in suggesting that the precontact populations of Panama descended, for the most part, from late-glacial and early-Holocene colonists, rather than from waves of more recent immigrants from continental areas. In later prehistory (after about A.D. 700) three broad cultural units can be identified on the basis of pottery distributions: Gran Chiriquí, Gran Coclé, and Gran Darién. Their internal and external boundaries were tenuous, however, and waxed and waned over time and space in response to shifting economic emphases and, probably, the consequences of population fission and fusion. None can be related with confidence to modern ethnic groups or languages. But it is very likely that polities encountered by the Spanish when they arrived on the isthmus represented, in part or in whole, antecedent segments of the much-reduced population that survived conquest and assimilation and currently lives on or very near the isthmus of Panama.

Richard Cooke

References

Bird, R. McK. 1980. "Maize Evolution from 500 B.C. to the Present." *Biotropica* 12: 30–41.

———. 1984. "South American Maize in Central America?" In *Pre-Columbian Plant Migration*, 39–65. Ed. D. Z. Stone. Papers of the Peabody Museum of Archaeology and Ethnology 76. Cambridge, MA: Harvard.

Cooke, R. G. 1984. "Archaeological Research in Central and Eastern Panama: A Review of Some Problems." In *The Archaeology of Lower Central America*, 263–302. Ed. F. W. Lange and D. Z. Stone. Albuquerque: University of New Mexico Press, School for American Research.

————. 1985. "Ancient Painted Pottery from Central Panama." *Archaeology* July-August: 33–39.

————. 1992. "Prehistoric Nearshore and Littoral Fishing in the Eastern Tropical Pacific: An Ichthyological Evaluation." *World Archaeology* 6: 1–49.

————. 1998. "Cupica (Chocó): A Reassessment of Gerardo Reichel-Dalmatoff's Fieldwork in a Poorly Studied Region of the American Tropics." In *Recent Advances in the Archaeology of the Northern Andes,* 91–106. Ed. J. S. Raymond and A. Oyuela. UCLA Institute of Archaeology Monograph 39. Los Angeles.

Cooke, R. G., and A. J. Ranere. 1999. "Pre-Columbian Fishing on the Pacific Coast of Panama." In *Pacific Latin America in Prehistory: The Evolution of Archaic and Formative Cultures,* 103–122. Ed. M. Blake. Pullman: Washington State University Press.

Ford, J. A. 1969. "A Comparison of Formative Cultures in the Americas." *Smithsonian Contributions to Knowledge* 11. Washington, DC.

Galinat, W. C. 1980. "The Archeological Maize Remains from Volcan, Panama—A Comparative Perspective." In *Adaptive Radiations in Prehistoric Panama*, 175–180. Ed. O. F. Linares and A. J. Ranere. Peabody Museum Monographs 5. Cambridge, MA: Harvard University Press.

Haberland, W. 1984. "The Archaeology of Greater Chiriquí." In *The Archaeology of Lower Central America,* 233–254. Ed. F. W. Lange and D. Z. Stone. Albuquerque: University of New Mexico Press.

Linares, O. F. 1976. "Garden Hunting in the American Tropics." *Human Ecology* 4: 331–349.

————. 1977a. "Adaptive Strategies in Western Panama." *World Archaeology* 8: 304–319.

————. 1977b. "Ecology and the Arts in Ancient Panama: On the Development of Rank and Symbolism in the Central Provinces." *Studies in Precolumbian Art and Archaeology* 17, Dumbarton Oaks, Washington, DC.

Linares, O. F., and A. J. Ranere, eds. 1980. *Adaptive Radiations in Prehistoric Panama.* Peabody Museum Monographs 5. Cambridge, MA: Harvard University Press.

Linares, O. F., P. D. Sheets, and E. J. Rosenthal. 1975. "Prehistoric Agriculture in Tropical Highlands." *Science* 187: 137–145.

Lothrop, S. K. 1937. "Coclé: An Archaeological Study of Central Panama, Part 1." *Memoirs of the Peabody Museum of Archaeology and Ethnology* 7.

————. 1938. "Coclé: An Archaeological Study of Central Panama, Part 2." *Memoirs of the Peabody Museum of Archaeology and Ethnology* 8.

Pearson, Georges. 1999. "Isthmus Be Here Somewhere." *Anthropology News* 40, 6: 22.

Ranere, A. J. 1975. "Toolmaking and Tool Use among the Preceramic Peoples of Panama." In *Lithic Technology,* 173–210. Ed. E. S. Swanson. The Hague: Mouton.

Ranere, A. J., and R. G. Cooke. 1991. "Paleo-Indian Occupation in the Central American Tropics." In *Clovis: Origins and Adaptations,* 237–253. Ed. R. Bonnichsen and K. L. Turnmire. Corvallis, OR: Center for the Study of the First Americans.

————. 1996. "Stone Tools and Cultural Boundaries in Prehistoric Panama: An Initial." In *Paths to Central American Prehistory,* 49–77. Ed. F. W. Lange. Niwot: University Press of Colorado.

Uhle, M. 1924. "Cronología y relaciones de las antiguas civilivizaciones panameñas." *Boletín de la Academia Nacional de Historia, Quito* 9: 24–26.

Willey, G. R. 1971. *An Introduction to American Archaeology,* vol. 2, *South America.* Englewood Cliffs, NJ: Prentice-Hall.

Wing, E. S. 1980. "Aquatic Fauna and Reptiles from the Atlantic and Pacific Sites." In *Adaptive Radiations in Prehistoric Panama,* 194–215. Ed. O. F. Linares and A. J. Ranere. Peabody Museum Monographs 5. Cambridge, MA: Harvard University Press.

Paphos

An area on the flat lands near the sea in the modern Cypriot city of Paphos has been designated a world heritage site because of the quality and quantity of archaeological material, primarily from the Hellenistic and Roman periods, to be found there. Large rock-cut tombs of the Hellenistic period (the so-called tombs of the kings) demonstrate architectural links with Alexandria. Nea Paphos was the administrative center of CYPRUS in the Roman period. Excavated public buildings of this period include an odeon with adjacent agora, a temple of Asklepios, and a theater. Villas of the period, excavated by a Polish team under A. W. Daszewski, are decorated with fine mosaics. One of these (the house of Theseus) may have been the villa of the Roman governor. Recent expansion of the modern city and hotel construction in the area have placed severe stress on the archaeological resources, so the Department of Antiquities is constantly engaged in rescue excavations and related mitigation programs.

Palaepaphos, 15 kilometers east of Nea Paphos, was an important center in earlier periods and the center of the ancient cult of Aphrodite. This area has been extensively explored by a long series of archaeologists, including some working for the Cyprus Exploration Fund (1888), T. B. Mitford and J. H. Iliffe (1950–1953), and David Rupp's long-running Canadian Palaepaphos Survey Project. Material from a late–Bronze Age sanctuary at the site was reused in the construction of the Roman Temple of Aphrodite and subsequently in the building of a medieval sugar mill. Excavations since 1966 by F.-G. Maier have covered a variety of sites, including the siege mound used by the Persians when they besieged and took the city in the fifth century B.C.

David Frankel

Papua New Guinea and Melanesia
Historical Background
One of the central theaters of anthropological research for a century, Melanesia has been systematically explored archaeologically only since the 1950s. Before that time, collections of Melanesian material culture were made, sometimes haphazardly, by explorers, sailors, missionaries, government officials, and anthropologists. Such collections sometimes included archaeological materials, which have subsequently taken on great scientific value. These materials have formed, with written descriptions of traditional Melanesian behavior by the same explorers and anthropologists, a rich ethnographic background on which some of the central themes of Melanesian archaeology have been predicated.

The University of Auckland in New Zealand was influential in opening up archaeology in the eastern Melanesian islands in the 1950s, and there is a similar connection between the 1960s development in Australian universities of formal archaeology courses and research into Australian archaeology and the development of ar-

chaeological research in western Melanesia. Fundamental to these developments was the appointment of JACK GOLSON to the Australian National University in the early 1960s. Within a couple of years of arriving in Australia, Golson, already experienced in Pacific archaeology from a previous appointment at the University of Auckland, had graduate students working in the New Guinea Highlands, the Bismarck Archipelago, and further afield in New Caledonia and Tonga.

In the Melanesian islands a compelling theme for investigation already existed, comprising some disparate and dated threads of evidence that had recently come together: decorated potsherds collected in the early 1900s by a German missionary on Watom Island, off the coast of New Britain, and deposited in the Musée de l'Homme in Paris; a 1920s expedition to Tongatapu in western POLYNESIA where similar pottery excavated by American archaeologist W. C. McKern from midden sites went unrecognized; and the recovery of more of this pottery in the 1940s on the Île des Pins off New Caledonia by J. Avias, who recognized the similarity of the designs on his material and those on the Watom shards.

Not long afterward, E. W. Gifford, from the University of California, led archaeological expeditions to Fiji and then to New Caledonia where he excavated more decorated pottery from a site called Lapita, first reported in 1917 by Frenchman M. Piroutet. Charcoal from the site was submitted for dating by the new radiocarbon technique and produced surprisingly old dates of 2500–3000 B.P. Gifford recognized that a distinctive, highly decorated, and almost identical form of pottery, now called Lapita after Gifford's New Caledonian site, occurred in sites stretching from the Bismarck Archipelago to Tonga.

It was a small and inevitable step to link evidence from Lapita sites to long-standing questions concerning Polynesian origins first posed by English explorer Captain James Cook. Golson, himself involved in Lapita research in the second half of the 1950s from his Auckland base, proposed in 1961 that a "community of cultures," stretching the length of Melanesia and recognized by the commonality of Lapita pottery in the sites, could be identified as the ancestors of the historic western Polynesian cultures. Accordingly, to further substantiate this view, Golson, now at the Australian National University, dispatched graduate students to Watom, the Île des Pins, and Tonga to carry out more detailed excavations.

A second thread of Melanesian archaeology was simultaneously evolving in Papua New Guinea. In 1959, the anthropologist Ralph Bulmer worked in the New Guinea Highlands with his archaeologist wife, Sue Bulmer, and it was she who conducted the first professional excavations in that country. The combination of an archaeologist and an anthropologist interested in biology and ecology as well as prehistory resulted in their seminal joint article, "The Prehistory of the Australian New Guinea Highlands," in a special issue of *American Anthropologist* in 1964. Meanwhile, the first Pleistocene date for human occupation in Australia had been announced. New Guinea, part of the same landmass during lowered Pleistocene sea levels, was one potential route of human entry onto this huge continent. Researchers set out to develop spatial and chronological frameworks for humans in the highlands, a direct counterpart to similar exploratory archaeology being initiated in northern Australia at that time.

In 1968, Ralph Bulmer became Foundation Professor of Anthropology at the newly formed University of Papua New Guinea, and he appointed Jim Allen to a lectureship in prehistory the following year. Sue Bulmer and Allen began projects delineating the prehistory of Port Moresby, which helped facilitate a further series of Australian National University graduate projects along the south Papuan coast. By the end of the 1970s, this area was, archaeologically, the best known region in Papua New Guinea.

From the beginning, systematic archaeology in Melanesia separated along colonialist lines, with Australian scholars taking the lead in Papua New Guinea, the French in New Caledonia and Vanuatu (then the New Hebrides), and the New Zealanders in the Solomon Islands and Fiji. Of course, such a generalized division of interests always has exceptions, and a smattering of

American and other scholars also contributed. Today, the territorial prerogatives have fragmented as indigenous archaeologists have taken over the responsibility for their histories through a strong system of museums and cultural centers in each of the Melanesian nations. Outside archaeologists interact with them and each other on the basis of specialized research interests facilitated by regular specialized conferences within the region. Several large-scale projects, such as the Southeast Solomons Culture History Project of the early 1970s and the Lapita Homeland Project of the mid-1980s, have shown the value of multipersonnel approaches to this geographically disparate region, and a number of current projects are now using the same team-based and interdisciplinary strategy.

Such a developmental process of research has not yet produced a coherent regional prehistory for Melanesia. Lapita, an exception, is a recognizable archaeological horizon that makes archaeological sense and comprehensible narrative history, factors that explain the time and effort put into Lapita research and the emphasis put on it in syntheses of Pacific prehistory. Post-Lapita archaeology, on the other hand, too often consists only of lists of poorly described ceramic types and other artifacts from sites that frequently depend heavily on local ethnographies for coherence. If there are behavioral themes linking the later archaeologies of the separate island groups, they are yet to be convincingly articulated. At the same time, a number of researchers have sought to come to terms with the particular constraints of their oceanic world by developing theoretical perspectives, whether culture-historical, sociopolitical, economic, or ecological, that are quite advanced for the relative infancy of their subject.

Pre-Lapita

Modern humans crossed from ISLAND SOUTHEAST ASIA into the Australasian region some time before 40,000 B.P. *Homo erectus* had reached Java a million years earlier but had failed to cross the water barriers further east. The biogeographical boundary called the Wallace line separated the primates, carnivores, elephants, and ungulates of Asia and the terrestrial marsupial fauna of

Australia and New Guinea. Claims that humans have lived in Australia for well in excess of 40,000 years are currently under scrutiny, but a continuous sequence of occupied sites in both Australia and New Guinea only occurs from about 40,000 B.P. onward. Although some people think one entry route might be a move from Timor to the western Australian shore, continuities between plant species and tropical marine faunas suggest New Guinea as the "logical biotic pathway" of initial colonization.

The themes of Pleistocene and early-Holocene archaeology are dictated by the diverse environmental backgrounds of western Melanesia. The continental island of New Guinea is dominated by a steep central cordillera rising in some places to 4,000 meters. Because of rainfall patterns and cloud cover, Pleistocene colonists likely settled the series of intermontane valleys that range between 1,200 and 2,400 meters. These settlers encountered many plants and animals foreign to people accustomed to the tropical coasts, as variations in altitude produced distinct vegetational zones, each with distinctive floral and faunal distributions. The subsistence patterns reflected in excavated sites like the Nombe rock shelter reflect a strategy of hunting and collecting across these different zones.

Although the oldest site on the New Guinea coast, on uplifted coral terraces on the Huon Peninsula, has yielded dates of ca. 40,000 B.P. or a little older, the earliest evidence of humans in the highlands is later, ca. 30,000 B.P., which may reflect the profound behavioral shifts required to colonize these uplands. The forests and grasslands contained mainly small game animals, but Pleistocene New Guinea was also home to a small number of large mammals, all now extinct. At Nombe, four megafaunal species—all forest browsers—existed between ca. 25,000 and ca. 14,000 years ago, but the excavator is ambivalent as to whether the bones are in the site through human action or whether the animals died there by natural causes.

In contrast to game species, the New Guinea Highlands possesses a huge array of plants, including about 200 that today are used for food. Little direct evidence exists for the development of artificial microenvironments to promote the growth of useful plants, plant processing, and perhaps plant storage, but these processes probably developed from the beginning of settlement. The Huon Peninsula site, Nombe, Kosipe, and a range of other early sites have produced a variety of tanged, waisted, and grooved axes, both flaked and ground. These tools were arguably used to thin forest patches by trimming and ring barking in order to promote the growth of useful plants. Early forest burning reflected in the pollen records supports this interpretation.

There are thus hints of a long progression that culminated in a distinctive highlands agriculture that appeared around 9000–6000 B.P. at Kuk in the Wahgi Valley in the highlands of New Guinea. A series of evolutionary stages of garden technology has been developed for the site, each stage reflecting sophisticated hydraulic practices involving both drainage and irrigation, and the series culminated in the familiar root crop/arboriculture systems present in the highlands today. Associated pig husbandry is reflected in the archaeological record between 5000 and 6000 B.P. with some claims going back to 10,000 B.P.

Apart from the obvious physical contrasts between montane and island settlement, the movement into the Bismarck Archipelago first involved humans in adapting to the simplified terrestrial ecology of an oceanic world. New Guinea today supports a total of fifty-two terrestrial mammals of sufficient size to represent potential game; the number shrinks to six in New Britain and New Ireland, of which at least two were probably carried there by humans. Bird and plant numbers also reduce dramatically. People were dependent upon a restricted range of natural resources, the majority of them coastal, which could not support more than low numbers of humans in the long term.

The initial colonists adopted strategies that compensated for this reduced range of edible plants and terrestrial animals by high mobility across a large territory. Such mobility was predicated on safe, durable, and maneuverable watercraft, which took people to the scattered resources rather than moving such resources to the people. However, as population, local resource

Prehistoric drainage ditches for gardens in swampland in the Wahgi Valley, Papua New Guinea. Excavations at the Kuk site have yielded evidence of hydraulic controls for horticulture ca. 9000 B.C. (J. Golson)

knowledge, and extractive efficiencies increased, moving resources to the people increased.

Tectonic uplift and deep submarine contours along the north coast of New Ireland allow a rare glimpse into late Pleistocene coastal adaptations in the region. Two limestone cave sites, Buang Merebak and Matenkupkum, about 140 kilometers apart, were initially occupied ca. 32,000–35,000 years ago. Both have extensive marine-shell midden deposits, and both contain fish bones that date from the beginning of occupation. Shell-fishing strategies from both sites indicate that initially, people targeted the larger species, which provided the best returns, and it is clear that periods of human absence were sufficiently long to allow for regeneration of the species. Later, a more intensive use of the shell resources diminished the availability of these larger species, which were then supplemented by a greater variety of smaller species.

People moved both inland and further east. About 36,000 years ago, outcroppings of limestone cherts (a kind of sedimentary rock used

for making stone tools) were quarried at two locations in the vicinity of Yombon, about thirty kilometers inland from the southwestern coast of New Britain, which reflects the systematic discovery and exploitation of useful resources in the region at an early date. Kilu Cave in the northern Solomons Island chain was occupied sporadically between 29,000 B.P. and ca. 20,000 B.P. Stone tools from this site carry residues of *Colocasia* and *Alocasia* taro in quantities sufficient to suggest that cultivated taro forms with large tubers, the product of prior human selection, were being processed.

Reaching the Solomon Islands required a sea journey about twice that of any prior necessary crossing between mainland Southeast Asia and the Bismarck Archipelago. This journey was also the first without two-way intervisibility—at a point in the journey the voyagers were unable to see where they were going or where they had been. But by 21,000 B.P., people had reached Manus Island in the Admiralties group, and this voyage, over 200 kilometers whether attempted from New Guinea or New Ireland, required that 60 to 90 kilometers be traversed totally out of the sight of any land. This is apparently the earliest known example of true seafaring anywhere in the world.

By 20,000 B.P., the change to moving resources to people is reflected in the appearance of obsidian from a New Britain source 350 kilometers away in two New Ireland sites. An introduced animal, the cuscus (*Phalanger orientalis*), also occurred in both sites at this time. This marsupial, which became an established species on New Ireland and an important food source, is the earliest of a series of animal translocations in the region and raises the possibility that useful plants and nut-bearing trees were also moved about well before the end of the Pleistocene period.

The sporadic use of caves in New Ireland in the early-Holocene period raises the contentious question of whether people were more dependent on cultivated plants and were settling down there around 8,000–10,000 years ago, as in the New Guinea Highlands. Lacking the complex evidence of later Lapita sites, some researchers continue to dismiss the various strands of supporting evidence that have emerged. These include further residues of taro and yam on various stone tools, including elaborate stemmed and hafted obsidian and chert items; the presence of domesticated *Canarium* nut shells in various island sites where wild forms were not endemic; several sites where up to twelve nut species indicate the presence of arboriculture; increasingly extensive distributions of obsidian from its several sources both east in the Bismarck Archipelago and west along the north coast of New Guinea; the appearance of stone and edge-ground axes, earth ovens in several sites, and pig remains in two lowland sites; and changing settlement patterns involving beachside, coastal, and inland open sites as well as caves and rock shelters on smaller offshore islands and atolls. It is thought that the model of gradual economic intensification reflected in these developments requires more substantial food productive systems than those provided solely by hunting and gathering.

Lapita

Beginning about 3500 B.P., an influx of Austronesian language speakers bringing exotic items of material culture from Southeast Asia transformed the history of the Melanesian peoples. The distinctions between the Lapita and what preceded it are so great that early researchers saw this migration of Polynesians-to-be as having little interaction with existing Melanesians other than bringing them agriculture, sailing technology, pottery, complex shell technologies, obsidian trading, prestige exchange, the pig, the chicken, and other benefits of their more complex society. Some researchers still hold such a view, but others now propose more interactive and integrative models that suggest the success and spread of Lapita depended on a greater economic and organizational parity between the indigenous groups and the new arrivals than previously thought. However, the new material culture, so dominant archaeologically, has acted to mask the prior levels of indigenous development. The island populations were ready for and receptive to the changes brought by Lapita. The mainland culture of New Guinea seems to have been bypassed or was more resistant since no Lapita-type sites occur there.

Lapita people almost immediately breached the previous barrier to Pacific expansion at the end of the main Solomons chain to occupy outlying islands in the southeastern Solomons, settle Vanuatu and New Caledonia, and reach Fiji, Tonga, and Samoa. The implication that a new sailing technology existed, specifically the double-hulled canoe, is strong. In any case, new spheres of influence beyond the Bismarck Archipelago added new dimensions of oceanic distance to Melanesian relationships, distances that provided the basis for the diversity that would develop in Melanesian societies.

An increased number of sites from this period may reflect higher populations, more-sedentary settlements in coastal and inland sites, a higher visibility of sites with pottery, or combinations of all three possibilities. The introduced technology of pottery-making looms large in all assessments of Lapita. Apart from a single claim for earlier Melanesian pottery from

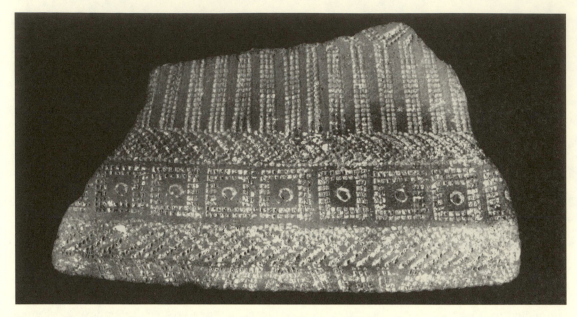

Dentate-stamped shard of Lapita pottery from Babase Island, New Ireland Province, late second millennium B.C. (G. Summerhayes)

the Sepik area of New Guinea, Lapita pottery is the first introduction of this technology to Melanesia. However, while characteristics of Lapita pottery can be found in Southeast Asia, such similarities are at present more generic than specific, not clearly antecedent in time, or both. Any clear Lapita pottery trail into the Pacific begins in the Bismarck Archipelago. Plain and decorated pots occur, with decoration being so elaborate that its presence in sites separated by thousands of miles must reflect a historically related and almost certainly socially interactive group, especially when much of the pottery seems to have been produced on a local or island level. If the pots themselves did not move far, the trading of obsidian was more extensive (although perhaps no more intensive) than in earlier times and appears to reflect a local continuity in both production and exchange.

Despite claims for Pleistocene house sites in the New Guinea Highlands, Lapita sites provide us with the first clear archaeological indications of villages. No Lapita open sites have earlier preceramic deposits, and several have revealed evidence of stilt houses built over lagoons. Typically, Lapita sites contain extensive and diverse types of shell tools and ornaments, including adzes, fishhooks, vegetable peelers, armshells,

and beads. Some sites have yielded diverse plant remains, and pig, dog, and fish and shellfish are typically present. Although the Lapita people were fishing agriculturists, they did not transfer rice cultivation from Southeast Asia, remaining instead dependent on root crops and fruit and nut trees.

Very little is known of Lapita social organization, and the few Lapita burials known are without grave goods. Arguments have been made for Lapita shell ornaments representing items of prestige exchange, and linguistic reconstructions suggest that some form of hierarchical structure existed. Strong and lasting social frameworks able to function at a distance seem fundamental to the transformation represented by Lapita.

Post-Lapita

Conventionally, the Lapita tradition is thought to have ended by about 2000 B.P., although various researchers have argued for both earlier and later terminal dates because the Lapita period was not static. Its stamped pottery is most elaborate in both decoration and vessel form in the earliest centuries in western Melanesia, subsequently simplifying through time and across space. The range of pot shapes diminishes, dentate stamping becomes coarser, and gradually this decoration technique is replaced by incising and appliqué techniques and, more frequently, undecorated pots, although the latter always formed some component of the Lapita pottery style, even in its earliest period. Fluctuations in the nature and extent of the overseas movements of obsidian from sources in the Manus and New Britain and other goods also occurred during the Lapita period. Put most simply, an initially large areal system gradually became a series of more-localized and probably more-specialized areal systems that gradually disconnected from each other.

Throughout island Melanesia, subsequent widespread incised and applied relief pottery traditions demonstrate local evolution. In some areas pottery technology eventually disappeared altogether, whereas in other areas particular villages or groups of villages became specialized pottery producers. In some localities the earliest local styles of incised and applied relief pottery may be directly descended from Lapita; in others they appear disconnected.

The south coast of Papua provides one example of local development. There, the people remained steadfastly aceramic throughout the Lapita development, but about 2000 B.P. Austronesian settlers occupied beaches, headlands, offshore islands, and even some inland locations along 800 kilometers of coastline. In something of a Lapita replay, the earliest sites were linked by similar elaborately decorated pottery, obsidian from Fergusson Island in the D'Entrecasteaux Group to the east, stone adzes, and a range of elaborate shell and bone artifacts. Over the next 800 years, successive related ceramic styles occurred at various points along the coast, although local developments gradually took separate paths, and in 1200 B.P., new and different pottery styles appeared and the extent of the obsidian trade diminished.

The occupants of the small offshore island of Mailu not only gradually monopolized pottery production in their area but, by the time of European contact, engaged in warfare to monopolize the use of large trading canoes—and thus long-distance trade—in the region. A similar but distinct specialized trading system developed around Port Moresby, an area of low seasonal rainfall and infertile soil. There, the Motu people in different villages specialized in pottery and shell bead manufacture and traded year-round up and down the coast and inland, with both Austronesian and non-Austronesian villages alike, in order to satisfy their subsistence requirements. The largest expedition each year shipped up to 20,000 clay pots 400 kilometers to the Papuan Gulf to exchange for hundreds of tons of sago and canoe hulls unavailable in the expedition's own district. This specialized system developed over some 400 years and involved coastal villages that ranged in size from several hundred to more than 1,000 people, all operating without hereditary or hierarchical social systems.

By the time of European contact, trading systems such as the one just described not only circled the coastline of New Guinea but also linked many small island groups throughout island Melanesia. Most of the systems fulfilled the dual functions of providing subsistence and social prestige for traders and recipients alike. Although Melanesia is known anthropologically for its less-structured big-man systems, hierarchical structures with hereditary chiefs are also known both ethnographically and archaeologically.

In the late 1960s and early 1970s, the French archaeologist Jose Garanger reconstructed the late, aceramic period of Vanuatu history by excavating chiefs' burials remembered in local oral histories. One of the most dramatic was that of Chief Roy Mata, possibly a Polynesian immigrant, who arrived on the island of Efate 400 to 600 years ago and subjugated the local populations there and on nearby islands. He was buried on the small nearby island of Retoka with great ceremony, together with near relatives and members of clans owing him allegiance. Some apparently sacrificed themselves; others were sacrificed by force. The exact number of retainers buried with him is not clear, but there were at least fifty. The excavations tallied closely with oral traditions. Roy Mata's body was surrounded by individuals and embracing couples, all highly decorated with shell valuables, pigs tusks, whale-tooth beads, and crocodile-tooth and calcite pendants. There were also secondary burials, which suggests that deceased clansmen were re-interred with their chief.

Whether the lack of rigid hierarchical social structures over large parts of Melanesia prevented the dense populations of agriculturists, like those in the New Guinea Highlands, or complex maritime traders, like those in island Melanesia, from achieving the transformation to city-states as elsewhere in the world remains a matter of debate. In neither case did any particular group control both a stable agricultural base and access to wealth accumulation through trade, which some people believe are requisites for such transformations. Especially in the case of island Melanesia, the emergence of maritime societies followed a gradual and logical adaptation to an oceanic world that had more limited terrestrial resources than homelands to the west. This evolution was clearly aided and added to by movements of people and technologies into the region from further west, coupled with increasing local complexity and specialization if not long-term stability.

Jim Allen

References

Spriggs, M. 1997. *The Island Melanesians.* Oxford: Blackwell.

Parrot, André (1901–1980)

André Parrot first studied theology and then, as a result of art history lessons at the École du LOUVRE, became interested in the ancient Near East. He spent a year at the École Biblique et Archéologique in Jerusalem and then excavated at Nerab in northern Syria in 1926. In 1927, he excavated at Balbeck in Lebanon, and in 1931, he worked at the Sumerian site of Telloh, where he was director of excavations from 1931 to 1933.

Parrot began excavating Tell Senkere, the site of ancient Larsa, in 1933, but political problems with the Iraqis caused him to begin to excavate the Mesopotamian site of Mari in southeastern Syria instead; he was to direct excavations there until 1961. Mari was a city founded in the early third millenium and had a long settlement history until the late first millenium B.C. Parrot discovered major temple and palace complexes

and major archives from the Old Babylonian period of the early-eighteenth century B.C.

Parrot's association with the Louvre continued throughout his career. He was appointed conservator, then chief conservator, of the Department of Near Eastern Antiquities, and during his time there, he completely reorganized the Near Eastern galleries. He was appointed director of the museum in 1965. He published on the history of art and biblical history, demonstrating links between the biblical world and other Near Eastern civilizations.

Tim Murray

See also French Archaeology in Egypt and the Middle East

References

Parrot, André. 1976. *L'Archéologie.* Paris: Seghers.

Peabody Museum of Archaeology and Ethnology

The Peabody Museum, a part of Harvard University in Cambridge, Massachusetts, has been an active sponsor of field archaeology since its founding in 1866. It has undertaken significant field research in the Maya area, lower Central America, the southwestern and southeastern sections of the United States, and the early prehistory of Europe and Asia. The first academic department to grant a Ph.D. in archaeology in North America, the Peabody Museum has provided an institutional base for the development of culture-historical archaeology and the direct historical approach.

The Peabody Museum helped shape the discipline of archaeology in North America. Its initial constitution called for special attention to "the early races of the American Continent," an orientation reflected in its original name, the Peabody Museum of American Archaeology and Ethnology. Forty years were to pass before the museum undertook serious archaeological exploration outside the Americas, and during that time, the museum underwent significant changes in organization that were of fundamental importance both to its changing orientation and to its impact on training in archaeology in the United States.

Curtis Hinsley (1985) argues that the museum began as a platform at Harvard University for Darwinian evolution, a concept that was resolutely resisted by Louis Agassiz of Harvard's Museum of Comparative Zoology. When Agassiz refused an endowment from the businessman George Peabody, O. C. Marsh, Peabody's nephew, persuaded Peabody to support the founding of a new museum for the study of American archaeology and ethnology. From 1866 to 1887, the Peabody Museum occupied an uneasy position vis-à-vis its institutional host. Although it was affiliated with Harvard, it was neither a teaching body nor fully incorporated into the university. It suffered from the lack of a disciplinary base within the university—or even in the United States in the days before academic archaeology developed. Hinsley notes that Jeffries Wyman, the first curator of the museum, refused an appointment to the professorship funded by the original endowment, an act that delayed the museum's development of a teaching presence in a community defined by teaching.

One of the major factors in the movement of the museum toward greater integration, and hence status, within the university was the appointment in 1874 of FREDERIC WARD PUTNAM as curator, the chief executive position in the museum. A former student of Agassiz who had split with his professor over the theory of evolution, Putnam overcame the resistance of Agassiz's supporters and became the first Peabody Professor of American Archaeology and Ethnology in 1887. His appointment made it possible to teach archaeology, and supervise graduate students, just as financial support for the museum was growing.

During its early years, the Peabody's trustees represented the social and business circles of eastern Massachusetts but not the leaders of Boston society. Hinsley identifies the appointment of F. M. Weld, a prominent Bostonian, to head the first visiting committee for the museum in 1889 as a turning point in drawing support from the more influential members of the community. Among the new patrons was Charles Pickering Bowditch, who encouraged and financially supported programs of research on Central America. In 1896, the legislature of Massachusetts approved the transfer of the assets of the Peabody Museum to Harvard and thus the museum became fully integrated into the university.

The Peabody's archaeological research programs responded to changes through time in the museum's academic staffing and support from the community and the growth it fostered in the discipline of archaeology. Under its first curator, research was restricted to the eastern United States and relied on independent research affiliates with no formal ties to the museum and variable training. Putnam ushered in a period of extension of fieldwork efforts. Still, the staff of the museum was limited, and much of the fieldwork was carried out by affiliates. With Putnam's appointment to teach in 1887, greater control over training became a possibility, and during the remainder of Putnam's tenure as curator, students gradually displaced affiliated researchers as the supervisors of the Peabody's archaeological work.

On its fiftieth anniversary in 1917, the Peabody was poised to dominate archaeology in the United States. It had in place a full complement of specialists in world prehistory and a corresponding presence in field archaeology throughout the world. As the earliest degree-granting institution in U.S. archaeology, the museum spread its methodological approaches and theoretical orientations to other institutions staffed by Harvard graduates. The change in the title of the chief officer of the museum from curator to director in 1913, which J. O. Brew (1966) notes, coincided with the construction of a new building and paralleled the growth in the roster of curators who came to spearhead the teaching and fieldwork of the museum. Putnam's successors had less influence over the direction of the museum's research, which was now controlled by the professional staff. These specialists pursued largely independent concerns dictated by the different emphases in their own subfields. As a result, the Peabody Museum became an increasingly global institution whose research efforts were only loosely linked together by the dominant approach that has come, in retrospect, to be called culture history.

Jeffries Wyman had, through the sponsorship of research affiliates, involved the Peabody as a participant in the intense controversy surrounding the identity of the builders of earthen mounds throughout the Ohio River Valley and southeastern United States. When Putnam assumed the direction of the museum, he worked on mound sites in the eastern United States and encouraged affiliated researchers to investigate the same field. Putnam was conscious of setting standards for a new generation of archaeologists in his approach to field excavation and documentation. He was also deeply involved in the search for evidence for the early peopling of the Americas, in effect, trying to develop a long prehistory like the European Paleolithic. From 1875 to 1913, the museum sponsored affiliated research directed toward this goal, which Hinsley notes was received poorly within the emerging archaeological profession.

Putnam also expanded the scope of the museum's field research, with affiliates conducting excavations in the western United States, MEXICO, and Nicaragua. Although the use of affiliated researchers allowed the museum to expand the sphere of its activities, these independent explorers were not trained in Putnam's methods, and their availability was usually a chance offshoot of other activities. Development of the museum's own research program lagged until the establishment of an academic department with Putnam's professorial appointment in 1887. The financial support Charles Bowditch offered at the same time determined that the archaeology of the Maya would be an early focus of the program.

At first, the financial resources supported affiliated researchers, beginning with Edward H. Thompson, who worked for the museum between 1888 and 1908, but by 1891, Putnam had a trained graduate student, John G. Owens, and sent him to head a project to investigate the site of Copan in Honduras. Owens's death while at the site placed the project engineer, George Byron Gordon, in charge and delayed the full realization of the goal of having Harvard-trained researchers conduct Central American fieldwork. Still, the precedent had been established.

Curtis Hinsley (1984) has reviewed the long search for a student who could carry out the goals Bowditch and Putnam envisaged for the museum in the Maya area, a search that culminated in selection of Alfred M. Tozzer. After 1905, the Peabody's exploration of the Maya area was taken over by a generation of students that included Tozzer, SYLVANUS G. MORLEY, Herbert J. Spinden, and R. E. Merwin. The mandate they worked under was Bowditch's desire to illuminate the writing and calendar systems of the ancient Maya, which led to an emphasis on the exploration of sites that yielded inscribed monuments.

Bowditch's resources made the orderly development of a research program in Central America possible. The patronage of Mary Hemenway, although more limited, was of similar importance to the museum. A fellowship funded by Hemenway was added to the museum's endowments in 1890, and according to Edwin Wade and Lea McChesney (1980), Hemenway's interests included both living cultures and archaeological sites of the U.S. Southwest. After her death in 1894, a collection of archaeological and ethnographic Pueblo pottery purchased with her funding in 1892 was left to the museum, and parts of the collection were placed on exhibit and thus available for study by the first generation of Harvard students to specialize in the cultures of the Southwest. Among these was ALFRED V. KIDDER, who supervised the first Peabody field research on the Pueblos from 1908 to 1914. From 1914 through 1929, the Peabody maintained a presence in the Southwest with excavations directed by Kidder and the museum's assistant director, S. J. Guernsey. Peabody's archaeology in this area stressed continuity between past and present and contributed to the developing culture area and direct historic approaches of U.S. archaeology.

Although the Americas were both the original focus and the strength of the museum, the Peabody made its first foray outside the Americas in 1900, and new research efforts were launched by museum staff members between 1914 and 1916 in England, the Near East, and Egypt. J. O. Brew notes that World War I cut short the development of the Peabody's presence in these areas, and when the research was renewed, it was in cooperation with the American School of Prehistoric Research (ASPR), which was founded in 1921.

Perhaps because of the financial support provided by Bowditch, the Peabody's work in Central and South America was the first to fully integrate student training and research. The establishment in 1914, under Sylvanus Morley's direction, of a program in Maya research by the Carnegie Institution of Washington, D.C. (CIW) provided opportunities for students trained by A. M. Tozzer to work in the Maya area but also effectively prevented the Peabody from continuing its own field research there. A precedent for work in lower Central America had been set by the museum's sponsorship of work in Nicaragua in the 1870s and 1880s and non-Maya Honduras in the 1890s.

Between 1917 and 1929, Peabody researchers undertook exploratory trips to COSTA RICA, Nicaragua, Honduras, and areas of GUATEMALA and MEXICO not directly under investigation by the CIW. As Hinsley notes, the Maya had given the museum a suitably civilized, and hence worthy, subject for research. The discovery of spectacular burials at the site of Sitio Conte in PANAMA provided another object of study, a Central American civilization that boasted a rich tradition of gold working. Under Tozzer, the Peabody expanded its efforts in Central and South American prehistory, from non-Maya Honduras to the Andes, through work by students and curatorial associates, themselves usually ex-students. Tozzer's central concern was to establish chronologies, exemplified in his own study of the site of CHICHÉN ITZÁ employing stylistic seriation. His students sketched the outlines of culture-historical sequences for much of Central and South America.

Even without the strong presence that Tozzer had exercised and the patronage support that Bowditch had provided, the archaeology of Europe and Asia developed as a new strength of the Peabody after 1921. Brew credits the ASPR with revitalizing the Peabody's interest in this field, noting that it provided field opportunities for students. Among them were the later principal investigators of Peabody-sponsored projects between 1929 and 1939 in southeastern Europe, the Middle East, and India. A stable institutional base for European archaeology within the museum was provided by curator Hugh

O'Neill Hencken, who directed projects in Ireland and ITALY beginning in 1931.

The Peabody's original interest in North American archaeology was also supported by new curatorial and professorial staff active in the 1930s and 1940s. J. O. Brew carried out research in the western United States beginning in 1931, especially in the Pueblo area, that served as a training ground for students. Philip Phillips institutionalized the museum's involvement in the archaeology of the Southeast, establishing the Lower Mississippi Survey (LMS) in 1933. The LMS took a systematic regional approach to site location and the construction of culture history.

In 1937, students working in the western United States reopened for the Peabody the long dormant issue of the antiquity of human occupation of the Americas. Undoubtedly this development owed some of its inspiration to a new acceptance of the topic sparked by the early dating of the Folsom tradition in 1926, which made respectable the concerns that Hinsley notes had been an embarrassment for Putnam at the turn of the century. It also reflected the influence of a global approach in archaeological training at the Peabody. The Peabody's specialist in Old World PALEOLITHIC ARCHAEOLOGY, Hallam Movius, began his research on early sites for the museum in Burma and Java in 1937. Following World War II, he continued his research with investigation of Mousterian sites in Uzbekistan and of the Abri Pataud in FRANCE. Familiarity through his teaching with the outlines of the European and Asian record facilitated the approach by students of the prehistory of the Americas to what had long been an ignored issue.

The Peabody Museum, by providing training for a substantial proportion of the academic archaeologists working in North America before 1950, effectively acted as one of the forces providing coherence to the discipline. This coherence was given literal form with the publication in 1953 and 1955 of sections of what became GORDON WILLEY'S and Philip Phillip's *Method and Theory in American Archaeology* (1958). The work of Tozzer's successor in the Central American field and the Peabody's curator for the southeastern United States, the book systematized the framework of North American archaeology, then experiencing institutional growth in the postwar expansion of anthropology.

Although begun as a challenge on the doorstep of North America's most influential anti-Darwinian scientist, Peabody's archaeology was remarkably free from overt evolutionary theory. Instead, the museum explored continuity between archaeological and contemporary cultures in Central America and the Southwest. This research thus exemplified the contradictions in the culture-historical approach that Bruce Trigger has identified in *A History of Archaeological Thought* (1978). A historian of archaeology, Trigger points to the influence on American archaeology of anthropologist Frans Boas's resistance to evolutionary anthropology, conjoined with an increasing awareness of the particularity of local archaeological remains, in fostering a preoccupation with classification, definition of culture areas, and construction of chronologies. As in U.S. archaeology generally, when the Peabody's archaeology grew to cover a global reach, the collation of culture-historical sequences substituted for an analysis of change.

A similar critique had been made from within Harvard by WALTER W. TAYLOR, whose dissertation was based on Peabody-sponsored fieldwork in northern Mexico in 1938 and 1939, in *A Study of Archaeology* published in 1948. Trigger argues that Taylor was one of several scholars to move at about the same time toward being more concerned with functional and behavioral questions. Such questions were part of a general trend in U.S. archaeology toward a renewed concern with process and with cultural evolution that gained support in the 1950s and became widespread in the 1960s. In the development of what came to be called "new archaeology," the formerly dominant voice of the Peabody was remarkably quiet. Like other anthropology departments with institutional roots in museums, Harvard persevered in its established practice of investigating the spatial and chronological extent of archaeological cultures. The carefully amassed collections, representative of different culture areas from around the world that formed the core of the museum, were installed for the benefit of advanced students in world prehistory. They were not suitable for the concerns of the systemic and functional studies launched under the new banner and awaited a new generation of archaeologists concerned with issues, such as materials sourcing and symbolic analysis, that could be addressed with individual objects.

Rosemary Joyce

See also Maya Civilization; United States of America, Prehistoric Archaeology

References

Primary Sources

The object collections of the Peabody Museum, including over 2 million (estimated) archaeological items, are accompanied in collections files by documentation of both the original acquisition and the later study of the collections. The object collections are complemented by a photographic collection of over half a million items. The Peabody Museum Archives include papers from a number of the central characters in the history of the museum and papers from various research expeditions sponsored by the museum. The archives also include all the records of the Maya program of the Carnegie Institution of Washington, D.C., which were turned over to the museum following the termination of the program. Other papers relating to the early history of the Peabody Museum, including the papers of Frederick Ward Putnam, are in the archives of Harvard University.

Secondary Sources

Brew, J. O. 1966. *People and Projects of the Peabody Museum, 1866–1966.* Cambridge, MA: Peabody Museum.

Brew, J. O., ed. 1968. *One Hundred Years of Anthropology.* Cambridge, MA: Harvard University Press.

Hinsley, C. 1984. "Wanted: One Good Man to Discover Central American History." *Harvard Magazine* 87, no. 2: 64A–64H.

———. 1985. "From Shell-heaps to Stelae: Early Anthropology at the Peabody Museum." In *Objects and Others: Essays on Museums and Material Culture,* pp. 49–74. Vol. 3 of *History of Anthropology.* Ed. G. Stocking. Madison: University of Wisconsin Press.

Wade, E., and L. S. McChesney. 1980. *America's Great Lost Expedition: The Thomas Keam Collection of Hopi Pottery from the Second Hemenway Expedition, 1890–1894.* Phoenix: Heard Museum.

Peake, Harold John Edward (1867–1946)

The son of a church minister, Harold John Edward Peake was trained in estate management and developed an interest in changes in the history of land tenure and land use. He spent some time on a ranch in British Columbia, CANADA, where he studied prehistoric pastoralism, and he then studied art and ceramics in JAPAN and CHINA.

Peake returned to England in 1899 and became curator of the Newbury Museum, which became well known for its prehistory exhibits of implements, pots, potsherds, and maps. Peake's catalog of 17,000 prehistoric British bronze implements was deposited in the British Library in recognition of its significance. Peake was interested in the evidence of the human past in relation to the environment of the time and its impact on people. His book *The Bronze Age and the Celtic World* (1922) attempted to link archaeology and linguistics while *The English Village,* published in the same year, was a study of social evolution. He regularly contributed to the Royal Anthropological Institute's journal.

Peake became well known for his literary collaborations with Professor HERBERT J. FLEURE, such as the ten-volume *Corridors of Time,* written between 1927 and 1936, which provided economic interpretations of the archaeological record. In these volumes, Peake contributed specifically to the debate about the beginning of cereal cultivation in northern MESOPOTAMIA during the Neolithic period and to questions on the origins of metallurgy.

Peake was a member of the council of the Royal Anthropological Institute and president of the institute between 1926 and 1928. He received the Huxley Medal in 1940.

Tim Murray

Pei Wenzhong (1904–1982)

Pei Wenzhong was born in Hebei Province in northern CHINA, the son of a primary schoolteacher who was involved in local anti-illiteracy campaigns. As a young man, Pei became politically active in the areas of better education and wholesale reform of China's traditional social institutions.

In 1921, Pei was admitted to Beijing University to study geology, and in 1927 he graduated with a major in paleogeology. The following year he went to work in Hebei Province at the site of Pleistocene fossiliferous fissures at Zhoukoudian, where an international team of scientists had been endeavoring since 1921 to uncover evidence of some of China's earliest human occupants. Beginning in 1929, Pei became field supervisor of the Zhoukoudian excavations, and at the end of the year made the most important discovery of his long career—the first skull of *Homo erectus* found on Chinese soil. This specimen, later known popularly as Peking man, formed the basis for a thorough reinterpretation of human evolution in eastern Asia.

At Zhoukoudian, Pei was influenced by such scholars as the Canadian anatomist Davidson Black, the U.S. anthropologist Franz Weidenreich, the French Jesuit archaeologist HENRI BREUIL and geologist and vertebrate paleontologist Pierre Teilhard de Chardin, and the Swedish archaeologist J. GUNNAR ANDERSSON. The Zhoukoudian excavations from 1921 to 1937 became, in fact, a model not only of multidisciplinary science but also of multinational collegiality.

Pei's discovery of the *Homo erectus* cranium at Zhoukoudian catalyzed his lifelong interest in China's Pleistocene prehistory, and from 1929 to 1935, under his guidance, many important localities at Zhoukoudian were discovered and excavated. These included the earliest archaeological material at the site (500,000 years old), the first unequivocal stone artifacts in association with fossil humans in China, and evidence of the use of fire dating back more than 300,000 years. In 1935, Pei enrolled at the University of Paris to study for his doctorate under Breuil's direction. Pei completed his degree, returned to Beijing in 1937, and took charge of the Cenozoic research laboratory there. In 1938, he joined the Communist Party.

From 1949 until 1953, Pei was head of the museums division of the Bureau of Social and Cultural Affairs under the Ministry of Culture in the new People's Republic of China. In 1957, he transferred to the Chinese Academy of Sciences and assumed the title of reseacher in the academy's Institute of Vertebrate Paleontology and Paleoanthropology. In 1963, he was appointed director of the Paleoanthropological Research Laboratory, and from 1979 until his death he was chairman of the Beijing Natural History Museum. During the 1950s and 1960s, Pei excavated sites and analyzed archaeological material from all over China—including the Upper Pleistocene site of Dingcun in Shanxi Province, the Paleolithic site of Guanyin cave in southern China—and from all periods, including the Neolithic and dynastic. These expeditions not only generated much of the information on which the current understanding of early Chinese prehistory rests, they also provided opportunities for the training of most of China's cadre of professional paleoanthropologists until the 1970s.

John Olsen

References

For references, see *Encyclopedia of Archaeology: The Great Archaeologists, Vol. 1*. Ed. Tim Murray (Santa Barbara, CA: ABC-CLIO, 1999), pp. 449–450.

Pengelly, William (1812–1894)

Born in Cornwall, England, the son of a sea captain, William Pengelly was the product of a village school and self-education. He began teaching, opened his own school, and was involved with the politics of improving education and ensuring universal access to it. He helped to found the Mechanics Institute (1837) and the Natural History Society (1844), both in his home town of Torquay, and the Devonshire Association for the Advancement of Literature, Science, and Art (1862). He became a private tutor of mathematics and geology and a popular public lecturer on those subjects.

Pengelly's principal interest was in the geology of Devonshire, early human history, and the antiquity of humanity, and he published articles on these subjects in the journals of the Royal Society, the Geological Society of London, and the British Association for the Advancement of Science. In 1846, Pengelly began to reexplore the prehistoric cave site at KENT'S CAVERN, which had been excavated by amateur archaeologist Father MacEnery in 1825, where Paleolithic artifacts and the remains of extinct animals had

been found beneath an undisturbed stalagmite floor. Pengelly systematically reexcavated the cave floor and found large numbers of stone and bone tools. Although the results converted Pengelly to the belief in a longer period for human antiquity, they were discounted by others.

In 1858, he explored and excavated BRIXHAM CAVE with the paleontologist HUGH FALCONER under the auspices of the Royal and Geological Societies of London. They unearthed the bones of several extinct fossil animals and flint knives and thus provided convincing proof of high human antiquity. Pengelly became a fellow of the Geological Society in 1850 and received its Lyell Medal in 1886. In 1863, he was elected to the Royal Society.

Tim Murray

Persepolis

Situated 58 kilometers from Shiraz in southwestern IRAN, Persepolis was developed mainly by the Persian king Darius I around 500 B.C. and destroyed by Alexander the Great in 330 B.C. Long visited by travelers and explorers, Persepolis was first systematically excavated by Ernst Herzfeld from 1931 to 1939 and later studied by E. F. Schmidt for the ORIENTAL INSTITUTE OF CHICAGO. Subsequent work has been undertaken by the Iranian Archaeological Service, directed by Andre Godard initially and then by Ali Sami. The site is an architectural masterpiece made up of a series of terraces, gateways, palaces, and staircases, the most famous of which contains exquisite carvings of people (from all parts of the Persian Empire) bearing tribute to the "Great King"—Darius I. At the head of this staircase is the Gate of All Nations built by Xerxes I, but the most magnificent structure is the Apadana (or Hall of Audience) built by Darius I and Xerxes I. Excavations and restoration work continue at the site today.

Tim Murray

See also French Archaeology in Egypt and the Middle East

Detail of carvings on the palace of the Persian king Xerxes I (Image Select)

Persia

See Iran

Peru

Investigation into Peru's pre-INCA past began during the early colonial period in the sixteenth century. The writings of Pedro Cieza de León record his visit around 1550 to the Guamanga Valley, now called Ayacucho, where he observed and described the ruins of Huari. The Indian residents of the area ascribed the ruins to an ancient race of people who had lived in the area long before the Inca conquest. Cieza, a very observant chronicler, noted that the walls of the ruins were deteriorating and showed signs of great age. Additionally, he noted that the plans of the buildings were distinctly different from those of the Inca constructions. Later, when he visited the ruins of Tiahuanaco at the south end of Lake Titicaca, Cieza drew similar conclusions about the antiquity of that now-famous site and proposed that Huari and Tiahuanaco were part of a culture that existed in the Andes before the

Incas. In linking these two sites, Cieza anticipated what is commonly accepted among Andean scholars today, but his thinking was not recognized for another 400 years.

It was not until the middle of the nineteenth century that scholars again took more than a fleeting interest in Peru's prehistory. Tschudi, visiting Peru from Switzerland between 1848 and 1852, became interested in the many ruins to be found everywhere in the valleys of the Peruvian coastal desert. He was particularly attracted to the massive adobe-walled structures of CHAN CHAN, the capital of the Chimu empire, and one of those structures now bears his name in honor of his pioneering work at the site.

In 1850, Antonio Raimondi, a famous figure in Peruvian history, arrived in Peru from Italy. During the many years that Raimondi spent in Peru, he traveled widely and explored nearly every part of Peru's very diverse geography. He wrote copiously about what he observed, and much of what he wrote was published in 1874 in his book *El Peru*. In the course of his travels he encountered many archaeological sites, the

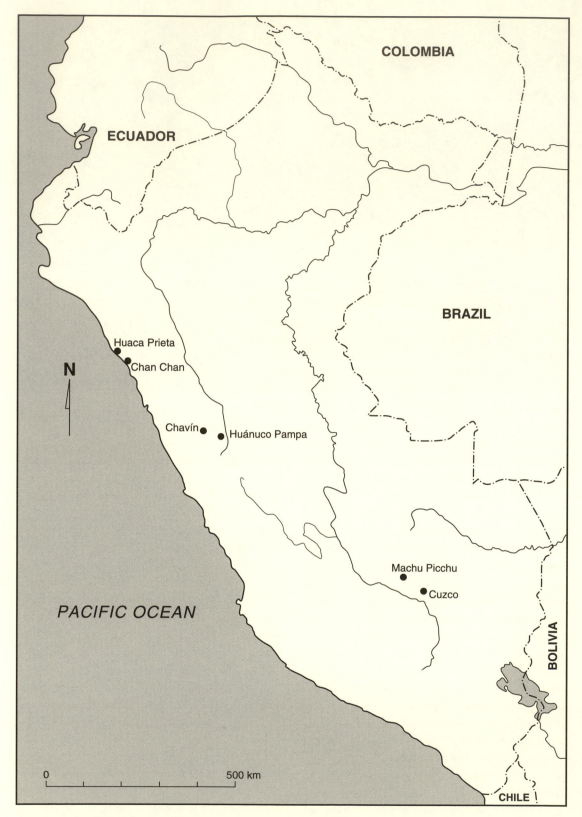

Peruvian Archaeological Sites

most noteworthy of which was the now-famous site of Chavín de Huantar, and one of that site's most important monuments is called the Raimondi Stone.

Contemporary with Raimondi, E. George Squier arrived in Peru in 1863 as cultural attaché to the U.S. embassy there. Squier, an archaeologist and the former publisher of a newspaper, was known in North America for his publications on mounds of the eastern United States, and his duties at the embassy were apparently very light, as he found time to travel widely throughout much of Peru. He visited many of the archaeological sites along the coast of Peru, including Chan Chan and Pachacamac, but his most extended journey took him from the far southern coast of Peru up to the Altiplano surrounding Lake Titicaca, north to Cuzco, and then back to Lima. His 1877 account of his journeys, *Peru: Incidents of Travel and Exploration in the Land of the Incas,* is richly illustrated with detailed drawings of the many sites he visited and descriptive narratives of his observations.

The first systematic excavations in Peru were carried out in the 1870s by two German geologists, W. Reiss and A. Stübel, who salvaged the destructive activities of grave robbers (*huaqueros* in Peru) at the site of Ancón just north of Lima. During his stay in Peru, Stübel traveled to Bolivia and visited Tiahuanaco and recorded the architecture and stone sculptures there. Back in Germany, MAX UHLE, eventually to be regarded by many as "the father of Peruvian archaeology," studied Stübel's notes and established that the Tiahuanaco style not only preceded the Inca conquest of the Altiplano, as Cieza had proposed, but was also older than the kingdoms that the Incas conquered.

Uhle arrived in Peru in the 1890s and began his prolific career. His early work focused on archaeological sites near Lima, notably the site of Pachacamac. This huge urban center, whose Inca temples had been an early target of Spanish vandalism, was known as the most important Inca center on the coast. Uhle's 1896 excavations at Pachacamac revealed earlier periods of construction and occupation, and in defining a ceramic chronology for the site Uhle recognized ceramics that bore Tiahuanaco-style design ele-

Gold Chimu mask from Peru (Image Select)

ments. Through further analysis he was able to define a four-phase chronology: pre-Tiahuanaco, Tiahuanaco, post-Tiahuanaco, and Inca. The Inca and Tiahuanaco styles, he argued, reflected broadly distributed horizon styles in the central Andes. Uhle's chronology constitutes the basic framework of the chronology still used today in Peru.

Beginning in 1900, much of Uhle's research in Peru was financed by the University of California as well as some other institutions in the United States. With such support he excavated in the MOCHE Valley, principally at the Huaca de La Luna site; on the south coast near Ica; and on the central coast at Ancón and in the area surrounding Lima. In each region he defined ceramic styles and used these to build chronological sequences, most of which have stood the test of time. Uhle's connection with Berkeley brought him into contact with American anthropologist Alfred Kroeber, who became fascinated with the ceramic assemblages that Uhle deposited in the museum at Berkeley. The elaborate art styles from coastal Peru, organized chronologically, gave Kroeber an excellent basis for examining some of his ideas about the development of art and civilization. This interest eventually took Kroeber to Peru, where he became involved in field research on both the south and north coasts.

Although Uhle is often referred to as "the father of Peruvian archaeology," many archaeologists, especially those of Peruvian birth, would give that title to JULIO C. TELLO. Tello, of humble origins from the Peruvian highlands, began his career in the early decades of the twentieth century and eventually became director of the Museo Nacional de Antropología y Arqueología in Lima, the most prestigious position for an archaeologist in Peru. Though sometimes criticized for a lack of scientific rigor, Tello brought an intelligent, imaginative mind to Peruvian archaeology. He was more concerned with the big picture of Peruvian prehistory and less with the minutiae of the chronology.

Tello was the first to appreciate the widespread distribution of CHAVÍN art and iconography. Because of its early date, Tello proposed that Chavín was the oldest of Peru's civilizations and that it constituted "the mother culture" from which all later Peruvian civilizations developed, a perspective eventually accepted by most Andean scholars. Tello also identified tropical forest creatures in Chavín iconography, which he used to bolster his argument that Peruvian civilization derived more from the eastern Andes and upper Amazon than it did from the coastal setting.

The University of California, Berkeley, continued to be deeply involved in Peruvian archaeology through the 1930s and 1940s, sustained by Kroeber's interest and that of his students, several of whom, notably Anna Gayton, Lila O'Neal, and WILLIAM DUNCAN STRONG, became involved in field research and museum studies. In the mid-1940s, with support from the newly founded Institute for Andean Research, Strong, now a professor at Colombia University, brought together several prominent archaeologists to carry out an intensive cooperative project in the VIRÚ VALLEY of Peru.

The list of participating archaeologists reads like a page from who's who in American archaeology of the time: Strong, JUNIUS BIRD, Donald Collier, Wendell Bennett, GORDON WILLEY, JAMES FORD, and Clifford Evans. The project benefited from the influence, support, and hospitality of Rafael Larco Hoyle, a wealthy landowner and avocational archaeologist from the north coast of Peru. Larco had amassed a huge private collection of north coast antiquities (many now on display at the Larco Herrera

Museum in Lima), and one of Larco's interests was to try to infer daily life among the ancient populations of the north coast through a detailed study of the scenes depicted on the pottery. With the encouragement of the archaeologists participating in the Virú project, however, he turned his attention to chronology and developed a chronological seriation of Moche stirrup-spout bottles, which with some refinements stands today as the core chronology for that period on the north coast.

Larco hosted a Chiclín conference in 1947 that brought together the participants of the Virú project and resulted in an edited volume, *A Reappraisal of Peruvian Archaeology,* published as a memoir of the SOCIETY FOR AMERICAN ARCHAEOLOGY in 1948. The aspects of the Virú project that had the most long-lasting impact were the Virú Valley survey and settlement pattern study carried out by Gordon Willey, widely regarded as a seminal work, and Junius Bird's excavation of Huaca Prieta, which for the first time revealed the existence of preceramic, sedentary fisher-farmer settlements on the coast of Peru. The complete report of Bird's findings was not published until after his death, but his discovery stimulated research on the Peruvian preceramic by Edward Lanning, Thomas Patterson, and eventually Michael Moseley, who proposed that Peruvian civilization was founded on a maritime economy.

As important as the Virú Valley project was the meticulous, detailed research on south coast ceramic styles carried out by a group of scholars at Berkeley under the direction of John Rowe. Building on the work of Uhle and Kroeber, by the end of the 1950s this group had worked out detailed chronological seriations for the south coast, which, they argued, allowed them in some cases to discriminate fifty-year segments of time. Using this seriated sequence and the horizon styles worked out by Uhle, John Rowe produced a six-period master sequence for Peru in 1962, and it continues to be used today as the favored chronological framework.

By the late 1950s, the broad outline of Peruvian culture history had been laid out. Most of the research, however, had been carried out on the coast, so despite the fact that both the Huari and Inca empires had their capitals in the high-

A tomb of one of the last of the Mochicas (Gamma)

lands, the prehistory of the highland region was interpreted through a coastal filter. Tello had tried to turn the attention of archeologists toward the highlands and the tropical forest regions. Indeed, in the 1930s he rediscovered the site of Huari, and in the late 1940s, Willey, Collier, and Rowe visited the site and published a short note on their perceptive observations. In addition, Bennett carried out test excavations in 1953 and produced a general map of Huari.

It was not until the 1960s and 1970s, however, that a substantive understanding of Huari and its connection to Tiahuanaco began to emerge, thanks to the research of Luis Lumbreras, Menzel, Isbell, and others. Chavín, despite its possible role as the founding civilization of Peru, was known almost entirely from its coastal manifestations—though Bennett and Tello had each carried out investigations at Chavín de Huantar. Again, excavations in the 1960s and 1970s began to redress this imbalance. John Rowe carried out a study of meaning and stylistic change in stone sculpture at Chavín de Huantar; Lumbreras and Amat carried out excavations at Chavín de Huantar; archaeologists from the

University of Tokyo carried out extensive surveys and excavations in the upper Huallaga Valley; Lathrap, together with students from the University of Illinois, initiated a program of research in the tropical forest regions; and Richard Burger completed further investigations at Chavín de Huantar and the surrounding region.

Surprisingly, almost no archaeological research on Inca sites had been carried out, the exceptions being Uhle's excavations at Pachacamac and Rowe's survey of Inca sites around Cuzco. In the mid-1960s, however, the Huanuco project was initiated, and it integrated ethnohistoric research carried out by John Murra and archaeological survey and excavations under the direction of Donald Thompson and Craig Morris. This project, for the first time, provided insight into the functioning of a provincial Inca administrative center.

Many research projects were carried out during the latter half of the twentieth century, despite the fact that much research was curtailed by the terrorist activities of the Sendero Luminoso (Shining Path) group. Notable for the size and number of people involved were the

Moche–Chan Chan project directed by Michael Moseley and the Ayacucho botanical project under the direction of Richard MacNeish. Looting of the rich, accessible coastal sites continues, despite international efforts to stop it, and like the drug trade, it will almost certainly continue as long as there is a market in North America and Europe for Peruvian antiquities.

J. Scott Raymond

References

Burger, Richard. 1989. "An Overview of Peruvian Archaeology: 1976–1986." *Annual Review of Anthropology* 18: 37–69.

Isbell, William, and Gordon McEwan. 1991. "A History of Huari Studies and Introduction to Current Interpretations." In *Huari Administrative Structure: Prehistoric Monumental Architecture and State Government*, 1–17. Ed. W. Isbell and G. McEwan. Washington, DC: Dumbarton Oaks.

Rowe, John Howland. 1954. *Max Uhle, 1856–1944: A Memoir of the Father of Peruvian Archaeology*. Berkeley: University of California Press.

Petrie, Sir William Matthew Flinders (1853–1942)

William Matthew Flinders Petrie's father, William Petrie, was a civil engineer, and his mother was the daughter of the explorer Matthew Flinders. Delicate as a child, Petrie was educated at home in England and showed early precocity in science and mathematics. As a boy he collected Greek and Roman coins, and in his teens and early twenties made triangulation surveys of earthworks and hill forts and, with his father's help, measured Stonehenge. His first visit to Egypt was in 1880. Living in a rock tomb and undertaking, almost single-handedly, a survey of the entire pyramid field, Petrie's meticulous measurement of the interior of the Great Pyramid disproved a current theory that it had been built under divine inspiration.

In 1884, Petrie was employed by the recently formed EGYPT EXPLORATION SOCIETY (then the Egypt Exploration Fund; EEF) to dig for that group. For his excavations of Tanis (1884) and Naucratis and Daphnae (1885–1886) he adopted an entirely new approach to Egyptian archaeology. Excavators had hitherto employed forced-labor gangs, driven by overseers, and had been concerned only with recovering monumental pieces, inscribed blocks, and museum exhibits—everything else was discarded. Petrie chose and supervised his own workforce, rewarding workers for their finds—which otherwise might have gone to dealers.

Maintaining that pottery was a key to the age of a deposit, and that much could be learned from hitherto discarded objects even if broken, he began to assemble his own collection, the nucleus of what was to become a teaching museum. From 1888 to 1890 he dug in the Fayyum in Lower Egypt, penetrating the pyramids of Illahun and Hawara. Among his finds were many mummy portraits of the Roman period and a workmen's village with a wealth of domestic objects. In June 1890 he excavated Tel el Hesy for the Palestine Exploration Fund, and for the first time he dated strata of occupation by the pottery, some of which he was familiar with from Egypt. Back in Egypt, important finds at Meydum (1891) and Tell EL AMARNA (1892) brought him his first honorary doctorate.

As a result of the will of Amelia Edwards, founder of the EEF and a novelist who had been his friend and supporter, Petrie became the occupant of the first Chair of Egyptology in Great Britain, at University College, London, in 1892. He was expected to excavate in Egypt every winter, training students in archaeological method. With his first student, James Quibell, he found archaic statuary of a hitherto unknown type at Coptos in 1893. The next year they dug the first predynastic cemetery in Egypt (later Petrie was to devise a chronological sequence for the graves by a remarkable statistical method of his own). After three years in ABYDOS (1900–1904), where he excavated the royal tombs of the earliest dynasties, and a winter in the copper-mining area of Sinai, he left the EEF's employment for the second time and founded the British School of Archaeology in Egypt. His wife, Hilda, whom he married in 1896, was his constant companion and right hand in the field, and she labored at home to raise funds and find new subscribers for their work; their camps, run on a shoestring, were a byword for spartan living.

Sir William Matthew Flinders Petrie (Image Select)

During the 1914–1918 war, Petrie remained in London arranging and partly cataloging his museum. This large collection, augmented every year by objects found or bought in Egypt, had been bought by University College in 1913. As the Petrie Museum, it is today a teaching collection without rival. In 1920, Petrie returned to Egypt to dig for a few years more; in 1926, he moved his work to Palestine, where he excavated between 1926 and 1934 three large tells near the Egyptian frontier. In 1934, at the age of eighty-one, he retired from the chair at University College and two years later went to live in Jerusalem, where he died. He had dug over 50 sites and written over 100 books and over 1,000 articles and reviews. He held five honorary doctorates, was made a fellow of both the Royal Society (1902) and the British Academy (1904), and was knighted in 1923.

Margaret S. Drower

See also Egypt: Dynastic; Egypt: Predynastic
References
For References, see *Encyclopedia of Archaeology: The*

Great Archaeologists, Vol. 1, ed. Tim Murray (Santa Barbara, CA: ABC-CLIO, 1999), pp. 231–232.

Peyrony, Denis (1869–1954)
Originally a school teacher, Denis Peyrony became the excavator of major French Paleolithic sites such as la Ferrasie, LAUGERIE HAUTE, and LE MOUSTIER. Peyrony used a version of the type-fossil approach to lithic classification to establish relative chronologies in French stone tool technology, which did not always accord with the linear evolutionary sequences proposed by ÉDOUARD LARTET and GABRIEL DE MORTILLET. Indeed, Peyrony's argument that the Aurignacian and the Perigordian lithic traditions were contemporaneous was a major step toward identifying the existence of geographical (if not "cultural") variability in Paleolithic technologies.

Tim Murray

See also France; Lithic Analysis
References
Ministère de la Culture. 1990. *Lartet, Breuil, Peyrony, et les autres.* Paris: Ministère de la culture.

Philippines

The Philippines, lying at the eastern margin of mainland Asia (see Map 1), has been a crossroad for the movements of peoples and ideas from the mainland to the Pacific islands since prehistoric times. Manila likewise has been the key entrepôt of maritime trade and commerce, notably during the almost 250 years (from 1564 to 1815) when the Manila galleons sailed the Pacific Ocean between Manila and Mexico.

Philippine archaeological resources, both on land and under water, are abundant and phenomenal. Archaeological sites range from the earliest indirect evidence for the presence of man in Cagayan Valley, northern Luzon, during the Middle Pleistocene to sixteenth-century dugout wooden coffin burials in northeastern Mindanao. Recent archaeological finds in the country also indicate the existence of complex societies in the northern, central, and southern Philippines, the latter dating as early as the ninth century A.D.

Important archaeological discoveries also include a flotilla of plank-built and edge-pegged wooden boats found in a waterlogged environment that range in date from the fourth to the thirteenth centuries A.D. Throughout Southeast Asia and, indeed, the world at this time, only in the Philippines are such prehistoric boats known to exist.

The history of archaeology in the Philippines elucidates the rich and varied archaeological wealth of the country, as well as the pivotal roles that pioneering individuals played in the evolution, history, and growth of archaeology in the country. For convenience, this updated history is presented in periods that parallel the political administrations of the archipelago from the sixteenth century to the present: the Spanish Period (1521–1898); the American Period (1898–1946); the post–World War II era and the 1950s; the 1960s; the 1970s; the 1980s; and the 1990s to the present. Space limitations allow the inclusion of only the most important archaeological discoveries since the 1960s.

The Spanish Period (1521–1898)

Although Ferdinand Magellan reached the Philippines on March 16, 1521, Spanish colonization of the archipelago did not begin in earnest until 1565. The Spanish explorers and colonizers noted the variety of Philippine cultures and languages. The early Spanish chroniclers of Philippine society and culture were generally members of religious orders; they primarily wrote ethnographic reports intended for Spain's ruling monarch or their own religious superiors.

The early Spanish writings were mostly descriptive in character, depicting, in varying details, the physical appearances and lifeways of the Filipinos as observed by the writers. At a later time a great deal of linguistic studies were conducted and subsequently published together with the ethnographic reports. Several chroniclers reported on archaeological discoveries, including Antonio de Morga, the vice–governor general of the Philippines in the seventeenth century who, in his *Sucesos de las Islas Filipinas,* noted ancient artifacts found by farmers in Luzon.

The only recorded important archaeological reconnaisance undertaken in the archipelago during the Spanish period was conducted in 1881 by Alfred Marche, a French archaeologist who systematically explored the central Philippines and discovered numerous sites. He collected varied archaeological specimens, mainly porcelains and stonewares recovered primarily from burial caves. The majority of his collections are now kept at the Musée de l'Homme in Paris. Marche's exploration activities at Marinduque Island (see Map 2) became "the most successful Philippine archaeological expedition recorded from Spanish times" (Beyer 1947, 260).

An Austrian, professor Ferdinand Blumentritt, also published a series of articles about the Philippines and its people around this time. Cursory exploration of caves and open archaeological sites were undertaken in several areas in the Philippines between 1860 and 1881, including those by the German traveler Feodor Jagor in 1860 and J. Montano and Paul Rey between 1879 and 1881.

In 1894 José P. Rizal, the national hero of the Philippines, reported on polished stone tools that he encountered and correctly identified at Dapitan, Mindanao, the place where he was ex-

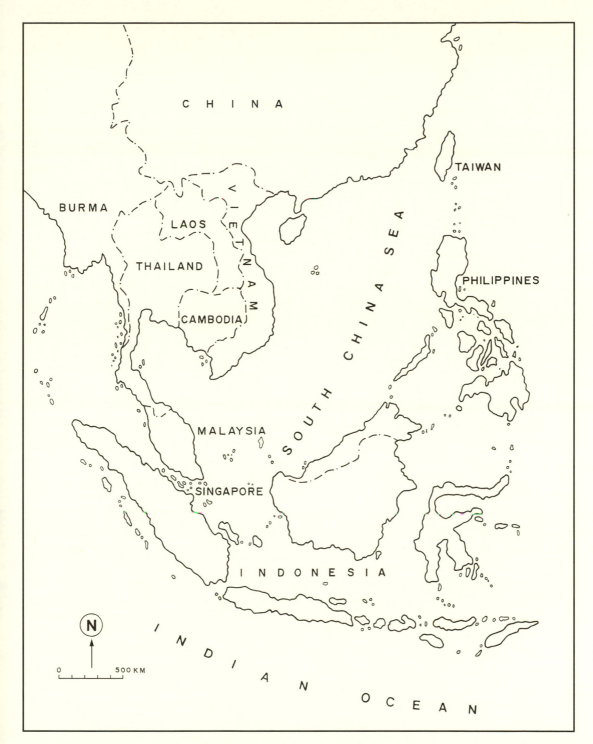

Map 1. The Philippines in their Southeast Asian setting

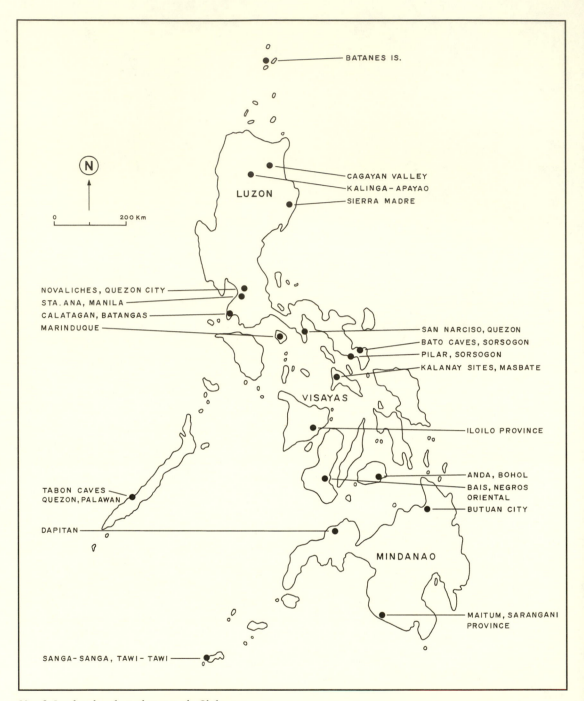

Map 2. Land archaeological sites in the Philippines

iled by the Spanish authorities in Manila. Having become acquainted with early works in scientific archaeology while he was studying in Spain and Germany (Evangelista 1962; Solheim 1981), he appropriately noted that these tools had been used by the prehistoric ancestors of the Filipinos.

The American Period (1898–1946)

The Philippines were occupied by the United States in 1898, and the U.S. administration of the archipelago began a year later. President William McKinley created the Taft Commission in 1900 in an attempt to craft proper legislation for the Philippines. The commission, in turn, established the Bureau of Non-Christian Tribes.

This bureau, which changed names through the years, was placed under different institutions and was eventually abolished.

In 1901 the first government museum was created, designated as the Insular Museum of Ethnology, Natural History, and Commerce, and was placed under the Bureau of Non-Christian Tribes. In the course of its existence the museum went through various changes, but it was never abolished. Today, it is a government bureau within the Department of Education, Culture, and Sports and is now officially called the National Museum.

Considered the founder of Philippine archaeology, HENRY OTLEY BEYER (1883–1966), an American from Iowa, arrived in Manila in 1905 to join the civil service. His pioneering works resulted in much of what was known about Philippine prehistory. Three years with the Philippine Bureau of Education found him among the Ifugao of northern Luzon, serving as a schoolteacher and documenting their lifeways. In 1914 he founded the Department of Anthropology at the University of the Philippines, and his first writing on Philippine archaeology came out in 1921. As head of the anthropology department, Beyer studied the racial and cultural history of the country.

From 1922 to 1925 Carl Guthe from the University of Michigan led an archaeological expedition to the central Philippines. Guthe was the first trained archaeologist to work in the archipelago, and his exploration activities focused on the collection of ceramics in the hope that these materials would shed light on the early maritime trade between the Philippines and mainland Southeast Asia. He identified 542 archaeological sites and collected more than 30 cubic tons of archaeological specimens, which are now are kept at the University Museum of the University of Michigan.

Early 1926 saw Beyer's first involvement in field archaeology, via the accidental discovery of major prehistoric sites at Novaliches during the construction of a dam for the water supply of Manila. Beyer's ensuing investigation was to be the start of the Rizal-Bulacan Archaeological Survey. By the middle of 1930 excavation activities had also reached Bulacan Province, and in

five years of work a total of 120 sites had been identified, with the collection of almost half a million specimens.

Personnel of the National Museum conducted surveys and excavations during the 1930s. In 1934 Ricardo E. Galang, the first Filipino-trained archaeologist, spent two months excavating fourteenth- to fifteenth-century sites at Calatagan, Batangas. In 1938 he investigated a jar burial at San Narciso, Quezon. He recorded a total of six jar burial and midden sites in the area and recovered associated materials of shell bracelets, beads, and ceramics.

In 1938 Generoso Maceda, another staff member of the National Museum, identified a jar burial site in Pilar, Sorsogon Province, in southern Luzon. Twenty-four jars containing artifacts were excavated in three sites (Evangelista 1962, 21). In 1940 Olov Janse, a Swedish-American archaeologist with support from Harvard University, conducted archaeological excavations in the Calatagan sites. Working in three sites, he excavated a total of sixty-six graves, the results of which were published in the annual report of the SMITHSONIAN INSTITUTION (Janse 1946).

There was a complete cessation of archaeological activities during the Japanese occupation of the archipelago (1941–1945). Beyer, who was under conditional internment, was assisted by Tadao Kano, a Japanese civilian assigned to protect museums in the Philippines. The Japanese allowed Beyer to continue working at the museum of the University of the Philippines and at the Institute of Ethnology and Archaeology, which enabled him to pursue his research writing and complete the final sections of his major postwar publications (Evangelista 1962; Jocano 1975; Solheim 1981).

Post-World War II and the 1950s

An increased interest in the beginnings of Philippine society and culture developed in the years after World War II, and archaeology as a course was included in the curriculum at the University of the Philippines. Beyer's research writings during the war years resulted in two important publications, his "Outline Review of Philippine Archaeology by Islands and Provinces" and his *Philippine and East Asian Archaeology, and Its Rela-*

tion to the Origin of the Pacific Islands Population (Beyer 1947, 1948). These major works are invaluable as references for archaeologists working in the Philippines to this date.

Archaeological exploration and excavation activities resumed in the l950s, led by two Americans, Wilhelm G. Solheim II and Robert B. Fox. Both were pivotal in arousing the interest of a number of Filipinos to pursue careers in archaeology. With an M.A. in anthropology from the University of California, Solheim published his first work on Philippine prehistory and archaeology in 1951. He conducted archaeological excavations from 1951 to 1953 in Masbate Island with two Filipino students, Alfredo E. Evangelista and E. Arsenio Manuel. Archaeological data generated from the excavations there were collated with the archaeological materials from the Guthe collection recovered in the 1920s from the central Philippines, resulting in *The Archaeology of the Central Philippines: A Study Chiefly of the Iron Age and Its Relationships* (Solheim 1964).

Fox (1918–1985) wrote avidly and extensively about Philippine ethnology, archaeology, and natural history from the late 1940s until 1973. He stayed in the Philippines after his service with the U.S. Navy during the war. With B.A. and M.A. degrees in anthropology, Fox was active in Philippine ethnography before focusing his attention on the archipelago's prehistory.

Major fieldwork in the 1950s was undertaken through the National Museum under the direction of Fox, working with Evangelista and several other members of the museum staff. In 1956 Fox and Evangelista excavated the Sorsogon Province of southern Luzon. A jar burial/stone-tool assemblage was encountered; the sites range in date from 2900 to 2000 B.P.

The most extensive archaeological project in the middle of the 1950s was the Calatagan, Batangas, Archaeological Project south of Manila led by Fox. Over 500 pre-Spanish graves were excavated in a number of burial sites, resulting in the recovery of thousands of trade ceramics—Chinese and Siamese porcelains and stonewares of the late-fourteenth to early-sixteenth centuries A.D. Extended primary burials were revealed as well as secondary burials in jars, with some graves exhibiting evidence of teeth filing and ornamentations. It is unfortunate that the 1950s excavations at Calatagan would witness the start of widespread pothunting activities, which continue to this day.

The 1960s

Fox led major archaeological activities for the National Museum from 1962 to 1966 in a number of caves along the west coast of Palawan, known collectively as the TABON CAVES. Work in this area resulted in the discovery of late-Pleistocene human fossil remains and associated stone implements. Going back to over 30,000 years ago, six successive periods of prehistoric occupation were found. The C-14 dates available for the Tabon Caves range from 30,500±1100 B.P. and 9250±250 B.P. At nearby Manunggul Cave an earthenware burial jar was found with incised and hematite-painted designs about the shoulder and cover (the latter having a ship-of-the-dead motif dating from 890 to 710 B.C.); it is now one of the country's National Cultural Treasures.

The preliminary results of the archaeological work at the Tabon Caves were published by Fox in 1970. This work included information on human bone fragments that, although recovered from a disturbed area of the caves, have been dated from 22,000 to 24,000 years ago—still the earliest evidence for *Homo sapiens* in the Philippines.

In 1966 significant archaeological sites were discovered right in the city of Manila. Known as the Santa Ana Sites, they exhibited both habitations and burials that "date more than 400 years before the arrival of the Spaniards in Manila" (Fox and Legaspi 1977, 1). The main burial site excavated was originally an archaeological mound on which the present Santa Ana Church was built, and the associated tradeware ceramics recovered from the burials date from the late eleventh to the fourteenth centuries A.D.

In 1967 cursory underwater archaeological activities were undertaken by the National Museum and the Times-Mirror-Taliba, a now-defunct newspaper outfit, in Albay, 500 kilometers south of Manila (see Map 3). Believed to be a Spanish galleon, the ship was found 40 to 65 meters below the surface. In addition to two large

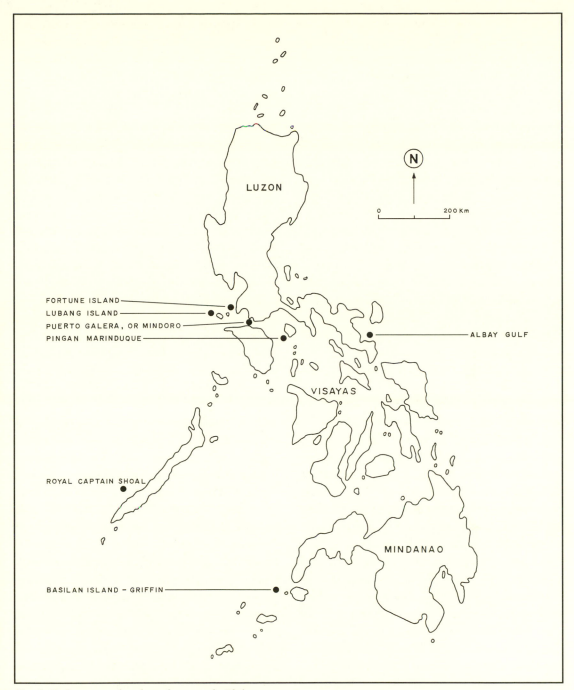

FORTUNE ISLAND
LUBANG ISLAND
PUERTO GALERA, OR MINDORO
PINGAN MARINDUQUE
ALBAY GULF
LUZON
VISAYAS
ROYAL CAPTAIN SHOAL
MINDANAO
BASILAN ISLAND – GRIFFIN

Map 3. Underwater archaeological sites in the Philippines

anchors with a forging date of 1649, each weighing about 3 tons, other items recovered included a bronze butterfly hinge, pottery sherds, copper plates and nails, chain links, capstans, plankings and the center bolt of an auxilliary mast (Lopez 1967). Underwater archaeological activities by the National Museum were not started again until 1982 (*see* The 1980s, below).

In 1969 limited archaeological excavations of the SHELL MIDDENS at the Balobok Rockshelter, Sanga Sanga, Tawi Tawi Province in the southern Philippines were undertaken by Alexander Spoehr of the University of Pittsburgh (Spoehr 1973). Recovered at this site were polished shell adzes made from the giant clam *Tridacna gigas* and red-slipped earthenware shards with impressed designs. C-14 dating of shells recovered from this site resulted in dates ranging from 8000 to 6500 B.P. Shell adzes were also noted from Duyong Cave, Palawan, in the Ryukus Islands, and on other Pacific islands.

The 1970s

The 1970s saw a profusion of archaeological research undertaken by both Filipino and foreign archaeologists. The elephant fossil sites in Cagayan Valley, northern Luzon, which had previously been reported, were explored and excavated in the 1970s by the National Museum. Led by Fox, the research uncovered hundreds of fossilized remains of mammals such as elephas, stegodon, rhinoceros, crocodile, giant tortoise, pig, and deer, as well as flaked and cobblestone tools (Fox and Peralta 1972). The first three large mammals in this group are now extinct in the Philippines.

Encumbered by geological problems in the open sites of Cagayan Valley, Richard Shutler Jr., then with the University of Iowa, was crucial in sending to the country a succession of geologists and geomorphologists from Iowa State University. Led by Carl Vondra in 1977, these researchers defined the Plio-Pleistocene terrestrial sequence in the Cagayan Valley basin, demonstrating the in situ association of artifacts and Pleistocene fauna, the age of artifacts, and the Plio-Pleistocene environments in the valley. Geological research has since solved the majority of the problems of the Pleistocene geology of the area, but the debate over the age of the artifacts still continues.

In 1972 Solheim and A. M. Legaspi led an archaeological survey of coastal southeastern Mindanao, a joint project of the National Museum and the University of Hawaii (Solheim, Legaspi, and Neri 1979). The Talikod rock-shelter sites, where flaked shell and stone tools were recovered, are the earliest sites recorded from the survey, with dates ranging from 7620 ±120 B.P. and 3950±90 B.P.

Two ethno-archaeology studies were undertaken in the 1970s. The first was conducted by Bion and Agnes Griffin among the Agta Negritos in the Sierra Madre range of northeastern Luzon from 1974 to 1976. With the goal of providing models for adjustments to hunting and gathering in wet and seasonal environments, the researchers hoped that the results of the study might be utilized for an archaeological understanding of hunters in tropical settings.

William Longacre of the University of Arizona directed an ethno-archaeological study in pottery-making villages in Kalinga Apayao, northern Luzon. Designed to provide data directly relevant to archaeological methods for inferring patterns of behavior and organization of peoples who lived in the past, the project, now in its third decade, has revealed significant insights into the manufacture, distribution, uses, breakages, and discarding of ceramics and how these and other material culture relate to human behavior.

From 1977 to 1978 archaeological surveys and limited excavations were undertaken in Iloilo Province, Panay, in the central Philippines. Australian archaeologists from the Victoria Archaeological Survey, led by Peter Coutts, focused their research on the establishment of a regional sequence, on the study of tradeware ceramics on Panay Island, on the recording of local pottery-making traditions and their trading networks, and on the collection of osteological materials for comparative studies.

While the geologists were working out the problems at the open sites at Cagayan Valley, the National Museum archaeologists concentrated their research activities in Penablanca, about 15 kilometers east of the Pleistocene open sites. Led by Wilfred Ronquillo and R. A. Santiago, exploration activities in the limestone area resulted in the recording of over 100 caves and rock shelters, eight of which have since been excavated. Basically aimed at elucidating the structure and distribution of the stone-tool industries in the area, the technological and functional analyses of the lithic flaked tools and debitage recovered from the excavations of Rabel Cave (ranging from 4900 to 3000 B.P.) indicated the generalized functions of the flake tools, which made them ideal for use as maintenance tools; the manufacture of the stone flaked tools involved a percussion method without core preparation.

In 1977 Barbara Thiel, then a graduate student at the University of Illinois, excavated two caves at Penablanca, Cagayan Province—Arku

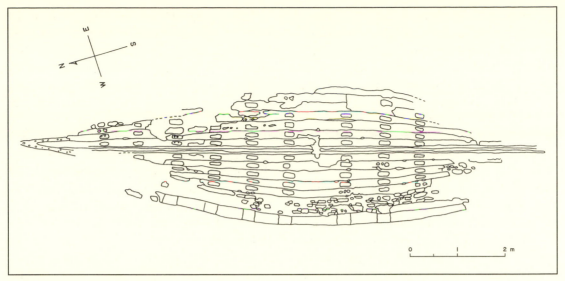

Excavation plan of Bhutuan boat 5

and Musang Caves. Arku Cave, a burial site with six different types of secondary burials, has an earliest date of 3300 B.P. Musang was both a habitation and a burial site, but the dating from this site is problematic.

In 1978 Richard Shutler conducted limited excavations at Andarayan, Solana, Cagayan Province, where he discovered direct evidence for early rice cultivation in the Philippines. Used as tempering material for the pottery, the rice husks and stem portions were dated through the use of accelerator mass spectrometry (AMS), resulting in a date of 3240±160 years B.P. The context of the discovery suggests that it is a product of dry cultivation. Studies by rice expert T.T. Chang of the International Rice Research Institute in the Philippines indicate that the samples are intermediate between cultivated rice (*O. sativa*) and its immediate wild relatives (*O. rufipogon* Griff. or *O. nivara* Sharma and Shastry).

Cagayan Valley is also known to have extensive shell-midden archaeological sites, extending from the mouth of the Cagayan River to a distance of 45 kilometers upriver. The shell-midden sites are found in varied locations, such as along the Cagayan River bank, in limestone hills, in inland areas, and in coastal sand dunes. Led by Japanese archaeologists Y. Aoyagi, H. Ogawa, and K. Tanaka, the Cagayan Shell Midden Project was undertaken jointly with archaeologists from the National Museum.

In late 1976 one of the most important finds in Philippine archaeology was made in Butuan City, Agusan del Norte, in northeastern Mindanao. As a result of illegal pothunting activities, prehistoric wooden boats were found and subsequently recovered and conserved. To date, a total of eight such boats are known to exist.

The first two Butuan boats recovered date to A.D. 320 and A.D. 1250, respectively; the third dates to A.D. 990. All the boats recovered thus far average 15 meters in length and 3 meters across the beam. The excavated boats exhibit the characteristic edged-pegged method of construction, which is typical of Southeast Asian boat-making technology. The planks are of one continuous piece, carved to shape and made of hardwood. The planks are pegged to the keel every 12 centimeters by hardwood pins or dowels (see drawing above).

The location of the two wooden boats appears to have been a former shoreline. Initially, two boats were excavated, and a third was retrieved in 1986. The most distinctive feature of the wooden planks is a succession of flat and rectangular protrusions or lugs that were carved from the same wooden plank on the upper side, that is, on the inside of the boats. Placed exactly opposite one another on each plank, these lugs are 78 centimeters apart and have holes along their edges through which cords or lashings can be passed. The use of these lugs was confirmed by the recovery of cordage of palm fibers. Their presence indicates that an older ship-building method was used. The Butuan archaeological assemblage points to a complex society in this area, indicated by craft specialization (such as wood, bone, and shell working, pottery manufacture, bead reworking, and metallurgy—specifically gold working) and the capability to participate in long-distance trade.

In 1979 an archaeological program led by Karl Hutterer of the University of Michigan started an interdisciplinary project focused on the prehistoric social and cultural development of a small geographical area in Negros Oriental. Known as the Bais Anthropological Project, the research, participated in by graduate students from Michigan, generated archaeological, ethnographic, biological, and geological data used to provide an overall understanding of prehistoric and present-day societies in Negros.

The 1980s

Archaeologists from the National Museum were busy during the 1980s. Although limited in manpower, the museum is the only institution that undertakes full-time archaeological research activities in the country. One of its priority activities is rescue archaeology, which involves the investigation of caves prior to the mining of bat droppings for use as fertilizer.

In 1981 archaeological exploration activities started at the limestone formation of Anda, in the island province of Bohol in the central Philippines. Designed to explicate the island adaptation of prehistoric man, this project, led by Santiago, resulted in the discovery of over 130 caves and rock shelters, the majority of which are archaeological sites. A number of caves exhibit wooden coffin burials as well as rich prehistoric habitation and burial sites.

Museum archaeologists were active in various areas in the country, such as Laurel, Batangas; Ma-ug, Prosperidad, Agusan del Norte; and Polillo Island, Quezon Province. Important archaeological data were generated from the continuation of the excavations at the Butuan sites in northeastern Mindanao, where primary extended burials indicate teeth filing and blackening.

Laura Junker, Hutterer's former student and now a professor of anthropology at Vanderbilt University, did research in Tanjay, Negros Oriental, in the central Philippines. Concentrating on the operation of control over the distribution of prestige goods, tradewares, and earthenware ceramics, Junker used archaeological and ethnohistoric data to test the hypothesis that early Philippine chiefdoms' participation in Southeast Asian luxury goods trade during the tenth to the sixteenth centuries A.D. was strongly linked to centralized control of a complex intraregional system of production, exchange, and resource mobilization.

In the 1980s numerous underwater archaeological sites were worked by the National Museum. The various shipwrecks found in Philippine territorial waters include Spanish, English, American, and Asian craft, usually with portions of the cargo still intact. The tradeware ceramics help date the ships and cargo. The associated archaeological materials have added new insights into the history of the trade from the ninth to the eighteenth centuries, as well as the nature of the trade and the societies that produced, bartered, and used the goods.

In the majority of cases the sites explored and excavated were worked as joint ventures with private entities. The shipwrecks studied include: one believed to be a merchant boat, found in 1982 on the southeast coast of Marinduque Island, about 150 kilometers south of Manila; a probable local watercraft found in 1983 at Puerto Galera, Mindoro Island; and a sixteenth-century wreck found in 1985 at the Royal Captain Shoal, a coral reef west of Palawan Island. The archaeological materials recovered from this site include porcelain plates, saucers, bowls, cups; boxes and box covers; blue-and-white, pear-shaped, terra-cotta bottles; jarlets; jars; over 200 beads; 33 identical gongs; and bronze, iron, and copper objects. The tradewares recovered from the wreck point to the Wan Li period (1573–1620).

It was also in 1985 when the *Griffin,* an East India Company vessel, was excavated northwest of Basilan Island in the southern Philippines. Along with numerous Chinese tradeware ceramics, the few metal objects found include iron ingots used as ballast, iron tools in the form of adzes, cannonballs, lead sheets used to line the wooden tea crates, lead musketballs, teapots, a Chinese coin of copper alloy, shoes and belt buckles of copper alloy and gilt bronze, and other objects used for daily life on board the ship.

In 1986 the exploration for the sunken galleon *San José* was started off the waters of Lubang Island, Mindoro Province. Only portions of the ship's planks, numerous shards of blue-and-white chocolate cups, and fragments of bronze, iron, and copper materials were recovered.

The 1990s to the Present

Important archaeological discoveries were made in the 1990s. In 1991 earthenware potteries with covers exhibiting anthropomorphic motifs were excavated at Ayub Cave, Pinol, Maitum, Sarangani Province. Led by E. Z. Dizon, the analysis of the potteries, designed and formed like human figures with varied and distinct facial expressions, indicates that they were used as covers for multiple secondary burial jars. Typologically the jars and the associated materials found date to the Metal Age period in the Philippines, around 500 B.C. to 500 A.D.

The year 1991 also marked the start of an archaeological survey for the Spanish warship *San Diego,* which sank off Fortune Island on December 14, 1600. A joint project of the National Museum and World Wide First, Inc., the excavation found the wreck at a depth of about 50 meters below the sea's surface. Two seasons of underwater archaeological excavation were undertaken, resulting in the recovery of over 34,000 archaeological items, including tradeware porcelains and stonewares, earthenware vessels, metal artifacts, and various organic materials.

The archaeological materials recovered from the *San Diego* site include more than 500 blue-and-white Chinese ceramics in the form of plates, dishes, bottles, kendis (spouted water containers), and boxes that may be ascribed to the Ming dynasty, specifically to the Wan Li period; more than 750 Chinese, Thai, Burmese, and Spanish or Mexican stoneware jars; over seventy Philippine-made earthenware potteries

influenced by European stylistic forms and types; parts of Japanese samurai swords; 14 bronze cannons of different types and sizes; parts of European muskets; stone and lead cannonballs; metal navigational instruments and implements; silver coins; 2 iron anchors; animal bones and the teeth of pigs and chickens; and seed and shell remains of prunes, chestnuts, and coconut.

Noteworthy among the metal finds are a navigational compass and a maritime astrolabe. Also retrieved from the site is a block of hardened resin that was noted in historical accounts to have been used for caulking and for making fire in stoves. A summary of the excavations and finds is presented in C. Valdes's *Saga of the San Diego,* published in 1993.

In the northernmost islands of the Philippines, the Ijangs (megalithic structures situated in elevated hills, indicating evidence of fortification) were confirmed through archaeological explorations and limited excavations. Led by Dizon and Santiago, the cursory archaeological activities indicate that the structures closely resemble the castles reported from Okinawa and date to the twelfth century A.D. These recent finds may prove crucial in the understanding of the formation of sociopolitical complexities in the Philippines.

This concise history of archaeology in the Philippines records the fascinating story of the search for the prehistoric beginnings of the archipelago, which is inextricably linked with mainland Southeast Asia and the Pacific islands. Although it may seem that archaeological activities in the country are adequate, there are still countless archaeological sites in the country that need proper assessment, excavation, and management. Unfortunately, these important and nonrenewable components of the country's cultural resources are also subject to plunder, nearsighted exploitation, and vandalism. Properly managed and protected, these archaeological resources have educational, recreational, and tourism potential. Without doubt, they are worth protecting for the enrichment and enjoyment of succeeding generations.

Wilfredo P. Ronquillo

See also Island Southeast Asia

References

Aoyagi, Y. 1983. "General Survey in Northern Luzon." Pp. 69–87 in *Batan Island and Northern Luzon*. Kumamoto: University of Kumamoto, Faculty of Letters.

Aoyagi, Y., M. L. Aguilera Jr., H. Ogawa, and K. Tanaka. 1986. "The Shell Midden in the Lower Reaches of the Cagayan River." *Journal of Sophia Asian Studies* 4: 45–91.

Aoyagi, Y., and K. Tanaka. 1985. "Some Problems of the Shell Mound Potteries Found in the Lower Reaches of Cagayan River, Northern Luzon." *Journal of Sophia Asian Studies* 3: 81–129.

Beyer, H. O. 1936. "The Prehistoric Philippines." *Encyclopedia of the Philippines*. 8: 21–62.

———. 1947. "Outline Review of Philippine Archaeology by Islands and Provinces." *Philippine Journal of Science* 77, nos. 3 and 4: 205–374.

———. 1948. *Philippine and East Asian Archaeology, and Its Relation to the Origin of the Pacific Islands Population*. Bulletin 29. Quezon City: National Research Council of the Philippines.

———. 1956. *New Finds of Fossil Mammals from the Pleistocene Strata of the Philippines*. Bulletin 41. Quezon City: National Research Council of the Philippines.

Coutts, P. J. F. 1983. *An Archaeological Perspective of Panay Island, Philippines*. Humanities Series No. 13. Cebu City: University of San Carlos Publications.

———. 1986. "Survey of the Griffin Wreck Site." Manila: Ms. National Museum.

Cummins, J. S., ed. and trans. 1971. *Sucesos de las Islas Filipinas by Antonio de Morga, 1559–1636*. Second Series No. 140. London: Hakluyt Society at the University Press.

Dizon, E. Z. 1988. "An Iron Age in the Philippines? A Critical Examination." Ph.D. diss., Department of Anthropology, University of Pennsylvania. Ann Arbor, MI: University Microfilms International 8816166.

Dizon, E. Z., L. Bauzon, A. P. Bautista, J. M. Aguilera, R. Paular, A. Orogo, and A. de la Torre. 1992. "Second Status Report on the Archaeological Project in Placer, Surigao Del Norte, N.E. Mindanao, Philippines." Manila: Ms. National Museum.

Dizon, E. Z., and R. A. Santiago. 1994. "Preliminary Report on the Archaeological Explorations in Batan and Sabtang Islands, Batanes Province, Philippines." Manila: Ms. National Museum.

Evangelista, A. E. 1962. "Philippine Archaeology up to 1950." *Science Review* 3, no. 9: 17–22.

———. 1967. "H. O. Beyer's Philippine Neolithic in the Context of Postwar Discoveries in Local Archaeology." Pp. 63–87 in *Studies in Philippine Anthropology*. Ed. Mario D. Zamora. Quezon City: Alemar Phoenix.

Fox, R. B., and A. Legaspi. 1977. *Excavations at Sta. Ana*. Manila: National Museum of the Philippines.

Fox, R. B. and J. T. Peralta. 1972. "Preliminary Report on the Palaeolithic Archaeology of Cagayan Valley, Philippines and the Cabalwanian Industry." Pp. 100–147 in *Proceedings of the First Regional Seminar on Southeast Asian Prehistory and Archaeology*. Manila: National Museum.

Hutterer, K. L., and W. K. MacDonald, eds. 1982. *Houses Built on Scattered Poles*. Cebu City: University of San Carlos.

Janse, O. R. T. 1946. "Archaeology in the Philippine Islands." *Smithsonian Institution Annual Report*: 345–360. 15 plates.

Jocano. F. L. 1975. *Philippine Prehistory: An Anthropological Review of the Beginnings of Filipino Society and Culture*. Diliman, Quezon City: Philippine Center for Advanced Studies, University of the Philippines System.

Junker, L. 1990. "Long-Distance Trade and the Development of Socio-Political Complexity in Philippine Cheifdoms of the First Millennium to Mid-Second Millennium A.D." Ph.D. diss., Department of Anthropology, Michigan University. University Microfilms.

Longacre, W. A. 1981. "Kalinga Pottery, an Ethnoarchaeological Study." Pp. 49–66 in *Patterns of the Past: Studies in Honour of David C. Clarke* Eds. I. Hodder, G. Isaac and N. Hammond. Cambridge: Cambridge University Press.

Lopez, P. T., Jr. 1967. *Marine Archaeology in the Philippines*. Manila: Ms. National Museum.

Nicolas, N. C. 1986. "Preliminary Report: Griffin Underwater Archaeological Excavation Project." Manila: Ms. National Museum.

Ogawa, H. 1993. "Lal-Lo Shell Middens on the Lower Cagayan River, Northern Luzon, Philippines." *Journal of Southeast Asian Archaeology* 13. Tokyo: Japan Society for Southeast Asian Archaeology.

Ronquillo, W. P. 1981. "The Technological and Functional Analyses of Lithic Flake Tools from Rabel Cave, Northern Luzon, Philippines." Anthropological Papers No. 13. Manila: National Museum.

Ronquillo, W. P., and R. A. Santiago. 1977. "Archaeological Cave and Open Site Explorations at Penablanca, Cagayan Province." Manila: Ms. National Museum.

Solheim, W. G., II. 1964. *The Archaeology of Central Philippines: A Study Chiefly of the Iron Age and Its Relationships*. Monograph 10. Manila: Monographs of the National Institute of Science and Technology.

———. 1981. "Philippine Prehistory." Pp. 17–83 in *The People and Art of the Philippines*. Los Angeles: Museum of Cultural History, University of California, Los Angeles.

Solheim, W. G., II, A. M. Legaspi, and J. S. Neri. 1979. *Archaeological Survey in Southeastern Mindanao*. Monograph 8. Manila: National Museum.

Spoehr, A. 1973. *Zamboanga and Sulu: An Archaeological Approach to Ethnic Diversity*. Ethnology Monograph 1. Pittsburgh, PA: Department of Anthropology, University of Pittsburgh.

Thiel, B. 1980. "Excavations in the Pinacanauan Valley, Northern Luzon." *Bulletin of the Indo-Pacific Prehistory Association* 2: 40–48.

Valdes, C., ed. 1993. *Saga of the* San Diego. Manila: Concerned Citizens for the National Museum, Inc.

Pieridou, Angeliki (1918–1973)

Angeliki Pieridou studied archaeology at the University of Athens and worked for many years in the Cyprus Museum. She was involved in a variety of archaeological projects in CYPRUS, especially of later antiquity. She was especially important in pioneering research on Cypriot folk arts and crafts.

David Frankel

References

Iacovou, M. 1996. "Angeliki Pieridou 1918–1973." *Chronologio-Ergographia*. Nicosia.

Piette, Edouard (1827–1906)

One of the most influential French Paleolithic archaelogists of the nineteenth century, Edouard Piette gained fame as the excavator of the major cave site of LE MAS D'AZIL in the French Pyrénées, where a single sequence linking the Upper Paleolithic and the Mesolithic was identified for the first time. He named the linking assemblage Azilian (after the site). A keen student of Paleolithic art, Piette acquired a great collection of portable art (i.e., art that was moveable as opposed to Paleolithic art on cave walls), particularly the bones of animals that had been incised. He gave this collection (as well as his collection of ancient stone tools) to the French Museum of Antiquities at Saint Germain-en-Laye, where it is displayed as a unity.

Tim Murray

See also Lithic Analysis

References

Musée des Antiquités Nationales. 1964. *Collection Piette: Art mobilier préhistorique*. Paris: Editions des musées nationaux.

Piggott, Stuart (1910–1996)

Stuart Piggott is one of a small group of extremely influential archaeologists who began their careers between the First and Second World Wars and who went on to dominate British and European archaeology in the decades after 1945. The breadth of his interests are exceptional, and although his views have been the subject of considerable criticism in recent years, his work is still valued today.

Piggott's initial area of interest was the Neolithic period of Great Britain, and between 1930 and 1950 he defined the principal monument and artifact types, the chronological sequence, and the regional characteristics of the period. This work culminated in his definitive account of the period, *Neolithic Cultures of the British Isles* (1954). His approach in this work was distinctive and was characterized by detailed description, accompanied by very fine illustration, and a minimalist approach to social interpretation. It was an attempt at objectivity designed to extract accurate information for a scientific understanding of prehistoric societies. Piggott acknowledged the influence of O. G. S. CRAWFORD and Alexander Keiller in his early development, and the scientific rigor of both of those methodical Scotsmen clearly influenced Piggott's approach.

World War II was a turning point in Piggott's career. It marked an end to his employment as Keiller's research assistant at AVEBURY and a broadening of his archaeological interests. During the war he was sent to India, and when not working on aerial photographic interpretation he was able to do a considerable amount of research on the early prehistory of the subcontinent, which resulted in the publication of several books and papers.

On returning to Britain, he became the new Abercromby Professor in Edinburgh, a post that brought with it a commitment to fieldwork in Scotland and an incentive to research the broader field of European archaeology. The former resulted in the excavation of several important Neolithic sites. The latter led to the publication of a synthetic study of ancient Europe, which examined themes covering prehistory from the introduction of agriculture.

Ultimately, these two imperatives changed the direction of Piggott's interests. He became more interested in later prehistory and, in particular, the development of wheeled transport and the significance of Celtic art and religion. Interest in wagons, chariots, and horses was a theme that brought together many of his European interests, charting the movement of peoples and the rise and fall of political elites.

Piggott continued as the Abercromby Professor in Edinburgh until his retirement in 1978. After that time, he carried on writing, and a large number of books and papers appeared on many subjects, not just those discussed above. He also developed his interest in the history of British archaeology. In this area, he originally focused on the figure of WILLIAM STUKELEY, an individual with an important role in the understanding of the Neolithic period at Avebury, but he later expanded his work to cover the antiquarian imagination of the sixteenth, seventeenth, and eighteenth centuries.

As his career progressed, Piggott became more and more aware of the limits of archaeological inference. He realized that much of his earlier speculation on the Neolithic period was inaccurate, which was emphasized by the radiocarbon revolution that undermined the typological chronology he had striven so hard to construct. He therefore narrowed the range of his interests in the later part of his career to emphasize the history of archaeology and the technological development of transportation.

Niall Sharples

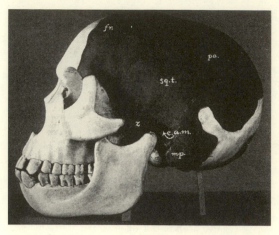

Model of the Piltdown "skull," in fact a re-creation from parts of two animals (Ann Ronan Picture Library)

References
For references, see *Encyclopedia of Archaeology: The Great Archaeologists, Vol. 2,* ed. Tim Murray (Santa Barbara, CA: ABC-CLIO, 1999), pp. 630–633.

Piltdown Forgery

The Piltdown man, one of the most famous forgeries in the history of paleoanthropology, was a composite of a skull and associated skeletal remains discovered in a gravel pit in East Sussex, England. The skull (named after Piltdown Common where it was found) was first unveiled at a meeting of the Geological Society of London in 1912 by Charles Dawson, the discoverer, and Arthur Smith Woodward of the British Museum of Natural History, the professional paleontologist who backed its legitimacy and importance. Based on excavations made at the site by Dawson, Smith, Woodward, and others, crude stone tools (or *eoliths*) were thought to have been found in association with the remains of an animal that had a large brain but an apelike jaw with "modern" teeth. Coming at a time when skeletal evidence of the physical evolution of human beings was extremely rare, especially from really remote antiquity, the Piltdown discovery gained great notoriety.

As Frank Spencer (1990) has noted, however, from the very first the Piltdown remains were regarded as problematic by some people, but a clear understanding of just how problematic they really were was only gradually revealed. As time passed, and other discoveries of fossil hominids were made in Asia and Africa that were dramatically different from Piltdown, the English remains came to be seen as being anomalous rather than of very great interest. It was not until 1953 that the Oxford physical anthropologist J. S. Weiner reanalyzed the remains and concluded that the braincase and jaw were from separate animals—a suspicion confirmed by fluorine testing. Further analysis demonstrated that the jaw was that of an ape and that the teeth had been deliberately altered and stained to match the color of the braincase fragments. By 1955, the entire Piltdown collection was rejected as fraudulent.

Of course, the revelation of fraud requires the identification of the forger, and this topic has become one of the most enduring detective stories in the history of physical anthropology. The list of suspects ranges from the obvious (such as Dawson) to the truly surprising (eminent physical anthropologist Sir Arthur Keith) and has included most of the people who were in any way associated with the forgery. In the absence of a signed confession by the forger, we are left with a range of probabilities. Although these may not be enough to obtain a conviction in a court of law, there is every reason to believe that there was a greater purpose to the forgery than to simply hoax the scientific community.

Tim Murray

References

Spencer, Frank. 1990. *Piltdown: A Scientific Forgery.* London: Oxford University Press.

Pincevent

The site of Pincevent in FRANCE lies near the village of Montereau in the southeastern part of the Paris basin. It is situated on the River Seine, between its confluence with the river Yonne and its confluence with the river Loing, in a landscape of high plateaus and wide valley systems. Its immediate surroundings were quarried for gravel from 1926 onward, but its archaeological potential was recognized only thirty years later when occasional finds began drawing the attention of local collectors.

Between 1956 and 1964, volunteers made several attempts at recording and salvaging some of the abundant remains from both prehistoric and historic times. In 1963, several Magdalenian hearths were unearthed, provoking the local suspension of gravel extraction through the intervention of the Association Française pour L'étude du Quaternaire and the Société Préhistorique Française in 1964. The site was acquired by the Ministère des Affaires Culturelles, which enabled a team from the Centre de Recherches Préhistoriques of the University of Paris to initiate a comprehensive archaeological investigation, which was partly subsidized by the Centre National de la Recherche Scientifique. The excavations at Pincevent have become famous for their detailed and rigorous execution, setting a precedent for archaeological fieldwork that is still valid today. They were directed by ANDRÉ LEROI-GOURHAN until 1985 and continued by his team, including, among others, Pierre Bodu and Claudine Karlin.

Although finds suggest that the locale of Pincevent was the setting for human activities during at least parts of the late Pleistocene and the Holocene periods, research has focused on the Magdalenian remains. These assemblages owe their excellent preservation to a gentle incorporation into a two-meter-thick sequence of clays and silts deposited through the occasional flooding of the river Seine. They consist of scattered lithics, bone fragments, and clasts (archaeological debris) punctuated by hearths and are generally interpreted as representing a number of activity sites created by Magdalenian people in the context of (possibly seasonal) reindeer hunting. Two assemblages, those of habitation number one and section thirty-six, are the focus of two major publications.

The archaeological phenomenon of Pincevent is very much a product of the history of the discipline of French archaeology and of the persons involved in the excavations and subsequent research. Leroi-Gourhan's background in ethnography and anthropology, and his belief that material culture is as meaningful a cultural manifestation as linguistic expressions, led him to adopt an ethnographic approach to the Magdalenian remains at Pincevent. The excavations, consisting of extensive horizontal exposures, were designed to obtain information on site structure, which was treated as representing a number of settlement floors. Casts were made by Michel Brézillon of entire excavation surfaces, replicating the spatial arrangements of the archaeological remains. Ethnographic case studies were employed to illuminate butchery patterns, and the lithics were subjected to technological analysis and refitting studies to gain insight into the *chaînes opératoires* ("operational sequences"). These were taken to be forms of expression of mind and language and were therefore of vital importance for the study of cognitive evolution.

In the last decades, many researchers have been involved in analyzing and (re)interpreting aspects of the Magdalenian remains from Pincevent. Refitting and technological studies have been claimed to yield information on the age, gender, and social contexts of the Magdalenian people that visited Pincevent. Several spatial analyses have been conducted; most notably, the hut structures that were tentatively reconstructed by the excavator are now rejected by many archaeologists. Raw material analyses have provided insight into the movement of material, placing Pincevent within a wider regional framework.

Since excavation commenced at the site of Pincevent, it has increasingly acquired a model status, the influence of which reaches far beyond the boundaries of both French and PALEO-LITHIC ARCHAEOLOGY. The meticulous excavation through extensive horizontal exposures and the detailed recording practices have become models for archaeological fieldwork, and the interpretations of the structure of the site have become models for the interpretation of site structure elsewhere. Above all, however, the site of Pincevent has become the archetypal archaeological site. It has provided archaeologists with a template of what an ideal archaeological site looks like and has been used to judge the interpretative potential of other sites. Particular importance is assigned to archaeological configurations stemming from limited time spans of activity owing to rapid burial and to

minimal postdepositional disturbance as a result of gentle burial in fine-grained sediments. This template betrays an enduring preoccupation with the ethnographic analysis of archaeological sites. However, discrepancies between the ethnographic approaches applied to it and the structure of the site, despite its excellent preservation and excavation, make Pincevent an important locus for a critique of current frameworks for archaeological interpretation.

Josara de Lange

References
Leroi-Gourhan, André, and Michel Brézillon. 1966. "L'habitation magdalénienne no. 1 de Pincevent près Montereau (Seine-et-Marne)." *Gallia Préhistoire* 9, no. 2: 263–385.
———. 1972. *Fouilles de Pincevent: Essai d'analyse éthnographique d'un habitat magdalénien.* Seventh supplement to Gallia Prehistoire. Paris.

Pitt Rivers, Augustus (1827–1900)

Augustus Pitt Rivers was born Henry Lane Fox, and it was when he succeeded to the large estate of his cousin that he took the Pitt Rivers name. He began his career in the army in 1845 and thus traveled to Malta and Scutari in the Crimea during the 1850s, to Canada during the American Civil War in 1861, and to Ireland from 1862 to 1866, where he was assistant quartermaster-general in Cork.

Pitt Rivers's interest in archaeology, and in ethnography and collecting ethnographic material, was initially stimulated by the Great Exhibition of 1851 in London and his own collection became his life's passion. He was part of an upper-class, well-educated group of people who interacted socially with, or were related to, the scientists and social scientists of the day, such as Herbert Spencer and John Stuart Mill. Pitt Rivers was an an early convert to Darwinism and through membership in the Ethnological Society of London became friends with the antiquarian and politician Sir John Lubbock (LORD AVEBURY), later his son-in-law, and the philosopher and politician Thomas Henry Huxley.

While stationed in Ireland, Pitt Rivers explored and surveyed the local historic circular forts or raths, promontory forts, ogham stones

(stones with Celtic inscriptions), and some medieval antiquities, and in 1864 he was elected fellow of the SOCIETY OF ANTIQUARIES OF LONDON. On his return from Ireland three years later, he began his archaeological fieldwork in earnest, and for the next thirteen years he surveyed and excavated in Yorkshire and at the hill forts and in the flint mines of Sussex Downs. He field-walked in Oxfordshire and Wiltshire, he discovered Paleolithic implements and animal bones in the drift gravels of the Thames Valley, and he excavated barrows at Guildford and Brighton in southern England. He also traveled abroad and undertook archaeological fieldwork in FRANCE and DENMARK.

Pitt Rivers joined the Anthropological Society of London in 1865 and in 1868 was general secretary of the International Archaeological Congress that met at Norwich and London. In 1871, he helped to form the Anthropological Institute—he was later to serve as its president—and he became a fellow of the Royal Society in 1876. By 1874, his collection of ethnographic material had grown to 14,000 pieces, which he loaned to the British Museum of Natural History to educate the public. In 1884, this collection was given to Oxford University and became the basis of the Pitt Rivers Museum. In 1880, on his inheritance of Lord Rivers's estates, he visited Egypt, where he met SIR WILLIAM MATTHEW FLINDERS PETRIE and discovered Paleolithic remains in the drift gravels of the Valley of the Kings.

In 1882, General Pitt Rivers retired from the army. For the remaining years of his life, his archaeological work was divided between a notable series of excavations at Cranborne Chase, mostly on his own property, and his official duties as the first inspector of ancient monuments. Lubbock's Ancient Monuments Protection Act of 1882 provided for an inspector to effect the legislation, and Pitt Rivers undertook seven journeys of inspection between 1883 and 1889, primarily in highland Britain, surveying and sketching monuments.

At Cranborne Chase, Pitt Rivers supervised the excavations of a Neolithic barrow, several round barrows, and Bronze Age enclosures; the hill fort of Winkelbury; the Romano-British settlements of Woodcutts and Rotherley; the linear ditches Bokerley Dyke and in Wiltshire, Wansdyke; and the medieval King John's house, Tollard Royal. Several exercises in experimental archaeology were also carried out, accounts of the excavations were published, and a public museum was established at Cranborne Chase detailing the excavations and finds.

Pitt Rivers's fame has rested at different times on his abilities as an excavator, a builder of typologies, and a theorist. He was one of the finest excavators of his generation, and his care in recording information in plan and section drawings rivals modern practice, but he could be inconsistent in its use. In the evidence that he chose to record, Pitt Rivers was far in advance of his contemporaries. He kept most of the potsherds and animal bones that others usually discarded, arguing for their importance for dating a site. He was not a good field archaeologist and not adept at seeing relationships between earthworks, but Pitt Rivers probably did more than anyone in his generation to promote the establishment of a sound chronology for British archaeology through his work behind the scenes in the ROYAL ARCHAEOLOGICAL INSTITUTE and more particularly by the creation of typologies for field monuments as well as portable artifacts. He should perhaps also be assessed as an administrator, as one who bridged the gap between anthropology and archaeology believing that they were inseparable elements in the system of cultural evolution, and as an educator who had strong views on museum design and display and accessibility to the public. He was also present at, and instrumental in, the first faltering steps of the heritage preservation movement in England.

Mark Bowden

See also Britain, Prehistoric Archaeology

References
For References, see *Encyclopedia of Archaeology: The Great Archaeologists, Vol. 1*, ed. Tim Murray (Santa Barbara, CA: ABC-CLIO, 1999), pp. 138–139.

Plymouth, Massachusetts

Plymouth, Massachusetts, was a seventeenth-century colony settled by English religious dissenters, or Pilgrims. The excavation of Plymouth Colony domestic sites began with J. Hall's 1864 exploration of the Miles Standish home in Duxbury. Excavations were undertaken in the 1940s by H. H. Hornblower at the "R. M. site" in Plymouth and the Edward Winslow site in Marshfield; in 1938, S. Strickland excavated the Joseph Howland site in Kingston; in the 1950s, R. W. Robbins did so at the John Alden site in Duxbury; and in 1959–1966, JAMES J. F. DEETZ worked at the Joseph Howland and William Bradford sites in Kingston and the Isaac Allerton and William Bartlett sites in Plymouth.

The results of these excavations have contributed to an interpretation of Pilgrim life at Plimoth Plantation (a living-history museum) and to synthetic studies of New England culture and material life by Deetz. Research has focused on the transference of traditional culture and its transformation as settlers adapted to new environmental and social conditions. Archaeological evidence indicates that houses were timber-framed, single-cell or cross-passage in plan, partially cellared, and of post-in-the-ground construction or with sills set on stone foundations. Artifacts recovered included tin-glazed and coarse earthenware (of Low Countries, Iberian, north Devon, Midlands, and southern England in origin as well as locally made); German stoneware in forms for dairying, storage, and communal drinking; weaponry and gun parts; utensils; personal effects; and building hardware. Faunal remains indicate consumption of both domesticated and wild animals such as deer and bear.

In the 1970s, Deetz excavated the 1690–1740 Samuel Smith Tavern site at Great Island in Wellfleet and portions of a 1792–1840 African American settlement at Parting Ways in Plymouth, moving beyond the home sites of the seventeenth-century "Pilgrim fathers" of English descent to consider cultural change and ethnic diversity. The Wellfleet tavern assemblage, with high proportions of smoking pipes and drinking vessels, differed markedly from the typical domestic assemblages. At Parting Ways, Deetz found the African heritage of the site's occupants expressed in traditional West African ar-

chitecture, pottery forms, foodways, and mortuary practices.

Mary C. Beaudry

See also United States of America, Prehistoric Archaeology

References

Beaudry, M. C. 1984. "An Archaeological Perspective on Social Inequality in 17th-Century Massachusetts." *American Archeology* 4, no. 1: 55–60.

Beaudry, M. C., and D. C. George. 1987. "Old Data, New Findings: 1940s Archaeology at Plymouth Reexamined." *American Archeology* 6, no. 1: 20–30.

Bowen, J. V. 1976. "The Parting Ways Site: A Preliminary Report on Foodways." Report on file, Plimoth Plantation, Plymouth, MA.

Brown, M. R. 1972. "Ceramics from Plymouth, 1621–1800: The Documentary Record." In *Ceramics in America,* 41–74. Ed. I. M. G. Quimby. Charlottesville: University Press of Virginia.

Deetz, J. 1960a. "Excavations at the Joseph Howland Site (C5), Rocky Nook, Kingston, Massachusetts, 1959: A Preliminary Report." *Supplement to the Howland Quarterly* 24, nos. 2–3: 1–12.

———. 1960b. "The Howlands in Rocky Nook: An Archaeological and Historical Study." *Supplement to the Howland Quarterly* 24, no. 4: 1–8.

———. 1968. "Late Man in North America: Archeology of European Americans." In *Anthropological Archeology in the Americas,* 121–130. Ed. B. J. Meggers. Washington, DC: Anthropological Society of Washington.

———. 1969. "The Reality of the Pilgrim Fathers." *Natural History* 78, no. 11: 32–44.

———. 1970. "Plymouth and the Pilgrims." *Collier's Encyclopedia Yearbook.*

———. 1972. "Ceramics from Plymouth, 1620–1835: The Archaeological Evidence." In *Ceramics in America,* 15–40. Ed. I. M. G. Quimby. Charlottesville: University Press of Virginia.

———. 1976. "Black Settlement: Plymouth." *Archaeology* 29, no. 207.

———. 1977. *In Small Things Forgotten: An Archaeology of Early American Life.* Garden City, NY: Anchor Books.

———. 1979. "Plymouth Colony Architecture: Archaeological Evidence from the Seventeenth Century." In *Architecture in Colonial Massachusetts: A Conference Held by the Colonial Society of Massa-*

chusetts, September 19 and 20, 1974, 4–59. Charlottesville: University Press of Virginia for the
Colonial Society of Massachusetts.

Ekholm, E., and J. Deetz. 1971. "The Wellfleet
Tavern Site." *Natural History* 80, no. 8: 48–57.

Hornblower, H. H. 1943. "The Status of Colonial
Archaeology in Massachusetts in 1941." *Massachusetts Archaeological Society Bulletin* 4: 41.

———. 1950. "Pilgrim Sites in the Old Colony
Area." *Eastern States Archaeological Federation
Bulletin* 9: 9–10.

Landon, D. B. 1991. *Zooarchaeology and Urban
Foodways: A Case Study from Eastern Massachusetts.*
Ph.D. dissertation, Boston University. Ann Ar-
bor, MI: University Microfilms International.

———. 1993. "Testing a Seasonal Slaughter Model
for Colonial New England Using Tooth Cemen-
tum Increment Analysis." *Journal of Archaeological Science* 20: 439–455.

Robbins, R. W., and E. Jones. 1969. *Pilgrim John
Alden's Progress: Archaeological Excavations in
Duxbury.* Plymouth, MA: Pilgrim Society.

Poland

The interest in antiquity in Poland dates back to
the thirteenth century, as evidenced in the
records of mounds called "giants tombs." In the
fourteenth century Jan Długosz, in his *Historia
Polonica,* mentioned clay vessels rooted into the
ground, which he considered to be the work of
nature. The author who correctly identified
those clay vessels as cinerary urns was John Jonston (1605–1675), a doctor and naturalist of
Scottish origin from Szamotuły (in the
Wielkopolska region). At the same time, Jacob
Mellen provided the first detailed description of
excavation works in the graveyard of the Lusatian culture in Śmigiel (also in the Wielkopolska
region). The sixteenth and seventeenth centuries brought discoveries of the first archaeological artifacts, such as box graves, urns, and
coins. Of special note in the eighteenth century
were the activities and initiatives of the last Polish king, Stanislaus Augustus Poniatowski, a
great lover of antiquity. The first private collections of archaeological materials were founded
in that period. At the end of eighteenth century
Count Jan Potocki (1761–1815) drew public attention to archaeological artifacts as sources of
knowledge about the history of the Slavs. Con-

sidered the pioneer of historical and archaeological studies on the Slavs and their culture, he
was the first to formulate a hypothesis about the
autochthony of Slavs and authored such important works as *Recherches sur la Sarmatie* and *Histoire primitive des peuples de la Russie.*

The year 1795 was a tragic one for Poland,
for it was the year in which the country lost its
political independence and was divided between
RUSSIA, Prussia, and AUSTRIA. For 123 years,
therefore, until Poland regained its independence in 1918, the Polish interest in antiquity and
then in prehistory developed independently in
each of the occupied areas. The first institution
to take on archaeological studies was the Warsaw Royal Society of Friends of Sciences,
founded in 1800. One of its initiatives was to organize lectures, mainly on history, religion, art,
or the beginnings of writing among the Slavs.
The society also emphasized the importance of
collecting archaeological materials, thus contributing to the formation of the nucleus of the
collection of the future Museum of Prehistory.
At the same time, state and private collections
expanded, for example, those of the Włyńskie
Lyceum in Krzemieniec, the Museum of the
Czartoryskis in Lvov, the Płock Scientific Society, and the Dukes Czartoryski in Puławy.

The true turning point in the studies of prehistory was a work by Adam Czarnocki (1784–
1825) (whose pen name was Zorian Dołęga
Chodakowski) entitled *On the Slavonic Lands before Christianity* (1818). Written in the romantic
spirit, Czarnocki's work comprised ethnographic, archaeological, and linguistic elements;
it described a program for a systematic study of
prehistoric monuments and argued for comprehensive research on Slavdom. It also recognized
the unique function and importance of archaeology in the study of the past, with particular
emphasis on the prehistory of the Slavs. This interest in the past of Slavdom was inspired by patriotism, which for Poles was closely linked
with the loss of statehood. During the whole
period of romantic archaeology, that is, until the
1870s, the attention of archaeologists was almost entirely focused on the history of Slavs. In
1848 a four-faced statue of Światowid (a Slavic
deity)—made of sandstone and 2.7 meters

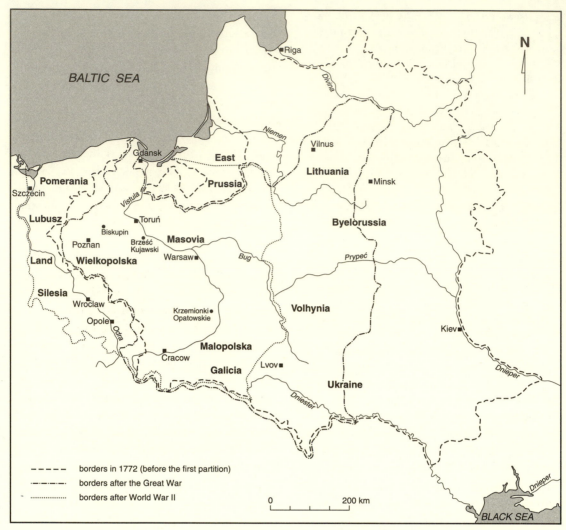

Poland, showing changing borders: (1) 1772, before the first partition; (2) 1918, after World War I; and (3) 1945, after World War II

high—was discovered in the Ukrainian River Zbrucz. Since then the Światowid has been considered the symbol of Slavdom.

The well-known historian, geographer, and numismatist Joachim Lelewel (1786–1861) mentioned archaeology as a subdiscipline of historiography. For the first time variation among archaeological material was acknowledged, and issues of chronology, imports, and regional differences were recognized. This laid the foundations of later regional studies. Archaeological monuments were seen as sources of knowledge about the past, and hence the need to collect and describe them was emphasized.

The dynamic development of the study of antiquity was interrupted by the collapse of the November Uprising in 1831 and the resulting Russian repressions. Conditions favorable to the study of antiquity emerged under Prussian occupation, particularly in Wielkopolska as well as in the Vilna region. Papers on the antiquity and prehistory of the Slavs were published in *Przyjaciel Ludu,* one of the first Polish illustrated magazines, founded in Leszno in 1834. In this magazine in 1843, Wojciech Morawski published an article that used C. J. THOMSEN's and Lisch's THREE-AGE SYSTEM.

In 1840 in Szamotuły (in the Wielkopolska region), on the initiative of Jędrzej Moraczewski, the Society of the Gatherers of Native Antiquities was founded as the first prehistoric society in Poland. Its goals were to collect archaeological artifacts, through excavation and retrieval from private collections, and the material remains of old Polish culture (including written sources) and to establish a library.

The most outstanding prehistorian of the late nineteenth century was Eustachy Tyszkiewicz (1814–1873), who conducted systematic excavations in Vilna. His papers, published after 1843, clearly indicate that he had a thorough knowledge of the three-age system, which he studied during his stay in DENMARK. He systematically applied a comparative-ethnological method, involving the explanation of archaeological phenomena by analogy with contemporary tribal peoples. During this time the concept of archaeology was used alternately with the study of antiquity to denote not only archaeological but also numismatic and ethnographic materials, as well as those connected with art history (painting, sculpture, tombstones, garments, and furniture).

In 1850 the Archaeological Department of the Cracow Scientific Society was opened (in 1851 it became the Section of Archaeology and Fine Arts). The society ensured that the Małopolska region played a dominant role in the development of archaeology between 1850 and 1875. Under German and Russian occupation and due to Polish patriotic insurrections and the resulting repressions, institutions conducting prehistoric studies found it difficult to survive, let alone continue their work. These years are characterized by the institutionalization of efforts focused on the study of antiquity and by large achievements in the areas of organization and methods. At the same time, an archaeological commission was set up in Vilna, and a separate Society of Friends of Sciences was established in Poznań in 1857, with the department of historical and moral studies, of which archaeology was a part. The period was also marked by the foundation of specialist museums in Cracow (1850), Vilna (1856), Poznań (1878), and Toruń (1860), evidence that archaeology had moved out of private collections and into public institutions. The foundation of museums was accompanied by the formulation of guidelines on collecting archaeological materials, which were addressed not just to ar-

chaeologists but also to the whole of society. Józef Łepkowski (1826–1894), from Cracow, created an archaeological map for registering, making inventories of, and, as the result, interpreting the archaeological artifacts of Powiśle. Large exhibitions of antiquities were held in Warsaw (1856) and Lvov (1861), which greatly contributed to the popularization of archaeology. The greatest achievements in this area were two exhibitions of antiquities in Cracow (in 1858 and 1872) that attracted broad public interest. The main organizers were Karol Rogawski and Łepkowski. French scientist Georges Cuvier's assertions that natural history methods were indispensable to archaeological research became widely recognized. In addition, important excavation programs were launched, such as those in Ostrów Lednicki in the Wielkopolska region and the Ojców Caves in the Małopolska region.

In the context of educating new researchers, Łepkowski's postdoctoral thesis in the field of medieval archaeology was significant. A graduate of the Jagiellonian University in Cracow in 1863, he became the leader of his institute in 1874. His lectures initiated the study of archaeology as a university discipline. In 1866 he organized the Archaeological Room, where he collected archaeological artifacts and artworks.

Polish archaeologists maintained good relationships with foreign researchers, evidenced by their participation in congresses of prehistoric anthropology and archaeology—for example, in Copenhagen (1869), Bologna (1871), and Brussels (1872)—and at archaeological conferences in Antwerp (1867) and Bonn (1868). During the congress in Bologna, Aleksander Przeździecki described his project of archaeological mapping, which was seen as an important and innovative initiative. Przeździecki and Edward Rostawiecki become the founding members of the Royal Society of Northern Antiquity in Copenhagen and also participated in excavation studies abroad; Konstanty Tyszkiewicz took part in the excavation works under French archaeologist JACQUES BOUCHER DE PERTHES in Abbeville in FRANCE and was involved in archaeological investigations at sites beside Lake Hallstatt in Austria.

Impressed by Austrian laws on the preservation of monuments, the first two positions for keepers of artistic and cultural monuments were created in the Małopolska region in 1853. In 1873 the positivist revolution began; critical of Slavonic archaeology, it was closely linked with Romanticism and the growing interest in the origins of humankind and human culture. Archaeology assumed a naturalist and evolutionist bias, and it became a profession.

In Cracow in 1872, the Society of Friends of Sciences was replaced by the Academy of Learning, a scientific institution whose primary objective was to stimulate the development of many disciplines. At the same time, both the Archaeological and the Anthropological Commissions were set up, which signaled the collapse of a broadly based archaeology. The field was divided into prehistory, anthropology, and ethnography, labeled "anthropological sciences." A modern program of joint archaeological and anthropological studies was set up by Izydor Kopernicki, secretary of the Anthropological Commission. This commission propagated a positivist evolutionist approach, whereas the Archaeological Commission continued the traditions and historical approach of Romantic archaeology. Fundamental archaeological works by John Lubbock (LORD AVEBURY), LEWIS H. MORGAN, H. Spencer, and E. B. Taylor were translated into Polish between 1864 and 1898. As a result the typological method originating in evolutionism was introduced, as was the stratigraphic method in excavation, which allowed for the classification of an increasing number of source materials.

In 1873 the first Polish archaeological journal, *Wiadomości Archeologiczne* (Archaeological News), was founded by private researcher Count Jan Zawisza. It has continued to publish ever since. The end of the nineteenth century was marked by many achievements and the extraordinary activities of a few outstanding prehistorians. Among these was Godfryd Ossowski (1835–1897), who studied the Paleolithic caves near Cracow and Ojców and excavated unique Magdalenian artifacts from the Maszycka Cave near Ojców. Ossowski also studied prehistoric Pomerania, Ukraine, and Volhynia and authored the first written attempts to synthesize the prehistoric cultures of Galicia (1890). Jan Nepomucen Sadowski researched Greek and Roman trade routes, using topographic information to map the extensions of imported goods. Zawisza, owner of the Prądnik Valley, continued to study caves with Paleolithic material. Józef Przyborowski and Zygmunt Gloger studied Mesolithic sandhill deposits.

Attempts to map and inventory prehistoric monuments were undertaken by Sadowski for the Wielkopolska region (in 1877), by Ossowski for the region of Pomerania (between 1880 and 1881), and by Władysław Przybysławski for eastern Galicia (in 1906). Bolesław Erzepki, director of the Museum of the Society of Friends of Sciences in Poznań, made significant contributions in this area. The landed gentry were also significantly involved, an example being Count Albin Węsierski from Wróblewo (in the Wielkopolska region), who was a well-known collector of archaeological artifacts. Activity in the regions centered around the local scientific societies, the most enterprising of which were those in Poznań and in Toruń.

The last decade of the nineteenth century was marked by a slowing down or even a break in what had been a vigorous development of archaeology, primarily due to a generation gap. Both the societies and the archaeological journals were in a state of crisis. Archaeology itself suffered from an identity crisis, trying to find its place between the humanities and natural sciences. Ludwik Krzywicki introduced the distinction between prehistoric archaeology and proto-historic archaeology.

The work and achievements of Erazm Majewski (1858–1922) had a large impact on the development of late-nineteenth-century Polish archaeology. Majewski was interested not only in archaeology but also in ethnography, sociology, economics, and the philosophy of civilization. He was the author of a four-volume work entitled *The Science of Civilization* (1908–1923), and in 1899 in Warsaw he started publishing the archaeological journal *Światowit*. He also founded his own museum, which quickly assumed a dominant position in Polish archaeology. He gathered around himself a group of committed collaborators, who became the outstanding archaeologists of the interwar period. These included Ludwik Sawicki (1893–1972), STEFAN KRUKOWSKI (1890–1982), and LEON KOZŁOWSKI (1892–1944). Majewski funded a program of field research just for them, thus becoming one of the major contributors to the revival of Polish archaeology. He also published a number of scientific papers, some of them concerning the methodology of conducting excavations. It was through Majewski's support that the Warsaw Center assumed a dominant role in Polish archaeology from the end of the nineteenth century until 1918, when Poland regained its independence.

Meanwhile, Cracow University had produced an outstanding prehistory researcher by the name of Włodzimierz Demetrykiewicz (1859–1937). The author of a modern regional synthesis of the archaeology of Galicia (1896), in which a wider cultural context was considered and a typological method was applied, Demetrykiewicz was the first Polish archaeologist to write the Paleolithic prehistory of Poland. He defended his postdoctoral dissertation at the Jagiellonian University in Cracow in 1905 and in 1919 was granted the title of professor. He became the founder of a renowned archaeological center. Among his most successful students were Michał Drewko, Tadeusz Reyman, Józef Żurowski, and, indirectly, JÓZEF KOSTRZEWSKI and Leon Kozłowski. At the same time, the Lvov Center was led by Karol Hadaczek (1873–1914), a professor of prehistory and classical archaeology.

The improvement of the political situation under Russian occupation led to the foundation of prehistory departments at some regional museums, for example, in Płock, Włocławek, Kalisz, Piotr-ków Trybunalski, Kielce, Lublin, Sandomierz, Radom, and Łowicz. Private collections were still popular and numerous, and some were quite large. Vigorously developing museums were a precondition to the development of Polish prehistory. They bridged the gap in its development, providing research collections and training and stimulating interest, until it became possible to study archaeology at the university level.

In the Wielkopolska region, which remained under German occupation, German archaeology dominated. The Provincial Museum (from 1904 known as the Kaiser Friedrich Museum) in Poznań was the center of archaeological activities. The Polish Museum of the Society of the Friends of Sciences was led, at that time, by Bolesław Erzepki. Four volumes of the *Album Zabytków Przedhistorycznych* (The Catalog of Prehistoric Monuments) for the Poznań region were issued by Erzepki, Klemens Koehler, and Zygmunt Zakrzewski. In 1914 the position of the director of the Polish Museum was occupied by Kostrzewski (1885–1969), who had just defended his doctoral dissertation in Berlin under GUSTAF KOSSINNA. In the same year he wrote a synthesis of the history of the Wielkopolska region. The main characteristic of the first two decades of the twentieth century was the appearance of regional syntheses (e.g., about Galicia, Eastern Galicia, Wielkopolska, Gdańsk [Danzig], and Danzig Pomerania, as well as an attempted one for LATVIA).

Poland regained its political independence in November 1918, and the state of Polish archaeology changed dramatically. An independent Poland created conditions conducive to the unrestricted development of science. In addition to the already operating university institutes of archaeology in Cracow (under Włodzimierz Demetrykiewicz) and in Lvov (under Leon Kozłowski), new departments were founded in Warsaw (under professor Erazm Majewski and, after his death in 1922, Włodzimierz Antoniewicz) and at Poznań, in the newly founded university in 1919 under professor Józef Kostrzewski. Subject to the law on the preservation of monuments issued by the new Polish government in 1918, keepers of prehistoric monuments for particular regions of Poland were appointed. These were united in the Group of Keepers of Prehistoric Monuments, a central body whose objective was to protect and create an inventory of archaeological monuments. The law officially acknowledged the importance of archaeological monuments to the national heritage of Poland.

In 1920 the Polish Prehistoric Society was set up in Poznań, and its ranks grew. Regional soci-

Biskupin (Klandyna Kucharska / Archiwum Fotograficzne Museum Archeologicznego)

Biskupin reconstructed (Arkadiusz Marciniak)

eties became more active and took up research. The founding of an independent Archaeological Commission within the Polish Academy of Learning was evidence of the emancipation of archaeology as an independent research discipline. This move was an attempt to separate archaeology from the Ethnographic and Anthropological Commission. In the first years after independence many new Polish archaeological journals emerged, the most significant of them being *Przegląd Archeologiczny* (Archaeological Review) and *Z Otchłani Wieków* (From the Abyss of Ages), both published in Poznań. Of the old ones, *Wiadomości Archeologiczne* and *Światowit* were still published.

Excavation become more extensive, and the most spectacular discoveries of this time were made in Złota, KRZEMIONKI OPATOWSKIE, BRZEŚĆ KUJAWSKI, Gniezno, and Poznań, including the most significant site—the early Iron Age Hallstatt castle in BISKUPIN, discovered in 1933. It became obvious that accurate pictorial and photographic documentation was indispensable. The importance of surface studies also increased. Archaeology was still between the natural and the historical sciences. A number of regional monographs were written (on Wielkopolska, Silesia, and Pomerania by Kostrzewski, on southeastern Poland by Kozłowski, on Volhynia by Włodzimierz Antoniewicz and Helena Cehak Hołubowiczowa, and on Pomerania by Tadeusz Waga). Monographic syntheses of particular prehistoric periods were written as well, the most significant being the works by Kozłowski on the Paleolithic, Neolithic, and Bronze Ages.

In 1928 Antoniewicz published the first complex synthesis of Polish prehistory, *Archeologia Polski* (Archaeology of Poland). The interwar period ended with the successive synthesis of the prehistory of Polish land, *Prehistoria Ziem Polskich* (The Prehistory of the Polish Lands), written under the auspices of the Polish Academy of Learning by Krukowski (for the Palolithic Age), by Kostrzewski (from the Neolithic Age to the great migration period and the Roman period), and by Jakimowicz (for the early Middle Ages). Due to the outbreak of World War II, the work was not published until 1948. It was a classic study that incorporated such concepts as industry, culture, and type as fundamental categories for chronological and spatial classification and for the interpretation of archaeological material.

Other significant influences on the archaeology of this period were the anthropogeographic and the culture-historical schools. Kozłowski indicated the significance of typological method to distinguish particular archaeological cultures; in fact, most of the cultures were identified in the Polish prehistory by this method, and the distinctions remain valid today. Research concentrated mainly on the analysis of archaeological sources and their typology and chronology. Prehistoric archaeology was considered to be part of the history of material culture.

Between the World Wars Polish archaeologists were involved in an academic-political debate with Germans about the ethnic interpretation of certain archaeological cultures, particularly of the Lusatian culture. The dispute was concerned mainly with the origin and beginnings of Slav and German peoples. Archaeologists such as Kostrzewski, Kozłowski, and Tadeusz Sulimirski (1898–1983) argued that the Lusatian culture's roots were Slavonic. These discussions became particularly fervent after 1933, when Adolf Hitler came into power in Germany.

Museum collections were nationalized to guarantee their stability, and they became the main centers of research. In 1924 the Wielkopolskie Museum, with a large section on prehistory, was founded as the result of the fusion of the Mielżyński's Museum and the Provincial Museum (Kaiser Friedrich Museum) in Poznań. Four years later the State Archaeological Museum in Warsaw became the central archaeological museum of Poland.

World War II was a catastrophe for Polish archaeology. Approximately 25 percent of Poland's archaeologists were killed, and many museum collections and libraries were destroyed. The political situation after the war, when Poland was incorporated in the Soviet zone of influence, ideologized academia, entailing the obligatory acceptance of the doctrine of dialectical materialism. This tendency was particularly strong in the first postwar decade (until 1956), and it did not spare archaeology. The years between 1949 and 1955 were the period of the greatest political and police terror. Ideologizing markedly decreased after 1956 and had disappeared almost completely by the 1970s. From the Marxist perspective, archaeology was considered to be the history of material culture, which was reflected in the reform of archaeological studies. Historical materialism imposed a belief in the primacy of the material conditions of human life. Postwar archaeology became a purely historical discipline focused on progress that hypothetically took place in subsequent periods of prehistory.

The first years after the war were mainly devoted to the reconstruction of ruined research centers. Some were reconstituted on so-called regained territories in the west (Silesia, the Lubusz Lands, and Pomerania). New departments of archaeology were founded at the Universities of Lublin, Łódź, Toruń (which continued the traditions of the University of Vilnus), and Wrocław (which was a continuation of the University of Lvov). Both Vilnus and Lvov did not fall within the borders of postwar Poland.

Witold Hensel (Arkadiusz Marciniak)

In 1946 the Institute for the Research on Slavonic Antiquities was established. It was a product of the growing interest in the prehistory of Slavdom, and it included, as well as archaeology, the disciplines of anthropology (the works of Jan Czekanowski), linguistics (Tadeusz Lehr-Spławiński), ethnology (Kazimierz Moszyński), and history in general (Kazimierz Tymieniecki). This field of interest proved to be one of the most important areas of contact between archaeologists from Slavonic socialist countries, and the new journal *Slavia Antiqua* was founded in 1948 primarily for the sake of promoting such contact. An encyclopedic *Dictionary of Slavonic Antiquities,* including information from prehistory, history, and ethnography, has been published since 1961. In 1952 WITOLD HENSEL published the monumental *Early Medieval Slavdom,* which has since had four editions. These interests culminated in the International Congress of Slavonic Archaeology, held in 1965 in Warsaw, and other such congresses have been organized every five years since then. Another result was the foundation of the International Union of Slavonic Archaeology.

Next to the reestablishment of journals founded before the war, new ones appeared,

many of them published under the auspices of museums. Another important moment in the development of the Polish archaeology after World War II occurred in 1966, a consequence of the celebration of the millennium of the Polish state and the Christianization of Poland by Prince Mesco I. A special institution was founded to coordinate all the undertakings in this area. In 1949 the Management of Studies of the Beginnings of the Polish State was established under the supervision of Aleksander Gieysztor. This move was the beginning of the biggest research program in the history of Polish archaeology, in which almost all active archaeologists in Poland participated. The result was an enormous increase in the number of publications concerning the early Middle Ages.

The central archaeological body, the Institute of the History of Material Culture of the Polish Academy of Sciences, was established in 1953 and inaugurated on January 1, 1954. Initially the institute focused its research projects on the millennium of the Polish state. For many years (from 1954 until 1989) it was directed by Witold Hensel. In 1991 it was renamed the Institute of Archaeology and Ethnology. As a state academic institution following official political priorities, the institute soon became the main center for archaeological research in Poland. Since 1957 it has published the journal *Archeologia Polski* (Archaeology of Poland), which is currently the most important Polish periodical in the field. *Archeologia Polona,* published in the main European languages to make the achievements of Polish archaeologists available to a foreign audience, was founded a year later.

Strong efforts were made to promote Marxist archaeology, but it was never widely accepted. The whole postwar period has been dominated by a positivist approach, concentrating on the classification of material and the study of its chronology and systematics. However, there were other attempts to problematize archaeological research, such as those by Jan Żak (1923–1990), who defined prehistory as the study of the development of the conscious and purposeful activity of prehistoric human communities intended to reduce their dependence on nature. His works focused on the issue of so-called discontinuity, the discontinuation of social existence.

There were a number of spectacular excavations during the postwar period, such as those in Nowa Huta related to the construction of huge steelworks just east of Cracow. This site was in a fertile agricultural area, and its settlements dated back to the Neolithic period. Polish archaeologists also took part in a number of successful excavations abroad, especially in the 1960s. These included a program that researched the deserted villages of France, studies on the beginnings of Venice and the Longobard settlements in northern ITALY, as well as research in Algeria, Egypt, Ethiopia, SPAIN, India, Cuba, Sudan, Tunisia, and in other countries of the former USSR.

A list of the most outstanding postwar scholars includes Włodzimierz Hołubowicz (1908–1962), Konrad Jażdżewski (1908–1985), Zdzisław Rajewski (1907–1974), Tadeusz Wiślański (1931–1989), and Jan Żak, as well as Zbigniew Bukowski, Waldemar Chmielewski, Kazimierz Godłowski, Witold Hensel, Janusz Krzysztof Kozłowski, Stefan Karol Kozłowski, Zofia Kur-

natowska, Lech Leciejewicz, Jan Machnik, Andrzej Nadolski, Jerzy Okulicz, Romuald Schild, Stanisław Tabaczyński, and Jerzy Wielowiejski.

By 1980 there were some 700 Polish scholars active in archaeology, and this resulted in an intensification of the field research. For instance, in the 1960s there was seasonal fieldwork on some 300 sites. The areas of major interest became the early and late Middle Ages and the Modern Age. Prehistoric archaeology has been more and more distinctly supplemented by the archaeology of historical periods.

The so-called Archaeological Photograph of Poland (Archeologiczne Zdjęcie Polski), started in 1979 as a continuation of the nineteenth-century archaeological maps, has been particularly interesting. The project, which is still in progress, covers the whole territory of Poland, and an immense database is now being gradually computerized.

Among the important books published during this period is Konrad Jażdżewski's *Prehistory of Central Europe* (1981), also published in German as *Urgeschichte Mitteleuropas* (1984). Other significant syntheses of the prehistory of Polish lands, such as the *Prehistory of Poland* (1965) by Józef Kostrzewski, Waldemar Chmielewski, and Konrad Jażdżewski, have been published as well. Another important work is the five-volume *Prehistory of the Lands of Poland* (1975–1981), published under the general supervision of Witold Hensel.

Since World War II the number of Polish archaeologists has increased dramatically, and research was grown increasingly specialized. A more detailed account of changes in the discipline would have to focus on each of the existing research centers and/or the specific characteristics of the study of particular periods of prehistory.

Arkadiusz Marciniak

See also Lithuania

Polynesia
Polynesia Defined

The term *Polynesia* was an invention of the European Enlightenment, a direct consequence of the great voyages of Pacific exploration associ-

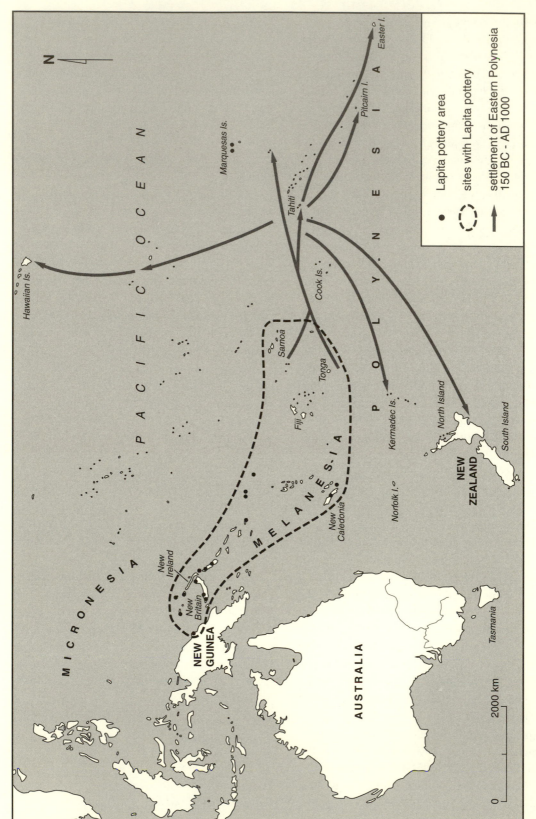

Legend

Lapita pottery area

sites with Lapita pottery •

settlement of Eastern Polynesia 150 BC – AD 1000

Map labels

N

PACIFIC OCEAN

MICRONESIA

MELANESIA

POLYNESIA

Marquesas Is.

Tahiti

Pitcairn I.

Easter I.

Hawaiian Is.

Cook Is.

Samoa

Tonga

Fiji

New Caledonia

New Ireland

New Britain

NEW GUINEA

AUSTRALIA

Tasmania

Norfolk I.

Kermadec Is.

North Island

South Island

NEW ZEALAND

2000 km

0

Pacific Islands

ated with such famous navigators as Louis de Bougainville, James Cook, George Vancouver, and La Pérouse. The first use of the term (derived from the Greek words for "many" and "island") is generally attributed to De Brosses in his 1756 *Histoire des navigations aux terres Australes,* where it applied to all of the islands of the "Great South Sea." The modern definition of *Polynesia,* as the islands found within the vast triangle subtended by Hawai'i in the north Pacific, New Zealand in the southwest, and EASTER ISLAND (Rapa Nui) in the far southeast, dates to the French explorer Sebastien Dumont d'Urville (1790–1842). In his 1832 *Notice sur les Iles du grand océan,* he set Polynesia apart from Melanesia, the islands of the southwestern Pacific from New Guinea to Fiji, and from Micronesia, the islands north of the equator ranging from the Marianas and Palau in the west to the Marshall Islands in the east. This tripartite segmentation of Oceania continues to have geographic salience, even though its value for historical understanding has been greatly diminished.

Culture historians such as ROGER C. GREEN (1991) have recently recognized that a more meaningful way to partition Oceania is between *Near Oceania* (comprising New Guinea, the Bismarck Archipelago, and the Solomon Islands) and *Remote Oceania* (comprising all of Micronesia, the Melanesian archipelagoes of Vanuatu, the Loyalty Islands, New Caledonia, Fiji, and all of Polynesia). This distinction recognizes the deep history of the Pleistocene human occupation of Near Oceania (beginning at least 40,000 years ago) and the relatively late expansion of Austronesian-speaking peoples into Remote Oceania (after about 2000 B.C.). Nonetheless, the term *Polynesia* retains considerable salience, for the island cultures found within this vast triangle (along with a few Polynesian "outliers" scattered to the west of the triangle proper) do cohere as a single cultural region.

The high degree of relatedness among the peoples of Polynesia was first recognized, on the basis of language similarities, by Enlightenment voyagers such as J. R. Forster, the naturalist of Captain Cook's second voyage, who published a comparative table of Polynesian words in 1778. Modern historical linguistic studies confirm that the thirty-six documented Polynesian languages form a single branch of the great Austronesian language family. They can all be traced back to a proto-Polynesian language, for which more than 4,000 words have now been reconstructed (Kirch and Green in press). As biological populations the Polynesian islanders also exhibit considerable phenotypic homogeneity and common genetic markers. Recent studies in molecular biology suggest that the Polynesian ancestors passed through a "genetic bottleneck" at some point in their early history, quite probably associated with the initial colonization the Fiji-Tonga-Samoa region.

Ethnographically Polynesia is generally subdivided into two major sectors: *Western Polynesia,* which includes Tonga, Samoa, Futuna, 'Uvea, and a few smaller islands in this region, and *Eastern Polynesia,* including both the central-eastern archipelagoes of the Cooks, Australs, Societies, and Marquesas and the more isolated islands of Hawai'i, Easter, and New Zealand. The formal distinction between Western and Eastern Polynesia was first defined on comparative ethnographic evidence by Edwin G. Burrows in 1939. Archaeological research has subsequently demonstrated that Western Polynesia was settled first, around 1000–900 B.C., and was the geographic homeland of the ancestral Polynesians (the speakers of proto-Polynesian language; see Kirch and Green in press). Subsequent dispersals out of this homeland region, to the east, north, and southwest, led to the settlement of Eastern Polynesia. Dating the settlement of Eastern Polynesia remains a controversial matter, but scholars would agree the process began sometime after 500 B.C. and was completed by A.D. 800–1000.

Nineteenth-Century Scholarship

As already noted, the late-eighteenth-century voyagers recognized the coherence of Polynesia (Captain Cook wrote of the "Polynesian Nation"), and they began to advance theories of Polynesian origins, generally suggesting that the Polynesians were related to similar peoples found in the Malay Archipelago (modern INDONESIA). Again, linguistic similarities provided key evidence.

By the early decades of the nineteenth century the islands of Polynesia were becoming the targets of increasing European interest, first by itinerant traders, followed by various missionary sects and, by mid-century, imperial efforts at colonization. The French annexed Tahiti and surrounding archipelagoes, and the British took political control of Aotearoa (New Zealand) from the indigenous Maori (but not without a protracted war of resistance). Somewhat later Samoa fell to German and then U.S. and British interests, and the legitimate Hawaiian government was overthrown by a cabal of U.S. expatriates in 1893. As was typical in other parts of the colonized world, scholarly interests in the newly subjugated populations followed missionary and imperialist expansion. The origins of modern anthropology and prehistoric archaeology, as many have argued, are closely intertwined with global European expansion.

Many missionaries and colonial officials who found themselves in Polynesia conducted pioneering ethnographic and linguistic research and used the data to construct theories of Polynesian origins and history. Although a few archaeological ruins were studied (such as the Hawaiian temple, or *heiau,* sites recorded by Thomas Thrum in Hawai'i), archaeology per se figured little in these nineteenth-century endeavors. Rather, great emphasis was placed on indigenous Polynesian oral traditions and narratives, by such scholars as Sir George Grey, Abraham Fornander, and S. Percy Smith. Their particular accounts varied, but these authors generally traced Polynesian origins back to Asia, with protracted migrations through the western Pacific into the Polynesian triangle. Fornander's *Account of the Polynesian Race* (1878) remains a classic of this genre, tracing the Polynesians back to "the Vedic family of the Arian race" that was eventually "driven out of India" and gradually spread into Indonesia and beyond.

In New Zealand, however, direct archaeological evidence in the form of prehistoric stone implements (flake tools and ground-stone adzes) came to the fore when they were found in association with the bones of several species of giant, extinct, ostrichlike birds known as moa. As early as 1872 Julius Von Haast was excavating "moa-hunter" sites in the South Island of New Zealand and using such evidence to argue for a race of Paleolithic hunter-gatherers who had preceded the classic Polynesian Maori in these southern islands.

By the fin-de-siècle, such ad hoc scholarship was giving way to more formal academic enterprises, associated with the founding of museums, universities, and other institutional bases from which ethnological and archaeological research would henceforth be sponsored. The POLYNESIAN SOCIETY was established in New Zealand in 1892 to promote such research, and the *Journal of the Polynesian Society* remains a prominent publication today. The Otago Museum and Dominion Museum in New Zealand and the Bernice P. Bishop Museum in Hawai'i became leading centers for archaeological and ethnographic research. The Bishop Museum, in particular, would come to play the dominant role in Pacific archaeological research throughout the first half of the twentieth century.

The Problem of Polynesian Origins

In the first decades of the twentieth century archaeology began to come into its own in Polynesia. Katherine Scoresby Routledge, a remarkable woman and scholar, led a three-year private expedition to Easter Island to investigate its enigmatic, giant stone statues. Routledge combined archaeological survey and mapping of the ruins with ethnographic inquiries among the surviving Rapa Nui people to arrive at the conclusion that the statues and the temples upon which they stood were "the work of the ancestors" of the Polynesian-speaking Rapa Nui themselves, not the vestiges of some vanished race (Routledge 1919, 291). In Hawai'i, John F. G. Stokes carefully surveyed the remains of stone temple sites on Hawai'i and Moloka'i Islands to determine whether a sequence of temple forms could be inferred and possibly correlated with Hawaiian oral traditions of religious change. Stokes also conducted stratigraphic excavations on the island of Kaho'olawe and found a succession of fishhook types in the Kamohio rock shelter, although the significance of his results would remain unappreciated for nearly fifty years.

The greatest impetus to Polynesian archaeology, however, occurred in 1920 when geologist Herbert E. Gregory acceded to the directorship of the Bishop Museum in Honolulu, convened the first international Pan-Pacific Science Conference, and proclaimed that the study of Polynesian archaeology and anthropology should be a major research priority (Kirch 2000, 20–24). Gregory, who continued to hold a professorship at Yale University, had important connections with the East Coast establishment in the United States and was able to secure major funding for a series of research expeditions to several Polynesian archipelagoes. The Bayard Dominick Expeditions of the Bishop Museum, from 1920 to 1922, were designed to implement the emerging Americanist vision of a holistic anthropology, combining multiple lines of evidence from ethnography, archaeology, ethnobotany, and physical anthropology (somatology). Research teams combining these disciplines were dispatched to Tonga, the Austral Islands, the Marquesas, and Hawai'i to carry out parallel investigations designed to address the overarching problem of Polynesian origins.

In retrospect, however, archaeology played a subordinate role in the Bayard Dominick Expeditions, leaving the field to be dominated by the comparative ethnologists. In the Tongan expedition, for example, archaeologist William C. McKern (later to become famous for his work on North American ceramic taxonomy) focused most of his efforts on the mapping of large stone monument sites, making only limited excavations in a few caves and kitchen middens (McKern 1929). McKern did recover an elaborately decorated form of pottery in these excavations, but lacking any method for direct DATING, he interpreted this as a late-prehistoric variant of Fijian trade ceramics. Only decades later would his shards be properly recognized as part of the Lapita cultural complex, dating to the early part of the first millennium B.C. and associated with the first human settlement of Polynesia.

In the Marquesas Islands Ralph Linton (best known for his later ethnographic work in Africa) directed the archaeology but completely failed to recognize the potential for stratigraphic excavations. Without even bothering to test excavate, Linton simply concluded that "no opportunity was afforded for the gradual accumulation of stratified deposits" and that "no kitchen midden or shell heaps exist in the islands" (1925, 3). Thus he focused entirely on the mapping of late-prehistoric and early-postcontact monumental structures, interpreting these strictly within the context of a static, ethnographic reconstruction of "traditional" Marquesan culture. Even the possibility of cultural change or time depth (long periods of time) was thereby eliminated.

Consequently, despite a renewed emphasis on modern, scientific methods of archaeological survey (and sometimes excavation), the interpretation of Polynesian prehistory from the 1920s until World War II was largely dominated by comparative ethnology. The failure of archaeology to take hold partially resulted from the absence of any evident method for direct (or even relative) dating. Radiocarbon dating was still a thing of the future, and the methods of seriation being developed in North America and elsewhere for generating relative chronologies were seen as not applicable in Polynesia, given the general absence of pottery. Thus the stone structures and stone tools mapped and recorded by archaeologists in Polynesia were fitted into a largely static, ethnographic reconstruction and subsumed under the rubric of "material culture." To be sure, a great deal of fundamental survey work was carried out during these years, such as that done by Kenneth P. Emory in the Society Islands (Emory 1933) and elsewhere or that of Wendell C. Bennett (1931) on Kaua'i Island (Bennett would later make his mark in Andean archaeology). This was archaeology, but it was not prehistory.

Migration Theories of the Early Twentieth Century

With the failure of archaeology to provide a real temporal framework for culture change and culture-history in Polynesia, the interpretive field was left to the comparative ethnologists, who adduced the new archaeological survey data only rarely. Dominant among this group of scholars was Edward S. Craighill Handy, who had led the Marquesas party of the Bayard Dominick Expeditions in 1920. Handy's theoretical perspective was closely allied to that of the European Kulturkreise (culture-circle) school (see, e.g., FRITZ GRAEBNER 1905), in which the origins of a particular people or culture were sought through a comparison of trait lists with neighboring or even far-flung cultures. Thus Handy developed an elaborate theory of Polynesian origins and migrations in which Polynesian cultural traits were correlated with "Brahmanical" and "Buddhistic" cultures ranging from India to CHINA (Handy 1930). Rather than seeing variations among the Polynesian cultures as deriving from a lengthy process of cultural change in situ, he interpreted all variation as the outcome of successive "waves" of migration.

A more influential theory of Polynesian origins was promulgated by the Maori scholar Te Rangi Hiroa (also known as Sir Peter Buck), who had succeeded Gregory as director of the Bishop Museum in 1936. Hiroa was a seasoned ethnographer, with experience throughout much of Polynesia. He had, however, little use for archaeology, finding it a "dry subject." Hiroa relied more upon the salvage ethnographic work of Bishop Museum scientists to develop a migration theory that traced the route of Polynesian voyages into the Pacific not via the large archipelagoes of Melanesia but through the small coral atolls of Micronesia. In his widely read book, *Vikings of the Sunrise*, Hiroa argued that "the master mariners of the Pacific [the Polynesians] must be Europoid for they are not characterized by the woolly hair, black skins, and thin lower legs of the Negroids nor by the flat face, short stature, and drooping inner eyefold of the Mongoloids" (1938, 16). Hiroa's racially charged theory can be understood in retrospect in light of the severe racial prejudice he himself suffered at the hands of the dominant white academic society and in terms of the racial pigeonholing that characterized much of anthropology in the early twentieth century (Kirch 2000, 24–27). His theory was, however, a highly forced contrivance, and archaeology later in the twentieth century lent no support whatsoever to the concept of a Micronesian migration into Polynesia.

Within the genre of migrationist theories of Polynesian culture-history, mention must also be made of the highly influential writings of Thor Heyerdahl, a Norwegian zoologist and adventurer who captured the world's attention in 1947 with his daring *Kon Tiki* raft voyage from South America to the Tuamotu Islands. World War II had already focused much attention on the Pacific islands, and Heyerdahl now claimed to have a theory that explained the Polynesians as deriving from successive migrations not from Asia but from the Americas. The full theory was published in a massive volume a few years after the *Kon Tiki* voyage (Heyerdahl 1952), and Heyerdahl funded his own archaeological expedition to Easter Island and other Eastern Polynesian islands in 1955 and 1956 in an effort to prove his origins theory. His hypothesis has not survived the test of modern archaeological research, but Heyerdahl must be credited with helping to spur a reinvigoration of Polynesian archaeology in the period immediately following World War II.

Stratigraphic Archaeology and Culture-History

After several decades of being relegated to a minor supporting role in Polynesian studies, archaeology suddenly emerged in the aftermath of World War II as the primary source of data on Polynesian culture-history. This intellectual transformation can be traced to several developments. One was the heightened scientific interest in the Pacific islands generated in the wake of the war itself (a number of influential U.S. anthropologists and scientists had worked closely with military intelligence in the Pacific theater). Thus, in the later 1940s, renewed archaeological studies in the Pacific were initiated by such scholars as Edward W. Gifford of Berkeley in the Fiji archipelago and Alexander Spoehr of the Field Museum in the Marianas Islands (Gifford 1951; Spoehr 1957). Rather than continuing with surface surveys of monumental architecture, which had dominated prewar field research, these new efforts emphasized a return to stratigraphic excavations. Significantly, both Gifford and Spoehr, working outside of Polynesia proper in island groups where pottery had been manufactured and used by the indigenous inhabitants, were able to demonstrate sequences of material cultural change, primarily in ceramic styles. As a result materially documented time depth and culture change were finally shown to exist in Oceanic archaeology. Within Polynesia proper Kenneth Emory of the Bishop Museum also began a program of excavations in Hawaiian archaeological sites, beginning about 1950. The prehistoric Hawaiians had never used pottery, but Emory and his colleagues Yosihiko Sinoto and William Bonk realized that they could apply the methods of seriation to changing styles in bone and shell fishhooks, thus outlining a culture-historical sequence for the Hawaiian Islands (Emory, Bonk, and Sinoto 1959).

Equally important to the reapplication of stratigraphic methods were the discovery and implementation of radiocarbon dating by WILLARD LIBBY, beginning in the late 1940s. Emory, Gifford, Spoehr, and others were quick to take advantage of Libby's offer to date samples from various parts of the world, and by the early 1950s a number of radiocarbon dates had been published for sites ranging from Hawai'i to New Caledonia and the Marianas. The significance of this technological development cannot be underplayed, for it provided an independent means of assessing chronology, and the dates themselves left no doubt that the time depth of Polynesian prehistory could now be counted in thousands—not hundreds—of years. As Emory put it, radiocarbon dating "opened up undreamed of possibilities for reconstructing the prehistory of [Polynesia]" (Emory, Bonk, and Sinoto 1959, ix).

By the mid-1950s there was a veritable resurgence of field archaeology throughout Polynesia. In New Zealand the pioneering excavations of ROGER DUFF (1950) at Wairau Bar were followed by a series of careful excavations conducted by JACK GOLSON, a young Cambridge-trained archaeologist who had been appointed to a faculty post at the University of Auckland (Golson 1959). As mentioned earlier, Thor Heyerdahl privately financed and led his own Norwegian Archaeological Expedition to Easter Island and other Eastern Polynesian locales in 1955 and 1956, with excavations conducted by four professional archaeologists (Heyerdahl and Ferdon 1961, 1965). Their work also put the statue cult of Easter Island within a radiocarbon framework. At the same time, Robert Suggs of the American Museum of Natural History took up where Ralph Linton had left off in the Marquesas Islands, quickly demonstrating that the latter's assumptions about a dearth of stratified sites had no empirical justification. Suggs found a wealth of artifact-rich deposits, and his monograph outlined one of the first well-defined culture sequences for a Polynesian archipelago (Suggs 1961).

Coming less than two decades after Hiroa's migrationist theory had been at the fore, the new outpouring of archaeological results inspired a radical rethinking of Polynesian culture-history. Suggs (1960) wrote the classic synthesis of this period, *The Island Civilizations of Polynesia*, not only debunking the older ethnographic theories of Handy, Hiroa, and their peers but also attacking the rival Heyerdahl theory of American origins. Suggs's synthesis privileged the material evidence of "dirt archaeology," but it also drew widely upon newly emerging linguistic and human-biological research. Polynesian origins were now traced back to a Southeast Asian homeland, with a dispersal route through the Melanesian archipelagoes (not Micronesia, as Hiroa had advocated), this latter evidenced by a ceramic style that would shortly come to be named Lapita. The Western Polynesian archipelagoes of Tonga and Samoa were now argued to be the immediate Polynesian homeland, with subsequent voyages of colonization to the Marquesas and Society Islands and thence to the farthest islands of Eastern Polynesia.

Settlement Archaeology in Polynesia

The rejuvenation of stratigraphic archaeology in Polynesia and its expansion beyond Polynesia into the western Pacific was initially driven by a strong culture-historical orientation, encouraged by rapid success in defining considerable time depth and sequences of material culture change (whether in ceramic styles or in fishhooks and stone adzes). Under this culture-history paradigm, the emphasis in fieldwork was on a few selected sites chosen for extensive excavation because they contained well-stratified deposits and were rich in diagnostic artifact types. Classic sites of this type in Polynesia, excavated during the 1950s and 1960s, include the Pu'u Ali'i and Waiahukini sites in Hawai'i, the Wairau Bar site in New Zealand, and the Ha'atuatua and Hane dune sites in the Marquesas.

A significant shift in archaeological research priorities, accompanied by a reorientation of field methods, began in the early 1960s. This was, in essence, a broadening of the Polynesian research agenda beyond narrow concerns with culture-historical sequences and the long-standing question of "Polynesian origins"; the agenda would now encompass questions of cultural change and evolution, of the nature of prehistoric societies and political systems, and of their ecological and economic contexts. This shift in research orientation naturally did not occur in a vacuum, and it was part of the broader reorientation in Anglo-American archaeology from a culture-historical to a "processual" approach (Trigger 1989). To a large degree in Polynesia, this involved not a complete rejection of the older culture-historical orientation but rather a broadening of the research agenda to incorporate extensive efforts at the reconstruction of prehistoric culture.

In Polynesia this shift can first be detected in Suggs's Marquesan research, in which, despite a continued emphasis on key stratified sites, the research questions encompassed such issues as demographic, economic, and sociopolitical change in Marquesan society. More influential, however, was the introduction of the "settlement-pattern" approach to Polynesian archaeology by ROGER GREEN, who had been trained in this approach by its main proponent in the United States, GORDON WILLEY of Harvard University. Green first applied a comprehensive, settlement-pattern survey methodology in his study of the 'Opunohu Valley on Mo'orea Island (Society Islands), in which *all* sites in a valley landscape were recorded and treated as a record of nonportable artifact variability (Green et al. 1967). As Green summarized the perspective of settlement-pattern archaeology, "[With] increasing concern with delineating the social aspect of the data recovered from sites . . . the day has passed when such monuments or their structural features can afford to be treated only as contexts for portable artifacts and not as artifacts in their own right" (1967, 102).

A settlement-pattern orientation soon came to dominate archaeological research throughout Polynesia, particularly as investigations were expanded to such islands and archipelagoes as Samoa (Green and Davidson 1969, 1974), New Zealand (Groube 1965), the Marquesas (Bellwood 1972; Kellum-Ottino 1971), Easter Island (McCoy 1976), and Hawai'i (Kirch and Kelly 1975). Although initially designed to elucidate aspects of precontact Polynesian sociopolitical organization, such settlement-pattern studies soon came to include a strong research orientation toward economic and ecological questions. Thus in Hawai'i, for example, much work in the 1970s and early 1980s was focused on the field evidence for variability in prehistoric agricultural systems, both dryland field systems and irrigated pondfield terraces (Kirch and Kelly 1975; Yen et al. 1972). This research was by no means limited to surface survey and mapping, and it included new methods of excavation and analysis, such as the interpretation of agricultural soils (Kirch 1977). Similar concerns prompted major research projects elsewhere in Polynesia, such as the Palliser Bay research of B. Foss and Helen Leach (1979) and the study of the Polynesian outlier of Tikopia by P. V. Kirch and D. E. Yen (1982).

This extension of settlement-pattern archaeology to encompass economic and ecological aspects of precontact Polynesia societies also began to open up issues of the dynamic relationships between Polynesian populations and their island ecosystems. Under the older culture-historical paradigm, the island environment had been viewed largely as a static context for human settlement. The settlement-pattern approach, by contrast, put humans on the land as active agents of change. The accumulation of much zooarchaeological evidence for changes in island faunas, combined with interdisciplinary work between archaeologists, geomorphologists, palynologists, and other natural scientists, led to a considerable rethinking concerning the dynamism of island ecosystems. Although the human role in the extinction of New Zealand's giant moa birds had long been documented (Anderson 1989), it became increasingly clear that there had been major episodes of human-induced avian extinctions throughout tropical island of Polynesia (Steadman 1995). Combined with evidence for deforestation, erosion and valley alluviation, and the widespread conversion of natural communities to highly anthropogenic landscapes, our view of island ecosystems and the role of indigenous peoples in shaping their landscape histories has been entirely transformed (Kirch and Hunt 1997).

A further outgrowth of the settlement-pattern reorientation in Polynesia throughout the 1960s, 1970s, and 1980s was a concern with wider theoretical issues in processual archaeology. The Polynesian societies had been taken as a virtual "type" instance for the concept of the chiefdom, which was regarded by many processual archaeologists as a key intermediary stage in the evolution of human societies from simpler band and tribal levels of sociopolitical organization to fully state-level polities. This made the study of variation and cultural change within Polynesian chiefdoms a topic of some theoretical import. T. Earle (1978, 1997), for example, drew upon his research on Kaua'i, Hawai'i, both to test Wittfogel's "hydraulic hypothesis" regarding the role of irrigation in the rise of complex societies and more generally to test notions of "how chiefs come to power." Kirch (1984) integrated ethnohistorical and archaeological approaches to construct a broad model of the evolution of Polynesia chiefdoms, arguing that the trend toward increased hierarchy and social control in certain Polynesian societies was substantially constrained by a constellation of demographic, ecological, and economic parameters. In a later study Kirch (1994) argued that a fundamental dichotomy between "wet" and "dry" agricultural landscapes strongly constrained the evolution of hierarchy and power.

New Views on Polynesian Origins and Dispersals

Perhaps because the question of how a "Neolithic" people managed to discover and colonize the most isolated islands on earth remains such an intrinsically compelling issue, the matter of Polynesian origins and dispersals did not disappear with the paradigm shift from culture-historical to processual archaeology. Rather, this question has received renewed scrutiny and been the subject of invigorated debate since the 1970s, as a result of several developments. One impetus was the expansion of modern archaeological work into Melanesia, a region that had been almost entirely neglected prior to World War II. In particular, the realization that a widespread early-ceramic horizon—the Lapita cultural complex—linked the initial stages of human settlement in both Polynesia and eastern Melanesia provoked a fundamental rethinking of Polynesia origins (Green 1979). The earliest Polynesian cultures are now seen to be a direct development out of an early eastern Lapita culture, itself the eastward extension of a process of Lapita expansion that had commenced in the Bismarck Archipelago around 1500 B.C. (Kirch 1997).

Equally important has been a rethinking of the process of dispersal and colonization of islands within the Polynesian triangle itself, where the longest voyages of discovery involved distances of as much as 3,000 kilometers against generally prevailing winds and currents. Computer simulations of the probabilities of accidental drift voyaging first led to a new realization of the high degree of intentionality in early Polynesian voyaging (Irwin 1992). But it is the dramatic experimental voyages of the replicated voyaging canoe Hokule'a that have particularly forced a new model of Polynesian colonization (Finney 1994). These voyages, conceived as a kind of "experimental archaeology," have taken the double-hulled, 19-meter Hokule'a on journeys between many Polynesian archipelagoes without the aid of instrument navigation, the most dramatic being a voyage from Mangareva to remote Easter Island in 1999.

The investigation of voyaging and interaction between Polynesian islands and archipelagoes has also been spurred by the application of new archaeometric techniques, especially X-ray fluorescence sourcing of basalt artifacts such as adzes. M. I. Weisler and Kirch (1996) demonstrated the transport of stone adzes between

Samoa and the Cook Islands, a distance of some 1,600 kilometers, and more recently Weisler (1998) has tracked the movement of adzes from the Marquesas to the Society Islands. Equally innovative has been the work of E. Matisoo-Smith and colleagues (1998) using studies of mitochondrial DNA variation in Pacific rats (*Rattus exulans*) to show patterns of interisland contact.

Contemporary Archaeology in Polynesia

Polynesian archaeology continues to change and evolve. The very practice of archaeology has been significantly affected by changing institutional and sociopolitical contexts. Throughout the first six decades of the twentieth century, archaeology fell almost exclusively within the institutional purview of a few museums and universities. This situation began to change dramatically in the 1970s with the rise of "public archaeology" or, as it has come to be labeled in Americanist contexts, "cultural resource management" (CRM) archaeology. In Hawai'i, for example, most contemporary archaeological work is carried out not by research institutions but by private (for-profit) archaeological contractors. Thus the very definition of field projects has shifted from areas selected strictly on the basis of their research potential to specific locations subject to impact from highway construction, resort development, and the like (Graves and Erkelens 1991; Kirch 1999). Similarly, in French Polynesia much archaeological work is now undertaken to mitigate the adverse effects of "development," such as in the large-scale Papeno'o Valley project where the construction of hydroelectric dams was the main consideration. Although it has generated significant new funding sources for fieldwork, this shift to CRM archaeology also led to the production of a very large "gray literature" of archaeological reports not published in the usual academic journals and monographs—a serious problem for the long-term archiving and preservation of archaeological evidence.

The sociopolitical context of Polynesian archaeology is also rapidly evolving. Once almost exclusively the purview of white, expatriate scholars (Te Rangi Hiroa was a major exception), archaeology in the islands has begun to in-corporate significant numbers of indigenous practitioners. As Polynesians themselves are trained in the theory and methods of archaeology and begin to take up professional posts in museums, universities, historical preservation agencies, and CRM firms, they bring new questions and concerns to the field. There is, for example, a renewed interest in the potential integration of indigenous oral traditions and narratives with archaeological evidence (Cachola-Abad 1993). Heightened cultural sensitivity toward the archaeological record has also changed the nature of archaeological practice. This is evidenced, for instance, in the complete reburial of several thousand human skeletal remains that had been excavated from Hawaiian archaeological sites, a direct outcome of the Native American Graves Protection and Repatriation Act in the United States.

These and other influences will continue to modify the ways in which archaeology is practiced in Polynesia and elsewhere in the Pacific islands. Certainly, however, there is no sign that interest in Polynesian archaeology is abating. The long-term history of the islands and their indigenous peoples has engaged scholars for more than two centuries, yet new questions continually emerge even as older issues receive renewed scrutiny from fresh approaches and methods.

Patrick V. Kirch

See also Papua New Guinea and Melanesia
References
Anderson, A. 1989. *Prodigious Birds: Moas and Moa-Hunting in Prehistoric New Zealand.* Cambridge: Cambridge University Press.
Bellwood, P. 1972. *Settlement Pattern Survey, Hanatekua Valley, Hiva Oa, Marquesas Islands.* Pacific Anthropological Records 17. Honolulu: Bernice P. Bishop Museum.
Bennett, W. C. 1931. *Archaeology of Kauai.* Honolulu: Bernice P. Bishop Museum Bulletin 80.
Burrows, E. G. 1939. *Western Polynesia: A Study in Cultural Differentiation.* Ethnological Studies no. 7. Gothenburg, Sweden.
Cachola-Abad, C. K. 1993. "Evaluating the Orthodox Dual Settlement Model for the Hawaiian Islands: An Analysis of Artefact Distribution and Hawaiian Oral Traditions." In *The Evolution and Organization of Prehistoric Society in Polynesia,*

13–32. Ed. M. W. Graves and R. C. Green. Monograph 19. Auckland: New Zealand Archaeological Association.

Duff, R. 1950. *The Moa Hunter Period of Maori Culture* (2d ed.). Wellington, New Zealand: Government Printer.

Earle, T. 1978. *Economic and Social Organization of a Complex Chiefdom: The Halelea District, Kaua'i, Hawaii.* Anthropological Papers no. 63. Ann Arbor: Museum of Anthropology, University of Michigan.

———. 1997. *How Chiefs Come to Power: The Political Economy in Prehistory.* Stanford, CA: Stanford University Press.

Emory, K. P. 1933. *Stone Remains in the Society Islands.* Bulletin 116. Honolulu: Bernice P. Bishop Museum.

Emory, K. P., W. J. Bonk, and Y. H. Sinoto. 1959. *Hawaiian Archaeology: Fishhooks.* Special Publication 47. Honolulu: Bernice P. Bishop Museum.

Finney, B. R. 1994. *Voyage of Rediscovery: A Cultural Odyssey through Polynesia.* Berkeley: University of California Press.

Fornander, A. 1878. *An Account of the Polynesian Race.* London: Trubner.

Gifford, E. W. 1951. *Archaeological Excavations in Fiji.* Anthropological Records 13: 189–288. Berkeley: University of California Press.

Golson, J. 1959. "Culture Change in Prehistoric New Zealand." In *Anthropology in the South Seas,* 29–74. Ed. J. D. Freeman and W. R. Geddes. New Plymouth, New Zealand: Avery.

Gräbner, F. 1905. "Kulturkriese und Kultur schichten in Ozeanien." *Zietscrift für Anthropologie, Ethnologie und Urgeschichte* 37: 28–53, 84–90.

Graves, M. W., and C. Erkelens. 1991. "Who's in Control?: Method and Theory in Hawaiian Archaeology." *Asian Perspectives* 30: 1–18.

Green, R. C. 1967. "Settlement Patterns: Four Case Studies from Polynesia." In *Archaeology at the Eleventh Pacific Science Congress,* 101–132. Ed. W. G. Solheim II. Asian and Pacific Archaeology Series no. 1. Honolulu: Social Science Research Institute, University of Hawaii.

———. 1979. "Lapita." In *The Prehistory of Polynesia,* 27–60. Ed. J. Jennings. Cambridge, MA: Harvard University Press.

———. 1991. "Near and Remote Oceania: Disestablishing 'Melanesia' in Culture History." In *Man and a Half: Essays in Pacific Anthropology and Ethnobiology in Honour of Ralph Bulmer,*

491–502. Ed. A. Pawley. Auckland, New Zealand: Polynesian Society.

Green, R. C., K. Green, R. Rappaport, A. Rappaport, and J. Davidson. 1967. *Archaeology on the Island of Mo'orea, French Polynesia.* Anthropological Papers 51, 2. New York: American Museum of Natural History.

Green, R. C., and J. Davidson, eds. 1969. *Archaeology in Western Samoa,* vol. 1. Bulletin of the Auckland Institute and Museum 6. Auckland, New Zealand: Auckland Institute and Museum.

———. 1974. *Archaeology in Western Samoa,* vol. 2. Bulletin of the Auckland Institute and Museum 7. Auckland, New Zealand: Auckland Institute and Museum.

Groube, L. M. 1965. *Settlement Patterns in New Zealand Prehistory.* Occasional Papers in Archaeology no. 1. Dunedin, New Zealand: University of Otago.

Handy, E. S. C. 1930. *The Problem of Polynesian Origins.* Bernice P. Bishop Museum Occasional Papers 9: 1–27. Honolulu: Bernice P. Bishop Museum.

Heyerdahl, T. 1952. *American Indians in the Pacific: The Theory behind the Kon-Tiki Expedition.* London: Allen and Unwin.

Heyerdahl, T., and E. N. Ferdon Jr., eds. 1961. *Reports of the Norwegian Archaeological Expedition to Easter Island and the East Pacific.* Vol. 1, *Archaeology of Easter Island.* Monographs of the School of American Research 24, 1. Santa Fe, NM: School of American Research.

———. 1965. *Reports of the Norwegian Archaeological Expedition to Easter Island and the East Pacific.* Vol. 2, Miscellaneous Papers. Monographs of the School of American Research 24, 2. Santa Fe, NM: School of American Research.

Hiroa, T. R. [P. H. Buck]. 1938. *Vikings of the Sunrise.* New York: Frederick Stokes.

Irwin, G. 1992. *The Prehistoric Exploration and Colonisation of the Pacific.* Cambridge: Cambridge University Press.

Kellum-Ottino, M. 1971. *Archéologie d'une vallée des Iles Marquises.* Publications de la Société des Océanistes 26. Paris.

Kirch, P. V. 1977. "Valley Agricultural Systems in Prehistoric Hawaii: An Archaeological Consideration." *Asian Perspectives* 20: 246–280.

———. 1984. *The Evolution of the Polynesian Chiefdoms.* Cambridge: Cambridge University Press.

———. 1994. *The Wet and the Dry: Irrigation and Agricultural Intensification in Polynesia.* Chicago: University of Chicago Press.

————. 1997. *The Lapita Peoples: Ancestors of the Oceanic World.* Oxford: Blackwell Publishers.

————. 1999. "Hawaiian Archaeology: Past, Present, and Future." *Hawaiian Archaeology.*

————. 2000. *On the Road of the Winds: An Archaeological History of the Pacific Islands before European Contact.* Berkeley: University of California Press.

Kirch, P. V., and R. C. Green. In press. *Hawaiki, Ancestral Polynesia: An Essay in Historical Anthropology.* Cambridge: Cambridge University Press.

Kirch, P. V., and T. L. Hunt, eds. 1997. *Historical Ecology in the Pacific Islands.* New Haven: Yale University Press.

Kirch, P. V., and M. Kelly, eds. 1975. *Prehistory and Ecology in a Windward Hawaiian Valley: Halawa Valley, Molokai.* Pacific Anthropological Records 24. Honolulu: Bernice P. Bishop Museum.

Kirch, P. V., and D. E. Yen. 1982. *Tikopia: The Prehistory and Ecology of a Polynesian Outlier.* Bernice P. Bishop Museum Bulletin 238. Honolulu: Bernice P. Bishop Museum.

Leach, B. F., and H. Leach, eds. 1979. *Prehistoric Man in Palliser Bay.* National Museum of New Zealand Bulletin 21. Wellington, New Zealand: National Museum of New Zealand.

Linton, R. 1925. *Archaeology of the Marquesas Islands.* Bernice P. Bishop Museum Bulletin 23. Honolulu: Bernice P. Bishop Museum.

Matisoo-Smith, E., R. M. Roberts, G. J. Irwin, J. S. Allen, D. Penny, and D. M. Lambert. 1998. "Patterns of Prehistoric Human Mobility Revealed by Mitochondrial DNA from the Pacific Rat." *Proceedings of the National Academy of Sciences, USA* 95: 15145–15150.

McCoy, P. C. 1976. *Easter Island Settlement Patterns in the Late Prehistoric and Proto-Historic Periods.* International Fund for Monuments, Easter Island Committee, Bulletin 5.

McKern, W. C. 1929. *Archaeology of Tonga.* Bernice P. Bishop Museum Bulletin 60. Honolulu: Bernice P. Bishop Museum.

Routledge, K. S. 1919. *The Mystery of Easter Island.* London: Sifton, Praed.

Spoehr, A. 1957. *Marianas Prehistory: Archaeological Survey and Excavations on Saipan, Tinian, and Rota.* Fieldiana: Anthropology 48. Chicago: Field Museum of Natural History.

Steadman, D. W. 1995. "Prehistoric Extinctions of Pacific Island Birds: Biodiversity Meets Aooarchaeology. *Science* 267: 1123–1130.

Suggs, R. C. 1960. *The Island Civilizations of Polynesia.* New York: Mentor Books.

————. 1961. *Archaeology of Nuku Hiva, Marquesas Islands, French Polynesia.* Anthropological Papers of the American Museum of Natural History 49, part 1. New York: American Museum of Natural History.

Trigger, B. 1989. *A History of Archaeological Thought.* Cambridge: Cambridge University Press.

Tuggle, H. D., and P. B. Griffin, eds. 1973. *Lapakahi, Hawaii: Archaeological Studies.* Asian and Pacific Archaeology Series no. 5. Honolulu: Social Science Research Institute, University of Hawaii.

Von Haast, J. 1872. "Moas and Moa Hunters." *Transactions of the New Zealand Institute* 4: 66–107.

Weisler, M. I. 1998. "Hard Evidence for Prehistoric Interaction in Polynesia." *Current Anthropology* 39: 521–532.

Weisler, M. I., and P. V. Kirch. 1996. "Inter-island and Inter-archipelago Transport of Stone Tools in Prehistoric Polynesia." *Proceedings of the National Academy of Sciences, USA,* 93: 1381–1385.

Yen, D. E., P. V. Kirch, P. Rosendahl, and T. Riley. 1972. "Prehistoric Agriculture in the Upper Makaha Valley, Oahu." In *Makaha Valley Historical Project: Interim Report No. 3,* 59–94. Ed. D. E. Yen and E. Ladd. Pacific Anthropological Records 18. Honolulu: Bernice P. Bishop Museum.

Polynesian Society

Formed in Wellington, New Zealand, on 8 January 1892, the Polynesian Society has been publishing a quarterly journal ever since. The *Journal of the Polynesian Society* (*JPS*) is one of the oldest continuously published anthropological journals in the world and has always been the preeminent journal of its kind in the Pacific region. The journal and the society's other publications, including fifty memoirs, are the primary record of the society's activities. A bibliography of the journal was compiled by Dorothy Brown (Brown 1993), and a centennial history by M. P. K. Sorrenson (Sorrenson 1992) was published by the society. Most of the society's papers are held at the Alexander Turnbull Library in Wellington, and the remainder are in the society's office in the Maori Studies Department of the University of Auckland.

Ethnographic recording of the culture of the

Pacific Islands began when the first European navigators entered the region, but it was not institutionalized until the late nineteenth century when some European scholars became alarmed that, because of a decline in and possible extinction of the Pacific peoples, their traditional lore would be lost. This concern led a small band of enthusiasts, headed by the surveyor-general of New Zealand, Stephenson Percy Smith, to form a society and publish a journal to record the lore, languages, and cultures of the Maori and other Pacific peoples.

Although their morbid prognosis did not prove true and the Maori and other Polynesian populations have gradually recovered, the Polynesian Society also survived, though it has never flourished. Its membership has never exceeded 1,500, and it has relied for the most part on voluntary contributions from a few active members. For the first forty years the society and journal were managed by the founders: Smith himself, who was usually president of the society and editor of the journal until his death in 1922; then by a fellow surveyor, W. H. Skinner; and later by Elsdon Best, New Zealand's preeminent ethnologist. Smith was mainly interested in the publication of Maori lore and traditions, and Best, who had carried out extensive fieldwork among the Tuhoe Maori of the Urewera country, published articles about them and about general Maori ethnography. Both men were competent in Maori and even recruited some of their Maori informants as members of the society and contributors to the journal. They were also interested in archaeology, particularly with that great obsession of nineteenth-century scholars of the area, whether it was the Maori or some earlier race who had known and exterminated the flightless bird, the moa. However, it was not until the 1920s that New Zealand archaeology began to progress beyond the realm of speculation and general exploration.

Although the Polynesian Society and its journal remained New Zealand based, coverage extended well beyond the Maori branch of the Polynesian peoples. Smith was assiduous in recruiting overseas members for the society, particularly in Hawaii, and some prominent overseas scholars were corresponding members or contributors to JPS. Queen Liliuokalani of Hawaii was the first patron of the society until after she was deposed in 1893. She was replaced by New Zealand's governors-general until 1981 when another Polynesian queen, Dame Te Ariki-nui Te Atairangikaahu of New Zealand, became patron.

Smith made several tours of the Pacific, including a trip to the Cook Islands in 1897 where he collected migration traditions, and he traced Maori and Polynesian origins to India and used genealogies from New Zealand and the Cook Islands to calculate the dates of the supposed Maori/Polynesian migration from that subcontinent. His findings were published first in JPS and later in a celebrated book, *Hawaiki: The Original Home of the Maori, with a Sketch of Polynesian History* (1904). Such findings seem ridiculous today, but Smith, Best, and others were merely following the lead of renowned European scholars. Moreover, they should not be condemned as mere amateurs since there were no opportunities, at least in New Zealand, for professional training in anthropology.

That professionalism was to become influential in the society and journal after World War I. The first professional anthropologist to become involved was H. D. Skinner, son of W. H. Skinner and a graduate in anthropology from Cambridge University, who was appointed as a part-time lecturer in anthropology at Otago University in 1919. Skinner and several of his students, including the archaeologist ROGER DUFF, were frequent contributors to JPS. Skinner was briefly a co-editor of the journal and later president of the society, but he was never a dominant force since the journal and the society were still under the sway of amateurs. The most notable leader was Best's understudy, Johannes Andersen, who was librarian at Wellington's Alexander Turnbull Library, the largest repository of Maori and Pacific material in the country. The association between the library and the society was continued by his successors at the library, especially Clyde Taylor, who was at times both editor of the journal and secretary of the society. The society also benefited from another Wellington-based organization, the Maori Purposes Fund Board, formed largely through the lobbying of the politician Sir Apirana Ngata.

Ngata was a leading Maori scholar in his own right, a longtime member of the society and later its president, and a frequent contributor to *JPS*. The board subsidized the society's publications and other activities.

Although Maori scholarship remained the main focus of the society's work and publications, the wider Pacific was not ignored. An important figure in this regard was Ngata's friend and former political colleague, Te Rangihiroa (Peter Buck), who first became a research fellow at the Bishop Museum in Hawaii in 1927. He subsequently became its director. Buck remained in frequent contact with Ngata, as can be seen by their extensive correspondence, published as *Na To Hoa Aroha* (Sorrenson, ed. 1986–1988). He was also in touch with Andersen, sometimes contributed to the *JPS,* and solicited copy from his Bishop Museum colleagues, including E. C. S. Handy and Kenneth Emory. Nevertheless, the bulk of the material for the *JPS* still came from enthusiastic amateurs.

The professional takeover of the journal and eventually the society did not occur until after World War II and the establishment of an Anthropology Department at the University of Auckland in 1950, when Bill Geddes, JACK GOLSON (the first archaeologist to be appointed to a New Zealand university), Murray Groves, and Bruce Biggs took turns as editor of *JPS*. They also infiltrated the Wellington-based council of the society. The editorship of the *JPS* has remained with the Auckland Anthropology Department, and the Auckland editors have given the journal a thoroughly professional appearance and content, drawing most of their material from academic colleagues at New Zealand universities and from abroad.

Most of the articles have been on social anthropology, linguistics, and archaeology, and the balance between New Zealand and Pacific material has gradually tilted in favor of the latter as the Pacific peoples, several of them in the process of gaining independence, became the focus of intense academic interest. A notable case was PAPUA NEW GUINEA, the anthropologists' last frontier. But old perennials, like the quest for Polynesian origins, have continued to tease scholars and fill the pages of the society's publications. That subject got a new lease of life when the society published Andrew Sharp's controversial *Ancient Voyagers in the Pacific* in 1956, and there have been numerous subsequent contributions published in *JPS* or as separate memoirs. The subject is far from exhausted, even today.

With the later establishment of Maori studies departments in most New Zealand universities, there was a greater involvement of Maori scholars in the journal and the society. In 1979, Bruce Biggs, the first professor of Maori studies at Auckland, became president of the society, and in the following year, the society's office was shifted from Wellington to Auckland, where it remains. In 1999, Biggs surrendered the presidency to his successor in the Maori studies chair, Sir Hugh Kawharu.

The society ended its first century as it had begun: a small band of dedicated scholars, now mainly university academics, who in their "spare" time continue to put together a journal that remains preeminent in its field.

M. P. K. Sorrenson

See also Polynesia; New Zealand: Historical Archaeology

References

Brown, Dorothy. 1993. *Journal of the Polynesian Society Centennial Index, 1892–1991.* New Zealand.

Sorrenson, M. P. K. 1992. *Manifest Duty: The Polynesian Society over 100 Years.* Auckland, N.Z.: Polynesian Society.

Sorrenson, M. P. K., ed. 1986–1988. Na To Hoa Aroha: *The Correspondence Between Sir Aprirana Ngata and Sir Peter Buck, 1925–50.* 3 vols. Auckland, N.Z.: Auckland University Press.

Pompeii

No archaeological site has captured the popular imagination like Pompeii, a prosperous Roman town on the Bay of Naples, some 200 kilometers south of Rome. It was effectively discovered in 1748; inscriptions and other finds made during the construction of an aqueduct between 1594 and 1600 had failed to raise interest. Destroyed by the eruption of Vesuvius in A.D. 79, ancient Pompeii covered 66 hectares within the city walls, with villas, cemeteries, and other in-

An arch and walkway in the ancient Roman city of Pompeii (Image Select)

stallations scattered around the perimeter. The site has been intensively excavated for 250 years, with work only occasionally overshadowed by that at other sites nearby, particularly HERCULANEUM. Some one-third of Pompeii remains unexcavated.

Excavations in the eighteenth century uncovered the theater, the Temple of Isis, and a number of other important structures in the western part of the town. The first plan of the site was produced in 1778, and Pompeii was firmly incorporated into the itinerary of the grand tour. Complaints about the conduct of the excavations began almost immediately (and have continued virtually unabated). The worst excesses probably occurred in the first half of the nineteenth century, when teams of up to 1,500 men began vast clearances. The excavations and the works of art they produced were sources of great pride for the Bourbon kings of Naples and were used extensively for political purposes. The main public areas emerged in this period (the Forum, the amphitheater), along with a number of luxurious houses. The houses were often cleared to a point at which the final uncovering of the wall paintings and mosaics could take place in the presence of visiting dignitaries, after whom the houses might then be named. These excavations were not conducted stratigraphically, and the documentation (especially regarding the objects found in the structures) was poor.

Some methodological improvement arrived in 1860, when the Bourbon kings were ousted and Giuseppe Fiorelli was appointed director of excavations for the newly unified Italian state. Although some contemporaries criticized Fiorelli's methods as lacking the appropriate intellectual and aesthetic ambition, the director's general approach and his establishment of a school of archaeology in Pompeii brought a new professionalism to the excavations. It was Fiorelli's idea to pour plaster into the cavities left by perishable material, which decayed only after volcanic ash had hardened around it, allowing the recovery of the shapes of humans, animals, furniture, and even tree roots. It has been estimated (though not very reliably) that 2,000 people perished in the eruption of A.D. 79 at Pompeii. Many residents escaped, and the town may already have been partially abandoned as the result of seismic activity in the decades preceding the final eruption. Pompeii is now regarded rather less like a time capsule than it was in the past.

In the twentieth century Vittorio Spinazzola (working from 1910 to 1923) and Amadeo Maiuri (from 1923 to 1961) cleared an enormous area of Pompeii, especially along one of the main streets of the town, the so-called Via dell'Abbondanza. Publication lagged badly behind, and Pompeii's structures suffered disastrously (especially from 1940 onward) from pollution, theft, tourism, earthquakes, bombardment during World War II, and, most particularly, neglect. Since 1980 the pace of excavation has slowed considerably, and a large-scale restoration program has been undertaken using mainly traditional materials, rather than the inappropriate modern materials used in the past. The most recent projects have concentrated on previously excavated structures, documenting what remains of the buildings and decorations in an attempt to recover the finds and their contexts; to better understand the building history of the structures and the urban development of Pompeii, digging often extends below the A.D. 79 level.

Ted Robinson

References

Descoeudres, J.-P. 1994. *Pompeii Revisited: The Life and Death of a Roman Town.* Sydney, Australia.

Etienne, R. 1992. *Pompeii: The Day a City Died.* London: Thames and Hudson.

Wallace-Hadrill, A. 1994. *Houses and Society in Pompeii and Herculaneum.* Princeton, NJ: Princeton University Press..

Zanker, P. 1998. *Pompeii: Public and Private Life.* Cambridge, MA: Harvard University Press.

Popenoe, Dorothy Hughes (1899–1932)

Trained as a botanist and a pioneer in the determination of cultural chronology in Honduran prehistory, Dorothy Hughes Popenoe conducted independent fieldwork in Honduras and sought the advice and sponsorship of A. M. Tozzer of the PEABODY MUSEUM at Harvard University. Her major works, published posthumously, dealt with the sites of Playa de los Muertos and Tenampúa in Honduras.

A brief memoir by Thomas Barbour, issued as an introduction to her posthumously published study of Antigua, GUATEMALA, and an obituary by Alfred M. Tozzer in *Maya Research* provide sketchy details of Popenoe's early life. She was born in Great Britain, and following World War I she worked as a technical illustrator at Kew Gardens in London. She developed enough expertise to establish new species of grasses in the scientific literature. Her relocation to Washington, D.C., in 1923 as an employee of the U.S. National Herbarium led to her marriage to Wilson Popenoe. Accompanying him to Honduras in 1925, after he accepted a position with the United Fruit Company, she began a brief but highly active career that was ended prematurely by her accidental death.

Popenoe's earliest work, published with her husband in 1931, was the report of a site uncovered during construction of a botanical station at Lancetilla, near Tela on the Caribbean coast of northern Honduras in 1925. The report mixes a scientific format, a description of each category of data, with a speculative vignette about life at the site on the eve of Spanish conquest. Since both Wilson and Dorothy Popenoe were accomplished botanists, it is no surprise that they attempted to present the archaeological data according to the standards of the time, including the use of general taxonomies of material culture, especially of lithics, that implied time depth. But the site could not be placed in any real context because of a paucity of available literature on Honduran archaeology.

Dorothy Popenoe's interest in archaeology was apparently engaged by this chance discovery. According to Barbour, she was determined not to be idle after her transfer to Honduras and had begun historical and ethnographic investigations. Following the Lancetilla excavations, she took a major step forward in archaeology by initiating excavations at Tenampúa in the Comayagua Valley in 1927, a fortified hilltop site that had been reported over fifty years earlier by American archaeologist E. G. Squier. Popenoe's Spanish-language report (1928), reissued in English after her death by the SMITHSONIAN INSTITUTION (1936), is most notable for drawing on sixteenth-century ethnohistoric documents in an attempt to identify the site.

Following her work at Tenampúa, Popenoe ranged widely in Honduran archaeology. In 1927, she began work at the hilltop site of Cerro Palenque on the Ulua River. Unfortunately, her field notes were lost, and she produced no report, although photographs in the Peabody Museum document the area of the site at which she worked. According to DORIS STONE, a contemporary who also worked in Honduras, Popenoe believed Cerro Palenque was a sixteenth-century fortress related to Tenampúa. An unpublished typescript on copper bells in the collections of the Tozzer Library at Harvard University may relate to otherwise undocumented work at La Majada caves in the Department of Santa Barbara, suggested by the donation to the Peabody Museum of bells with this provenience in 1930.

A report in 1910 by A. H. Blackiston had described a metal cache from a cave in the same region as probably the goods of a wandering Mexican Toltec trader and smith. It is likely that Popenoe was familiar with this report, as she cited another paper by Blackiston in the same journal. This paper had described burials eroding into the river at a site Blackiston called Playa de los Muertos, or "beaches of the dead." Popenoe chose the same name for the site of the burial excavations that initiated her collaboration with the Peabody Museum. She identified it as one of the locations explored in the 1890s by G. B. Gordon for the Peabody Museum, documenting her familiarity with his report as well.

Popenoe's published account of her excavations at Playa de los Muertos says that she broke off work at Cerro Palenque when reports of burials washing into the Ulua River a few miles downriver reached her in 1928. Her salvage of burials that season sparked her interest in the site, to which she returned the following year. By then she had made contact with Alfred M. Tozzer of the Peabody Museum, to whom she looked for guidance in her subsequent work. Although documentation for her initial introduction to Tozzer is lacking, later correspondence suggests that Thomas Barbour, who was a naturalist at the Museum of Comparative Zoology at Harvard and a member of the Peabody Museum's governing board, may have put Popenoe in contact with his archaeological colleague.

Tozzer supported the continuation of Popenoe's research in Honduras beginning with her second season of work at Playa de los Muertos. Correspondence relating to the collections from this site in the Peabody Museum shows that he encouraged her to use the work as an opportunity to clarify the relative chronological placement of monochrome and polychrome pottery in Honduras. The existence of two separate pottery complexes in the Ulua Valley had been established by G. B. Gordon, who felt they represented two separate cultures. Tozzer, who supervised George Vaillant's seriation of Mayan pottery, including the Ulua polychromes, believed the pottery types represented distinct time periods and urged Popenoe to seek burials, the contexts he believed best suited to establish chronological relationships, containing monochrome and polychrome pottery.

Popenoe exposed a series of burials at Playa de los Muertos now known to date to the middle formative period, preceding the Ulua polychromes of the classic period. Because she did not also find polychrome burials there, Popenoe continued to search for other sites with both ceramic complexes. Her excavations in 1930 and 1931 at Siguatepeque and along the Ulua River, described in manuscripts at the Peabody Museum and represented by collections deposited there, produced evidence of stratigraphic superposition. She describes her approach to these excavations as "the horizontal," or "onion-peel" method, resulting in identification of surfaces with dispersed remains of single vessels. She correctly interpreted the stratigraphy she isolated and related it to her results from Playa de los Muertos.

It was at this juncture that she unexpectedly died in 1932. Accounts of the cause of death cite accidental ingestion of poisonous akee, planted at the Lancetilla station. After her death, Tozzer prepared her Playa de los Muertos report for publication, framing it with a paper by George C. Vaillant that used the data from Playa de los Muertos to address the wider question of the origins of formative period culture. Although the Playa de los Muertos report is thus usually cited as the basis for the definition of the so-called Q complex, Popenoe's own discussion was quite different. It dealt with what today would be considered site formation processes, examining environmental data to explain the sedimentation and recutting of the site.

During a brief period of residence in Antigua, Guatemala, in 1930–1931, Popenoe came in contact with institutional archaeology through an acquaintance with Oliver and Edith Bayles Ricketson, who were directing the Carnegie Institution's research at Uaxactún. Her scientific training as a botanist and her willingness to follow the advice of specialists like Tozzer and the Ricketsons created for her the possibility of an alliance with professional archaeologists. But as an outsider, Popenoe did not automatically view her research through the lenses of those questions that had been established as important by the authorities. R. A. Joyce argues in *Women in Archaeology* (1994), that Popenoe virtually disappeared from subsequent archaeological literature primarily because she wrote from a standpoint outside the emerging academy.

Like other women with informal affiliations during this period, Popenoe was able to practice as a field archaeologist because of her freedom from the need for economic support. A recent commentary on her life by Daniel Schávelzon (1991) obscures her unique position, describing her as representative of "that so-peculiar group of archaeologists that came out of" the United Fruit Company. Schávelzon assumes that Popenoe was part of a "closed and select circle of the United Fruit Company" with Doris Stone, the other female pioneer in Honduran archaeology. This quite natural assumption is contradicted by correspondence as late as 1932 in which Tozzer comments on the fact that the Popenoes had never met Samuel Zemurray, Stone's father, and sketches an introduction for Stone herself. By subsuming Popenoe under the institutional aegis of the banana company, and by an apparently unsupported description of her as "rich and aristocratic," Schávelzon overemphasizes the ways that privilege would have smoothed her way.

It would be a mistake to underestimate the difficulties Popenoe faced in carrying out her groundbreaking basic research. Not only did she travel to sites that were accessible only on horseback, without the accompaniment of her husband, but during the few short years she worked in the field, she gave birth to four of her five children. Self-trained, she nonetheless adhered to high standards of excavation and documentation for the time. Her work at Playa de los Muertos remains one of the crucial sources for the early prehistory of Honduras.

Rosemary A. Joyce

References

Barbour, T. 1933. "Introduction." In D. H. Popenoe, *Santiago de los Caballeros de Guatemala*, vii–xii. Cambridge, MA: Harvard University Press.

Joyce, R. A. 1994. "Dorothy Hughes Popenoe: Eve in an Archaeological Garden." In *Women in Archaeology*. Ed. C. Claassen. Philadelphia: University of Pennsylvania Press.

Popenoe, Dorothy H. 1928. *Las ruinas de Tenampúa.* Tegucigalpa, Honduras: Tipografía Nacional.

———. 1934. "Some Excavations at Playa de los Muertos, Ulua River, Honduras." *Maya Research* 1: 62–86.

———. 1936. *The Ruins of Tenampúa.* Annual Report for 1935, pp. 559–572. Washington, DC: Smithsonian Institution.

Popenoe, W., and D. H. Popenoe. 1931. "The Human Background of Lancetilla." *Unifruitco Magazine* August: 6–10.

Rosengarten, F., Jr. 1991. *Wilson Popenoe: Agricultural Explorer, Educator, and Friend of Latin America.* Lawai, Kauai, HI: National Tropical Botanical Garden.

Schávelzon, D. 1991. "Dorothy H. Popenoe y la arqueología de Mesoamérica (1899–1932)." *Cuadernos de arquitectura mesoamericana* 14: 93–95.

Tozzer, A. M. 1934. Untitled obituary of Dorothy H. Popenoe. *Maya Research* 1: 86.

Portugal

The first Portuguese contacts with the Stone Age came through the navigators who reached the coasts of Africa, South America, and Asia in the fifteenth and sixteenth centuries. By A.D. 1500 these contacts had already resulted in the production of the first reports on such peoples as the Guanche of the Canary Islands, the San (Bushmen) of Southern Africa, and the Indians

ATLANTIC
OCEAN

Braga - Braccara Augusta
Citânia de Briteiros

Coa

Conimbriga

Abrigo do
Lagar Velho

Furninha
Casa da Moura

Zambujal
Muge

Salemas

SPAIN

Anta Grande do Zambujeiro

Tróia

N

Castro da Cola

0   100 km

Portugal

of BRAZIL, including accurate descriptions of polished stone axes and other tools. However, these descriptions failed to produce any impact on sixteenth- and seventeenth-century humanists and scholars who studied Roman and pre-Roman antiquities.

By the end of the eighteenth century archaeology had become an established discipline. The first scientific excavations in Portugal were undertaken at the time by Friar Manuel do Cenáculo, in the Iron Age settlement of Cola (Alentejo). Several descriptions and inventories were published of dolmens, which were correctly interpreted as pre-Roman monuments but generally thought to be altars, not burial chambers. And, as elsewhere in Europe, it was not until the mid-1800s that the concept of the remote antiquity of humanity was finally accepted, mainly as a result of developments in the geological sciences.

Beginning in 1848 several organizations were created to survey the geology of the country, and prominent members of their staffs, such as Carlos Ribeiro and Joaquim Filipe Nery Delgado, became interested in the problem of human origins. Ribeiro's work on the eolith problem and the possible existence of people in Europe in the Tertiary era is well known. It led scholars of the time to agree to convene the 1880 session of the Congrès International d'Anthropologie et d'Archéologie Préhistoriques in Lisbon in order to be able to inspect his sites and finds.

Delgado's work is not as well known but is of greater general methodological relevance. He was appointed to the Geological Survey in August 1857 at the age of twenty-two, but his first independent work was the geological mapping of the Peniche area. This project eventually led him to the excavation of the Casa da Moura cave site, which he began on January 19, 1865. The results obtained after initial testing led to the almost immediate publication of an extensive bilingual (Portuguese and French) monograph whose title, The Existence of Man on Our Soil in Very Remote Times Proved by the Study of Caves, leaves no doubt as to the research design that drove him in this early stage of his scientific career.

At that time the evidence from caves was re-garded as untrustworthy. It was the fluvial deposits of the Somme Valley that played a key role in the establishment of the remote antiquity of humans. They, in turn, were used to validate some of the associations between artifacts and extinct fauna found in various caves of Germany, England, FRANCE, and BELGIUM. Several objections had been raised against such evidence. Some argued that deposits of very different ages could easily be intermixed during the flooding to which caves are often submitted; others contended that the use of caves by people to bury their dead may have caused the occurrence of human bone in apparent association with extinct faunas; and still others suggested that although the deposits might have been originally undisturbed, mixing could arise from careless investigation.

Since his work was wholly based on the exploration of caves, Delgado had to deal with these objections, which probably explains the most remarkable characteristic of his monograph: the fact that it represents an integrated geo-archaeological approach to site-formation processes. Moreover, the great detail with which he recorded stratigraphic observations (the correctness and precision of which have since been demonstrated by reexcavation of the residual deposits at Casa da Moura) was intended to avoid any objections that his conclusions were based on careless excavation.

His most important find was a carefully described and measured human skull and mandible, which were enveloped in a matrix of concreted red sands just like the ones that composed the in situ lower deposit of the site. This cranial material was clearly of Pleistocene age and should therefore be counted, alongside better-known fossils such as the Engis adult skull and the Red Lady of Paviland, as one of those early findings of Upper Paleolithic human fossil remains that took place before the 1868 discovery of the Cro-Magnon burials. However, unlike the material at Paviland and Engis, the Casa da Moura material's age was correctly recognized and established by the discoverer.

Later revision of the Paleolithic artifacts from the cave identified Gravettian and Solutrean components. At that time, however, investigations in France had only just begun to address the question of the periodization of Quaternary human artifacts. Both ÉDOUARD LARTET's chronology, based on fauna, and GABRIEL DE MORTILLET's, based on lithic types, were presented to the first meeting of the Congrès International d'Anthropologie et d'Archéologie Préhistoriques, which was held in Paris in 1867, the year in which Delgado published his results. In this theoretical context, therefore, the only question that made sense was whether the lower deposit (and the skull derived from it), now known to date to the Upper Paleolithic, could be considered of Quaternary age.

The criteria used at the time to assess such an antiquity were twofold: paleontological, or the secure association of human remains or artifacts with extinct faunas, and geological, or secure association with deposits indicative of an earth not yet "modern in form"—that is, association with the "extensive and general deposits of loam and gravel" for which WILLIAM BUCKLAND coined the term *diluvium*. Later, after the abandonment of the equation between such deposits and the great deluge, loam and gravel deposits also became known as *drift*. Drift was unequivocally recognized as a distinctive stratigraphic unit, regardless of the debate that animated mid-nineteenth-century geology over whether it owed its genesis to flooding or glaciation. However, this unit was generally considered to be associated with the extinct faunas; hence "anterior to the [earth's] surface assuming its present form" then meant both modification of the earth's topography and faunal extinctions.

Since Delgado was unable to identify any representatives of clearly extinct species among the animal bones recovered in the lower deposit at Casa da Moura, he was obliged to resort mainly to geological arguments in order to try to establish its chronology. Noting that the matrix of this deposit was very similar to the diluvial sands that covered the surrounding plateau and filled its karstic fissures, he thought that the sediments in Casa da Moura had been derived from these surficial deposits and were therefore more recent. Yet they were older than the last geomorphological changes that had affected the area, since they contained no pottery. The fact that the absence of pottery could be used as an indicator of an earth "not yet modern in form" was demonstrated by the finding of shards in the lacustrine tuffs into which one of the small rivers of the plateau had cut its bed.

To complete his geological reasoning, Delgado also resorted to comparative analysis of the archaeological materials found in the lower deposit. In this context he noted that the primitive character of the artifacts and the absence of pottery indicated that they should predate the Danish *kjokkenmoddings* (kitchen middens). At the time, these were thought to be of late-Quaternary age. The resemblance of some of the flaked flints to similar materials reported by Carlos Ribeiro from diluvial deposits of the Tagus Valley further reinforced this argument. But Delgado also compared a rhomboidal bone fragment thought to be intentionally pointed, with the rhomboidal bone sagaie points found by Lartet at Aurignac. Although this last parallel is certainly ill founded, Delgado's suggestions proved to be generally correct. The lower deposit of Casa da Moura does belong to the same (Upper Paleolithic) period as Aurignac and does predate the Epipaleolithic shell middens.

The fact that geological and archaeological reasonings could be combined to produce chronological assessments was clearly dependent on the assumption of the integrity of the in situ lower deposit. Unless the integrity of these red sands could be demonstrated, the statement that the artifacts and the sediments that contained them were contemporary and undisturbed by subsequent events could come under attack on the grounds of Buckland's theories. Therefore, Delgado had to address the question of how the red sands were laid down. The discussion of this problem, embedded in an exposition of current knowledge on how caves were themselves formed, is a major and most interesting section of the monograph.

He determined that the lower deposit in Casa da Moura had not been washed in by floodwaters because the artifacts, bones, and charcoal it contained were not present in similar "diluvial" deposits found outside the cave, from which the interior deposits were presumably derived. Moreover, such a flooding process could not have produced the sorting of the different parts of the skeletons of the animals whose remains were found in the lower deposit. Other possible agents of accumulation, such as carnivores, could not account for the presence of charcoal and flaked flint in the deposit.

Given these factors, Delgado concluded that there was no known natural cause that could account for the mixed accumulation inside the cave of sands, éboulis, bones, and artifacts. He therefore developed his own alternative explanation. He viewed the formation of the deposit as a gradual and slow process, not as the result of one or several catastrophic flooding events. Otherwise, he thought, it would be impossible to explain either the presence of bone at all depths or the vertical and horizontal discontinuities in the concretion of the sands at all levels. He therefore thought that the remains of human dwellings suggested by the association of the animal bones, charcoal, and artifacts had gradually been incorporated into the deposit as it built up. The provenience of the sandy matrix was thought to be the diluvial deposits outside the cave. Since no natural process was identified by geological authorities at the time as a possible cause for such a gradual filling of a cave by external sediments, Delgado attributed this process to human action: the sands were thrown in to elevate the floor of the cave and thus facilitate human access through its vertical entrance. Although this explanation is certainly wrong in terms of the specific agency invoked, it is certainly much closer to modern ideas regarding the nature of the process described than the theories current in his time.

Another remarkable feature of Delgado's monograph is the attention given to the discussion of taphonomic (site formation) issues. Taphonomic observations were instrumental in rejecting the action of flooding waters as an explanation for the origin of the lower deposit, and they also played an important role in sustaining Delgado's evaluation of its faunal content. For instance, rabbits and birds were represented mainly by mandibles (jawbones) and broken long bones. There were far fewer vertebrae and pelvises than could be expected given the number of individuals represented by the

mandibles, and ribs were almost completely absent. The minimum number of rabbits, based on the counting of mandibles, was over 1,000. As for the larger mammals, Delgado observed that spongy bones were generally lacking and that the bones richest in marrow were the most fractured. But unlike the herbivore bones, the carnivore bones were generally intact and did not show any signs of having been transported by water, which was another argument against the flooding hypothesis as an explanation for the deposit's origin. Carnivores were also mostly represented by mandibles, and the majority of the animals found were young individuals. Delgado interpreted these observations as confirming his conclusion that humans were the agents responsible for the bone accumulation. At that time there was no known natural cause that could account for the apparent sorting of the different skeletal parts and the differential preservation of herbivore and carnivore bones.

With the benefit of hindsight, we now known that Delgado's conclusions are not completely correct. The variety of large, medium, and small carnivores (especially wolves) identified from the deposits suggests that the cave was also a carnivore lair. The important point here, however, is that in order to substantiate his behavioral interpretation, Delgado took what would now be considered the correct scientific approach. He tried to derive from the characteristics of the bone assemblage itself objective criteria that might lead to the identification of the agent or agents responsible for its deposition and modification. What was lacking at the time was a set of actualistic reference studies that might provide the patterns against which it would be possible to validate such identifications. This and Delgado's predisposition to favor human action as the explanation for the site's characteristics (an understandable inclination, given the research design that drove him) probably biased his diagnosis.

Delgado reported on the Neolithic human bone remains from the cave's upper deposit with a similar taphonomic approach. Their great fragmentation, the sorting of the different parts of the skeleton, and the fact that some bore what he thought to be marks of cutting by tools led him to conclude that the action of carnivores alone could not explain this set of characteristics and that they were evidence of cannibalism. In his era this behavior was commonly attributed to the "Celtic" peoples who inhabited Europe in pre-Roman times, as Delgado pointed out by extensively quoting such recognized authorities as JACQUES BOUCHER DE PERTHES, Laying, or Huxley and Spring, whose excavations at Chauvaux had led to similar conclusions.

He would develop this argument further based on the results of his later excavations at the Middle Paleolithic and Neolithic cave site of Gruta da Furninha, which he reported to the 1880 Lisbon conference. Applying a taphonomic approach to the issue of cannibalism, he completely excavated the deposit, carefully sieving all the sediments and taking note of the spatial distribution of the bones inside the cave. This enabled him to present quantified observations and to substantiate his arguments on differential body part representation with a statistical table of the counts for each skeletal part from each of the loci discriminated during the excavation. These showed, for instance, not only that several bones were not represented in the proportions they have in the human skeleton but also that such differential preservation was true for the distal and proximal parts of the same bone. Delgado conceded that there could be sample bias in the case of the smaller skeletal elements and that the low representation of spongy bones could be due to their greater perishability. However, he thought the other features of the assemblage, together with the breaks, burns, and supposed cut marks on the bones, could only be explained by human action. He therefore concluded that the deposit comprised the remains of cannibal meals.

Although this conclusion was accepted by some of the authorities present at the congress and subsequently proven true through chemical analyses showing that the bones had indeed been burned, the majority of the committee appointed by the congress to settle the issue did not agree with Delgado. Among his opponents were de Mortillet and EMILE CARTAILHAC. The latter rightly objected that the evidence instead suggested that people had been buried in the cave, not eaten there. Similar phenomena had been observed in dolmen burials and could be easily accounted for by the action of carnivores or the practice of successive burial, which would disturb and damage the bones from previous interments. However, the point to note once more is that, right or wrong, Delgado had pushed observation beyond the practices current in his time. This was recognized by the committee itself, which recorded in its proceedings a unanimous appreciation of the rigorous methodology of his work and of the statistical treatment of his data that it allowed, in an attempt to establish specific characteristics of bone assemblages that could be correlated with specific animal or human behaviors. Coupled with experimentation and extended to ethnoarchaeological contexts, this is what archaeozoologists and taphonomists still do today. Delgado therefore deserves to be more widely recognized not only as one of the earliest excavators of Upper Paleolithic sites and first finders of Upper Paleolithic human fossils but also as a pioneer in the geo-archaeological study of cave deposits and in those related fields that play such an important part in contemporary PALEOLITHIC ARCHAEOLOGY.

The tradition begun by Ribeiro and Delgado of doing Paleolithic research within the framework of the normal mapping activities of the Geological Survey was not continued until the middle of the twentieth century. The onset of World War II took HENRI BREUIL to Portugal, where, accompanied by Zbyszewski, a geologist of Polish origin who would settle in the country, he undertook a systematic survey of the Quaternary deposits along the coast and the main river valleys. As a result they produced a detailed cultural stratigraphic scheme of the Portuguese Paleolithic.

This scheme contained several weaknesses. On the one hand it was based on a strictly altimetric interpretation of both the raised beaches and the river terraces. On the other hand it was largely based on the type fossil system of interpreting certain kinds of artifacts as representative of whole industries. Furthermore, almost all of the sites studied consisted of surface scatters or mixed colluvial deposits in which different assemblages were distinguished, dependent upon the amount of patina the artifacts had developed. Artifacts with similar patina were thought to have been deposited at the same time and were sorted as kinds of stratigraphic units of a physicochemical nature. The assemblages thus distinguished were organized in a chronological sequence, the oldest being those presenting the most-developed surface weathering. In the decades that followed, the few new accidental finds that were made were accommodated to this scheme, whose methodological foundations were not questioned until quite recently. As a result, Quaternary geology and Paleolithic archaeology in Portugal did not participate in the enormous progress that was made elsewhere in Europe in the postwar period.

Breuil and Zbyszewski's scheme dealt mainly with the Lower and Middle Paleolithic. The Upper Paleolithic was largely ignored because of the dearth and poverty of cave assemblages, including the new sites excavated and studied by Jean Roche and O. da Veiga Ferreira in the 1950s and 1960s, such as Gruta das Salemas. Roche attributed this poverty to the fact that in the coastal areas of Portugal, the climate was temperate and humid during the Upper Paleolithic. This concept has been proven false by recent paleoenvironmental research, but it led Roche to believe that people lived mainly in the open and would only have used caves in exceptional circumstances. He may have been influenced by the fact that Manuel Heleno, then director of the National Museum of Archaeology, had discovered and excavated in the late 1930s and the early 1950s numerous open-air Upper Paleolithic sites in the Rio Maior and Torres Vedras areas.

However, these discoveries were never published, except via very short notices. Heleno was not an archaeologist in the modern sense of the word but a historian who wanted to establish the background of the "Portuguese nation." Therefore, he was mainly interested in establishing, using the equation

type fossil = Paleolithic industry = Paleolithic people

that such a background was European, not African. This question had become relevant be-cause of University of Oporto anthropologist A. Mendes Corrêa's suggestion of a common background between the peoples of the Capsian and those of the Muge shell middens, where hundreds of Mesolithic burials had been excavated from the mid-nineteenth century onward. Corrêa's concept of a *Homo afer taganus* as the origin of the Portuguese also had significant political implications during World War II, given the possibility of a German invasion and occupation of Iberia. In this context the identification of supposedly diagnostic lithic types among the assemblages recovered allowed Heleno to state that Aurignacian, Gravettian, Solutrean, and Magdalenian were indeed all represented in the country. This was enough to establish the European affiliation of the Upper Paleolithic of Portugal, as he had hoped, making it unnecessary, from the point of view of his research design, to publish extensively on the sites he had excavated.

Paleolithic research in Portugal gained a new momentum only after 1975. The major political and economic changes experienced by the country since that time have helped to transform what was until then a field largely dominated by amateurs and a few university professors into an almost exclusively professional activity, most of whose practitioners are now in private consulting and in the heritage departments of the central and municipal administrations. With regard to the Paleolithic, this progress was mostly the result of the development of the careers of professionals who originally came together as a group of university students—the Grupo para o Estudo do Paleolítico Português (GEPP)—and of the establishment of collaborative projects with different French and U.S. colleagues. The work of a new generation fully integrated with the international mainstream of the discipline rapidly bore fruit. Among the recent and most spectacular products of this collaboration were, in 1994, the discovery of the Côa Valley complex of open-air Paleolithic rock-art and habitation sites, included in the World Heritage List in 1998, and the pivotal role played by Portuguese sites (especially the Lagar Velho child burial) in the debates about Neanderthal extinction and modern human origins in Europe.

In spite of the fact that, currently, these Paleolithic finds have become Portugal's internationally best-known archaeological sites, most archaeology practiced in the country since 1800 has dealt principally with the later prehistoric periods and the era of Roman rule. Extensive excavations were carried out beginning in the mid-nineteenth century in the numerous *castros* (Iron Age hill-forts) of northern Portugal, the pioneer work of Martins Sarmento in the Citânia de Briteiros being of paramount importance in this regard. Other approaches tried to bring together archaeology, ethnography, and linguistics to procure a better understanding of the pre-Roman peoples of Portugal, and it was under the influence of such a program that the National Museum of Archaeology was founded, in the late 1800s, by J. Leite de Vasconcelos. Several fortified sites from the Copper and Bronze Ages were also extensively excavated in the twentieth century in central and southern Portugal. A good example is the site of Zambujal, first excavated by H. Schubart in the 1960s, which also well illustrates the role played by German archaeologists in this research (a delegation of the DEUTSCHES ARCHÄOLOGISCHES INSTITUT existed in Lisbon for some thirty years, until 1998), in the wake of the megalithic inventories made by Georg and Vera Leisner in war and postwar times. The most important methodological innovation of the postwar period, however, the introduction of SIR MORTIMER WHEELER's grid method, is due to E. Cunha Serrão, an active amateur who eventually would become the president of the Associação dos Arqueólogos Portugueses, founded in 1863.

Given the richness of the empirical record, including some of the largest dolmens known (such as the Anta Grande do Zambujeiro), megalithic research has been pursued by many Portuguese archaeologists and has become a popular research topic since 1970. As a result and although the clarification of chronological issues is still a major concern, attention has progressively shifted toward issues of spatial and landscape archaeology. Attempts at integrating the study of the funerary and other ritual monuments (menhirs and cromlechs) with the survey for and investigation of the contemporary settlement sites are commonplace in current Neolithic research. Indigenist views of the development of megalithic phenomenon as part of the increasing complexity of the first agricultural societies of Europe have also been completely removed from the debate. These comprised interpretations, common until the 1970s, that related it to oriental influences. But the issue of colonization is far from being settled, especially with regard to the large Copper Age hill-forts that spread through central and southern Portugal in the third millennium B.C.

Until quite recently in Portuguese archaeology, however, most efforts and resources were dedicated to the study of Roman antiquities. The most consistent archaeological project throughout the twentieth century was the excavation of the city of Conimbriga, and this was largely due to the commitment of the Institute of Archaeology of the University of Coimbra. Other sites, major by Portuguese standards but of relatively minor importance by international standards, have also been investigated, albeit to a lesser extent. Tróia, one of the largest industrial complexes connected to the processing of fish in the Roman world, is still largely unknown after 150 years of very discontinuous research. Since 1980 the development of salvage archaeology in urban environments has led to a major broadening of our knowledge of the Roman cities of Portugal, and this is especially the case with Braga (*Bracara Augusta*), but most of this work remains unpublished. Largely as a result of the same phenomenon, medieval archaeology and especially the archaeology of the period of Islamic rule are currently undergoing an explosion in terms of finds and resources devoted to their study. The same is true with underwater archaeology, and the fact that preliminary surveys have become mandatory in harbor works and humid areas has led to significant discoveries. These comprise, in continental Portugal as well as in the Azores, fifteenth-century vessels and their cargo; as a result, for the first time, the physical documentation of the construction of the caravels that pioneered European overseas expansion has been possible.

Several universities offer training in archaeology within the framework of their depart-

House of the Fountains at Conimbriga (Archivo Iconografico, S.A. / CORBIS).

ments of history, and the degree given at the end of study generally combines history and archaeology. Integration with geography and the natural sciences is still very weak, but recent efforts by the central administration are designed to change this situation through the creation of independent research units specifically devoted to the study of archaeology as human ecology. The growing number of professionals, however, is still insufficient to meet the market demand for salvage and contract work. Largely as a result of this, the main weakness of Portuguese archaeology these days is that scientific publications are seriously lagging behind. Yet the fact that the pressing needs of dealing with the material record on the ground fully occupy most professionals also has a positive side effect. Postprocessualism has not really had an impact, and, theoretically, traditional cultural-historical and processual approaches continue to dominate a field in which the main concern for many years to come should continue to be pursuing a thorough, high-quality documentation of a rapidly disappearing empirical record.

João Zilhão

References

Choffat, Paul. 1908. "Notice nécrologique sur J. F. Nery Delgado (1835–1908). *Jornal de Sciencias Mathematicas, Physicas e Naturaes,* 2nd series, 7, 8: 1–14.

Correia, A. A. M. 1947. "Histoire des recherches pré-historiques en Portugal." *Trabalhos de Antropologia e Etnologia* 9, 1–2: 115–170.

Delgado, J. F. N. 1867. *Da existência do homem em tempos mui remotos provada pelo estudo das cavernas,* vol. 1, *Notícia àcerca das grutas da Cesareda.* Lisbon: Comissão Geológica de Portugal.

———. 1884. "La grotte de Furninha à Peniche." In *Congrès International d'anthropologie et d'archéologie préhistoriques: Compte-rendu de la neuvième session à Lisbonne (1880),* 207–279. Lisbon: Académie Royale des Sciences.

Fabião, C. 1997. "Percursos da arqueologia clássica em Portugal: Da Sociedade Archeologica Lusitana (1849–1857) ao moderno projecto de Conimbriga (1964–1971). In *La cristalización del pasado: Génesis y desarrollo del marco institucional de la arqueología en España—Actas del II Congreso de Historiografía de la Arqueología en España (siglos XVIII a XX), 27 al 29 de noviembre de 1995 (Madrid),* 105–124. Ed. G. Mora and M. Díaz-Andreu. Málaga: Universidad de Málaga.

Ribeiro, C. 1873. "Sur la position des silex taillés découverts dans les terrains Miocène et Pliocène du Portugal." In *Congrès International d'Anthropologie et d'Archéologie Préhistoriques, Compte-Rendu de la 6ième session, Bruxelles 1872,* 95–100.

Zilhão, J. 1993. "As origens da arqueologia paleolítica em Portugal e a obra metodologicamente precursora de J. F. Nery Delgado." *Arqueologia e História,* series 10, 3: 111—125.

Potocka Zijalka

Potocka Zijalka is an alpine Paleolithic cave site in SLOVENIA, approximately 1700 meters above sea level, on the southern edge of the Karavanke mountain ridge on the Slovenian-Austrian border. The site was discovered by SRECKO BRODAR in 1928 and was systematically excavated until 1935.

The archaeological record comprises numerous cultural layers all belonging to the Wurm I–II phase of the Aurignacian period, around 34,000 years ago. Brodar's excavation revealed numerous finds, the most outstanding among them being 133 bone points of the Mladec, or elongated oval-shaped, type (also Lautscher type), the largest known collection of points of this type found in one site. Some of them have traces of the earliest known ornamentation of parallel incisions while others seem to be the prototype of a needle and a simple flute with three holes made from the cave bear's mandible. The total artifact assemblage consists of more than 100 tool types.

The vast majority (99 percent) of the faunal remains belong to the cave bear (*Ursus speleaus*) with the more poorly represented other species being musk ox (*Ovibus moscatus*), wolf (*Canis lupus*), and smaller mammals (*Micromammalia*). Several hearths containing charcoal of tree species *picea* and *pinus* were detected some 20 meters from the entrance to the cave. Owing to the extreme altitude and the artifact richness of the site, Brodar proposed that Olschevien (called after Olseva, the location of the Potocka Zijalka) was a distinctive cultural phase of the alpine Aurignacian hunters and gatherers. However, his proposal has not been accepted.

Drasko Josipovic

References

Bayer, J., and S. Brodar. 1928. "Die Potocka Hohle, eine Hochstation der Aurignacschwankung in die Ostalpen." *Prahistorica* (Vienna) 1.

Brodar, S., and M. Brodar. 1983. "Potocka zijalka, visokoalpska postojanka aurignacienskih lovcev." *Dela SAZU 24, class I and IV,* Ljubljana.

Poverty Point

Brought to public attention in 1873 by Samuel Lockett, Poverty Point is one of the most significant sites in North America, located near the Mississippi River in northern Louisiana. It is most closely linked to the work of JAMES A. FORD, who began research there in 1953. Constructed between 1730 B.C. and 1350 B.C. by a preagricultural people, the site features complex earthworks undertaken on a massive scale. The central construction is composed of six rows of concentric ridges, which are thought to have been 1.3 meters high originally. The five aisles and six sections of ridges created by this construction take the form of a wheel; the diameter of the outermost ridges measures three-quarters of a mile. Scholars believe that these ridges served as foundations for dwellings, although little evidence of structures has been found. However, features and midden deposits uncovered during excavations offer some support for this theory. Large earth mounds were also constructed on the site; among them are Poverty Point Mound, which measures about 210 by 195 meters at its base and is 21 meters high, and Mound "B," which is conical in shape.

We know quite a bit about the people who lived at Poverty Point. For example, they imported stone for projectile points from as far away as the Ouachita and Ozark Mountains. Indeed, the evidence indicates that Poverty Point was part of a major trading network that spanned the eastern United States.

Tim Murray

See also United States of America, Prehistoric Archaeology

References
Gibson, J. L. 1996. *Poverty Point: A Terminal Archaic Culture of the Lower Mississippi Valley.* Louisiana Archaeological Survey and Antiquities Commission.

Powell, John Wesley (1834–1902)

John Wesley Powell grew up in the midwestern portion of the United States, fought in the American Civil War, and later became an explorer of the Colorado River canyons. He began fieldwork among the Soshone, Ute, and Paiute Native American Indian peoples of the Great Basin and Grand Canyon regions. He founded the SMITHSONIAN INSTITUTION's Bureau of American Ethnology (BAE), which he directed from 1879 until 1902.

As an early anthropologist, geologist, and member of the Anthropological Society of Washington, D.C., Powell was an evolutionist. Greatly influenced by Charles Darwin, Herbert Spencer, and LEWIS HENRY MORGAN, he envisaged a rigid framework for human development. As director of the BAE, he supported the Cyrus Thomas Survey of North American Indian mounds and sponsored the fieldwork of archaeologists FRANK CUSHING and WILLIAM HENRY HOLMES, among others. He also supported the preparation of the 1891 linguistic map of North American native peoples and the collection of Native American Indian vocabularies.

Powell argued for applied government anthropology to improve reservation conditions; for federal government support of linguistic, archaeological, and ethnographic fieldwork; and for the preservation of antiquities such as Great Serpent Mound in Ohio and CASA GRANDE in Arizona. The publication of his own fieldwork was not realized until a century after his death; however Powell contributed many essays to the BAE's annual reports as its director.

Tim Murray

See also Mason, O. T.; United States of America, Prehistoric Archaeology

References
Zernel, J. J. 1983. *John Wesley Powell: Science and Reform in a Positive Context.* Ann Arbor: University Microfilms.

Prescott, William Hickling (1796–1859)

Born in Salem, Massachusetts, and educated at Harvard University, the partially sighted William Hickling Prescott became a prolific writer with a particular interest in Spanish history. *A Chronicle of the Conquest of Granada* (1829) and *History of the Reign of Ferdinand and Isabella the Catholic* (1838) were followed by *History of the Conquest of Mexico* (1843) and *History of the Conquest of Peru* (1847). The last two multivolumed works portrayed the AZTEC and INCA as civilized peoples and remain the standard authorities on the Spanish conquistadores in the New World. Both works brought Prescott widespread recognition in Europe.

Tim Murray

See also Mexico; Peru

Prestwich, Sir Joseph (1812–1896)

Born in London and educated at University College, London, Joseph Prestwich abandoned a career in chemistry to work in his father's wine merchant business. He took up geology and became particularly interested in stratigraphical analysis. His papers on the Tertiary geology of southeastern England and on Quaternary geology published in the mid-1840s and 1850s established his reputation and his place among the elite of British science. In 1874, Prestwich finally retired from business and took up the chair of geology at Oxford University.

In 1858, Prestwich was a member of the committee of the Geological Society of London that presided over the excavation of BRIXHAM CAVE by WILLIAM PENGELLY, but Prestwich agreed with Richard Owen and geologist SIR CHARLES LYELL that the evidence was not enough to establish greater human antiquity. In 1859, HUGH FALCONER insisted that Prestwich visit French archaeologist JACQUES BOUCHER DE PERTHES in France and examine the evidence of human antiquity that he had found in the Somme River gravels. Prestwich was persuaded of the validity of this evidence, and from then on he supported the notion of a high human antiquity and the value of the discoveries at Brixham Cave.

Prestwich was elected fellow of the Royal Geological Society in 1833 and fellow of the Royal Society in 1853. He was knighted in 1896.

Tim Murray

References
van Riper, A Bowdoin. 1993. *Men among the Mammoths.* Chicago: University of Chicago Press.

Prinsep, James (1799–1840)

If any person in addition to ALEXANDER CUNNINGHAM can be called a founding father of Indian archaeology, the honor should go to James Prinsep. He was the assay master of the East India Company mints and was posted first to Varanasi and then to Calcutta. Prinsep initiated the tradition of field investigations by members of the company and other European officials in various parts of the country where they traveled in their private capacities. Prinsep became the secretary of the Asiatic Society of Bengal in the 1830s and began the new and regular publication of the society, which continues even today: the *Journal of the Asiatic Society of Bengal* first appeared under his editorship in 1832. His stimulation and encouragement of the antiquarian interests of his European contemporaries in India has been well expressed by Abu Imam (1966, 21–22): "A new breed of officers arose who interested themselves in the mysterious remains of the country's past, although preoccupied with their official duties. . . . On their various rounds in the four corners of India, these officers began to shower on Prinsep coins, inscriptions and rubbings in profuse numbers. . . . Soon both the collectors and the interpreters were acting in a spirit of friendly competition."

Prinsep's own special fields of study lay in coins and inscriptions. He studied and cataloged a large series of north Indian coins, beginning with Roman coins in "upper India" (Prinsep 1832). His study of Greek coins in the possession of the Asiatic Society (Prinsep 1833) was the first study of the Indo-Greek phase of history in the northwestern part of the subcontinent. He was also astute enough to realize the significance of the nameless early historic coins of northern India, and in the Indian area he was certainly the first to appreciate the dating value of coins in archaeological contexts (Prinsep 1834).

It is, however, principally for his decipherment of the ancient Brahmi script of the Asokan inscriptions of the third century B.C. and of the similarly dated Kharoshti script (confined principally to the northwest) that Prinsep is most famous. The study of the late form of Brahmi script began in the late eighteenth century on the basis of its resemblance with the script form of late medieval Bengali and related manuscripts in eastern India. The task of decipherment then proceeded from the known to the unknown and culminated in Prinsep's reading of the Asokan inscriptions around 1837 (Prinsep 1837). He achieved this task between 1834 and 1838. The main source of study of the Kharoshti script for Prinsep was a series of Indo-Greek coins bearing royal names both in Greek and Kharoshti, which made the task of decipherment comparatively easier.

Pinsep's spirit comes through when, writing about the framework of archaeological researches in India, he advocates "the need of an independent pursuer of the object for its own sake; or for his own amusement and instruction" (Prinsep 1835, 623).

Dilip Chakrabarti

References

Imam, Abu. 1966. *Sir Alexander Cunningham and the Beginnings of Indian Archaeology.* Dhaka.

Prinsep, James. 1832. "Roman Coins in Upper India." *Journal of the Asiatic Society of Bengal* 1: 27–41.

———. 1833. "On the Greek Coins in the Cabinet of the Asiatic Society." *Journal of the Asiatic Society of Bengal* 2: 27–41.

———. 1834. "Note on the Coins Found by Captain Cautley at Behat." *Journal of the Asiatic Society of Bengal* 3: 227–228.

———. 1835. "On the Connection of Various Hindu Coins, etc." *Journal of the Asiatic Society of Bengal* 4: 623.

———. 1837. "Facsimiles of Ancient Inscriptions." *Journal of the Asiatic Society of Bengal* 6: 218–223, 278–288, 663–682, 869–887.

Proskouriakoff, Tatiana (1910–1985)

Tatiana Proskouriakoff was one of the greatest scholars of the MAYA CIVILIZATION. She made major contributions in the areas of Maya art and architecture as well as in the decipherment of Maya hieroglyphics.

Proskouriakoff was born in Russia in 1910 and emigrated to the United States with her family while still a child. She graduated from university with a degree in architecture just as the Great Depression set in. She was a wonderful artist, and her talents were spotted by Linton Satterthwaite, who at the time was excavating the classic Maya site of Piedras Negras, GUATEMALA, as part of a University of Pennsylvania project. He hired her as staff artist for the project, and her superb reconstruction drawings of ancient Maya sites and temples caught the attention of scholars working for the Carnegie Institution of Washington, D.C., at the time the largest and best-funded institution working in the Maya area. Proskouriakoff was hired by the Carnegie Institution in 1940 and spent the rest of her career as one of its staff archaeologists, working at sites such as Copan, Uaxactun, and Mayapan in Central America.

In 1946, Proskouriakoff published *An Album of Maya Architecture,* which is a compendium of her reconstruction drawings of classic Maya buildings. In 1950, she published *A Study of Maya Art,* a brilliant analysis of the motifs and details contained in Maya sculptural art that contained as a major component a technique for "style dating" monuments that had no legible dates. These two books immediately became "classics" in Maya studies.

But Proskouriakoff did not stop there and focused her attention on Maya hieroglyphs. In 1960 she published an article that is perhaps the most important in all of Maya studies. Cogently, and in great detail, she deciphered the dynastic sequence of Piedras Negras, identifying a 200-year succession of kings and their birth and accession dates at the site. Such work might not seem particularly earthshaking, but the article must be seen in the context of the then-current views on ancient Maya society. Increasingly over the previous thirty years or so, Mayanist scholars had come to the conclusion that classic Maya society was not ruled by secular kings but was made up of a peaceful rural peasantry overseen by a priestly class that lived almost as ascetics in otherwise unoccupied "ceremonial centers." Proskouriakoff's article changed this view overnight, and since the 1960s there has been a tremendous advance in the understanding of classic Maya society and politics. Scholars can now decipher Maya hieroglyphic inscriptions almost completely, and the intricacies of Maya politics within and between kingdoms are increasingly understood.

Proskouriakoff continued leading that aspect of Maya research until the Carnegie Institution withdrew from the field of Maya studies in the 1960s. By this time she was living in Cambridge, Massachusetts, and was affiliated with the PEABODY MUSEUM at Harvard University. Even in retirement, Proskouriakoff continued to make major contributions to the field: for instance, in 1974 she published a major study of the thousands of jade objects thrown into the sacred well at CHICHÉN ITZÁ, Yucatán, once one of the principal centers of the Maya.

Peter Mathews

See also Maya Epigraphy; Mesoamerica
References
Proskouriakoff, T. 1963. *An Album of Mayan Architecture.* Norman: University of Oklahoma Press.

Pueblo Bonito

Pueblo Bonito is the largest Anasazi site of CHACO CANYON in northwestern New Mexico. It is located on the north side of Chaco Canyon, between Chaco Wash and the canyon wall. Built in the Pueblo III style during the early tenth century, Pueblo Bonito has 800 rooms in a D-shaped complex over three acres, with evidence of earlier settlements underneath the remaining structure. Approximately 1,000 residents were accommodated by this site. Pueblo Bonito is characteristic of the southwestern Anasazi sites of the Pueblo III period, with Black-on-red pottery; rectangular pit houses; multistory, multiroom pueblos; and well-developed kivas.

Among the many sites of Chaco Canyon, Pueblo Bonito is remarkable for offering scientists a chance to accurately date the structures. Besides being the largest and most outstanding site of the time, Pueblo Bonito contains many wooden support beams. The wood was well preserved in the southwestern climate of dry heat and affords a uniquely precise insight into the timeline of the building. Dendrochronology, a DATING technique developed using tree rings to measure time, was used very successfully to pinpoint the age of the building. Pueblo Bonito has been accurately dated to between A.D. 919 and A.D. 1130 through tree-ring dating of the large number of wooden beams.

The structure itself is the most impressive site in the entire Southwest at this time for several reasons. It is the largest masonry structure; and judging by its sameness throughout was most likely planned as a unit. It contains many kivas (large meeting or ceremonial rooms), and is similar to pueblos nearby, but the scale of Pueblo Bonito is very large in many aspects. The walls are very thick and the rooms much larger than other pueblos. The walls are rubble-filled, with a shaped sandstone exterior that encloses an inner court. Pueblo Bonito is three to four stories high at the back, with one great kiva and several smaller kivas.

The site has advanced architecture and similarly complex cultural traits. This conclusion is reached, according to Lister and Lister, because of the social organization needed to create such a large and planned village. The site shows evidence of population increase, localization of the population, and craft specialization. All these factors represent a complex, stable social organization. Most likely the Pueblo Bonito site was influenced by the CASAS GRANDE sites in Mexico.

In an 1877 visit to Chaco Canyon William H. Jackson drew a map of the Pueblo Bonito site and a reconstruction. Pueblo Bonito was first photographed by Victor Mindeleff in 1888. From 1897 to 1899, George H. Pepper and Richard Wetherill cleared 189 rooms and several kivas, published in their field notes. Neil M. Judd completed excavation of the rest of Pueblo Bonito between 1921 and 1927. The more significant reports were published by *National Geographic Magazine.* Gordon Vivian of the National Park Service worked on stabilizing and opening more rooms in the 1930s. Judd and ANDREW E. DOUGLASS collected tree-ring specimens for dating, as did Deric O'Bryan at Gila Pueblo. Tree-ring dates range from A.D. 828 to 1130. Construction and minor reconstruction continued between two main building periods, first in the early tenth century, after A.D. 919, and the second in the second half of the eleventh century.

Many of the Pueblo Bonito rooms contained burials and funerary items, but do not contain remains of the entire population. Many rooms excavated were previously undisturbed, and had intact floors and ceilings which preserved artifacts that would normally deteriorate, such as wood, basketry, cordage, and shell. Pueblo Bonito is the most studied of sixteen great towns built in the Pueblo III era.

Danielle Greene

See also United States of America, Prehistoric Archaeology

References

Lister, Robert H., and Florence C. Lister. 1981. *Archaeology and Archaeologists: Chaco Canyon.* Albuquerque: University of New Mexico Press.

McGregor, John C. 1965. *Southwestern Archaeology.* Urbana: University of Illinois Press.

Ortiz, Alfonso, vol. ed. 1979. *Handbook of North American Indians: Southwest, Volume 9.* Washington, DC: Smithsonian Institution.

Thomas, David Hurst. 1989. *Archaeology.* Fort Worth: Holt, Rinehart and Winston.

Pumpelly, Raphael (1837–1923)

Raphael Pumpelly was born in CANADA, lived in the United States, and studied to be a mining engineer in Freiberg, Germany. In 1859 he returned to the United States to mine silver in Arizona, and in 1861 he went to San Francisco where he was appointed geologist for the Japanese government. When this job finished in JAPAN in 1863, Pumpelly traveled to CHINA and then, in 1865, made his way overland to Europe via central Asia and Siberia.

Pumpelly returned to the United States in 1869 and began to explore the copper and iron deposits of Michigan; in 1871, he became that state's state geologist. Ill-health caused him to resign, and he returned to the eastern states. In 1884, he began working for the New England Division of the U.S. Geological Survey under JOHN WESLEY POWELL. In 1903, the Carnegie Institution of Washington, D.C., hired him to organize and conduct expeditions to central Asia to look for prehistoric sites and evidence of climatic changes. His excavation of the site of Anau in Russian Turkistan led Pumpelly to propose an "oasis theory" for the origins of food production during the Neolithic period. This theory was based on the fact that as the Near East became drier after the last Ice Age, its hunter-gatherers were forced to group around water sources and domesticate wild animals and crops in order to survive. SIR GRAFTON ELLIOT SMITH, HAROLD JOHN EDWARD PEAKE, and HERBERT J. FLEURE popularized this theory during the two decades after Pumpelly's death, and VERE GORDON CHILDE was especially influenced by it.

Tim Murray

See also United States of America, Prehistoric Archaeology

Putnam, Frederic Ward (1839–1915)

After early training under Henry Wheatland at the Essex Institute in Salem, Massachusetts, Frederic Ward Putnam studied with Louis Agassiz and Asa Gray at Harvard University. After the revolt of Agassiz's students in 1863, Putnam returned to Salem, where he had been born, and founded and published *The American Naturalist,* directed the new (1868) Peabody Academy of Science, and pursued a career in ichthyology and herpetology.

Upon the death of Jeffries Wyman in 1874, Putnam returned to Cambridge, Massachusetts, as director and curator of the PEABODY MUSEUM of American Archaeology and Ethnology at Harvard. He became Peabody Professor of Anthropology as well in 1887, and he held all three positions until retirement in 1909. He served as permanent secretary of the American Association for the Advancement of Science (AAAS) from 1873 to 1898 and president of AAAS from 1898 to 1899. He was a founding member of the ARCHAEOLOGICAL INSTITUTE OF AMERICA in 1879 and was largely responsible for its early work in the Western Hemisphere. From 1891 to 1894, he served as chief of the Department of Ethnology of the World's Columbian Exposition in Chicago, directing the work of anthropologists Franz Boas, Alice C. Fletcher, Zelia Nuttall, Marshall Saville, George Byron Gordon, George A. Dorsey, Warren K. Moorehead, and many others. From 1894 to 1903, he served as curator of anthropology at the American Museum of Natural History in New York. He and Boas supervised the Jesup North Pacific Expedition and the Hyde expeditions to the American Southwest in the late nineteenth century. In

1903, he founded the Department of Anthropology at University of California, Berkeley, and served as professor of anthropology and director of the Anthropological Museum there until 1909. He was elected to the National Academy of Sciences in 1884.

A major institution-builder in early American anthropology, Putnam's significance derived primarily from his organizational abilities, his support for and influence on younger men and women (especially Boas and Alfred M. Tozzer), his pioneering work in preserving Serpent Mound in southern Ohio and other sites, and his popularization of North American archaeology. He and Boas jointly trained the next generation of anthropologists in the four-field tradition by dividing the labor: archaeology at Harvard, linguistics and ethnography at Columbia, physical (biological) anthropology at both.

His own archaeological fieldwork of the 1880s in southern Ohio (preceded by explorations in Kentucky and Tennessee and followed a decade later by work in California) established field methods on a new plane, with emphasis on attention to context (spatial, stratigraphic) of specimens, careful recording of the excavation process, viewing each site as a complex unit for purposes of study, and conservative excavation techniques. Deeply embroiled in the controversies of his generation over "ancient man" in North America, Putnam cautiously supported the claims of Charles C. Abbott and others for a presence of 10,000 or more years. Permanently influenced by his early zoological training under Agassiz, Putnam always evinced a preference for close description of the artifactual base and a reluctance to make broader generalizations.

Curtis Hinsley

See also United States of America, Prehistoric
  Archaeology

References

For References, see *Encyclopedia of Archaeology: The Great Archaeologists, Vol. 1,* ed. Tim Murray (Santa Barbara, CA: ABC-CLIO, 1999), pp. 152–154.

Q

Qatar

See Arabian Peninsula

Quatrefages, Jean Louis Armand de (1810–1892)

Jean Louis Armand de Quatrefages studied medicine at the University of Strasbourg and practiced as a doctor in the southwestern French city of Toulouse until 1840 when he moved to Paris to become a scientific writer and illustrator. De Quatrefages was a talented draftsman and began to work for the National Museum of Natural History in Paris while publishing extensively on invertebrate biology and classification.

In 1850, he was appointed to a university chair of natural history, but in 1855 he returned to the museum to take up the chair of anthropology (formerly anatomy and human natural history) and his research and publications became focused on anthropological issues. He was strongly opposed to Darwinian evolutionary theory and to the theories of English scientist Thomas Henry Huxley, and he remained firmly convinced that mankind had not evolved from apes but was a separate entity in the rest of the animal world. He was also against polygenism and an opponent of the French anthropologist Paul Broca.

Although a conservative, de Quatrefages was an early believer in the idea of human antiquity, which, allied with his anti-evolutionist views, explains why he was such an ardent supporter of the authenticity of the MOULIN-QUIGNON Jaw. De Quatrefages's major publication, *Crania ethnica* (1882), produced jointly with colleague Theo-

dore Hamy, followed the rejection of his arguments concerning the validity of the Moulin-Quignon fossil. The book stands as his most significant contribution to the debate about the nature of human physical evolution in Europe.

Tim Murray

See also Falconer, Hugh; French Archaeology in
the Classical World
References
Hamy, E. T. 1870. *Précis de paléontologie humaine.*
Paris: Ballière.

Quebec

In Quebec, it is said that everything began in 1960 with the outburst of what has been called the Quiet Revolution. This was the time when the people of Quebec decided to change their country, to cast aside fear and silence, to shake the traditional basis of social power, and to share in urbanized North America's every positive move toward success and efficiency. The gradual results of this changed perspective had quite an impact on archaeology.

In 1960, the 1,540,680 square kilometers of Quebec was perhaps the largest archaeological *terra incognita* in the whole western world. There were no university training programs, no governmental sponsorship of archaeological studies, and no professional archaeologists. The word *archaeology* itself had almost no meaning. It was culturally irrelevant.

Certainly several artifacts had been found since the establishment of Europeans in the area. For instance, Samuel de Champlain dug through a prehistoric Amerindian site in 1608 when he set the foundations of his trading post in Quebec City and the Jesuits found old Indian burials, as did many settlers. There is even a private collection of prehistoric artifacts assembled around 1700. However, such accidental meetings with relics of the past had little to do with the discipline of archaeology.

Early colonists in Quebec had just divorced European history and it took some time before they would call for a history of their own. They were busy creating the present, fighting for existence, and articulating a new way of life. They really had no time for history until the English told them they had none. To show that the English were wrong, the colonists of Quebec created throughout the nineteenth century a true database of their colonial history—but they did not use archaeology as it is now defined (Gagnon, 1978).

The database included miscellaneous collections from individuals who found material traces of missionary establishments on the shore of Lac St-Jean, excavated a Jesuit burial place in Quebec City, reported old French forts on the North Shore, and discussed whether some of the remains were left by Jacques Cartier's visits or where Champlain's burial place was, but these were unconnected events of no lasting value.

The archaeology of American Indians fared no better. The wild people had been both friends and foes of Quebec colonists during the earlier European occupation. They were considered interesting in as far as they had interacted in some ways with the settlers but, in the nineteenth century, although they were still of some importance to missionaries, fur traders, and some travelers, they were not interesting to most of the inhabitants of Quebec.

Some accidental discoveries were talked about for some time during the nineteenth century. The most important one was the Iroquoian site found in 1859 near the campus of McGill University and described by John William Dawson, principal of the university. Indian burials were also found in Trois-Rivieres and Valleyfield. Robert Sellar reported other chance findings in southwestern Quebec in 1888 and Montpetit talked about the discovery of Indian tomahawks on Pointe-du-Buisson. Joseph

Charles Tache collected antiquities from Huronia and other places but only one man became involved in the meaning of these material traces. He was a lawyer from Montreal, William Douw Lighthall (1857–1954). He went as far as to write a book on prehistoric Montreal in 1929 but never succeeded in publishing it.

Four years earlier, A. Gagnon had published his *Études archéologiques* (1925) but he had nothing to say about Quebec antiquities in this book, in which he confessed that his best friends told him that his interests in the past were useless. At about the same time, William J. Wintemberg (1876–1941) made a productive survey of southern Quebec (1927), but he never returned from Ottawa to excavate the sites he had located. One of these, the Lanoraie site, was excavated in 1932 by A. Beaugrand-Champagne but there exists no record of what he found.

Until 1940, only one small-scale but problematic excavation had taken place in Quebec, in 1915 in Tadoussac by the American ethnologist Frank G. Speck. In the following years a few more experts came to Quebec (Rogers and Rogers, Burger, Bradley, Ridley, and Taylor) and collected some artifacts. By 1960 the whole bibliography of published papers on archaeology in Quebec amounted to less than twenty titles, and these were of limited value (Martijn and Cinq-Mars 1970; Martijn 1974, 1978; Cinq-Mars and Martijn 1981; Clermont 1982, 1987).

From 1955 to 1960, archaeology developed as a topic of some interest within Quebec's regional communities. Gordon Lowther, Albert Gérin-Lajoie, Rene Lévesque, Gilles Boulet, Michel Gaumond, and others began to dream about some kind of involvement in Quebec Archaeology. This came about in the 1960s.

In the 1960s, avocational archaeologists such a Rene Lévesque, W. L. Bancroft, Rene Ribes, J. Henri Fortin, Thomas Lee, Robert Simard, Joseph Bérubé, James Pendergast, Clyde Kennedy, and others proved that good archaeological sites were to be found everywhere in Quebec. The Université de Montréal initiated a general program of archaeology in 1961. A Service d'Archéologie was created in the same year by the Ministry of Cultural Affairs. Gilles Boulet set up a Museum of Archaeology at Trois-

Archaeologists dig at the site of St. James Bay in Quebec (Dave G. Houser/Corbis)

Rivieres and launched the first archaeological review in the province with Rene Ribes. Roger Marois became the first graduate student in Quebec archaeology and major excavations were done at Côteau-du-Lac, Morrison's Island, Allumette Island, Pointe-du-Buisson, Batiscan, La Martre, Bourassa, Beaumier, Berry, Mistassini-Albanel and many other sites. SAPQ (Société d'Archéologie Préhistorique du Québec) and Parcs Canada did especially good jobs. Regional societies became active and historic archaeology also became important at Ile aux Noix, Place Royale, Côteau-du-Lac, and Forges du Saint-Maurice.

The new interest in archaeology in Quebec was due to negative feelings of being late and left behind in this field of knowledge and to a more positive articulation of self within CANADA. A new desire to know exactly what had happened in the past replaced authoritative and uncritical judgement by the people of Quebec about themselves, about others, and about the past. At the same time that archaeology developed, the need for good ethnology and for a

new kind of history developed as well. This important ideological shift and the development of archaeology was part of Quebec's new involvement with science. While being pleased by and involved with this new flow of knowledge, would-be archaeologists also had to learn how to contribute in a positive way to these trends. They focussed on obtaining facts, leaving no time for analysis and interpretation.

By the 1970s the Université de Montreal had created a special program of Quebec Archaeology (1973) along with a summer field-school (1977). The Université du Quebec à Montreal (UQAM) also presented an undergraduate program in archaeology, as did McGill University. The Ministry of Cultural Affairs organized a more efficient direction for archaeology and ethnology, passing a new law on cultural heritage (1972). When large hydro-electricity developments were launched in northern Quebec in 1972, there were summer jobs for all archaeologists surveying and excavating before the sites were covered by water. Out of this, students created private companies to survey the area and to salvage the most important sites. With archaeological data piling up in files and on shelves, some major publications appeared, proving that Quebec territory was no longer *terra incognita.*

Among both historic and prehistoric archaeologists there were important meetings about the orientation and the management of field archaeology. The new topical review *Recherches Amérindiennes au Québec,* created in 1971, published important research results. Other publications included the state collections of *Dossiers, Civilisation du Québec, Cahiers du Patrimoine,* and *Activités archéologiques* and other collections such as *Paléo-Québec,* Mercury series. In 1979 a new archaeological association was founded. At the end of this decade of work, Quebec archaeology was securely included within the prehistoric and historic research that was being done in Northeastern North America.

In the 1980s, Quebec archaeology moved into fieldwork programs, rescue interventions, publications, a centralized inventory, public diffusion, and so on. Cultural history, reliable sequencing, paleoethnography, and inventories of material culture were the dominant objectives of research. Quebec is as large as FRANCE, SPAIN, ITALY, and GREECE put together. It contains a large range of ecology, from northern tundra to southern closed deciduous forests. Barren land Inuit, boreal forest Algonquian hunting groups, and horticultural Iroquoian societies were all using this land when Europeans arrived, and the lifestyle of each of these groups was the result of long regional cultural developments. A single generation of archaeologists only had the time to sample this huge diversity, and to sketch what had happened in it since the end of Pleistocene.

The first synthetic overviews of Quebec archaeology, *Archeologia,* edited by Chapdelaine in 1978, and writings by Wright in 1979, soon became obsolete and have not been updated. The reason is that the fast-growing data bank on Quebec archaeology can no longer be easily and simply summed up. In the 1980s it became obvious that the study of archaeology in Quebec was bound to be an endless task. This was because Quebec's territory was so huge, there were only a handful of archaeologists,

and cultural development within it proved to be complicated.

The archaeologists of Quebec did not let these obstacles overcome their curiosity and desire for knowledge. Although overburdened and calling for assistance, Quebec archaeologists continued their work throughout the 1980s and the 1990s with undiminished enthusiasm.

New research has focussed on zooarchaeology (Osteotheque Inc.) and on restoration. A center for archaeological investigation and formation opened in Chicoutimi (UGAC). Long-term studies in Ungava, southwestern Quebec, the James Bay area, the Gaspe Peninsula, Cap Tourmente, Tadoussac, Tracy, Downtown Quebec City, Chambly, the lower North Coast of St. Lawrence, Lake St-Jean, Temiscouata, and many eastern townships have proved to be very productive.

Quebec archaeology has reached international standards of quality and professional productivity. There has never been a lack of sites, and the standards of academic outcome are as good as any. New theoretical problems about the origins of Iroquoian agriculture, Dorset-Thule cultural articulation, long-distance exchange of material goods, demographic archaeology, zooarchaeology, adaptation, methods of colonization, industrial impact, Basque implantation, and many other topics are discussed. Cooperation with other specialists in many other fields is a day-to-day occurrence.

Looking back to the early 1960s, Quebec archaeologists are proud of how far they have come, but are still dissatisfied. Full-time archaeologists undertaking fieldwork, analysis, and interpretation of Quebec antiquities are few. Eight archaeologists work in universities, four in museums, and fifteen in their own contract archaeology companies, which hire students for summer work. About twenty others have jobs in administration, heritage advising, or college education. All in all, fewer than fifty archaeologists are involved full time with archaeology in Quebec. The ratio of archaeologists to the population is less than one to 140,000 and to available land is less than one to 30,000 square kilometers. Approximately fifty more archaeologists work part time, especially in the summer.

Quebec archaeology has mostly been written in French and is easily available in local publications. Unfortunately very few English-speaking archaeologists have ever had access to this literature.

As early as 1943, Ringuet called for a Quebec commitment to archaeology in his book *Un Monde etait leur empire*. There is not much that remains relevant in this book today, except as ideological evidence. Anything that happened in the long history of humankind is important and relevant to archaeologists because it is a way to share in the inquiry about the development of this world. Quebec is part of and a contributor to this world history of mankind. Quebec archaeologists work abroad in MEXICO, ECUADOR, France, the Near East, the West Indies, and Carthage as part of important archaeological research programs.

Now a whole new generation of Quebec archaeologists are discovering information about the different groups who came to and shared this country over the last 10,000 years. Their contributions are already promising, refreshing, and welcome. Until the 1960s, English-speaking archaeologists had been the most active scholars in Quebec, but since then French speaking archaeologists have become the most numerous. It is hoped that Amerindians will be part of the next generation.

Norman Clermont

References

Archeologia, ed. 1978. *Le Canada depuis l'origine*. Paris: Dossier de l'Archéologie 27.

Clermont, N. 1982. "Quebec Prehistory Goes Marching In." *Journal Canadien d'Archéologie* 6: 195–200.

Clermont, N. 1987. "La préhistoire du Quebec." *L'Anthropologie* 91, 4: 847–858.

Chapdelaine, C., ed. 1978. *Images de la prehistoire du Québec*. Montreal: Recherches Amerindiennes au Québec, vol. 15: 1–2.

Cinq-Mars, J., and C. Martin. 1981. "History of Archaeological Research in the Subarctic Shield and MacKenzie Valley." In *Handbook of North America Indians, volume 6, Subarctic*: 30–34. Ed. J. Helm. Washington, DC: Smithsonian Institution.

Gagnon, S. 1978. *Le Québec et ses historiens de 1840 à 1920*. Quebec: Presses de l'Université Laval.

Martijn, C. 1974. "Etat de la recherche en préhistoire du Quebec." *Revue de géographie de Montréal* 28, 4: 428–441.

Martijn, C. 1978. "Historique de la recherche archéologique au Quebec." In "Images de la préhistoire du Québec," 11–18. *Recherches Amerindiennes du Quebec* 15, 1–2. Ed. C. Chapdelaine. Montreal.

Martijn, C., and Cinq-Mars. 1970. "Aperçu sur la recherche préhistorique au Québec." *Revue de géographie de Montréal* 24, 2: 175–188.

Wright, J. V. 1979. *Quebec Prehistory*. Toronto: Van Nostrand Reinhold.

R

"Race" and Ethnicity, Archaeological Approaches to

Concepts of race and ethnicity have played an important role in the production of archaeological knowledge throughout the history of the discipline. One of the first questions that antiquarians and archaeologists have asked of the physical remains that they deal with is, Who was responsible for these creations? The answers have almost always been sought in terms of named groups of people, and embedded in these attributions are theories about the nature of the groups concerned. Here, the concepts of race and ethnicity have taken center stage, alongside the related concepts of culture, nation, and tribe. Yet despite their apparently straightforward role in the initial naming and classification of archaeological remains, race and ethnicity have a checkered history within the discipline. Their complex and overlapping meanings and uses have changed dramatically over time, as have the different theories surrounding them. They have also been implicated in some of the major epistemological shifts within the discipline. Finally, archaeological interpretations of race and ethnicity have been intricately bound up with the construction of modern ethnic, national, and racial identities, adding greater weight and urgency to the development of critical approaches to these concepts within the discipline.

Race, Culture, and Language

During the nineteenth century the study of archaeological remains became intertwined with the task of defining the "races" of humanity. A complex range of theories and definitions developed over this time, but a number of general trends can be observed. Race was thought to be *the* primary basis of human differentiation. Other concepts that later became associated with very different forms of group identity—concepts such as nation, ethnic group, and tribe—were often used interchangeably, but they were all heavily racialized. Races were regarded as discrete, objective entities, each possessing its own unique character. Scholars attempted to identify and describe the different races of humanity on the basis of empirical criteria. Physical and anatomical features were given a primary role in the definition of races, but language, psychology, and cultural and intellectual ability were also seen as important. Indeed, racial theories posited a direct relationship between biological and cultural capabilities, and it was argued that physical features such as cranial shape and size determined cultural and intellectual ability. Research was also devoted to explaining the origins of different races, which entailed the study of the historical and evolutionary relationships between them. Many different disciplines were involved in the study of race, including anthropology, archaeology, philology (historical linguistics), biology, psychology, and anatomy, and the individual scholars often moved between two or more disciplines. Recent historiographical studies of nineteenth-century theories of race include George Stocking's *Culture and Evolution* (1968), Michael Banton's *The Idea of Race* (1977), and I. Hannaford's *Race: The History of an Idea in the West* (1996).

Archaeological research played an important role in the development of racial typologies and in historical and evolutionary theories of race.

Johann Friedrich Blumenbach (1752–1840) is often called the father of physical anthropology and the first to develop a scientific concept of race. He divided the human race into five types: Caucasian, Mongolian, Malay, Ethiopian, and American. (Image Select)

Likewise, theories of race had an important impact on the development of archaeological theory and method. Human remains from archaeological sites provided evidence for the definition of racial types on the basis of metric analyses of skeletal components. In the European context the most common mode of racial classification was based on measurements of the shape and size of the skull, and the distinction between the dolichocephalic (longheaded) northern races and the brachycephalic (roundheaded) southern races became particularly significant in debates about European prehistory. Human skeletal remains were especially important sources of evidence in debates concerning the longevity of specific races and disputes about the permanence or fluidity of racial traits and groups.

Archaeologists, for their part, often used direct associations between material culture and skeletal material as the basis for the attribution of racial categories to specific archaeological cultures. However, the widespread claim that cultural capabilities were directly tied to racial heritage meant that archaeologists could apply racial attributions to their evidence even in the absence of skeletal remains. During the late nineteenth century broad similarities in forms of technology, subsistence, architecture, and art were used as means of distinguishing the so-called lower and higher races according to an evolutionary scale ranging from savagery through barbarism to civilization. There was little concern with the history of particular racial groups; rather, the focus was on the establishment of a universal history of race through the comparative study of both ethnographic and archaeological material culture. Good examples of such an approach can be found in the work of Gen. AUGUSTUS PITT RIVERS (see, for instance, *The Evolution of Culture* [J. L. Myres, ed., 1906]) and John Lubbock (LORD AVEBURY)(see, for instance, *Pre-historic Times* [1865]). For a recent overview of such work, see Bruce Trigger's *A History of Archaeological Thought* (1989).

By the early twentieth century the emphasis in both archaeological and anthropological research was starting to shift away from an overarching concern with social evolution and toward an interest in the particularistic histories of specific racial groups. Strong resemblances between material culture assemblages were regarded as de facto evidence for a shared racial heritage or, as it was often phrased, an "affinity of blood." One of the forerunners of this approach in Europe was the German scholar GUSTAF KOSSINNA, who developed and applied the method of "settlement archaeology." His approach was based on the axiom that sharply delineated archaeological culture areas coincide with clearly recognizable peoples largely conceived of in racial terms. To trace the history of present-day racial groups, he argued for a retrospective approach whereby the historically attested settlement of a specific group could be traced back into prehistory on the basis of a continuity in associated styles of material culture. Historical linguistics also provided an important source of evidence, as race, language, and culture were assumed to be closely interrelated and coeval with one another. On the basis of this methodology he claimed that it was possible to identify major prehistoric racial groups, such as the Aryans and the Slavs, and trace their relationships through time. The work of others, such as the early archaeology of VERE GORDON CHILDE, although of a very different political persuasion, was embedded in similar concepts and methodology, as exemplified in Childe's book *The Aryans* (1926). The conflation of race, language, and culture in the study of archaeological remains can be confirmed by a glance though the volumes of any early archaeological journals. For more recent historiographical overviews see Colin Renfrew's *Archaeology and Language* (1987), K. Sklenár's *Archaeology in Central Europe* (1983), and Siân Jones's *Archaeology of Ethnicity* (1997).

The Politics of Race

Racial typologies and classifications remained all-pervasive throughout the nineteenth century and the first few decades of the twentieth century, penetrating many aspects of social life and informing ideological and political debates. The idea that the physiological characteristics of particular races determined cultural and intellectual ability, allied with evolutionary theories, provided a convenient way to justify relationships of power in the context of slavery and colonialism. For instance, applied to colonial America or Africa, such approaches placed the indigenous inhabitants lower down on the evolutionary ladder and members of European "civilization" at the top. Archaeologists maintained this idealized evolutionary racial hierarchy by going to great lengths to attribute "sophisticated" sites and assemblages to migrating races of European or Near Eastern origin (despite evidence to the contrary) rather than to the supposedly backward non-European races. For classic examples see Peter Garlake's *Great Zimbabwe* (1973) and R. Silverberg's *Mound Builders of Ancient America* (1968). Recent historiographical studies highlighting the politics of racial theory and the role of archaeology more generally include Bruce Trigger's *A History of Archaeological Thought* (1989) and "Archaeology and the Image of the American Indian" (*American Antiquity* 45,

1980), Martin Bernal's *Black Athena* (1980), and K. Sklenár's *Archaeology in Central Europe* (1983); further case studies are provided by contributions to a number of books in the One World Archaeology Series (Routledge), in particular *Archaeological Approaches to Cultural Identity* (S. J. Shennan, ed. [1989]) and *Social Construction of the Past: Representation as Power* (G. C. Bond and A. Gilliam, eds. [1994]).

The concept of race played an equally important role in European politics of the nineteenth and early twentieth centuries. Nations were conceived of in racial terms, and states justified their actions toward one another and their own populations on the basis of racial theory. Once again archaeology's role in legitimizing and informing contemporary political thought concerned historical relations between races, in particular the evolution of European civilization. Archaeological evidence was employed in the competition between nation states as to whose racial pedigree was superior and which nations had played a decisive role in the development of European civilization. The most notorious case in this regard is the way in which the Nazi regime used the work of archaeologists, including Kossinna, to support its misplaced claims about the superiority of the Germanic race, contributing to the ideological apparatus that supported the destruction of millions of Jews in the Holocaust. Other European nations also employed archaeological evidence in support of racial theories that would be used to legitimate their relationships with others. The English, for instance, used archaeological evidence to emphasize their Roman and Anglo-Saxon heritage and to justify their superiority over the Welsh, the Scottish, and particularly the Irish, all of whom were considered to be racially inferior. For an overview of the German case see Bettina Arnold's "The Past as Propaganda: Totalitarian Archaeology in Nazi Germany" (*Antiquity* 64, 1990); for an analysis of the English case see Richard Hingley's *Roman Officers and English Gentlemen* (2000).

Culture-History and Typology

The political importance of race in contemporary society goes some way toward explaining why the concept was so all-pervasive and persistent until the 1920s and 1930s. However, race politics also contributed to the demise of race within the social sciences because those in contemporary institutions abhorred the notion of race and the practices associated with it. By the 1930s a critique of the concept of race was emerging in archaeology, just as it was in social and cultural anthropology, as expressed in J. S. Huxley and A. C. Haddon's *We Europeans: A Survey of Racial Problems* (1935). This critique consisted less of an attack on the concept of race per se than of a dismantling of the correlation of cultural and physical groupings and a questioning of the appropriateness of the concept of race for archaeological analysis. For instance, in "Races, Peoples and Cultures in Prehistoric Europe" (*History* 18, 1933), Childe argued that any confusion between cultural-linguistic and physiological similarity should be studiously avoided, as culture is a "social heritage" that has no direct link to the physical traits acquired through heredity. Writing in the early 1930s, Childe was concerned with the political implications of archaeological research, most notably the political use of Kossinna's claims about the superiority and the purity of the Nordic Aryan race. This concern to distinguish race from cultural forms of differentiation was heightened following World War II and the ensuing outrage over the political appropriation of the past under the Third Reich. Racial-ethnic labels, such as the "Germani," the "Aryans," and the "Indo-Europeans," were avoided by many due to their political associations. Following the rejection of the grand evolutionary schemes of the late nineteenth century, the empiricist trend that emerged was consolidated, at least in Europe. However, the emphasis now was on the description of empirical evidence in terms of artifact "types" and "archaeological cultures," rather than on past peoples.

By the mid-twentieth century the definition of culture areas had become the principal means by which prehistory was delineated in space and time, producing a mosaic of discrete peoples and cultures. But despite the uncoupling of race and culture, the culture concept carried over many associated ideas about the nature of human groups, in particular their holistic, bounded, and homogeneous character. The normative theories of culture that were employed were based on the idea that within a given group, cultural practices and beliefs tended to conform to prescriptive ideational norms or rules of behavior. Further, these norms were said to be maintained by regular interaction within the group and the transmission of shared cultural norms to subsequent generations through the process of socialization. A culture was therefore regarded as the product of a particular society or ethnic group, and at the same time it was assumed to provide the distinguishing characteristics of that group. Within an archaeological framework such ideas led to the assumption of a fixed and one-to-one relationship between material types and particular past peoples, even if they were no longer referred to as races. Thus, as Ulrich Veit argued in "Ethnic Concepts in German Prehistory" (in *Archaeological Approaches to Cultural Identity*, S. J. Shennan, ed. [1989]), the term *archaeological culture* became merely a quasi-ideology-free substitute for the terms *race* and *ethnic group*. Peoples of the past still lurked behind the apparently neutral archaeological cultures. Useful summaries of the place of culture-history in the archaeological traditions of various European countries can be found in contributions to *Archaeological Theory in Europe* (I. Hodder, ed. [1991]). For a discussion of developments in other regions of the world see the contributions to *Theory in Archaeology: A World Perspective* (P. J. Ucko, ed. [1995]).

Recent Approaches and Debates

During the 1960s and 1970s a concerted shift occurred in archaeological theory and method with the emergence of the "New Archaeology" (later more widely referred to as "processual archaeology"). The normative concept of culture that had dominated traditional archaeology was overturned within New Archaeology. It was argued that culture constitutes an integrated system, made up of differently functioning subsystems such as subsistence, exchange, politics, ideology, and religion. Consequently, it was argued, archaeological remains must be regarded as the product of a variety of past processes, rather than simply a reflection of ideational norms. Hence any one-to-one link between cultural variation and past peoples (ethnic groups, tribes, races) was broken. Cultural variation could arise from numerous social processes, often linked to functional and adaptive requirements. The identification of cultures became regarded as a preliminary stage in archaeological research—the necessary classification of archaeological "facts" prior to interpretation. However, descriptive historical reconstructions of past cultures and peoples were no longer considered to be the primary objective of archaeological interpretation.

There are a number of exceptions to this general picture, all of which are rooted in a reconceptualization of ethnicity as an aspect of social organization, rather than a passive reflection of normative culture. Work in social anthropology—for instance, *Ethnic Groups and Boundaries* (F. Barth, ed. [1969]) and *Urban Ethnicity* (A. Cohen, ed. [1974])—emphasized that the recognition and expression of group identity or ethnicity are social processes usually related to economic and political relationships between groups. Ethnic identity, it was argued, involves the active maintenance of cultural boundaries in the process of social interaction, rather than a passive reflection of cultural norms. Ethnicity thus becomes an aspect of social process and yet another component of the social system (alongside subsistence, economics, politics, religion, and so on) that requires processual analysis. Recent overviews of anthropological approaches to ethnicity are provided by Thomas H. Eriksen in *Ethnicity and Nationalism* (1993) and by Banks's *Ethnicity: Anthropological Constructions* (1996).

Following these developments, two main areas of research can be identified in the archaeological literature of the 1970s and 1980s. The first comprised studies concerned with the relationship between material culture and ethnic symbolism. For instance, on the basis of ethnoarchaeological research in Baringo, Kenya, I. Hodder (*Symbols in Action* [1982]) argued that there is rarely a one-to-one correlation between cultural similarities or differences and ethnic groups. He demonstrated that the kinds of material culture involved in ethnic symbolism can vary between different groups and that the expression of ethnic boundaries may involve a limited range of material culture, even as other material forms and styles may be shared across group boundaries. Others studies include R. Haaland's research on Sudanese Nubia (*Norwegian Archaeological Review* 10, 1977), A. Praetzellis and colleagues' examination of Chinese-American identity (in A. Saski, ed., *Living in Cities* [1987]), and R. Larick's analysis of Loikop Sanbura spears (*World Archaeology* 18, 1986).

The second main area of research concerned the role of ethnicity in the structuring of economic and political relationships. Thus, for instance, Hodder also showed how the maintenance of ethnic boundaries in the Baringo District related to modes of subsistence and control over resources. Drawing on this ethnoarchaeological research, he and others attempted to examine similar processes in late–Iron Age Britain (see Blackmore et al. in B. C. Burnham and J. Kingsbury, eds., *Space, Hierarchy and Society* [1979]). A rather different example is provided by E. M. Brumfiel's analysis of ethnicity in the AZTEC state (in E. M. Brumfiel and J. W. Fox, eds., *Factional Competition and Political Development in the New World* [1994]). State representations of identity, Brumfiel argues, were fashioned to suit the needs of particular political factions. The Aztecs sought to override particularistic ethnic identities within regional elites, but at the same time they promoted derogatory ethnic stereotypes that served to reinforce the superiority of the civil state culture.

These studies clearly situated ethnicity as an active social process, rather than a passive reflection of shared cultural norms. Nevertheless, they perpetuated the idea of ethnic groups as discrete, coherent wholes. Since 1990, however, archaeologists have started to challenge the very existence of ethnic groups in the form of bounded, monolithic, territorially based entities. Instead, it is argued that the construction of ethnicity (and cultural identity in general) is a situational and dynamic process that can take diverse forms in different contexts of social interaction. The material world both informs such processes of identity construction and is used in the communication of similarity and difference, which ethnicity inevitably entails. Thus, from an archaeological perspective, it cannot be assumed that there is any fixed relationship between particular material types and particular identities. And furthermore, rather than consisting of neat, coherent cultural entities, the resulting pattern is more likely to be a complex web of overlapping styles of material culture relating to the repeated realization and transformation of ethnicity in different social contexts. Examples of such an approach to ethnicity are provided by Stephen Shennan in his introduction to *Archaeological Approaches to Cultural Identity* (S. J. Shennan, ed. [1989]) and by Siân Jones in *Archaeology of Ethnicity* (1997). Peter Wells's analysis entitled "Identity and Material Culture in the Later Prehistory of Europe" (*Journal of Archaeological Research* 6, 3, 1998) provides a convincing application of such an approach. Other general studies of cultural identity that reach similar conclusions include Julian Thomas's *Time, Culture and Identity* (1996) and Andrew Jones's "Where Eagle's Dare" (*Journal of Material Culture* 3, 3, 1998). Studies focusing on the discourses involved in the construction of identity, particularly the role of myth and tradition, are also becoming common; for instance, see Jonathan Hall's *Ethnic Identity in Greek Antiquity* (1997).

Conclusions: The Present Past

Recent research focusing on ethnicity in archaeology has overturned many traditional assumptions about the discrete, bounded, and homogeneous nature of cultures and the straightforward link between culture and identity that is central to culture-historical archaeology. But studies focusing on ethnicity still tend to be sporadic. The relationship between cultures and ethnic groups remains a problematic area of archaeological analysis. There is, therefore, a pressing need for further research, at the very least because of the role of archaeological knowledge in the construction of modern ethnic and national identities. Of all the recent developments concerning identity in archaeology, perhaps the most significant in terms of its impact on the discipline as a whole is the concern with the role of archaeology in the construction and legitimation of na-

tional identities. The 1980s and 1990s witnessed an increasing body of conferences, symposia, and publications devoted to this topic. (Examples include the contributions to *Nationalism and Archaeology in Europe,* M. Diaz-Andreu and T. C. Champion, eds. [1996]; *Nationalism, Politics and the Practice of Archaeology,* P. L. Kohl and C. Fawcett, eds. [1995]; *Nationalism and Archaeology,* J. Atkinson et al., eds. [1996]; and Philip Kohl's overview entitled "Nationalism and Archaeology" in *Annual Review of Anthropology* 27, 1998.) Clearly, traditional approaches to race and ethnicity have enabled history, place, and people to be tied together in an exclusive and monolithic fashion, reinforcing essentialist representations of ethnic and national identity in the present. The challenge for archaeologists is twofold. First, they must recognize the relationship between present constructions of group identity and our interpretations of the past. And second, rather than abandon the study of ethnicity and identity altogether, they must pursue more sophisticated analytical and interpretive approaches in order to ensure that essentialist perspectives are not merely imposed on the past.

Siân Jones

References

Specific references have been included in the preceding text. Here, only overviews, syntheses, or compilations of articles are listed.

For discussions of early approaches to race and ethnicity and their relationship to other developments within the discipline, see K. Sklenár, *Archaeology in Central Europe* (Leicester, UK: University of Leicester Press, 1983); B. Trigger, *A History of Archaeological Thought* (Cambridge: Cambridge University Press, 1989); and P. Ucko, ed., *Theory in Archaeology: A World Perspective* (London: Routledge, 1995).

For overviews of recent research into ethnicity in archaeology, see S. Jones, *The Archaeology of Ethnicity* (Routledge, 1997); R. H. McGuire, "The Study of Ethnicity in Historical Archaeology," *Journal of Anthropological Archaeology* 1 (1982); B. Olsen and Z. Kobylinski, "Ethnicity in Anthropological and Archaeological Research: A Norwegian-Polish Perspective," *Archaeologia Polona* 29 (1991), as well as other articles in the same volume; and G. Emberling, "Ethnicity in Complex Societies: Archaeological Perspectives," *Journal of Archaeological Research* 5, 4 (1997).

For studies of the role of archaeology in the construction of colonial and national identities, see B. G. Trigger, "Alternative Archaeologies: Nationalist, Colonialist, Imperialist," *Man* 19 (1984); P. Kohl, "Nationalism and Archaeology," *Annual Review of Anthropology* 27 (1998); contributions to G. C. Bond and A. Gilliam, eds., *Social Construction of the Past: Representation as Power* (London and New York: Routledge, 1994); M. Diaz-Andreu and T. C. Champion, eds., *Nationalism and Archaeology in Europe* (University College, London, 1996); P. L. Kohl and C. Fawcett, eds., *Nationalism, Politics and the Practice of Archaeology* (Cambridge: Cambridge University Press, 1995); and John A. Atkinson, Iain Banks, and Jerry O'Sullivan, eds., *Nationalism and Archaeology* (Glasgow: Cruithne Press, 1996).

Friedrich Ratzel (Science Photo)

Ratzel, Friedrich (1844–1904)

Born in GERMANY and educated at Munich University, Friedrich Ratzel originally studied zoology. After graduating in 1869 he spent six years traveling before returning to Munich to study for a doctorate in geography. He is one of the most important figures in the development of nineteenth-century geography, and he contributed to the development of ethnology as a separate discipline in the German-speaking world.

Ratzel's work focused on the influence of the environment on human life and on political geography. He also supported German colonialism, inventing the word *lebensraum* ("living space"), used later by the Nazis as a means of justifying territorial expansion in the 1920s, 1930s, and 1940s. Ratzel also coined the term "anthropogeography," which was used during the nineteenth century to distinguish the discipline now known as human geography.

With colleagues FRITZ GRAEBNER, Leo Frobenius, and Wilhelm Schmidt, Ratzel founded the cultural-historical school of anthropology. His concept of a culture area (*Kulturkreis*) was widely used within both German and American anthropology and in describing cultural regions such as Melanesia and Mesoamerica, becoming one of the common concepts within the disci-

pline. Ratzel taught for most of his life at the University of Leipzig and wrote about diffusion and diffusion routes, another fundamental interest of the cultural-historical school.

Tim Murray

References

Heine-Geldein, R. 1964. "One Hundred Years of Ethnological Theory in the German-Speaking Countries: Some Milestones." *Current Anthropology* 5: 407–418.

Ravdonicas, Vladislav I. (1894–1976)

A member of the Communist Party and a theoretician, Vladislav I. Ravdonicas led the movement to create a new Marxist archaeology in the Soviet Union during the 1920s and 1930s. In a paper, "For a Soviet History of Material Culture," Ravdonicas criticized the theoretical positions of such prominent Russian archaeologists as Aleksandr Miller and VASILIY GORODCOV, which in some cases led to their being dismissed and exiled. The State Academy for the History of Material Culture, led by the Stalinist Nicolay Marr, ensured that Ravdonikas's protégés occupied leading positions within the discipline.

Although this approach to archaeology had dire consequences and many limitations, it also resulted in some interesting interpretations and directions within the discipline. Because Russian archaeologists had to concentrate on how ordinary people lived, they undertook large-scale excavations of settlements, camps, and work sites and therefore collected important data in the areas of Paleolithic and Neolithic houses and settlements in particular.

Tim Murray

See also Russia

Rawlinson, Sir Henry Creswicke (1810–1895)

Henry Creswicke Rawlinson was born in England the son of wealthy middle-class parents. He took up a military cadetship in the East India Company in 1827 and while serving in that capacity met the governor of India, Sir John Malcolm, a diplomat and oriental scholar who inspired and encouraged the young Rawlinson's prodigious interest in languages. In 1839, he was sent to Persia (now IRAN) to help reorganize the Persian army by raising regiments from frontier tribes in order to prevent the spread of Russian influence toward India. Also in 1839, he helped with the crisis in Afghanistan, becoming a British political agent in Kandahar where he raised Persian cavalry that fought in subsequent battles with the Afghanis.

Rawlinson continued to study throughout his military career, and his language and leadership abilities were so exceptional that he was appointed to explore unknown areas of the subcontinent, central Asia, and the Middle East. These included Susiana (now southwestern Iran) in 1836, and in 1838 he explored Persian Kurdistan for the Royal Geographic Society, for which he was awarded the society's gold medal. It was during this trip that he first became interested in cuneiform inscriptions. In 1843, Rawlinson became a political agent for the East India Company in Turkish Arabia, as well as becoming a British consul in Baghdad, and combined his new interests in epigraphy and archaeology with his diplomatic career.

Henry Creswicke Rawlinson (Hulton Getty)

He began to locate and copy, decipher, and translate Persian cuneiform inscriptions and to publish them in the *Journal of the Royal Asiatic Society*. At the same time that he was working in Iraq and Iran, several other scholars of philology in England and Ireland were endeavoring to decipher cuneiform from the direction of its vowel systems. All of the independent translators, including Rawlinson, were given an undeciphered inscription to test their ability. The results so closely resembled each other that cuneiform was officially recognized as deciphered—an epigraphic triumph similar to that by the great French philologist JEAN-FRANÇOIS CHAMPOLLION in the field of Egyptian hieroglyphics. But it was Rawlinson's translations of inscriptions "in the field" that were the most important contribution—and earned him the title of the first successful decipherer of cuneiform.

Rawlinson returned to England in 1849 and was commissioned by the BRITISH MUSEUM to excavate in Babylonia for the benefit of that institution's collections. In 1851, Rawlinson was asked by the British Museum to revise the second half of the early cuneiform texts brought back by SIR AUSTEN HENRY LAYARD from NIMRUD. From this work he published *Inscriptions of Assyria and Babylonia* (1850) and *Outline of the History of Assyria as Collected from the Inscriptions by A. H. Layard* (1852). He remained involved with Layard's collection and oversaw the publication of six volumes of inscriptions between 1861 and 1880.

In 1856, Rawlinson resigned his diplomatic position and returned to England for good to become a member of Parliament. He became a trustee of the British Museum in 1876 and remained one until his death. He continued to be involved in the Royal Asiatic Society and was its president from 1878 to 1881, and he was president of the Royal Geographic Society 1871–1872 and 1874–1875. Rawlinson helped with the state visits of the shah of Persia in 1873 and 1889 and was a royal commissioner for the Paris Exposition of 1878 and the India and Colonial Exhibition of 1886. He was made a baronet in 1891.

Tim Murray

See also Mesopotamia
References
Lloyd, S. 1980. *Foundations in the Dust: The Story of Mesopotamian Exploration.* 2d ed. London: Thames and Hudson.

Reinecke, Paul (1872–1959)

A German pre- and proto-historian and chief curator at the museum in Munich, Paul Reinecke contributed to European archaeology for over fifty years while remaining independent of the influential archaeologist GUSTAF KOSSINNA and the German cultural-historical school under FRIEDRICH RATZEL and FRITZ GRAEBNER.

Reinecke's interests ranged from the Neolithic to Roman provincial archaeology, but he is best known for his studies of and interest in categories of objects, such as metal helmets and fibulae from the late Bronze and early Iron Ages. It was Reinecke who named the later Bronze/early Iron Age period "Halstatt" after the cemetery and mining site excavated in AUSTRIA on Lake Halstatt. The later Iron Age was named "LA TÈNE" after a site in SWITZERLAND. De-

tailed typological analyses of these objects and of funeral rites and rituals of this period enabled him to differentiate between northwestern German and Scandinavian developments and to propose his own southern German Iron Age regional variations.

Tim Murray

See also Celts; Germany

Reisner, George Andrew (1867–1942)

George Andrew Reisner was an eminent Egyptologist, a pioneer in the archaeology of NUBIA and the Sudan, and the organizer of the world's first archaeological salvage project. He was born in 1867 into a German-American family in Indianapolis, Indiana. A youthful interest in the ancient Near East led him to study Assyriology and Semitic languages at Harvard, where he graduated in 1889 and took a Ph.D. in 1893. He then went abroad for further study in GERMANY, at that time the world center for Near Eastern research. While in Berlin, however, he fell under the spell of the great Egyptologists Adolf Erman and Ludwig Borchardt, who diverted the young American's interests from the Near East to Egypt. In 1897, he accompanied Borchardt to Egypt and assisted him for two years in the enormous task of cataloging the collections in the Egyptian Museum of Antiquities.

Reisner began fieldwork in 1899 when he led a University of California expedition excavating at Naqa el-Derr in Middle Egypt. In 1903, the expedition transferred its activities to the enormous necropolis of Giza, in the shadow of the Great Pyramids, the area that was the major focus of Reisner's activities for the rest of his life. When funding from the University of California was discontinued in 1905, Reisner organized the Harvard-Boston Expedition, a joint enterprise of Harvard University and the Boston Museum of Fine Arts, and remained its director for nearly forty years.

The Harvard-Boston Expedition was originally designed to work only in Egypt, but a development in 1907 resulted in a major enlargement of its focus. The first Aswan Dam (now often called the Low Dam) was then under construction in southern Egypt, and when completed, it was destined to flood nearly 100 miles of the Nile Valley. The threatened region was politically a part of Egypt, but ethnically and historically it was the most northerly part of Nubia (usually called lower Nubia), a land whose culture and history had always been different from those of Egypt. In anticipation of the threatened destruction of archaeological sites, the Egyptian director-general of antiquities persuaded the Egyptian Survey Department to undertake the Archaeological Survey of Nubia and invited Reisner to be its director. It was, in fact, the world's first major archaeological salvage campaign.

The Archaeological Survey of Nubia was active from 1907 to 1911. Reisner served as its director only in the first season, 1907–1908, but during that time he developed the field methodology that was to be followed in all subsequent seasons as well as by later expeditions in Nubia for almost half a century. The expedition confined its attention almost wholly to cemetery sites, bypassing town sites, because they mostly appeared to be of recent date, and bypassing temples, which were later to be studied by epigraphic specialists. In the excavation of graves, however, Reisner was thorough and systematic. Encountering almost at once the remains of several previously unsuspected Nubian cultures, he developed a chronological sequence for them that has generally stood the test of time, as well as typologies of the various grave and pottery types encountered.

Most important, he introduced for the first time the use of standard recording forms in the field to replace the unsystematic daily diary that was the usual method of documentation among Egyptologists. During the course of a brief return to Harvard in 1908, Reisner gave a course in archaeological field methods, based mainly on his Nubian experiences. It was attended by ALFRED V. KIDDER, SYLVANUS MORLEY, and other budding American archaeologists, who later credited Reisner with teaching them the use of standardized recording procedures.

The directorship of the Archaeological Survey convinced Reisner that a rich and largely unexplored field of investigation was awaiting the archaeologist in Nubia. In 1913, therefore, he began a series of excavations that would eventually encompass nearly all of the most monumental sites in the more southerly portion of Nubia, which then lay within Anglo-Egyptian Sudan. Over a period of twenty years, the Harvard-Boston Expedition excavated the great early Nubian necropolis of Kerma; most of the huge brick fortresses that Egyptian pharaohs had built in Nubia; a complex of Kushite temples at Napata; and all of the royal tombs of the Kushite monarchs and their queens, both at Napata and at Meroe. This work resulted in the development of a chronological framework that is still basic to the understanding of Nubian prehistory and history.

Notwithstanding the monumental importance of his work in Nubia and the Sudan, Reisner's first love was apparently always Egypt. The Harvard-Boston Expedition ceased its activities in the Sudan after 1932 but continued at Giza until the director's death a decade later. The Giza excavations were models of excavation methodology and recording for their time, and they furnished the enormously rich Egyptian collections that are now found in the Boston Museum of Fine Arts. The single most spectacular discovery was the tomb of Hetapheres, the mother of Khufu of Great Pyramid fame. Given the amount that was already known about Egyptian archaeology and history, however, Reisner's overall contribution in this field was not on the same scale was his work in the Sudan, where his name and work still stand preeminent.

Reisner's fieldwork and his publications exhibit a concern for systematics that was decidedly rare for his time. He developed not only a chronological sequence for the prehistoric Nubian cultures that he had first discovered but also a detailed chronology for all of the seventy-odd rulers of the empire of Kush, and for their queens, based mainly on the typological study of their royal tombs. In Egypt also he worked out the early development of tomb types, again based on seriational methods. Although there have been some subsequent modifications in these schemes, their major outlines remain unchallenged. For each of the culture periods that he investigated, Reisner also developed formal typologies of pottery and other artifacts. Finally, his introduction of the use of standard grave-recording forms has already been mentioned. He was fond of saying that a well-conducted excavation should be recorded in such a way that future scholars could reconstruct every detail of the conditions found by the original diggers. His British colleague, Herbert Winlock, asserted that Reisner was the greatest excavator of Egyptian antiquities then alive, while WALTER B. EMERY went so far as to assert that he was the greatest archaeologist America had ever produced.

Although from 1910 onward Reisner held appointments both as professor of Egyptology at Harvard and as curator of Egyptian Art at the Boston Museum, he was quintessentially a field man. He spent nearly the whole of every year in the Nile Valley, digging in Egypt in the summer and in the Sudan in the winter, and returned only intermittently to give courses at Harvard and to attend to his curatorial duties at the museum. His later years were plagued by poor health and failing eyesight, which eventually forced him to give up his university appointment, but he remained active as director of the Harvard-Boston excavations until the end of his life. He died in his field camp on the Giza Plateau on 6 June 1942.

Because of his almost single-minded dedication to fieldwork, Reisner published final reports on only a few of his excavations. After his death, final reports on most of his Sudan excavations were published by his longtime assistant and colleague, Dows Dunham, and William Kelly Simpson published individual reports on many of the Giza tombs.

William Y. Adams

See also Africa, Sudanic Kingdoms; Egypt:
    Dynastic; Egypt: Predynastic

References

Dunham, D. 1958. *The Egyptian Department and its Excavations.* Boston: Museum of Fine Arts.

Wilson, J. A. 1964. *Signs and Wonders upon Pharaoh.* Chicago: University of Chicago Press.

Remote Sensing

Remote sensing has been defined as the science and art of obtaining information about an object, area, or phenomenon through the analysis of data procured by indirect means. In other words, information is obtained by the use of a device that is not in direct contact with the subject under investigation. In the broadest sense, different techniques can be considered as remote sensing. These range from subsurface sensing methods, such as ground-penetrating radar, seismometer, and soil resistivity, to the analysis and interpretation of the electromagnetic energy radiated from the surface of the earth, recorded on air- and spaceborne platforms in the form of aerial photography, and satellite and radar imagery. This article deals only with the latter forms.

Basic Principles of Electromagnetic Energy

In simple terms, electromagnetic energy is the energy that is emitted or reflected from all objects. The emission of this energy is picked up by special airborne or spaceborne sensors and is processed in photographic or digital form. In reality, only the sun emits strong enough electromagnetic energy to be picked up by the sensors; the remaining objects on the earth's surface will reflect the energy they receive from the sun. Visible light is the most common form of electromagnetic energy, but other familiar forms of electromagnetic energy are heat, ultraviolet rays, radio waves, microwaves, and X-rays.

Electromagnetic energy radiates in waves that travel in harmonic sinusoidal movements. The length of the waves varies, and in the process gives place to a range of wavelength variation known as the electromagnetic spectrum. The part of this spectrum that we are more familiar with is the optical wavelength, which is divided into several bands for remote sensing purposes. The visible light that can be perceived by the human eye forms a fraction of the optical wavelengths. It comprises the blue, green, and red bands with a wavelength range that goes from about 0.4 to 0.5 μm, 0.5 to 0.6 μm, and 0.6 to 0.7 μm, respectively. Outside the visible range adjoining the blue band is the ultraviolet band (UV), which has a wavelength

The still-enigmatic Nazca geoglyphs in Peru were not discovered until the 1920s, when planes began to fly over the desert; the glyphs, often over 100 meters in diameter, are visible only from the air. (Marilyn Bridges / Corbis)

ranging from 0.3 to 0.4 μm. On the other end, following the red band, are three different categories of infrared (IR) waves: near-IR (.07–1.3 μm), mid-IR (1.3–3 μm), and thermal-IR (less than 3 μm).

Length of wave is of prime importance in remote sensing because it will determine the type of interaction that electromagnetic energy will have with the objects sensed from the earth's surface. For example, the blue band is able to penetrate water bodies; thus it is particularly useful in coastal mapping. The red band is useful for sensing chlorophyll absorption and, hence, in differentiating vegetation cover from nonvegetation, including cultural features, while the near-IR has proved useful for determining vegetation types.

On the other side of the spectrum, we have the microwave radiation of electromagnetic energy, which consists of radio waves that range from 1 millimeter to 1 meter in length, and it cannot be recorded by standard optical means but it can be recorded by special radar. Radar is the acronym for *radio detection and ranging,* and

as its name suggests, it uses radio waves to detect the presence of objects and determine their position. Radar imagery, then, is rather different from aerial photography or satellite imagery. The latter are passive sensors that depend on the sun as the source of electromagnetic energy and can therefore use only the visible and infrared wavelengths of the spectrum to create images. Radar is an active sensor that emits its own electromagnetic energy in the form of radio waves to create images.

Aerial Photography

Remote sensing in the form of aerial photographs has been used in archaeology since at least the early 1900s. J. Capper is credited with having taken the first photographs of an archaeological site, Stonehenge, from a hot air balloon in 1906. These photographs, however, were more a novelty than a conscious archaeological venture. The first conscious use of aerial photography for archaeological purposes was in 1913 when Sir Henry Wellcome took photographs of his excavations in the Sudan using a box kite. And between 1919 and 1921, there occurred the first systematic application of aerial photography by European and American archaeologists, working in MESOPOTAMIA and the Cahokia Mounds, Illinois, respectively.

Since many archaeological sites leave no traces detectable at ground level but can produce distinctive soil patterns that are easily discernible from the air, archaeologists saw the clear advantages that aerial photography offered and readily embraced this new tool. The decade of the 1920s witnessed a boom in the use of aerial photography in archaeology. In 1925, Poidebard traced ancient caravan routes that led to Roman fortifications in Syria, and ALFRED KIDDER and Charles Lindbergh photographed a series of archaeological sites while flying over the Yucatán Peninsula and the American Southwest.

The onset of World War II in Europe not only did not stop the use of aerial photography, it virtually furthered its development. For obvious reasons, aerial photography was perfected during this period, both by technological innovations in aircraft and cameras and by further developments in its interpretative principles. In this process archaeologists played a leading role; some, such as GLYN DANIEL, were even recruited by the military as photo interpreters.

The success of these early ventures and the developments in the technique that followed World War II secured a place for aerial photography in archaeology. However, the differences between the European and North American academic traditions, along with differences in the nature of the archaeological sites per se, resulted in very distinct approaches in the use of this new method of archaeological survey. European archaeologists were more concerned with a classical-historical approach and centered their efforts on site detection. North American archaeologists, on the other hand, who by this time had been greatly influenced by JULIAN STEWARD's cultural-environmental approach, put the emphasis on more regional approaches.

These theoretical orientations had an important effect on the preferred method of aerial photography that was adopted. In Europe, where the main interest was the architectural characteristics of spectacular sites, oblique photography was favored because of the better perspective that it produced. This method assisted European archaeologists in the discovery of thousands of sites throughout the countryside. In the Americas, where archaeologists put greater emphasis on anthropological issues such as subsistence activities, vertical photography was the preferred method because it facilitated regional mapping in which the location of archaeological sites was considered in relation to resource areas. Examples of this type of project are Ralph Solecki's 1952 Missouri River survey and GORDON WILLEY's 1953 seminal settlement pattern study of the VIRÚ VALLEY in PERU.

But interpreting aerial photography to locate sites and/or resource areas is just the initial stage in archaeological research. Regardless of the method applied—oblique or vertical photography—the archaeologists' final intent is to map the features that are of relevance to their research. The application of reliable methods to measure the observed features with the intent of producing a map is a subject covered by photogrammetry. Through the application of the principles of photogrammetry, the photo interpreter can quantify—in terms of location and extent—the interpreted features on the surface of the earth. Thus, the quantification process complements the information obtained by the initial interpretation and is geared toward identifying what features are present in the photograph, where they are on the ground, and over what areal extent.

With the advent of more sophisticated methods of remote sensing, such as satellite and radar imagery, the new developments in aerial photography technology have centered more on photogrammetry computer applications, image enhancing, and digital photography. Nevertheless, because of its lower cost, greater scale, and extensive coverage, the traditional black-and-white aerial photography still remains a favored methodological tool in archaeological research.

Satellite and Radar Imagery
Remote sensing from space has its origins with the development of the first meteorological satellites, which in 1960 transmitted back to earth the first coarse images of the earth's sur-

face along with cloud patterns. Throughout the 1960s, when the Mercury, Gemini, and Apollo space programs were launched by the U.S. National Aeronautics and Space Administration (NASA), thousands of photographs of the earth's surface were taken from space. The level of technological sophistication of the cameras used increased through time, and in 1969, during the Apollo 9 space mission, the first multispectral photographs of the earth's surface were taken. The clear advantages that the use of space imagery offered to monitoring the earth's natural resources encouraged NASA and the U.S. Department of the Interior to create a spatial observations program for that purpose, and in 1967, the Earth Resources Technology Satellites (ERTS) international program began. This space program would successfully launch into the earth's orbit the first unmanned satellites, which we now know as the Landsat series.

These developments, however, also took place in the midst of the cold war, and when the need to monitor the Soviet bloc's movements became apparent after the Cuban missile crisis in the early 1960s, high-resolution spy satellites were sent into the earth's orbit to keep track of any military buildup. Nevertheless, civilian-run programs represent the more important suppliers of satellite imagery. Along with the Landsat series, other important satellite series are the NOAA and GEO series along with the French SPOT satellites.

Information about earth's resources is also being obtained at an increasing rate from sensors that operate at the microwave level, that is, from radar sensors. Radar imagery can be produced from airborne or spaceborne platforms, and several series of the latter have been in operation since the late 1970s. These are the shuttle-imaging radar (SIR) A, B, and C series launched by the United States, and the Almaz-1, ERS-1, JERS-1, and Radarsat systems launched by the former Soviet Union, the European Space Agency, Japan, and Canada, respectively.

NASA has grown aware of the value that remotely sensed data may have to social scientists and has made great efforts to establish a reachout program. More and more satellite and radar imagery has been declassified and made available to civilian researchers, and archaeologists have used Landsat images to trace ancient levee systems in Mesopotamia, map prehistoric roads in the CHACO CANYON in New Mexico, and detect 2,500-year-old footpaths in the Arenal region of COSTA RICA. So far, the most successful application of satellite and radar imagery in archaeological research has taken place in MESOAMERICA, where the analysis of Landsat and radar images has resulted in the discovery of an extensive network of prehistoric farm fields and settlements on the Yucatán Peninsula and the discovery of "lost" cities and a complex network of causeways and platforms in the Maya lowlands. Radar imagery has also assisted archaeologists in the detection of previously unseen structures in Angkor, CAMBODIA.

Satellite imagery, however, has some disadvantages that may constrain its applicability in archaeology. First, the spaceborne optic sensors carried in the Landsat, SPOT, and NOAA satellites depend on solar radiation to image, for instance, daylight. Second, because of the wavelength of the optical part of the electromagnetic spectrum, atmospheric phenomena like cloud formations, smoke, dust, and fog and vegetation cover represent actual barriers that prevent the sensors from distinguishing cultural features that may be underneath. Third, the level of ground resolution varies significantly depending on the sensor used by the satellite systems. The Landsat series, for example, can go from 240, 120, 80, 30, to 15 meters; SPOT satellites have a ground resolution of 10 to 20 meters; and the NOAA series has a ground resolution of 1.1 kilometer. These characteristics may pose a problem depending on the type of features the archaeologist is interested in detecting and the availability of the images.

From this perspective, radar imagery has several advantages over satellite imagery. First, because they are active sensors, they provide their own illumination (the radar pulses), which means that, unlike optical sensors, they can image any time of day or night regardless of sun illumination. Second, because microwaves—the wavelength in which radar operates—are much longer, they can penetrate cloud cover, fog, dust, smoke, and even tree canopy and soil and thus provide images for targets that cannot be seen with the other platforms.

These characteristics have proved to be of great value not only for the detection of archaeological features situated underneath a tree canopy or other covering but also for the detection of subsurface archaeological features. One SIR-A radar image made over the Sahara revealed a prehistoric river system located between one and four meters beneath the sand. Subsequent excavation yielded human artifacts dating back to the Paleolithic period and other archaeological data that indicated a moister environment.

The complex nature of the archaeological data, comprising cultural and environmental elements, requires archaeologists to take advantage of all the available methodological tools. With the changing emphasis in archaeological research, which has shifted from site-oriented problems to more-regional approaches, the adoption of remote sensing along with other new technologies such as GEOGRAPHIC INFORMATION SYSTEMS makes perfect sense. Although still in its early stages, remote sensing provides an excellent means of gathering data that describe the biophysical context where human groups developed. The growing access to affordable computer power along with the increasing availability of satellite and radar images will soon consolidate the position of remote sensing as an essential component of the archaeologist's tool kit.

Armando Anaya Hernández

See also Crawford, O. G. S.; United States of America, Prehistoric Archaeology

References
Ebert, J. I. 1984. "5 Remote Sensing Applications in Archaeology." In *Advances in Archaeological Method and Theory* 7:293–362. Ed. Michael B Schiffer. New York: Academic Press.
Lillesand, T. M., and R. W. Kiefer. 1991. *Remote Sensing and Image Interpretation.* 3d ed. New York: John Wiley and Sons.
Liverman, D., E. F. Moran, R. R. Rindfuss, and P. C. Stern. 1998. *People and Pixels.* Washington, DC: National Academy Press.

Rock Art

The study of rock art in all its various forms has no specific point of origin. Indeed, rock art was never really "discovered" at all with the obvious exceptions of caves blocked since the Ice Age, sites buried by deposits (which had to be excavated), and areas no longer frequented by humans (deep jungle, remote desert). Local people always knew the rock art was there, often believing it to be the work of devils, evil spirits, sorcerers, or fairies, and would sometimes point it out to visiting explorers or scholars. Most early "scholarly discoveries" of rock art came about accidentally as traveling missionaries or explorers reported on anything of interest that they encountered.

It was not until the late nineteenth or early twentieth century that systematic searches for rock art began. Naturally, early reports had no concept of the art's age (even today, most rock art remains undated) since archaeology had not yet become an established discipline and there was as yet no idea of the antiquity of humankind or of the very concept of prehistory.

It seems that it was the Chinese who were the pioneers, since the earliest known written reports of rock art are to be found in *Han Fei Zi,* a book written 2,300 years ago by the philosopher Han Fei (280–233 B.C.). In the fifth century A.D., Li Daoyuan, a geographer of the northern Wei dynasty (A.D. 386–534), wrote a famous geography book called *Shui jing zhu* (Notes on the Systems of Rivers), which consists mostly of his personal experiences and describes places he had seen. He mentions a score of places with rock art in about half of CHINA's provinces and states that he had also heard of rock art in India and Pakistan. The book also describes techniques (painting and engraving) and subjects (tigers, horses, goats, and chickens as well as divinities and masks, footprints, and hoofprints).

The earliest known reference to rock art in Europe occurred 1,000 years after Li Daoyuan's book when, in 1458, Calixtus III, one of the Borgia popes from Valencia, forbade the Spanish to carry out cult ceremonies in a cave with horse pictures—presumably a decorated cave of Ice Age date—showing the persistence of beliefs attached to prehistoric images. Only two years later, one traveler, Pierre de Montfort, wrote a letter to his wife that mentioned the Vallée des Merveilles in the Alps as "an infernal place with figures of devils and a thousand demons carved everywhere on rocks." In the sixteenth century, Onorato Lorenzo, a priest from the same region wrote a large unpublished manuscript called "Accademio dei Giordani di Belvedere" that contained information obtained from shepherds, and this manuscript mentions the "Meraviglie" and provides a long list of rock-art motifs and subjects.

The earliest known documentation of rock carvings in Europe occurred in SWEDEN when some seventeenth-century drawings of petroglyphs at Backa Brastad near TANUM, Bohuslän (at that time part of Norway, itself linked to DENMARK) were made by Peder Alfssön, a schoolmaster from Kristiania (Oslo), and sent to one OLE WORM, the king of Denmark's doctor. Worm, a renowned polymath and founder of museums, had sent out questionnaires to educated people in the provinces, mainly priests, asking them to notice the location, setting, and dimensions of ancient monuments and, if possible, to make drawings, investigate how the monuments were constructed, and ascertain what the local people said or believed about them. Alfssön produced freehand wash drawings and accompanying text, which, amazingly, still survive in Copenhagen, having escaped several wars and great fires (they remained forgotten until published as small copperplate engravings by P. F. Suhm in 1784). It is not known exactly when the drawings were made, but they were made a part of the Copenhagen archives in 1627, which makes them the oldest known drawings of rock art in the world.

Alas, Worm made no mention of rock art in his 1643 book on ancient Denmark, and Alfssön, of course, had no inkling of the art's antiquity. The latter believed that the carvings—including a large human figure subsequently nicknamed *Skomakeren* ("the shoemaker")—were medieval graffiti by apprentice stonemasons working on the construction of a church in the vicinity. It was only in the eighteenth century that scholars came to realize that such carvings were very old, though at first it was believed they depicted historical events such as battles between Viking ships.

In the Alps, a French historian, Abbé Pietro Gioffredo, wrote *Storia delle Alpi Marittime* (ca. 1650) and based his somewhat fanciful account of the Vallée des Merveilles on Onorato Lorenzo: "Various stones of all colours, flat and smooth, decorated with engravings of a thousand imaginary subjects, representing quadrupeds, birds, fish, agricultural or military mechanical instruments dating from several centuries, and . . . the authors of such merry jokes were shepherds trying to avoid boredom."

In RUSSIA, petroglyphs (*pissanye kamni,* or "written stones") were mentioned in the notes made by travelers, ambassadors, and merchants during the seventeenth and eighteenth centuries. For example, a Moldavian prince, Nikolai Milesku Spafarii, an ambassador for Czar Alexei Romanov, traveled through Siberia to China in 1675 and mentioned petroglyphs in the Yenisey Valley in his travel notes. Tomskaya Pisanitsa in Siberia was described in a Russian chronicle of the seventeenth century as a big stone with the images of animals, birds and people, and in 1692, the Dutch traveler and scientist Nicolaas Witsen, a friend of Peter the Great, published a book *Nord und Ost Tartaray* (North and East Tartary) in Amsterdam (2d ed., 1705). In effect, that work was the first Siberian encyclopedia, and it contained descriptions of "ancient paintings," including rock pictures on the River Irbit in the Ural Mountains.

Developments in the New World

The major development of the sixteenth century occurred in the New World where "inscriptions" of various kinds were spotted, and sometimes described and illustrated, by conquering Europeans exploring the interior of Brazil. During the first centuries of the conquest, members of various religious orders also penetrated the interior of Amazonia. The earliest known information on rock art in this area is attributed to Ambrósio Fernandes Brandão, who, in 1598, recorded the existence of rock engravings in the present state of Paraíba on the Araçai River. In 1618, Brandão published drawings of motifs in

Brazilian petroglyphs in his *Diálogos das Grandezas do Brasil,* probably the world's earliest known reproductions of rock art.

Also during the sixteenth century, some Spanish missionaries in Latin America realized that certain rock art sites were religious in nature and remained sacred to the native population: for example, a late-sixteenth- or early-seventeenth-century document from MEXICO, written by Padre Andrés Pérez de Ribas, mentions that a cleric in the northern part of Sinaloa saw a native stop in front of a sculptured stone decorated with some crude figures and make some demonstrations of reverence. Consequently, the clerics either destroyed such images or engraved crosses in high or prominent places at the sites to demonstrate the superiority of Christianity. In some cases, they actually superimposed crosses on the rock art, for example, at Peña Escrita in the Andean zone of Santa Cruz, Bolivia.

The earliest mention of rock art in Mexico is in the sixteenth-century book *Monarquía Indiana* by Juan de Torquemada, who linked examples of rock art with the chief TOLTEC and AZTEC god, Quetzalcoatl: "Quetzalcoatl arrived at another place, a hill near the village of Tlalnepantla, two leagues from this city of México, where he sat down on a stone, and placed his hands on it, and left their imprint there, of which traces can still be seen today . . . and at present it is called Temacpalco, which means, in the palm of the hand."

The first investigations of Bolivian rock art began early in the colonial period. The priest Alonso Ramos Gavilán, in his book *Historia de Nuestra Señora de Copacabana* (1621), mentioned four rock art sites. In three of them, the Spanish found engraved "footprints" in the rock, but instead of attributing them to Quetzalcoatl, as in Mexico, they assumed them to be the traces of a Christian saint—an idea that fit their theory that there had been a Christian missionary in the Andes in pre-Columbian times. Some of them believed the missionary to have been St. Thomas, who was said to have preached on the South American continent and to have left his footprints when he moved on. The fourth site was described as having "letters written on a rock"—early explorers often saw rock art as ancient writing.

In a document of 1615, Padre Rodrigo de Cabredo wrote to the padre general telling of a legend that circulated in the area of the bay of Banderas in the southwestern part of the state of Nayarit, Mexico: On a crag of a sierra here "there is sculpted a most devout Christ, and below it some lines of ancient characters; and the letters . . . contained many little dots, and must be Hebrew. . . . [I]n these mountains can be seen a little crag on which, in the manner of a ladder, there are imprinted the tracks of this saintly man [i.e., a preacher called Matias or Mateo]."

A. de Calancha, in *Crónica moralizada de la Orden de San Agustin en el Perú* (1638), published a drawing of petroglyphs on a rock at Calango, near Lima, including a footprint that he believed was that of a saint and other motifs that he saw as keys, an anchor, and letters. He reported that because the stone was still the object of superstitious worship on the part of the Indians, Hispanic visitors had the figures ground down and a cross placed at the head of the rock. De Calancha felt that this was enough to eliminate any superstition and that the perpetrators were wrong to "erase a footprint that was so worthy of veneration, but perhaps it was an impulse from heaven."

In 1695, a remarkable book appeared in Amsterdam, Adriaan van Berkel's *Amerikaansche Voyagien, behelzende een Reis na Rio de Berbice etc.,* which refers to an Indian tribe in Guyana called the Acquewyen (Akawai): the book describes near their trading place many cliffs upon which can still be seen the marks of the Spaniards who first discovered the coast and penetrated the river. Once again, therefore, petroglyphs were explained as being marks by people from the Old World.

The first reports also emerged from North America at this time. In 1673 a Jesuit father, Jacques Marquette, who was exploring the upper Mississippi River in the United States, noted in his journal hideous, painted winged monsters high on a cliff near Alton in modern state of Illinois. Unfortunately, Marquette's original drawing of the figure was lost when his canoe capsized on the St. Lawrence River as he was returning from the Mississippi area. Other discoveries soon followed: on the east bank of the Taunton River in Massachusetts, the first drawing of Native American petroglyphs on Dighton Rock (a large rock covered with deeply incised abstract designs and highly stylized human figures) were made by colonists in 1680—although the markings have been attributed by some people on the fringe of archaeology to Norsemen, Phoenicians, Scythians, and Portuguese explorers. The pictograph site of La Roche-à-l'Oiseau on the Outaouais River in QUEBEC was mentioned in 1686 in connection with Indians throwing down offerings of tobacco when they passed close to the rock.

The Age of Enlightenment

In the eighteenth century, a time when so many fields of inquiry began to be transformed into serious topics of study, a more profound and sustained interest began, and rock art was reported on two more continents. As yet, however, serious study developed very sporadically and slowly.

For instance, in Ireland, Newgrange and the other decorated tombs were frequently described and illustrated in the eighteenth and nineteenth centuries, and "rude carvings" at Killin, County Louth, were reported by Wright in 1758. Regarding Scandinavian rock art, a letter from a superintendent of the Swedish-Norwegian border written in 1751 mentions carvings in Bohuslän: "In the parish of Tanum, not far from the sea, I have also visited a sloping rock, where a man with spear in his hand is cut, and about whom is said that a Scottish commander had been killed in his flight during a military campaign and that the position of his dead body was reproduced in the rock." The letter's plea for an inventory to be started in the parish fell on deaf ears.

Also in the mid-eighteenth century, the great cairn of Kivik in Skane, southern Sweden, was discovered, and the carved figures on the stone slabs of its central cist were drawn in very professional fashion by Carl Gustaf Hilfeling, an antiquarian who specialized in depiction and description. The much-traveled Hilfeling also visited Bohuslän, and his travel books published after 1792 include several drawings of monuments and rock carvings in that region. He produced measured drawings done to scale, not freehand sketches, and his pictures are full of comments on size, distance, and location. Unfortunately, he had a tendency to see nonexistent runic inscriptions on some rocks.

In 1719, Czar Peter the Great sent a young doctor and naturalist, Daniel-Gotlieb Messerschmidt, to lead a scientific expedition to study the nature and population of Siberia. In Tobolsk, Messerschmidt met Philip Johann Tabbert von Strahlenberg, a Swedish officer who was a prisoner in Siberian exile, and together they carried out the first scientific excavations in the region. In 1722, Messerschmidt made a drawing of a rock with symbols, images of animals, and a man. He also discovered runic inscriptions on rocks that were determined to be old Turkic in 1893; earlier, they conjured up romantic ideas about Vikings and Germans and led Messerschmidt to investigate ancient rock images more closely and make copies of them.

In his diary entry for 23 February 1722, he reported that by the Yenisey River, not far from the village of Birjusa, near Krasnoyarsk, there were all kinds of "characters" and figures, written in red, to which the locals ascribed all kinds of meanings because the motifs were quite high above the river on smooth, steep rocks so the locals could not understand how people could have made them there. He also noted that the locals called them *pisannyj kamen*. On 18 August of the same year, Messerschmidt saw numerous Scythian graves bearing stones covered with figures, some of which he published as drawings. His diary entry for 26 September mentions that at the Gordovaja stena he once again saw characters and figures about eight and a half meters above the river level that were made with a crimson and indelible color.

In 1730, liberated and back home in Sweden, von Strahlenberg published a book (*Das Nord- und Östliche Theil von Europa und Asia*), the first scientific publication about the archaeological monuments of the Yenisey region (Siberia), including petroglyphs. Other expeditions to Siberia followed, and these also examined the archaeology and rock art of the region. For example, the historian Gerhard-Friedrich Mueller produced a book in 1750 in Russian (*Opisanie Sibirskogo carstva*) in which he refuted the supposition that these ancient rock drawings could be taken as a special form of writing. In this work, which was later also published in German, he published sketches of some figures.

Further Work in the New World

Discoveries of rock art continued to be made in the Americas. In 1711, Father Eusebio Kino described and mapped "the painted rocks"—actually engravings—near Gila Bend, Arizona. In Quebec, the Nisula site on Lac de la Cassette was mentioned on Father Pierre-Michel Laure's maps, drawn between 1731 and 1733 during the French regime in Canada and showing the so-called Domaine du Roy in Nouvelle FRANCE, where it says "Pepéchapissinagan [the stone thing on which there are paintings] naturally painted figures can be seen on the rock." Heads, or faces, carved at the foot of the great falls on the Connecticut River in the village of Bellows, Vermont, have been commented on by travelers and researchers since 1789, the petroglyphs being described variously as Indian chiefs, families, symbols of male authority, memorials of noteworthy events, idle artwork, and the work of shamans recording vision experiences.

In the eighteenth century, a Jesuit missionary called Schabel visited Pedrazza, Venezuela, and thought the petroglyphs there to be engraved by "angelic hands." Alexander von Humboldt himself saw many petroglyphs during his travels through South America at the end of the century, and he put forward some interpretations of petroglyphs in the Orinoco region. Father Pedor Lozano, in about 1730 to 1760, interpreted the abundant engravings and paintings of COLOMBIA, BRAZIL, Paraguay, and PERU as tracing the itinerary of St. Thomas, with all footprints being attributed to the saint as usual (conversely, red handprints were often attributed to the devil in Latin America). But Filippo Salvadore Gilii, another Jesuit missionary in Venezuela, reported in 1781 that, according to the Tamanaco Indians, rock inscriptions there had been made by the creator-god Amalivaca.

There was a great deal of activity in Mexico in the eighteenth century. For example, a 1792 compilation commissioned by the Spanish viceroy of New Spain, Conde Revilla Gigedo, contained a natural history of Baja California that was attributed tentatively to the Jesuit Juan Bautista Mugazábal, who died in 1761. If correct, the compilation would be the oldest known reference to rock art on the peninsula, and it describes a clear attempt to obtain relevant ethnographic information:

> In all of civilized California, from south to north, and particularly in the caves and smooth cliffs, rustic paintings can be seen. Notwithstanding their disproportion and lack of art, there can be easily distinguished the likenesses of men, fish, bows and arrows, and diversely assembled lines in the fashion of written characters. The colours of these paintings are four: yellow, red, green and black. The majority of the images are painted in very high places, and from this, some infer that there is truth in the constant tradition of giants among the ancient Californians. . . . It has been impossible to ascertain what these figures, lines and characters mean, despite extensive questioning of the California Indians. The only thing which has been determined from what they say, is that they are from their ancestors, and that they have absolutely no knowledge of their significance.

An eighteenth-century Jesuit missionary, the Spaniard Miguel del Barco, wrote hundreds of pages about California that were not published until 1972 by Miguel Leon-Portilla in *Historia natural y crónica de la Antigua California*. This account contains an extended reference to the great murals of Baja California, and it quotes Joseph Mariano Rothea, a missionary at San Ignacio from 1759 until 1768:

> I happened to investigate several painted caves. . . . one would be about 30 to 35 feet long, about 16 feet wide. . . . From top to bottom it was all painted with various figures of men, women, and animals. . . . The colours were the same that are found in the volcanoes of the Tres Virgenes: green, black, yellow and flesh-coloured. The durability of these colours seemed notable to me; being there on the exposed rock in the inclemencies of sun and water where they are no doubt struck by rain, strong

wind or water that filters through these same rocks from the hill above, with all this, after much time, they remain highly visible. . . . Without scaffolds or other implements suitable for the purpose, only giant men would have been able to paint at so much height.

Hence, the Cochimí, the local people, had legends disassociating them and their ancestors from the painters, and the missionaries thought the paintings impressively old. Del Barco also wrote:

The people of this land say that the giants were so large that, when they painted the ceiling of a cave, they lay on their backs on the ground and that even thus they were able to paint the highest part. An enormous fable that, for its verification, would necessitate those men to have a height of at least thirty feet, unless we imagine extremely long paint brushes in their hands! . . . It is simpler to persuade oneself that, for this work, they found and conveyed to the cave, or caves, some wood with which to form a scaffold.

Africa and Australia

The eighteenth century also saw the first discoveries of rock art in AFRICA. The earliest reference is from 1721, when an ecclesiastic in the Portuguese colony of Mozambique mentioned paintings of animals on rocks in a report to the Royal Academy of History in Lisbon. In 1752, explorer Domingo van de Walle de Cervellón reported engravings in the cave of Belmaco on Las Palmas in the Canary Islands. These meandering pecked motifs were considered to be mere doodles, produced by chance or the imagination of the ancient barbarians. That same year, explorers led by Ensign August Frederick Beutler, who were more than 200 miles from their Capetown base, noticed rock paintings in the valley of the Great Fish River in the Eastern Cape, which they recognized to be the work of "the little Chinese" (bushmen).

The first known copies of rock art in the region were made in 1777–1778 by an expedition to the Sneeuwbergen ("snowy mountains") of the Eastern Cape led by Governor Joachim van Plettenberg. The copies were made by Colonel Robert Jacob Gordon and his draftsman servant

Johannes Schumacher—the latter had already copied probable petroglyphs or rock paintings (he called them *teekeningen*) in 1776 on an expedition to the western area area of the Cape that had been led by H. Swellenberg. In 1790–1791, on an expedition led by Grosvenor, Jacob van Reenen noted in his diary that "on a rocky cliff the Bushmen had made a great many paintings or representations of wildebeeste, very natural, and also of a soldier with a grenadier's cap."

The French traveler Le Vaillant published a book on South Africa at this time in which he dismissed the bushman paintings as "caricatures" and said of pictures in a cave in the Eastern Cape, "the Dutchmen believe them to be a century or two old and allege that the Bushmen worship them, but though it is quite possible, there is no evidence to show it."

One of the first people who made an attempt to understand the rock art of southern Africa was Sir John Barrow, who was excited to see rock paintings on his journeys through Cape Colony and beyond in 1797 and 1798. He was filled with wonder that they could have been produced by people described by one writer in 1731 as "troops of abandon'd Wretches" lacking laws, fixed abodes, and religion: "In the course of travelling, I had frequently heard the peasantry mention the drawings in the mountains behind the Sneuwberg made by the Boujesmans; but I took it for granted they were caricatures only, similar to those on the doors and walls of uninhabited buildings, the works of idle boys; and it was no disagreeable disappointment to find them very much the reverse."

The art's beauty made him think that the San (bushmen) had been rendered "more savage" by the conduct of the European settlers. He was especially interested in the aesthetic aspects of the art, which he assumed was indeed "art" in the European sense. On inquiring about their age, he was told that some paintings were known to be new while others had been present since the first settlement of this part of the colony.

The other new continent whose rock art was "discovered" in this period was AUSTRALIA. There had been a report in 1678 by J. Keyts, a Dutch trader, of rock paintings on a cliff face in Speelmans Bay, western New Guinea (Irian Jaya), but

A San (bushman) in South Africa standing by an example of ancient rock art (South African Tourist Board)

it was ignored at the time. European discoveries in Australia began during the first months of colonization in 1788 and continued sporadically over the next century as explorers and pioneers pushed further into the country. At first, very few sites were discovered or documented, and the colonizers made little effort to inquire about the meaning of motifs and designs. The art was considered to be childish attempts by primitive people to produce paintings and radically inferior to the European art of the period.

The first known European discovery of Australian rock art was made in Bantry Bay, near Sydney, by Governor Arthur Phillip, the commander of the First Fleet and of the first settlement at Port Jackson, in 1788, when he led short expeditions into the surrounding area. The expedition surgeon's journal describes how, on 16 April 1788, "We saw . . . some proofs of their ingenuity in various figures cut on the smooth surfaces of some large stones. They consisted chiefly of representations of themselves in different attitudes, of their canoes, of several sorts of fish and animals; and considering the rudeness of the instruments

with which the figures must have been executed, they seemed to exhibit tolerably strong likenesses."

In his first dispatch of 15 May 1788 to Lord Sydney, Phillip wrote: "In Botany Bay, Port Jackson and Broken Bay we frequently saw the figures of men, shields, and fish roughly cut on the rocks; and on the top of a mountain I saw the figure of a man in the attitude they put themselves in when they are going to dance, which was much better done than I had seen before, and the figure of a large lizard was sufficiently well executed to satisfy every one what animal was meant."

The Nineteenth Century

By the end of the eighteenth century, therefore, prehistoric rock art was being noticed and even copied with increasing frequency, though no great accuracy. In the next century, a turning point was to be reached, not only in numbers of discoveries but also in the realization that some of the art was of great antiquity. Just as archaeology became established by the mid-nineteenth century, when the great antiquity of humankind and the concept of prehistory were accepted, so, too, did the study of rock art gradually begin to grow more widespread, more systematic, and better documented.

In Australia, discoveries multiplied in different areas. It was Matthew Flinders, a British navigator and explorer, who, while exploring and mapping the coastline, made the first discovery of rock shelters with paintings and stencils—on Chasm Island near Arnhem Land on the coast of Northern Territory—on 14 January 1803 during the first circumnavigation of the continent. His account describes the location, identifies some figures, considers the materials used, and even attempts an ethnographic interpretation with generalized meaning.

Some eighteen years later, Allan Cunningham made further discoveries on Clack Island, off Queensland, which he compared to those of Flinders. On 22 June 1821, Cunningham found a major collection of rock paintings, the first in Queensland. Flinders's images had been produced with a burned stick, "but this performance, exceeding a hundred and fifty figures . . . appears at least to be one step nearer refinement than those simply executed with a piece of charred wood."

Tasmania was next. On 4 September 1830, George Augustus Robinson, protector of the aborigines in Tasmania and Victoria, found an engraved circle surrounded with dots on the island's northwestern coast. Three years later, in the same region, he "saw large circles cut on the face of rocks done by natives. Some of them were a foot and eighteen inches in diameter."

The first Wandjina galleries of the Kimberley region in northern Western Australia were seen by the British explorer George Grey on 26 March 1838: "On looking over some bushes, at the sandstone rocks which were above us, I suddenly saw from one of them a most extraordinary large figure peering down upon me. Upon examination this proved to be a drawing at the entrance to a cave, which, on entering, I found to contain besides, many remarkable paintings." Although Grey interpreted the patterns on the figure's "halo" as an oriental script in his journals of two expeditions of discovery in northwestern and western Australia (1841), he was a true pioneer in that he made a great effort to produce detailed descriptions, measurements, and colored sketches of some panels at the site over the next few days.

In 1891, the explorer Joseph Bradshaw found an entirely different kind of rock art in the Kimberley area, the delicately painted figures that were to become known as "Bradshaws": "numerous aboriginal paintings which appeared to be of great antiquity, and I do not attribute them to the presentations of the Black race." He, too, published sketches.

The earliest report of the rock paintings in Arnhem Land was made by Ludwig Leichhardt in 1845; his first discovery was a rock shelter containing an image of a long-necked turtle. However, it was only with the incursion of European buffalo shooters into Kakadu in early 1880s that this area's paintings became better known. In the 1870s, on a voyage in the McCluer Gulf (now Berau Bay), the Dutch trader T. B. Leon came across some rock paintings in New Guinea that he took to be Hindu symbols, and photographs were taken of New Guinea rock art in 1887.

Discoveries soon occurred in POLYNESIA as well. In NEW ZEALAND, a surveyor, Walter Mantell, made the first record of rock drawings at the Takiroa rock shelter (North Otago) on the south island of N.2 in 1852—elaborate and apparently nonfigurative designs in red and black. In Hawaii, William Ellis observed petroglyphs in 1824:

> Along the southern coast, both on the east and west sides, we frequently saw a number of straight lines, semicircles, or concentric rings, with some rude imitations of the human figure, cut or carved in the compact rocks of lava. They did not appear to have been cut with an iron instrument, but with a stone hatchet, or a stone less frangible than the rock on which they were portrayed. On inquiry, we found that they had been made by former travellers, from a motive similar to that which induces a person to carve his initials on a stone or tree, or a traveller to record his name in an album, to inform his successors that he had been there.

He recorded the meaning of some motifs in what is one of the few existing firsthand accounts recorded anywhere in the world during a period when petroglyphs were still being made.

As for EASTER ISLAND, its hundreds of giant statues were obviously seen and mentioned by the first known European discoverers—the Dutch in 1722—and by all subsequent visitors, but its rock engravings and paintings were not noticed, or at least not mentioned, until a four-day visit by a German vessel under the command of Lietenant-Captain Wilhelm Geiseler in 1882, which included a study of the painted slabs inside some houses, bas-relief petroglyphs of "the god of the seabird eggs," and carvings of "the feminine sex" that adorn the rocks around the ceremonial cliff-top village of Orongo.

In various parts of Africa, rock art was, understandably enough, the first evidence of the past that attracted the attention of explorers: for example, in 1816, at the mouth of the River Congo (Zaïre), J. Tuckey, a British captain, observed a rock with engravings in what is now Angola; he named it Pedra do Feitiço (Fetish Rock) and published a detailed description of its human figures, animals, and various objects such as boats, rifles, and palanquins.

Sir James Alexander, another Briton, was traveling in 1835 near modern Oudtshoorn in South Africa and was taken to see overhanging rocks with paintings. In his 1837 book *A Narrative of a Voyage of Observation among the Colonies of Western Africa,* he included three copies of these paintings, which had been made by his guide, Major C. C. Mitchell, a civil engineer and surveyor general in the Cape. Like Barrow before him, Alexander was surprised to find "that these rude attempts of uncivilized artists are not utterly devoid of merit; and that although defective in proportions, there is more resemblance in them to the human figure than is ever seen imparted by persons, however educated, who have a total negation of graphic talent. This, indeed, is rendered most evident on the spot, by sundry miserable attempts at figures, made beside them by some civilized bungler."

Alexander noticed that some of the art must be ancient, stating that Mitchell had made copies of all of the drawings that still remained uninjured by time and the weather. He noted that the color of the drawings seemed to have been produced by a preparation in which iron rust formed a principal ingredient. He believed the figures to be narratives and tried to "read" them.

A geologist, George Stow, made copies of rock art in the Orange Free State and Eastern Cape beginning in 1867, and in 1870, he said in a letter:

> I have been making pilgrimages to the various old Bushman caves among the mountains in this part of the Colony and Kaffraria; and as their paintings are becoming obliterated very fast, it struck me that it would be as well to make copies of them before these interesting relics of an almost extinct race are entirely destroyed. . . . I have fortunately been able to procure many facsimile copies of hunting scenes, dances, fightings, etc., showing the modes of warfare, the chase, weapons, disguises, etc.

However, most of his copies, including watercolors and pencil tracings, were not published until 1930.

Stow was very selective, often ignoring hundreds of figures of animals and humans doing ordinary things and only copying some small part that he imagined to represent a ceremony. He also displayed typical Victorian prudishness, omitting some details presumably because they were unsuitable for publication. His method was to make a preliminary copy on rough paper, then trace from it onto art paper. Sometimes his lack of paper seems to have led him to reproduce together figures from different parts of a site or even from different shelters. The tracings on art paper were then colored, using as paints the original bushman pigments that he had picked up from the shelter floors. By the end of his life, he had amassed a dossier of seventy-four plates, and he tried to interpret them by asking bushman acquaintances what they meant.

Another pioneer copier was Joseph Orpen, a colonial administrator in the 1870s who published some of his drawings in color and who listened to bushmen talking about the art, especially one called Qing. Orpen's work, in turn, acted as a great stimulus to Wilhelm Bleek, the German philologist who, in the 1870s, together with his sister-in-law Lucy Lloyd, spent years investigating the languages and cultures of the South African bushmen, recording verbatim 12,000 pages of testimony about bushman life, rituals, and beliefs; he also appealed for faithful copies of rock art to be made, backed up by photography, so that the art could be understood in terms of its folklore. Unlike earlier writers who had adopted a somewhat patronizing or simplistic view of African rock art, he urged that one should consider the paintings "not as the mere daubing of figures for idle pastime, but as an attempt, however imperfect, at a truly artistic conception of the ideas which most deeply moved the Bushman mind, and filled it with religious feelings."

Copies of paintings were produced by enthusiasts in the Cape and shown to bushmen for explanation and comment. Lucy Lloyd bought Stow's drawings after his death, later willing them to Bleek's daughter Dorothea, who finally managed to get them published in 1930, almost fifty years after Stow's death.

Rock images had also been observed by Europeans in North Africa, the Sahara, and the Nile Valley by the mid-nineteenth century. The weathered appearance, alien style, and exotic subjects of the rock images suggested that they must be of some antiquity and had possible associations with vanished peoples. The first discoveries of rock art in these regions were made in 1847 by two soldiers (François Félix Jacquot and Captain Kook of the Foreign Legion) who were part of General Cavaignac's expedition against tribes in the Ksour Mountains of northwestern Algeria. The soldiers reported seeing large engravings of animals (elephants, lions, antelopes, ostriches, gazelles) and humans with bows, and thanks to the costumes and scenes depicted, they had no doubt whatsoever that these were ancient works, dating from an era before the Arab invasion of the middle ages but after the time of Carthage in the second century B.C. (in 1847 the concept of prehistory had not yet become established). They assumed that the engravings were the work of idolaters believing in fetishes who had been brought to the oases of southern Oran in caravan expeditions from the south of Africa; they believed the

artists to have been members of the nomadic Tuareg people.

In 1848, J.-J. Ampère mentioned the engravings of NUBIA on the banks of the Nile in his *Voyage et recherches en Egypte et en Nubie,* as did the 1842–1845 expedition of KARL LEPSIUS. Ampère focused on the engraved rocks on the west bank near Philae: "These signs are not hieroglyphs and bear no resemblance to the letters of any known alphabet." Among the figures he noticed were the symbol of life and various animals "grotesquely drawn"—lions, giraffes, elephants, ostriches. He also mentioned some not very artistic (and often indecent) depictions of humans.

In 1849, the German explorer Heinrich Barth set out from the Libyan port of Tripoli on a four-year trip and was the first to discover a large number of rock engravings, including the now-famous site of Tilizzaghen (Telizzharen), and the first engravings in Fezzan, Libya. He included some reproductions in a series of five volumes published in Gotha in 1857 and 1858 *(Reisen und Entdeckungen in Nord und Central Afrika in den Jahren 1849 bis 1855)* and noted that some parts of the figures seemed unfinished, especially the lower extremities of animals' limbs. He interpreted some scenes as allegories and noted differences in quality and technique among engravings, which he saw as being of chronological significance. The fauna represented, especially the herds of cattle, led him to the conclusion that climatic conditions had once been very different in that desert region.

A Frenchman, Henri Duveyrier, set out in 1859 on a journey that took him to western Tripolitana and the eastern Algerian Sahara in North Africa; in 1865, he published copies of rock engravings in Tassili, a North African location discovered during this expedition, in *Les Touaregs du Nord* and concurred with Barth about allegorical interpretations and about the existence in earlier times of abundant pastures and water resources. Rabbi Mardokhai-Abi-Sourour, on a journey of exploration in southwestern Morocco in 1875, discovered numerous rocks bearing animal figures and inscriptions and was the first explorer, in that part of the world at least, to make stamped copies by pressing a thin layer of clay, contained between two sheets of paper, onto the reliefs and depressions of the rock surface (by coincidence, in 1874–1878, the famous Finnish linguist and ethnographer Matias-Alexander Castren was working in the Yenisey Valley in Siberia and likewise developed a mechanical stamping method for copying rock drawings and inscriptions).

Some sixty-eight stamps, including forty-six of engravings, were sent by the rabbi to the Société de Géographie de Paris where they were studied by Duveyrier. They featured depictions of elephant, rhinoceros, horse, giraffe, fox, birds, etc., as well as objects such as harnesses and shields. Duveyrier noted a difference between lines drawn deeply and clearly, which had been made with a metal point, and lines that were broad and blurred, which had been made by percussion or rubbing with a hard stone. Still, he attributed everything to a single period because, as he was working from a uniform stamped impression, he could not see differences in patina and weathering. Rejecting an attribution to modern people, Portuguese merchants, Romans, or Phoenicians, he eventually ascribed the figures to an indigenous black race, "the Ethiopians-Daratites" mentioned by the Romans in their histories.

It was in 1882 that V. Reboud became the first person to suggest that the North African engravings might be prehistoric; and in 1889, Bonnet of the Paris Natural History Museum, while on a botanical expedition in Algeria, was the first to note the presence of worked flint tools near some of the rock-art sites. Indeed, Bonnet is especially important for his archaeological observations: he noticed prehistoric weapons and tools around the engraved rocks on the ground surface—worked flints, arrowheads, knives, scrapers, etc.—and he supposed that it was probably with a fragment of worked flint that "the primitive artists engraved this gigantic page of their history." He was thus able to concur with Reboud that the figures were prehistoric, particularly those depicting pachyderms or ruminants that had already left the region for Central Africa by Roman times.

It was in the second half of the nineteenth century that India, too, was placed on the rock art map, in particular by one astonishing and farsighted pioneer, Archibald Carlyle (or Carlleyle), first assistant to the Archaeological Survey of India, who discovered rock paintings in shelters at Morhana Pahar above the Ganges Valley in the 1860s. He wrote in his notebooks:

> Lying along with the small implements in the undisturbed soil of the cave floors, pieces of a heavy red mineral colouring matter called geru were frequently found, rubbed down on one or more facets, as if for making paint—this geru being evidently a partially decomposed haematite. . . . On the uneven sides or walls and roofs of many of the caves or rock shelters there were rock paintings apparently of various ages, though all evidently of great age, done in the red colour called geru. Some of these rude paintings appeared to illustrate in a very stiff and archaic manner scenes in the life of the ancient stone chippers; others represent animals or hunts of animals by men with bows and arrows, spears and hatchets. . . . With regard to the probable age of these stone implements I may mention that I never found even a single ground or polished implement, not a single ground ring-stone or hammer-stone in the soil of the floors of any of the many caves or rock shelters I examined.

Since Carlyle found only stone tools and bits of pottery in the vicinity, he attributed the paintings to various periods, including that of the makers of thousands of microliths. His recognition that some of the paintings must be prehistoric had no precedent in Europe and was probably the first in the world. But, alas, he published nothing about the paintings; he merely placed some notes with a friend, and these were published in 1883 by one A. Smith. It is known from the index books of Carlyle's microlith collections that he prepared copies and tracings of rock pictures, but unfortunately these have never been found.

The first scientific article on Indian rock art was published in 1883 by John Cockburn, a government agent who gave "a short account of the petrographs [rock drawings] in the caves or rock-shelters of the Kaimur range in the Mirzapur district." He had found paintings of rhinoceroses and boars, and in the "exceedingly numerous" rock shelters containing drawings in red pigment of "men, women and animals, weapons, utensils, symbols of religion, etc." In the Sorhow ghat cave he found pieces of haematite and a pointed pencil of chalk. On grinding these up with oil—in what may be the first piece of experimental archaeology related to rock art—Cockburn was able to produce colors exactly like those used in the cave drawings. He did not consider them to be more than six or seven centuries old. In 1899, he published an account of all his finds and compared the drawings with those found in Australia, South Africa, and North and South America. He made tracings of several pictures using paper made transparent by petroleum.

In the Americas, major developments took place in the north—as the West was won and frontiers were pushed back, like in Australia—but comparatively little happened further south. In Mexico, for example, nobody in the nineteenth century seems to have taken much notice of the great murals of Baja California until 1882. Shortly afterward, in 1888–1890, Teobert Maler visited the MAYA cave of Loltun, in Yucatán, and made drawings and photographs of its rock engravings and paintings.

Historical accounts from 1816 describe "human footprints" found in limestone at the edge of the Mississippi at St. Louis. Three years later, the footprints were removed to Indiana by Rappites, members of a German religious group. In an intriguing echo of the early missionaries' interpretation of such prints, they were associated with the Angel Gabriel. Some early visitors, including Henry Rowe Schoolcraft, the famous American explorer and ethnologist, discussed whether these were actual footprints in solidified mud or petroglyphs, but a geologist eventually proved that they were definitely the work of humans. In 1853, Schoolcraft published a drawing given to him by Chingwauk, his informant in the Agawa Bay area of Lake Superior—he had hired Chingwauk in 1822 to teach him the meaning of pictures on birch-bark scrolls and stone—of pictures from two rock-art sites, one on the south shore and the other on the north shore (which he called Inscription Rock); Schoolcraft also supplied a reading.

On the Northwest coast, petroglyph carving continued in British Columbia until the nineteenth century. Newcombe learned this fact from Indian informants near Beecher Bay in the 1860s and 1870s while anthropologist Franz Boas observed an actual petroglyph carving ceremony among the Kwakiutl in 1895.

The earliest major American pioneer was Garrick Mallery, a U.S. army colonel in command of Fort Rice on the upper Missouri River who retired in 1879 and collected and interpreted a vast amount of material. His first account, *Pictographs of the North American Indians* (1866), contained only 21 pages on rock art, but he followed this volume with his definitive work, *Picture-Writing of the American Indians* (1893), which contained no fewer than 150 pages on the subject. In it, he noted that "one of the curious facts in connection with petroglyphs is the meager notice taken of them by explorers and even by residents other than the Indians, who are generally reticent concerning them" (p. 36).

It was in Europe, however, that by far the most momentous developments in the study of prehistoric art were to occur during the nineteenth century as the existence of paleolithic portable and parietal art was discovered, authenticated, and eventually accepted. In parallel with those events, though, more-recent rock art continued to be found or studied. For example, the French doctor François-Emmanuel Fodéré mentioned the petroglyphs of the Vallée des Merveilles (Monte Bego) in 1821 when referring to Hannibal's passing through the region—he thought them to be blocks prepared for the construction of a monument that the makers never had the time to erect. There were several studies of these engravings in the 1860s and 1870s before two major figures came on the scene: in 1877, Emile Rivière was the first to recognize that the petroglyphs were prehistoric, and the English amateur botanist Clarence Bicknell carried out the first systematic studies of Monte Bego from 1881 onward.

The earliest mention of SPAIN's famous Levantine rock paintings came in 1892 in a book called *Los toros de La Losilla* by J. E. Marconell, which concerned the white rock paintings of the Sierra de Albarracín, although the author did not realize they were prehistoric. As for Spain's megalithic art, the first description of decoration in a stone monument is that of Santa Cruz, Cangas de Onis, in 1871, followed by others in the 1870s. In Brittany, the earliest known drawings of the decorated stones called Les Pierres Plates and La Table des Marchands were done in 1814 by Maudet de Penhoët. Many such sites were also reported in Ireland in the nineteenth century, including Loughcrew in the 1860s.

In BRITAIN, stones called Calderstones, in a chambered tomb in Liverpool, were noted in 1825, although these sandstone blocks were already well known and had been referred to in a boundary dispute as early as 1568—however, there is no indication that the spirals, cupmarks, and feet pecked into the slabs were aboveground at that time, as the stones' decoration was first described in 1825. The decorated stones of Orkney were also discovered by excavation in the nineteenth century. The first person to describe English rock art was George Tate in 1864—he mentioned fifty-five sites. Sir James Simpson, Queen Victoria's physician in Scotland, wrote a book called *Archaic Sculpturings* (1867) about some Scottish cup and ring marks.

The Lake Onega engravings in Russia were discovered in 1848, and their earliest (fanciful) publication by P. Schwed was in 1850. Other nineteenth-century discoveries were made in the Urals and Siberia. In Scandinavia, some copies of rock carvings were made by Carl George Brunius in the early nineteenth century, though it was only after the clergyman Axel Emanuel Holmberg began his work in 1843 that really useful catalogs of the art were put together. Homberg's *Skandinaviens hällristningar* (Rock Carvings of Scandinavia), published in 1848, was illustrated with 165 drawings, only a small part of his collection. The most outstanding work is considered to be that of a Danish art teacher, Lauritz Baltzer, who published two volumes of prints, *Hällristningar fran Bohuslän, I, 1881–1890* and *II, 1891–1908,* that contained 248 drawings and descriptions, all of great accuracy. Plaster casts of rock engravings were made as early as the mid-nineteenth century by the great Danish prehistorian JENS JACOB WORSAAE.

Brunius was one of the greatest pioneers of rock-art recording, though his name remains largely unknown outside Scandinavia. Born in 1792 in the parsonage of Tanum in western Sweden to a clergyman father who had an interest in antiquities, Brunius was surrounded throughout his childhood by the wealth of ancient monuments and rock art in the region and showed early talent as a draftsman. He carried out fieldwork in Bohuslän in the three summers from 1815 to 1817, which led him to write a book, *Hällristningslära* (A Doctrine of Rock Art), in 1818 that was translated into French and titled *Rapport succinct sur les hiéroglyphes trouvés sur les rochers de la Province de Bohus* (A Short Report on the Carvings Found on the Rocks of the Province of Bohus) but for financial reasons was never printed—the many plates made it very expensive. Nonetheless, it comprised the first professional record of sixty-five rock-art sites in his part of the world. The drawings are preserved in Stockholm's Topographical Archives.

Brunius thought of petroglyphs as hieroglyphics and could see that they were older than the alphabet, so he assumed that they were older than runes—especially as they are not mentioned in the Icelandic sagas. Since the petroglyphs were located far from the present coast, he thought they might be several thousand years old if they had originally been cut next to the shore (presumably the dominance of ship motifs suggested this idea as well as his observation of several ancient beaches and inland SHELL MIDDENS). Brunius argued like a natural scientist and even used weathering processes as indicators of antiquity. However, he had no comparable studies from which to work: for his somewhat simple narrative interpretations (seeing the figures as memorials, a kind of picture writing, depicting fighting, embarkation, etc.) he used classical sources such as Tacitus and Pytheas and also the emerging ethnography of the Eskimo, for example, by drawing on knowledge of Greenland canoes and some Siberian carvings on rocks published earlier by von Strahlenberg.

Brunius also left a detailed account of his working methods, and those methods reveal what a true pioneer he was. He proclaimed that careful and true observations create better conditions for interpretation.

> The earth on the carvings was taken away, the mosses were scratched off by an iron scraper, the water was led another way and the bedrock was cleaned and washed somewhere. If the figures were small and unclear, I had to—in order to be sure—visit the place at that hour of the day when the sun was shining so that a separation of the figures was possible by light and shadow. It is possible to have the same effect after the sun set by the help of a lantern. If the observation was difficult I had to revisit the place. On these occasions chalk was brought to make contours. It was also rewarding to use the finger tips to know if a line was natural or artificial.

To produce his drawings, Brunius laid a grid system over the rock surface and copied the figures onto a corresponding grid paper, all within a controlled scale. Figures that were hard to identify were visited several times in different conditions—as mentioned in the above quotation, in oblique sunlight, by night lantern, or after a rain. The figures were marked on the rock with chalk and drawn onto paper with pencil in such a way that a darker line denoted a deeper carving. Finally, he also discussed the location, age, and significance of the figures; noted differences in their condition, from intact to almost totally disappeared; and looked at the sites' environs, their setting in the landscape, and the presence of monuments nearby.

Since Brunius was such a pioneer, he had very little comparative material to help him with interpretation. He also had a moral problem in his documentation—should the impressive sexual organs of the male figures be depicted or not? He therefore referred to other tribes such as the Lapps or the Huns as the creators of the rude customs shown on the rocks and claimed that the original Nordic people were above this cultural level.

The bombshell of Paleolithic (Ice Age) art came after decades of sporadic and misunderstood finds. Its existence was first established and accepted through the discovery, in the early 1860s, of engraved and carved bones and stones in a number of caves and rock shelters in south-western France, particularly by ÉDOUARD LARTET and his English associate HENRY CHRISTY. These objects were found with Paleolithic stone and bone tools and the bones of Ice Age animals, which proved their great age—in particular, the famous engraving from LA MADELEINE of a mammoth on a piece of mammoth tusk. There followed a kind of "gold rush," with people plundering likely sites for ancient art treasures.

Some French scholars had noticed art on cave walls in the 1860s and 1870s but had not realized its age or significance. The pioneer who did make the crucial mental leap was a Spanish landowner, Marcelino Sanz de Sautuola, who noticed in 1879 that the bison figures painted on the ceiling of the cave of ALTAMIRA, near the north coast of Cantabria, were closely similar in style to the figures in Paleolithic portable art. Unfortunately, most of the archaeological establishment refused to take his published views seriously, dismissing him as naive or a fraud. One prehistorian who did accept Altamira, however, was EDOUARD PIETTE, who, in the late 1880s, was to find the famous painted pebbles in the cave of LE MAS D'AZIL in the French Pyrenees, a discovery the establishment found equally hard to swallow. One of the doubts raised about Altamira was that the cave was too humid and the rock too friable to have preserved painting for so long, but the stratigraphic position of the Azilian pebbles finally proved that ocher could adhere to rock for millennia.

It was in southwestern France once again that the final breakthrough occurred when engravings were found, in 1895, in a gallery of the cave of La Mouthe in the Dordogne region. Since the gallery was blocked by Paleolithic deposits, it was obvious that the engravings must be of the same age. Other discoveries soon followed in other caves in southern France, culminating in those of Les Combarelles and Font de Gaume in 1901, which served to at last establish the authenticity of Paleolithic cave art.

The Twentieth Century: A Splintering of Approaches

In the twentieth century, the discoveries made involved not just individual sites but whole classes of art and brought more countries onto the map of prehistoric art. For example, it was in 1903 that the first scientific discovery of a site of Levantine art in Spain was discovered—red paintings of three deer and aurochs at Roca dels Moros at Calapatá, Teruel—by Juan Cabré y Aguiló, a photographer. He did not dare publish his findings until 1907, mindful of the ridicule and furor caused by Altamira in 1880, but eventually his find aroused national interest. The same year, the Roca dels Moros at Cogul, Lérida, was reported by the local parish priest, Ramón Huguet, and published in 1908, although the locals had always known of them and attributed them, like all ancient things, to the Moors, who had brought so much culture to Spain in earlier times. Elsewhere in Europe, the rock art of VALCAMONICA in the Italian Alps was first pointed out by a shepherd in 1914.

One might think that the rock-art map of Europe was now well established, but not only do new decorated caves continue to turn up every year in France and Spain, and new petroglyph sites in the Alps and elsewhere, but thousands of petroglyphs have been discovered in the far north of Norway (especially around Alta) since 1973 while major collections of hundreds of open-air Paleolithic engravings and petroglyphs have been found in Spain and Portugal since 1980 and especially in the 1990s.

In Asia, Thailand became of interest to the rock-art world thanks to a French military surveyor, L. L. Lunet de Lajonquière, who was in the area from 1903 to 1909. His descriptive records, published in 1912, include references to painted rock-art sites, notably Khao Kian (Mountain of Paintings), a shallow cave containing geometric designs and naturalistic animals. More sites were found in the 1920s and later. In China, an engraving in Hong Kong had been mentioned in newspapers in 1819, but the first real research in that country, which took place in 1915, consisted of work on the engravings in Fujian Province after Professor Hua Zhongjin was informed of them by villagers. In 1927, the Swedish archaeologist Bergman found engravings in Inner Mongolia and filled them with white powder to take photographs.

Amazingly, it was not until the 1980s that rock-art research really got under way in earnest

in China and that the outside world learned of the country's enormous wealth in this regard. Major discoveries have continued there—for example, scores of rock-art sites with thousands of figures were discovered in Tibet only during the 1990s. Meanwhile, in India, research flourished throughout the century, with the result that we now know of more than 1,000 rock shelters with paintings in over 150 sites; there is rock art in almost all the states of India.

In Australia, the first clues that the rock art might be really ancient came in 1929 when excavations of the Devon Downs shelter on the Murray River exposed engraved art on the rock face, the earliest of which was associated with debris four meters below the surface. In the last few decades of the twentieth century the dates were pushed back—for example, 13,000 years for engravings at the Early Man Shelter in Queensland. Claims have been made for an age of more than 40,000 years for organic material trapped in varnish on top of simple petroglyphs at Wharton Hill and Panaramittee South in South Australia, although the validity of such dates from organic material in an "open system" remains highly uncertain and controversial. In some areas, such as the Kimberley, more than 100 new sites per year were found in the 1990s, and a large number of previously unsuspected decorated caves were also discovered.

In North America, there was relatively little interest in rock art until JULIAN STEWARD wrote a work on the subject that was published by the University of California at Berkeley in 1929. He was the first person to use the terms "petroglyph" and "pictograph," and he shunned the use of ethnographic data as speculative, preferring to focus on defining a series of rock art "areas." In more recent years, it has been found that the New World has one of the world's richest and most diverse bodies of prehistoric art, with whole new areas still being put on the rock-art map, especially in vast territories like Brazil, where, for example, the hundreds of decorated rock shelters of the Piauí region have become known only since the 1970s.

The continent on which rock art was perhaps the most transformed in the course of the twentieth century is Africa. In East Africa, the first discovery of rock art occurred in 1908, when some missionaries on the western shore of Lake Nyanza in Tanzania found red figures in rock shelters. The first decorated cave in the Central African Republic was found in 1912, and engravings were discovered in Cameroon in 1933. In North Africa, rock paintings (as opposed to engravings) were not documented until 1933 when a camel-corps officer, one Lieutenant Brenans, ventured into a deep canyon of the Tassili n' Ajjer during a police operation; as he rode slowly on his camel, he saw strange figures on the cliffs of the wadi: the animal and human engravings of Oued Djerat. He also saw very delicate paintings, the first European to do so. New discoveries continue to be made in Africa; for example, the first rock art (in this case, engravings) in Gabon was found only in 1987.

Concerning Ice Age art, the huge majority of discoveries were made in the twentieth century, not only of caves (an average of one per year, including such major sites as Niaux, Les Trois Frères, Pech Merle, LASCAUX, and Chauvet) but also of thousands of pieces of portable art. In recent decades, it has become apparent that art of the same age also exists outside Europe, indeed, on every other continent. The subject was dominated by ABBÉ HENRI BREUIL until his death in 1961; renowned for his tracings of cave and portable art (primarily in Europe but also in southern Africa), he was less noted for his interpretations, which remained firmly entrenched in simplistic notions of hunting and fertility magic based on selected ethnographic analogies.

Breuil was one of the towering figures in Old World prehistory during the first half of the twentieth century. He trained as a priest in his youth but was allowed to devote all his energies to prehistory: he undertook virtually no religious duties and made almost no contribution to the reconciliation of prehistory's findings with religious teachings. He had the supreme good fortune, as a young man with a talent for drawing animals, to make the acquaintance of Piette and EMILE CARTAILHAC, two of France's greatest prehistorians at the turn of the twentieth century, when they needed help with the study and illustration of Paleolithic portable art

and cave art, respectively. Breuil consequently became the world's leading authority on Paleolithic art. He discovered many decorated caves or galleries himself and copied their art—by his own reckoning, he spent about 700 days of his life underground. Although now seen as excessively subjective and incomplete, his tracings are nevertheless recognized as remarkable for their time. In some instances, they constitute our only record of cave figures that have since faded or disappeared.

Breuil's concept of two phases in the development of Paleolithic art (two essentially similar but independent consecutive cycles, each progressing from simple to complex forms in engraving, sculpture, and painting) was inconsistent and unsatisfactory and was eventually replaced by ANDRÉ LEROI-GOURHAN's four "styles," themselves now being abandoned. Breuil thought of Paleolithic art primarily in terms of hunting magic, thanks to a simplistic use of selected ethnographic analogies, and he generally considered decorated caves to be accumulations of single figures, unlike Leroi-Gourhan who saw them as as carefully planned compositions.

Breuil's legacy of publications and tracings has been found to contain many errors and misjudgments, but his work also contains an abundance of profound insights that are only now being supported by new finds; for example, new direct dates and pigment analyses in European caves often tend to support Breuil's views rather than André Leroi-Gourhan's.

After Breuil's death, the field was dominated by Leroi-Gourhan, who undertook no tracing but revolutionized interpretation by rejecting ethnography and conducting a structuralist analysis of the content of cave art. He found a basic dualism—i.e., the art was dominated by horses and bison—which he interpreted as male and female symbols, respectively, and he also saw the art's nonfigurative "signs" in sexual terms. He believed that caves were not simple collections of individual images (as Breuil had thought) but carefully planned homogeneous compositions laid out according to a preconceived blueprint. Since Leroi-Gourhan's death in 1986, approaches to this subject have splintered, and it has become apparent that no single all-embracing theory can hope to account for such a widespread, long-lasting, and varied phenomenon.

One can generalize from the experience of Paleolithic art that during the early decades of the twentieth century, attention focused on discovering and copying prehistoric art, interpreting it in fairly simple and literal terms—often distorting or selecting facts to fit a preselected pet theory derived from ethnography—and great effort was devoted to building up regional chronologies based on styles, techniques, and superimpositions. This was the period when searches became systematic, although accidental discoveries continued to be made and, indeed, are still being made.

In those early days, the study of rock art was akin to that of stone tools or any other artifacts in that it was based on stratigraphy (i.e., superimpositions) and typology (i.e., styles) with the primary aim of developing a classificatory framework. The regional stylistic sequences that were built up were equivalent to the geological and artifactual sequences of other fields. Interpretations were simplistic, drawn largely from the history of religion, and uncritically incorporated elements from a wide array of places, periods, and cultures.

During the second half of the century, attention was devoted to developing more complex (and no doubt more accurate) interpretations. Some of these were based on structuralism, most notably the interpretations of Leroi-Gourhan, and researchers such as FRED MC-CARTHY in Australia and Patricia Vinnicombe and Tim Maggs in southern Africa urged that the rock-art corpus should be recorded as objectively and comprehensively as possible and placed great emphasis on quantification.

However, counting and listing require enormous amounts of time and labor and do not reveal much about meaning—they merely provide the raw material on which hypotheses can be based (although they can lead to fascinating insights, as shown by current wide-ranging studies based on the tens of thousands of figures traced accurately by Harald Pager in the Brandberg mountains in what is now Namibia in southern Africa).

Most recently, therefore, there has been a move toward environmental and spatial studies, examining the art in its landscape, for one of the fundamental features of rock art is that it is located precisely where the artist chose to place it and much can still be learned from this placement. At the same time, greater efforts have been made to integrate rock art with contemporary archaeological data and cultural contexts (where its date can be at least estimated). Some researchers have even attempted a semiotic approach, treating rock art as conveying complex, symbolic messages. There has also been renewed interest in ethnographic information, with an avowed intention (not always successful) to avoid the simplistic and all-embracing explanations for which ethnography was misused in the past and with a renewed ability to tell new kinds of stories about the figures and scenes in the art. Currently, there are numerous attempts to "read" the art in terms of shamanism and trance, attempts that usually owe more to the predilections and wishful thinking of the interpreters than to an objective and respectful assessment of the ethnographic record.

As in archaeology itself, since the 1960s there has also been a desperate desire to find some new approach to the study of rock art, some fresh fashion to adopt, and every other discipline imaginable has been trawled for any useful titbits of theory or insight. So, in rapid succession we have passed through structuralism, processualism, poststructuralism, structural Marxism, and contextualism. Overall, there has been a diversification of approaches, which can only be healthy, and a new emphasis on the nonmaterial, the ideological, and the social aspects of prehistoric art. For example, Scandinavian ships are now seen by some researchers as ambiguous symbols of social interaction and unity, and it is thought that rock-art sites containing such symbols mark social boundaries or ownership of places and resources.

More serious, and far more important, has been the growing realization that indigenous people have rights that need to be respected. Just as it came as a profound shock to archaeologists and anthropologists in the late 1970s and 1980s to find that some indigenous people objected vociferously to having their ancestors or sacred objects excavated and stored in museums without their knowledge or permission, so rock-art researchers in several parts of the world (especially Australia) have had to modify their procedures and outlook after aboriginal groups campaigned for control of their own culture and provided input into (and demanded feedback from) research into their art. It is safe to say that, today, nobody in Australia would dream of beginning a study of rock art without consulting the aboriginal custodians of the region in question.

On the technical side, photography was adopted quite early—the first photograph of an African rock painting was taken in 1885—but the procedure became commonplace within a decade. Much later, color photography began to be used, at first by pioneers such as Alex Willcox in South Africa beginning in 1951, and technology such as digital cameras, video, and computer enhancement is now coming into its own. In the last few years of the twentieth century, new techniques of direct DATING began to revolutionize (in some cases) or at least fine-tune (in others) the traditional chronologies built up over decades, and newly dated rock art at last joined the already well-dated portable art in being embraced by mainstream archaeologists as data worthy of attention. It remains to be seen in what new directions the latest technology and the impending discoveries of the twenty-first century will take rock-art studies, especially as the field is one of ever-increasing popularity in many parts of the world.

Paul G. Bahn

References

Bahn, P. 1998. *The Cambridge Illustrated History of Prehistoric Art*. Cambridge: Cambridge University Press.

Bahn, P. G., and Jean Vertut. 1988. *Images of the Ice Age*. New York: Facts on File.

Chippindale, C., and P. S. Tacon, eds. 1998. *The Archaeology of Rock-Art*. Cambridge: Cambridge University Press.

Romania

Romania is rich in archaeological discoveries because of its geographical location in southeastern Europe, through which important roads used since ancient times have passed, and because of its temperate climate (*Istoria României* 1 1960; *Istoria României* 2 1962). Its diverse landscape includes thick forests and mountainous areas that afforded natural protection from invaders, and broad plains where native populations could live during peaceful times, allowing them to survive for millennia on Romania's plentiful natural resources.

In the early nineteenth century, amateur archaeologists began to collect artifacts from ancient settlements, which led to the founding of the first museums: in Sibiu in 1817, the National Museum in Bucharest in 1834, the Historico-Natural Museum in Iași also in 1834, and another in Cluj in 1859. In the late nineteenth century, these amateurs began to unearth and study some Neolithic and Geto-Dacian settlements. In 1880 Grigore Tocilescu published a paper entitled "Dacia before the Romans," and in 1912 Ion Andrieșescu published the "Contribution to Dacia before Romans." These publications encouraged Vasile Pârvan, with the aid of Ion Andrieșescu, to train some young scholars to specialize in archaeology, and Romanian archaeological research blossomed. Young researchers started their fieldwork with university scholars such as Ion Nestor in Bucharest, Constantin Daicoviciu in Cluj, and Mircea Petrescu-Dâmbovița in Iași; all over the country, archaeologists began prospecting and excavating and publishing the results in the journal *Dacia*, which was translated into several languages. Other museums based on small collections were founded in counties, towns, and villages (mostly small collections). Between 1926 and 1948, sites representing all historical periods were systematically excavated (Nestor 1933). Since 1950, the Institute of Archaeology in Bucharest has published *Studies and Research of Ancient History and Archaeology* (in Romanian) in addition to the internationally translated *Dacia* and numerous monographs. In the last few decades of the twentieth century, dozens of specialized periodicals were being published (almost every one of Romania's forty-one counties has its own journal).

In addition to the excavations carried out on sites from all historical epochs, prospecting expeditions have mapped out a detailed archaeological picture of Romania. Nicolăescu-Plopşor (1938, 41–107) and Păunescu (1970, 11–34, 107–148) made notable discoveries concerning the Paleolithic era. Others found implements dating back to the Pebble culture, located in the south of Romania between the Olt and Argeş rivers. Objects made with the Abbevillo-Acheulean technique were found. Clactonian implements were discovered in Oltenia, Muntenia, and northern Moldavia (historical provinces). Mousterian settlements such as the one at Ripiceni, which has been studied in detail, were identified. In caves and on terraces, Aurignacian complexes were found, and evidence of the Gravetian culture was discovered in several zones. Archaeologists also discovered settlements dating back to the archaic Campignian, Swiderian, Romanello Azilian, and Tardenoisian epochs. The northwestern Tardenoisian of Romania was connected with eastern-central Europe, whereas the northeastern is linked with the north Pontic area (Pontus Euxinus is the Black Sea).

Since the mid-twentieth century, aspects of the Neolithic epoch have been studied extensively. Many Neolithic cultures have been found in Romania (Berciu 1961; Comşa, E. 1987), including the previously undiscovered cultures of Cârcea-Gura Baciului (in Oltenia and Transylvania), Starčevo-Criş (in Banat, Oltenia, Moldavia, Muntenia, and Transylvania), and Ciumeşti (in Maramureş). In the area close to Portile de Fier, studies were done of some complexes that did not contain ceramics but had some tools such as little hoes, leading to the conclusion that the people who lived there belonged to a protoneolithic culture. During the Neolithic period, people began using tools made of flint, obsidian, and horn. They were also acquainted with metals (copper and gold). At first they made simple implements, but toward the end of the epoch they were making large copper tools (such as axes), golden figurines, and jewels. They practiced a fertility re-

Neolithic figurine discovered in Romania (AAA)

ligion represented by feminine figurines of clay, bone, copper, and gold, and their funeral rite was inhumation (with most corpses placed in the fetal position with or without an accompanying burial inventory).

The earliest Neolithic culture was Cârcea-Gura Baciului, which existed in Oltenia from south of the Danube to western Transylvania, followed by the Starčevo-Criş communities, which came from the southwest but spread across almost all of Romania. Both of these cultures were known for their painted ceramics. In the northwest, the Ciumeşti communities used incised decorations on their ceramic vessels. At the end of the early Neolithic period, the Dudeşti culture brought incised ceramics (ladder, net, spiral) from the south into Muntenia and Oltenia. Into northern Moldavia came the communities with linear ceramics (incised lines and graphics that looked like heads of musical notes), spreading into northeastern Muntenia and southern Transylvania. The linear ceramic cultures mixed with the Dudeşti culture to form the Boian culture in Muntenia with its various phases (Bolintineanu, Giuleşti, Vidra, and transitional) of excised pottery containing encrusted white lines. At the end of the Giuleşti phase, the Boian population penetrated southeastern Transylvania and southern Moldavia. In the same epoch, the Hamangia culture of southern origin developed in Dobroudja, which was distinguished by ceramics decorated with groups of incised lines and dots. In southeastern Oltenia, the Vădastra culture developed, while in western Oltenia and in Banat the Vinča culture thrived, with canelled decoration on ceramics fired red and black. In neighboring southwestern Transylvania lived the people of the Turdaş culture, who were closely related to the Vinča.

During the middle Neolithic epoch, the population of southern Romania had scanty settlements comprising few dwellings, mostly earth huts built below agricultural terraces. Those communities had a less stable life than the previously mentioned ceramic cultures, practicing primitive agriculture with little hoes, breeding cattle, hunting, and fishing. In the Giuleşti phase in the southern territories, the people gradually began to use ploughs pulled by animals, creating an essential change in farming techniques. In time, the Giuleşti communities penetrated southeastern Transylvania and southern Moldavia, where, by mixing with late linear ceramic cultures, they formed the pre-Cucuteni culture, whose area extended far to the northeast. At the same time in southern Transylvania lived the Petreşti culture (which made painted ceramics), and in the west the Tisa culture. Until the end of the epoch, these communities made continual progress toward more settled existence in southern Romania. Settlements comprising surface dwellings and protective walls were even constructed on high terraces surrounded by steep slopes. Some such settlements have been exhaustively excavated (Hăbăşeşti, Truşeşti, and Târpeşti in Moldavia; Radovanu and Căscioarele in Muntenia).

A period of significant development took place during the last decades of the Neolithic era. In Muntenia and Dobroudja, the Gumelniţa culture was descended directly from the Boian culture, and in Oltenia the Sălcuţa culture developed. Bowls, some with graphite painted decoration, are identified with both cultures. The Cuceteni culture developed out of a pre-Cucuteni culture in Moldavia, distinguished by ceramic vessels with painted decoration (white, red, and black) that were fired in improved ovens. The Cucuteni communities attained an advanced stage of development, with some settlements comprising over 1,000 dwellings. The Româneşti and Gorneşti cultures have also been identified with the late Neolithic era in western Romania. During the Neolithic epoch, an ethnic and cultural continuity can be traced for over two millennia in the Dudeşti, Boian, and Gumelniţa cultures in Muntenia and in the linear ceramics pre-Cucuteni and Cuceteni cultures in Moldavia.

At the end of the Neolithic era, semi-nomadic populations of Yamnaia shepherds who lived in the eastern and southern plains of Romania spread from the steppes into areas north of the Black Sea (identified by tumuli burials, with ochered corpses placed on their backs instead of their sides). This migration defined a period of transition from the Neolithic to the Bronze Age (Morintz and Roman 1973, 259–295). In the southern territories, the Cernavoda I culture in Dobroudja, southern Muntenia, and southern Oltenia developed and was characterized by ceramics made of paste mixed with ground shells. Ceramic vessels from the Celei complex in southeastern Oltenia and the Cernavoda II culture in eastern and southern Muntenia were shaped like sacks and made of paste containing sand and ground shards and ornamented with incised lines or relief bands. Cernavoda III (related to Cernavoda I and Gumelniţa), in Dobroudja and southwestern Muntenia, was also known for its vessels made of paste with ground shells. Simultaneously, the Horodiştea I communities lived in Moldavia and the local Cucuteni population mixed with eastern shepherd tribes to form the Folteşti I culture. These nomads rarely painted their ceramics, but used incised or corded decorations. Soon, globular amphorae began to appear from the north and along the Carpathian mountains, along with spherical corded vessels and the practice of burying their dead in "stone cists." The Foltești II culture developed in Moldavia, and the Coțofeni culture covered Banat, Crișana, Oltenia, and Transylvania. These communities, which were located in mountains, foothills, and on the plains, bred cattle as well as practicing agriculture. Their vessels were characterized by overturned handles and ornate incised decorations. Yamnaia shepherds from the east continued to penetrate Romania throughout this transition period from the Neolithic to the Bronze Age, and all of the above-mentioned cultures continued to develop in their respective regions.

The Bronze Age, which took place from around 2000 to 1200 B.C., featured the Glina III communities in Muntenia, Oltenia, southeastern Transylvania, and southeastern Banat, identified by pottery containing "hollow-button" decoration (Morintz 1978). During the Middle Bronze Age, in western Dobroudja and southeastern Transylvania, the Tei populations (rushian zolniki) built settlements on river terraces. Their pottery vessels consisted of short pots with just one handle (later with two), with white encrusted spiral decorations. These communities were contiguous with those of the Monteoru culture from northeastern Muntenia and southern Moldavia. The latter built their fortress-like settlements on hilltops and terraces and were known for richly ornamented two-handled pots. They used polished stone implements and sometimes bronze daggers or spear points. At Sărata Monteoru four burial sites were found containing crushed skeletons. Although inhumation dominated burial rites during this period, cremation was also practiced. Burial inventories were rich, consisting of ceramic vessels, stone axes and weapons, and bronze daggers. Women's graves contained bracelets, bronze necklaces, amber beads, and bronze and gold rings.

Also during the Bronze Age, the Verbiciora communities established lasting settlements in Oltenia, protected by ditches. This culture was known for handled ceramics and incised decoration. Burials were characterized by inhumation earlier in the period and later by crema-

tion. The Gârla Mare populations in southern Oltenia had cremation burial sites containing richly decorated urns and female figurines. In southern Banat, the Cruceni culture also practiced cremation. Contemporaries of the Verbiciora were the Vatina in western and southwestern Banat and the Periam-Pecica on the Lower Mureș, with tell (mound) settlements. These two cultures both had ceramics with incised geometric ornaments and practiced the inhumation of crouched corpses. Meanwhile, the Wietenberg populations inhabited mostly unprotected settlements in the central Mureș area, using vessels decorated with bands and triangles, axes, and some bronze Micenian-type swords. In western Romania, the Otomani culture built fortress-like settlements and made large decorated pots. Funeral rites in both of these latter cultures evolved from inhumation to cremation. In the northwest, the Suciu de Sus culture decorated pottery with spirals and practiced cremation as well.

At a great distance from Moldavia and Transylvania lived the Noua communities. They bred cattle, used two-handled pots decorated in the hollow button style, and practiced inhumation in flat necropolises. The Noua culture was related to the Sabatinovka and the Coslogeni cultures, who lived in southeast Romania and were known for their use of two-handled vessels. These populations practiced inhumation of crouched corpses, occasionally using tumuli burials. Near the end of the Bronze Age, the Zimnicea-Plovdiv populations (who buried their dead in the fetal position with undecorated two-handled jars) penetrated southwestern Muntenia and developed bronze metallurgy, making weapons and jewelry. The influx of shepherds from the east into Dobroudja, Moldavia, and across the Romanian steppes continued throughout the Bronze Age.

The early Iron Age in Romania, called the Hallstatt period, lasted from about 1200 B.C. to 450 B.C. (Laszlo 1976, 89–98; Vasiliev 1988, 83–102; Vulpe 1974, 1–21). Bronze metallurgy was prevalent at the beginning of the period and gradually gave way to iron metallurgy. Existing populations mixed with each other, forming what became known as the Thracian communities. These complex societies have been studied extensively by the Romanian Institute of Thracology, an interdisciplinary school of anthropology, archaeology, ethnoarchaeology, ethnology, ethnomusicology, and linguistics that publishes the journal *Thraco-Dacia*. In the beginning of the Hallstatt period in western Romania, the Gava, Susani, and Insula Banului cultures thrived, making black pottery. The Insula Banului spread east along the Danube River, contributing to the formation of the Babadag culture in Dobroudja and the Cozia-Brad culture in Moldavia, characterized by imprinted pottery. These communities practiced agriculture and bred cattle; some had burial rites of inhumation (supine corpses) and others cremation; their necropolises were either flat or tumuli. Later, in Moldavia and Transylvania, came the Mediaş and Reci cultures. In the middle Hallstatt, the Basarabi culture covered a great expanse of territory in southwestern Romania; it was identified with bitronconic vessels, jars, and dishes, all with spiral ornaments. Simultaneously, the Babadag culture continued to develop in Dobroudja, with settlements of earthen huts protected by ditches and walls, and with black and incised white encrusted pottery.

In the late Hallstatt period, the local population flourished under the influence of the southern Thracians. In Moldavia, fortress-like settlements point to the existence of some well-organized tribes of Thracians known as Gets or Dacians, depending on the archaeological source. Greek colonies on the Black Sea coast also played an important role in the development of Thracian culture. Histria was founded in 657 B.C. and issued silver and bronze coins beginning around the middle of the fifth century B.C.; arrowheads were sometimes used as currency in neighboring areas. The Thracian culture occupied the hilly southern area of Bârseşti-Ferigile, with tumuli cremation burial sites that contained some Scythian weapons (akinakes, axes, and rare vessels made on pottery wheels). Nomadic Scythians had invaded from the north Pontic steppes. They spread to Moldavia and along the Danube plain and also from the west into Transylvania, where the Agathirsies culture has been docu-

mented (Vasiliev 1980). However, outside the Carpathian region, their forays are believed to have been only temporary.

In all Romanian provinces, archaeologists have discovered complexes dating to the late Iron Age, or LA TÈNE, period (Berciu 1967; Daicoviciu, C. 1945; Daicoviciu, H. 1965; Pârvan 1926). The Geto-Dacians, who built these settlements, were direct ancestors of the present-day Romanian people. The Geto-Dacians experienced several other invasions. As early as the first half of the fourth century B.C., Celtic communities invaded from the west (Crişan 1971, 149–164; Zirra 1971, 171–238). At the same time, western Oltenia and part of Banat came under the rule of Scordisci Celts. The Gets, under the leadership of Dromichaites, defeated the Macedonian army led by Lisimach, who was taken prisoner. At the end of the third century B.C., the Bastarns, a Germanic people, penetrated Moldavia from the north, creating the Poieneşti-Lukaşevka culture. Celtic rule lasted in the area until the end of the second century B.C. However, by the first century B.C., the Geto-Dacians had achieved superior tribal organization in the south, with fortresses (dava) and military chieftains, and by the middle of the first century, they had established a center in southwestern Transylvania under King Burebista. During that period, the Geto-Dacians conquered a wider territory and Dacia extended from the Middle Danube to the Black Sea littoral (between Apollonia and Olbia) and from present-day Slovakia's mountains to the Balkan mountains.

The Geto-Dacians maintained two social classes: tarabostes (aristocrats) and comati (common people). An aristocratic "council" and great priest helped the king rule the population. The Geto-Dacians practiced various occupations; predominantly agriculture on the plains and cattle breeding in the foothills and mountains. Hunting, fishing, pottery making, metallurgy (iron, silver), salt extraction and processing, viticulture, arboriculture, and beekeeping were also known (Vulpe 1976, 19–21). The Geto-Dacians used diverse tools (plows, scythes, sickles, axes) and weapons (swords, spears, knives, lances) made of iron. Many settlements were built on high terraces or mountaintops and defended by ditches and walls. These complexes have been studied extensively (for example, in Moldavia: Poiana, Răcătău, Bradu, and Piatra Neamţ; in Muntenia: Tinosul, Zimnicea, Popeşti, Cârlomăneşti, and Piscu Crăsani; in Oltenia: Polovragi, Ocniţa, and others; in Transylvania: Covasna, Jigodin, Simleul Silvaniei, and Pecica). The most important site is that of Sarmisegetusa, the capital of Dacia near Grădiştea Muncelului in southwestern Transylvania (Daicoviciu, C. and Daicoviciu, H. 1963). This site was surrounded by a series of fortresses with stone walls and other edifices, including quadrilateral sanctuaries (composed of three to six rows of stone or wooden columns) as well as circular ones (with stone columns or wooden pillars) in which to worship the deity Zamolxis. The complex contained various types of dwellings made respectively of earth, wooden pillars, and stone bricks. Ceramics were found in great quantities in all Geto-Dacian settlements. Common ware (jars, lamps, storage pots) was made of rough paste and decorated with outlined belts of round indentations or notches. Fine pottery was usually thrown on a wheel, with carefully polished surfaces fired gray or black. Vessels primarily consisted of dishes with various kinds of rims, single-handled tall pots, or pots with feet, decorated with polished strips (horizontal or waved) or notched motifs. The Geto-Dacians also used Greek pottery (amphorae, cups) obtained in trade, some of which was imitated by local artisans (for example, the megorian cups).

Dacia was conquered by the Romans and became their province (Macrea and Tudor 1960, 345–467), which included Banat, Oltenia, western Muntenia, and Transylvania. The Romans built camps along the border. The Romans also occupied southern Moldavia and Muntenia, where they built several camps, which they deserted during the reign of Emperor Hadrian. Within Dacia the Romans established numerous towns and fortresses containing many buildings and temples (Daicoviciu, C. 1945). The following complexes have been studied by archaeologists: Apulum, Napoca, Porolissum, Sarmizegetusa Ulpia Traiana, and Cumidava in Transylvania;

Drobeta, Sucidava, and Buridava in Oltenia; and Tropaeum Trajani, Capidava, Dinogetia, Noviodunum, and others in Dobroudja. Many colonists came to Dacia from different provinces of the Roman Empire. The Romans tried to seize as many of Dacia's riches as possible, especially the gold and other metal deposits as well as the salt. Battles with the Romans took a heavy toll on the Dacian population, but not all of them were exterminated. The Romans needed the native labor for agriculture and cattle breeding. The continuity of the local population has been corroborated by archaeological research. At Roman sites, pottery specifically identified with the Dacians has been continuously present, and cremation was maintained as the funeral custom during the entire Roman occupation.

Roman colonists mixed with local Dacians and the Romanian culture began to form, with its language's origin in Latin. This process lasted for several centuries because some indigenous people remained isolated in the foothills and mountains, which Roman immigrants avoided, keeping to the roads along the plains. In the year 271 A.D., during the reign of the Roman Emperor Aurelian, the Roman legions and some of the colonists retreated from Dacia because of the many Barbarian attacks. Some Romans remained, as certified by the archaeological evidence. Life continued, for better or worse, within the small and large Roman centers, as demonstrated by archaeological evidence of continuing Roman farming and mining techniques.

After the retreat of Roman authorities and legions from Dacia, free Dacians and Carps began to immigrate from the east. At the same time, remaining Romans and Romanized populations spread into neighboring regions. Consequently, the invasion of the Gots (after 320 A.D.) began the gradual integration of the Carps, Geto-Dacians, and Sarmathians into the Sântana-Cerneahov culture under the rule of the Gots (Mitrea 1972, 81–94), which spread into Transylvania. Archaeologists include the indigenous material culture outside the Carpathian region in the Santana-Cerneahov culture, whereas in Transylvania the Sântana-Cerneahov elements appear to have been assimilated by Roman provincial culture. During the reign of

Emperor Constantine the Great, the Gots became citizens of the Roman Empire; consequently, Constantine the Great took control of a significant part of the former Dacia. During the same period, some of the Romans in the former Roman province of Dacia became Christians (Moga 1974, 259–266). Christianity played a significant role not only in maintaining Roman influence north of the Danube but also in assimilating newcomers. A time of unrest ensued, during which many different migrating peoples penetrated Romania's territory from the east, north, and west. Some of them crossed the Danube into the Roman Empire; others settled in the lowlands for some time, a few of them going into Transylvania. One of these invading groups was the Huns, who in ca. 375 or 376 A.D. exterminated the Sântana-Cerneahov culture in Romania. However, in turn, the Roman Empire defeated the Huns and took control of lands north of the Danube, establishing camps along the river.

The Gepids invaded northwestern Romania and destroyed the surviving Roman centers in the area. To escape these conquerors, some of the local people crossed the Carpathian mountains to Moldavia and Muntenia. The Gepids coexisted with the remaining natives (Horedt 1975, 111–122), sharing the settlements and burial grounds. The two communities were distinguished from one another by dwelling type and funeral rituals. The settlement at Moreşti, in Transylvania, is one example of a Gepid settlement. It contained shared burial grounds and earthen huts surrounded by a defense wall and a ditch. Also dating back to this period are several Christian basilicas in Dobroudja, Oltenia, and Transylvania. The Christian influence in Dacia can be traced through Latin Christian terminology preserved in the Romanian language. In the year 568, the Avars invaded western Romania and took political power from the Gepids (Comşa, M. 1987, 219–230; Rusu 1975, 123–154).

The first known populations of Slavs appeared in southern Romania around 527 A.D., with other Slavic groups following until about 680 A.D. (Comşa, M. 1975, 171–200; Nestor 1973, 29–33; Rusa 1975, 123–154; Teodor 1975, 155–170). By the end of the sixth cen-

tury A.D. in Muntenia, the valleys of the Dâmboviţa and Lower Argeş rivers were shared by Romanic and Slavic populations under rulers such as Dauridas, Ardogast, and Piragast, along with Mosikios, chieftain of the area along the river Buzău. The Suceava "Sipot," a settlement consisting of rectangular earthen huts containing hearths bordered with stone, is the earliest Slavic complex discovered by archaeologists. Handmade ceramics and jewelry were found there, including digitated fibula dating to the eighth century (Matei 1960, 374–394). The burial ground at Sărata Monteoru (Buzău County), comprising over 1500 cremation burial sites, was also a significant discovery. Human ashes were placed either in a pit or in an urn, with burial inventories of digitated fibulae, beads, jewels, knives, and flint tools (Nestor and Zaharia 1961, 513–515). The existence of a Slavic group in northwestern Romania during the eighth and ninth centuries A.D. is indicated by the cemeteries at Nuşfalău and Someşeni, characterized by tumuli cremation burials. The burial grounds at Nuşfalău held wooden tombs where ashes were stored with funeral inventory such as pottery, wooden pails, knives, and jewelry. Taking into account the types of vessels and the burial inventory, these complexes were connected with the western Slavs. Some necropolises in Dobroudja, such as Castelu and Satu Nou, held ashes in urns, some bordered with stone slabs forming a cist, a practice that connects the population with the southern Slavs. Slavs came into contact with the native population of the former Dacia and in time were assimilated into a population that shared the Romanic language (Comşa, M. 1975, 171–200).

The continuity of the Romanic population from the end of the seventh century through the tenth century A.D. is evidenced by types of dwellings, pottery thrown on wheels, and styles of jewelry. South of the Carpathian mountains at Cândeşti, Ciurel, and Ipoteşti, autochthonous settlements that came under Romano-Byzantine influence have been discovered by archaeologists. These populations practiced agriculture, cattle and sheep breeding, and in certain regions, viticulture and arboriculture. Many agricultural terms of Latin origin were preserved in the Romanian language, along with a few such words of Slavic origin. The indigenous valley populations and Slavic communities merged in time, so that by the ninth century A.D., Romanian or Romanian-Slavic communities already existed, their natural progress interrupted only by the extension to the north of the first Bulgarian tzarate under Krum and Omurtag (Comşa, M. 1960, 395–422). The Bulgarians instituted a kind of suzerainty where taxes (in the form of natural products) were paid by the local chieftains to the Bulgarian Chans. On some ceramic vessels dating back to the ninth and tenth centuries, names of "jupani," or chieftains, were inscribed; for example, at Sânnicolau Mare in Banat, pots contained the names Bouilla and Boutaul, and at Mircea Vodă, a mid-tenth-century A.D. vessel was inscribed Dimitrie and another one at Basarabi was inscribed Gheorghe; both were found in Dobroudja.

At the end of the ninth century, the Hungarian migration into Romania began. These semi-nomadic shepherds, along with a few farmers and artisans, were resisted by the Bulgarians and they moved on to the northwest and crossed the northern Carpathian mountains over Verecke Pass, spreading into the Tisa Valley, which was inhabited by Bulgarians, Slavs, and "Vlachs," or Romanians. After that, the Hungarians started gradually to conquer neighboring territories (Pascu 1972, 28–36). They attacked the dukedoms under the rules of Menumoruth in Crişana and of Glad in Banat. Both these rulers, under conditional capitulation, managed to maintain autonomy from Arpad, the Hungarian chieftain, for themselves as well as for their descendants. A third dukedom existed in Transylvania and was ruled by Gelu, "the duke of Valachians." Led by Tuhutum, the Hungarians attacked him as well and, after several battles, Gelu was defeated and killed. At the same time, in the first half of the tenth century, the Pechenegs came from the east to the steppes of Moldavia and Muntenia (Pascu 1972, 81–88), and in the eleventh century the Ouzs and the Cumans followed. Some crossed the Danube while others settled in southern Transylvania. In 1241 and 1242 A.D., the great Tartar invasion took place through two routes into Romania: one across the plains (resisted by the Miscelau in Muntenia and Berezem-ban in Oltenia), and also through Transylvania (Constantinescu, Daicoviciu, and Pascu 1969, 125). The Hungarians continued their migration into Transylvania between the tenth and the thirteenth centuries, despite resistance from the local population.

In certain mountainous and forested regions, difficult to access, Romanian populations continued to live under autonomous political leadership, keeping their traditional customs. Thus, during the thirteenth century in Transylvania, several important Romanian centers, which are now of intense interest to archaeologists, existed, such as Breaza (Făgăraş County, thirteenth to fourteenth centuries); Strei Sângeorz (Hunedoara County, twelfth to fourteenth centuries); Voievozi (Bihor County, thirteenth century); and Giuleşti and Cuhea (Maramureş, thirteenth to fourteenth centuries), among others. Similar political entities existed also south of the Carpathians in southern and northern Moldavia (for example, Slon in Prahova County). In the first half of the thirteenth century, Romanian chieftainships were led by Litovoi in the region of the Upper Jiu and Haţeg Land, Seneslau in northwestern Muntenia, Farcaş in Vâlcea,and Ioan in southeastern Oltenia (Giurescu 1981, 104–120). In the same period, a settlement called "Banat" was ruled by Oslu and located in parts of present-day Banat and western Oltenia. Archaeologists have also found evidence of a similar political formation in Moldavia near the town of Piatra Neamţ.

By the first half of the fourteenth century, many chieftains had joined together to form the Romanian feudal states of Moldavia and Valachia. The unification of the populations south of the Carpathians was done under the reign of Basarab I, who ruled over Banat, Muntenia, and Oltenia. In 1330, after defeating the Hungarians at Posada under the leadership of Carol Robert of Anjou, Basarab I obtained the independence of Valachia from the kingdom of Hungary. The unification of Moldavian populations was achieved between 1343 and 1353 by Dragoş, and in 1359, under Bogdan, they obtained independence from Hungary. Their descendants during the fourteenth century managed to occupy all of the territory of the feudal state of Moldavia (between the eastern Carpathians, Dniestr, and the Black Sea). Dobroudja, having long been under the occupation of the Byzantines, at the end of the fourteenth century was ruled by Mircea cel Bătrân, the prince of Valachia (Giurescu 1981, 118–120). The two states of Moldavia and Valachia, in which lived people with the same language and traditions, unified with each other in 1859, and in 1918 they were joined by Transylvania and Bessarabia, thus constituting the nation of Romania. Because of close relations among Romanians in Dobroudja, Moldavia, Transylvania, and Valachia, the Romanian language of Latin origin, the traditional customs, and some other elements of archaic material culture have been preserved even into the twenty-first century.

Eugen Comša

References

Berciu, D. 1961. *Contribuții la problemele neoliticului in România in lumina noilor cercetări.* Bucharest: Editura Academiei Republicii Populare Romîne.

———. 1967. *Romania before Burebista.* London: Thames and Hudson.

Comşa, E. 1987. *Neoliticul pe teritoriul României.* Considerații. Bucharest: Editura Academiei Republicii Socialiste România.

Comşa, M. 1960. "Die bulgarische Herrschaft nördlich der Donau während des IX. und X Jh. im Lichte der archäologischen Forschungen." *Dacia* 4: 39–422.

———. 1975. "Socioeconomic organization of the Daco-Romanic and Slav Populations of the Lower Danube during the Sixth to Eighth Centuries. In *Relations between the Autochthonous Population and the Migratory Populations of the Territory of Romania,* pp. 171–200. Ed. Miron Constantinescu et al. Bucharest: Editura Academiei Republicii Socialiste România.

———. 1987. "Slawen und Awaren auf rumänischen Boden ihre Beziehungen zu der Bodenständigen romanischen und späteren frührumänischen Bevölkerung." *Die Völker Südosteuropa im 6. bis 8. Jahrhundert* 17: 219–230.

Constantinescu, M., C. Daicoviciu, and Ş. Pascu. 1969. *Istoria României.* Compendiu. Bucharest.

Crişan, I. H. 1971. "Contribuții la problema celților din Transilvania." *Studii şi cercetări de istorie veche* 22, no. 2: 149–164.

Daicoviciu, C. 1945. *La Transylvanie dans l'antiquité.* Bucharest.

Daicoviciu, C., and H. Daicoviciu. 1963. Sarmizegètusa: *Les citadelles et les agglomérations dacique des monts d'Orǎştie.* Bucharest.

Daicoviciu, H. 1965. *Dacii.* Bucharest: Editura enciclopedica româna.

Giurescu, D. C. 1981. *Istoria ilustrată a Românilor.* Bucharest.

Horedt, K. 1975. "The Gepidae, the Avars, and the Romanic Population in Transylvania." In *Relations between the Autochthonous Population and the Migratory Populations of the Territory of Romania,* pp. 111–122. Ed. Miron Constantinescu et al. Bucharest: Editura Academiei Republicii Socialiste România.

Istoria României I. 1960. Bucharest.

Istoria României II. 1962. Bucharest.

Macrea, M., and D. Tudor. 1960. "Dacia în timpul stăpâninii romane." *Istoria României* 1: 345–467.

Matei, M. 1960. "Slavianskie poseleniia v Suceave." *Dacia* 4: 374–394.

Mitrea, B. 1972. "Die Goten an der unteren Donau-einige Probleme im III.IV. Jahrhundert." *Studia Gotica:* 81–94.

Moga, M. 1974. "Vestigiile paleocreştine în Banat." In *In memoriam Constantini Daicoviciu,* pp. 259–266. Cluj.

Morintz, S. 1978. *Contribuții archeologice la istoria tracilor timpurii.* Bucharest.

Morintz, S., and R. Roman. 1973. "Übergangsperiode vom Äneolithikum zur Bronzezeit in Rumänien." Symposium Baden. *Bratislava:* 259–295.

Nestor, I. 1933. *Der Stand der Vorgeschichtsforschung in Rumänien.* 22 Berrgk, Frankfurt am Main.

———. 1973. "Autochtones et Slaves en Roumanie (aux VIe-IXe siècles)." In *Les Slaves et le monde méditerranéen Vie-Xie siècles,* 29–33. Sofia: BAN.

Nestor, I., and E. Zaharia. 1961. "Săpăturile de la Sărata Monteoru." *Materiale şi cercetări archeologice* 7: 513–515.

Nicolăescu-Plopşor, C. S. 1938. "Le paléolithique en Roumanie." *Dacia* 5–6: 41–107.

Pǎrvan, V. 1926. *Getica, o protoistorie a Daciei.* Bucharest: Editura Meridiane.

Pascu, Ş. 1972. *Voievodatul Transilvaniei* 1. Cluj: Dacia.

Pǎunescu, A. 1970. *Evoluția uneltelor şi armelor de piatră cioplită descoperite pe teritoriul României.* Bucharest.

Rusu, M. 1975. "Avars, Slavs, and the Romanic

Population in the Sixth to Eighth Centuries." In *Relations between the Autochthonous Population and the Migratory Populations of the Territory of Romania,* pp. 123–154. Ed. Miron Constantinescu et al. Bucharest: Editura Academiei Republicii Socialiste România.

Teodor, D. 1975. "Natives and Slavs in the East Carpathian Regions of Romania in the Sixth to Tenth Centuries. In *Relations between the Autochthonous Population and the Migratory Populations of the Territory of Romania,* pp. 155–170. Ed. Miron Constantinescu et al. Bucharest: Editura Academiei Republicii Socialiste România.

Vasiliev, V. 1980. *Sciţii Agatirşi pe teritoriul României.* Cluj: Dacia.

———. 1988. "Problèmes de la Chronologie du Hallstatt sur le territoire de la Roumanie." *Apulum* 25: 83–102.

Vulpe, A. 1974. "The Cultural Unity of the North Thracian Tribes in the Balkano-Carpathian Hallstatt (Seventh–Eighth Centuries)." *Journal of Indo-European Studies* 1 (1974): 1–21.

———. 1976. "Nouveaux points de vue sur la civilisation géto-dace: L'apport de l'archéologie." *Dacia* 20: 19–21.

Zirra, V. 1971. "Beiträge zur Kenntnis des keltischen La Tène in Rumänien." *Dacia* 15: 171–238.

Rouse, Irving Benjamin (1913–)

Born in Rochester, New York, Irving Benjamin Rouse went to Yale University in 1930 with the intention of studying botany, but some cataloging work at the Peabody Museum began his interest in archaeology. He went on to study for his doctorate in archaeology and received it in 1939.

Rouse spent the whole of his career at Yale University: at the Peabody Museum as an assistant curator of anthropology from 1938 to 1947, associate curator of anthropology from 1947 to 1954, research associate and affiliate from 1954 to 1962 and 1975 to 1977, curator of anthropology from 1977 to 1984, and curator emeritus. His fieldwork during this long period added substantially to the Peabody's research collections in the Caribbean area, giving it one of the premier Caribbean archaeological collections in the world. At the same time, Rouse worked in the Department of Anthropology from 1939 to 1943 as instructor, from 1943 to 1948 as associate professor, and from 1954 to 1970 as professor. He was appointed Charles J. McCurdy Professor of Anthropology in 1970, a post he held until his retirement in 1984. He played a significant role in the education of a number of students who have gone on to prominence of their own in archaeology, including Robert C. Dunnell, Patrick V. Kirch, and Bruce G. Trigger.

Rouse's primary area of interest has been the Caribbean. He has excavated in Puerto Rico, Cuba, Florida, Venezuela, Trinidad, Antigua, Guadeloupe, the Bahamas, the Dominican Republic, the Virgin Islands, and Jamaica. This tremendous breadth of first-hand experience, coupled with the fact that Rouse constructed the chronologies of many key areas in the region and his proclivity for synthetic writing, guaranteed Rouse a central position in Caribbean archaeology, a position he still holds. Many of Rouse's publications synthesize Caribbean culture-history, or aspects of it, and he has often been called upon to summarize Venezuela and/or the Caribbean area in large syntheses, such as the *Handbook of South American Indians* (1948), and in several synopses of current work in the *Handbook of Latin American Studies.* He has contributed chapters to many of the significant books about settlement patterns, chronologies, and biogeography in archaeology, and some of his more influential pieces were journal articles: masterful areal syntheses such as "Prehistory of the West Indies," published in *Science* in 1964, and "Pattern and Process in West Indian Archaeology," in *World Archaeology* in 1977.

His interest in early human culture developed initially as a result of his Caribbean research but then expanded well beyond it, and his most recent research has focused on contact-era and postcontact inhabitants of the region. He has continued his culture-historical research as well, which culminated in the publication of *Migrations in Prehistory* in 1986.

Rouse's level of activity and methodological contributions have garnered an impressive array of awards and honorific positions. He served as editor of AMERICAN ANTIQUITY from 1946 to 1950, and he served on the executive board of the American Anthropological Association from 1950 to 1953 and was that assocation's president in 1967–1968. His honors and awards include the Viking Fund Medal in Anthropology (1960), election to the National Academy of Science (1962), and the Distinguished Service Award from the American Anthropological Association.

Robert C. Dunnell

See also Caribbean; Florida and the Caribbean Basin, Historical Archaeology in

References

For references, see *Encyclopedia of Archaeology: The Great Archaeologists, Vol. 2,* ed. Tim Murray (Santa Barbara, CA: ABC-CLIO, 1999), pp. 674–679.

Royal Archaeological Institute

The Royal Archaeological Institute (RAI) is one of the older archaeological societies in Great Britain and has a tradition based on the broadest study of the past, a study that encompasses aspects of the art and architectural history of Britain and adjacent areas as well as the full temporal range from the Paleolithic to the early modern periods.

In December 1843, a group of people with a passionate interest in the past came together to form a new national organization to promote their antiquarian interests, which were becoming increasingly popular at the time. They acted out of disillusionment with the only existing national body, the SOCIETY OF ANTIQUARIES OF LONDON, which was by then effectively moribund. The new group was drawn from a wider social spectrum than the members of the Society of Antiquaries, but it remained largely drawn from the London establishment.

The organization was founded as the British Archaeological Association and organized the first national archaeological congress, which was held in Canterbury, England, in 1844. The meeting was a major success, but there was a serious dispute over the rights to the publication of the congress, which led to a split in the membership. The result was the birth of two separate organizations: one kept the name British Archaeological Association; the other styled itself the Archaeological Institute of Great Britain and Ireland but retained ownership of the journal that had been established—the *Archaeological*

Journal has been published annually ever since). The latter organization became the Royal Archaeological Institute of Great Britain and Ireland in 1866, and in 1962, it received a royal charter and dropped the reference to Great Britain and Ireland from its title.

Through the nineteenth century, the RAI became firmly established as the center of archaeology and antiquarian studies in Britain. Its members were eclectically drawn from the British establishment and, at times, included influential politicians and thinkers. The pattern of meetings established in the early years continues today. Through the winter, there are monthly meetings in London, at which lectures and reports on research in archaeology and architectural history are presented. In the summer, there is a residential meeting, lasting a week, for which participants travel to a locale, visit key buildings and monuments, and listen to talks about them. In more recent years, these activities have been supplemented by day-long excursions at other times of the year. The institute also has a long tradition of sponsoring fieldwork and research. Most notably, it engaged in a broad-based project to study the origins of the medieval castle during the 1960s. Some of the most distinguished of British archaeologists (e.g., Sir Alfred Clapham, Dame Joan Evans, CHRISTOPHER HAWKES, Sir John Lubbock [LORD AVEBURY], and SIR MORTIMER WHEELER) have served as officers of the organization over the years.

One of the enduring legacies of the institute is its publications. The *Archaeological Journal* has appeared annually since the 1840s, and a series of other volumes have appeared as well. The proceedings of the summer meetings, sometimes printed in the *Journal,* otherwise as separate volumes, represent a key source for understanding the topography, archaeology, and buildings of the British Isles. Equally, the articles in the earlier volumes of the *Journal* represent a prime source for understanding the emergence of the discipline, its concepts, and its methods of study. During the twentieth century, the *Journal* published a variety of key articles for understanding the archaeology of Britain. For many years until 1978 the *Journal* attempted to provide an annual review of research progress across the full range of British archaeology. In more recent years, as archaeology has become more compartmentalized, the journal has developed a reputation as one of the few places where multiperiod sites can sensibly be published.

As the twenty-first century begins, the RAI remains one of the few archaeological societies in the United Kingdom that has a mixed membership of both interested members of the public and professional archaeologists. It also retains a broadly based organization catering to people who have a truly catholic interest in Britain's past.

Martin Millet

See also Britain, Prehistoric Archaeology

References

Ebbatson, L. 1994. "Context and Discourse: Royal Archaeological Institute Membership, 1845–1942." In *Building on the Past: Papers Celebrating 150 Years of the Royal Archaeological Institute,* 22–74. Ed. B. Vyner. London.

Evans, J. 1949. "The Royal Archaeological Institute: A Retrospect." *Archaeological Journal* 106: 1–11.

Wetherall, D. 1994. "From Canterbury to Winchester: The Foundation of the Institute." In *Building on the Past: Papers Celebrating 150 Years of the Royal Archaeological Institute,* 8–21. Ed. B. Vyner. London.

Russia

Historiographic Literature

General surveys of the history of Russian archaeology were written only during Soviet times, and only one of them encapsulates the whole history—the chapters written by A. V. Arcikhovsky and published in a collective work of the history of historic disciplines in the USSR (Arcikhovsky 1973). His chapters are primarily factual and are carefully filtered to correspond to the Marxist and nationalist demands of the state ideology of the time.

The rest of the literature may be divided into two parts. One part comprises books describing prerevolutionary times, and the other part books dealing with Soviet times. The first accounts (Ravdonikas 1932; Khudyakov 1933), issuing from Marxist dogmatists, are too nihilistic in their evaluations of the prerevolutionary past, and few are objective (Formozov 1961). The most complete historiographic work (Lebedev 1992) is subjective and disordered.

Books describing Soviet times are often very critical (Miller 1956). Although written in freedom and abroad, Miller's book was not particularly competent because he was a provincial archaeologist, and the essence of great scholarly debates eluded him. In contrast, the apologetic book by A. L. Mongait (1956) was written inside the country, and it is not so much a history of the discipline as a survey of its state during Soviet times. Two later books are also apologetic: V. F. Gening's book (Gening 1961) was written in the framework of militant dogmatism, but A. D. Pryakhin's work (Pryakhin 1986) is more moderate and factual. Pryakhin tried to present a more objective and frank exposition, as much as that was possible, first abroad in some articles in English (in 1977 and 1982) and then in a book published in Russian and Spanish in 1993 and later in German and English.

In the works of V. I. Ravdonikas and M. V. Khudyakov, the history of archaeology is viewed as a series of changing class approaches to archaeological activity: feudal, bourgeois, and proletarian (Marxist) archaeology. In A. A. Formozov's work (1961), the history of Russian archaeology is divided into periods according to the changing place of archaeology among disciplines and to the shifts in its interests: geographic, art criticism, and historic (but not ethnographic). G. S. Lebedev has maintained that Russian archaeology experienced a change of paradigms "à la Kuhn" (in the sense used by the philosopher of science Thomas Kuhn) and that these determined the methodological character of the study of antiquities. These paradigms were antiquarian, encyclopedic, applied-arts, and everyday-life-describing. The last, according to Lebedev, was developed in Russia instead of an evolution paradigm.

Russian Society and the Knowledge of Antiquities

The attitude toward antiquities in the days before Czar Peter the Great, before the beginning of the eighteenth century, was one of traditionalism and negligence. The Tatar yoke hampered the development of Russia and kept it separate from the rest of Europe. In Russia, there was no Renaissance, no Reformation, and certainly no Crusades or Inquisition. Hence, until Russia was "Europeanized" by Peter the Great, there was no antiquarian tradition as in the rest of Europe.

Some kinds of antiquities were revered not because of curiosity about or sympathy for ancient culture but because of sacred and religious reasons. There was a special reverence for Greek Christian culture rather than for Greek pagan culture, which was revered in Western Europe. For Russia, Greek Byzantine civilization was the source of the Russian Orthodox religion, and some antiquities were esteemed as insignia of power or attributes of rulers and heroes. So "Monomach's cap," the Russian crown, was revered as a Byzantine article even though, in reality, it had been made during the time of the Golden Horde. In Pskov, "the sword of Litvanian Count Dovmont," the defender of the city, was saved and respected. It was to save such treasures that the czars created a state armory in the Kremlin in Moscow. First mentioned in documents in 1504, the armory still exists as a museum today.

The attitude toward other antiquities was utilitarian and not always good for the monuments. People extracted saltpeter from ancient earthworks, and barrows were simply robbed. In Siberia, special bands of barrow robbers, called bugrovshchiki (from bugor or "hillock," the local term for "barrow"), made their living pillaging ancient monuments, and hundreds of the monuments disappeared. Observing the robbery of ancient graves and the melting down of treasures from them, the Dutchman Vitsen, who visited Russia during the time of Peter the Great, wrote that the Russians did not like antiquities. The collecting of classical antiquities had begun in Italy the late fifteenth century, in England in the sixteenth century, and in France in the seventeenth century, but it did not occur in Russia before the early eighteenth century.

Czarist Antiquarianism: The First Forms of Scholarly Attitude to Antiquities, 1696–1762

The development of antiquarianism in Russia was a result of the enlightened absolutism of Pe-

ter the Great. In the last years of the seventeenth century he traveled incognito throughout Europe, and on his return in 1698, he began to reform the whole of Russia based on European standards. These reforms involved changed attitudes to antiquities as well. Peter demanded that ancient numisma (coin collections) and other finds, as well as all kinds of curiosities and rarities, be sent to him from all over Russia. Between 1715 and 1716, a Uralian factory owner, Demidov, and Count Gagarin sent him collections of golden antiquities that had been taken away from the bugrovshchiki. In 1718, Peter created the Kunstkammer Museum in the newly founded capital of Saint Petersburg and issued a special edict ordering that everything that was very old and unusual was to be sent there. In 1721, he ordered that the curious things that were being found in Siberia were to be sent to him, and so the well-known Siberian collection of Scythian and Sarmatian gold, which is now in the Hermitage Museum, was established.

Under Peter the Great, scientific expeditions to Siberia began. In the 1720s, the German naturalist Messerschmidt was sent there for seven years to study Siberian natural resources and folk art and to buy and collect antiquities. The Russian Academy of Sciences, created by Peter and consisting in part of foreigners, took over the organization of the primary expeditions to Siberia only after Peter's death. The great Siberian expedition of 1733–1743, led by Justus Bering, opened the strait between Asia and North America, and the archaeological survey of this expedition was conducted by the Germans Gerhard Miller and I. Gmelin.

Sentimental Opening of Classical Heritage, 1762–1812

After 1762, the German-born queen Catherine II ruled Russia. She was educated in the spirit of the French Enlightenment and corresponded with the French encyclopedists and the French writer François-Marie Voltaire. The cult of the civil ideals that grew out of the Enlightenment was connected with an interest in classical antiquity and with fashionable sentimentality, and the purchase of classical antiquities from elsewhere became common. In 1768, just a year af-

Shards of pottery from a Siberian barrow (Image Select)

ter the death of the great art historian JOHANN JOACHIM WINCKELMANN, the new Hermitage Museum opened in Saint Petersburg. Built near the Winter Palace of Russian czars, it was established especially for the royal collections of classical art and Renaissance European paintings.

The treaty that concluded the war between Russia and Turkey from 1768 to 1774 gave Russia the northern shores of the Black Sea and part of the Crimea, which included sites of ancient Greek colonies. Russia finally had its own piece of classical antiquity, and the main focus of scientific and collecting expeditions shifted from the extreme north to the extreme south of the country. In the early nineteenth century, two books of travelers' tales about expeditions to Taurida (the ancient name of the Crimea) were published, and both authors—Pavel Sumarokov and Ivan Muraviev-Apostol—had been charmed by the monuments of classical antiquity. Antiquities other than those of classical times were neglected and damaged. "For all the Russian antiquities I wouldn't give even a Grosh [the smallest piece of money]" wrote the well-known Russian poet Batyushkov in a pri-

vate letter. "Quite another thing Greece, quite another Italy!"

Romantic and Patriotic Insights into Russia's Past

As in many other European countries, Napoleon's invasion, national humiliation by the French, and the ensuing patriotic war of 1812 produced a burst of nationalist sentiment in Russia and awakened interest in the ancient past of the Russian people. This impulse was part of a broader romanticism based on political and social discontent, and the regard for antiquities manifested itself in two different ways.

First, the passion for classical antiquities did not cease and became even more popular, but its character changed. Sentimentality and enlightenment for their own sake disappeared, and antiquities now endowed their owners with prestige and profits. Museums needed collections to help educate society and to help artists depict the ancient world, and the latter was the aim of a prominent archaeologist of the time, Olenin, the president of the Academy of Arts. The archaeological study of Scythian monuments and the Greek jewelry found in them also became popular. In the first decade of the nineteenth century, the French emigré Paul Dubruxe, a low-ranking official, began excavating the Crimean city of Kerch, and in the second decade, the governor of Kerch, Stempkovsky, a retired colonel, encouraged serious archaeological work there.

The second result of the romantic movement and the wave of patriotic feeling in Russia was the birth of interest in Slavic and Russian antiquities. This interest was stimulated by the publication of the "History of Russian State" by the well-known writer and official state historiographer Nikolay Karamzin. According to Karamzin, Russian autocracy was the result of the long development of the Russian peoples' national peculiarities. Russia's grand and attractive beginnings were obvious in the study of its monarchy, written language, and orthodoxy.

The Polish enthusiast Zorian Dolega-Chodakowsky (pseudonym of Adam Czarnocky), who was fighting for recognition of the great Slavic past, was the first to show a substantially different interest in antiquities. He argued that written history was distorted by clerical chronologists for the sake of the church and monarchic power and that only folklore and material monuments revealed the truth about the past. He was interested in paleoethnography and, more particularly, in the pagan and premonarchic Slavic past.

In 1822, at the site of the medieval principality of Ryazan, which had been destroyed by the Mongol ruler Batu Khan in the thirteenth century A.D., a hoard of ancient Russian ornaments was found by chance. This find caught the imagination of the Russian people and increased their interest in Slavic-Russian antiquities. During the government of the comparably liberal Czar Alexander I, the enthusiasm for Slavic-Russian antiquities was still not very different from an interest in classical archaeology, and the Slavic past was adjusted to fit the classical model. However when Czar Nicholas I suppressed the Decembrist rebellion in 1825 to become "the gendarme of Europe," so-called Kvass Patriotism (something like jingoism) prevailed in Russia. The czarist administration be-

gan to promote Russian traditions and values as an antidote for the European spirit of free-thinking, a defensive idea that was expressed by the minister of enlightenment, Count Sergey Uvarov, as *autocracy, orthodoxy, nationality*. Thus, the disciplines of classical and medieval archaeology, which in the rest of Europe were formed at different times, stimulated by different interests, and developed by different groups of scholars, were in Russia born simultaneously; governed by the same interests, both applied aesthetic and political; and conducted by the same scholars.

The young Count ALEXEY UVAROV, a son of the notable minister formerly mentioned, was fascinated by archaeology and studied at St. Petersburg, Heidelberg, and Berlin Universities. At the last, he was taught by Eduard Gerhard, the founder of the DEUTSCHES ARCHÄOLOGISCHES INSTITUT (German Archaeological Institute), who transferred Winkelmann's ideas on style in the analysis of classical sculpture to the analysis of classical vase painting. Between 1851 and 1854, the young count and the archaeologist and orientalist Savelyev excavated 7,759 barrows. The results were published thirty years later.

At the same time that excavations were beginning, there was an upheaval in the aristocratic-bureaucratic Russian Archaeological-Numismatic Society in Saint Petersburg. The leadership of the society, created some years earlier, was seized by patriotic members who collected folktales and also fabricated "folk" frauds with a monarchic ideology. These members not only changed the direction of the society's activities, they also renamed the group the Russian Archaeological Society and began publishing in Russian instead of in French.

Prehistoric archaeology was not very popular at the time. In the journals of the 1820s and 1830s, occasional notes about European discoveries of "pre-flood" people appeared. In 1826, however, censorship instructions declared, "Every harmful theory, such as for instance, on the prehistoric bestial state of man as if natural . . . is not to be allowed to [be] printed," and nothing of that kind appeared in print in the 1840s and early 1850s.

Crystallization of Archaeology during the Epoch of the Great Reforms, 1855–1881

In 1855, Czar Nicholas I, unable to bear Russia's defeat in the Crimean War, died. The defeat was partly the consequence of a delay in the reformation of the country's archaic social order, a point the new czar, Alexander II, understood. He began the necessary all-embracing reforms, such as the abolition of the serfdom and changes to laws, and one of his first reforms concerned archaeology. In February 1859, the Archaeological Commission (AC) was created by the Ministry of the Court as the central state office to control archaeological excavations, the collection of data on antiquities, the stimulation of their studies, and expert knowledge of them. All archaeological finds from state and municipal land, i.e., not in private ownership, came under the authority of the AC. The Hermitage was also under the Ministry of Court, so the AC was closely connected to it and the most valuable finds went to the Hermitage. The AC published annual reports of its studies and activities, which listed all archaeological finds and their fates.

In 1864, in addition to the archaeological institutions in Saint Petersburg, two were created in Moscow—the Moscow Archaeological Society (MAO) and the Society of Amateurs of Natural Science, Anthropology, and Ethnography (OLEAE). The founder of MAO was Count Alexey Uvarov, now thirty-seven years old and an archaeologist. Beginning in 1869, MAO organized the all-Russian archaeological congresses, held every three (later four) years, each in a different town. Ivan Zabelin, a venerable Moscow archaeologist, was for many years invited to work in Saint Petersburg in the AC. Zabelin had no university education, in fact no education at all, and he obtained his great knowledge from practice. He was the real head of the Historical Museum founded by Uvarov in Moscow.

Uvarov's and Zabelin's methodological articles reveal their interest in Slavic archaeology, mainly with the ethnic identification of monuments and the widely understood *byt* (everyday life and equipment) of ancient peoples, i.e., their cultures. The two men did not separate archaeological sources of information into a special branch, instead considering it side by side with ethnographic evidence from the field, museum observations, and written sources. They included all of these sources of information into the study of archaeology. They separated the discipline of archaeology not by specific sources but according to two criteria: practically, as a period not enlightened, or poorly enlightened, by chronicles, and theoretically, not by events but *byt* (culture). Archaeology for them, from the beginning, was something like paleoethnography.

In 1874, when the participants in the Third (Kievan) Archaeological Congress went to see the Sophian Cathedral, its dean, according to the historian Kostomarov, asked them, "Haven't you come in order to search for arguments in favor of the origin of man from the ape?" Count Uvarov, leading the archaeologists, reassured the archpriest, "We do not march into such a distance."

However, some Paleolithic discoveries were made in Russia, especially in the late 1870s and early 1880s. These included the excavations of KOSTENKI near Voronezh on the Don River by Polyakov, the exploration of Crimean caves by Merezhkovsky, and even the discovery of a Paleolithic site in Karacharovo, on Uvarov's own land. The main explorers of these sites were naturalists, not humanists. In Uvarov's book *Archaeology: The Stone Age* (1881), there is no long chronology, and Darwin is not mentioned. Uvarov really did not march "into such a distance."

Separation of Archaeology into a Special Discipline, 1881–1917

Liberalization ended when Czar Alexander II was assassinated by a terrorist in 1881. The majority of the archaeologists were on the side of the counterrevolution, and there were many aristocrats and priests in archaeology. Countess Praskovia Uvarova, who replaced her husband as the head of MAO after his death, once said that archaeology is knowledge for the rich.

In 1889, as part of a general centralization, the AC received the monopoly on issuing permits for excavations. Count Bobrinsky, a well-known Saint Petersburg archaeologist and the head of the AC, began to issue permits with great fervor. Uvarova and her colleagues at MAO protested, initiating a long quarrel between Saint Petersburg and Moscow archaeologists. The split mirrored the competencies of the two main schools and centers for archaeology in Russia, each with its own tradition. The Saint Petersburg school, with the Hermitage and state support, stood for a more professional approach, preferring the detailed study of material and strong methodology. The Moscow school was more open to amateurs, and its members had broader interests and more often made generalizations and historical inferences.

At the end of the nineteenth century, two very great and influential archaeologists were growing up—ALEKSANDER SPITSYN in Saint Petersburg and VASILIY GORODCOV in Moscow. Their eventual profession was not their only similarity. Both came from the provinces, both were of middle-class origin (Spitsyn was a teacher's son; Gorodcov, the son of a deacon). Neither attended a school of archaeology, and both contributed greatly to the development and systematization of Russia's archaeology.

Classical archaeology continued along traditional lines with a preference for the analysis of the art of antiquity. The most prominent representative of this school was NIKODIM KONDAKOV, a Muscovite originally, who created his own school of archaeology in Odessa and then moved with it to St. Petersburg, together with his pupils Farmakovsky and Rostovcev.

Catastrophe and Change
of Structures, 1917–1924

At first, the 1917 Revolution had no impact on the content of archaeological studies, but it did cause a sharp decrease in excavations and the complete breakup of all the old institutions of archaeology. The AC and the Hermitage were subsumed into the Ministry of the Court, but both the ministry and the court suddenly disappeared. The majority of the members of the MAO, mainly from the nobility and clergy, were suppressed and lost their influence and possessions. Archaeology had developed in Russia as "knowledge for the rich," and there were now no rich in the country. Private collections were partially robbed and annihilated, and what was left was nationalized and put into the large museums.

At the same time, the new government tried to give a civilized form to its power. In November 1917, the new Peoples Commissariat (ministry) of Enlightenment asked the people to save their cultural monuments. On 19 September 1918, a decree concerning the state registration of monuments was issued, and on 10 October 1918, the exporting and selling abroad of any artifacts of Russian art and history was forbidden.

A new central institution, the Academy for History of Material Culture in St. Petersburg, was created to replace the AC. The academy was a more powerful, centralized, and all-embracing institution that studied history, linguistics, ethnography, and the arts and later concentrated on archaeology. There was only a section of this academy in Moscow. The head of the academy was Nikolay Marr, half-Georgian, half-Scot and a linguist by profession. He was a talented man but emotionally unbalanced and not self-critical. Although his education was very narrow, his pretensions were enormous. He applied his revolutionary ideas to linguistics, declaring, for instance, that Caucasian languages (Japhetic in his terminology) were previous stages of Indo-European languages not only in structure but also in substance. For him, the main process was not the splitting of languages but their fusion. Linguists closed their ears to his wild ideas, hoping that he would adopt cultural studies and archaeology, while archaeologists excused his evident ignorance of archaeology and regarded him as a great linguist. In 1923, Marr finished formulating his "new learning on language" (or Japhetic theory), which, as yet, had no influence on archaeology.

There was another important institutional novelty, the teaching of archaeology at universities where faculties of social sciences were opened. However, these new structures were unstable, the revolutionary impulse was not exhausted, and they were constantly reconstructed and reorganized. Before the Revolution there were as many as 150 museums in Russia, and this number increased five times after 1917, mainly owing to the founding of small local museums. The development of archaeology was considerably damaged by the emigration of many of its great scholars, such as Kondakov, Rostovcev, Shtern, Bobrinsky, and Uvarova.

Revolution in Archaeology:
Muscovian Control, 1924–1929

Even before Lenin died, in 1924, Joseph Stalin took over the reigns of political power, and after Lenin's death, Stalin soon got rid of any opposition and "the Lenin guard" to become the sole ruler of Russia. This change meant a very different style of government, the end of any private-sector economic freedoms, and an increasing ideological monopoly, with Moscow-based organizations dominant.

In 1926, the Russian Academy based in Moscow (RAIMK) modified its title to encompass all of the USSR and was renamed the State Academy (GAIMK). From 1924 on, to centralize control, all the scholarly institutions of archaeology were united into the Russian Association of Research Institutes of Social Sciences (RANIION). This framework facilitated the reeducation of scholarly cadres in the ways of the new communist spirit.

In Moscow the well-known Bolshevik sociologist and art critic Friche surrounded himself with a group of Gorodcov's students, who, under his influence, became very keen on Marxism and on building a Marxist archaeology. These students were Arcikhovsky, Bryusov, Kiselev, and Smirnov, and all of them later became well-known Soviet archaeologists. They fought against another group of young Moscow archaeologists from Zhukov's paleoethnological school. Zhukov was Anuchin's pupil, and he was interested in the impact of the natural environment on cultures and ethnic development. His pupils were Bader, Tolstov, and Voevodsky—they, too, became well-known Soviet archaeologists. Eventually, Zhukov was arrested and the paleoethnological school dispersed. However, Archikhovsky's "Marxist archaeology" did reign supreme in Russia before it was demolished by colleagues from Leningrad (formerly St. Petersburg).

Revolution in Archaeology:
Leningrad Campaign, 1930–1934

In 1930, Stalin had finished with any opposition to his power and was ostensibly the dictator of Russia. Lenin's new economic policy (NEP) was rejected, and the revolutionary ideas of freedom, internationalism, and annihilation of state apparatus were anathema to the tyrant. His slogan, "dictatorship of the proletariat," aimed at building socialism in the country by increasing the power of the state and exacerbating the class struggle. Resistance was ruthlessly suppressed. The collectivization of agriculture was accompanied by the mass deportation of well-to-do peasants to Siberia, and the church, the peasants' main spiritual support, was suppressed as well. Local archaeological and folklore studies were forbidden, and organizations were disbanded if they were sympathetic to and protective of old customs and church buildings.

The old archaeological cadres were badgered and accused of "creeping empiricism," of "naked artifactology," and of controlling archaeology with formal typological studies. If their work reflected idealism, nationalism, or other -isms, they were even worse off and forced to make public renunciations and repentances.

Bolsheviks from the Communist Academy (not to be confused with Academy of Sciences) came to help Marr at GAIMK, and their careers provide a study in the politics of the times. Sergey Bykovsky was a mathematician prior to the Revolution, a commissar during the civil war, a member of the Red Army's secret political security service, and then a historian in the Communist Academy. Fedor Kiparisov was a philologist and had earlier worked as a trade-union organizer. SERGEY SEMENOV was a young secret political security investigator when he began his postgraduate study of stone tools using modern criminological techniques at GAIMK. Marr became a member of the Communist Party, and his courses became obligatory.

In 1930, in Leningrad, Spitsyn's pupil VLADISLAV RAVDONIKAS developed a work program according to orders from the Bolshevik rulers of GAIMK even though he himself was not a member of the Communist Party. Called "the Marxist history of material culture," not of archaeology, it contained sharp criticism of many contemporary archaeologists for their unwillingness to work in the new way. The use of the new term *material culture* instead of archaeology was significant. Bykovsky and other Marxists favored a model that divided material culture in general, not by its sources or its methods of manufacture, but by epochs and their socioeconomic formation. This division was later rejected.

RANIION, because of its own reconstruction, had not caught up with all the new ideas and was dismissed. Some Moscow archaeologists joined GAIMK and built a little Muscovite department. Inspired by Marr, Leningrad archaeologists Ravdonikas and Krichevsky transferred ideas from the "new learning on language" to archaeology and built the theory of stadial (i.e., stages of history) development. This theory ignored the national specifics of cultures and their migrations and emphasized their fusions and sharp changes from epoch to epoch. It supported the current Soviet policy with regard to the maintenance of power in the multinational state inherited from the Russian Empire.

In the GAIMK periodicals of the time, theoretical articles and reviews (usually crushing) composed 47 percent of the contents, particular research themes 35 percent, and field reports 17.5 percent. However the enthusiasm for theory did not last long.

Soviet Archaeology: In the Service of Stalin's State, 1934–1956

On 1 December 1934, Sergei Kirov, the ruler of Leningrad, the second-ranking person in the Communist Party and state hierarchy, and Stalin's competitor, was killed. His murder was probably organized by Stalin, and in any case, Stalin used it as a pretext for a campaign of mass terror across the country. Stalin introduced Draconian laws, and all members of "Lenin's guard" were annihilated along with hundreds of the participants in the Sixteenth Party Congress and nearly all of the army's general officers. Terror was used initially against the top members of the Party, but it spread to involve ordinary people simply to bring the whole population under control. The cult of Stalin was introduced.

The repressions affected many archaeologists. Some, like Zhukov, had been eliminated even earlier; some, like Miller and Borovka, perished in detention; others, like Rykov and Teploukhov, committed suicide; and still others, including Rudenko, Latynin, Gryaznov, Bonch-Osmolovsky, and Sychev, languished in prisons and prison camps or were deported. It became

very dangerous to have any scholarly position, and theoretical studies ceased immediately. Sociology was abolished, and sociological interests, described as "sociologization," were regarded as harmful. Marr's successors, Bykovsky and Kiparisov, were both shot.

There was a section of archaeology at the Institute of Ethnography at the Academy of Sciences in Moscow, which included the archaeologists Ravdonikas, ALEKSEI P. OKLADNIKOV, Zamyatnin, and Bibikov. The section was allowed to issue the serial *Sovetskaya Arkheologiya* (later a journal) and then fused with GAIMK to form the Institute for the History of Material Culture (IHMK) within the framework of the Academy of Sciences. The mighty GAIMK became a demoted institution.

Archaeologists were advised to stick to the empirical facts, to stay close to the "real" history written by Soviet historians, and to use the same methods as the historians, which were based on historical materialism. With this in mind, Muscovite archaeologists, former builders of the "Marxist archaeology," reoriented their archaeology from sociology toward history, aiming their studies at historical reconstructions on the basis of known archaeological facts and written sources. Arcikhovsky described archaeology as "history armed with the spade." There were about 300 archaeological expeditions under way at this time. Knowledge about the former provinces of the Russian Empire greatly increased, and the monuments of Urartu, the barrows of Pazyryk and Trialeti, and the ancient center of Parthia Nissa were discovered in Russian Central Asia.

World War II (1941–1945) delivered yet another blow to the development of archaeology in Russia. Expedition activity ceased, and many archaeologists perished in the fighting. The German invasion annihilated many museum collections while others were taken to Germany and destroyed there. As a result of the siege of Leningrad, IHMK archaeologists Zhebelev, Podgaecky, Zograf, Rydzevskaya, Degen-Kovalevsky, and Golmsten starved to death, and others were evacuated in an emaciated state. After the war, the institute established a department in Leningrad, but its headquarters were transferred to Moscow. By this time, Stalin's long-term suspicion that the people of Leningrad secretly longed for their city to be the capital again meant that he did the opposite and centralized most government institutions in Moscow. He also dismissed and then executed some of what was left of the Leningrad elite.

The inglorious Soviet-Finnish War (1939–1940) and the defeats in the first year of the Patriotic War (1941–1945) revealed the weakness of Stalin's brand of socialism, which was in reality equal to the old feudal order with elements of slave ownership. Stalin was forced to resort to the patriotic feeling of the people of the USSR, and more particularly to the patriotic feeling of the Russian people, because Russian soldiers were the basis and the majority of the Soviet army. Soviet archaeologists glorified the national character of the Russian people and some other peoples of the Soviet Union, tracing their noble ancestors and their ethnic peculiarities back in antiquity and searching for their ethnic territories and broadening their boundaries during the remote past in order to justify any new "historic claims" on territory.

Marr's position was no longer fashionable, and his theories were dismissed personally by Stalin in a public discussion in 1950 in the party newspaper *Pravda*. Stalin declared that Marr was not a Marxist, and Indo-European linguistic studies were restored. The theory of staged development was rejected as well, and another detachment of scholars was forced to publicly repent. Although the repression this time was not as dramatic as earlier, it still existed, and "cosmopolites" (mainly Jews) became "antipatriotic critics" and "slanderers" and were expelled from scholarly organizations.

Soviet Archaeology: From Thaw to Moderate Frosts to Stagnation, 1956–1991

Nikita Khrushchev's speech during the Twentieth Party Congress exposed Stalin as a despot and took power from his nearest associates. It was a kind of liberalization, and the writer Ilya Erenburg coined the word "thaw" for it. The dictatorship of the proletariat was repudiated, and normalization of relations with the West began.

All of this change led to some shifts in archaeology. Gradually, the concern for "historic rights" on maps disappeared, the details of local origins were no longer so important, and archaeologists were able to argue for migration in their explanations of cultural change. Slavic archaeology began to be as well regarded as other branches of the discipline, and ethnogenesis lost its priority. However, the new ruler of Russia neither understood humanist intellectuals nor had any special sympathy for them.

In 1956, Boris Rybakov, a specialist in Slavic-Russian archaeology, was appointed as head of the IHMK, which was shortly renamed the Institute of Archaeology. Rybakov earlier had made his name by encouraging patriotic ideals in archaeology, specifically by the glorification of ancient Russian handicrafts.

In the middle of the 1960s, Khrushchev, whose political experiments were considered dangerous for the regime, was demoted by a palace revolution. To justify this change in policy, it became necessary to introduce objective and reliable methods in all disciplines. Archaeologists seized this opportunity to develop theoretical studies, their relationships with western non-Marxist scholars became more positive and respectful, and debates took place. However, the new scholarly freedom that led to the invasion of Prague by Russian troops in the spring of 1968 badly frightened the Brezhnev oligarchy, and debate and discussion, even critiques of Stalin, ceased.

Archaeological activity continued to grow enormously. In 1985 there were some 700 expeditions; more recently, it has been estimated that every two years 8,000 archaeological books and articles are published in the USSR, i.e., as much as was published between 1918 and 1940. Using state donations, planned economy, and centralized organization, Rybakov managed to initiate the twenty-volume edition *The Archaeology of the USSR,* and although only a small number of the volumes have been published, hundreds of other volumes entitled *Corpus of Archaeological Sources* have appeared.

Russian Archaeology in the Struggle for Survival since 1991

In 1985, Mikhail Gorbachev's rise to power initially caused considerable liberalization and the introduction of moderate freedoms. But in archaeology nothing changed during the period of *"perestroika"* (reconstruction), except for the destruction of the socialist camp and then the fall of all the socialist regimes in Europe. Glasnost (quite considerable freedom of the press) and intensive contacts with the West increased the amount of information available to the Soviet people, and their preference for capitalism became evident.

Real transformations began in 1991 when Boris Yeltsin was elected president and the Soviet Union fell to pieces as a result of an attempt to overthrow the government in August. Communist power broke down completely, and the new government began radical economic reforms. The disintegration of the old economic system without a new system to take its place, and the disruption of old economic connections among national republics, were the very painful consequences of democratization and growing capitalism. They were also very destructive with respect to archaeology.

Independent national archaeological programs emerged in the Ukraine, Belorussia, Moldavia, all the Transcaucasia, central Asia, and the Baltic areas. The monuments that had been studied for a long time by many Russian scholars were now located in countries other than Russia. Archaeology was decentralized, and the role of local centers increased. The Institute of Archaeology was split into two independent institutes in Moscow and St. Petersburg (formerly Leningrad, now St. Petersburg once again), and in the latter, the name Institute for the History of Material Culture (IHMK) was restored.

Another consequence for archaeology has been a sharp decrease in state allocations of funding for academic disciplines, including money for archaeology. The lack of state ideology has also deprived archaeologists of any material support. They have been forced to search for new sources of funding from western foundations, local sponsors, or their own earnings. The amount of foreign literature in specialist libraries decreased as the availability of foreign currency decreased.

On the positive side, communications with foreign colleagues have intensified, and the choice of methodology and direction in archaeology appears to be completely free now. The main journal has changed its name to *Archaeology of Russia,* but attempts to rebuild professional archaeological societies have not met with much success. The milieu that gave the societies their members and made them strong and influential has disappeared, and new sources of support for archaeology have not been formed as yet. Russian archaeology is at another turning point in its history.

The Development of Archaeological Thought

Antiquarianism

Peter the Great's enthusiasm for antiquities as rarities was undoubtedly antiquarian in character. Although an interest in antiquarianism came to Russia two a half centuries later than it had come to Italy, two centuries later than to England, and a century later than to France, it took the same forms. Antiquities were sampled and connected at random with ancient peoples known from written chronicles. Scholarly activity proceeded in newly annexed or explored territories on the periphery—Siberia, the Urals, northwestern Russia—and the study of antiquities was seen as a part of geography and as part of broad encyclopedic interests, as they were in other countries. However Russian antiquarianism was different in two respects.

First, Russian antiquarian interest was originally directed toward local antiquities—at colonial antiquities—rather than toward classical Greek or Roman antiquities. This difference was connected with ethnographic interests. Classical antiquities attracted attention later, when Russia received part of the lands around the Black Sea where there were ancient Greek colonies, and Russian-Slavic antiquities received attention later still.

The second distinction existed because the motivating force in Russian antiquarianism was the czar and the state. In other European countries, collecting antiquities was initially a bourgeois intellectual hobby that was later taken up by the aristocracy. Antiquarianism in Russia spread, from the very beginning, from above as one of the important aspects adopted by the Russian state from the western European way of life.

Under the influence of the German art historian Winckelmann, classical antiquities were considered everywhere, including in Russia, as the greatest monuments of art and as an ideal. This sentimental attitude was an important part of antiquarianism, and it was alive and well in Russia until the beginning of the Soviet era, for example, in Zhebelev's *Introduction to Archaeology,* published in 1923. The final demise of these values was recognized in Marr's statement: "Down with Venus of Milos, long live the hoe!"

Romantic Ethnography
The romantic movement gave birth to a widespread interest in local medieval monuments all over Europe, and Russian romanticism was especially patriotic because it developed as a result of the war against Napoleon's invasion in 1812. In the early nineteenth century, this interest was best expressed by Chodakovsky's program of scholarly travels. He was as carried away by hill forts, as was WILLIAM STUKELEY by megaliths in England—and like Stukeley, Chodakovsky suspected that his hill forts were sacred places. Passek had the same passion for barrows, but both men were interested in the ethnography of these monuments.

Passek's investigations of barrows occurred during the middle of the nineteenth century and were inspired by the grand excavations of barrows by Uvarov and Savelyev. Uvarov published the results of these excavations in 1871 and described the barrows as belonging to the Merya (a Finnish people), although later it became clear that they were, in fact, ancient Slavic monuments. This episode shows that leading Russian archaeologists still did not have means to properly identify ancient peoples with the peoples of today and thus identified them ethnically. It also shows that at least some Russian scholars had no nationalist subplot they were trying to justify via archaeology and that they did not try to widen the ancient territories of the Russian people to this end. Their national self-esteem was not dependent on the past.

Archaeology was considered to be the simple expansion of ethnography into the distant past. The same scholars undertook both the archaeological and the ethnographic exploration of a region. The principle that every people had distinct peculiarities of culture and distinct material or types of things seemed quite natural and was the view that the German archaeologist RUDOLF VIRCHOW and other German scholars of his circle took.

The best example of this point of view can be found in an 1899 article by Spitsyn, "The Distribution of Ancient Russian Tribes According to Archaeological Data," in which he established that the territory of Russian "tribes" (as they were called in the chronicles Polyane, Drevlyane, and Vyatichi) reflected the area of their temple ring types, i.e., each "tribe" had its own type of ring. Spitsyn's work resembles that of the twentieth-century German archaeologist GUSTAV KOSSINNA in his article "On the Decorated Iron Lanceheads as Attribute of Ancient Germans" (1905). However free Spitsyn was of Kossinna's nationalist and racist overtones, he could still get carried away by the possibilities of migrations. The notion of archaeological culture also originated in Russia at this time and has been used widely since 1901.

Migrations were only one part of Kossinna's overall concerns and not really central to them. For central Europe, where the Germans lived, Kossinna preferred to argue for local and continuous development so that, in fact, the central part of his argument was autochthonism. This concept was more widely held in Russia than migrationism. Within the framework of the "*byt*-descriptive" (everyday-life-descriptive) approach developed by Zabelin and Samokvasov, there was also an argument for a very long and continuous development of the Russian state and culture from the same territories as Kievan Rus, which must have originated from the Scythians ("the noble ancestors"). Despite the cold reception this hypothesis received and numerous critiques, it remained tenacious and was revitalized again and again. In the middle of the twentieth century (from the 1930s to the 1970s), Boris Grekov and Boris Rybakov built a scheme for Russian state development that was still longer than that of Zabelin and Samokvasov, as they included not only Scythians but also Tripolye agriculturists, from the Eneolithic period. There are many weak points in this concept, and its political and nationalist motivations help to explain its popularity during the Soviet period. Paradoxically, it now receives new support—from Ukrainian ideologists.

Progressivism

The THREE-AGE SYSTEM made its way into Russia, as in the rest of Europe, from Scandinavia. For its establishment, it was necessary to elaborate on the Enlightenment idea of progress that declared that the contemporary was a higher cultural state than the ancient classic ideal. This idea was in harmony with the reforms of Czar Peter the Great, whose ideals were contemporary Europe and European civilization. Thus, as distinct from Germany, in Russia there was fertile soil for the idea of progress. In the middle of the nineteenth century, a series of translations (including the writing of Danish archaeologist JENS JACOB WORSAAE) acquainted Russian archaeologists with the achievements of Scandinavian progressivists. In 1881, the leader of Russian archaeologists, Count Uvarov, based his book *Archaeology: The Stone Age* on the three-age system. Thus, the basis for archaeological periodization was introduced.

The corresponding ethnographic periodization in three steps (savagery, barbarism, civilization) was merely elaborated by American anthropologist LEWIS HENRY MORGAN in the evolutionary spirit. However, it had been advanced earlier by Vedel-Simonsen, and in his version it was properly a progressivist scheme and was adapted by Fredrich Engels into the basics of Marxist revolutionary ideology.

Evolutionism

Created in England, France, and Sweden, archaeological evolutionism became known in Russia comparably early—through reviews, surveys, expositions, and, later, translations of Lubbock and GABRIEL DE MORTILLET's work. It had an impact on Russian ethnography but little impact on Russian archaeology. Russian archaeologists were more conservative than Russian ethnographers (some of whom were deported as revolutionaries), and archaeologists were confused by the connection of archaeological evolutionism with the ideas of Charles Darwin.

The revolutionist periodization of de Mortillet was transferred to Russia by Fedor Volkov, who studied in France, and by his pupil Petr Efimenko, whose fundamental work on the Paleolithic was published in 1934. In that work's exposition of data, the periodization of the Stone Age was elaborated in the spirit of de Mortillet's evolutionism at a time when, in France, much of de Mortillet's approach was being revised by HENRI BREUIL and others. Russian archaeologists first learned about the methodological elaborations of Swedish archaeologist OSCAR MONTELIUS in the first volume of Ravdonikas's *History of Primordial Society* (1939).

In the first half of 1930s, the theory of stadial development rejected the primacy of the *Ursprache* ("ancestor language") as well as the importance of ethnic boundaries and insisted on the mixing, crossing, and fusion of peoples. Nevertheless, it retained the autochthonistic principle of a gradual, slow sojourn of peoples in places. To substantiate the theory, Kruglov and Podgaecky, in their book *The Clan Society of East-European Steppes* (1935), introduced a correction into the concept of a revolutionary replacement of stages (the break of continuity) by using the concept of "stadial transitions," i.e., connecting chains or intermediate types, in what was an evident retreat from revolutionary phraseology to evolutionism. Gradual evolutionism began to mark the Irkutsk school of Soviet archaeologists, especially Teploukhov and his pupil Gryaznov. For them, development occurred independently at each place, and an archaeological culture was considered identical to its period.

Anthropogeographism (Paleoethnological Trend)

Anthropogeographism, named after FRIEDRICH RATZEL's school of Anthropogeography, rejected the evolutionary aspects of ancient cultures and moved the center of consideration to territorial aspects—development in the space and distribution of culture complexes, which were considered as very steady and unchanging. A large role was given to the interaction of the sciences of man with geography and, in general, with the sciences of the natural environment.

In Russia, this trend developed independently of western anthropogeography and had a closer contact with evolutionism. One of the originators of this trend in Russia was Dmitriy Anuchin, a pupil of the founder of Russian physical anthropology, Anatoliy Bogdanov. Anuchin was Bogdanov's successor and led the Institute of Anthropology at Moscow University from 1880 to 1884. Anuchin viewed anthropology as the science that embraces both the biological and the cultural sides of man, and he simultaneously created in Russia his own schools of geography and ethnology. He was busy with archaeology, too, and in his works on the history of material culture, archaeological and ethnographic data were combined as Uvarov and Zabelin had done previously. Unlike the German anthropogeographers, who were humanists, Anuchin was a naturalist, an avowed Darwinist, and consequently a partisan of the theory of evolution. He collaborated with de Mortillet in France, but Anuchin distinguished himself from the evolutionist approach by his attention to the diversity of cultural phenomena and to the estimation of geographical factors.

One of Anuchin's pupils at the Institute of Anthropology, Bunak, continued the tradition in physical anthropology; another, Kuftin, worked in ethnography, later transferring to archaeology; and Zhukov became the head of the Moscow paleoethnological school of archaeology. The name of the school itself shows that its adherents considered archaeology to be a continuation of ethnology into the depths of time. Paleoethnologists tried to differentiate particular groups of peoples, to distinguish them in antiquity, and therefore they paid special attention to the formal and technological analysis of pottery. They conducted interdisciplinary ("complex") expeditions and aimed to complete the survey of a territory. In a cultural complex (the combination of elements in a culture), they stressed correlation, and correlation in dynamics, in development. In Russian archaeology, paleoethnologists were the first to implement statistics and correlation. In 1930, Zhukov was arrested and died, and the school fell to pieces.

If one searched in the West for a most likely analogy to the Moscow paleoethnological school, it would appear to be not the French archaeologists but the Americanist archaeologists, dubbed "taxonomists" by critic WALTER TAYLOR in the 1960s and described by Bruce Trigger as followers of an American culture-historical approach. They shared with the Russians a discontent with the indeterminacy of the concept of "archaeological culture," a stress on the formal classification of ceramics, and emphasis on the survey of entire regions. However, the Americans developed their approach approximately at the same time (1924–1939) without hindrance.

The paleoethnological trend existed in Leningrad, too. As in Moscow, it developed there under French influence and was characterized by an approach to archaeology as a natural discipline—as part of a broadly understood anthropology and also as a continuation of ethnology into the depth of time. This trend was connected to a strong interest in ethnic problems—identifying ethnic peoples in the past and revealing the roots of contemporary peoples.

Although in Moscow at least the founder of the trend was friendly with de Mortillet, not all of the main figures of Saint Petersburg/Leningrad were so immediately connected with the evolutionists. The leader of the Leningrad trend was Fedor Volkov (his Ukrainian name was Khvedor Vovk). He was a contemporary of Anuchin's, the discoverer of the Paleolithic site of Mezin, and a believer in the evolutionist ideas of de Mortillet. Volkov's pupils included the Leningrad Ukrainians Petr Efimenko and Sergey Rudenko. Efimenko was one of the first to work on correlation, applying it to the Ryazan Slavic-Russian barrows and the Russian Paleolithic from a remnant evolutionist position using the theory of stadial development. Still later, he became the director of the Kievan Institute of Archaeology. Rudenko discovered the permanently frozen Pazyryk graves before he was politically repressed and deported to the extreme North. After liberation, he studied the impact of nature on culture and welcomed the geographical approach of English archaeologist O. G. S. CRAWFORD, writing a laudatory preface to the translation of Crawford's book. His pupil Lev Gumilev, the son of glorified Russian poets, continued this tradition and became more and more interested in biological determinism.

The other influential figure among the

Leningrad paleoethnologists was Alexandr Miller, who studied in the École Anthropologique in Paris after the death of de Mortillet and was friendly with Breuil and HUGO OBERMAIER GRAD. Miller published very little but trained very strong pupils—Artamonov, Piotrovskiy, Iessen, Passek, Latynin, Kruglov, Podgaecky, and Krichevsky. Miller was also arrested in the 1930s, and his pupils were encouraged to maintain an interest in ethnic problems rather than any paleoethnological directions.

This trend in Russia was strangely unlucky, but there was a logic to its bad luck. During the time of the czars, in the 1880s, the Department of Anthropology at Moscow University was closed and what survived was transferred as the Department of Ethnography from the historical-philological faculty to the natural sciences faculty in order to hinder the intrusion of naturalist scientific ideas into humanist studies. During Soviet times, it was dangerous for social scientists to look for explanations in natural factors instead of socioeconomic ones or (in the early period) to have an interest in ethnic problems. The attitude of paleoethnologists, whether consciously or not, was opposed to the historicizing and politizing of archaeology and to its Marxist directions. Thus, the heads of both schools of paleoethnology—Moscow and Leningrad—were arrested and annihilated, and some members of the schools also "visited" prisons and camps. Paleoethnology remained disorganized and broken.

After interests in ethnogenesis were allowed, and even encouraged, again in the USSR, the pupils of paleoethnologists who had survived started to research ethnogenetic questions. The leading figures in this respect were Artamonov, the pupil of Miller; Tretyakov, the pupil of Efimenko; and Tolstov, the pupil of Zhukov.

Diffusionism

An interest in cultural influences first appeared in Russia in the late nineteenth century in a paper by Anuchin entitled "On Cultural Influences on the Prehistoric Soil of Russia" (1880). Yet the proper bearer of the diffusionist concept in Russia became, partly as a result of the influence of Anuchin, Vasiliy Gorodcov. His generalizing works were built on the idea of *ex Oriente lux* (out of the East comes light). He sought the origins of any novelty in a given culture—as an invasion or borrowing. He attentively observed the activity of the prominent European diffusionist SOPHUS MÜLLER, especially his remarkable excavations of Jutland barrows, and in 1901–1903 exactly copied those excavations in the Izyum and Bakhmut districts of the Ukraine, discovering the pit-grave, catacomb-grave, and framework-grave cultures. Gorodcov's "typological method" was opposed to that of Montelius, mainly because Müller was an opponent of Montelius.

The controversy between Gorodcov and the head of the Moscow paleoethnological school, Zhukov, is characteristic of these different points of view. Zhukov built the periodization isophenomenologically, that is, he divided material into periods exclusively according to typological similarities and distinctions regardless of time. Gorodcov did so isochronologically, that is, he divided the periods into chronological sections regardless of material types. If some leading regions entered the Bronze Age, all others were considered as being in the Bronze Age; contacts were held to be more important than the level of development.

Some particular manifestations of Gorodcov's approach existed after World War II (Foss in 1949 stuck to such a periodization, as did Bryusov in part), but all in all, diffusionism did not continue in Russia, even though Gorodcov had many well-known pupils, Arcikhovsky, Bryusov, Smirnov, and Kraynov among them. They continued his interests in classification but not his diffusionism.

Combinationism

The designation of the term *combinationism* is not well known and belongs only to the historiographer, the author of this article, who formed a special school for it (Klejn 1977). All the main schools of archaeology tried to answer the question of why there were breaks of continuity in the development of culture, because there had to be continuity in terms of process between past and present for the present to be understandable. The question of why or how cultures change requires us to limit the two notions of heredity and continuity with innovations. Some western scholars in the late nineteenth and early twentieth centuries stated ideas about the importance of joining various traditions together. The French historian Tarde defined invention as "logical copulation." The German ethnologist Leo Frobenius described cultural creation as the "coupling of cultures." In the second and third decades of the twentieth century, the English anthropologist AUGUSTUS PITT RIVERS clearly believed that new cultural elements emerged as a result of the fusion and crossing of the old elements of culture.

In Russian archaeology at the turn of the century, Kondakov, who moved from the University of New Russia in Odessa to St. Petersburg and studied ancient art on the basis of archaeological records, advanced the idea that anything new in art emerged out of the crossing of old forms. For instance, he stated that ancient Russian art was the result of a fusion of Byzantine, nomad, and local elements. In the first decades of the twentieth century, his methodological ideas were further developed by his pupils—Rostovcev on the example of the Bosporus and Scythia and Farmakovsky on the materials of the archaic culture of the Caucasus. In the first case, the Iranian ethnic element crossed with the Greek one; in the second, the Ionian crossed with the Oriental. After the Russian Revolution, Kondakov and Rostovcev emigrated. Another pupil of Kondakov, Zhebelev, remained in Soviet Russia and managed to publish Rovtovcev's *Scythia and Bosporus,* in Leningrad in 1932. Rostovcev became a widely known specialist in the economic history of Hellenistic culture.

The ideas of the Russian combinationists influenced the development of stadialism. The idea of cultures crossing was adapted by Soviet archaeologists from the linguistics school of Marr (see below). The impact of this approach in archaeology was first made by Kondakov and Rostovcev. It was based on combinationism and a broad trend of Euro-Asianism that became very popular among Russian emigrants abroad. They believed that the Russian people were the result of a crossing of European and Asian cultures. However this trend was even more popular in history than in archaeology.

Stadialism

In the first decades of the Soviet period, the director of RAIMK/GAIMK, the main archaeological institution of the country, was Academician Nikolay Marr, a linguist and orientalist. In the middle of the 1920s he formulated his "new learning on language" (Japhetic theory), which completely rejected the concept of an Indo-European *Ursprache* ("ancestor language"), a concept that had been well elaborated by many generations of linguists, and explained the close similarity of languages, not by affiliation (common origin), but by their mixing and crossing. This theory depicted the history of speech as a series of language revolutions within the melting pot of one language family that are instantly transformed into languages with quite another structure and substance without any alien intrusion. There was no serious substantiation of these assumptions, but the revolutionary phraseology and defaming of Indo-European studies as "bourgeois" gained Marr the support of Communist Party ideologists.

This linguistic theory was picked up by some young archaeologists, especially those of the Leningrad school (such as Ravdonikas, Krichevsky, and Okladnikov), and transformed into an archaeological theory—that of stadial development. Ethnic cultures were placed under languages, and the whole of their history was depicted as a series of leaps from one stage to another—leaps in which the ethnic nature of the culture was instantly transformed. The theory resolved some of the most difficult problems of ethnogenesis as it became possible to derive any culture from any other. Such a large role was assigned to the interaction of cultures that the question of roots, of ancestors, simply no longer arose. All peoples appeared mixed, the ancestors of all of them being similar and, to some extent, common. All had behind them the various and finely crumbled mixture out of which modern peoples were formed by gradual junctions or crossings and mainly by sudden stadial transformations.

The first observable realization of this theory was Ravdonikas's work "The Cave Towns of Crimea and the Goths Problem in Connection with Stadial Development of the Northern

Black Sea Region" (1932). In it, Ravdonikas suggested that the reader believe that Cimmerians who had populated the region earlier were Japhetides, i.e., they were related in language to the Caucasians of today, that they turned as the result of revolutionary transformations into Iranian-speaking Scythians, that they in their turn became German-speaking Goths, and that the Goths became Slavs. Nobody came from the outside into Crimea; everything evolved within it. Language and culture changed sharply and abruptly. Why? Because the sharp transformations are the dialectical law of being and because language and culture are connected with social structures, which, of course, went through revolutions.

In 1934 and 1935, Efimenko attempted to represent the development of the Paleolithic through stages and in 1935 Kruglov and Podgaecky postulated a series of stages in the Bronze Age of the steppes. In their work, however, the ethnic aspect was completely absent. They timed the stages according to technical shifts, to steps in the development of production, and while showing the revolutionary character of these shifts they tried to allot all of the phenomena of culture, including "superstructional" (projective) ones, to these steps. This work looked more realistic than the fantastic transformations of languages and peoples, but the more realistic it looked, the less it retained of the theory of stadial development. Because the essence of that theory was miraculous transformations, it resisted explanations that were logical and that proposed any continuity of development. However, stadial development depends on logic and on intermediate chains— "stadial transitions" as they were called by Kruglov and Podgaecky.

During the Patriotic War (World War II in Russia), considerable mass opposition against Stalin began, which forced the state to reconsider the patriotic feelings and nationalist temper of the peoples of the Soviet Union, especially the Russian people. Ethnic groups within the USSR were encouraged to take pride in their independent origins and to search carefully for their roots. Marr's Japhetic theory contradicted this activity. In 1951, there was a multiweek linguistic discussion in the central Communist Party newspaper *Pravda* in which Stalin personally took part. He argued against Marr's works, and both the Japhetic theory and the theory of stadial development were rejected.

It was now possible to criticize Marr. He was described as a bad linguist and really not an archaeologist at all—not even knowing that there was no metal in the Paleolithic period. Despite the lack of arguments, the theory of stadial development did bring some fresh ideas into the explanation of the most difficult problems of archaeology. It insisted that archaeologists begin to consider the sources of transformations in each society, i.e., to the importance of socioeconomic shifts for the transformation of culture, to leaps that are really inherent in every development. Later, such ideas began to be discussed seriously in many archaeological schools of the West, especially those interested in "the new archaeology."

Marxist Sociohistoricism

After the victory of the Bolsheviks in Russia, Marxist doctrine and its values were imposed on the entire scholarly world, and young archaeologists began to search for methodological ideas that could distinguish their activity from "bourgeois" archaeology. One of the first to be proposed, "the complex method" (Nikolskiy 1927) was a dim conglomerate of ideas, and it was understood variously as a demand to consider things as being associated in assemblages, which was not a new idea in Europe at all. It also argued for the involvement of many source-studying disciplines in complete historic reconstruction and for the organization of "complex," that is, multidisciplinary, expeditions.

In the middle of the 1920s, a group of young archaeologists in Moscow, disciples of Gorodcov, proceeded to engage in reeducation under the guidance of the Marxist sociologist Friche. They tried to superimpose Marxist concepts and principles onto archaeological material—to study the development of implements and to show how this development conditioned the whole appearance of economy and culture—and they tried to search for a connection between dwelling forms and the economy and socioeconomic structure of society. For a Marxist reconstruction of the past on the basis of material remains they invented "the method of ascending." Supposing that Marxism gives absolutely reliable schemes for a one-to-one correlation of implement types with the socioeconomic structures of society, these archaeologists believed it possible to "ascend" in reconstruction from implements of labor as a fundamental aspect of social building to economic structures (in Marxism, the basis of society) and even further to social as well as ideational relations (in Marxism, superstructures). As this process of "ascending" came to be regarded as completely plausible, there appeared to be no need to address oneself to neighboring disciplines—such as ethnography and linguistics—or even to written sources. Archaeology itself appeared as history, a history that was more trustworthy than the written one, for material records were considered as more objective evidences of the past, free from subjective distortions and admixtures.

True, history supposes an interest in personalities and particular events that is mostly inaccessible to archaeologists. Yet in the Marxist view, another notion about history dominated in which "collectives" (societies, masses) and processes acted instead of personalities and personalities figured only as "products" and "markers" of social relations. This type of history could be "built" by archaeologists.

Later on, the theoretical basis of "the method of ascending" was not further developed by its creators (Arcikhovsky, Kiselev, Smirnov, and Bryusov), who became prominent and authoritative Soviet archaeologists. However, those same students and their pupils used the method in their work and considered the whole of archaeology as another history—a "history armed with the spade" (Arcikhovsky). That idea became the initial premise of this approach. Arcikhovsky became the head of the Department of Archaeology at Moscow University and the editor of the main archaeological journal, and his younger associate and disciple Rybakov acted for three decades in the post-Stalin era as the head of the leading archaeological institution of the country and all of Russian archaeology. Given the problematics of ethnogenesis, these students preferred local development (in Russia, this preference is called "autochthonism"), and in that respect they did not diverge from Marr's ideas. After those ideas had been discredited, they restored the argument of the old Russian autochthonists Zabelin and Samokvasov and combined it with Marxist discourses on the inner sources of the state origins in each society.

This trend corresponded more than the others to Soviet ideology and was skillfully adjusted to it. It appeared to be very tenacious. In the last decades of the Soviet regime, Vadim Masson in Leningrad advanced methodological elaborations in the spirit of sociological historicism (1976, 1990), and Vladimir F. Gening in Kiev put forward a detailed methodological substantiation of "sociological archaeology" as he understood it—quite in the spirit of the 1930s. Masson's recommendations do not go beyond searching for stereotyped correlations to social structures in archaeological materials, and the expansive works of Gening are distinguished by dogmatism and scholastics. Thus, one can say the trend has been exhausted. However, analogous interests have started to appear in the West (the "sociological archaeology" of Colin Renfrew among others), so it appears that Russian archaeologists initiated a worldwide movement.

Sequention of Cultures
The views and interests of Efimenko and Artamonov were formed in the Leningrad paleoethnological school. Efimenko first studied Slavic-Russian barrows and then the Paleolithic period before moving from Leningrad to Kiev to become the head of the Institute of Archaeology there. Artamonov dealt with many branches of prehistoric archaeology—from the Bronze Age to Scythian and Slavic-Russian antiquities—as well as heading the Leningrad University Department of Archaeology and serving as the director of the Hermitage. After World War II, when the dogmatic settings of the stadialist theory were first weakened and then dismissed entirely, Efimenko and Artamonov, their pupils, and the pupils of their pupils began to reconstruct migrations in any direction, including invasions into the territory of the country of the researcher. This was not migrationism, for they

did not seek explanations for any novelties in the migrations. Simply, the fact was recognized that peoples moved in the past and the ethnic frontiers changed. Elsewhere, these searches have been called "submigrationist" (Klejn 1994).

The interests of these students were mainly in the problems of ethnogenesis. They opposed the autochthonism of the stadialists and the ultrapatriotic autochthonism of the state glorifiers; nor did they believe in the necessity of "archaeological right"—of the deep antiquity of habitation that was necessary to substantiate the right of a people to live where they did. Their reconstructed migrations, therefore, were a kind of challenge to the then-dominate doctrine—and to official politics.

However, their position did have some scholarly basis. In order to study culture-historical processes correctly, one needs first to establish the channel by which the development proceeded, and such a channel does not necessarily occur only in the cultures of one country. Cultural traditions are transferred, not through the earth, but through human contacts. From time to time, the human masses begin to move themselves, sometimes by jerks and sometimes for great distances.

Scientism

The scientific and technical revolution in archaeology did not occur in Russia until the post-Stalin period, later than in the West. Chemical, metallographic, and petrographic analyses, and the techniques of scientific DATING, began to be used more intensively in archaeological research, and many archaeologists started to look to these methods for clues to the solutions to the main problems of archaeology. It was believed that it was possible to separate archaeological cultures and epochs by material attributes that could be more easily discovered with scientific methods and technological analyses and to search for evolution and hereditary continuity in this way.

However, the founder of the functionalist-traceological method (the investigation of implement traces with a binocular microscope) in the 1930s to 1950s, Semenov, proposed his method of typology (i.e., the determination of

the function of an implement by its form) as the proper scientific method. Later on, the baton of this method passed to the archaeologists who utilized mathematical methods in the service of archaeology—especially statistics and combinatorial mathematics—Yakov Sher, Boris Marshak, Vera Kovalevskaya, the German Fedorov-Davydov, and Igor Kameneckiy. In the main, they developed methods that had already been developed in the West, but the first attempts of this kind emerged in Russian archaeology in the work of Efimenko and Gryaznov in the 1930s, even earlier than in the West.

Computers began to be used by Russian archaeologists much later than they began to be used in the West, but some decades earlier Russian archaeologists, observing computerization in the West and trying to keep up with it with the help of perforated cards, had grasped that computerization demands a theoretical restructuring of all of archaeology. More measuring, more exactness in descriptions, a strictness of determinations, and an elaboration of algorithms is needed. *Descriptive archaeology* became the phrase used by Kameneckiy, Marshak, and Sher and the Gening school in Kiev.

Relativist Subjectivism

After Marxism was discredited, and with it objectivist optimism in general, the dizzying successes of science and the superb perfectness of computer programs led archaeologists to believe that research implements were all important and that research results were completely dependent on those who possessed those implements. The crisis of positivist and postpositivist methodology pushed researchers to the opposite extreme—to the absolute freedom of the researcher's intelligence in the interpretation of sources and to an exaggeration of the role of the subjective factor in the reconstruction of the past. In addition, the recent cases of Soviet and Nazi scholarship have shown how dependent the inferences of archaeologists and historians are on social conditions and the position of the scholar is on his subjective bias. By contrast, the Marxist type of sociological analysis, which became very influential in archaeology in the West ("the critical theory"), provided the basis of the general applicability to this idea and distributed it into analysis of other concepts.

In archaeology in the West, some scholars (such as J. O. Brew and JAMES A. FORD in the United States and MATS P. MALMER in Sweden) advanced a concept according to which grouping of material and inferences were fully dependent on the investigator's will and arbitrariness—on the definitions, methods, and criteria chosen by the investigator. In the last decades of the Soviet regime, this concept also appeared in archaeology, although sporadically (in Paleolithic studies in the work of Gennady Grigoryev). Recently, this has also developed into a broader concept (in general theory in the works of Evgeny Kolpakov).

Leo Klejn

References

"Arcikhovskiy, A. V." In *Great Soviet Encyclopedia.* Ed. A. M. Prokhorov. 31 vols. (1973–1983). New York: Macmillan.

Formozov, A. A. 1961. "Ocherki po istorii russkoy arkheologii." *Akademiya nauk SSSR.*

Gening, V. F. 1982. *Ocherki po Istorii Sovetskoy Arkheologii.* Kiev: Naukova Dumka.

Khudyakov, M. V. 1933. "Dorevolyucionnaya russkaya arkheologiya na sluzhbe ekspluatatorskikh klassov."

Klejn, L. S. 1977. "A Panorama of Theoretical Archaeology." *Current Anthropology* 18: 1–42.

———. 1994. *Fenomen Sovetskoy Arkheologii.* SPb, Farn.

Lebedev, G. S. 1992. *Istoriya otechestvennoy arkheologii.*

Miller, M. O. 1956. *Archaeology in the USSR.* London and New York: Atlantic Press.

Mongait, A. L. 1956. *Archaeology in the USSR.* Moscow: Foreign Languages Publishing House.

Pryakhin, A. D. 1986. *Istoriya Sovetskoy Arkheologii.* Voronezh: VGU.

Ravdonikas, V. I. 1932. "Za marksiskuyu istoriyu materialnoy kultury." *Izvestiya GAIMK* 7: 3–4.

S

Salamis

Salamis, an Iron Age and classical site on the east coast of CYPRUS, has a long history of archaeological work. The Cesnola family worked on the site in the mid-nineteenth century, but fortunately they found too little to encourage further depredations on their part. Toward the end of the nineteenth century, M. Ohnefalsch-Richter and others excavated on behalf of various British institutions.

In the 1920s and 1930s, small-scale work was carried out by the Department of Antiquities, Cyprus. After World War II, work was resumed under the direction of VASSOS KARAGEORGHIS, who excavated at Salamis between 1953 and 1974. During that time, the Department of Antiquities cleared and restored large areas of the classical city, including the gymnasium and the theater. French archaeologists, including J. Pouilloux and M. Yon, worked at several sites together with the Department of Antiquities between 1964 and 1974. Further work has been precluded by the Turkish occupation of northern Cyprus. In a nearby Iron Age necropolis, tumuli cover the built tombs of the eighth century, some of which have horse-and-chariot burials and luxury grave goods (such as a bronze cauldron and ivory furniture fittings).

David Frankel

References

Karageorghis, V. 1999. *Excavating at Salamis in Cyprus, 1952–1974.* Athens: A. G. Leventis Foundation.

Sankalia, Hasmukh D. (1908–1989)

For many years Hasmukh D. Sankalia was a professor of archaeology at the Deccan College, Pune (Poona) in India, and he was also director of the college for some time before his retirement. Initially, he undertook surveys in Gujarat, his home state, and published, among other things, an analysis of the ancient historical geography of the region. Subsequently, he excavated Langhnaj, a Mesolithic to early-historical site in northern Gujarat.

At Deccan College, he initiated a well-coordinated field-based program of Ph.D. studies covering areas that included the modern states of Rajasthan, Gujarat, Nadhya Pradesh, Naharashtra, Andhra, Earnataka, Orissa, and Uttar Pradesh (the Son Valley and the Kumaun Hills). The emphasis was on area surveys and on prehistory and proto-history. He and his colleagues excavated major proto-historic sites from Rajasthan to Karnataka—Ahar, Navdatoli, Kayatha, Somnath, Nasik, Jorwe, Nevasa, Sanganakallu, Tekkalakota, Inamgaon, and others. In each case, the emphasis was on horizontal exposures, and the plethora of details on the proto-historic village life of the region is entirely owing to a range of excellently conducted and published excavation reports. In each case, there was also emphasis on the scientific analysis of materials, especially in the identification of animal, plant, and human remains.

Sankalia did not extensively excavate many historical sites except Brahmapuri in the southern part of Naharashtra. He was ever receptive to the changing ideas of archaeology and more keen than anybody else of his generation about the establishment of archaeology as an inde-

Step pyramid at Saqqara (Image Select)

pendent academic subject in its own right in the Indian universities. An austerely religious man, he lived, in the true sense, the ideals of an ancient Indian teacher—a guru who lives only for his subject and his students. Some of his ideas were disputed in later years, especially his tendency to see "western Asia" and "Aryans" in the proto-historic record. However, he dealt with even those who criticized him academically, and they never forgot to touch his feet and seek his blessings. A list of his publications may be found in the Indian journal *Man and Environment* (1989 14, no. 2).

K. Paddayya

See also South Asia

References

For references, see *Encyclopedia of Archaeology: The Great Archaeologists, Vol. 2.* Ed. Tim Murray (Santa Barbara, CA: ABC-CLIO, 1999), pp. 588–589.

Saqqara

Saqqara is one section of the great necropolis of Memphis, the capital of the Old Kingdom in Egypt. Most of the kings of the First and Second Dynasties were buried there. Though it is best known for the Step Pyramid built by Imhotep for King Djoser of the Third Dynasty, the site is also famous for mastaba tombs (low, rectangular, flat-roofed tombs with a shaft to the burial chamber), the Serapeum, and the numerous private tombs that date between the Old Kingdom and Greco-Roman times.

Saqqara has been under virtually continuous excavation since the nineteenth century and is particularly associated with French archaeology in Egypt, especially the work of AUGUSTE MARIETTE, who founded the Egyptian Antiquities Service and excavated the Serapeum. The Serapeum was a funeral complex where the mummified sacred Apis bulls were entombed. It was a place of pilgrimage.

Tim Murray

See also French Archaeology in Egypt and the Middle East; Egypt: Predynastic

References

Lauer, J. P. 1976. *Saqqara: The Royal Cemetery of Memphis: Excavations and Discoveries since 1850.* London: Thames and Hudson.

Šašel, Jaroslav (1924–1988)

A Slovenian archaeologist, epigrapher, and specialist in ancient history, Jaroslav Šašel studied at Ljubljana University, received his Ph.D. in 1969, and specialized at Graz University, the French School in Athens, and the Institute of Advanced Study at Princeton in the United States. Between 1951 and 1961, Šašel was an assistant in the Department of Archaeology, University of Ljubljana, and from 1961 to 1988, he was a research fellow at the Institute of Archaeology of the Slovenian Academy of Arts and Sciences. He was a member of many academies and learned societies: for example, a member of the DEUTSCHES ARCHÄOLOGISCHES INSTITUT (German Archaeological Institute), visiting member of the Austrian Archaeological Institute, honorary member of the Society of Antiquaries, and correspondent member of the Slovenian Academy of Arts and Sciences.

At first, Šašel's research focused on the archaeology of major Roman towns in SLOVENIA (Ljubljana, Ptuj, and Celje), but later he was more interested in Roman epigraphy. His numerous works include studies in epigraphy (writing/inscriptions), prosopography, ancient history, Roman military history, the ancient economy, and the historical topography of northeastern ITALY and the Roman provinces in the Balkans (Pannonia, Noricum, Dalmatia, Moesia). Together with his wife, Ana Šašel, he published the supplement to the *Corpus inscriptionum Latinarum* in three volumes (1963, 1978, and 1986). In his onomastic studies, he analyzed the structure and distribution of some Roman family names, and together with colleague P. Petru, he initiated research on the late Roman limes on the northeastern border of Italy.

Šašel also contributed to the *Tabula Imperii Romani* (1976), *Pauli-Wissowa Real Encyclopadie der klassischen Altertums-Wissenschaft, Princeton Encyclopedia of Classical Sites* (1976), *Der drosse Plotz* (1980), and the archaeological map of Slovenia *(Arheoloska najdisca Slovenije)*, in which he published a synthesis on Roman roads. He was also the editor of numerous Slovenian and Yugoslav archaeological journals and publications.

Milan Lovenjak

References
Šašel J. 1989. "Opera selecta." *Situla* (Ljubljana) 30. Reprint of his most important studies.

Saudi Arabia
See Arabian Peninsula

Schele, Linda (1942–1998)

One of the greatest Mayanist scholars of the late twentieth century, Linda Schele began her academic career as a studio art teacher. A tourist trip to Yucatán with her husband, David, changed her life. She was fascinated by the amazing ruins that she saw and the beauty of Maya art, and she resolved to learn more about them.

In the early 1970s Schele began to study Mayan hieroglyphic writing. By this time the basic structure and some of the content of Maya inscriptions were understood, but more precise details were still unclear. Over the following quarter century that situation was to change, and Schele was at the forefront of efforts aimed at "breaking the Maya code," as one scholar has put it.

In 1973 Schele attended the first round table conference at PALENQUE in MEXICO. At this, her initial professional conference, she and colleague Peter Mathews presented a proposed king-list (chronology of rulers deciphered from Maya inscriptions) of Palenque. Over the following fifteen years she worked not only on the inscriptions of Palenque but also on those of other classic Maya sites. In the studies she conducted during these years, she was indefatigable in her attempts to evaluate the archaeological sequence in conjunction with the epigraphic history of individual sites—an approach that has paid huge dividends. At Copán, Honduras, she worked with a number of other epigraphers and archaeologists conducting excavations in and around that site, and the result was a detailed synthesis of the archaeology, architectural sequence, and history of Copán, which is now one of the best understood of all classic Maya centers.

By the early 1980s Schele was a recognized leader in the field of Maya studies. She and a colleague from Yale University, Mary Miller, were asked to prepare a major exhibition of Maya art and to write the descriptive catalog to accompany it. The exhibition, called "The Blood of Kings," was a tour de force. For the first time masterpieces of Maya art from collections in both Europe and North America were exhibited together. The accompanying catalog was much more than a series of descriptive paragraphs about individual objects, preceded by a brief introduction: in addition to describing the exhibition pieces in detail, the book also contained essays by Schele and Miller on several great themes in Maya art, ranging from kingship to warfare to bloodletting. These essays were major statements on various aspects of elite life among the classic Maya, and *The Blood of Kings* represented an important step in Maya studies, in which art, hieroglyphs, and archaeology were brought together to arrive at an exciting new interpretation of classic Maya society.

Schele's next book, written with David Freidel, continued in this same vein. Entitled *A Forest of Kings,* it was an ambitious look at Maya history, combining the archaeological sequence with history gleaned from the glyphs. It did so in such a detailed way that the classic Maya elites almost leaped off the page: for the first time the "mysterious" Maya were becoming more accessible to twentieth-century readers.

Schele was a great popularizer of the ancient Maya. One of her lasting contributions to the field of Maya studies was the development of public workshops on how to read Maya hieroglyphs. Over the years she presented many such workshops, most notably the "Texas Workshops" held in Austin, where she was based. The audience regularly included many of the major scholars in the field of Maya studies, as well as several hundred members of the general public, all of whom were as captivated by Schele's infectious enthusiasm as they were by new discoveries about the ancient Maya. With another colleague, Nikolai Grube, Schele also conducted workshops for the Maya themselves in GUATEMALA and MEXICO. This was her proudest achievement: as she put it, she was giving back to the Maya people their own history, which had been taken from them in the years and centuries following the Spanish conquest.

In all her work Schele displayed rare analytic and synthetic skills in making groundbreaking discoveries herself and leading her field to still others. She was not afraid to try new approaches, and with her brilliant insights her efforts were more often than not rewarded. By fostering the same attitudes among her many students, she ensured that her intellectual heritage would survive her untimely death from cancer in 1998.

Peter Mathews

See also Maya Civilization; Maya Epigraphy; Mesoamerica

References
Schele, L., and D. Freidel. 1990. *A Forest of Kings: The Untold Story of the Ancient Maya.* New York: Morrow.

Heinrich Schliemann (Ann Ronan Picture Library)

Schliemann, Heinrich (1822–1890)

Heinrich Schliemann was born in northern Germany and became a sailor, shopkeeper, and merchant; he taught himself fluent French, Dutch, Greek, Russian, and English. A short visit to California in the gold rush days and a longer period trading in RUSSIA consolidated his personal fortune, and he began to travel extensively and to write about his experiences. He also became interested in history and archaeology, learned Latin and Greek, and was inspired by the successful careers and the great fame of famous archaeologists SIR AUSTEN H. LAYARD, SIR HENRY RAWLINSON, and AUGUSTE MARIETTE.

In 1866, Schliemann began to study at the Sorbonne in Paris and became interested in the debates about the veracity of Homer's legends. In 1868, he visited the places in GREECE and TURKEY mentioned by Homer, taking the same route as Odysseus to Turkey, and published a popular account of his travels. In 1869, he divorced his Russian wife and married a young Greek woman who was as passionate about Homer as he was and well connected within Athenian society.

In 1870 Schliemann began to excavate at Hissarlik, the small Turkish village believed to be the site of Homer's Troy. Although he found many antiquities and architectural features, it took two years and a deep trench to get to the bottom of the site and find what he considered to be a wall of the Trojan city. The next year he unearthed what he claimed to be "Priam's hoard" (a collection of artifacts supposedly belonging to the King of Troy during the Trojan War). It is clear that the material was assembled over time and from several different sites to resemble a Trojan treasure, which he then smuggled out of Turkey and used as proof that he had uncovered Homer's Troy. He had, in fact, found remains older than Troy, but to get to them he had destroyed some of what he had thought he was looking for.

In 1876, Schliemann began to excavate within the citadel at Mycenae in central GREECE where he unearthed graves packed with gold comprising more than 100 pounds of artifacts including masks, diadems, goblets and other ornaments, gem-encrusted bronze swords, silver perfume bottles, and painted earthenware vessels. Schliemann believed he had found the graves of Agamemnon and his retinue, but the graves proved to be about three centuries older than the period of the Trojan War. In 1878, Schliemann returned to Hissarlik to correct the errors of the earlier work there with new, more methodical and systematic excavations and to halt criticism by journalists and archaeologists. During this season, the German anthropologist RUDOLF VIRCHOW visited and offered advice to Schliemann and lent credibility to the work.

In 1880, Schliemann moved back to Greece to excavate Orchomenos, where the legendary King Minias and the Minoan people had lived. He hired WILHELM DORPFELD, a young architect and a secretary at the DEUTSCHES ARCHÄOLOGIS-CHES INSTITUT (German Archaeological Institute) in Athens, whom he had met years earlier at ERNST CURTIUS's excavations at Olympia. It was the beginning of a collaboration that gave Schliemann the archaeological credibility he needed. Two years later, Schliemann took Dorpfeld to Hissarlik for a third season of excavation there. Dorpfeld quickly sorted out the stratigraphy of the walls and when they had been built and rec-

Schliemann at the excavation of Mycenae (Ann Ronan Picture Library)

tified Schliemann's mistakes; he also discovered a continuation of the city in a valley outside the walls. In 1884, Schliemann began excavating in Greece again, this time at Tiryns, and continued doing so for the next two years to develop a clearer picture of Mycenaean culture.

In subsequent years, Schliemann reflected less on the rehabilitation and confirmation of Homer and more on the civilization that came to light through Homer's epic. In 1883, he defended Dorpfeld and himself from criticism by the amateur archaeologist Ernst Botticher, and in 1889, he rushed to Paris to repeat his defense at the Anthropological Congress held there, which resulted in a large number of archaeologists inspecting the excavations at Hissarlik in 1890 with Schliemann and Dorpfeld as their guides. It would be the last time he would visit the site—he died later that year. All of Athenian high society, including the king of Greece, was present at his burial in Athens.

Schliemann was more treasure hunter than model archaeologist, and he can be accused of many faults—arrogant naiveté, general carelessness, precipitate identifications, wholesale destruction of archaeological material, and fraud—but his contribution to archaeology was enormous. First and foremost, he discovered the Trojan and Mycenaean civilizations at Ilios, Mycenae, Orchomenos, and Tiryns. Scholars had doubted their existence, and the unearthing of that world was one of the great moments of archaeology, and because of it, Homer's epic poetry and mythology became sources of historical information. Schliemann enriched Greek history by bringing 2,000 years into the historic record, and his findings linked classical, oriental, and prehistoric archaeology in a new way. Finally, Schliemann brought public attention to archaeology and raised the profile of the discipline through his discoveries, his publications, and his extraordinary success.

Leo Klejn

References
For references, see *Encyclopedia of Archaeology: The Great Archaeologists, Vol. 1*. Ed. Tim Murray (Santa Barbara, CA: ABC-CLIO, 1999), pp. 124–125.

Schmerling, Philippe Charles (1790–1836)

Born in Delft in the NETHERLANDS, Philippe Charles Schmerling served as a medical officer in the Dutch army from 1813 to 1816. In 1825, he completed a degree in medicine at the University of Liège, but during his four years of study Schmerling became interested in paleontology and geology after being given presents of fossils collected by workers in a nearby quarry. Beginning in 1829, he systematically explored over forty caves in and around the Liège region of BELGIUM and became professor of geology at the University of Liège in 1835.

Schmerling's published finds (especially in his *Recherches sur les ossemens fossiles* [1833–1834]) included more than sixty extinct fossil animal species, but it is for his discoveries of human remains that he has gained lasting fame. Schmerling excavated at the caves of Engis and Engihoul, Chokier and Fond-de-Foret, and under a layer of brecchia he found human remains in association with the bones of extinct fossil animals and with what he described as stone and bone tools. He also found an infant skull that, in 1935, was proved to be that of a Neanderthal

child. Although Schmerling's work attracted the cautious interest of the English geologist SIR CHARLES LYELL, the latter was unable to accept the possibility of high human antiquity until HUGH FALCONER and others had conclusively demonstrated the case at BRIXHAM CAVE and had argued for the validity of French archaeologist JACQUES BOUCHER DE PERTHES's discoveries in the gravels of the Somme Valley in 1859.

Tim Murray

References
van Riper, A. Bowdoin. 1995. *Men among the Mammoths: Victorian Science and the Discovery of Human Prehistory.* Chicago: University of Chicago Press.

Semenov, Sergei Aristarkhovich (1898–1978)

Sergei Semenov was a Soviet archaeologist and author of *Prehistoric Technology* (1957), in which he determined the uses of prehistoric stone and bone tools by identifying the processes that caused the use-wear patterns found on them. His approach followed the USSR's Marxist interest in production methods and a historical view of the past. The translation of his book had a large impact on the profession of archaeology in the West. Semenov's techniques became the basis of modern use-wear studies (particularly on stone tools from the Paleolithic), which have unlocked much new information about the use of ancient technology.

Tim Murray

See also Russia
References
Semenov, S. A. 1957. *Prehistoric Technology: An Experimental Study of the Oldest Tools and Artifacts for Traces of Manufacture and Wear.* Translated by M. W. Thompson. London: Cory, Adams, and Mackay.

Shanidar

Shanidar is a major cave site in the foothills of the Zagros Mountains, in northeastern Iraq, excavated by Ralph Solecki from 1957 to 1961. The site is considered to be particularly significant due to the excavation of the remains of nine Neanderthal adults and children, but there is a strong sequence exemplifying technological evolution from the Mousterian (between 60,000 and 40,000 years ago) through to Upper Paleolithic industries dating to about 25,000 years ago. Most attention has been focused on the Neanderthal skeletons, one of which shows evidence of a disabling disease from which the individual must have suffered for a considerable time before death. The prolonged care this individual received has been taken as evidence of the social bonds existing among Neanderthals. Some researchers have also claimed that flowers were placed in one of the burials—an indication, according to some interpretations, of sentiment among these people. Although the claim has been disputed, novelists have nonetheless readily incorporated this notion in their imaginative reconstructions of everyday life among the Neanderthals.

Tim Murray

See also Mesopotamia
Reference
Trinkaus, E. 1983. *The Shanidar Neandertals.* New York: Academic Press.

Sharma, Govardhan Rai (1919–1986)

Govardhan Rai Sharma was one of the most effective university teachers of archaeology in postindependence India. He built up a strong tradition of field research in the Department of Ancient History and Archaeology at Allahabad University, where he served throughout his working life. His early years were spent excavating the historic city site of Kausambi, in northern India, on which he published two major excavation reports (Sharma 1960, 1969).

However, his work in the fields of prehistory and proto-history in the neighboring Vindhyan Hills brought him more prominence in Indian archaeology. The easternmost section of the Vindhyas touches the Gangetic Plain near Allahabad, and although the prehistoric potential of the region had been known since the nineteenth century, it was Sharma who rigorously built up a section profile from the Acheulean to the Mesolithic Periods and excavated a number of what he called "advanced Mesolithic" sites both there and in the Pratapgarh area of the adjacent plain. At the site of Koldihawa in the same area, he found evidence of cultivated rice in the context of sixth–fifth millennia B.C. (Sharma et al. 1980). Between Varanasi and Allahabad, especially in the Mirzapur section of that stretch, he found a large number of Megalithic burials and painted rock shelters in association with microliths. Finally, in collaboration with J. DESMOND CLARK of Berkeley, Sharma extended his prehistoric sequence up to the Son Valley in Madhya Pradesh (Sharma and Clark 1983).

Sharma had a strong personality, which did not make him popular with his colleagues (some of whom disputed his claims after his death), but the field team he built up in Allahabad is unquestionably among the best in India.

D. Chakrabarti

See also South Asia
References
Sharma, G. R 1960. *The Excavations at Kausambi.* Allahabad, India: Department of Ancient History, Culture, and Archaeology, University of Allahabad.
———. 1969. *Excavations at Kausambi 1949–50.* Memoirs of the Archaeological Survey of India no. 74. Delhi: Manager of Publications.
Sharma, G. R., and D. Clark. 1983. *Palaeoenvironments and Prehistory in the Middle Son Valley.* Allahabad, India: Abinash.
Sharma, G. R., V. D. Misra, D. Mandal, B. B. Misra, and J. N. Pal. 1980. *Beginnings of Agriculture.* Allahabad, India: Abinash.

Shaw, Charles Thurstan (1914–)

One of the pioneers of West African archaeology, Charles Thurstan Shaw, or Thurstan Shaw as he has always preferred to be known, was born on 27 June 1914 in Plymouth, England. Shaw was educated at Blundell's School in Tiverton, England, and Sydney Sussex College, Cambridge, where his main archaeological teachers were Miles Burkitt and GRAHAME CLARK. In 1937, Shaw joined the staff of Achimota College in the Gold Coast (now Ghana), then one of the nearest things to a university in sub-Saharan Africa. There, in addition to his teaching duties, he was in charge of the Anthropology Museum at the college and found time to conduct archaeological research in the south of the country, the most notable being his excavations at Bosumpra rock shelter and at a midden mound at Dawu. Shaw left the Gold Coast in 1945, but his work subsequently led, during the 1950s, to both the creation of the Ghana National Museum and the establishment of a Department of Archaeology in the University of Ghana, which grew out of Achimota College.

From 1945 to 1963, Shaw held educational posts at Cambridge University and continued to publish on African archaeology. In 1959–1960, he was invited by the Nigerian Federal Department of Antiquities to excavate at Igbo-Ukwu in eastern Nigeria, and there he uncovered important evidence for the emergence of social complexity, the development of sophisticated metallurgical skills, and the growth of long-distance trade by the late first millennium A.D. This work, together with his previous publications, led to his being appointed in 1963 to a research professorship in archaeology at the University of Ibadan in Nigeria, which he held until his retirement in 1974.

During his time at Ibadan he did further work at Igbo-Ukwu as well as excavating a rock shelter at Iwo Eleru in the Nigerian rain forest. From the latter site he recovered evidence of late–Stone Age occupation from about 10,000 B.C. to about 1500 B.C., including a human skeleton from the earliest deposits that was proto-negroid in character and the earliest such evidence in West Africa. At Ibadan, he built up a successful research team that supported not only his own work but also that of fellow archaeologists Graham Connah, Steve Daniels, and Adebisi Sowunmi. Shaw not only researched and published widely but founded and edited the *West African Archaeological Newsletter* and the *West African Journal of Archaeology,* which subsequently replaced it. His most important contribution to the future of African archaeology, however, was his creation in 1970 of a teaching Department of Archaeology in the University of Ibadan that could train some of the future generation of African archaeologists.

Following retirement, Shaw did further excavation in the Kaduna Valley of northern Nigeria and also continued to publish extensively. He lives quietly near Cambridge, England, having donated his library and papers to the Institute of Archaeology in the University of London.

There can be no doubt that Shaw's contribution to West African archaeology, and indeed to African archaeology as a whole, was an important one. His career straddled the change from colonial to independent rule in black Africa, and his vision and hard work, in his search for West Africa's past, contributed significantly to Africa's rediscovery of itself.

Graham Connah

References
For references, see *Encyclopedia of Archaeology: The Great Archaeologists, Vol. 2,* ed. Tim Murray (Santa Barbara, CA: ABC-CLIO, 1999), pp. 740–741.

Shell Midden Analysis

After stone artifact scatters, archaeological deposits dominated by shell are the most commonly encountered evidence of the past, yet the infrequency of published accounts of midden analyses in the current archaeological literature suggests that archaeological deposits of shell contribute little to our understanding of human history. In this brief history of midden analyses, I locate the source of this contradiction in shifting explanatory paradigms in archaeology in general.

A shell midden is any archaeological site with a visible quantity of mollusks, which indicates the human consumption of shellfish. Shell is durable, and the preservation of shell middens is high when compared to other faunal material. That fact, combined with the generally large number of shells in a midden site, makes them highly visible in the landscape and easily recognized. Shell deposits also provide a matrix in which other kinds of cultural material, both artifacts and bone, are preserved. In this article, the focus is on shell middens that come under the rubric of "hunter-gatherer sites," that is, sites that reflect behavior associated with non-agricultural peoples for whom marine resources probably constituted a seasonal or year-round food source.

The modern analysis of midden sites owes much to the earliest systematic midden excava-

Artist's impression of an encampment of "kitchen middeners" (Ann Ronan Picture Library)

tion undertaken on "kitchen middens" in DEN-MARK in the early to mid-nineteenth century. JENS JACOB WORSAAE, Denmark's first professional archaeologist, led the interdisciplinary research team that excavated these coastal midden sites. The analysis not only demonstrated the human origin of the middens but reconstructed the local environment at the time of their creation (Trigger, ed. 1986). Activities at the site were identified through a spatial analysis of the hearths and artifactual material found in the midden. Publication of the results of Worsaae's excavations in the 1850s stimulated shellmound research outside Europe, particularly in the Americas (Trigger, ed. 1986; Waselkov 1987, 139). However, investigators elsewhere focused not on Worsaae's pioneering research interests in paleo-reconstruction and midden formation but on the artifacts found in midden sites, and this focus would continue for the next century.

European explorers had noted large accumulations of shell in the late eighteenth and early nineteenth centuries on the east and west coast of the Americas, Pacific islands, and the east coast of Australia (Beaglehole 1962, 427). Indigenous people were observed collecting and eating shellfish, which provided an ethnographic explanation for the origin of the middens. The recovery of artifacts such as ceramics and shell and stone tools in early midden excavations in the Americas and Australia confirmed their cultural origin. Valerie Attenbrow (1999) reported on the first scientific excavation of shell middens in Australia that took place in Sydney in the late 1800s, an excavation that was stimulated by an interest in stone tools and the antiquity of aboriginal culture. Through the first half of the twentieth century, middens in the Americas (Moffet 1951), Australia (McCarthy 1943a, 1943b), and the Pacific (Duff 1950; Yawata and Sinoto 1968) provided a source of stone, ceramic, and shell artifacts used to construct morphological typologies to delineate cultural chronologies. Concern with the shell itself remained limited to the publication of species lists.

In the 1960s, archaeologists became interested in past behavior as represented in archaeological evidence. Radiocarbon DATING, introduced in the late 1950s, enabled the independent dating of cultural deposits and a shifting of emphasis away from establishing culture histories to questions about how people utilized resources in the past. The effect of this shift to an economic prehistory in Europe or "new archaeology" in North America (Trigger 1989) is reflected in the large number of journal articles in the 1970s that were devoted to coastal archaeology. In these, midden analysis was central to investigating marine economies or adaptations, and central to this focus on adaptive behavior was the development of explanatory models for the patterning of archaeological evidence using ethnographic data and actualistic or experimental studies.

The economic approach is perhaps most clearly represented in the work of English archaeologist G. N. Bailey. In one work (Bailey 1975), he describes his investigation of the importance of shellfish in the precontact diet of aboriginal groups using midden excavations on the north coast of New South Wales. He used present-day yields and distribution of shellfish species, the estimated daily energy needs of modern aboriginal people, and historic demographic data to interpret the excavated shell assemblages. Bailey concluded that although the frequency and size of shell middens suggest that they are a major food resource, shellfish made up only a small percentage of dietary intake and midden sites represent only seasonal or short-term occupation.

In the 1960s and 1970s, archaeologists recognized the potential for paleoenvironmental reconstruction through midden analysis. Shellfish species are associated with discrete marine habitats, and therefore shellfish populations are susceptible to small environmental changes. As a consequence, species present in dated midden deposits reflect the coastal morphology at the time of their collection (Shackleton 1983). Judith Shackleton interpreted the changes in shell species through time from stratified midden deposits in southern GREECE in order to reconstruct the paleo-shoreline adjacent to the cave (Shackleton and van Andel 1980). Variability in the midden deposits reflected the changes in the shoreline that resulted from rising sea levels at the end of the Pleistocene period.

Oxygen isotope analysis of midden shells became popular in the 1970s in order to measure paleo-temperature change and to establish midden chronology through radiocarbon dating of shells (Shackleton 1971, 411). Oxygen isotope analysis was also useful in determining the season of death of the shellfish and therefore whether or not the use of midden sites was seasonal (Deith 1983; Godrey 1988).

An environmental determinism underpinned the economic approaches of the 1960s and 1970s. Human behavior was viewed as being shaped more or less exclusively by nonhuman constraints, and middens were interpreted as reflecting shell species availability rather than choice. Countering these economic approaches, social explanations for temporal and spatial variability became a popular form of archaeological analysis in the late 1970s (Lourandos 1977, 1983), and the strength of the social explanations owed much to ethnographic data. Betty Meehan (1982) observed that the Anbarra people on the northern Australian coast targeted particular shellfish species rather than randomly collecting all available species; Sandra Bowdler (1976) argued for a gendered approach to shellfish analysis using ethnographic data to show that traditional shellfish collection was women's work.

In the early 1980s, competing social and environmental explanations were offered for the pattern of increased site density and the intensity of coastal resource use in the late Holocene record of North America and Australia. Australian archaeologist Harry Lourandos argued that an intensification of economy and settlement evident in sites in southeastern Australia could be explained as increasingly complex social networks, possibly in response to population increase, possibly owing to rising sea levels in the early Holocene period. In contrast, S. Perlman (1980) used the environmental determinism of the optimal foraging theory to argue that similar changes apparent on the eastern coast of North America reflected the appearance of highly productive coastal resources following sea level stabilization. These resources were capable of supporting increasing numbers of hunter-gatherers attracted by the ease with which these resources could be exploited.

Prior to the early 1980s, little account had been taken of the postdepositional processes affecting midden structure. As part of the general trend toward identifying noncultural factors influencing the pattern of archaeological evidence, midden analysts began to incorporate the effects of dynamic coastal processes on the archaeological record. Although the influence of postdepositional factors such as storm activity had been recognized since the early 1970s (Hughes and Sullivan 1974), it was not until the early 1980s that the impact of geomorphological processes on sites brought the earlier behavioral explanation into question. Mike Rowland (1983) suggested that the spatial distribution of midden sites in eastern Australia, their internal structure, and their contents are as much a product of geomorphological change owing to coastal processes of erosion and deposition as of human behavior. Associated with geomorphological considerations, methodological issues of sampling and quantification (Bowdler 1983) and taphonomic studies such as differential preservation of shell species (Stein 1982) also became popular in midden analysis.

By the mid-1980s, regional approaches to coastal archaeology had largely replaced the behavioral interpretation of individual sites (Attenbrow 1999), and the change led to the inclusion of open midden sites in research. Open sites, in particular shell scatters with no associated artifactual material, had hitherto been largely overlooked in favor of stratified in situ deposits— in part because noncultural processes such as storm activity (Beaton 1985) and birds also create midden scatters. The need to identify open midden scatters of cultural origin led to the development of sets of criteria for establishing their cultural origin (Bowdler 1983). These criteria looked at the range, habitat, and size of the species present and provided a systematic means of assessing midden sites for the purpose of cultural heritage management (Attenbrow 1992).

The number of published midden analyses declined rapidly through the early 1980s. This decline may have been a reaction to the acknowledgment of the effect of noncultural processes on the structure and pattern of middens in the present, and the limits that this effect places on understanding past behavior. This fact, coupled with the shift away from site specific analyses and, at least in Australia, an emphasis on Pleistocene archaeology, appears to have sidelined midden archaeology in Australia, Europe, and the Americas. In contrast, the late 1980s and early 1990s saw a resurgence in midden archaeology in the southwestern Pacific owing to the excavation of a large number of midden sites as part of the Lapita homeland project (Allen and Gosden 1991). Deposits excavated in island Melanesia provided the first detailed evidence of a Pleistocene colonization of the Pacific along with associated marine economies and shell artifact technology (Smith and Allen 1999).

During the 1990s, issues of cultural heritage management were the main focus of shell midden archaeology. Midden recording and excavation were, and are, primarily undertaken in response to the demands of increasing development in coastal areas. Midden deposits are likely to be directly impacted by the development process and indirectly affected by the altering of coastal processes as a consequence of development (Smith 1998). In Australia, the involvement of aboriginal owners in the management process has emphasized the cultural significance of middens in the present.

The key issues for midden analysts are still those of Worsaae in the nineteenth century— how can a human origin be established for a midden deposit and what human behavior does the midden deposit reflect? The history of midden analysis is, therefore, not a story of increasing knowledge about the past so much as an increasing recognition of the complexity of processes creating archaeological deposits in general.

Anita Smith

References

Allen, J., and C. Gosden, eds. 1991. *The Report of*

the *Lapita Homeland Project*. Canberra: Department of Prehistory, RSPAS, Australian National University.

Attenbrow, V. 1992. "Shell Bed or Shell Midden?" *Australian Archaeology* 34: 3–21.

———. 1999. "Archaeological Research in Coastal Southeastern Australia: A Review." In *Australian Coastal Archaeology,* 195–210. Ed. J. Hall and I. McNiven. ANH Publications, RSPAS. Canberra: Australian National University.

Bailey, G. N. 1975. "The Role of Mollusca in Coastal Economies: The Results of Midden Analysis in Australia." *Journal of Archaeological Science* 2: 45–62.

———. 1978. "Shell Middens as Indicators of Postglacial Economies: A Territorial Perspective." In *The Early Postglacial Settlement of Northern Europe,* 37–63. Ed. P. Mellars. Pittsburgh: University of Pittsburgh Press.

Beaglehole, J. C., ed. 1962. *The Endeavour Journal of Joseph Banks, 1768–1771.* Vol 1. Sydney, Australia: Angus and Robertson.

Beaton, J. M. 1985. "Evidence for a Coastal Occupation Time-lag at Princess Charlotte Bay (North Queensland) and Implications for Coastal Colonisation and Population Growth Theories for Aboriginal Australia." *Archaeology in Oceania* 20: 1–20.

Bowdler, S. 1976. "Hook Line and Dilly Bag: An Interpretation of an Australian Coastal Shell Midden." *Mankind* 10: 248–258.

———. 1983. "Sieving Seashells: Midden Analysis in Australian Archaeology." In *Australian Field Archaeology: A Guide to Techniques,* 135–144. Ed. G. Connah. Canberra: Australian Institute of Aboriginal Studies.

Deith, M. R. 1983. "Seasonality of Shell Collecting Determined by Oxygen Isotope Analysis of Marine Shells from Asturian Middens in Cantabria." In *Animals and Archaeology 2: Shell Middens, Fishes, and Birds.* 183: 67–76. Ed. C. Grigson and J. Clutton-Brock. Oxford, England: BAR.

Duff, Roger. 1950. *The Moa-Hunter Period of Maori Culture.* Bulletin no. 1. Wellington, New Zealand: Canterbury Museum.

Godfrey, M. C. S. 1988. "Oxygen Isotope Analysis: A Means for Determining Seasonal Gathering of the Pipi (*Donax deltoides*) by Aborigines in Prehistoric Australia." *Archaeology in Oceania* 23: 17–21.

Hughes, P. J., and M. E. Sullivan. 1974. "The Redeposition of Midden Material by Storm Waves." *Royal Society of New South Wales Journal and Proceedings* 107: 6–10.

Lourandos, H. 1977. "Aboriginal Spatial Organisation and Population: South Western Victoria Reconsidered." *Archaeology and Physical Anthropology in Oceania* 12: 202–225.

———. 1983. "Intensification: A Late Pleistocene-Holocene Archaeological Sequence from Southwestern Victoria." *Archaeology in Oceania* 18: 81–94.

McCarthy, Fred. D. 1943a. "An Analysis of the Knapped Implements from Eight Eloura Industry Stations on the South Coast of New South Wales." *Records of the Australian Museum* 21, no. 3: 127–153.

———. 1943b. "Trimmed Pebble Implements of Kartan Type from Ancient Kitchen-Middens at Clybucca, New South Wales." *Records of the Australian Museum* 21, no. 3: 164–167.

Meehan, B. 1982. *Shell Bed to Shell Midden.* Canberra: Australian Institute of Aboriginal Studies.

Moffet, R. 1951. "The Rose Site: A Stratified Shell Heap on Cape Cod, Massachusetts." *American Antiquity* 17: 98–107.

Perlman, S. M. 1980. "An Optimum Diet Model, Coastal Variability, and Hunter-Gatherer Behaviour." *Advances in Archaeological Method and Theory* 3: 257–310.

Rowland, M. J. 1983. "Aborigines and Environment in Holocene Australia: Changing Paradigms." *Australian Aboriginal Studies* 2: 62–77.

Shackleton, J. C. 1971. "Marine Mollusca in Archaeology." In *Science in Archaeology. A Survey of Progress and Research,* 407–414. Ed. D. Brothwell and E. Higgs. London: Thames and Hudson.

———. 1983. "An Approach to Determining Prehistoric Shellfish Collecting Patterns." In *Animals and Archaeology 2. Shell Middens, Fishes, and Birds.* 183: 77–85. Ed. C. Grigson and J. Clutton-Brock. Oxford, England: BAR.

Shackleton, J. C., and T. H. van Andel. 1980. "Prehistoric Shell Assemblages from Franchthi Cave and Evolution of the Adjacent Coastal Zone." *Nature* 288: 357–359.

Smith, A. 1998. "Preliminary Results from a Midden Excavation at Arrawarra Beach, Mid-north Coast NSW." *Australian Archaeology* 47: 61–62.

Smith, A., and J. Allen. 1999. "Pleistocene Shell Technologies: Evidence from Island Melanesia." In *Australian Coastal Archaeology,* 291–298. Ed. J. Hall and I. McNiven. Canberra: ANH Publications, RSPAS, Australian National University.

Stein, J. K. 1982. "Geologic Analysis of Green River Shell Middens." *Southeastern Archaeology* 1: 22–39.

Trigger, Bruce. 1989. *A History of Archaeological Thought.* Cambridge: Cambridge University Press.

Trigger, Bruce., ed. 1986 *Native Shell Mound of North America: Early Studies.* New York: Garland Press.

Waselkov, G. A. 1987. "Shellfish Gathering and Shell Midden Archaeology." *Advances in Archaeological Method and Theory* 10: 93–210.

Yawata, I., and Y. Sinoto, eds. 1968. *Prehistoric Culture in Polynesia.* Honolulu: B. P. Bishop Museum Press.

Silcott, Washington

Located on the lower Snake River, eight miles downstream from Lewiston, Idaho, Silcott was a bustling little farming and ranching hamlet in the early twentieth century. White settlement began in 1861, and in 1888, Alpowa City was platted, but it eventually became known as Silcott. By 1930, the town was extinct, largely because of automobiles and better roads, which allowed people to travel and shop in nearby towns.

In 1972, three field seasons were conducted in Alpowa under the direction of Frank C. Leonhardy of Washington State University. David R. Brauner directed the excavation of Alpowa's prehistoric and historic Nez Percé sites, and Timothy B. Riordan investigated the migrant-worker sites. William H. Adams directed the excavations of Silcott, including Bill Wilson's General Store, Cliff Wilson's General Store, Trapper Wilson's House, the Ireland Place, the Ferry Tender's House, and the Weiss Ranch Dumps. These sites dated from 1890 to 1930, and their excavation marks the first time that archaeologists intentionally excavated twentieth-century sites.

The project used a multifaceted ethnoarchaeological approach involving in-depth informant interviews, documentary research, and excavations combined synergistically into an historical ethnography of the community. Using oral history to cross-verify documentary and archaeological data was innovative and provided a model for future work. The study pioneered the use of a broader context—the community—instead of focusing on individual sites. The study also represented a shift in historical archaeology away from sites associated with famous people and events and toward a broader understanding of American culture.

William H. Adams

References

Adams, W. H. 1977. *Silcott Washington: Ethnoarchaeology of a Rural American Community.* Pullman: Washington State University Press.

Sipán

Sipán is a MOCHE site in northern PERU, near the coastal city of Chiclayo (Lambayeque). It consists of a lavish tomb complex that was discovered in 1987 by looters. Four tombs have been explored, and in 1988 Peruvian archaeologist Walter Alva excavated the tomb of the "Lord of Sipán," which was so extraordinarily rich that it is now popularly known as the tomb of "the King TUTANKHAMUN of the Americas." Without doubt, the scale of the offerings, which include masks, necklaces, earrings, and other elaborate jewelry, make this the most spectacular tomb discovered in Peru and excavated by archaeologists. The tomb was built by the Moche, who ruled the northern coast of Peru between the first and sixth centuries A.D. These people are justly famous for their pottery, and the tomb of the lord of Sipán clearly demonstrates the quality of Moche metalwork in gold, copper, and silver.

Tim Murray

References

Alva, W., and C. B. Donnan. 1993. *Royal Tombs of Sipán.* Los Angeles: Fowler Museum of Cultural History, UCLA.

Situla Art in Slovenia

Situla art is an artistic style peculiar to the Veneti and Illyrians between the seventh and fourth centuries B.C. It is named after the figural ornamented vessels (Latin *situlae*), the most common and popular objects of this art.

The main centers of situla art production were in the region of the middle and lower Po

Valley (Este and Bologna), in the alpine foothills and Alto Adige, and in central SLOVENIA. In addition to *situlae,* objects such as helmets, belt plates, vessel lids, and shields were also decorated in the same style. Situla art represents the most refined and elaborate art pieces of the eastern early Iron Age Hallstatt cultures. All known objects of situla art have been found in rich male graves (often princely graves), and are considered among the most precious grave goods, which demonstrates the high status of the dead. All objects are normally made of hammered sheet bronze and decorated in the repoussé technique. The design was initially drawn on the interior and then hammered with punches. Some details were later also engraved. *Situlae* and other more-complex objects were bent and riveted together.

The first component (geometrization) in situla art is primarily rooted in the art and craftsmanship of the native Urnfield tradition. The second component (the orientalizing Etruscan, Greek, and Levantine elements) can be found in iconography and many other decorative elements foreign to the Hallstatt cultures (sphinxes, palmettos, lions, etc.).

The development of situla art in Slovenia can be divided into three main phases. In the earliest phase (seventh–sixth century B.C.) only a few objects (helmets, vessel lids) and almost none of the *situlae* were decorated, and the motifs were usually simple (isolated figures, animals, and floral ornaments). The classical phase of situla art belongs to the fifth century B.C., and the most frequent objects are the *situlae* with very developed and complex composition and iconography. Classic examples have normally tripartite zonal division of the scenes, and the motifs are not isolated figures any more but represent the feasts of the Hallstatt aristocracy—horse riding, symposia, boxing for a trophy, drinking precious potions, dancing, etc. The decline of situla art occurred in the fourth century B.C. Feasting and collective scenes and figural representations of men gradually disappeared, and the most frequent motifs were once again animals and floral ornaments.

The sites with the richest examples of situla art in Slovenia are the barrow cemeteries of the princely hill forts: STIČNA, Vace, MAGDALENSKA GORA, NOVO MESTO, etc. The most classical and famous object from Slovenia is a bronze bucket from Vace, which is 23.8 centimeters high and dates to the sixth century B.C.

Predrag Novakovic

See also Celts
References
Kastelic, J., K. Kromer, and G. Mansuelli. 1965. *Situla Art.* Belgrade: Jugoslavijan Publishers.
"Umetnost Alpskih Iliroy." 1962. In *Yenetoy (Situla Art between the Po and Danube).* Exhibition Catalogue. Ljubljana: National Museum.

Skara Brae

Skara Brae is one of the most notable Neolithic village sites in the British Isles. Located in a sand dune on one of the Orkney Islands off the north coast of Scotland, the site was inhabited between 3200 B.C. and 2200 B.C. and comprises eight houses with stone "furniture" of beds and storage areas. The houses are connected by covered passageways. Archaeological evidence testifies to the inhabitants keeping sheep and cattle, fishing and growing cereal crops. The site was exposed during a violent storm in 1850 and was excavated by VERE GORDON CHILDE between 1928 and 1930.

Tim Murray

References
Childe, V. G. 1931. *Skara Brae: A Pictish Village in Orkney.* London: Kegan Paul, Trench, Trubner & Co.

Škocjan

Škocjan is a series of prehistoric sites in a complex of caves near the village of Škocjan in southwestern SLOVENIA. The majority of the sites were excavated by Carlo Marchesetti (1850–1926) of the Trieste Museum at the end of nineteenth century and the beginning of the twentieth. In the same period, J. Szombathy of the Naturhistorisches Museum in Vienna excavated the cave sites Musja Jama (other names Fliegehohle, Grotta delle Mosche) and Skeletna Jama (Knochenhohle, Grotta degli Scheletri), and some caves and the Škocjan hill fort itself were excavated by R. Battaglia, also of the Trieste Museum, after World War I. Test excavations were carried out in the caves of Roska Spilja and Tominceva Jama by SRECKO BRODAR and F. Leben after World War II.

Archaeological evidence from the late Upper Paleolithic to the Bronze Age was documented in the cave sites of Roska Spilja, Tominceva Jama, and Pecina v Sapendolu. The most important late prehistoric settlement is the hill fort of Škocjan, occupied from the late Bronze Age to the Roman period. There are four recorded cemeteries from this period, the largest (containing some 325 graves) being the flat cremation cemetery at Brezec dated to the late Bronze Age (twelfth–eighth centuries B.C.) Some very rich burials from the tenth–eighth centuries B.C., comprising sword graves, the earliest presence of iron from the tenth century, have been discovered in this cemetery.

The large ritual hoard found at the bottom of the vertical cave Musja Jama belongs to the late Bronze Age. Among other things, the hoard contained 244 bronze and 10 iron spearheads, 1 iron and 19 bronze swords, and many fragments of bronze helmets and vessels. The objects and ritual offerings were mostly fragmented and destroyed by fire. According to typological analysis, this ritual center functioned between the twelfth and eighth centuries B.C. Analogies for the metal finds can be found in the Pannonian Plain in central ITALY and on the Balkan peninsula.

The hoard and the Brezec cemetery are evidence of a well-stratified society intensively incorporated in long-distance exchange systems at the time of transition from the late Bronze Age to the early Iron Age. Iron Age graves found in three smaller cemeteries demonstrate a certain decline in comparison with the previous period, but two major exceptions should be mentioned: another ritual hoard (Tesoretto di San Canciano), found in the Škocjan hill fort, and a rich burial with a situla with an inscription in the Venetic language found in Skeletna Jama. Both examples are dated in the fifth century B.C.

Peter Turk

See also Celts

References
Ruaro Loseri L., G. Steffe de Piero, and S. Vitri. 1977. *La necropoli di Brezec*. Monografie di Preistoria no. 1 Trieste.
Szombathy J. "Altertumsfunde aus Hohlen bei St. Kanzian im osterreichischen Kustenlande." *Mittheilungen der Prahistorischen Kommission 2*, no. 2: 127–190.

Slovenia

The term *Slovenian archaeology* in the sense of a national institutional framework can only be fully applied for the period after 1918. In that year parts of the former Austrian provinces of Carniola, Styria, and Carinthia and the region of Prekmurje were united and joined the newly established Kingdom of Serbs, Croats, and Slovenes (renamed the Kingdom of Yugoslavia in 1929). Prior to that period, archaeology in Slovenian lands (i.e., Austrian provinces) was part of the Austrian institutional framework organized on the provincial level and governed by central institutions and scholarly societies in Vienna.

Antiquarian Background

The beginnings of studies on ancient history and antiquities in Slovenian lands can be traced to the fifteenth and sixteenth centuries A.D. The first such attempts developed in the coastal towns of northern Istria (Koper/Capodistria, Izola/Isola, and Piran/Pirano—Slovenian/Italian names respectively), which were under Venetian rule and predominantly settled by a population that spoke a Romance language. The first known text on local ancient history is *De situ urbis Iustinopolitanae* [About Ancient Aegida/Koper] by Pier Paolo Vergerio the Elder (1370–1444). Another important early work is a topographic essay entitled *Del sito de Listria* (*The Ships of Listria*), published in Venice 1540 and written by the famous cartographer and geographer Pietro Coppo (1469/1470–1555/1556).

The establishment of the bishop's court in Ljubljana in the late fifteenth century gave a strong boost to the development of the Austrian province of Carniola (the central Slovene province) and to Ljubljana, the provincial capital. The central figure in this regard was August Prygl (also known as Tyffernus) (1470–1535), a scholar who, after studying at Padua, was an ecclesiastical diplomat, an architect, a chancellor to the bishop, and the first known researcher of Roman epigraphy in the Austrian lands. He produced a two-volume manuscript on Roman inscriptions from CELEIA, Poetovio, and other sites from the Inner Austrian Provinces. The records from Prygl's manuscript were included in Theodor Mommsen's *Corpus Inscriptionum Latinorum* (CIL), together with the inscriptions collected by Antiquus Austriacus, supposedly another sixteenth-century antiquary from Carniola and Styria but later identified with as Prygl.

In the seventeenth century, essays on ancient history were frequently included in major geographic and topographical studies. Giacommo Filippo Tommasini, bishop of Novigrad/Cittanova (1595–1654), wrote an updated description of the history and geography of Istria (*De commentarii storici-geografici della provincia dell'Istria libri otto con appendice*), and he was the first to attempt to reconstruct Istria's ancient geography on the basis of analyses of written sources, archaeological monuments, place-names, and oral history. In 1689 Janez Vajkard Valvazor (1641–1693), a nobleman from Carniola, a topographer, and a member of the Royal Society in London, published *Die Ehre des Herzogthums Crain,* a fifteen-volume synthesis with 528 graphics on the geography, topography, history, ethnography, and antiques of Carniola. For almost two centuries this was the most complete and influential work in the field of geography and history in Slovenia. At the same time, during the seventeenth century, two other historians and antiquaries worked in Ljubljana: Janez Ludvik Schönleben (1618–1681) and Janez Gregor Dolničar (Thalnitscher) (1615–1719). In 1681 Schönleben, a theologist, philosopher, and professor of rhetoric in Linz, Vienna, and Ljubljana, published *Carniola antiqua et nova sive annales sacroprophani,* a work on the history of Carniola from the prehistoric period to the year 1000. Dolničar, a jurist, historian, and member of many Italian learned societies, was also the author of the first manuscript on the history and antiquities of Ljubljana (*Antiquitates Urbis Labacensis*) published in Ljubljana in 1693.

In the eighteenth century historical and antiquarian studies were particularly intensive in Istria. Due to the excellent preservation of monuments there, especially in Pula/Pola, many foreign scholars went to Istria to study the Roman architecture and antiquities. Among these scholars were some of the most famous architects and antiquaries of their times, such as Andrea Palladio (1508–1580), the Venetian architect; Indigo Jones (1573–1652), the English architect; Jacob Spon, the antiquarian from Lyon; Gianbattista Piranesi (1720–1778), the Italian graphic artist and painter; Julian David Le Roy (1724–1803), the French architect; and Robert Adam (1728–1792), the English architect to the king. One of the most influential local scholars was Gian Rinaldo Carli (1720–1795), an economist and historian who authored *Delle antichità di Capodistria* (Venice 1743) and *Antichità Italiche* (*Italian Antiquities,* 1788–1791) and conducted the first recorded excavation of the Roman amphitheater in Pula.

The first studies on national history appeared at the end of the eighteenth century, in the context of the "national rebirth" of Slovenes. Anton Tomaž Linhart (1756–1795), a writer and historian, published a study on the history of Carniola and of the southern Slavs in AUSTRIA, *Versuch einer Geschichte von Krain und der übrigen südlich Slaven Österreichs* (1788–1791). This work was the first study to define the Slovene nation on the basis of a common history in the medieval period. The chapters in which Linhart presented prehistoric and Roman period geography and historical developments prior to the arrival of the Slavs are particularly important for the history of archaeological thought in Slovenia.

Valentin Vodnik (1758–1819), a priest, poet, grammarian, and historian, applied Linhart's concept of the Slovene nation in his book *Geschichte des Herzogthums Krain, des Gebietes von Triest und der Grafschaft Görz* (Vienna 1809). Vodnik was also engaged in archaeological projects: he copied the famous Roman itinerary the *Tabula peuntingeriana* in Vienna, and he excavated the Early Iron Age (EIA) hill-fort at STIČNA, together with Žiga Zoiss (1747–1819), an industrialist, a member of the Académie Celtique from Paris, and the most influential promoter of sciences and arts in Carniola. The idea for the excavations came from Ettiene Marie Siauve (?–1813), a French archaeologist who was a member of the Académie Celtique as well as the French military commissioner in the Illyrian Provinces. Vodnik recorded these activities in his *Itineraria* (1809). Siauve himself published a book on the ancient history and antiquities of the Slovene lands, entitled *De Antiquis Norici viis, urbibus et finibus epistola* (Verona 1811).

Beginnings of the Scientific Discipline of Archaeology

A decisive step forward was the establishment of the museums and heritage protection service in the Austrian Empire in the first half of the nineteenth century. Provincial museums, which covered the territory of Slovenia, were located in Graz in 1811 around Styria, in Ljubljana in 1821 around Carniola, and in Klagenfurt in 1844 around Carinthia. Local museums were established later in Celje (1893), Ptuj (1893), Maribor (1909), and Koper (1911). The Littoral Province was left without a provincial museum, but the role was filled by the Trieste municipal museum (1875).

The Provincial Museum at Ljubljana played a decisive role in the development of the archaeological discipline in Slovenia. Although the museum was established in 1821, its archaeological activities did not start until the mid-1870s with the excavations of the prehistoric pile-dwellings in the LJUBLJANSKO BARJE (Iron Age sites in Carniola). Challenged by the discoveries of pile-dwellings on Swiss lakes and encouraged by the Anthropological Society from Vienna, DRAGOTIN DEZMAN (1821–1889), the curator of the museum, directed the first large excavation in the history of Slovene archaeology, from 1875 to 1877.

Dezman's close collaboration with the Anthropological and Prehistoric Societies in Vienna proved to be decisive for further developments of this discipline in Slovenia, and in less than fifteen years (from 1875 to 1889) he succeeded in providing a firm basis for its disciplinary framework. Dezman, being a zoologist, botanist, and geologist, developed an anthropological and evolutionary concept of prehistoric archaeology; contrary to the long tradition of antiquarian and historical research in Slovenia. In this short period he excavated a series of sites (Ljubljansko Barje) and published the first synthesis on the prehistory of Carniola ("Prähistorische Ansiedlungen und Begrabnisstätten," in Krain I. Bericht, *Denkschriften der k.k. Akademie der Wissenschaften, Matematisch-naturwissenschaftliche Classe* 42, 1–54 [Vienna 1880]; "Zur Vorgeschichte Krains," in *Die österreichisch-ungarisch Monarchie in Wort und Bild, Kärnten und Krain,* 305–324 [Vienna 1891]). He tried to apply the most recent developments and standards in prehistoric science in his work. For example, he defined the LA TÈNE period in Slovenia only a few years after O. Tischler had proposed the division of the Iron Age. His research results were highly esteemed by his colleagues in AUSTRIA. The Austrian Anthropological Society was very interested in his work and held its annual meeting in Ljubljana in 1879. At the end of his career Dezman succeeded in lobbying for a new museum palace (opened in 1888), whose archaeological collections and museum guide (*Führer durch das Krainische Landes-Museum Rudolfinum in Laibach* [Ljubljana 1888]) became the pride of the scientific community in Carniola.

Alfons Müllner (1840–1918) succeeded Dezman in the museum in 1889. Müllner had already published some important archaeological and historical works in the period prior to his transfer to the museum. These included *Archaologische Excurse durch Steiermark und Krain* (1878, 1880), the first topographic work in Slovenian archaeology, and a monograph on the Roman site of EMONA (1879). Despite the fact that he was also a naturalist, Müllner applied a different concept of archaeology in the museum—that of typological and chronological principles of artifact analysis—and he rearranged prehistoric collections accordingly. He published *Typische formen aus der Sammmlungen des krainischen Landesmuseums "Rudolphinum" in Laibach* (1900), a catalog of key forms of artifacts for prehistoric Carniola. However, in rearranging the collections, Müllner did not keep records on contexts, and a great deal of contextual data was irreparably lost.

Walter Schmid (1875–1951), who studied in

Graz and became the first professionally trained archaeologist in Carniola, was the curator of the museum from 1905 to 1909. He introduced the concept of archaeology as historical science and understood the discipline's importance in revealing major historical and cultural processes. Instead of artifact classifications, Schmid considered systematic topography, settlement excavations, and the analysis of settlement processes on the regional level as the most important direction in archaeological research. A good example of his approach is his study of prehistoric hill-fort settlements in the Pohorje region of northeast Slovenia ("Die Ringwälle des Bacherngebietes," *Mitteilungen des Prähistorischen Kommission* 2, 3 [1915], 239–305). This work retained its importance in settlement studies in Slovenia for more than fifty years. Schmid also conducted the first large-scale excavations in Emona and several smaller excavations on other Roman towns in Slovenia and Austria. Last but not least, he published the pioneering study on Slavonic archaeology in Slovenia ("Altslovenische Gräber Krains," *Carniola* 1, 17–44 [1908]).

In 1909 Schmid was not reelected to the position of curator, and he moved to the Provincial Museum of Styria in Graz. However, in spite of his short service in Ljubljana and only occasional research in Slovenia between the two world wars, his role in Slovenian archaeology was crucial, particularly in the fields of settlement studies and the archaeology of the Roman province of Noricum.

The Central Commission (established in 1850) was the second component of the institutional framework in the Austrian Empire. Its provincial offices, responsible for the territory of Slovenia, were located in Trieste, Ljubljana, and Graz. Though its major role was the protection of sites and monuments, the commission also encouraged archaeological research, particularly topographic studies, and the production of archaeological maps.

P. Kandler (1805–1872), conservator for the Littoral and historian, produced an archaeological map of Istria (*Carta archeologica dell'Istria*) in 1864. Unfortunately, it remained unpublished and was consequently lost. However, many scholars from that region (including Carlo Marchesetti) based their research on Kandler's records.

Simon Rutar (1851–1903), the conservator for Carniola (1889–1903), was a historian, geographer, and classical philologist who started his archaeological career in Split, working with Don Frane Bulić, the famous Croatian researcher of Roman Dalmatia. Rutar's most important archaeological work (written with A. Premerstein) was the survey of the Roman roads and fortresses in Carniola, *Römische Strassen und Befestigungen in Krain* (Vienna 1899). He was also an influential historian and is considered one of the founders of modern national historiography.

The history of the archaeological map ("Sites and Monuments Record") in Carniola started in 1862 when P. Radics published *Archäologische Karte von Krain* (Ljubljana 1862). This map contained records on some 150 Roman sites known from literature. In 1865 F. Pichler published a map of numismatic finds from Styria (*Repertorium der Steirischen Münzkunde* [Graz]), which was later completed with descriptions of other archaeological sites (*Text zur archaeologischen Krate von Steiermark* [Graz 1879]). On the initiative of the Central Commission, A. Globočnik published a more detailed archaeological map of Carniola ("Die archäologische Karte von Krain," *Mitteilungen des Musealvereines für Krain* 2, 263–264 [1889]) in 1882.

In other Slovene provinces archaeological research at the turn of the twentieth century was particularly intensive in the Littoral. There, the leading role was played by the Trieste Natural History Museum and its director, Carlo Marchesetti (1850–1926), a naturalist and prehistorian who systematically researched the prehistory of the province. Marchesetti conducted a series of large excavations (e.g., Licia, SKOCJAN) and smaller trial excavations, and he published the results relatively promptly. He produced a very influential topographic study on Karst and Istrian hill-forts (*I castellieri preistorici di Trieste e della regione Giulia* [Trieste 1903]), which is still considered a reference text for the prehistory of the Littoral and Istria. Ptuj was the major local center of archaeological research in Styria. The town already had a lapidarium (gemstone collection) in 1830, and the museum was established there in 1893. Large excavations of the Roman cemeteries in the area took place in the first decade of the twentieth century.

In Search of a National Framework of Archaeology (1918–1945)

In 1918, after the collapse of the Austrian Empire, the regions of Upper and Inner Carniola, Lower Styria, southern Carinthia, and Prekmurje were united in Slovenia in the Kingdom of Serbs, Croats, and Slovenes. The Littoral, Istria, and the western parts of Carniola were annexed by ITALY, and central and northern Carinthia remained in Austria. Such a radical change left archaeology in Slovenia almost without any institutional framework; of the provincial museums, only the one in Ljubljana lay in the territory of Slovenia. A new framework had to be constituted almost from scratch, but in the newly formed state, with different traditions and priorities, this was not an easy task.

Nevertheless, the new state provided a political context for some decisive steps toward the national emancipation of the Slovenes. For the first time national institutions were established, and among those important for archaeology were the University of Ljubljana (1919), the NATIONAL MUSEUM OF SLOVENIA (1921, formerly the Provincial Museum of Carniola), and the Slovene Academy of Arts and Sciences (1938).

Generally, the period from 1918 to 1945 was marked by a decline in archaeological research as compared to the "Austrian" period, and the National Museum was left without a professional archaeologist for the first ten years. The only notable exception in this regard during these years was Mihovil Abramić (1884–1962), the former director of the Archaeological Museum of Aquilea (from 1913 to 1919) who researched Poetovio in the 1920s and published the results in *Poetovio: Führer durch die Denkmäler der römischen Stadt* (Vienna 1925).

Archaeology was introduced into the university curriculum in 1924, and Vojeslav Mole (1886–1973) was appointed the professor of classical archaeology in Ljubljana. However, his role in archaeology was minor, and two years after his appointment he moved to Krakow University in POLAND.

The contributions of Balduin Saria (1893–1974), a historian and epigrapher, the curator of the National Museum of Belgrade, and a professor at Belgrade University (1922–1926), were much more important. From 1926 to 1942 Saria was a professor of ancient history at Ljubljana University, and he published major works on Roman epigraphy and Roman military history: *Antike Inschriften aus Jugoslawien, Noricum und Pannonia Superior* (Zagreb 1938), and "Doneski k vojaški zgodovini naših krajev v rimski dobi" [Contributions to the Military History of Slovenia in the Roman period], *Glasnik Muzejskega drusťva za Slovenijo* 20, 115–151 (Ljubljana 1939). He was also very active in the organization of the Archaeological Map of Yugoslavia project, for which he designed criteria and standards. In 1936 he published a model map for the region of Ptuj (*Archäologische Karte von Jugoslawien: Blatt Ptuj* [Belgrade-Zagreb 1936]) and, together with JOSIP KLEMENC, the map for the region of Rogatec (*Blatt Rogatec* [Belgrade-Zagreb 1938]).

In 1929 RAJKO LOZAR (1904–1985)) became the first archaeologist employed in the National Museum, twenty years after Schmid. Since he was the only professional archaeologist in Slovenia, he had to cover a vast array of activities, and it was only from the late 1930s that he succeeded in publishing some important works. Lozar, who was also an art historian, was the first to try to provide a conceptual framework for the history of archaeology as a national science in Slovenia, including the earlier (provincial) traditions within it, with an essay on history and conceptual issues in Slovene archaeology ("Razvoj in problemi slovenske arheološke vede," *Zbornik za Umetnostno Zgodovino* 17: 107–148 [1941]). His study on Slavic and medieval pottery production (*Staroslovansko in srednjeveško lončarstvo v Sloveniji, Glasnik Muzejskega društva za Slovenijo* 20: 180–225 [1938]), also attempted to push forward this branch of archaeological research, which he considered the primary task of archaeology in Slovenia.

Although somewhat apart from major developments in central institutions in Ljubljana,

SRECKO BRODAR (1893–1987), a naturalist and schoolteacher in Celje, was able to lay foundations for Paleolithic archaeology. In 1928 he excavated the POTOČKA ZIJALKA Cave, and the results proved to be crucial for the interpretation of the glaciation in the Alps (see J. Bayer and S. Brodar, "Die Potočka Höhle, eine Hochstation der Aurignacschwankung in die Ostalpen," in *Prähistorica*, vol. 1 [Vienna 1928]). In the 1930s he extended his research to other sites in Slovenia and Yugoslavia (see S. Brodar, "Das Paläolithikum in Jugoslawien (The Palaeolithic in Yugoslavia)," *Quartar* 1: 140–172[1938]).

Reconstruction of Archaeology and Definite Establishment of the National Disciplinary Framework (1945–)

Political and Social Conditions and New Beginnings

After 1945, when the king's rule in Yugoslavia was abolished, the Yugoslav Communist Party took over the government and started the process of "rebuilding the society" on a new, Marxist-Leninist basis. Another important political change was the annexation of the Littoral and Istria back from Italy to the Yugoslav Republics of Slovenia and Croatia.

These political and ideological changes had important consequences for archaeology. Lozar was a political opponent of the Communist-controlled Liberation Front during World War II, and he left the country in 1945. Mole, who had returned from Poland in 1942 and accepted a professorship at the Italian-controlled University of Ljubljana, also left in 1945. And Saria, an ethnic German who has been openly sympathetic to the German greater national cause, went to Graz, in Austria, immediately after the Italian occupation of Ljubljana in 1941. There were also experiences entailing Italian and German abuses of archaeology in Slovenia in the prewar and war years. The Italian annexation of the Littoral and Istria (from 1918 to 1943) and subsequent occupation of western Slovenia (from 1941 to 1943) were "justified" with claims about the allegedly historical borders of Roman Italy, and many individuals in Italian institutional archaeology in these regions were involved in providing "scientific" evidence for such claims.

And during World War II Germans conducted several excavations in northern Slovenia in order to prove the existence of early medieval Germans south of the Alps and to provide a supposedly scientific basis for Adolf Hitler's project of ethnic cleansing and the annexation of Styria to the Third Reich.

The almost complete absence of professional archaeologists and the lack of an infrastructural framework demanded an urgent and complete reform of archaeological science in Slovenia. The leading scholars from the Faculty of Arts at the University of Ljubljana and from the Slovene Academy of Arts and Sciences played a prominent role in renewing the institutional framework. Two new institutions were established—the Department of Archaeology in the Faculty of Arts at the University of Ljubljana, begun in 1946, and the Archaeological Commission of the Slovene Academy of Arts and Sciences, which was founded in 1947 and later known as the Institute of Archaeology. The first two professors of archaeology were appointed in 1946 and 1947: Klemenc for classical and Roman archaeology and Korosec for prehistoric and Slavic archaeology. PALEOLITHIC ARCHAEOLOGY also entered the curriculum with the 1946 appointment of Brodar as professor for Quaternary studies in the Faculty of Mathematics and Natural History, all at the University of Ljubljana. Klemenc and JOSIP KOROSEC were also among the founders of the Archaeological Commission, together with Milko Kos, a historian and chancellor of the University of Ljubljana, and France Stele, an art historian and conservator. A new generation of scholars also took leading positions in the National Museum. JOŽE KASTELIC, a classical philologist, became the director of the museum in 1945, and STANE GABROVEC, an archaeologist and classical philologist, started to work in the Archaeological Department there in 1948.

The problem of repairing and maintaining monuments was even more urgent, particularly because of the war damage. In August 1945 an Office for the Protection and Scientific Research of Cultural and Natural Monuments was established (later renamed the Office for the Protection of Natural and Cultural Heritage), and a series of government bills secured the protection and management of monuments from 1946 to 1948. This was the first integrated solution in the field since the abolition of Austrian legislation in 1918. Another important move was the establishment of the *Arheološki Vestnik* in 1949, designed to be the central archaeological journal; it was published by the Slovene Academy of Arts and Sciences.

It is interesting that the Communist authorities did not intervene to any great extent in the conceptual issues of archaeological research in the postwar period. Of course, all the scholars who were appointed to the leading positions had studied in the prewar period and were politically acceptable to the new regime, since they either supported the Liberation Front or were not compromised by collaboration with Germans or Italians. The official program of the Yugoslav (and Slovene) Communist Party encouraged the further emancipation of the Yugoslav nations (on a Marxist-Leninist basis, of course), and the development of a national cultural, scientific, and educational framework was part of this program. Had the new leaders in the field of archaeology been too rigidly selected on an ideological basis, the country would have lacked the cadre of intellectuals needed for the reconstruction.

The new ideology *was* expressed in various resolutions, manifests, and similar protocol documents presented at conferences, in new publications, and so on, but this had no operable effect on conceptual issues. Marxism could not anchor in archaeology as it could in historiography, philosophy, economics, and similar disciplines because the Yugoslav and Slovene Marxist ideologists were not capable of providing an applicable apparatus. Consequently, the positivist and culture-history paradigm in archaeology not only persisted but also further developed.

The late 1940s and 1950s were formative years that were decisive for the establishment of a stable archaeological institutional and conceptual framework. The formative process concluded in the mid-1970s when two networks were established: a network of regional Offices for Protection of Natural and Cultural Heritage and a network of regional museums. After that

point the institutional framework remained largely unchanged. Today, there are three national archaeological institutions (the National Museum; the Institute of Archaeology of the Slovene Academy of Arts and Sciences, Department of Archaeology, University of Ljubljana; and the Agency for Protection of Cultural Heritage, with seven regional offices) and ten regional museums. The stability of the institutional and conceptual framework can be seen in the developments after 1991. Although Slovenia underwent another radical political change and became an independent, democratic state, the functioning of archaeological institutional and the conceptual frameworks were not affected. In fact, the only notable change was the development of contract archaeology on a much larger scale.

Conceptual Issues

The 1950s and 1960s witnessed the first clear division of specialization in archaeological periods among Slovene archaeologists. Their field was organized in five subdivisions: Paleolithic and Mesolithic archaeology (traditionally the domain of the naturalist scholars); Neolithic and Eneolithic archaeology; Bronze and Iron Age archaeology; Roman archaeology (classical and provincial); and early Medieval and Slavonic archaeology. This structure is largely intact today.

The field's major effort in this period was the Archaeological Map of Slovenia project, coordinated by the Institute of Archaeology. In 1966, after almost fifteen years of intensive work, the data were collected, but it took another ten years to revise the data and publish *Arheološka najdišča Slovenije* (Ljubljana 1975). This gazetteer of sites and monuments contained more than 3,000 entries from the Paleolithic to the early Medieval period (nearly ten times more than any previous archaeological map). Particularly important was the series of syntheses on settlement history for each archaeological period, the first studies of this kind based on highly detailed information.

The archaeologies of the individual periods in Slovenia also needed new conceptual tools. Indeed, the only branch that was developed in the prewar period to a level comparable with archaeologies in neighboring countries was epigraphy. So in the 1950s and 1960s, Brodar, Kastelic, J. Korošec, P. Korošec, Klemenc, Gabrovec, and F. Osole, together with archaeologists from the first generations of postwar students (e.g., JAROSLAV ŠAŠEL, P. Petru, T. Bregant, F. Stare, I. Curk, M. Plesničar, and S. Pahič), invested a great deal of effort in developing regional studies, typologies, chronologies, and other tools needed for archaeological analysis and cultural interpretation.

This work arose from intensive fieldwork and analyses of artifacts from all the major archaeological sites in Slovenia: the Paleolithic and Mesolithic sites of Betalov Spodmol, Mokriška Jama, Ovčja Jama, and Špehovka; the Neolithic and Eneolithic sites at Ljubljansko Barje, Drulovka, Ajdovska Jama, and Ptuj; the Bronze Age sites of Brinjeva Gora, Bled, Pobrežje, Dobova, Ptuj, Ljubljana, and Ormož; the Iron Age sites of Stična, Tolmin, Saint Lucija, NOVO MESTO, and Križna Gora; the Roman sites of Emona, Celeia, Poetovio, Neviodunum, Šempeter, Hrušica, and CLAUSTRA ALPIUM IULIARUM; and the early Medieval and Slavonic sites of Dravlje, Ajdovski Gradec, Rifnik, Kranj, Bled, Ptuj, and Turnišče. In addition, there were intensive analyses of artifacts and data from sites excavated before 1918 that had been kept in Italian or Austrian museums. The results were discussed and evaluated, and further conceptual issues were addressed in several national conferences in Slovenia and Yugoslavia and published in *Arheološki Vestnik* (in 1962 and 1977 for the late–Iron Age archaeology, in 1965 for the late Roman, early Medieval, and Slavonic period, in 1970 for the Slavonic period, in 1970 for the Neolithic and Eneolithic, in 1972 for the early Iron Age, and in 1986 for the Bronze Age). Further evidence of conceptual growth can be seen in the large-scale settlement excavations that appeared from the mid-1960s onward. Among the most influential were Gabrovec's excavation of the EIA hill-fort at Stična (1967–1974), V. Šribar's excavation of the deserted medieval town of Gutenwert (1969–1979), and Bregant's excavation of the Eneolithic pile-dwelling at Maharski Prekop in Ljubljansko Barje (1970–1974). The latter involved the first application

of a series of scientific aids in order to reconstruct the paleoenvironment.

By the mid-1970s Slovenian archaeology was on a par with that in neighboring countries. Considering the circumstances and the amount and quality of the work they invested, the archaeologists of the first postwar generations in Slovenia and Yugoslavia were crucial to the establishment of the modern science of archaeology in these lands. Their ultimate triumph was the publication of a synthesis on prehistory in Yugoslav lands that filled more than 2,500 pages (*Praistorija jugoslavenskih zemalja*, 5 vols. [Sarajevo 1978–1987]).

Since 1980 other new concepts and tools have been introduced, particularly in the field of methodology: stratigraphic excavation techniques and Harris matrix recording systems, an intensive application of scientific aids in DATING and reconstructing paleoenvironments, the application of systematic survey techniques and sampling procedures, GEOGRAPHIC INFORMATION SYSTEMS (GIS) and other computer-aided techniques of description and quantitative analyses, aerial photography, and geophysics. Parallel to the developments in methodology, new archaeological fields have evolved—landscape archaeology, archaeology of the post-Medieval period, and environmental archaeology and archaeological theory. Most of these concepts and techniques resulted from the initiatives of a new generation of archaeologists from the Department of Archaeology at the University of Ljubljana, who cooperated closely with colleagues in U.S. and British archaeological schools.

Particularly active in this field was Božidar Slapšak of the University of Ljubljana, who contributed pioneering texts in the fields of landscape and settlement archaeology; he also conducted several joint projects with British and U.S. archaeologists in which new methods and techniques were introduced into archaeological practice and theory in Slovenia. In addition, the archaeological discipline at Ljubljana University has been considerably transformed since 1985 by, among other things, translations of important theoretical and methodological texts, guest lecturers from universities in the United States and the United Kingdom, grants for specialization at U.S. and British universities, and joint projects in Slovenia and elsewhere. These developments have also provided something of a counterpart and a challenge to the mainstream culture-history approach.

At the same time, the scholars who came from Gabrovec's school of prehistoric archaeology—Biba Teržan, Mitja Guštin (from the University of Ljubljana), and Janez Dular (from the Institute of Archaeology)—decisively contributed to the further development of a distinctive school of prehistoric research that is well respected on an international level.

In the 1980s and 1990s other fields of archaeological research also gained recognition on the international level. In numismatics, for example, A. Globočnik and P. Kos, after less than four decades of systematic work, were able to present rich collections on an exemplary level. Šašel's work became a reference for the epigraphy and ancient history of Roman Pannonia, Noricum, Dalmatia, and Venetia et Histria, and the very high standards he set are continued in the work of M. Šašel Kos.

Slavonic archaeology was established in a proper sense only after 1945, and in its first years it was beset by political problems arising from World War II, as well as conceptual disputes with historians about its interpretative potentials. Yet, despite all these constraints, it has matured admirably in recent decades and become a respected discipline with a developed critical apparatus.

Predrag Novakovic

See also Most na Soči

References

Gabrovec, S. 1971. "Stopetdeset let archeologije v Narodnem muzeju" [One-hundred and fifty years of archaeology in the National Museum]. *Argo* 10: 35–48.

Kastelic, J., S. Gabrovec, and T. Knific. 1987. "Arheologija" [Archaeology]. In *Enciklopedija Slovenije I,* Mladinska knjiga–Ljubljana, 100–105.

Petru, P. 1971. "Misli ob stopetdesetletnici Narodnega muzeja" [Some thoughts on the occasion of the one-hundred-fiftieth anniversary of the National Museum]. *Argo* 10: 3–34.

Slapšak, B., and P. Novaković. 1996. "Is There National Archaeology without Nationalism? Archaeological Tradition in Slovenia." In *Nationalism and Archaeology in Europe,* 256–293. Ed. M. Díaz Andreu and T. Champion. London: UCL Press.

Smith, Sir Grafton Elliot (1871–1937)

Born in Grafton, New South Wales, Australia, Smith graduated with a degree in medicine from the University of Sydney in 1895. He won a scholarship and traveled to Cambridge to further his anatomical research. In 1900 he became professor of anatomy in Cairo, Egypt, and returned to England in 1909 as anatomy professor at Manchester University. In 1919 he became professor of anatomy at University College London. He received a Fellowship of the Royal Society in 1907, a Royal Medal in 1912, and a knighthood in 1934.

During his time in Cairo, Smith was a major participant in the planning and completion of the Archaeological Survey of NUBIA. The creation of the Aswan Dam in 1902 had caused widespread flooding, which had destroyed many monuments and sites. When the Egyptian government decided the water level of the dam had to be raised another 7 meters, it was decided that this time they would record all threatened antiquities and examine and photograph all burials that would be destroyed by the new water levels—hence the survey. More than 10,000 burials were recovered and studied, the largest sample of burials ever excavated from an archaeological site. This was also the largest skeletal population ever studied and it revealed the prevalence of many interesting diseases and provided a detailed picture of everyday life and death in Egypt. The methods Elliot Smith and his colleagues developed during these studies changed the nature and significance of paleopathology forever.

Smith also contributed to the ongoing debate about primate evolution, believing that it was characterized by an increase in neurological sensory development in the areas of sight and hearing. He examined the Piltdown skull and declared it "the most primitive and most simian of human brains so far recorded," lending some credibility to this scientific hoax at the time of its perpetration.

Sir Grafton Elliot Smith (Image Select)

Elliot Smith's interests in and thoughts about ethnology and paleopathology, the results of his participation in the Archaeological Survey of Nubia, later led him to theorize that all cultural development—especially agriculture, pottery, clothing, monumental architecture, and kingship—had originated uniquely in Egypt, "the cradle of civilization," and then Egyptian merchants had carried Egyptian innovations and culture and spread them to the rest of the world. His books *The Migrations of Early Culture* (1915) and *The Ancient Egyptians and the Origin of Civilizations* (1923) elaborate these "hyper-diffusionist" ideas and were popular at the time of their publication.

Tim Murray

See also Piltdown Forgery; Reisner, George Andrew

References

Spencer, F. 1990. *The Piltdown Papers 1908–1955: The Correspondence and Other Documents Relating to the Piltdown Forgery.* London: Oxford University Press.

Smithsonian Institution

Although the Smithsonian Institution (SI) became operational in 1846, its foundation actually stemmed from an 1835 bequest by James Smithson, an Englishman who had never visited the United States. Smithson's gift of over half a million dollars created one of the most significant institutions in the history of U.S. archaeology as part of one of the world's leading museum organizations.

Under its first secretary, John Henry, the Smithsonian made a vital contribution to the archaeology of North America when it published Ephraim G. Squier and EDWIN H. DAVIS's *Ancient Monuments of the Mississippi Valley in 1848*. Its influence continued with the publication of Samuel Haven's *The Archaeology of the United States, or Sketches Historical and Biographical, of the Progress of Information and Opinion Respecting Vestiges of Antiquity in the United States* (1856). Both works had a significant impact on the history of prehistoric archaeology in North America.

The Smithsonian soon became an important element in the U.S. government's network of information sources, and its prominence in this arena remains undiminished. Not only would it become a storehouse of national knowledge, it would also use that knowledge in the service of government. In this sense the Smithsonian responded to a thirst for knowledge about the United States and through its work increased the desire for knowledge. This was especially true in the case of ethnology and archaeology. In 1861 the SI published "Instructions for Research Relative to the Ethnology and Philology of America" by George Gibbs, which mirrored the scope and purpose of the famous "Notes and Queries" produced by the British Association for the Advancement of Science. Gibbs's questionnaire, included in the instructions, was used by many of those undertaking primary ethnological and archaeological research, as well as others, such as missionaries and government agents, who sought a more direct understanding of indigenous Americans. In 1864, the SI sought to gather information about collections of artifacts derived from earthworked archaeological sites known as "mounds" and also about the "moundbuilders" who built them in order to make copies of such artifacts for their own collections. There was much discussion as to whether the mounds were the work of non-Native American peoples. A further example of the types of projects the SI pursued in its early years stemmed from the work of the Corps of Topographical Engineers and the various U.S. explorations in the West, first during the wars with the Mexicans in 1841 and then in the 1860s, particularly after the Civil War. These explorations had created an immense amount of geographic and ethnographic knowledge, and many of the collections and much of the information they produced eventually found their way into the Smithsonian.

Pioneers of Southwest archaeology, such as the ethnologists FRANK CUSHING and WILLIAM H. HOLMES, became associated with the Smithsonian through the dominating personality of JOHN WESLEY POWELL, who gained fame through his explorations down the Colorado River. Powell's first voyage (in 1868) was conducted on a shoestring budget, but the scale of the discoveries made soon persuaded Congress to fund the project for three years, beginning in 1869, under the direction of the Smithsonian.

Important as those voyages of exploration were, great strides were also made by Smithsonian correspondents and staffers who patiently accumulated systematic data through the application of questionnaires designed to gather ethnological evidence. In February 1878 the SI, through Professor OTIS T. MASON, from its Department of Ethnology, sought information about the nature and status of the archaeological remains of "American Indians" in order to update the earlier Squier and Davis study. Powell supported the great publication *Contributions to North American Ethnology* (which began with the Squier and Davis work); this series also served governmental ends in facilitating what was considered to be a more informed approach to the management of "Indian affairs." For example, in 1879 Congress earmarked $20,000 for the publication of *Contributions to North American Ethnology* on the proviso that all primary documents pertinent to indigenous North Americans (no matter which agency had created them) be lodged with the Smithsonian. The Bureau of Ethnology, with

Powell as the bureau's founder and leader, was created to analyze and publish this vast amount of information. Of course the bureau performed other government tasks as well, as when Powell was put in charge of taking the census of the Indians in 1880. It changed its name to the Bureau of American Ethnology in 1894 to emphasize the geographic limit of its interests.

Notwithstanding these duties Powell continued to be interested in promoting primary fieldwork. He recruited Cyrus Thomas in 1881 to his Ethnology and Mound Survey, funded by what at that time was a large grant of $25,000 for continuing ethnological research among the North American Indians. Significantly, $5,000 of this amount was designated for archaeological investigations relating to mound builders and prehistoric mounds, directed by Thomas while he was based in the Bureau of Ethnology. The Smithsonian continued its commitment to North American archaeology after Powell left the scene. Among other projects, it conducted the River Basin Surveys, which were begun in 1945 and continued until 1969.

Although the place of archaeology within its institutional structure changed after the great days of the late nineteenth century, the SI has been served particularly well by its head curators of anthropology. Some of the major figures of North American archaeology, such as William Henry Holmes, Frank M. Setzler, Waldo Wedel, Richard B. Woodbury, and William Fitzhugh, occupied this position (in addition to chairing the Department of Anthropology). The appointment of ROBERT M. ADAMS to the post of secretary in 1984 was an eloquent statement of the significance of the institution in that it could attract an archaeologist of Adams's caliber to such a post.

The Smithsonian continues to promote fundamental research into the archaeology of the Americas, and it is a major publisher of archaeological materials from around the world. But in recent years it has also been at the forefront of discussions in the United States about the repatriation of the indigenous cultural properties and skeletal remains in its collections. Although these discussions have provoked considerable soul-searching and anger (on both sides of the repatriation divide), the Smithsonian has been responsive to the interests and concerns surrounding the Native American Graves Protection and Repatriation Act (NAGPRA) legislation.

Tim Murray

See also Atwater, Caleb; Jefferson, Thomas; Moundville

References

Goode, George Brown. 1897. *The Smithsonian Institution, 1846–1896: The History of Its First Half Century.* Washington, DC: DeVinne Press.

Hinsley, Curtis M., Jr. 1994. *The Smithsonian and the American Indian: Making a Moral Anthropology in Victorian America.* Washington, DC: Smithsonian Institution Press.

Judd, Neil M. 1967. *The Bureau of American Ethnology: A Partial History.* Normal: University of Oklahoma Press.

Meltzer, David J., and Michael B. Schiffer. 1983. *The Antiquity of Man and the Development of American Archeology.* Vol. 6, *Advances in Archeological Method and Theory.* New York: Academic Press.

Meltzer, David J., and Robert C. Dunnell, eds. 1992. *The Archaelogy of William Henry Holmes.* Washington, DC: Smithsonian Institution Press.

Roberts, Frank H. H., Jr. 1946. "One Hundred Years of Smithsonian Anthropology." *Science* 104: 119–125.

———. 1961. "River Basin Salvage Program: After 15 Years." *Smithsonian Institution Annual Report for 1960,* 523–549. Washington, DC: U.S. Government Printing Office.

True, Webster P. 1946. "A Century of Smithsonian Publications." *Science* 104: 141–142.

Society for American Archaeology

The Society for American Archaeology, founded in 1934, is an organization of professional and avocational archaeologists devoted to the study and preservation of the archaeology of North and South America. The 1930s were a period of tremendous growth in American archaeology—many state archaeological societies were founded, and new regional conferences provided forums for local archaeological communication. The Great Depression actually led to a vast increase in archaeological fieldwork as a way to relieve unemployment, and the increased work led to new organizations, new journals, and a perceived need for greater communication among archaeologists on the national level.

Concurrent with the increased scientific archaeological activity was increased looting and vandalism of sites. A number of archaeologists felt the need for better communication and cooperation between amateurs and professionals as well as for more effective communication within the archaeological community. Since 1920, the Committee on State Archaeological Surveys (COSAS) of the National Research Council had served as a clearinghouse for U.S. archaeology—promoting the formation of state archaeological surveys, publishing guides to archaeological fieldwork and site recording, and organizing regional conferences. The American Anthropological Association (AAA) also served as a focus of archaeological communication through meetings and publications. *American Anthropologist* was the journal of choice for professional archaeological articles of national interest, and until 1932, it published an annual compilation of archaeological fieldwork in the United States. COSAS was quite successful in its endeavors, but its last chairman (1927–1937), Carl E. Guthe, realized that the committee's private funding would not be continued indefinitely. This fact, along with the unwillingness of the editor of *American Anthropologist* to continue publishing the annual archaeological fieldwork summary, created the need for a national organization.

In 1933, COSAS members approved the idea of a national archaeological organization, and in 1934, Guthe sent a prospectus to 192 interested individuals for comment. Response was positive enough that COSAS formed a subcommittee to write a constitution and bylaws, and an organizational meeting held in Pittsburgh, attended by 31 people, created the Society for American Archaeology on 28 December 1934 (Griffin 1985; Guthe 1967).

The society's activities originally were governed by an elected executive council consisting of a president, vice-president, secretary-treasurer, editor, and eight other members. As the years passed, the composition of the council (later called the executive committee and finally the executive board) changed with the needs of the society. A nominating committee has always selected candidates for all of the society's offices, but only the positions of president, vice-president (dropped in 1958), and council member have had more than one candidate.

The activities of the society were initially run out of the offices of the members of the executive council, but as membership grew, the need for a central office to handle some of the society's activities became imperative. In 1953, the office of the American Anthropological Association took over membership activities, and in 1973, the society voted to affiliate officially with the AAA. All business of the society was directed out of the AAA office in Washington, D.C., until 1983 when the society hired a part-time executive director to run its business in an independent office. In 1992, a full-time executive director was hired to handle the society's increasingly complex affairs.

The society's activities are financed primarily by membership dues and donations, although private and government grants have been received for special projects. Dues in 1935 were $3 per year, but primarily because of increased paper and printing costs and increased society activities, they rose to $6 in 1947, $15 in 1970, $50 in 1984, and $75 in 1990. Expenditures by the society were initially around $1,000 per year, most going toward the cost of the society's journal AMERICAN ANTIQUITY. By the late 1970s, the society was involved in many more activities, and less than 50 percent of its $100,000 budget went for publication. In 1992, only a third of the $544,000 budget was spent on publications, less than was spent on administration and management.

The principal method by which the executive committee accomplishes its tasks is through a number of standing, advisory, and ad hoc committees. In addition to the standard committees for things such as finance, membership, nominations, and publications, a variety of more specialized committees of varying duration have been created. They range in function from short-ranged ones—like the one in 1949 appointed to investigate whether the spelling of archaeology should be changed (it recommended that the second "a" remain)—to longer-sighted ones such as one on the status of women

in archaeology formed in 1974 and the Foundation for American Archaeology incorporated in 1990 to obtain outside funding for public education. By 1990, the society had thirty-three committees and other units, and its organizational chart resembled that of a small country.

Membership in the society has always been open to anyone interested in furthering the objectives of the society. Initially, two categories of membership were established—fellows, the professional archaeologists and avocationals who have conducted archaeological research, and affiliates, which included everyone else—but this stratification was dropped in 1942.

Although Guthe optimistically predicted 1,500 members when the society was formed, it did not reach that level until the 1960s. Initial membership was about 300 individuals and 100 institutions and rose quickly to between 600 and 800 individuals where it stayed until the early 1950s. A moderate growth rate began at that time and picked up in the 1960s. Between 1968 and 1971, the society's membership doubled to 3,800. Growth peaked around 1980 near 5,000 individual members and then began to drop, not returning to that level again until the late 1980s.

For the first quarter century of the society's history, avocational archaeologists made up a majority of the membership. With the growth of the profession in the 1960s and 1970s, the balance shifted toward professional archaeologists, and in a sample membership poll taken in 1986, less than 10 percent of the respondents considered themselves avocational archaeologists. Participation of avocationals in the society has always been low relative to their membership numbers. Avocationals have almost never been elected to positions in the society, and although participation in meetings is difficult to gauge, it, too, has probably been low. The principal area of avocational participation has been in publications. The first article in *American Antiquity* was by Paul F. Titterington, an avocational archaeologist from St. Louis who was a strong advocate for the formation of the society, and by the mid-1950s, about 13 percent of the major articles and 28 percent of the short comments were submitted by avocationals. With the vast growth in the discipline since the late 1960s, however, such contributions have almost disappeared from the journal.

Although nearly 20 percent of the signers of the society's constitution were women, the proportion of female members in the early years was about half that. Occasionally, women such as Frederica de Laguna and H. MARIE WORMINGTON were elected as low-level officers in the society, but the first woman president (Wormington) was not elected until 1968, and the first woman editor of *American Antiquity* (Dena Dincauze) was not elected until 1981. By the 1980s, more women held elected positions, and in some years, they held a majority of the elected posts.

Participation by women in the society's annual meeting and in the writing of journal articles began at an equally low level. Women were authors or coauthors of 10 percent or less of the papers at meetings until the 1970s, and it was not uncommon to have no papers by women. By 1983, the number had increased to one-quarter of the papers, and it had reached nearly one-third by 1992 (Feinman, Nicholas, and Middleton 1992). Of the most productive contributors to *American Antiquity* in its first thirty years only two (Betty J. Meggers and Nathalie F. S. Woodbury) were women (Rogge 1976).

Membership of the society has always been made up predominantly of U.S. citizens with small numbers from CANADA, MEXICO, and Europe and almost none from South America. One Canadian archaeologist (Diamond Jenness) and one Mexican archaeologist (IGNACIO BERNAL GARCIA) have been elected president over the years.

One of the primary purposes of the society was to increase communication among archaeologists, and to this end, a variety of regular and one-time publications have been published by the society. *American Antiquity* (1935 to the present), the society's quarterly journal, has been the principal medium for technical articles in American archaeology since its founding. The increasing need for a specialized journal for the archaeology south of the United States eventually led to the foundation of the bilingual *Latin American Antiquity* (1990 to the present).

Early on, there was a need for a less formal periodical to allow for the exchange of ideas among archaeological field-workers, both professional and avocational. The *Society for American Archaeology Notebook* (1939–1942), published in mimeographed form, contained letters from readers and brief notes on archaeological methods and terminology. Unfortunately, a lack of submissions forced the termination of this publication.

Copies of the *Memoirs of the Society for American Archaeology* (1941–1976), composed of monograph-length studies and symposia, were distributed free to members of the society. In almost all cases, the memoirs were published with outside financial assistance. The memoir series was replaced by the short-lived *SAA Papers* (1980–1986), which was made available to members for a charge. To promote the publication of data and other materials too expensive to print by normal methods, the society was a joint publisher, with the University of Wisconsin Press, of the *Archives of Archaeology* (1960–1966), which appeared in a microcard format. Increased publication costs and the availability of alternative publication led to the declining involvement of the society in the publication of monographs, collected volumes, and data. Recently, when symposia collections appropriate for the society's support have arisen, other publishers have been arranged. For example, the Smithsonian Institution Press published the proceedings of the society's fiftieth anniversary meeting (Meltzer, Fowler, and Sabloff 1986) and a three-volume set from symposia on the Columbian quincentennial, the profits of the latter going into the society's Native American Scholarship Fund.

Because of the lag between submission and publication, sometimes as long as fifteen months, *American Antiquity* was never an effective medium for announcements and news needing immediate attention. In the 1950s, the need for a society newsletter was recognized, but cost and administrative difficulties blocked the idea. In the 1970s, the society bought space for news in *the Anthropology Newsletter* of the AAA, but this practice soon ended because of cost. The SAA's increasing activism in federal legislation created a critical need to get information to members fast and efficiently, and the

Committee on Public Archaeology issued its own "Communications and Alerts" to members and legislators. Finally, in 1983, the *Bulletin of the Society for American Archaeology* (becoming the *SAA Bulletin* in 1987) made its long-needed appearance.

Abstracts of New World Archaeology (1959–1960) was instituted with private funding to bring together yearly summaries of articles, theses, and dissertations pertaining to archaeology in the New World. Although publication stopped after outside support ceased, this series did make the archaeological community aware of the usefulness of publishing article abstracts in journals, and *American Antiquity* began including abstracts of all articles in 1960.

When articles submitted to *American Antiquity* were thought by the editor or reviewers to be more appropriate for regional journals, authors were guided to the most appropriate one available. To help expand the range of such journals, the society, in an unusual move, provided a subsidy to initiate the *Mid-Continental Journal of Archaeology* in 1976.

Annual meetings (except 1937 and 1943) were envisioned by the society's founders as a major function of the society, and they are the principal locus of membership participation. In the early years, meetings were one- or two-day sessions with 10 to 20 papers and 50 to 100 attendees. By the 1950s, three-day meetings with 20 to 150 papers and 100 to 800 attendees were the rule, and since the 1970s, meetings have usually been three and a half days long with 400 to 1,000 papers and over 1,000 people attending. Until the late 1970s, meetings were run by students and other volunteers, but the increased size necessitated hiring personnel to operate them efficiently.

In the first decades of the society, meetings were commonly held in cities in the midwestern part of the United States, usually in conjunction with the Central States branch of the AAA (later the Central States Anthropological Association). This pattern provided a central location for members from either coast. During this same period, regional meetings, often on the east or west coasts, allowed members living in those areas to get together when they couldn't attend the annual meeting. As long-distance travel became faster and easier and the meetings grew in size, joint meetings and regional meetings ceased to occur, and the location of the annual meeting became more evenly spread around the United States and even included Mexico and Canada.

Attendance at the annual meetings is consistently around 20 percent of the membership, and, with a rejection rate for proposed papers of less than 5 percent, it is an important forum for students and for the initial presentation of data and ideas. Many papers later accepted for publication in *American Antiquity* or published in edited volumes were first presented at an annual meeting. Beginning in 1974, a formal job placement service was initiated at the annual meeting, which has always been an important place for initial contacts by job seekers.

Because of the citizenship of the majority of the members and the usual location of the meeting, papers on America north of Mexico have always predominated. Notwithstanding the Western Hemisphere focus of the society, papers on Old World archaeology often equal in frequency those on Latin America (Feinman, Nicholas, and Middleton 1992).

The society began during a period of large-scale government archaeology, but its role in that period was primarily as a medium of communication among archaeologists. Near the end of World War II, the society formed a committee to investigate the status and disposition of data that had been recovered by the Works Progress Administration (WPA). An index to WPA reports was one step that the committee suggested. At the same time, the enormous impact of dam construction activities along the Missouri River and elsewhere became apparent, and the society sent representatives to the American Council of Learned Societies' influential Committee for the Recovery of Archaeological Remains (1945–1976). In cooperation with the National Park Service, the SMITHSONIAN INSTITUTION, and other governmental agencies, the committee convinced archaeologists, universities, and museums to divert their archaeological research to sites that were to be impacted by construction or inundation. These river-basin survey projects conducted an immense amount of archaeology until termination of the program in 1969 (Fowler 1986).

The society's involvement in the federal legislation process began in 1956 when the Highway Archaeology Salvage Committee, chaired by Fred Wendorf, organized successful support for the inclusion of archaeology in the 1956 Highway Act. By the late 1960s, the society had become increasingly involved in historic preservation legislation and in fighting the illegal trafficking in foreign antiquities. Some members of the society, however, felt that enough action was not being taken, and in 1974, the American Society for Conservation Archaeology was formed to focus specifically upon resource preservation issues.

A particularly active subunit of the society is the Committee for the Public Understanding of Archaeology (later the Committee on Public Archaeology, COPA). Initially formed in 1967 to promote communication with the public, it evolved into the society's major body for communicating information on proposed federal legislation, trafficking in antiquities, and other issues through a network of state representatives.

When the Antiquity Act of 1906 failed to stand up in court in the late 1970s, some members of the society began to explore remedies. Frustrated by the Department of Interior's foot-dragging in getting new legislation introduced, they convinced the society to draft the legislation itself and to lobby the bill through Congress without the assistance of government departments. The process was successful and resulted in the powerful Archaeological Resources Protection Act of 1979 (Collins and Michel 1985).

The assistance of a professional lobbyist was critical in the legislation process regarding that act, and as the society had become the primary organization lobbying for archaeology in Washington by 1983, a lobbyist was retained to represent the society on a continuing basis. Of major significance at that time was proposed legislation regarding Native American human remains.

Although the first president of the society, Arthur C. Parker, was of part Native American descent, there have been few professional Native American archaeologists, and the society at first had little explicit concern for Native American interests. As a result of increased political activism, a deteriorating relationship between Native Americans and archaeologists was noted in the mid-1970s. The society initiated a dialogue with Native Americans to counteract this trend, and in 1985, the SAA cosponsored a conference on reburial that brought together Native Americans, archaeologists, and physical anthropologists. Although this conference revealed major differences between the groups represented, it also assisted in the process of finding common ground among them. When the Native American Graves Protection and Repatriation Act was passed by Congress in 1990, it had the support of both Native Americans and the SAA, which had worked closely with congressional committees on the wording of the bill and with government agencies on implementing it.

Closely related to the increased archaeological activism and employment outside academia was a concern with archaeological standards and ethics. As early as 1953, a subcommittee of the society was appointed to examine the question of professional qualifications. It came back with a rating scale of archaeological competence that was circulated to members but never officially adopted because of various objections. In 1961, another committee published "Four Statements for Archaeology" (*American Antiquity* 27: 2) that proposed basic professional standards, ethics, and qualifications. At the 1973 annual meeting, the idea of certification of archaeologists was raised, and in the following year, a committee was appointed to investigate the suggestion. The committee recommended a national register of professional archaeologists, and the recommendation was approved by a referendum of members. Because of problems of implementing the registry within the society, the committee made the controversial move to form a separate Society of Professional Archaeologists to maintain a registry of archaeologists.

SAA president and public archaeology advocate Charles R. McGimsey II proposed in 1974 a series of seminars on the future direction of archaeology. Funded by the National Park Service, the Airlie House seminars covered archaeology and the law, cultural resource management, guidelines for archaeological reports, communication, archaeology and Native Americans, and certification (McGimsey and Davis 1977).

The problem of site looting and vandalism was one of the factors that influenced the original founding of the society, and official activities of the society on this issue have usually been in the form of editorials in *American Antiquity*. Activities on the international level have included authorizing the use of society funds to assist in prosecuting an illegal antiquities case (1972) and a long-term effort leading to implementation of the UNESCO Convention on Cultural Property in 1983. On the national level, the society began a major antilooting project, Save the Past for the Future, in 1988.

During its more than sixty years, the SAA has evolved from a national learned society concerned principally with communication among scholars through meetings and publication to an international professional society concerned with influencing governmental activities and defining professional standards as well as including the interests of non–U.S. Americanist scholars. The archives of the society are located in the National Anthropological Archives of the National Museum of Natural History, Smithsonian Institution.

Andrew L. Christenson

References

Collins, Robert B., and Mark P. Michel. 1985. "Preserving the Past: Origins of the Archaeological Resources Protection Act of 1979." *American Archaeology* 5: 84–89.

Dyson, Stephen L. 1985. "Two Paths to the Past: A Comparative Study of the Last Fifty Years of *American Antiquity* and *American Journal of Archaeology*." *American Antiquity* 50: 452–463.

Feinman, Gary M., Linda M. Nicholas, and William D. Middleton. 1992. "Archaeology in 1992: A Perspective on the Discipline from the Society for American Archaeology Annual Meeting Program." *American Antiquity* 57: 448–458.

Fowler, Don. D. 1986. "Conserving American Archaeological Resources." In *American Archaeology Past and Future: A Celebration of the Society for American Archaeology 1935–1985*, 135–162. Ed. David J. Meltzer, Don D. Fowler, and Jeremy A. Sabloff. Washington, DC: Smithsonian Institution Press.

Griffin, James B. 1985. "The Formation of the Society for American Archaeology." *American Antiquity* 50: 261–271.

Guthe, Carl E. 1935. "The Society for American Archaeology Organizational Meeting." *American Antiquity* 1: 141–151.

———. 1967. "Reflections on the Founding of the Society for American Archaeology." *American Antiquity* 32: 433–440.

McGimsey, Charles R., III, and Hester A. Davis. 1977. "The Management of Archaeological Resources: The Airlie House Report." Society for American Archaeology.

Meltzer, David J., Don D. Fowler, and Jeremy A. Sabloff, eds. 1986. *American Archaeology Past and Future: A Celebration of the Society for American Archaeology 1935–1985*. Washington, DC: Smithsonian Institution Press.

Rogge, A. E. 1976. "A Look at Academic Anthropology: Through a Graph Darkly." *American Anthropologist* 78: 829–843.

Wilmsen, Edwin N. 1973. "Report of the Editor." *American Antiquity* 38: 521–523.

Society for Historical Archaeology

In early January 1967, an ad hoc Committee of Fifteen, made up of most of the leading historical archaeologists in the Americas, met in conjunction with an International Conference on HISTORICAL ARCHAEOLOGY in Dallas, Texas, and over a three-day period organized the Society for Historical Archaeology (SHA). The new society's origins can be traced back over three decades before the meeting in Dallas. Special symposia at both the SOCIETY FOR AMERICAN ARCHAEOLOGY (SAA) and the American Anthropological Association and the 1960 creation of the more-regional Conference on Historic Site Archaeology by Stanley South served as precedents. By the middle of the 1960s, the growing community of historical archaeologists realized that the SAA, which was dominated by New World prehistorians, could not represent their developing interests and that their numbers were now adequate to support an autonomous association.

Independence and formal organization led to visible success and rapid growth, with the SHA becoming the central social, and to some degree intellectual, base for the emerging discipline. By the 1990s, its annual meetings, held in January, had more than 1,000 attendees, and its quarterly journal, *Historical Archaeology,* and substantial *Newsletter* had gained international standing and distribution. Although fundamentally a scholarly association, the SHA has also served as an effective lobbying base, as is seen by its primary role in the passage of the 1987 Abandoned Shipwreck Act by the U.S. Congress.

Phenomenal growth has resulted in a 2,000 individual membership, which makes the SHA the second-largest association of anthropological archaeologists in the world. Nevertheless, these numbers have not created an economy of scale. Across its three-decade history, a small number of dedicated volunteers have preserved and nurtured the society. The terms of office of the journal editor, Ronald L. Michael (1978–2001), the recent book review editor, Roderick Sprague (1977–1997), secretary-treasurer, Stephanie H. Rodeffer (1978–2001), and newsletter editor, Norman Barka (1982–2001) highlight this unusual situation for a mature and national-international organization.

Even though the core of its membership is in North America, the SHA has always been international in its orientation. In 1967, scholars from CANADA and MEXICO joined their colleagues from the United States at the Dallas meeting, and during the 1960s and 1970s, the society built early linkages to both the Society for Post-Medieval Archaeology in Europe and the Australasian Society for Historical Archaeology in Oceania. The SHA is the only truly global organization in the field; it is also one of the few of these collateral associations to self-reflexively recognize its own disciplinary history. In 1981, it created the J. C. HARRINGTON MEDAL IN HISTORICAL ARCHAEOLOGY and followed that in 1989 with the Carol V. Ruppé Distinguished Service Award and in 1998 with the John L. Cotter Award. It also established the flexible and successful category of SHA awards of merit.

The Society for Historical Archaeology, and parallel organizations in North America (including the Advisory Council on Underwater Archaeology, long associated with the SHA; the

Society for Industrial Archaeology; the Council for Northeastern Historical Archaeology; and the former [1960–1982] Conference on Historic Site Archaeology) and similar scholarly associations overseas, have been pivotal in the history and growth of the discipline.

Robert L. Schuyler

See also Africa, South Historical; Australia, Historical; Caribbean; United States of America, Prehistoric Archaeology

Society of Antiquaries of London

The Society of Antiquaries of London, founded in 1707, is the oldest learned society in Great Britain and Ireland concerned with archaeology and history. The Elizabethan College of Antiquaries, with such scholars as WILLIAM CAMDEN, Sir Robert Cotton, and John Stow, disbanded in the reign of James I (van Norden 1946). The Royal Society, founded in 1660, had an early interest in historical monuments such as AVEBURY (Ucko et al. 1991) and published much material on archaeological finds in its *Philosophical Transactions,* but by the end of the eighteenth century, its attention was focused purely on science.

The Society of Antiquaries of London was founded by three friends—Humfrey Wanley, John Talman, and John Bagford—who met informally in various London taverns. At the time, people who were interested in the physical and documentary evidence of the past were called antiquaries. The society has a continuous history from 1717, when there were twenty-three members, and the first Articles of Association defined the purpose of the new society as making knowledge of British antiquities more universal (Evans 1956). The Society of Antiquaries of London's early *Minutes* recorded the discoveries and exhibits of members, often with drawings, and are still of great interest. The drawings by the director, Charles Frederick, of the Arreton Downs hoard on the Isle of Wight, found in 1734, has made it possible for a group of Bronze Age metalwork items, now widely dispersed, to be reconstituted by later scholars and given their true provenance (Needham 1986).

The first secretary after 1717, WILLIAM STUKELEY, made important discoveries at Stonehenge, Avebury, and Roman Chesterford and elsewhere and drew heavily on the society's *Minutes* for his own publications. (Piggott 1985). Engravings of monuments, coins, seals, and antiquities were issued regularly to members and were often seen as a reason for joining the society. In 1740, a large-format series of illustrations, later issued with substantial text, was given the name *Vetusta Monumenta,* and it continued to be published until the early twentieth century. The preservation of historical monuments has been a concern since the society paid to protect the thirteenth-century Waltham Cross in 1721.

The society had a membership of about 150 in 1751 when it was granted a royal charter by King George II, who became its patron, and its members became entitled to call themselves "fellows of the Society of Antiquaries" (or FSA). Its purpose was widened to cover the study of the past of other countries as well as that of Britain in order to encompass a current interest in classical antiquities, and a wide international outlook has been a feature ever since. A number of Italian fellows were elected soon afterward, including the artist Giambattista Piranesi (1720–1778). Once the society had been incorporated as a chartered learned society, bequests could be accepted, and the collections grew rapidly from the contents of a box in 1719 to about 3,000 books, 250 manuscripts, and 5,000 prints and drawings by the time of the first published catalog of books and manuscripts in 1816. In 1753, the society rented rooms in a former London coffeehouse in Chancery Lane, which provided a secure space for the library, but it soon outgrew those premises. In 1781, the Society of Antiquaries joined the Royal Society and the Royal Academy in spacious new accommodations with finely decorated rooms at Somerset House, which had been granted by their patron at the time, King George III.

Some commentators believe that the eighteenth-century antiquaries contributed little toward an understanding of the distant past (Piggott 1989). However, in the absence of any framework for DATING prehistoric remains, some fellows made perceptive comments. In a paper on stone hand-axes found at Hoxne, Suffolk, in 1797, JOHN FRERE claimed that they had been made at a very remote period, beyond that of the present world, which has caused him to be described as "the father of scientific archaeology" (Wymer 1999). His observations and others by fellows were published in the society's *Archaeologia,* (1770–), the longest-running archaeological journal in Great Britain and the world.

Nevertheless, the society's most notable contribution in the eighteenth century was toward the understanding of British medieval art and architecture. The commissioning of record drawings of medieval buildings was an important aspect of the society's work, and artists such as George Vertue and John Carter were appointed as draftsmen. The thirteenth-century murals at the Palace of Westminster and the sixteenth-century murals at Cowdray House, Sussex, were recorded and published by the society (both buildings were later destroyed by fire). A series of detailed engravings of English cathedrals was launched in 1792, and the first color illustrations of the Bayeux Tapestry were published between 1821 and 1825 in *Vetusta Monumenta.* Key manuscript sources for British history, such as the twelfth-century "Winton Domesday" and the mid-sixteenth-century "Inventory of Henry VIII," were purchased by the society although it was nearly 200 years before transcripts of them were published.

By the beginning of the nineteenth century, the society was considered fashionable, and members included leading politicians, noblemen, clergy, lawyers, and collectors and by 1812, it had 800 members. However, the society suffered from intrigues, poor financial management, and a lack of direction. Numbers declined, and papers read at meetings and publications concentrated on the literary sources of British history. Other national societies, such as the British Archaeological Association and the Archaeological Institute (later the ROYAL ARCHAEOLOGICAL INSTITUTE), were founded in the 1840s, and they were soon followed by county societies. These new organizations appealed to a wider public and a growing interest in archaeology and historical monuments.

The Society of Antiquaries of London remained a small, closed elite society, but it managed to raise its standing in the archaeological community by the vigorous efforts of several distinguished officers in the second half of the nineteenth century. Under Albert Way's directorship in the 1840s, the society began publishing its *Proceedings,* the predecessor of the present *Antiquaries Journal.* Way also compiled a classified catalogue of the society's museum collection, which then consisted of about 400 items (Way 1847). After 1852, local secretaries were appointed who reported on finds in their areas, and the record was published in the *Proceedings.*

When A. W. Franks, keeper of British and Medieval Antiquities at the BRITISH MUSEUM, was director of the society in the 1860s and 1870s, several important exhibitions were held in Somerset House, including a series on Paleolithic (1871), Neolithic (1872), and Bronze Age (1873) implements. Scholars with an international reputation, such as HEINRICH SCHLIEMANN, visited the society and addressed its meetings. The society's most outstanding resident secretary, William St. John Hope, was appointed in 1886, and he carried out some pioneering excavations of medieval ecclesiastical sites. Under the presidency of SIR JOHN EVANS (1885–1892), the society took the initiative to improve liaison between county archaeological societies by establishing the Congress of Archaeological Societies. In 1889, Evans established the research fund with a sizable donation from his own resources. Grants from the fund, the society's support, and the expertise of its fellows have made possible excavations at many important British sites from Silchester, Hampshire, in the 1890s to SUTTON HOO, Suffolk, in the 1980s.

The government's pressing need for accommodation for civil servants in Somerset House led to the learned societies there being offered alternative premises in the new Burlington House, Piccadilly, and when the antiquaries moved there in 1875, the society gained considerably more space for its growing library. The collections developed from a concentration on British topography into a major resource for the study of British and European archaeology, with complete series of all the main archaeological journals for the area helped by an extensive international exchange program. Purchases by the society and gifts by fellows and institutions enlarged the library to such an extent that it expanded into the former living quarters of the resident secretary when they became vacant in 1910.

The society has generally been more influential in private than in public in promoting the interests of British archaeology. In 1907, it encouraged the government to establish the Royal Commission for the Historical Monuments of England, and in 1944, it took an active part in the creation of the Council of British Archaeology to succeed the Congress of Archaeological Societies. Full reports of excavations of national importance could not be contained within the annual *Archaeologia,* and a separate series of publications, *Research Reports,* began with the results of the excavation of Wroxeter published in 1912. Most of the later titles also present the evidence from excavations supported by the society, and they include SIR MORTIMER WHEELER's classic studies of *Verulamium* (1936), *Maiden Castle* (1943), and *The Hillforts of Northern France* (1957).

In the twentieth century, the Society of Antiquaries grew to over 2,000 fellows. Women were admitted for the first time in 1921, and they now form about one-sixth of the total. Almost half of the members are professional archaeologists; the remainder work in museums, universities, libraries, record offices, or heritage management or are amateur experts in their field. To reflect the two main strands of the fellowship, the convention has arisen in recent years that the elected president alternates between an archaeologist and a historian. The premises are used for regular meetings of the society, those of many bodies with similar interests, and conferences on archaeological and art-history subjects. The papers of some conferences have been published in a new series of *Occasional Papers* since 1980. The society is a registered charity because of its library, support for publications, and awarding of grants. It is also a registered museum because of its collections and ownership from 1962 of the summer home of one of its fellows, the artist William Morris at Kelmscott in Oxfordshire. The society's interests are therefore multidisciplinary, but the contributions made by both the society and its fellows to archaeology over nearly 300 years have been considerable.

Bernard Nurse

See also Britain, Prehistoric Archaeology

References

Evans, J. 1956. *The History of the Society of Antiquaries.* Oxford: Oxford University Press.

Levine, P. 1986. *The Amateur and the Professional.* Cambridge: Cambridge University Press.

Needham, S. 1986. "Towards a Reconstitution of the Arreton Hoard: A Case of Faked Provenances." *Antiquities Journal* 66: 9–28.

Piggott, S. 1985. *William Stukeley.* London: Thames and Hudson.

———. 1989. *Ancient Britons and the Antiquarian Imagination.* London: Thames and Hudson.

Ucko, P., et al. 1991. *Avebury Reconsidered.* London: Unwin Hyman.

Way, A. 1847. *Catalogue of Antiquities . . . in the Society's Possession.* London.

Wymer, J. 1999. "A Memorial to John Frere." *Past* 33: 3–4.

Society of Antiquaries of Scotland

The second-oldest antiquarian society in Great Britain, the Society of Antiquaries of Scotland was founded in 1780. David Steuart Erskine, eleventh earl of Buchan, called a meeting of eminent historians and antiquaries at his home in St. Andrews Square in Edinburgh on 14 November, and the new society was formally constituted on 18 December. Its first meeting followed on 16 January 1781, and it set the pattern for years to come: an academic lecture and a display of items donated to the society's museum. In the terms of the charter granted in 1783, the aim of the society was "to investigate both antiquities and natural and civil history in general," and King George III and his successors were to be the society's patrons. The current laws of the society define its purpose as "the study of the antiquities and history of Scotland, more especially by means of archaeological research." The society was granted a coat of arms in 1827.

The publication of academic papers began in 1792 with the first volume of the *Transactions;* the name of the journal was changed with volume four in 1831 to *Archaeologia Scotica,* and its publication ceased with volume five in 1890. It was replaced by the *Proceedings of the Society of Antiquaries of Scotland,* the first volume of which was published in 1854, and it remains the primary journal of archaeological record in Scotland (Graham 1969–1970). The society's minute books and correspondence, together with original drawings and manuscripts of antiquarian interest, are in the National Museums of Scotland Library, and other manuscripts formerly belonging to the society are in the National Monuments Record for Scotland.

Initially, the society occupied a number of different properties in Edinburgh, and at one time it shared a building with the Royal Society of Edinburgh. As the collection grew in size and importance, however, concern about its long-term future led to the transference of responsibility for its housing and financing to the government in 1859, in return for which the society agreed to give the collection to the nation. In 1890, the museum was moved to a purpose-built museum and portrait gallery in Queen Street; an ornate building was designed by Rowand Anderson in the Italianate Gothic style.

The museum had become the National Museum of Antiquities of Scotland, and the society had rooms, including a splendid library, in the new building. An act of Parliament in 1954 relieved the society of the management of the museum, but the library remained mutual and the society continued to be housed by the museum. The name of the museum was changed to the Royal Museum of Scotland when it was amalgamated by an act of Parliament in 1985 with the Royal Scottish Museum under the overall title National Museums of Scotland. Before the end of the twentieth century, the Scottish collections were to be redisplayed in a new building in Chambers Street, and the society was to move into new rooms there.

Members of the society are known as fellows and are admitted by election. There were 50 fellows in 1780 and almost 3,000 in the 1990s. Membership is worldwide and includes both professional and amateur archaeologists and historians. There are also up to 25 honorary fellows, elected in recognition of their services to

Scottish or international archaeology and history. Office-bearers consist of a president, three vice-presidents, a treasurer, and an editor, and there is currently a professional staff of three, headed by the director of the society. The society celebrated its bicentenary in 1980 with special meetings and exhibitions, and a commemorative medal was struck in bronze for fellows and in silver as a presidential badge of office. A volume of essays about the society, the museum, and leading antiquarians was published to mark the bicentennial year (Bell 1981).

From the 1850s onward, reports of excavations featured strongly in the *Proceedings,* and the society sponsored its own excavations from the 1890s to the 1930s, including work on the Roman forts at Birrens, Ardoch, Inchtuthil, and Newstead; the native forts at Dunadd and Traprain; the broch at Gurness; and the Viking settlement at Jarlshof in the Shetland Islands. Although the society no longer conducts excavations today, it supports excavation and research through grants awarded from its research fund and through conferences.

A leading fellow of the mid-nineteenth century, A. H. Rhind, funded an annual lectureship that began in 1876–1878 with a series of lectures on Scottish ethnography by Sir Arthur Mitchell; these lectures were published as *The Past in the Present* (1880). The next series was given by Joseph Anderson, the keeper of the society's museum from 1869 to 1913. His lectures represented a milestone in Scottish archaeology because of their scientific analysis of sites and artifacts, and they were published in two volumes as *Scotland in Early Christian Times* (1881) and in another two volumes as *Scotland in Pagan Times* (1883–1886). The prestigious Rhind Lectures still continue to provide a platform for scholars to present the most up-to-date research in a wide variety of archaeological, historical, architectural, and ethnographical fields.

Apart from the *Proceedings,* there have been occasional publications such as the great tome *The Early Christian Monuments of Scotland* (1903) by J. Romilly Allen and Joseph Anderson, and since 1982, the society has published its own series of monographs, mostly recording excavations in Scotland. From its inception, the society has been consulted on important developments relating to Scottish history and archaeology, and it continues to have a powerful voice on matters concerning Scotland's heritage and the management of archaeology in Britain.

Anna Ritchie

References
Bell, A. S., ed. 1981. *The Scottish Antiquarian Tradition.* Edinburgh: John Donald.
Graham, A. 1969–1970. "Records and Opinions: 1780–1930." *Proceedings of the Society of Antiquaries of Scotland* 102: 241–284.

Society of Dilettanti

Founded in 1734 in London by a group of gentlemen who had taken the grand tour of Europe, the primary purpose of the Society of Dilettanti was to promote the study of classical antiquities. The society gained great fame during its history by funding research, the most important being a survey of Athenian monuments by James Stuart (artist) and Nicholas Revett (architect), which took place between 1751 and 1754, and a highly detailed survey of the ruins of Ionia by Richard Chandler beginning in 1765. The society sealed its place in the history of archaeology by publishing both surveys. Stuart and Revett produced the four-volume *Antiquities of Athens* (1762–1816), and Chandler brought out *The Antiquities of Ionia* (1769–1797).

Tim Murray

See also Elgin, Lord; Greece; Turkey
References
Schnapp, A. 1996. *The Discovery of the Past.* London: British Museum Press.

Solutré

Solutré, an open site in the Ardèche region of southeastern FRANCE, was selected in 1869 as the type site for the Solutrean industry. The site is located at the base of a cliff and dates from about 30,000 B.P. to 17,000 B.P. Solutré contains an excellent sequence of French Paleolithic industries from the Mousterian to the Magdalenian, but it is most famous for the presence of the distinctive laurel leaf points and shouldered points that are characteristic of the

Solutrean stone tool industry. The site is also notable because it contains the remains of many horse, reindeer, and bovids, giving rise to the interpretation that Solutré was a major ambush site (perhaps by chasing animals over the cliff to be killed and butchered below).

Tim Murray

See also Lithic Analysis

References

Lagardère, G. 1997. *Solutré: Musée Departmental de Préhistoire.* Consul General Sâone et Loire.

South Asia
Introduction

Considering the enormous geographical area involved, the number of its modern nation states, and the rich spectrum of its archaeology, one would expect the literature on the history of archaeology in South Asia to be fairly analytical and detailed. This is not the case. Straightforward narrative accounts, sometimes viewed in relation with contemporary government policies and other historical factors, are available for the period up to 1947 when the British rule of the subcontinent ended (*see* Roy 1953, 1961; Ghosh 1953; Allchin 1961; Imam 1966; Chakrabarti 1988a, 1988b; Possehl 1990; Mirsky 1977). These histories deal fully (*see* Roy 1961; Chakrabarti 1988a) or partly with the history of archaeology in British India, which was dominated almost exclusively by the official Archaeological Survey of India that came into existence, although tentatively, in 1861. But at least two other dimensions of this period remain unresearched. First, some major "native" states of the subcontinent that enjoyed varying degrees of autonomy during British rule, such as Hyderabad, Mysore, Travancore, Gwalior, Kashmir, Baroda, and Nepal, ran, on the British Indian model, their own archaeology departments. The history of these departments lies untouched. Second, the different nuances between archaeology and nationalism provide great scope for research, especially in view of the long struggle for Indian independence, but this is another field of study that remains neglected. The development of the concept of an Indian past among the different sections of Indian people is closely related to this issue. The main source of study in this case is the great amount of vernacular literature from the second half of the eighteenth century onwards in different parts of the country in different major languages. This concept has to be seen separately from the Western concept of the past of India. In any case, the interaction between these two major concepts of the Indian past should provide a separate field of study in itself.

After 1947 the history of subcontinental archaeology becomes the history of archaeology in its different nation-state components. For obvious historical reasons, one of which is the difference in majority religion between these countries (Hinduism in India and Nepal, Islam in Pakistan and Bangladesh, Buddhism in Bhutan), the concept of the past in these individual nation states need not exactly be the same. Still, the model of archaeological organization in them has a lot in common because of close ancestral links with the pre-1947 Archaeological Survey of India, and, more significantly, this possible difference in attitudes to the past has not changed the pattern of archaeological research in these countries. Also, the interaction between the Western concept of the past of South Asia and the concept of the past developed by South Asians themselves merits close study even in the post-1947 period, mainly to analyze the extent to which the hegemonic ideas of Western Indology still retain their grip over the intellectual tradition in a Third World region like South Asia.

The Beginning

The middle of the eighteenth century is as convenient a starting point for South Asian archaeological studies as any. At about this time Anquetil du Perron, a Frenchman with knowledge of Oriental languages, and Karsten Niebuhr, a Danish engineer and voyager, wrote about the need to open up India as a field of scientific inquiry. They also prepared measured drawings of the West Indian monuments of Elephanta and Kanheri, both easily accessible to Europeans because of their proximity to Bombay. In fact, these and other conveniently located monuments had been drawing the attention of Euro-

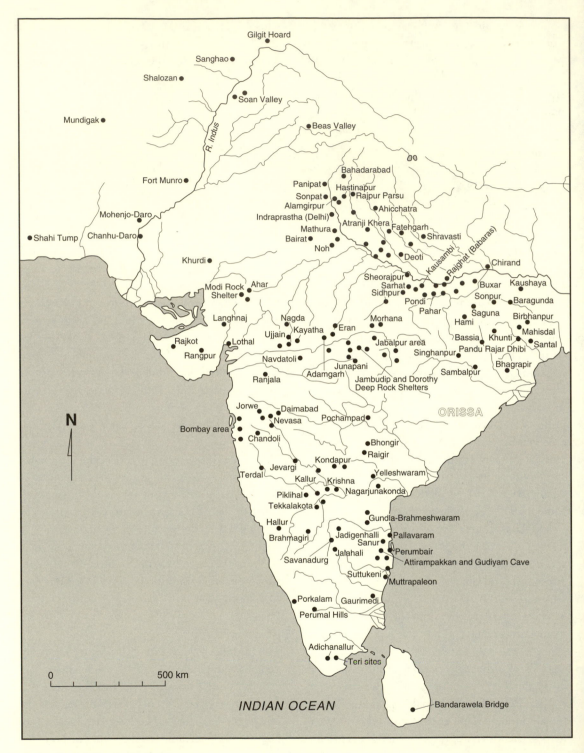

Gilgit Hoard

Sanghao

Shalozan

Soan Valley

Mundigak

Beas Valley

R. Indus

Bahadarabad

Fort Munro

Panipat
Hastinapur
Sonpat
Rajpur Parsu
Alamgirpur
Ahicchatra
Indraprastha (Delhi)
Atranji Khera
Mathura
Fatehgarh
Bairat
Shravasti
Noh
Deoti
Kausambi
Raighat (Babaras)

Mohenjo-Daro

Chanhu-Daro

Shahi Tump

Khurdi

Chirand

Modi Rock
Shelter
Ahar
Sheorajpur
Sarhat
Buxar
Kaushaya
Sidhpur
Sonpur

Langhnaj
Nagda
Morhana
Pondi
Pahar
Baragunda

Ujjain
Kayatha
Eran
Hami
Saguna
Birbhanpur

Rajkot
Bassia
Khunti
Mahisdal

Lothal
Navdatoli
Jabalpur area
Pandu Rajar Dhibi
Santal

Rangpur
Singhanpur
Bhagrapir

Junapani

Ranjala
Adamgarh
Sambalpur

Jambudip and Dorothy
Deep Rock Shelters

ORISSA

Jorwe
Daimabad

Bombay area
Nevasa
Pochampad

Chandoli

Bhongir

Kondapur
Raigir

Jevargi
Yelleshwaram

Terdal
Kallur
Krishna

Piklihal
Nagarjunakonda

Tekkalakota

Hallur
Gundla-Brahmeshwaram

Brahmagiri
Jadigenhalli
Pallavaram
Sanur
Perumbair
Savanadurg
Jalahali
Attirampakkan and Gudiyam Cave

Suttukeni
Muttrapaleon

Porkalam
Gaurimedi

Perumal Hills

Adichanallur

Teri sites

INDIAN OCEAN

Bandarawela Bridge

N

0   500 km

Archaeological Sites in South Asia

pean travelers and sailors since the sixteenth century, and although most of these descriptions were fanciful and deprecatory, some writers like the Italian Pietro della Valle of the seventeenth century insisted on some accuracy, aided in the case of della Valle by a few temple plans. There are two other reasons for selecting the mid-eighteenth century as our starting point. First, in 1753 J. B. D'Anville, a French geographer, published a book on Indian geography with detailed discussions of the locations of some ancient sites mentioned in classical writings on India. Second, in the writings of the French philosophers of Enlightenment, which attempted to move away from Judaeo-Christian thought, there was a strong emphasis on India as the original center of culture and religion (see Mitter 1977; Chakrabarti 1988a, 1–15).

The Asiatic Society of Bengal

An institutional focus of inquiry into the history and antiquities, the arts, sciences and literature of Asia was provided by the Asiatic Society of Bengal, established on 15 January 1784 in the contemporary British Indian capital of Calcutta with the Governor General Warren Hastings as its patron and William Jones, a senior judge, as the president. The ascending British supremacy in India, the trend of forming "societies" for scientific and other investigations in contemporary Britain, and a concern with "how far the products of India could be turned to account" explain the establishment of this institution. A major focus of interest was to understand Indian civilization in light of the contemporary notions of Universal History, which, because of its implicit acceptance of the biblical theory of creation, found no difficulty in believing that all human families were related and that one of the major tasks of historical investigation in India was to seek out proof of such relations. Having argued that the race he called Indian was descended from Ham, one of the three sons of Noah, Jones traced the ramifications of this concept in various fields of Indian endeavor, including Sanskrit, the speakers of which were supposed to have "had an immemorial affinity with the old Persians, Ethiopians and Egyptians, the Phoenicians, Greeks and Tuscans; the Scythians or Goths, and

CELTS; the Chinese, Japanese and Peruvians . . ." (Jones 1788). Interests in India both as the original center of civilization and for the identification of its ancient sites continued during this period. Among other things, Indian priests were supposed to have moved out of a climatically more equable central Asia, spreading civilization wherever they went (Chakrabarti 1976). In the field of historical geography there were some significant publications, notably those by James Rennell, whose *Memoir of a Map of Hindoostan,* which combined both modern and ancient data, "one illustrating and explaining the other," underwent three editions between 1783 and 1793 (Chakrabarti 1988a, 14, 16–18).

The Leadership of JAMES PRINSEP

Field archaeology gained no momentum until the 1830s, although some major archaeological sites were noticed by then in a few regional surveys (Roy 1953). The man who inspired field-archaeological studies was James Prinsep, Assay Master of the British mint in Calcutta, Secretary of the Asiatic Society of Bengal, and the principal decipherer, in collaboration with Indian traditional language scholars, of the ancient Indian scripts of Brahmi and Kharoshti. His attitude toward field research is clear from his statement, "What the learned world demands of us in India is to be quite certain of our data, to place the monumental record before them exactly as now exists, and to interpret it faithfully and literally" (Prinsep 1838).

One of the major developments of the period was the enumeration and excavation of Buddhist funerary remains, called stupas, in the northwestern part of the subcontinent. Leadership in this matter was given by some European army officers in the employ of the contemporary Sikh ruler of the region, Ranjit Singh, but nobody expressed it better than Alexander Burnes of the Bombay Army, who in his quest for the stupas and "Grecian remains" found himself referred from place to place "like one in search of the philosopher's stone" (Burnes 1833). None, however, was more extensive in his observations and collections in this region than Charles Masson (Possehl 1990), an alias for James Loews, who deserted from Bengal Horse

Artillery in 1827. In the southern part of the country there was a period of "barrow-hunting," when megalithic burials of various kinds were dug in their hundreds by British officials in the cool of the Nilgiri hills or literally in their backyards. At Jiwarji in the Deccan, Captain Meadows Taylor (1851) in his digging employed more care and precision than others. On the north Indian plains some major historical sites were identified or recorded during this period, the foremost coming from ALEXANDER CUNNINGHAM, a military engineer and a close associate of Prinsep. In the newly translated itineraries of the two famous Chinese pilgrims to India—Fa-Hian (early fifth century A.D.) and Hiuen-Tsang (the first half of the seventh century A.D.)—he found an important geographical base for conducting ground investigations. One could follow the pilgrims in their travels and mark out the places they reported. In 1843 he discovered the location of the early historic city-site of Sankisa in Uttar Pradesh by following this method (Cunningham 1843), but systematic surveys had to wait until 1861 when the government established an organization for the purpose, with Cunningham (then retired with the rank of Major General) at its head. In 1865 the Archaeological Survey of India was disbanded, to be reorganized in 1871 with Cunningham again in charge, this time with the services of two assistants, J. D. Beglar and A. C. L. Carlyle. Beglar left this job in 1880 and was succeeded by H. B. W. Garrick.

The Surveys of Alexander Cunningham (1861–1865, 1866–1885)

Cunningham conducted his surveys across the entire area between the northwestern hills and the Bengal delta, including the Vindhyan orbit in central India, eastern Rajasthan, the Chhotanagpur hills, and Orissa in eastern India. Some of the work was done by his assistants but the principal work was done by Cunningham personally. The results of these surveys were incorporated in twenty-three volumes published between 1871 and 1887 (Imam 1966).

> The standard features of a Cunningham report are the following: a ground survey studying the height, character and extent of the mounds, including their structural features and the plans and measurements of the more important of them; the record of their local traditions; the mention, if any, of the place in the ancient Indian literary texts; the description in Hiuen-Tsang's and/or Fa-Hian's records; an attempt to identify the various sacred spots, monasteries, stupas, etc. in Hiuen-Tsang's and Fa-Hian's account of the place with the various surviving features on the ground; and the mention of the still available coins, images and inscriptions at the place with notes on them. To do all these even in the context of a single site would require a strong measure of versatile scholarship and practiced eyes. What lends Cunningham's survey work great distinction is that he could set down these points for hundreds of sites of different types throughout north India. (Chakrabarti 1988a, 59)

The basic achievement of these surveys was the mapping out of sites on a large scale and this was something like the achievement of the Great Trigonometrical Survey of India, which mapped out the Indian landmass in considerable detail.

Archaeology as Architecture (1885–1901)

There was a sharp contrast in archaeological attitude between Alexander Cunningham and his successor James Burgess (1886–1889), who had considerable prior experience as an architectural surveyor in Gujarat and the Deccan and to whom archaeology was nothing but architectural study (Burgess 1905). The last quarter of the nineteenth century witnessed the publication of many studies of ancient and medieval monuments, principally by "provincial" surveyors, such as James Fergusson and R. L. Mitraand, under Burgess, and some by Burgess himself. At the same time the study of ancient Indian epigraphy was undertaken by a specially appointed government epigraphist and a curator of ancient monuments, to which Captain H. H. Cole (1880–1883) was appointed. This marked a departure from the earlier government attitude, reflected by its resolution to auction the Taj Mahal for the value of the marble of its construction—a resolution mercifully abandoned later. One of the significant field-archaeological investigations of this period was the exploration of the ancient city of Pataliputra, modern Patna, by L. A. Waddel of the Indian Medical Service. In the course of a hurried visit to Patna in 1892 he was surprised to find that not only was the ancient city practically intact but that "most of the leading landmarks of Asoka's palaces, monasteries and other monuments remained so very obvious" as to enable him "in the short space of one day to identify many of them beyond all doubt" (Waddel 1903). Excavations began at this site under the Public Works Department in 1894 and the general identifications, proposed by Waddel on the basis of his keen eye for the details on the ground and a close familiarity with the literary data on the topography of the place, were confirmed.

The John Marshall Era (1902–1944)

The fortunes of archaeological research in India changed considerably during the Viceroyalty of Lord Curzon, who took personal interest in such a non-revenue-earning matter as archaeology. Curzon imported the 26-year-old JOHN MARSHALL, an alumnus of King's College, Cambridge, with some archaeological experience in GREECE and TURKEY, and appointed him the director general of archaeology. As subsequent developments proved, he could not have chosen better. To begin with, various aspects of archaeology in India—explorations, excavations, conservation of ancient monuments, and epigraphy—were consolidated within the aegis of the Archaeological Survey of India. Archaeological research and the task of conservation came to be considered as permanent government responsibilities, which in itself was a very big step forward. The director general could now lay down clearly defined policies for his officers in various regions. Moreover, a system of publishing annual reports containing detailed accounts of the manifold activities of the survey was introduced right from the first year of Marshall's office (1902–1903). These volumes, the publication of which continued up to 1937, were substantial scholarly and administrative endeavors. Finally, there was a system of awarding annual research scholarships, one for Sanskrit and another for Persian and Arabic, to two students at Indian universities, enabling the induction of Indians at a superior level in the survey, which fostered over many years a strong core of primary scholarship. Epigraphical studies received much-needed impetus with the regular publication of *Epigraphia Indica*. On the whole archaeology was put on an even keel right from the early days of Marshall's director generalship.

In field archaeology the first great achievement of the Marshall era (notwithstanding his personal retirement in 1928–1929) lay in the excavations of major historical sites in virtually all areas of the subcontinent, which continued until 1944. It is true that many of them were mapped out by Cunningham but the details still needed working out with the help of physical excavation. From the Indian perspective, throughout the nineteenth century there was a constant discussion in vernacular literature on the theme of India's past, especially India's ancient past. This was primarily based on literature and partly on the study of standing monuments, but there was a need for the knowledge of archaeological details. Marshall's own early works were at Charsada in the northwest and Bhita and Rajagriha in the Gangetic valley, but after these he was mostly busy with excavations at Taxila, where the landscape reminded him of Greece and where there were numerous finds to illustrate the subcontinent's link with the West Asian and Mediterranean world. Marshall's personal report on Taxila (Marshall 1951) came out in three volumes in 1951, its earlier publication being reputedly prevented by the destruction of his notes during the London blitz. The people he recruited were busy at other sites, many of which enjoyed great reputation in the annals of early historic India—Pataliputra, Vaisali, Purushapura or Peshawar, Amaravati, Nalanda, Sravasti, Kusinara, and others. In each case, as in the case of Marshall's own work at Bhita, which arrived at stratigraphy based on floor levels, the work was largely horizontal and successful in offering a visual image of the famous cities and monuments of ancient India.

The second great field achievement of the period was the discovery of the INDUS CIVILIZATION, the first formal announcement on which was made in the *Illustrated London News* on 20

September 1924. This was based on D. R. Sahni's work at HARAPPA between 1920 and 1921 and RAKAL D. BANERJI's work at Mohenjo Daro between 1921 and 1922. It was Mohenjo Daro that received major attention, because a large section of the ruins at Harappa were destroyed by the brick-robbing activities of the contractors of the Lahore-Multan railway. The results of work at Harappa were published in 1940. However it was the three-volume *Mohenjodaro and the Indus Civilization,* edited by Marshall and including a long introduction and discussion by him on religion and art, chronology, and the like, that brought out the first integrated image of this civilization. Its town planning, its concern with water supply and sanitation, its excellently crafted glyptic art and well-ordered rows of short inscriptions on seals, the evidence of its internal and external trade, a distinct level of technological excellence, and an art and a religious system whose principal elements were carried into the later historic periods—all of these suggested to Marshall a strong factor of continuity between this Bronze Age civilization and modern India. The discovery of this unique civilization, as unique in its own way as the civilizations of Egypt, was a great achievement of the Archaeological Survey of India under Marshall. With independence in 1947, India, in the eyes of western scholarship, became part of the Third World. But Marshall never had the compulsion to denigrate India's unique antiquity, believing that the origins of historic India, including its major religion, Hinduism, could be traced back to the Bronze Age Indus civilization.

During the world Depression in the 1930s and World War II in the 1940s, archaeology survived somehow in India, although its budget was severely cut. N. G. Majumdar's surveys in Sind elucidating the antecedents and transformations of Indus civilization and the excavations by K. N. Dikshit at the major Buddhist monastery of Paharpur in eastern India belong to this period. In 1939 the government of India decided, for unexplained reasons, to seek the opinion of the famous British archaeologist LEONARD WOOLLEY of UR on the state of Indian archaeology. The resultant "Woolley Report," no worse and no better than many such pontificatory re-

ports on India by Western experts, suggested, among other things, prolonged excavations at a major historic site for "in-service" training of the survey officers and the appointment of another famous British archaeologist, SIR ERIC MORTIMER WHEELER, as the director general for four years.

Mortimer Wheeler (1944–1948)
Wheeler knew the value of vertical sequences established on the basis of layers, he appreciated archaeology as an academic discipline in its own right, and he fully understood the potential of the application of natural-scientific techniques in archaeology. His work at Taxila, where he operated a training school for survey recruits and university students, and at Harappa, Arikamedu, and Brahmagiri were exercises both in stratigraphic layer-based digging and in pursuing specific issues. In retrospect Wheeler's contribution to Indian archaeology lay in his determination to develop archaeology as an academic discipline in Indian universities, and this overall concern is obvious in his own writings during his stay in India in an annual publication he himself created, *Ancient India.* From the Indian academic point of view "he was no Elizabethan hero or a 'mad sahib' set among the natives to stampede them into a frenetic albeit well-ordered archaeological activity. . . . His role in India was basically that of a university teacher with firm, single-minded commitment to his subject" (Chakrabarti 1988a).

Prehistory until 1947
Until Wheeler organized a prehistory section in the survey, there was no official interest in prehistory, which had a checkered history of investigations in India since the early years of the twentieth century. During the second half of the nineteenth century, especially after the discovery of a hand-axe near Madras by Geological Survey of India officer ROBERT B. FOOTE, there were many prehistoric discoveries that were initiated almost exclusively by geologists. In 1923 an Indian teacher of anthropology at Calcutta University (Mitra 1923) published a book called *Prehistoric India.* In the 1930s, in the wake of stone tool discoveries in the outer Himalayan

region, H. de Terra, a geologist from Yale, and T. T. Paterson, an archaeologist from Cambridge (England) formulated a scheme of river terrace successions associated with lithic industries in the Soan River Valley of Panjab (now in Pakistan). The Soan terraces were related to the evidence of four glacial phases in Kashmir, which in turn were related to the four-fold glacial cycle in the Alps, thus bringing a sense of geochronology to Indian prehistoric studies. This work enjoyed influence for a long time and generated further interest in prehistoric studies in different parts of the country. In the 1940s STUART PIGGOTT, then in the Royal Air Force in India, studied protohistoric material from Baluchistan, arranging it into regional cultures with ties to central and west Asia. But on the whole prehistoric and protohistoric studies had to wait for an upsurge in interest until the postcolonial era.

The Post-1947 Situation

After 1947, the year of Partition and Independence from British rule, the history of South Asian archaeology becomes the history of archaeological research in five nation-states: India, Pakistan, Bangladesh, Nepal and Bhutan.

Bhutan and Nepal

There are no positive reports of early sites in Bhutan, and to the best of our knowledge there has been no detailed survey work either. The Himalayan kingdom of Nepal, on the other hand, has an established government archaeology department, complemented by archaeology and ancient history teaching at Tribhuvan University, Kathmandu. Considering the nature of sites in the Kathmandu valley and the tarai region of the country, the orientation of Nepalese archaeology has always been toward sites associated with the life of the Buddha and generally Buddhism (for a comprehensive survey, see Slusser 1982; for a representative excavation report, see Mitra 1971). At one point there was a great reluctance to come to terms with the fact that the site of Kapilavastu, the capital of the kingdom where the Buddha's father was king, was, as the discovery of Kapilavastu monastic seals by an Indian team showed, at Piphrawa on the Indian side of the Nepal-India border (Rijal 1979). The birthplace of the Buddha has always been, of course, on the Nepalese side of the border. The standard archaeological publication of Nepal is *Ancient Nepal,* officially published by the government department of archaeology.

Bangladesh

Bangladesh became an independent nation state in 1971 and archaeological research there between 1947 and 1971 was conducted by the Pakistan Department of Archaeology. The principal sites are the Buddhist monastery of Mainamati, which had its heyday in the seventh and eighth centuries A.D., and Mahasthangarh, one of the most imposing early historic city-sites of the subcontinent, dating back certainly to the third century B.C. when it was a provincial administrative center of the Mauryan empire, which stretched from south Afghanistan to Bengal. Buddhist monastery sites remain the focal point of contemporary Bangladesh archaeological research. Among its official publications *Bangladesh Archaeology,* of which regrettably only one issue has been published, must be considered the most important. Archaeology is taught at only one Bangladesh university, Jahangirnagar University near the nation's capital of Dhaka. The only evidence of Stone Age industry in Bangladesh is a late Acheulean/Upper Paleolithic industry made from the locally abundant fossilwood in the Lalmai hills (Chakrabarti 1993).

Pakistan

Archaeology in Pakistan has concentrated on protohistory and on the elucidation of the process of cultural development leading up to the development of Indus civilization. Initially Baluchistan received close archaeological scrutiny, notably with the beginning of a new phase of protohistoric research in this area by W. A. Fairservis, who was soon followed by a host of other researchers, notably B. de Cardi, G. F. Dales, and, more recently, J. Jarrige, who established the beginning of wheat-barley and cattle-sheep-goat domestication at around 7000 B.C. in the Bolan Valley site of Mehrgarh. From the point of view of subcontinental archaeology, the discovery of this level at Mehrgarh was a momentous event. French research in this part of Baluchistan has continued, and this and other activities in this region may best be seen as the continuation of a long preoccupation in archaeological literature to understand Baluchistan as an intermediate zone between the Gulf, Central Asia, Iran, Afghanistan, and the Indus valley. In the Indus valley itself the antecedents of the Indus civilization have been highlighted by excavations at a number of sites, notably Kot Diji and Amri. The steady sequence of development toward the Indus civilization has been traced through the excavation of the dried-up drainage system of the Ghaggar-Hakra to the east of the Indus valley in Bahawalpur. R. Mughal's work in this area has revealed not only the largest agglomeration of mature Harappan sites in a single area but also the successively earlier Kot Diji/early Harappan and Hakra Ware phases, the last one possibly going back to the fifth millennium B.C. The ramifications of different protohistoric levels all over Pakistan constitute the general theme of archaeological investigations in Pakistan, and excavations at sites such as Rehman Dheri in the Gomal valley, Jalilpur near Multan in the Indus valley, Saraikhola near Rawalpindi, Lewan, and Tarakai Qila and Sheri Khan Tarakai in Bannu, have contributed to our understanding of the protohistoric cultural picture of the subcontinent. Among the classic sites Mohenjo Daro, excavated further between 1964 and 1965 with some interesting results, formed the subject of intensive ground surveys and structural documentation in recent years. Harappa has an ongoing phase of excavations with specific targets in the eastern part of the ancient city. In the area between Swat and Chitral a sequence from the third millennium B.C. has been established and is best known for the distinctive grave assemblage known as Gandhara Grave Culture. Prehistoric studies gained some prominence in recent years with the claim of 2-million-year-old artifacts at Riwat to the south of Rawalpindi, and there are other finds in the Sukkur-Rorhi hills. Among the universities, Peshawar has a full-fledged teaching program in archaeology, with one or two other universities following suit. In addition to the central government department of archaeology, there are government archaeology departments in each province of Pakistan.

India

Continuity of the pre-1947 Archaeological Survey of India is most obvious in India, partly because of the rich diversity of archaeological remains and partly because of a much greater number of archaeology-teaching universities than in the other nation-states. Indian archaeologists began where Mortimer Wheeler left off. The building up of vertical sequences and the widening of the dimension of what was already known were pursued with great vigor, which was commensurate with other spheres of national activity, such as laying the base of industrialization. Within about twenty-five years of independence Indian archaeology had undergone a sea-change in terms of activities. Before the nature of some of these activities is outlined, it is necessary to emphasize the somewhat-changed character of the relevant institutional focus. Whereas the old survey went on opening more "branches" and "circles," now archaeology and museum directorates came up on state or provincial levels, each entrusted with the care of monuments and other archaeological activities within their own regional jurisdiction. In addition, from 1960 onwards a number of universities (twenty to twenty-five) began to offer postgraduate courses in archaeology leading up to master's and Ph.D. degrees in the subject. At about the same time, the Archaeological Survey of India began to run its own School of Archaeology for the training of university students and its own in-service officers. The universities that offered archaeology courses had usually their own excavation and exploration programs in the same way that the state departments ran their own field programs. A radiocarbon laboratory started functioning in the early 1960s. In the field of prehistory the initial cue was from the Terra-Paterson work mentioned earlier, and gradually the issues of prehistoric stratigraphy and geochronology came into focus. There was a great spurt in prehistoric discoveries, and in this field the survey was soon overtaken by the universities, where a new crop of Ph.D. students preferred to study regional prehistory and protohistory (see Sankalia 1974).

Stratigraphy and typology have formed the basic archaeological parameters of Indian prehistoric studies because that was what was needed first and because geoarchaeological techniques and the necessary adjunct of radiometric DATING remain undeveloped. In view of this there is an increasing emphasis on the "settlement-subsistence" approach, based on modern analogies (Paddayya 1978; Murty 1985; Nagar and Misra 1989; Misra 1989) or on the amalgamation of prehistoric data in the long-term settlement history of a geographical region (Chakrabarti 1993). Fossil evidence does not extend beyond the Mesolithic except in one case where a skull cap, presumably associated with late Acheulean artifacts and found in the cliff section of the Narmada river in central India, has been interpreted either as an Asian variety of *Homo erectus* or as an archaic *Homo sapiens*. Some cultural details are available from the Upper Paleolithic but earlier primary occupation sites associated with organic remains are still to be discovered, and their climatic background also remains to be worked out on a pan-Indian level, some regional efforts notwithstanding (*see* Agrawal 1992).

In the field of protohistory the discovery of Indus civilization sites on a large scale within Indian territory was among the primary archaeological targets after Independence, and the rapidity with which the vast space of Gujarat, Rajasthan, Haryana, eastern Panjab, and western Uttar Pradesh came to be dotted with "Harappan" sites of early, mature, and late denomination is enviable by any standard of archaeological research (for maps, *see* Joshi, Bala, and Ram 1984). Major excavations of Harappan sites in modern India include those at Rupar, Lothal, Kalibangan, Surkotada, Banawali, and Dholavira, all undertaken by the archaeological survey. Another major breakthrough in this context has been the discovery of a late Harappan phase in Maharashtra and Malwa. The regional protohistoric data are ever increasing in quantity. All major agricultural regions of India have their protohistoric antecedents, and again the discovery of this horizon is among the bright spots of archaeological research since 1947 (*see* Sankalia 1974).

Discoveries of the historical period have been no less abundant, and there is now a much clearer appreciation of early historic and later India as parts of the cultural development with protohistory and prehistory at its roots. Both civic and religious sites have been identified and excavated all over the country.

Dimensions of Archaeological Research in the Third World: Examples from Modern India

In any global survey of the history of archaeological research it would be invidious not to draw a distinction between the contexts of this research in the First and Third Worlds. Archaeological literature unconsciously hides this distinction because, generally speaking, data from the Third World are discussed primarily on the basis of the work done in those areas by experts from the First World and published in First World languages. However well meaning such archaeologists and their publications are, they have taken upon themselves the task of interpreting the past heritage of a very large number of people who belong to various nation states and who may themselves like to interpret their own past. No understanding of the context of archaeological research in India can be meaningful unless it is put firmly in the context of the broader framework of archaeological research in the Third World done by Third World archaeologists themselves. If Third World archaeology is to go anywhere, it must first learn how not to imitate the fashions and jargons of First World archaeology, with which, for various historical reasons, it cannot cope satisfactorily anyway. It has to pose problems that are meaningful and necessary in its own contexts and that can be pursued and solved by its own resources. To begin with, it has to be vigorously empirical and at least try to reach a position in which the basic questions regarding the past of the nation concerned can be answered in a way that will be understood by most of the population.

One of the unifying features of Third World archaeology is that there is far less money to spend on conservation and archaeological research. This paucity of money is glaringly manifest in the general absence of scientific analytical facilities in Third World archaeological and museum setups. As for India, there are only two radiocarbon laboratories in such a large and archaeologically rich country, and none of these laboratories are concerned only with archaeological samples. There is only one laboratory for thermoluminescent dating, and its impact is still marginal. Dendrochronology is an area where no research has been done. There has been no attempt to undertake radiometric datings on an organized basis. Electron Spin Resonance dating has been done in only one case. The metallography of ancient artifacts is a rarity and hundreds of old mineshafts are untouched. Only two laboratories undertake the identification of ancient plant remains. The identification of ancient animal bones has not made much headway. The term *geoarchaeology* is known but it has been unable to solve a single cardinal problem associated with Indian prehistory. The application of GEOGRAPHICAL INFORMATION SYSTEM technology is unknown, as is the application of various computer techniques. Appreciative noises have been made from time to time about "anthropological archaeology" or "new archaeology" (Paddayya 1990), but until there is a wide scientific base, Indian archaeology is unlikely to overcome its present, essentially history-oriented, limitations. To some extent the current situation is related to the paucity of funds to build up a proper infrastructure for such scientific investigations, but to a greater extent this is due to the lack of a correct perspective regarding the role archaeology can play in historical knowledge about the country.

Another major unifying feature of Third World archaeology is the place of archaeology in a nation's educational structure, and here also the Indian example may be instructive. In India, although archaeology is offered in the postgraduate programs of about 20 to 25 of her 180-odd universities and university-status institutions, it is offered as an adjunct of ancient Indian history, and that too without any undergraduate component. The absence of archaeology in the undergraduate teaching program, even as an adjunct of general historical studies, severely curtails both its educational scope and the job opportunities for those who specialize in it. By no

stretch of the imagination can archaeology be considered a part of mainstream Indian education, and until that is achieved it is futile to expect a rich intellectual contribution from it.

The third unifying feature of Third World archaeology is the deep-rooted neocolonialism of the historical educational system of most of these countries, India providing a classic example. India has a secure and widespread base of education, so why is archaeology not incorporated into the mainstream? There are two answers. First, Indian historical education, of which archaeology is a small and insignificant part, is basically neocolonial, concerned more with the study of history linked in various direct and indirect ways to Euro-America than with anything related to the grassroots level. This system of historical education dates from the colonial period but this is also something that the native inheritors of the colonial system have left unchanged for various selfish reasons, the most important of which is to perpetuate their own control over the vast, numerically overwhelming illiterate and semiliterate population. Another major reason is that this intellectually dominant class is eager to have access to the international network of fellowships, seminars, etc. Secondly, neocolonialism and the lack of archaeology in the mainstream are conditioned by the Indian notion of the past, which is all literary and peopled by various "races," among whom the image of the virile blue-eyed Aryans looms inordinately large. This model of the Indian past was foisted on India via hegemonic textbooks written by Western Indologists concerned with language, literature, and philosophy who were paternalistic at their best and racist at their worst. This image was also accepted by the Indian collaborating elite and freedom-fighters alike because they were beguiled into believing that some of them shared the same racial ancestry as their rulers and that those who were privileged to share this ancestry also stood racially aloof from the downtrodden non-Aryan autochthones at the lower end of the caste hierarchy. The study of Indian history with the Indian land as its main focus formed no part of this perception. In different forms this must be the general character of historical perception in the Third World as a whole. As long as this perception persists, archaeology is unlikely to join the mainstream of Indian education.

This brings us to another little-noticed but nonetheless major unifying feature of Third World archaeology. The results of archaeological research are published almost invariably in one of the dominant languages of the colonial period and are thus disassociated, right from the beginning, from a very large part of the nation as a whole. In India, for instance, it is doubtful if more than 2 percent of the population is familiar with English, but it is in English that almost the entire archaeological literature of India is written and whatever gets written in the major regional languages remains outside the mainstream of this literature. This simple fact puts archaeology beyond the horizon of about 98 percent of the Indian population, with the result that the tradition of conducting investigations and getting things reported first on the local level has never caught on. From this point of view, Bangladesh and Nepal are the only South Asian countries that have a substantial amount of primary archaeological literature in their own languages, Bengali and Nepali respectively.

Dilip Chakrabarti

References and Further Reading

Agrawal, D. P. 1992. *Man and Environment in India through Ages: An Interdisciplinary Study of the Indian Quarternary with Focus on North-West.* Delhi: Books & Books.

Allchin, F. R. 1961. "Ideas of History in Indian Archaeological Writing: A Preliminary Study." In *Historians of India, Pakistan and Ceylon.* Edited by C. H. Philips. London: Oxford University Press.

Burgess, J. 1905. "Sketch of Archaeological Research in India during Half-a-Century." *Journal of the Bombay Branch of the Royal Asiatic Society* (Centenary Memorial Volume): 131–188.

Burnes, A. 1833. "On the Topes and Grecian Remains in the Panjab." *Journal of the Asiatic Society of Bengal* 2: 308–310.

Chakrabarti, D. K. 1976. "India and the Druids." *Antiquity* 50: 66–67.

———. 1988a. *A History of Indian Archaeology from the Beginning to 1947.* New Delhi: Munshiram Manoharlal Publishers.

———. 1988b. *Theoretical Issues in Indian Archaeol-ogy.* New Delhi: Munshiram Manoharlal Publishers.

———. 1993. *Archaeology of Eastern India: Chhotanagpur Plateau and West Bengal.* New Delhi: Munshiram Manoharlal Publishers.

Cunningham, A. 1843. "An Account of the Discovery of the Ruins of the Buddhist City of Samkassa." *Journal of the Royal Asiatic Society* 7: 240–249.

Ghosh, A. 1953. "Fifty Years of the Archaeological Survey of India." *Ancient India* 9: 29–52.

Imam, A. 1966. *Sir Alexander Cunningham and the Beginnings of Indian Archaeology.* Dhaka: Asiatic Society of Pakistan.

Jones, W. 1788. "The Third Anniversary Discourse." *Asiatic Researches* 1: 415–431.

Joshi, J. P., M. Bala, and J. Ram. 1984. "The Indus Civilization Reconsideration on the Basis of Distribution Maps." In *Frontiers of the Indus Civilization.* Edited by B. B. Lal and S. P. Gupta. New Delhi: Published by Books & Books on behalf of Indian Archaeological Society jointly with Indian History & Culture Society.

Marshall, J. ed. 1951. *Taxila.* Cambridge: Cambridge University Press.

Mirsky, J. 1977. *Sir Aurel Stein: Archaeological Explorer.* Chicago: University of Chicago Press.

Misra, V. N. 1989. "Stone Age India: An Ecological Perspective." *Man and Environment* 14: 17–64.

Mitra, D. 1971. *Excavation at Tilaura Kot and Kodan and Exploration in the Nepalese Terai.* Kathmandu.

Mitra, P. 1923. *Prehistoric India: Its Place in the World's Cultures.* Calcutta: Calcutta University.

Mitter, P. 1977. *Much Maligned Monsters: History of European Reactions to Indian Art.* Oxford: Clarendon Press.

Murty, M. L. K. 1985. "Ethnoarchaeology of the Kurnool Cave Areas, South India." *World Archaeology* 17: 192–205.

Nagar, M, and V. N. Misra. 1989. "Hunter-Gatherers in an Agrarian Setting: The Nineteenth Century Situation in the Ganga Plains." *Man and Environment* 13: 65–78.

Paddayya, K. 1978. "New Research Designs and Field-Techniques in the Palaeolithic Archaeology of India." *World Archaeology* 10: 94–110.

———. 1990. *The New Archaeology and Its Aftermath: A View from Outside the Anglo-American World.* Pune: Ravish Publishers.

Possehl, G. L. 1990. "An Archaeological Adventurer in Afghanistan: Charles Masson." *South Asian Studies* 6: 111–124.

Prinsep, J. 1838. "On the Edicts of Piyadasi or

Asoka." *Journal of the Asiatic Society of Bengal* 7: 219–282

Rijal, B. K. 1979. *Archaeological Remains of Kapilavastu, Lumbini and Devadaha*. Kathmandu: Educational Enterprises.

Roy, S. 1953. "Indian Archaeology from Jones to Marshall (1784–1902)." *Ancient India* 9: 4–28.

———. 1961. *The Story of Indian Archaeology*. New Delhi: Archaelogical Survey of India.

Sankalia, H. D. 1974. *Prehistory and Protohistory in India and Pakistan*. Poona: Deccan College, Postgraduate and Research Institute.

Slusser, M. S. 1982. *Nepal Mandala, a Cultural Study of the Kathmandu Valley*. Princeton, NJ: Princeton University Press.

Taylor, M. 1851. "Ancient Remains at the Village of Jiwarji near Ferozabad on the Bhima." *Journal of the Bombay Branch of the Royal Asiatic Society* 2: 179–196.

Waddel, L. A. 1903. *Report on the Excavations at Pataliputra*. Calcutta: Bengal Secretariat Press.

Spain

The development of archaeology in the territory of the Spanish state has been marked by the long history (beginning in the fifteenth century) of that state's unity and by the discipline's strong dependence on state institutions. The latter factor enables us to link the general situation in Spain to the trajectory of archaeological practice in its various historical subdivisions (prehistoric, proto-historic, classical, medieval, American, Oriental). Thus, the history of Spanish archaeology can contribute to the debate on scientific neutrality by demonstrating the interdependence between science and society in a particular case.

The intellectual currents that marked Spanish archaeology's development are analogous to those in other European countries (Suarez Otero 1993, 331): (1) the antiquarianism and learning that largely inspired classical archaeology from the Renaissance to the nineteenth century; (2) the enlightened concern, linked with the natural sciences, with the antiquity of humanity and its early cultures that led to the origin of prehistoric archaeology in the last third of the nineteenth century, and (3) the ideologically motivated search for, and celebration of, national identity (Gilman 1988, 47–50) that influ-

enced all archaeological practice—more specifically, medieval (Salvatierra 1990, 71–72) and proto-historic (Ruiz Zapatero 1993a, 40)—as well as Spanish archaeological research abroad. In all these instances, the goals of research shift from the universal to the particular.

Preliminaries: Antiquarianism from the Fifteenth to the Eighteenth Centuries

During the classical period and throughout the Middle Ages, there were treasures (war booty, votive offerings) but no collections (Barril 1993, 39–42), but in the fifteenth century, collections acquired a scientific and educational value linked to humanism. The Greek and Roman world, natural wonders, and objects brought from the New World were at the center of attention. In Spain, a prominent collector was Cardinal Mendoza, counselor to the Catholic kings.

In the sixteenth century, Charles I and Philip II encouraged collecting, so the duke of Villahermosa wrote a treatise on Roman religion based on Roman antiquities, and other courtiers opened their collections to scholars such as Lucio Marinero Siculo, Ambrosio de Morales, and Antonio Agustín (sometimes dubbed the "first Spanish archaeologists"). In the seventeenth century, connections with foreign scientific circles to exchange, borrow, and acquire pieces became very important.

Those are the roots of eighteenth-century collecting. The monarchy and the enlightened aristocracy used archaeology to legitimize and give prestige to their power, to justify reforms (Mora 1991, 31), and to display and reinforce Spain's foreign image, which had been brought into question by other European powers.

This archaeology consisted of branches of classical erudition (epigraphy, numismatics, iconography, topography, mythology) that were secondary to literary sources. The monarchy created *gabinetes de antigüedades y de historia natural* ("cabinets of antiquities and natural history," which included archaeological remains), libraries, and academies. It financed archaeological excavations, scientific expeditions (Malaespina in 1789), and "literary journeys" inside the country itself. In addition, it gave legal protection to the country's antiquities. Some of these initiatives were in response to European educational thinking (Barril 1993, 44); others, to specific subjects, such as the study of the situation in the colonies or the defense of royal rights against the papacy (Mora 1991, 31).

The most prominent institutions were the private Sociedades de Amigos del País (Societies of Friends of the Country) and, among the public ones, the Real Academia de la Historia (Royal Academy of History, founded in 1738) the Real Academia de Bellas Artes de San Fernando (Royal Academy of Fine Arts of San Fernando, 1752), the Librería Publica (Public Library, 1716, the forerunner of la Biblioteca Nacional [National Library], which was founded in the nineteenth century), and the Gabinete de Historia Natural (Cabinet of Natural History, 1773), whose collections constitute the original nucleus of the present Museo Arqueológico Nacional, Museo Etnológico y Museo de America (National Museums of Archaeology, Ethnology, and the Americas).

The documentation and material preservation of archaeological monuments and finds were one of this period's great advances (Barril 1993, 45). Archaeological excavations were carried out to enlarge collections and to identify those ancient cities (Munda, Numantia, Segobriga, Saguntum) that had once contributed to the glory of the nation. In a sense, the appreciation of these ruins more for their aesthetic and picturesque than for their historical value prevented studies as broad as those that Charles III, as king of Naples, had sponsored at POMPEII, HERCULANEUM, and Stabia (Fernandez 1988, 384; Mora 1991, 32).

Beginnings of Scientific Archaeology

In the nineteenth century, archaeological research was carried out against a social background of civil and colonial wars and sharp conflict over the organization of the state. And it was carried out not by public sponsors, but by private initiatives. These initiatives, in the political and intellectual context of the times, were increasingly centered on local and national concerns. At the same time, isolation was broken by reading, contact with foreign researchers (Gran-

Aymerich and Gran-Aymerich 1991), participation in international congresses (Ayarzaguena 1991, 69), and universal expositions (Barril 1993, 50). Basic to this broadening of outlook was the establishment of the Institución Libre de Enseñanza by Francisco Giner de los Rios in 1876 (Moure 1993, 206–207), which had the patriotic goal of understanding and renewing Spain. Against Catholic conservatism, it represented a secular and innovative attitude and sought to renew Spanish secondary and university education by encouraging studies abroad and receptivity to French, British, and German pedagogical approaches (Jutglar 1971, 148–153).

Scholarly and scientific societies (numismatic, archaeological, and so on) began to be established early in the nineteenth century, and their publications, generally local, played a fundamental role in the popular and scientific spread of culture and education. Some demanded the protection and recovery of ancient monuments (Salvatierra 1990, 22); others participated in debates on evolution and prehistoric archaeology, topics censored until the Revolutionary Sexennium, a revolutionary period between 1868 and 1874 (Ayarzaguena 1991, 69). These initiatives, and those of booksellers, maintained the interest in knowledge of the past. The state sought to centralize that interest through institutions that would define a historic heritage common to the whole national territory: royal academies, museums, and (after 1900) universities, whose activities had hitherto been unimportant in the development of archaeology in Spain (Cortadella I Morral 1991, 161; Pasamar and Peiró 1991, 73).

The cabinets and royal academies were converted into public museums with ever more specialized collections. As a result of their participation in the *juntas cientifico-artisticas* ("scientific-artistic councils") and the *comisiones de monumentos provinciales y central* ("provincial and central monuments commissions") established to recover ecclesiastical properties after the disentailments decreed between 1835 and 1843 (Barril 1993, 47), the royal academies widened their work of protecting and collecting the cultural heritage. The Academy of History likewise devoted its efforts to the promotion of archaeological research and to the political and administrative needs of the liberal state. Thus, it encouraged the foundation of the Escuela Superior de Diplomatica (Higher School of Diplomacy, 1856–1900) for the technical training of historians, including the most important figures of the scholarly societies (Pasamar and Peiró 1991, 73). Interest in the recovery and preservation of antiquities, and in the organization of that heritage was also expressed in the foundation of the National Museum of Archaeology and of the *museos arqueológicos provinciales* ("provincial archaeological museums") in 1867 (Barril 1993, 48).

Collecting, which was encouraged because items acquired were considered investments (Barril 1993, 55–58), provided another link between private initiative and the state. Some collectors were members of the haute bourgeoisie (sometimes ennobled, like the marquis of Salamanca), but others were representatives of the middle class who were influential politically or intellectually (JUAN VILANOVA Y PIERA, for example). Scientifically motivated, they studied the ancient inhabitants of the Iberian Peninsula in the light of new information obtained in the rest of Europe, and the attention paid to Spanish evidence by some foreign scholars played a part in this study. Thus, from FRANCE, archaeologists ÉDOUARD LARTET and EMILE CARTAILHAC studied prehistory, Colonel Stoffel worked on the Roman period, and the German E. Hubner studied Latin epigraphy (Gran-Aymerich and Gran-Aymerich 1991). At the same time, some Spaniards (for instance, the marquis of Cerralbo) and foreign residents of Spain (such as Henri and Louis Siret, O. Sandars, and George Bonsor) financed their own excavations and carried out studies of their finds, subsequently giving or selling their data and finds to the state. These people were archaeologists more than collectors. A third group comprised local scholars. In other cases, the archaeological activities of foreign scholars in Spain (such as Pierre Paris and A. Engel, at the start of their careers) consisted of isolated travels to collect pieces and to know and popularize Spanish art (Marcos 1993, 80).

In the first third of the twentieth century, archaeological activity became structured legally, academically, and scientifically (Ruiz Zapatero

Painted limestone bust of the "Lady of Elche," from La Alcudia de Elche, fifth century B.C. (Image Select)

1993b, 47). The protective legislation (Ley de Excavaciones y Antiguedades [Law of Excavations and Antiquities] of 1911; Ley de Patrimonio Historico-Artistico [Law of the Historical and Artistic Heritage] of 1933) and administrative agencies (Junta Superior de Excavaciones y Antiguedades [Higher Board for Excavations and Antiquities], established in 1912, and its *actas* and *memorias*) that were instituted in this period have served as a reference point until the present (Barril 1993, 57).

In 1900, the Universidad Central (Central University) in Madrid received the responsibilities and resources of the Higher School of Diplomacy (Marcos 1993, 75). Three chairs in archaeology were established: Arabic archaeology (1912) for Manuel Gomez Moreno, primitive history of mankind (1922) for HUGO OBERMAIER GRAD, and pre-Columbian archaeology and American ethnography (1933) for Hermann Trimborn. At other universities, archaeological instruction was not separate from other branches of history, and professors of the discipline only joined their faculties later on, although Pere Bosch Gimpera's 1916 chair at the

University of Barcelona was an exception (Pasamar and Peiró 1991, 75).

Research became institutionalized at the national, regional, and local levels and, for a brief time, abroad. The Junta para la Ampliación de Estudios e Investigaciones Científicas (Board for the Expansion of Study and Scientific Research, 1907) had among its missions the establishment of scientific exchanges abroad. It created the Escuela Española de Historia y Arqueología en Roma (Spanish School in Rome for History and Archaeology, 1910), which did not outlast World War I, and sections on Spanish archaeology both within the Centro de Estudios Históricos (Center for Historical Studies, 1910) and the Comisión de Investigaciones Paleontológicas y Prehistoricas (Commission for Paleontological and Prehistoric Research, 1912). The commission had prestigious members (the marquis of Cerralbo, the count of la Vega del Sella, Juan Cabre, Eduardo Hernandez Pacheco, Hugo Obermaier Grad, Paul Wernert) and collaborators (Pere Bosch Gimpera, Hubert Schmidt, HENRI BREUIL) and carried out a vast program of systematic research and publication. Its foundation was encouraged by research in the region of Cantabria financed by Prince Albert I of Monaco.

The Servei d'Investigacions Arqueologiques (Archaeological Investigation Service, 1915) of the Institut d'Estudis Catalans (Institute for Catalan Studies, 1907) was established as part of the program of cultural modernization advocated by the Catalan bourgeoisie first through the Mancomunitat and later through the Generalitat (Cebria, Muro, and Riu 1991, 83; Dupre and Rafels 1991, 175). As in the case of analogous services established by provinces (Valencia and Sevilla) and cities (such as Madrid), the service represented the culmination of a process started the century before by local scholars and naturalists.

French research in Spain also became institutionalized. On Pierre Paris's initiative, the Escuela Francesa de Arte y Arqueología (French School of Art and Archaeology), or Casa de Velazquez, was established in Madrid in 1928 (Gran-Aymerich and Gran-Aymerich 1991, 117). In turn, German archaeology's great influence in Spain arose as the result of training that important Spanish archaeologists received in Germany and of work in Spain by scholars such as Georg and Vera Leisner on megaliths; Adolph Schulten on proto-history; Hans Zeiss on funerary archaeology of the Visigothic period; and Helmut Schlunk, who later became the first director of the Madrid branch of the DEUTSCHES ARCHÄOLOGISCHES INSTITUT (German Archaeological Institute), on late Roman and early medieval art and archaeology (Grunhagen 1979; Marcos 1993, 80).

As this period closed, only prehistory had succeeded in freeing itself from a philological and art-history perspective (Arce 1991, 209; Pasamar and Peiró 1991, 75; Rosello-Bordoy 1986, 8–9), which it had managed to do because of its empirical orientation and the national and international importance of discoveries in the Cantabrian region—ALTAMIRA by Marcelino Sanz de Sautuola in 1879—and the southeastern part of the peninsula—Los Millares, El Argar, and Villaricos by Louis Siret (Moure 1993, 207–210). In general, field archaeology did not involve stratigraphic controls or a detailed register of data, but enough evidence was available to permit Bosch Gimpera to create the first great federalist synthesis of pre- and proto-history, *Etnología de la Península Iberica,* in 1932 (Ruiz Rodriguez 1993, 308; Ruiz Zapatero 1993b, 47–48).

Meanwhile, classical and medieval archaeologists were concerned not so much with research as with the restoration of cities, ecclesiastical buildings, and large Islamic architectural complexes (Salvatierra 1990, 40–49). All of this initial structuring of Spanish archaeology was truncated by the Civil War of 1936–1939.

Institutionalization of the 1950s and 1960s
The Franco regime suppressed centers of debate and institutions of regional self-government but maintained other organizations (the network of provincial museums, universities) once their memberships had been purged. Academic institutions were particularly affected; for example, Pere Bosch Gimpera and Jose Miguel de Barandiaran were exiled, and Leopoldo Torres Balbas was compelled to retire. In other instances, such as Martin Almagro Basch's

becoming director of the Archaeological Museum of Barcelona or the creation of the Museum of the Americas in 1941 (which was provisionally placed in the National Archaeological Museum), the ideological content of an institution changed to serve the new political order (Cabello 1989, 49–50; Dupre and Rafels 1991, 175). The internal situation and the international context led some foreign researchers to leave the country, but strong ties with German research were maintained (Diaz Andreu 1993, 75).

New institutions were established immediately, proof of the new regime's interest in controlling culture. The earlier Board for the Expansion of Study was replaced by the Consejo Superior de Investigaciones Científicas (Higher Council for Scientific Research), and the Comisaría General de Excavaciones Arqueológicas (General Commissariat for Archaeological Excavations) replaced the Higher Board for Excavations and assumed state direction of archaeological policy through a new network of provincial, insular, and local commissions. The series Informes y Memorias (1942–1956) and Noticiario Arqueológico Hispanico (1953–1988) published the results of their commissioned work. At the same time, some provinces continued or founded their own services for prehistoric research.

The first volume of the *Historia de España* (1947), edited by Ramon Menendez Pidal, demonstrates the level of the new archaeological regime. Except for Martin Almagro Basch and Juan Maluquer de Motes, the work's authors had professional reputations that were established in the previous period (Eduardo Hernandez Pacheco, Luis de Hoyos Sainz, Alberto del Castillo, Juan de la Mata Carriazo, Antonio Garcia Bellido, Blas Taracena, and Julio Caro Baroja).

There was, however, an essential continuity in method and theory in archaeology before and after the Civil War. The goal was a system of classification that would permit the identification of ethnic-cultural entities and the reconstruction of their historical trajectories (Vicent 1994, 216–217). The French tradition was predominant in Paleolithic studies while the German tradition was paradigmatic in later prehis-

toric (ethnic interpretation) and classical archaeology (art-history perspective). Beginning in the 1950s, a new technocratic policy led to the opening up of the country toward the world and toward economic expansion (Spain-U.S. treaty in 1953; a stabilization program in 1959; tourism and emigration); and more interest was shown in archaeology, conservation, and restoration in Spain and abroad.

In 1947, Spain's only permanent research center abroad, the Spanish School for History and Archaeology in Rome, was established for a second time. It was attached to the Higher Council for Scientific Research and renewed its work in 1951 (Arce and Barrondo 1994, 5). In 1954, the Spanish section of the Instituto Arqueológico Alemán (German Archaeological Institute) in Madrid was established on a permanent basis (Grunhagen 1979, 143). Its excavations at later prehistoric, proto-historic, classical, and early Christian sites involved Spanish students and would prove to be fundamental in the modernization of archaeological field techniques. The international and multidisciplinary collaboration that was traditional in Paleolithic research was renewed in Cantabria and in Mediterranean Spain, with participation from the United States in the latter area (Maluquer de Motes 1958).

Archaeology was to be carried out by universities and the new centers of research. Throughout the country new professorships were founded in archaeology, epigraphy, numismatics, and prehistory, and the inclusion of prehistory as a required course in degree programs in philosophy and letters (1955) was a key step in the process. The publication of journals by university departments contributed to the consolidation.

In another direction, thanks to the reorganization of the academic world, prehistory occupied a position in the human sciences similar to that of other historical stages (Moure 1993, 216). In contrast, medieval archaeology was only a marginal part of university history programs that neglected Arabist studies and material culture and continued only because of the work of museum curators (Rosello-Bordoy 1986, 9–10).

The Higher Council for Scientific Research came to incorporate the Instituto Español de

Prehistória (Institute of Spanish Prehistory, 1958) and the Instituto Rodrigo Caro (Rodrigo Caro Institute, 1951) of classical archaeology, directed by Martin Almagro Basch and Antonio Garclia Bellido, respectively. These are still the only institutions of the central government specifically dedicated to archaeological research, and their journals, *Trabajos de Prehistória* and *Archivo Español de Arqueología,* have become among the most important in their respective specialties. As this period ended, Spain had a centralized administrative infrastructure responsible for the growing number of sites of all periods throughout its territory, and meetings of specialists and numerous publications made known the state of research. Antonio Beltran organized the Archaeological Congresses of Southeast Spain, which began in 1946, became national congresses in 1949, and have met biennially since then. In turn, the less regularly scheduled Symposia for Peninsular Archaeology established by Juan Maluquer de Motes in 1959 have served as important points of reference.

Academic Expansion and the "Science of Archaeology" in the 1960s and 1970s

Spain's general development in the 1960s and 1970s had very positive consequences for archaeology, such as the expansion of university education as the first members of the baby boom of the 1950s and 1960s came of age and an increase in funding both for university personnel and for archaeological field and laboratory research. In contrast, theoretical and methodological debate was tardy and scanty, and the centralization of archaeological policy, tied to the interests of an elitist academic community, limited the discipline's social impact.

During this period, Spanish archaeological missions were sent to Central and South America (Anonymous 1987) and to the Sudan, Egypt, JORDAN, and Syria (Perez Die 1983). The importance of universities to Spanish archaeology was reinforced by the general increase in the number of students and professors and, toward the end of the period, by the creation of specialized degree programs in prehistory or prehistory and archaeology in the larger universities (Ruiz Zapatero 1993b, 51). Museums were revitalized formally

and functionally as exhibits were remodeled and outreach programs were expanded. Martin Almagro Basch's directorship (1968–1981) of the National Museum of Archaeology exemplifies this pattern (Marcos 1993, 95). A very important monographic series, Excavaciones Arqueológicas en España, began to be published by the central government in 1962, and various university and museum journals appeared.

A strongly positivist research orientation characterized the first decade of this period, but at the end of the second, this orientation began to be questioned by a minority group of newly appointed university professors in Barcelona, Jaen, and Madrid. Fieldwork improved, with a better appreciation of stratigraphy and more detailed recording becoming prevalent. Prehistoric research increasingly (but other branches of archaeology only rarely) involved collaboration with the natural sciences. Meetings on scientific archaeology held in the late 1970s promoted the formation of the incipient Spanish infrastructure in this area (Chapa 1988, 137). In general, the role of biologists and archaeologists from Germany (M. Hopf, J. Boessneck, A. von der Driesch, E. Sangmeister, H. Schubart, W. Schule, W. Grunhagen, K. Raddatz, W. Hubener, T. Hauschild, H. Schlunk, T. Ulbert, Ch. Ewert) and France (Arlette and ANDRÉ LEROI-GOURHAN, FRANÇOIS BORDES, C. Domergue) was decisive in these developments, as was North American research on the Paleolithic period (C. Howell, K. Butzer, and L. G. Freeman at Torralba, Ambrona, and Cueva Morin) (Moure 1993, 217).

Throughout this period, Spanish archaeology was centered on the prehistoric and classical periods, and medieval archaeology was included in the National Archaeological Congresses only from 1971 on (Rossello-Bordoy 1986, 8). Americanist archaeological research developed completely independently from Old World archaeology, as the Museum of the Americas, with its own premises (subject to long closures) as of 1965 (Cabello 1989, 51–52), did not encourage a convergence.

At the end of the 1970s, several factors led to a reconsideration of the disciplinary tradition and laid the groundwork for future debate. The editorial work of the members of the Departamento de Antropología y Etnología Americanas (Department of American Anthropology and Ethnology) of the Complutense University of Madrid resulted in the publication of contributions on archaeological epistemology and European pre- and proto-history by LEWIS BINFORD, C. Renfrew, and DAVID CLARKE, and a new generation of archaeologists became aware of the enormous disproportion between the technical means of the discipline and the historical knowledge it had attained. At the same time, the increasing amount of radiocarbon DATING demonstrated the inconsistencies of traditional archaeological chronologies and weakened the authority of the theoretical approaches they embodied (Vicent 1994, 219). Finally, the greater intellectual freedom resulting from the new political situation—the end of the Franco regime and the transition to democratic government, the great increase in the number of university students and professors, and the generational turnover among the latter—favored the development of attitudes critical toward academic authority, which was generally elitist and conservative (Riu 1992, 10; Vicent 1994, 220).

Decentralization and Popularizing of Archaeology in the 1980s and 1990s

The restoration of democracy and the approval of the new constitution of 1978 led to the decentralization of the state. From 1979 on, responsibility for archaeological policy began to be transferred to the seventeen autonomous communities into which Spain was divided. The important Ley de Patrimonio Histórico Español (Law on Spanish Historical Heritage, 1985) responded to this new political reality and established the framework for the archaeological legislation of the autonomous governments (Garcia Fernandez 1989). This process coincided with the high points of the country's liberalization: joining the Common Market in 1985 and joining the North Atlantic Treaty Organization in 1986.

The new organization of the state had a pervasive effect on archaeological activity. It produced large differences in regional policies with respect to the legal and administrative frameworks for archaeology, the available infrastruc-

ture, and the degree of governmental intervention. Generally, the management, protection, and conservation of archaeological heritage, such as surveys, mapping, cataloging and restoration projects, and emergency excavations (Jimeno, Recio, and Moreno 1993; *Jornadas* 1991), particularly in urban areas (*Arqueología* 1985; *Primeras jornadas de arqueología* 1983), have taken precedence over research as such (long-term excavations, analyses, dating, publications). Public financing has increased but has focused on the management of archaeology, with the new "contract" archaeologist being responsible for its execution (Querol et al. 1994).

At the same time, the academic world has lost its previous position of almost exclusive dominance, precisely at the time when the increasing specialization of archaeology by historical periods, research projects, and theoretical and methodological outlooks has diversified and increased archaeological activities and their financial cost. A solution to this paradox has been sought through increased participation by research centers and, above all, universities; in projects funded by regional governments; and by an increased appeal to private or other public patronage (bodies responsible for landscape planning and public works).

The teaching of prehistory and classical archaeology still receives most funding, and the two fields had 145 and 62 permanent professors, respectively, by the mid 1990s. The greater influence of prehistory is owing to its role in the discipline's methodological renewal. American and Oriental archaeology have not seen their limited presence in universities compensated for by the possible impact of archaeological expeditions abroad. Those expeditions are either sporadic and strongly dependent on Spanish foreign policy or are organized by the National Museum of Archaeology (Perez Die 1993), which (given the current trend toward decentralization) does not have the administrative structure and the resources required to achieve an impact.

Medieval archaeology has become increasingly important in terms of practice, but its academic presence continues to be small. The increased importance of urban archaeology has led to its scientific consolidation, an association

An ancient aqueduct in Segovia (Corel)

of medieval archaeologists was founded in 1981, and the first national meeting on the subject was held in 1985. The traditional focus on architecture and art history has begun to be replaced by interest in urban and rural settlement patterns, in large part because of the work of A. Bazzana and P. Guichard of the Casa de Velazquez (Barcelo 1992, 245; Matesanz 1991; Rosello-Bordoy 1986, 12).

Present archaeological activity is characterized by varied, and sometimes coordinated, lines of research (*Primeras jornadas de metodología* 1984; Vicent 1993; Vila 1991). These include:

1. theoretical and methodological studies from culture-historical, functionalist, Marxist, and structuralist perspectives (Alcina 1991; Ruiz Rodriguez 1993; Vazquez and Risch 1991; Vicent 1994).
2. studies of ecology and economy based on faunal and paleobotanical analyses as well as sedimentology in the case of older sites (Moure 1992).
3. studies of settlement patterns, first from a functionalist "spatial" perspective (Arque-

ología 1984) and then from critical landscape perspectives based on structuralism (Criado, Rodriquez, and Viqueira 1986) or Marxism (Vicent 1991). The driving forces in this area have been specific research carried out by A. Gilman and J. B. Thornes (1985), the role of surveys as the principal means to carry out the archaeological policies of regional governments, and the incipient use of geographical information systems and remote sensing.
4. social archaeological studies based primarily on mortuary studies (Chapa 1991) and settlement patterns (Arqueología 1984).
5. studies of production and exchange based upon material analyses of ceramics, metals, and lithics (Bustillo and Ramos Millan 1991) and, to a lesser extent, experimental, use wear, and ethnoarchaeological research.
6. underwater archaeology (Martinez 1992).

No Spanish research center has the means to carry out all those lines of investigation, and resources are unequally divided. The principal victim of this situation is ARCHAEOMETRY, which is faced with unequal and unfair competition for access to laboratories with research in engineering and other scientific disciplines more favored by governmental priorities. Foreign collaboration in part mitigates this problem. The whole of Spain has one thermoluminescence and three radiocarbon-dating laboratories, eleven teams working on paleobotany (mainly palynology), seven working on paleontology, and two devoted to archaeometallurgy. The majority of these specialists and specialist laboratories were established in order to serve regional research favored by the ongoing administrative decentralization.

The Future of Spanish Archaeology: The Challenge of Decentralization

Archaeology was an element in all of the nationalist claims to legitimacy made in Spain from 1800 to 1936. As in other European countries, the *españolista* ("Hispanicizing," a term used to refer to an identification between what is Spanish and what is Castilian, in the broad sense of claiming a single historical tradition for all the peoples of Spain) oligarchy and the various regional elites (especially in the Basque country and Catalonia) traced their national roots at least to the peoples that resisted the Roman conquest (Ruiz Zapatero 1993a). This archaeologically justified nationalism was reflected in the literature (Olmos 1992a) and in the plastic arts. Modern events presented in ancient guise were combined with direct allusions to events in antiquity so as to glorify either Hispanic or regional individuality.

Archaeological cultures were used quite differently in the construction of each national identity. Thus, the Vascones would have avoided a Roman occupation of the Basque country, creating a clear break between that region and the rest of the peninsula, as it had been completely Romanized (Dupla and Emborujo 1991). This notion could be combined with a claim for the homogeneity and continuity of the Basque people from the Paleolithic period on (Diaz Andreu 1993, 79; Rua 1990, 207–209). For its part, Spanish Hispanicist nationalism appealed to antiquity to reinforce ideas such as independence, liberty, and heroism and to the Middle Ages and the Renaissance to promote key concepts such as unity, religion, and monarchy (Quesada

1994, 39), in line with traditionalist historical thinking. This defense of the essential continuity of the Spanish as defined by Catholicism established a trajectory from the late empire to the Catholic kings and the Habsburg empire by way of the Christian "reconquest" of the peninsula from the Arabs by the fifteenth century (Salvatierra 1990, 72–73). Meanwhile, Catalans emphasized their Greek roots, using Ampurias as an emblem (Guitart and Riu 1989, 28).

The governments of the Second Republic (1931–1936) were attuned to decentralizing, federalist political goals and assisted in the institutionalization of nationalist (regionalist) archaeologies, the most successful program being the Catalan Generalitat's (Dupre and Rafels 1991, 175). The Franco uprising put a violent end to this process, and the regime that emerged from the Civil War was characterized by a centralism and Hispanicism (Diaz Andreu 1993) that disappeared only after the restoration of democracy in 1975. During the 1940s and 1950s, all the nineteenth-century historical clichés were revived, illustrated, and incorporated in the textbooks (Prieto 1979; Valls 1993), and all other nationalist (regionalist) manipulations of the archaeological record were prohibited. In the years of nationalist Hispanicist self-assertion, the Iberian Iron Age was repeatedly interpreted as a precedent for leadership by a caudillo and as the origin of essential Spanish traits that were still part of the folklore and supposed national character (Olmos 1992b, 10–12). This ideological policy was most important in the years immediately after World War II when the Franco regime was internationally isolated and striving for self-sufficiency. In the later Franco years, Spanish archaeology gave greater emphasis to technical issues.

The present regionalization of archaeology has not led to a direct return to the process of inventing regionalist traditions interrupted by the Civil War. Other factors are more important, although the lack of specific studies on the most recent period could occasionally leave any interpretation open to question. On the one hand, interest in the social history of Spanish archaeology is still in its infancy and mostly oriented toward the early periods of the discipline's development. On the other hand, potential indicators of nationalist (regionalist) sentiments, such as the areas and periods studied in the various autonomous communities, do not exhibit clear patterns, are isolated, and/or are contradictory. Thus, the denounced historical biases (Gonzalez 1992, 25) or straightforward nationalist (regionalist) interpretations presented to the public (via temporary exhibits, museum posters, and popularizing publications) disappear or are diluted in academic presentations (Altuna 1990a, 1990b).

One must bear in mind that archaeology in Spain has become a regional science in two ways. It involves, of course, fundamentally descriptive and classificatory historical investigations, and its practice (excavations, surveys, study of museum collections) requires permission from the appropriate cultural authorities. Such permits, accompanied or not by public financing, are granted by each autonomous community (exceptions are the Basque country and the Balearic and Canary Islands). At the same time, practically all academic institutions have their base in the autonomous communities, and their archaeological research has tended to adjust itself to these divisions in order to simplify bureaucratic transactions, since almost all research funding is granted by the communities' cultural "ministries." In addition, the sponsorship of archaeological activity by the autonomous governments tends to favor the selection of projects presented by local centers and researchers. Throughout Spain these factors promote a regionalization that is only sometimes counterbalanced by the traditional involvement of teams from other regions of the country or from abroad (Gonzalez 1992). The adoption of the present administrative boundaries for the study of the past is a feature as characteristic of Spanish archaeology (Ruiz Zapatero 1988) as the endogamy of its institutions (Ruiz Zapatero 1991, 6).

The fact that these features are strongly marked throughout Spain suggests that they are not best explained as the result of regionalist nationalism. Even in those autonomous communities in which nationalist (regionalist) parties have a predominant political influence (the Basque country and Catalonia) heritage issues have not been the object of a systematic program. Even where such goals have been formulated, they have been quickly forgotten when they came into conflict with strong economic interests or the particular objectives of administrative bodies (Salvatierra 1994, 9). The cultural efforts of the regional nationalist parties have been directed more to the promotion of bilingualism and the reinterpretation of recent history than to a search for pre-Roman origins.

In short, the strong regionalization of archaeological activity in Spain is not the product of strong nationalist pressure (Gonzalez 1992; Vicent 1994, 221), as the political and administrative decentralization of the Spanish state has made it unnecessary for minority nationalities to archaeologically legitimatize their aspirations for self-government. Regional governments develop heritage policies as a function of political and administrative, not ideological, concerns. It is precisely for this reason that there is conflict between regional governments and academic bodies.

In spite of the varied policies developed in the seventeen autonomous communities, certain clear general tendencies are discernible. Regionalization is improving the conditions of archaeological research by sponsoring the creation of an infrastructure that sometimes includes research laboratories. Similarly, the professionalism and technical expertise of archaeologists have increased. At the same time, however, the uncertain publication of the results of archaeological work (Gonzalez 1992, 24) and the strong compartmentalization of Spanish archaeology constitute obstacles to the communication that is essential for scientific progress. Only a few of the autonomous communities have begun computerizing their data bases (Hernandez and Castella 1993), and these are not linked or standardized. The participation of academic centers in these efforts is also very uneven (Fernandez and Fernandez 1991).

In spite of these negative features, the future is heartening. The substitution of an authoritarian, centralized regime by one that is democratic and almost federalist has caused maladjustment, but in two decades the autonomous communities became established and the power conflicts promoted by regional or nationalist distrust were reduced. Spanish archaeologists have developed the critical perspectives required to recognize and to counterbalance the disadvantages associated with regionalism. At the same time, the effective monopoly that academic institutions had over archaeological work under the previous regime has disappeared. This has led to a public debate on the goals of archaeology, which has brought the discipline closer to its social base than in any other period of Spanish history. Likewise, it is undoubtedly positive that Spanish society has become more open to an international panorama in which the political, ideological, economic, and social implications of archaeology are subject to critical examination.

Isabel Martinez Navarrete;
translated by Antonio Gilman

Acknowledgments

My thanks go to Juan Vicent and Pilar Lopez (Dpto. de Prehistoria, Centro de Estudios Historicos, CSIC), to Teresa Chapa and M. Angeles Querol (Dpto. de Prehistoria, Universidad Complutense, Madrid), to Barbara Sasse Kunst (granted by the Deutsche Forschungsgemeinschaft) and Michael Kunst (Deutsches Archaologisches Institut, Madrid), and to Jose Alcina Franch (Universidad Complutense, Madrid) for their comments and advice, and to Antonio Gilman (Dept. of Anthropology, California State University, Northridge) for giving me his unique perspective as both insider and outsider to Spanish archaeology and for his translation of the Castilian original.

References

Alcina, J. 1991. "La arqueología en España: Una revisión critica de sus planteamientos teoricos." *Trabajos de Prehistoria* 48: 13–28.

Almagro Gorbea, M., et al. 1978. *C-14 y prehistoria de la Peninsula Iberica.* Serie Universitaria 77. Madrid:Ministerio de Educación y Ciencia, Dirección General del Patrimonio Artístico y Cultural.

Altuna, J. 1990a. "D. Jose Miguel de Barandiaran." In *Gure lehen urratsak, 1990, Odisea en el pasado: Homenaie a D. Jose Miguel de Barandiaran,* 2–24. Donostia-San Sebastian: Eusko Kultur Eragintza Etor, S.A.

———. 1990b. "D. Jose Miguel de Barandiaran: Notas biograficas, Munibe." *Antropologia-Arkeologia* 42: 7–9.

Anonymous. 1987. "El Departamento de Antropología de America de la Universidad Complutense de Madrid." *Anthropos* 68: 60–62.

Arce, J. 1991. "A. Garcia y Bellido y los comienzos de la historia antigua de España." In *Historiografia de la arqueología y de la historia antigua en España (siglos XVIII-XX),* 209–211. Ed. Javier Arce and Ricardo Olmos. Madrid: Ministerio de Cultura.

Arce, J., and E. Barrondo, eds. 1994. *Escuela española de historia y arqueología del Consejo Superior de Investigaciones Científicas en Roma: Memoria 1993.* Rome: Consejo Superior de Investigaciones Científicas.

Arqueología de las ciudades modernas superpuestas a las antiguas. 1985. Madrid: Ministerio de Cultura and Institución Fernando el Catolico (Consejo Superior de Investigaciones Científicas).

Arqueoloia, E. 1984. *Coloquio sobre distribución y relaciones entre los asentamientos.* 1. Teruel: Colegio Universitario de Teruel.

Ayarzaguena, S. Mariano. 1991. "Historiografía española referida a la Edad de Piedra desde 1868 hasta 1880." In *Historiografía de la arqueología y de la historia antigua en España (siglos XVIII-XX),* 69–72. Ed. Javier Arce and Ricardo Olmos. Madrid: Ministerio de Cultura.

Barcelo, M. 1992. "Quina arqueología per al-andalus?" *I Coloquio Hispano-Italianode Arqueología Medieval (Granada 1990):* 24–252.

Barril Vicente, M. 1993. "El proceso historico-social en la formaci6n de las colecciones del M.A.N." *Boletin de la A.N.A.B.AD* 43, nos. 3–4: 37–63.

Bustillo, Ma A., and A. Ramos Millan. 1991. *VI Flint International Symposium (Madrid, Bilbao, Granada, 1991):Abstracts.* Instituto Tecnolgico GeoMinero de España.

Cabello Carro, P. 1989. *Coleccionismo americano indigena en la España del siglo XVIII.* Madrid: Ediciones de Cultura Hispanica.

Cebria, A., I. Muro, and E. Riu, 1991. "La arqueología y la prehistoria en el siglo XIX: Actitudes y conflictos cientifico-sociales en la Cataluna de la Restauracion." In *Historiografia de la arqueología y de la historia antigua en España (siglos XVIII-XX),* 79–84. Ed. Javier Arce and Ricardo Olmos. Madrid: Ministerio de Cultura.

Chapa, T. 1988. "Perspectivas actuales de la arqueología española." *Revista de Occidente* 81: 135–142.

―――. 1991. "La 'arqueología de la muerte': Planteamientos, problemas, y resultados." In *Arqueología de la muerte: Metodología y perspectivas actuales,* 13–38. Cordoba: Universidad de Cordoba.

Cortadella I Morral, J. 1991. "La formación acade-mica de Bosch Gimpera: De la filología griega a la protohistoria peninsular." In *Historiografía de la arqueología y de la historia antigua en España (siglos XVIII-XX),* 161–166. Ed. Javier Arce and Ricardo Olmos. Madrid: Ministerio de Cultura.

Criado Boado, F., J. Ma Aira Rodriguez, and F. Diaz-Fierros Viqueira. 1986. *La construcción del Paisaje: Megalitismo y ecologia, sierra de Barbanza.* Arqueoloxia/Investigación no. 1. Coruna: Xunta de Galicia.

Diaz Andreu, M. 1993. "Theory and Ideology in Archaeology: Spanish Archaeology under the Franco Regime." *Antiquity* 67: 74–82.

Dupla, A., and A. Emborujo. 1991. "El Vasco-cantabrismo: Mito y realidad en la histori-ografía sobre el Pais Vasco en la antiguedad." In *Historiografía de la arqueología y de la historia antigua en España (siglos XVIII-XX),* 107–111. Ed. Javier Arce and Ricardo Olmos. Madrid: Ministerio de Cultura.

Dupre I Raventos, X., and N. Rafels I Fontanals. 1991. "La politica arqueológica de la generalitat de catalunya durante la republica." In *Histori-ografía de la arqueología y de la historia antigua en España (siglos XVIII-XX),* 173–176. Ed. Javier Arce and Ricardo Olmos. Madrid: Ministerio de Cultura.

Fernandez Martinez, V., and G. Fernandez Lopez. 1991. *Aplicaciones informaticas en arqueología.* En Complutum 1. Madrid: Ed. Complutense.

Fernandez Murga, F. 1988. "El rey y Napoles: Las excavaciones arqueológicas." *Carlos III y la Ilustración* 1: 375–384. Madrid: Ministerio de Cultura.

Garcia Fernandez, J. 1989. "The New Spanish Archaeological Heritage Legislation." In *Archae-ological Heritage Management in the Modern World,* 182–194. Ed. H. Cleere. London: Unwin Hyman.

Gilman, A. 1988. "Enfoques teóricos en la arque-ología de los ochenta." *Revista de Occidente* 81: 47–61.

Gilman, A., and J. B. Thornes. 1985. *Land-Use and Prehistory in South-East Spain.* London: Allen and Unwin.

Gonzalez Morales, R. M. 1992. "Racines: La justi-fication archeologique des origines regionales dans l'Espagne des communautes autonomes." In *The Limitations of Archaeological Knowledge,* 15–27. Ed. Shay and J. Clottes. Liege: Univer-site de Liege.

Gran-Aymerich, E., and J. Gran-Aymerich. 1991. "Les echanges franco-spagnols et la mise en place des institutions archeologiques (1830–1939)." In *Historiografía de la arqueología y de la historia antigua en España (siglos XVIII-XX),* 117–124. Ed. Javier Arce and Ricardo Olmos. Madrid: Ministerio de Cultura.

Grunhagen, W. 1979. "Zur Geschichte der Abteilung Madrid des Deutschen Archaologis-chen Instituts von 1929 bis 1979." *Das Deutsche Archaelogische: Institut Geschichte und Dokumente* 3: 117–170.

Guitart, J., and E. Riu. 1989. "Arqueología i cultura a la Catalunya contemporania." *L'Avenc* 124: 26–31.

Hernandez Herrero, G., and J. Castella I Camp. 1993. "Banco de datos e informatización del patrimonio arqueologico de Cataluna." In *Actas, inventarios, y caras arqueológicas: Homenaje a Blas Taracena, 50 aniversario de la primera Carta Arque-ológica de España: Soria 1941–1991,* 207–218. Ed. Alfredo Jimeno Martinez, Jesus M. Val Re-cio, and Jose J. Fernandez Moreno. Valladolid: Junta de Castilla y Leon.

Jimeno Martinez, A., J. M. Val Recio, and J. J. Fer-nandez Moreno, eds. 1993. *Actas, inventarios, y cartas arqueológicas: Homenaje a Blas Taracena, 50 aniversario de la primera Carta Arqueológica de España: Soria 1941–1991.* Valladolid: Junta de Castilla y Leon.

Jornadas Internacionales. 1991. *Arqueología de inter-vención (16–20 diciembre 1991 Palacio Miramar, San Sebastian).* Bilbao: Gobierno Vasco.

Jutglar, A. 1971. *Ideologías y clases en la España con-temporanea: Aproximación a la historia social de las ideas, II (1874–1931).* Madrid: EDICUSA.

Maluquer de Motes, J. 1958. "Las actividades de la Wenner-Green Foundation for Anthropological Research, en relación con España." *Zephyrus* 9: 250.

Marcos Pous, A. 1993. "Origen y desarrollo del Museo Arqueológico Nacional." In Museo Arqueológico Nacional, Madrid, *De Gabinete a Museo: Tres siglos de historia Madrid,* 21–99. Madrid: Ministerio de Cultura.

Martinez Diaz, B., ed. 1992. *Acta del primer semi-nario de Arqueología Subacuatica (1 al 31 agosto 1987, San Pedro del Pinatar Murcia), in Cuadernos* de *Arqueología Maritima*. I. Cartagena: Museo Nacional de Arqueología Maritima, Centro Nacional de Investigaciones Arqueológicas Subacuaticas.

Matesanz Vera, P. 1991. "Arqueología medieval cristiana despues de 20 anos: Confirmación de una realidad." *Boletin de la Asociación Española de Amigos de la Arqueología* 30–31: 291–301.

Mora, G. 1991. "Arqueología y poder en la España del siglo XVIII." In *Historiografía de la arqueología y de la historia antigua en España (siglos XVIII-XX)*, 31–32. Ed. Javier Arce and Ricardo Olmos. Madrid: Ministerio de Cultura.

Moure Romanillo, A.1993. "The Spanish Palaeolithic: Scientific Structure and Present Problematics." In *Theory and Practice of Prehistory:Views from the Edges of Europe*, 205–227. Ed. Isabel Martinez Navarrete. Cantabria: Universidad de Cantabria, Consejo Superior de Investigaciones Científicas.

Moure Romanillo, A., ed. 1992. *Elefantes, ciervos, y ovicaprinos: Economía y aprovechamiento del medio en la prehistoria de España y Portugal*. Cantabria: Servicio de Publicaciones de la Universidad de Cantabria. Fundación Jose Ortega y Gasset.

Nunez, D. 1969. *El darwinismo en España*. Madrid: Ed. Castalia.

Olmos Romera, R. 1992a. "Una mirada a la novela arqueológica de raiz decimononica." *Revista de Arqueología* 13, no. 140: 52–57.

———. 1992b. "El surgimiento de la imagen en la sociedad iberica." In *La sociedad Iberica a traves de la imagen*, 8–32. Madrid: Ministerio de Cultura.

Pasamar Alzuria, G., and I. Peiró Martin. 1991. "Los origenes de la profesionalización historiografica española sobre prehistoria y antiguedad (tradiciones decimononicas e influencias europeas)." In *Historiografía de la arqueología y de la historia antigua en España (siglos XVIII-XX)*, 73–79. Ed. Javier Arce and Ricardo Olmos. Madrid: Ministerio de Cultura.

Perez Die, Ma del C. 1983. "Excavaciones y restauraciones en oriente proximo y Africa del Norte (1960–1981)." *Indice Cultural Español* 11: 11–58.

Prieto, A. 1979. "El franquisme i la historia antiga." *L'Avenc* 18: 75–77.

Primeras jornadas de arqueología en las ciudades actuales (Zaragoza 14, 15, 16 enero 1983). 1983. Organizadas por la Delegación de Patrimonio Historico-Artistico del Excmo. Ayuntamiento de Zaragoza. Zaragoza.

Primeras jornadas de metodología de investigación prehistorica (Soria, 1981). 1984. Madrid: Ministerio de Cultura.

Querol, Ma A., L. Ma Cerdeno, I. Ma Martinez Navarrete, and F. Contreras. 1994. "El ejercicio profesional de la arqueología en España." *1o Congreso de Arqueología Peninsular Porto, 1993: Actas V. Trabalhos de Antropolología e Etnologia* 35, no. 1: 485–500.

Quesada Sanz, F. 1994. "La imagen del heroe: Los antiguos iberos en la plastica española del XIX." *Revista de Araueologia* 15, no. 162: 36–47.

Riu I Barrera, E. 1992. "Preambul: La mobilitzacio dels arqueolegs a Catalunya, entre assemblees i jornades (1978–1987)." In *I Jornades sobre la situacio professional en l'arqueología (Barcelona, 26–28 marc 1987)*, 9–15. Barcelona: Collegi Oficial de Doctors i Licenciats en Filosofía i Letres i en Ciencies de Catalunya. Diputacio de Barcelona.

Rossello-Bordoy, G. 1986. "Islam andalusi e investigación arqueológica: Estado de la cuestion." *Actas, I: Congreso de Arqueología Medieval Española Huesca, 1985* 3: 7–24.

Rua, C. de la. 1990. "Los estudios de paleoantropología en el Pais Vasco." *Homena.ie a D. Jose Miguel de Barandiaran Munibe* (Antropologia-Arkeologia) 42: 199–219.

Ruiz Rodriguez, A. 1993. "Present Panorama of Spanish Archaeology." In *Theory and Practice of Prehistory:Views from the Edges of Europe*, 307–326. Ed. Isabel Martinez Navarrete. Cantabria: Universidad de Cantabria, Consejo Superior de Investigaciones Científicas.

Ruiz Zapatero, G. 1988. "La prospección arqueológica en España: Pasado, presente, y futuro." *Seminario sobre Arqueología Espacial (Lisboa / Tomar 10–13 Marco 1988)* en Arqueología Espacial 12: 33–48. Teruel.

———. 1991. "Arqueología y universidad: La 'reproducción del sistema.'" *Revista de Arqueología* 12, no. 118: 6–7.

———. 1993a. "El concepto de Celtas en la prehistoria europea y española." In *Los Celtas: Hispania y Europa*, 23–62. Ed. Martin Almagro-Gorbea and Gonzalo Ruiz Zapatero. Madrid: Universidad Complutense.

———. 1993b. "The Organisation of the Archaeology in Spain." In *Theory and Practice of Prehistory:Views from the Edges of Europe*, 45–73. Ed. Isabel Martinez Navarrete. Cantabria: Universidad de Cantabria, Consejo Superior de Investigaciones Científicas.

Salvatierra C., Vicente. 1990. *Cien años de arqueología medieval: Perspectivas desde la periferia.* Jaen:
Universidad de Granada.

———. 1994. "Historia y desarrollo del modelo
andaluz de arqueología." *Trabajos de Prehistoria*
51, no. 1: 1–13.

Suarez Otero, J. 1993. "Prehistoria nórdica en el
Museo Arqueológico Nacional." In *Museo
Arqueológico Nacional, Madrid, De Gabinete a
Museo: Tres siglos de historia Madrid, 1993,*
326–334. Madrid: Ministerio de Cultura.

Valls, R. 1993. "La historia ensenyada a l'epoca
franquista." *L'Avenc* 169: 71–73.

Vazquez Varela, J. M., and R. Risch. 1991. "Theory
in Spanish Archaeology since 1960." In *Archaeological Theory in Europe: The Last Three Decades,*
25–51. Ed. I. Hodder. London: Routledge.

Vicent Garcia, J. M. 1991. "Fundamentos teórico-
metodológicos para un programa de investigación arqueogeografica." In *El cambio cultural
del IV al II milenios a.c. en la Comarca Noroeste de
Murcia.* Ed. Pilar Lopez Garcia. Madrid: Consejo Superior de Investigaciones Científicas.

———. 1993. "Department of Prehistory of the
Centre for Historical Studies (C.S.I.C.)." In *The-
ory and Practice of Prehistory: Views from the Edges of
Europe,* 19–35. Ed. Isabel Martinez Navarrete.
Cantabria: Universidad de Cantabria, Consejo
Superior de Investigaciones Científicas.

———. 1994. "Perspectivas de la teoría arqueológica en España." In *6 Congreso Hispano-Ruso
de Historia,* 215–223. Madrid: Fundación Cultural Banesto, Consejo Superior de Investigaciones Científicas.

Vila, A., ed. 1991. *Arqueología.* Madrid: Consejo
Superior de Investigaciones Científicas.

Spitsyn, Aleksander Andrevich (1858–1931)

Aleksander Andrevich Spitsyn was one of the first
archaeologists in RUSSIA to adopt the cartographic
method of research, that is, comparing information from both historic and archaeological
sources. He compiled and published systematized archaeological reviews of many Russian
provinces, and his chronologies are still used today. He was primarily concerned with the Bronze
Age, the Volga-Kama region, and Slavic peoples.

In 1892, he became an associate of the Ar-
chaeographic Commission, and in 1919, he
joined the Russian Association for the History of
Material Culture. At the Upper Paleolithic site
of KOSTENKI on the Don River in western Russia, the lowest level of Kostenki XVII, dating to
about 40,00–32,000 B.P., was named "the Spitsyn culture" in his honor. It was characterized
by burins, retouched blades and scrapers, and
some bone tools and ornaments.

Tim Murray

St. Acheul

St. Acheul, the type site for the Acheulean, an
early Paleolithic industry (dating roughly from
1.5 million years ago to about 100,000 years
ago), was first identified in the Somme River
gravels of northern FRANCE near Amiens. The
Acheulean stone tool industry has been found in
sites in western and central Europe, over much
of Africa, and in Asia as far east as India.

The area of St. Acheul has long been known
as a source of flint tools. As early as 1854, stone
tool finds were recorded in this area, and, consequently, in 1859, Albert Gaudry of the
Académie des Sciences commented very favorably on Amiens as a locality for studying early
human history. In recognition of this fact, in
1872 GABRIEL DE MORTILLET named the distinctive industry based around biface hand-axes the
Acheulean industry.

Tim Murray

See also Lithic Analysis

Steenstrup, Japhetus (1813–1907)

Danish zoologist and professor of zoology in
Copenhagen, Japhetus Steenstrup's major contribution to science concerned the study of the
octopus until, in an attempt to trace the changes
in Danish flora and fauna since the last Ice Age,
he excavated in the peat bogs of Zealand and
found artifacts there. He also discovered that
the initial pine forests of DENMARK corresponded with Stone Age occupations, while the
Bronze Age was contemporary with the succeeding period of oak forests and the Iron Age
with beech forests. In this he was providing
stratigraphic evidence for CHRISTIAN JÜRGENSEN

THOMSEN's theory of the THREE-AGE SYSTEM and, as importantly, showing that archaeologists could use environmental changes to help them understand social, technological, and cultural changes. Steenstrup, archaeologist JENS JACOB WORSAAE, and geologist J. Forchammer were members of the KITCHENMIDDEN COMMITTEE that excavated mounds of shells found in Denmark to ascertain their origin and, subsequently, contributed to the knowledge of the Mesolithic period in northern Europe.

Tim Murray

See also European Mesolithic; Shell Midden Analysis

References
Klindt-Jensen, O. 1975. *A History of Scandinavian Archaeology.* London: Thames and Hudson.

Sir Aurel Stein (Image Select)

Stein, Sir (Mark) Aurel (1862–1943)

Aurel Stein was born in Budapest. Educated there and in Dresden, Germany, and at the universities of Vienna and Leipzig, he received his Ph.D. in 1883 from the University of Tübingen, where he studied Persian and Indian archaeology. Between 1884 and 1887, he studied classical and oriental archaeology and languages at Oxford University and the British Museum, where he met, and was greatly influenced by, SIR HENRY RAWLINSON.

In 1888, Stein traveled to India to become the principal of the Oriental College at Lahore and registrar for the Punjab University. For the next ten years he spent his vacations on antiquarian and geographical research in Kashmir in northern India and on the North-West Frontier (now northern Pakistan and eastern Afghanistan) and his spare time learning and translating Sanskrit. He became well connected with the civil and vice-regal establishment of British colonial India.

In 1900, with the support from Lord Curzon (the viceroy of India) and the Survey of India, Stein led his first expedition into central Asia, where he was to lead three more in 1906–1908, 1913–1916, and 1930. He took different routes each time to and from Turkistan, surveying, exploring, mapping, and excavating as he went. He traveled huge distances and brought back to

India and England thousands of artifacts and, it is rumored, intelligence information for the British government. He became a naturalized British subject in 1904, and between 1910 and 1929 was directly employed by the Archaeological Survey of India. He was knighted in 1912. Stein's achievements were substantial—here was a whole area of the world that was unknown archaeologically, and its history was little known as well. Stein filled in this huge gap.

On his first expedition he explored the southern oases of the Taklamakan Desert, and at settlements in the Khotan region he discovered numerous documents in ancient Tibetan, Chinese, and Kharoshti. On the second expedition, he explored the dried-up Lop Sea bed and traced the long-used caravan route between CHINA and the West by following the trail of Neolithic implements, metal objects, beads, and ancient Han coins. He visited the watchtowers of the ancient Chinese frontier, and at the site of Miran in what is now Chinese Central Asia, which had been abandoned in the third century B.C., he found wall paintings of classical design. Stein's greatest find was not only the fabulous "Cave of the Thousand Buddhas" but the large number of documents and temple paintings at the same site, which had been undisturbed since the eleventh century A.D.

Stein's third expedition completed his circuit of the Taklamakan Desert via Russian territory, and he traced the Silk Route to Samarkand, returning south through eastern Persia to Baluchistan. The difficult political situation in central Asia between the two world wars prevented the completion of his fourth trip—but he did manage to travel 2,000 miles around the Taklamakan once more. The scientific record of Stein's trips was published in *Ancient Khotan* (1907, 2 vols), *Serindia* (1921, 5 vols), *Innermost Asia* (1928, 4 vols), and *Memoir on Maps of Chinese Turkistan and Kansu* (1923), and his narrative accounts of the same appeared in *Sand-Buried Ruins of Khotan* (1903), *Ruins of Desert Cathay* (1912, 2 vols), and *The Thousand Buddhas* (1921).

Difficulties traveling in central Asia led Stein to travel in Baluchistan and Persia between 1927 and 1936 to explore the connections between the INDUS CIVILIZATION, unearthed by SIR JOHN MARSHALL in what is now Pakistan, and the civilizations of the Euphrates in the Near East. He discovered extensive Chalcolithic and Neolithic remains and published *Archaeological Reconnaissances in North-Western India and South-Eastern Iran* (1937) and *Old Routes of Western Iran* (1940). In 1929, with the help of the Royal Air Force, Stein had carried out an aerial survey of the Roman frontier in Iraq and the Jezira, and he investigated these finds on the ground and in detail between 1938 and 1939.

As a consequence of his travels throughout the Near East and central Asia, Stein became interested in searching for traces of Alexander the Great's eastern campaigns between 331 and 323 B.C. He had already found some evidence of Alexander in southwestern Persia near PERSEPOLIS and in the Greco-Buddhist remains in the Swat Valley of northern Pakistan. In 1931, Stein traveled from Taxila east of the Indus River to the Jhelum River, where he located the site of the defeat of Poros and explained Alexander's tactics. In 1943, at the age of eighty, Stein's last expedition traced the retreat of Alexander's army through Baluchistan. He then went on to visit Kabul, in Afghanistan, where he died suddenly.

In many ways, Stein was the last of the great nineteenth-century explorers: physically tough, fearless, possessed of a brilliant intellect, a superb linguist, independent, and able to travel with only loyal and local colleagues and guides as companions. In other ways, he was unique in the breadth of his achievements. Stein was a nomad with no home base to speak of, and on his occasional visits to England he stayed at Corpus Christi College, Oxford. He never married, but he had many close friends and he supported relatives in Hungary after World War I. He left his estate to create the Stein-Arnold Fund to be used for the geographic and antiquarian exploration of central and southwestern Asia. He received the founder's gold medal from the Royal Geographical Society in 1904, the gold medal of the Royal Asiatic Society in 1932, that of the SOCIETY OF ANTIQUARIES OF LONDON in 1935, the Flinders Petrie Medal in 1928, the Huxley medallion, and honorary degrees from the universities of Oxford, Cambridge, and St. Andrews.

Tim Murray

See also Iran; South Asia
References
Walker, A. 1995. *Aurel Stein: Pioneer of the Silk Road.* London: John Murray.

Steno, Nicolas (1638–1686)

Born in Copenhagen, Nicolas Steno went to Amsterdam to study anatomy and became the physician of the grand duke of Florence, Ferdinand II, in 1665. Steno became interested in geology, and in 1669 he published a landmark geology book on basic crystallography in which he claimed that fossils were the remains of ancient living organisms and that many rocks were the result of sedimentation. He also proposed that the chronological history of the earth could be understood by studying the earth's strata (stratigraphy) and that landscape was the result of changes in the earth's crust. Although he believed that all of this change had occurred over a long time, he was restricted by religious dogma to only being able to estimate 6,000 years for the entire history of the earth.

Steno abandoned science and converted to Catholicism in 1667. He became a priest in

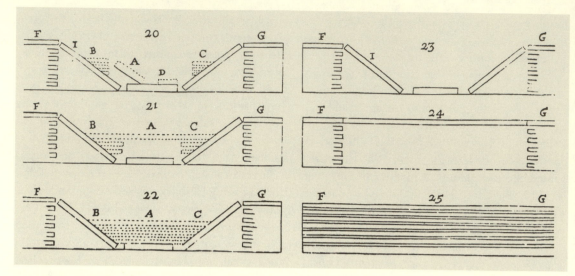

Drawing by Nicholas Steno in 1671, illustrating his theory of how rock strata can fold and produce different formations (Image Select)

1667 and a bishop in 1677 and died in Schwerin in Germany. His discovery of the parotid salivary duct was named "Stensen's duct" for him, as is his work on the faces and angles of crystals, which is known as "Steno's law."

Tim Murray

References

Schnapp, A. 1996. *The Discovery of the Past*. London: British Museum Press.

Stephens, John Lloyd (1805–1852)

John Lloyd Stephens was born in New Jersey and studied classics at Columbia College, after which, in 1822, he studied law. He was a successful lawyer in New York City for eight years until ill health caused him to embark on a two-year voyage to the Mediterranean and eastern Europe. He began to publish accounts of his travels, which were so successful that he became known as "the American traveler." He met and befriended the English architect and draftsman FREDERICK CATHERWOOD and collaborated with him on *Incidents of Travel in Egypt, Arabia, Petraea, and the Holy Land* (1837) and *Incidents of Travel in Greece, Turkey, Russia, and Poland* (1838). Both books proved to be popular and made Stephens enough money to finance his first expedition to Central America.

In 1839, with personal recommendations from U.S. President Martin Van Buren and in the company of Catherwood, Stephens traveled to BELIZE and then through the dense rainforest of the Yucatán to the site of Copán in western Honduras, which had to be cut out of the forest. He left Catherwood to draw the site and traveled on to GUATEMALA and EL SALVADOR, then to COSTA RICA AND NICARAGUA, and then back to Guatemala where he again met up with Catherwood. Together they traveled to MEXICO under difficult and dangerous circumstances via PALENQUE, a classic Maya site in Chiapas, and visited the ancient city of Uxmal. By this point, the health of both was dire and they were carried on stretchers to the boat back to New York. The resulting book, *Incidents of Travel in Central America, Chiapas, and Yucatan* (1841, 2 vols.), with text by Stephens and illustrations by Catherwood, became a best-seller.

Although Stephens was no archaeologist, he had seen enough archaeological monuments in Egypt, the Near East, and eastern Europe to understand that the New World sites were astounding and rivaled Old World sites in their artistic achievements. He was more than able to convey their power and significance and his own excitement, and his books attracted great interest in the United States.

In late 1841, Stephens and Catherwood returned to Uxmal to finish their work by taking new daguerreotypes, and they then visited the site of CHICHÉN ITZÁ. Once again, they had to clear a site in order to survey it. After Chichén Itzá it was on to Cozumel and Tulum before returning to New York where the two men published another book, *Incidents of Travel in Yucatán* (1843).

Stephens became the promoter and director of a steamship company and then became involved in building railways. Between 1849 and 1851 he helped to survey and prepare for the construction of the Panama railway, where the malaria he had caught during his earlier explorations flared up again and forced him to return in 1852 to New York City, where he died.

Tim Murray

Steward, Julian (1902–1972)

Born in Washington, D.C., Julian Steward studied zoology and geology at Cornell University. He completed a Ph.D. in anthropology in 1929 at the University of California, Berkeley, and then worked for the Bureau of American Ethnology at the SMITHSONIAN INSTITUTION.

Steward began his ethnographic career among the western Shoshone Indians, one of the most simple of societies, and moved on to study complex cultures such as those in Puerto Rico. By the end of his career he was managing a cross-cultural, worldwide inquiry into the modernization of peasant societies. In 1943, he became director of the Smithsonian's Institute of Social Anthropology; from 1946 to 1952, he was professor of anthropology at Columbia University; and from 1952 until he retired in 1970, he was professor of anthropology at the University of Illinois.

Steward is best known for his theories about "cultural ecology," which held that a society's environmental resources and available technology determine the kinds of labor used by them and, consequently, inform their entire social system—an ecological, neo-evolutionist, and materialist view of human behavior. He formulated a theory of "multilinear evolution," which described the ways in which societies progress toward greater complexity.

He was one of the few ethnologists of his time who was interested in archaeological data and its potential for contributing to the study of human behavior over long periods of time, and he had a great impact on the development of archaeology in the United States after World War II. He taught and supported a number of archaeologists, such as ROBERT BRAIDWOOD and Richard MacNeish, who undertook pioneering multidisciplinary research programs into the origins of food production in the Near East and MESOAMERICA. And he inspired many others, such as GORDON WILLEY, who initiated the use of settlement archaeology in the VIRÚ VALLEY in PERU.

Tim Murray

See also United States of America, Prehistoric Archaeology

References
Harris, M. 1968. *The Rise of Anthropological Theory.* New York: Crowell.

Stična

Stična (or Vir pri Sticni or Stiski cvinger, as it is also called) is an early–Iron Age site in lower Carniola, in SLOVENIA, a center for the Dolenjska (lower Carniola) group of the Hallstatt culture. The hill-fort type of settlement covers an area of more than 21 hectares.

The settlement was intensively excavated between 1967 and 1974 by STANE GABROVEC and several other collaborators. The excavations were limited to the hill-fort ramparts and revealed three main early–Iron Age occupation phases (contemporary with the nearby barrow cemetery) and a late–LA TÈNE phase. The cemetery was partly excavated during the twentieth century by the duchess of Mecklenburg (1905–1914), RAJKO LOZAR (1936), JOŽEF KASTELIC (1946, 1952–1953), and Gabrovec (1960–1964).

The burial rites are almost exclusively inhumations in earthen barrows. Approximately 125 barrows were documented in an area approximately 15 to 50 meters in diameter. The number of inhumations in a barrow varies from a few graves (e.g., in Mecklenburg's Glogovica barrow, 3 graves) to more than 150 graves (e.g., barrow 48 has 183 graves). On average there are 20–30 graves per barrow.

The cemetery covers the period between the eighth and fourth centuries B.C. The graves vary considerably in the amount of grave goods they contain, from very poor graves to warrior graves containing weaponry (mostly axes and spears) to so-called princely graves containing body armor, helmets, weapons, horse-riding equipment, decorated bronze vessels (situlae), buckets, and great quantities of personal ornaments and ceramic vessels. Grave goods, especially those imported from or influenced by the Etruscan culture, indicate a distinguished and well-stratified community with very rich individuals at the top that flourished between the seventh and fifth centuries B.C.

Peter Turk

See also Celts; Etruscan Archaeology

References

Wells, P. S. 1981. "The Emergence of an Iron Age Economy." *Bulletin of the American School of Prehistoric Research* 33.

Stone, Doris Zemurray (1909–)

Doris Stone was one of the pioneers of Central American archaeology. She was educated at Radcliffe College and conducted fieldwork in Honduras and COSTA RICA while she was research associate for the Middle American Research Institute of Tulane University and for the PEABODY MUSEUM, Harvard University.

Born the daughter of Samuel Zemurray, an early developer of the banana trade in Central America, Stone spent parts of her formative years in Honduras and Costa Rica. As an undergraduate at Radcliffe College, she was able to attend classes offered by Alfred M. Tozzer, Harvard's specialist in Mayan archaeology. She was not encouraged to continue studying archaeology after receiving her undergraduate degree in 1930 and returned to New Orleans, her home town.

Stephen Williams (1986) identifies an unpublished study of Ulua Valley figurines that was filed at Tulane University in 1930 as Stone's earliest known written work. In that same year, she donated a pottery figurine found near La Lima, Honduras, to Harvard's Peabody Museum. Williams speculates that the figurine paper was completed for Tozzer's senior research course. The date of the manuscript makes this theory plausible, but there is no sign of it in Tozzer's papers, now in the archives of the Peabody Museum, or in the manuscript holdings of the Tozzer Library at Harvard University. It was not until much later that Stone was actively encouraged by Tozzer. Her early research was sponsored by the Middle American Research Institute (MARI) at Tulane University, of which her father was a supporter, and she was appointed an associate there in 1930. By 1934, she was publishing field reports based on her own work in Honduras in the MARI-affiliated journal, *Maya Research*. MARI also published her landmark comparative study of the Ulua marble vases (Stone 1938) that was based on collections in multiple institutions, including both MARI and the Peabody Museum.

When Honduran archaeology received renewed attention during the 1930s, Stone, already in the country, was instrumental in encouraging the interests of first MARI and later the Peabody Museum. Stone's own approach centered on identifying linguistic groups described in the sixteenth century with archaeological remains, which encountered some resistance on the part of the director of the Peabody's Honduran expedition, WILLIAM DUNCAN STRONG. Despite the reservations of Harvard archaeologists about Stone, which is well documented in Tozzer's correspondence at the Peabody, by the end of the 1930s she had established herself as an authority on Honduran archaeology. Although Tozzer, in his "Foreword" to her first monograph on Honduran archaeology, went so far as to state that "her indefatigable energy, her enthusiasms and her intuitive impressions have, at times, been handicaps" (Stone 1941, v), he acknowledged that the handicaps he ascribed to her "have all contributed to the ultimate success of her work." He cited as the foundation of her strength as an authority on Honduran archaeology Stone's laboring "for long periods and in all possible seasons" in the country. The same claim to authority was featured by Stephen Williams in his introduction to her general study of Central American archaeology: "her numerous journeys on mule back . . . in pursuit of elusive sites in the Central American jungles were epic at a time when that sort of thing was not being done" (Stone 1972, vii). By successfully functioning in the field, Stone was able to prove herself to her former teacher and other academic archaeologists.

Her connections with the banana company and her sustained presence in Honduras resulted in her hearing of newly uncovered ruins at Travesía, a major center on the Ulua River. She excavated there in 1936, and in 1937, she enlisted Gerhardt Kramer of Tulane to undertake a second season of excavations. Most of the collections resulting from this stage of her research were donated to MARI, but in a letter to Tozzer in 1937, Stone reported that MARI did not have the financial resources to publish her Travesía paper and asked whether the Peabody might be interested in it. In the same year she thanked Tozzer for his frank critique of another paper she had decided not to publish in *Maya Research*. With these letters, the earliest correspondence preserved in the Peabody Museum between Tozzer and Stone, began the gradual process of Stone's re-affiliation with Harvard. From 1941 to 1953, she served as a trustee of Radcliffe College, and in 1954, the Peabody Museum appointed her a research associate.

Tozzer initially discouraged Stone about the prospects of publishing her Travesía study with the Peabody, establishing as a requirement that she take Strong's work into account. Stone complied with this request, welcoming the suggestions of both Strong and Samuel K. Lothrop for improvements in her manuscript. By 1939, with both expressing their appreciation for her work, even though they differed with her conclusions, Tozzer approved the study's publication by the Peabody. At about the same time, Stone was invited to contribute to *The Maya and Their Neighbors,* a Festschrift presented to Tozzer in 1940. She published some of her work on Travesía there as well as in her monograph *Archaeology of the North Coast of Honduras,* brought out by the Peabody Museum in 1941. Parallel with these developments, Stone donated her research materials from Honduras and from Costa Rica, where she began working in 1939, to the Peabody. As early as 1941, Stone had requested and received notes from Peabody-sponsored work in Honduras by Lothrop in 1917. She proposed a Peabody expedition in Comayagua, which resulted in excavations at Yarumela by Joel Canby, who completed his doctoral thesis in 1949. This region was the focus of Stone's *The Archaeology of Southern and Central Honduras* published by the museum in 1957.

Stone combined her firsthand knowledge of the archaeology of Honduras and Costa Rica to form the backbone of *Pre-Columbian Man Finds Central America,* which was published in 1972. This book highlighted the degree and nature of Mesoamerican contact as a crucial issue for the archaeology of these countries. The book benefited from a full adoption of stratigraphic succession, creatively combined with Stone's own interest in identifying the linguistic identity of archaeological cultures, and its success encouraged the Peabody Museum to publish *Pre-Columbian Man in Costa Rica* in 1977, the first English-language synthesis of Costa Rican archaeology. Stone's later publications emphasize broad synthetic themes that serve to place her fieldwork results in context with the continuing work of a new generation. An edited collection on cultivated plants (Stone, ed. 1984) resulted from a symposium at the International Congress of Americanists, and a co-edited volume on the archaeology of lower Central America stemmed from a seminar at the School of American Research (Stone and Lange 1984).

Stone's life has been the subject of preliminary research by Mary Ann Levine (1994), who notes that Stone's career epitomizes one alternative strategy for survival of women during the institutionalization of archaeology in the first half of the twentieth century. Obtaining training at what Levine calls "prestigious institutions in the East" paved the way for women like Doris Stone to become unpaid research associates working independently under the sponsorship of equally prestigious universities and museums. By virtue of her freedom from the need for economic support, Stone was able to pursue her archaeological concerns according to her own formulation of basic problems, and she proved herself to her male teachers and colleagues by her mastery of her chosen field. Although Stone downplays the difficulties she faced as a woman in archaeology, she has been a significant benefactor of women in academia, endowing a tenured position at Harvard and supporting Radcliffe's research centers, and thus ensuring others opportunities she did not have herself.

Rosemary A. Joyce

References

Andrews V. E. W., ed. 1986. *Research and Reflections in Archaeology and History: Essays in Honor of Doris Stone.* Middle American Research Institute Publication no. 57. New Orleans: Tulane University.

Levine, M. A. 1994. "Creating Their Own Niches: Alternative Career Styles among Women in Americanist Archaeology between the Wars." In *Women In Archaeology.* Ed. C. Claassen. Philadelphia: University of Pennsylvania Press.

Stone, Doris Z. 1938. *Masters in Marble.* Middle American Research Institute Publication, no. 8. New Orleans: Tulane University.

———. 1941. *Archaeology of the North Coast of Honduras.* Memoirs 9, 1. Cambridge, MA: Harvard University, Peabody Museum of Archaeology and Ethnology.

———. 1957. *The Archaeology of Southern and Central Honduras.* Papers 49, 3. Cambridge, MA: Harvard University, Peabody Museum of Archaeology and Ethnology.

———. 1972. *Pre-Columbian Man Finds Central America.* Cambridge, MA: Peabody Museum Press.

———. 1977. *Pre-Columbian Man in Costa Rica.* Cambridge, MA: Peabody Museum Press.

Stone, Doris E., ed. 1984. *Pre-Columbian Plant Migration.* Papers 76. Cambridge, MA: Harvard University, Peabody Museum of Archaeology and Ethnology.

Stone, Doris E., and F. W. Lange, eds. 1984. *The Archaeology of Lower Central America.* Albuquerque: University of New Mexico Press.

Williams, S. 1986. "Doris Stone: The Pathways of a Middle American Scholar." In *Research and Reflections in Archaeology and History: Essays in Honor of Doris Stone,* pp. 199–202. Ed. E. W. Andrews. Middle American Research Institute Publication 57. New Orleans: Tulane University.

Strong, William Duncan (1899–1962)

Born in Portland, Oregon, William Duncan Strong became a major figure in U.S. anthropology, distinguished in archaeological research as a theorist and as a teacher. After serving in the U.S. Navy in World War I, he went to the University of California, Berkeley, and received his B.A. in 1923. From an early interest in natural history he turned to anthropology as a result of the influence of Alfred A. Kroeber, with whom he worked on material excavated in PERU many years earlier by MAX UHLE. Strong's 1926 Ph.D. dissertation, "An Analysis of Southwestern Society," combined archaeological and ethnological data on the house-lineage-fetish complex.

He joined the staff of the Field Museum of Natural History in 1926 and took part in a fifteen-month expedition to Labrador where he spent a winter living with and studying the Naskapi Indians. In 1929, he moved to the University of Nebraska and began two years of archaeological research that completely revised the prehistory of the Great Plains. Instead of the mounted bison hunters of historic times being preceded only by nomads hunting and foraging on foot, he showed that there had been a long period of settled farming villages. Strong also excelled as a teacher, especially in informal, work-related settings, and several of his students at Nebraska went on to have distinguished careers in anthropology.

From 1931 to 1937, Strong was a member of the Bureau of American Ethnology of the SMITHSONIAN INSTITUTION and began archaeological research in Honduras. Like the Great Plains, this was a relatively neglected area, and he quickly identified key problems and laid the foundations for answers, particularly by establishing a firmer chronology of past occupations.

After Strong was appointed to the anthropology faculty of Columbia University in 1937, he turned again to Peruvian archaeology. In 1941, he headed one of ten field parties, under the sponsorship of the Institute for Andean Research, in a program of survey and stratigraphic excavation in lesser-known areas of Latin America. He worked at Pachacamac on the coast of Peru with GORDON WILLEY and John Corbett as student assistants. When he published the results of all ten field parties in 1943, he included a tabular presentation of cultural sequences for twenty regions from the United States to CHILE, aligned to permit continentwide comparisons of cultural development. This and later comparative studies by Strong reflect the change taking place in U.S. archaeology, with emphasis being placed on functional interpretations rather than local chronological sequences.

During World War II, Strong directed a new federal Ethnogeographic Board, which provided the military with information from anthropological sources on little-known parts of the world. In 1945, he returned to his teaching at Columbia, and he was in the field in Peru again the next year with the VIRÚ VALLEY program, a combined geographical, ethnographic, and archaeological study of a single Peruvian valley. It was a landmark in coordinated research and in introducing new concepts and improved chronology. His last work in Peru was in 1952.

Strong's career was cut short by his sudden death. His research combined the details of ceramic sequences with hemispheric comparative studies, and he was influential in moving archaeology toward greater concern with cultural growth and change.

Richard B. Woodbury

References

For references, see *Encyclopedia of Archaeology: The Great Archaeologists, Vol. 1,* ed. Tim Murray (Santa Barbara, CA: ABC-CLIO, 1999), pp. 422–423.

Stukeley, William (1687–1765)

William Stukeley can be regarded as the last of the great English antiquarians and the first of that country's reliable archaeologists. He was born in Lincolnshire, England, the son of a country lawyer and attended Cambridge University from 1704 to 1709. He then moved to London to train as a doctor and later practiced medicine in Boston, Lincolnshire. From 1710 until 1725, he undertook an annual antiquarian tour on horseback to different parts of England viewing churches, abbeys, remarkable buildings and gardens, and sites of historic interest. A competent draftsman, he made many drawings on these tours, and these were published in

William Stukeley (Science Photo)

1724 in a well-illustrated volume, *Itinerarium Curiosum* [List of Curiosities].

Stukeley returned to London in 1717 and became the secretary of the newly revived SOCIETY OF ANTIQUARIES OF LONDON. He became interested in stone circles and their association with the Druids after reading a copy of JOHN AUBREY's *Monumenta Britannica*. For the next few years, he applied himself to elucidating the many problems raised by megalithic monuments, effectively advancing the work that Aubrey had begun. He gathered notes on circles and allied monuments from all over the British Isles and undertook intensive fieldwork on the two major sites of Stonehenge and AVEBURY in Wiltshire. His work at Avebury was especially valuable because the local landowner had begun its wanton destruction, breaking up the great stones for building materials and lime. Without Stukeley's meticulous record of the location of every stone, and his perceptive tracing of depressions and contours, current knowledge of the monument would be greatly reduced.

Similarly, Stukeley carried out intensive fieldwork at Stonehenge over the same period.

He was able to identify that the stone circle was part of a much larger site comprising avenues and ditches and an earthwork enclosure. He was also the first to notice the significance of the orientation of Stonehenge and its potential astrological significance. Stukeley and his patron and friend, the earl of Pembroke, engaged in some limited excavations within the stone circle and learned that the monoliths had been levered into holes in the solid chalk floor of the plain and then packed in with flints for stability.

Accurate measurement, precise draftsmanship, intelligent understanding of the relationship of monuments to landscape, and an ability to make rewarding comparisons with similar sites and structures—all of these qualities made Stukeley a pioneer in field archaeology. He became a minister of the church in 1726 and gave up field archaeology to work on his books *Stonehenge* (1740) and *Avebury* (1743). His record of the sites as they stood in the early-eighteenth century were invaluable to archaeologists of the twentieth century.

Graham Parry

References

For references, see *Encyclopedia of Archaeology: The Great Archaeologists, Vol. 1,* ed. Tim Murray (Santa Barbara, CA: ABC-CLIO, 1999), p. 49.

Su Bingqi (1909–1997)

Su Bingqi was the major archaeological theoretician in the People's Republic of CHINA. Born in Gaoyang (Hebei Province), he graduated from Beiping Normal University in 1934 and then worked at the Society (after 1936, the Institute) for Historical Studies of the National Beiping Academy. As an assistant to the historian Xu Xusheng (Xu Bingchang, 1888–1976), who sought to substantiate archaeologically the then-novel theory that China's early dynasties each had different ethnic origins, Su had his first taste of fieldwork when he participated in excavations at Doujitai, Baoji (Shaanxi Province) in 1934–1937. After the academy had relocated to Kunming in Yunnan Province in southern China during World War II, Su wrote an archaeological report on the Doujitai tombs (published in 1948), applying the method of Swedish archae-

ologist OSCAR MONTELIUS in his meticulous typological analysis of ceramic vessels.

After the Communist takeover in 1949, the Beiping Academy was dissolved. In 1950, both Su and his teacher Xu Xusheng were appointed research fellows at the newly founded Institute of Archaeology of the Chinese Academy of Sciences (since 1977, the Chinese Academy of Social Sciences) in Beijing. Su participated for a time in the institute's fieldwork, and his chronology of late Zhou tombs at Luoyang (Henan Province), excavated in 1955, was long followed as the standard yardstick for cross-dating finds from all over China.

In 1952, Su was appointed professor in the History Department of Beijing University, where he founded mainland China's first academic archaeology program. He served as the program's chair until 1983, simultaneously maintaining his position at the Institute of Archaeology. In 1958, students targeted Su in their criticism of archaeology, which they found insufficiently concerned with real people and society. This spurred Su to conceptualize a new system for the study of prehistoric cultures, enriched with elements of Marxist social theory and an analysis of historical texts. The resulting "Chinese school of archaeology," tailor-made to accommodate the characteristics of Chinese history as well as contemporary political strictures, became widely influential.

Leading his students in excavations at Neolithic sites in Shaanxi Province in 1958–1959, Su first applied Montelian principles in working out the filiation of chronological and regional phases of the Yangshao culture. He subsequently worked out a general theory of simultaneously developing and interacting regional networks and sequences of cultures from which the Chinese civilization gradually emerged. In the 1980s and 1990s, Su traveled widely across China to inspect Neolithic and early–Bronze Age finds, refining and expanding this grand framework.

During the Cultural Revolution (1966–1976), Su was subjected to criticism and sent to perform manual labor in the countryside (1970–1972). Marginalized at the Institute of Archaeology because of differences with its director, XIA NAI, Su developed an independent power base with his former Beijing University students, many of whom came to occupy important positions in the provinces. As provincial-level archaeology became increasingly important in the course of China's economic reforms, their adoption of Su's ideas have shaped a new, regionalist discourse in Chinese archaeology.

Lothar von Falkenhausen

References

For references, see *Encyclopedia of Archaeology: The Great Archaeologists, Vol. 2,* ed. Tim Murray (Santa Barbara, CA: ABC-CLIO, 1999), pp. 597–599.

Sumerians

The Sumerians were the first recorded occupants of the southern half of MESOPOTAMIA; the northern half of this region was referred to as Akkad, with the line of demarcation at Nippur. Famous as the earliest literate society, the Sumerians were unknown until the decipherment of the cuneiform tablets in the nineteenth century revealed the existence of a language (Sumerian) that predated the languages of the Babylonians and Assyrians (which were related to Akkadian, the language of the people of Akkad). The Sumerians are thought to have migrated from the mountains of Elam, almost certainly before the fourth millennium B.C., to the swamps at the head of the Persian Gulf. They drained the swamps, developed means of using floodwaters for irrigation, and established agriculture in the region. Agricultural surpluses became a basis of Sumerian wealth and underpinned intensive participation in long-distance trade as far east as the Indus Valley. Although the Sumerians influenced areas far outside their borders in southern Mesopotamia (certainly through the use of writing), the core of the culture lay in the great city-states such as UR, Eridu, Lagash, Larsa, Nippur, and Uruk, which were often at war with each other. Notwithstanding shared language and strong cultural and religious ties, political volatility and instability were common threads through Sumerian history at least until the sacking of Ur in 2004 B.C.

Tim Murray

Gudea, ensi (governor) of Lagash, ca. 2100 B.C. (Image Select)

See also Indus Civilization; Woolley, Sir Leonard
References

Crawford, Harriet. 1990. *Sumer and the Sumerians.* Cambridge: Cambridge University Press.

Postgate, J. N. 1992. *Ancient Mesopotamia.* London: Routledge.

Sutton Hoo

Sutton Hoo, a site located in Suffolk, England, was the cemetery of the Anglo-Saxon kings of East Anglia. It has been argued that it is the burial of the sixth-century king Raedwald (A.D. 599–635). The site (which comprises two mounds) was excavated in 1938–1939, with the first mound being explored under the direction of archaeologist Charles Phillips. He found a large ship burial with spectacular grave goods. Of particular note are a helmet, sword, and shield, but the grave goods include items of personal adornment in gold and glass, gold coins, and an array of silver vessels. The grave goods, now part of the collection of the BRITISH

Anglo-Saxon helmet and mask from the Sutton Hoo burial site (Image Select)

MUSEUM, were not displayed until after World War II.

Tim Murray

See also Society of Antiquaries of London
References
Bruce-Mitford, Rupert L. S. 1975–1983. *The Sutton Hoo Ship-Burial.* London: British Museum Publications.

Swahili Coast of Africa
Introduction

The Swahili towns on the East African coast have attracted the attention of scholars for many years. Colonial accounts of the origins of this widespread complex of sites, with visible architectural features comprising tombs, mosques, and palaces and substantial subsurface deposits, underplayed the indigenous contribution to the growth and development of the Swahili civilization. Recent archaeological and historical scholarship has gone some way toward reestablishing

the urban identity of the peoples of the coast, and the Swahili are now recognized as centrally important in the western Indian Ocean system linking the Middle East, India, and the far interior of Africa.

The great majority of Swahili settlements and towns along the East African coast are found in a narrow coastal strip of sandy soils that support the Zanzibar-Inhambane vegetational mosaic (White 1983). In the northern zone, the Somali-Maasai mosaic provides a dry hinterland that is most suited to herding and hunting while to the south, the vast Zambezian forested areas provide resources for mixed agriculture and hunting and, of course, gold on the Zimbabwean plateau. The offshore island archipelago of the Comoros, which is partly volcanic, and northwestern MADAGASCAR, with its sheltered bays and richly forested interior, provide substantial opportunities for subsistence, trade, and urban development.

Hafun, near the Horn, which dates from the early centuries B.C. to about A.D. 200, is the earliest trading site yet located on the East African coast (Smith and Wright 1988)—quite possibly, it was one of the entrepôts mentioned in the Periplus of the Erythraean Sea (a document written ca. A.D. 50 in Greek and Egyptian, author unknown, describing contact with East Africa). Southward, the coastal zone is punctuated by a series of important rivers that provide access to the interior and often have trading sites at their mouths. The earliest town site in eastern Africa, that of Rhapta (known from the Periplus), has still not been located, but it was perhaps situated in the Rufiji delta where finds of early trade goods dated approximately 200 B.C.–A.D. 200 have been recently located by Felix Chami.

The existence of a town at that time might presuppose a settlement hierarchy of early farming community sites. Sites of the Kwale Matola tradition dating from the B.C.–A.D. transition to ca. A.D.400 are known to have existed in a great distributional swath along the coastal hinterland from Kenya down to southern Mozambique and into South Africa (Sinclair 1987; Soper 1971). The possibility that these early sites of iron-using farmers constituted a prestate settlement system is widely accepted and increasingly they are also believed to have had the potential to have undergone an urban transformation.

Archaeology on the East African coast from the 1950s through the 1970s was concerned mainly with visible architectural remains. The tombs, temples, and palaces of the Swahili coast were located stratigraphically through archaeological excavation, chronologically by using imported ceramics, and architecturally in relation to better known building styles from the Middle East and India. These often very impressive scholarly efforts were strongly influenced by colonial ideology, which tended toward invasionist interpretations based on ethnic definitions expressed in terms of "Africans," "Arabs," or "Austronesians" and often underestimated the creativity of the indigenous peoples of the coast. The limited excavations on the Kenyan coast of stone buildings of "the Arab city of Gedi" and Ungwana (Kirkman 1954, 1966) were superseded by investigations of the Portuguese Fort Jesus in Mombasa (Kirkman 1974) and extensive excavations of the mosque and palace complexes at the major urban site of Kilwa on the southern Tanzanian coast (Chittick 1974).

In the 1980s, extensive archaeological excavations by Chittick (1984) at Manda in the Lamu archipelago off the east coast of Kenya were followed by excavations at Takwa, a site off the coast in an archipelago (Wilson 1980; Wilson and Omar 1996, 1997). Detailed stratigraphic excavations by M. Horton (1996) at Shanga in the same archipelago provided fine resolution chronological sequences and spatial layout of mosque construction and house forms. G. Abungu (1989), working at Ungwana, extended previous work by J. S. Kirkman (1966) and followed the settlement pattern inland up the river Tana. Work at Pate (located again in the same archipelago) by T. Wilson and A. L. Omar (1996, 1997) produced new insights into urban structure.

On the southern Kenyan coast, work by Wilding and later by C. Kusimba (1996) at Mtwapa was carried out in conjunction with investigations at Mombasa. First steps to investigate the role of symbolic values in shaping architectural features, especially Swahili houses, were implemented by L. W. Donelly (1982) on the Kenyan coast. This cognitive approach was extended to the settlement level by S. Kus (1982) in highland Madagascar.

The central coast of Tanzania has been the focus of numerous recent excavations, notably those by Felix Chami of the University of Dar es Salaam, which have transformed our view of the first millennium A.D. chronology and external trading contacts of the early farming communities of this area (Chami 1994, 1998). On Zanzibar and Pemba, a series of surveys focused on stone-built sites have been carried out and followed by excavations (e.g., Clark and Horton 1985; Juma 1996; La Violette and Fleisher 1995). Recent excavations at Unguja Ukuu on Zanzibar have demonstrated trading contact with Roman Egypt as early as the mid-fifth century A.D. (Horton 1996; Juma 1996).

By the eleventh century, the Swahili settlements extended more than 3,000 kilometers along the coastal strip from Somalia to Mozambique, and more than 400 sites were occupied before the sixteenth century (Horton 1987). The settlement system also encompassed the Comoros and the northwestern coast of Madagascar (Vérin 1986, Wright 1984), which were important foci of East African urban development from at least the ninth century A.D. on. The subsistence economy was based on hunting, fishing, cultivation, and livestock and included pottery and ironworking. Trade commodities included slaves, ivory, salt, rock crystal, animal skins, and cloth as well as iron and also gold from the south.

The earliest architectural evidence for the adoption of Islam from the latter first millennium A.D. comes from Shanga in the Lamu archipelago (Horton 1996) and early mosque construction at Sima in the Comorian archipelago. The 1100s and 1200s A.D. saw the widespread adoption of Islam, and this period is marked by a marked increase in settlement area (Wright 1993).

The Offshore Islands
On the Comoro Islands, small fishing and farming communities were established in the late first millennium A.D. (Allibert, Argant, and Ar-

gant 1990; Wright 1984), and they maintained trading contact with the East African coast. Early settlements with stone mosques, for example, at Sima on Anjouan, developed into a network of stone-built trading towns. In northwestern Madagascar, traces of human activity occur from ca. A.D. 770.

A number of settlements were established, and these were at first called trading *échelles* by Pierre Vérin (1986) and later discussed in terms of being towns and city-states or part of larger states (Vérin 1992). At Mahilaka in Ampisindava Bay, one such settlement, established ca. A.D. 900, grew to be a large walled town greater than twenty hectares in extent in the thirteenth and fourteenth centuries. Mahilaka maintained extensive trading contacts and had an estimated population of 3,500 before it declined in the fifteenth century (Radimilahy 1998).

The Southern Swahili Coast

Far to the south, in Mozambique, a series of publications concerning work on Portuguese remains on the Sofala coast was produced by, among others, G. Liesegang (1972) and L. Barradas (1967). Further north, a number of Swahili towns and settlements have been recognized, particularly in the Querimba archipelago at Ilha de Mocambique, near Nacala (Duarte 1993), and at Angoche. Farming community sites of the coastal area and interior of Nampula have been extensively investigated, particularly by Adamowicz (Sinclair et al. 1993).

In Vilanculos Bay, the Bazaruto Islands provided safe settlement locations, such as at Ponta Dundo, while on the mainland, where the River Govuro runs parallel to the coast, a settlement and trading entrepôt developed at Chibuene. From at least about A.D. 650, Chibuene maintained contacts deep into the interior, furnishing imported pottery and glass beads from the Persian Gulf as far as Palapye in eastern Botswana and there is evidence of extensive ironworking activities at Chibuene (Kiyaga Mulindwa 1992; Sinclair 1982, 1987). Later, the settlements along the Mozambique coast played an important role in linking the states of the Zimbabwean plateau with Kilwa and other Swahili trading cities.

The Swahili settlements were established initially as small local farming and fishing villages at a number of different places along the coast and the offshore islands. With the growth of overseas trade and the consolidation of internal production sectors, they underwent major expansion until they culminated in the Muslim towns of the fourteenth and fifteenth centuries. Although most settlements remained small villages, several towns expanded greatly in size and population. The larger towns exceeded ten hectares and had buildings of coral rag stone and wood-and-daub houses. Examples of classic Swahili cut coral architecture are best known from spectacular major sites such as Kilwa and Gedi, but they occur more widely. The settlements were small by modern standards, and even at their peak, in the fifteenth century, few were larger than twenty hectares. Their populations must have been small; for example, in the fourteenth century, the important town of Shanga had 220 masonry houses within seven hectares and an estimated population of 3,000 (Horton 1996, 58).

The main towns developed into city-states and had very little political control over their hinterlands. These major towns, from the Lamu archipelago, Ungwana on Tana, Malindi, Gedi, Mombasa, and Tongoni, as well as the towns on the southern Tanzanian coast and islands of Zanzibar and Pemba, represented larger population centers on a quite densely populated coast with numerous smaller villages in between. Initial investigations of parameters of settlement location and a spatial analysis of settlement size by J. De V. Allen (1980) and T. Wilson (1982) established a site hierarchy, which is still in use today, consisting of isolated structures, hamlets, and small settlements of less than 2.5 hectares; medium-sized sites occupying about 2.5 to 5 hectares; larger stone town sites 5–15 hectares in size; and town sites greater than 15 hectares. The Comoros apparently had similar urban networks, and in northern Madagascar, at least one of the coastal settlements, Mahilaka, grew into a large, walled urban settlement with extensive trading contacts with other parts of the western Indian Ocean system.

Current Issues

In general, controlled stratigraphic excavations at major settlements on the East African coast, dated by imported ceramics, go some way toward providing a general framework for stone town urban development. They still fall short, however, of providing clear estimates of the volume and spatial extent of nonstone-built residential areas and the relation of the country towns to the archaeologically better known stone towns, for example, Shanga (Horton 1996). The recognition of clusters of coastal settlements, for example, by Abungu (1998), points to the need for a detailed investigation of an area larger than an individual site. The need is to establish the contemporary size and spatial layout of the sites that made up the settlement clusters, which might provide significant insights into subsistence, craft specialization, and the political organization of the Swahili city-states.

Trade and Urban Development

Interregional trade knowledge, which is often based on evidence of imported ceramics, has been seen as fundamental for the growth of towns in East Africa (Horton 1987; Kusimba 1999; Middleton 1992; Wright 1993). The limited concept of "the Swahili corridor" as a conduit of trade has been expanded with the recognition of a lattice of trading hubs linking the offshore islands and the East African coast extending far into the various interiors (Sinclair 1995). Wilson (1982) pointed out that Swahili town sites were situated, not only to facilitate trade, but also in terms of local agricultural potential. The distinction between coast and interior has begun to crumble with the progress of historical and archaeological research that focuses on local production and exchange (Haaland 1994–1995; Horton and Mudida 1993; Kusimba 1993; Mutoro 1998; Radimilahy 1998; Wright 1984). New methods of retrieval of evidence from archaeological excavations and computer-aided remote-sensing applications such as GEOGRAPHIC INFORMATION SYSTEMS (GIS) are being developed to better address these issues.

Socioeconomic and Political Organization

Although archaeological and documentary evidence tell us something about the physical characteristics of the Swahili towns, we still know very little about their socioeconomic and political organization prior to the nineteenth century. Using scattered travelers' accounts from the tenth century on, supplemented by Portuguese sources from the sixteenth and seventeenth centuries and ethnographic sources, numerous authors have attempted to reconstruct the sociopolitical and local and regional economic relationships of the Swahili (Allen 1993; Mazrui 1995; Middleton 1992; Nurse and Spear 1985; Pouwel 1987).

Current discussion focuses upon the difficulties encountered in trying to provide dynamic models of culture change and urban development. The roles of external-forcing mechanisms and human-induced environmental change in system collapse have also been the focus of recent discussion (e.g., Kusimba 1999; Sinclair 1995) as has been the suitability of different concepts of city and state in describing Swahili political organization (Kusimba 1999).

Paul J. J. Sinclair

References

Abungu, G. 1989. "Communities on the River Tana, Kenya." Ph.D. dissertation, University of Cambridge.

———. 1998. "City States of the East African Coast and Their Maritime Contacts." In *Transformations in Africa,* 204–218. Ed. G. Connah. London: Leicester University Press.

Ådahl, K., and B. Sahlström, eds. 1995. *Acta Universitatis Upsaliensis figura nova series 27.* Uppsala.

Allen, J. De V. 1980. "Settlement Patterns on the East African Coast c. 800–1900." In *Proceedings of the Eighth Pan African Congress of Prehistory and Quaternary Studies.* Ed. R. Leakey and B. Ogot. Nairobi: ILLMIAP.

———. 1993. *Swahili Origins.* London: J. Currey.

Allibert, C., A. Argant, and J. Argant. 1990. "Le Site de Dembéni (Mayotte, Archipel des Comores)." *Études Océan Indien* 11: 63–172.

Barradas, L. 1967. "A primitiva Mambone e suas immediacoes." *Monumenta* 3: 23–41.

Broberg, A. 1995. "New Aspects of the Medieval Towns of Benedir in Southern Somalia." In *Acta Universitatis Upsaliensis figura nova series 27,*

111–122. Ed. K. Ådahl and B. Sahlström. Uppsala.

Chami, F. 1994. *The Tanzanian Coast in the First Millennium A.D.* Studies in African Archaeology no. 7. Uppsala.

———. 1998. "A Review of Swahili Archaeology." *African Archaeological Review* 15, no. 3: 199–219.

Chanudet, C., and P. Vérin. 1983. "Une reconnaissance archéologique de Mohéli." *Études Océan Indien* 2: 41–58.

Chittick, H. N. 1974. *Kilwa: An Islamic Trading City on the East African Coast.* 2 vols. Azaria, 9: 159–205. Nairobi: British Institute in Eastern Africa.

———. 1984. *Manda: Excavations at an Island Port on the Kenya Coast.* Nairobi: British Institute in Eastern Africa, Mem. no. 9.

Clark, H. N., and M. Horton. 1985. *Zanzibar Archaeological Survey 1984/5.* Zanzibar.

Connah, G., ed. 1998. *Transformations in Africa.* London: Leicester University Press.

Donelly, L. W. 1982. "House Power: Swahili Space and Symbolic Markers." In *Symbols in Aetia,* 114–126. Ed. Ian Hodder. Cambridge and New York: Cambridge University Press.

Duarte, R. T. 1993. "Northern Mozambique in the Swahili World." *Studies in African Archaeology* (Uppsala) 4.

Freeman, Grenville, G. S. P. 1963–1976. "The Coast, 1498–1840." In *The History of East Africa,* 1: 129–168. Ed. R. Oliver. Oxford: Clarendon Press.

———. (Ed.). 1975. *The East African Coast: Select Documents from the First to the Earlier Nineteenth Century,* 2d ed. London: Collins.

———. 1988. *The Swahili Coast, Second–Nineteenth Centuries.* London: Variorum Publishers.

Haaland, R. 1994–1995. "Dakawa: An Early Iron Age Site in the Tanzanian Hinterland." *Azania* 29–30: 238–247.

Horton, M. 1987. "The Swahili Corridor." *Scientific American* 257 (September): 86–93.

———. 1996. *The Archaeology of a Muslim Trading Community on the Coast of East Africa.* London: British Institute in Eastern Africa.

Horton, M., and N. Mudida. 1993. "Exploitation of Marine Resources: Evidence for the Origin of Three Swahili Communities of East Africa." In *Archaeology of Africa: Foods, Metals, and Towns,* 673–693. Ed. T. Shaw, P. J. J. Sinclair, B. Andah, and A. Okpoko. London and New York: Routledge.

Jama, A. D. 1996. "The Origin and Development of Mogadishu, A.D. 1000–1850: A Case Study of Urban Growth along the Benedir Coast of Southern Somalia." *Studies in African Archaeology* (Uppsala) 12.

Juma, A. 1996. "The Swahili and the Mediterranean Worlds: Pottery from the Late Roman Period from Zanzibar." *Antiquity* 70: 148–154.

Kirkman, J. S. 1954. *The Arab City of Gedi: Excavations at the Great Mosque, Architecture and Finds.* London: Oxford University Press.

———. 1964. *Men and Monuments on the East African Coast.* London: Lutterworth Press.

———. 1966. *Ungwana on the Tana.* The Hague: Mouton.

———. 1974. *Fort Jesus, a Portuguese Fortress on the East African Coast.* Oxford: Clarendon Press.

Kiyaga Mulindwa, D. 1992. "Iron-working at Makodu in Eastern Botswana." In *Urban Origins in Eastern Africa, Proceedings of the 1991 Workshop,* 162–167. Ed. P. Sinclair and A. Juma. Stockholm.

Kus, S. 1982. "Matters Material and Ideal." In *Symbols in Aetia.* Ed Ian Hodder. Cambridge and New York: Cambridge University Press.

Kusimba, C. 1993. *The Archaeology and Ethnography of Iron Metallurgy on the Swahili Coast.* Ann Arbor.

———. 1996. "Spatial Organization at Swahili Archaeological Sites in Kenya." In *Aspects of African Archaeology,* 701–713. Ed. G. Pwiti and R. Soper. Harare: University of Zimbabwe Press.

———. 1997. "Swahili and the Coastal City-States." In *Encyclopedia of Precolonial Africa,* 507–513. Ed. J. O. Vogel. Walnut Creek, CA: Alta Mira Press.

———. 1999. *Rise and Fall of Swahili States.* Walnut Creek, CA; Alta Mira Press.

La Violette, A., and J. Fleisher. 1995. "Reconnaissance of Sites Bearing Triangular Incised (Tana Tradition) Ware on Pemba Island, Tanzania." *Nyame Akuma* 44: 59–65.

Liesegang, G. 1972. "Archaeological Sites on the Bay of Sofala." *Azania* 7: 47–159.

Mazrui, Al-Amin Bin 'Ali Al. 1995. *The History of the Mazru'i Dynasty of Mombasa.* London: James Currey.

Middleton, J. 1992. *The World of the Swahili.* New Haven: Yale University Press.

Mutoro, H. 1998. "Precolonial Trading Systems in the East African Interior." In *Transformations in Africa,* 186–203. Ed. G. Connah. London: Leicester University Press.

Nurse, D., and T. Spear. 1985. *Reconstructing the History and Language of a Society, 800–1500*. Philadelphia: University of Pennsylvania Press.

Oliver, R., and G. Mathew, eds. 1963. *The History of East Africa*. Vol. 1. Oxford: Clarendon Press.

Pearson, M. N. 1998. *Port Cities and Intruders: The Swahili Coast, India, and Portugal in the Early Modern Era*. Baltimore: Johns Hopkins University Press.

Pouwel, R. 1987. *Horn and Crescent*. Cambridge and New York: Cambridge University Press.

Pwiti, G., and R. Soper, eds. 1996. *Aspects of African Archaeology*. Harare: University of Zimbabwe Publications.

Radimilahy, C. 1998. "Mahilaka." *Studies in African Archaeology* (Uppsala) 15.

Raharijoana, V. 1988. "Etude de peuplement de l'espace d'une vallée des Hautes Terres Centrales de Madagascar: Archéologie de la Manadona (XVè–XVIè siecles), Vakinankaratra." Doctoral dissertation, Inalco, Paris.

Shaw, T., P. J. J. Sinclair, B. Andah, and A. Okpoko, eds. 1993. *The Archaeology of Africa: Foods, Metals, and Towns*. London and New York: Routledge.

Shepherd, G. 1982. "The Making of the Swahili: A View from the Southern End of the East African Coast." *Paideuma* 28: 129–148.

Sheriff, A. 1987. *Slaves, Spices, and Ivory in Zanzibar*. London: James Currey.

Sinclair, P. J. J. 1982. "Chibuene: An Early Trading Site in Southern Mozambique." *Paideuma* 28: 149–164.

———. 1987. *Space, Time, and Social Formation: A Territorial Approach to the Archaeology and Anthropology of Zimbabwe and Mozambique c. 0–170 A.D.* Uppsala: Societas Archeaological Upsaliensis.

———. 1995. "The Origins of Urbanism in Eastern and Southern Africa: A Diachronic Perspective." In *Acta Universitatis Upsaliensis figura nova series 27*, 99–110. Ed. K. Ådahl and B. Sahlström. Uppsala.

Sinclair, P. J. J., J. M. F. Morais, L. Adamowicz, and R. T. Duarte. 1993. "A Perspective on Archaeological Research in Mozambique." In *The Archaeology of Africa: Foods, Metals, and Towns*, 410–430. Ed. T. Shaw, P. J. J. Sinclair, B. Andah, and A. Okpoko. London and New York: Routledge.

Smith, M., and H. Wright. 1988. "The Ceramics from Ras Hafun in Somalia: Notes on a Clöassical Maritime Site." *Azania* 22: 115–141.

Soper, R. 1971. "A General Review of the Iron Age of the Southern Half of Africa." *Azania* 5: 5–37.

Spear, T. 1977. *The Kaya Complex: A History of the Mijikenda Peoples of the Kenya Coast to 1900*. Nairobi: Kenya Literature Bureau, 1978.

Strandes, J. 1971. *The Portuguese Period in East Africa*. Nairobi: East African Literature Bureau. First published in 1899.

Sutton, J. 1990. *A Thousand Years of East Africa*. Nairobi: British Institute in Eastern Africa.

Trimingham 1975. "The Arab Geographers and the East African Coast." In *East Africa and the Orient*, 115–146. Ed. H. N. Chittick and R. Rotberg. New York: Africana Publishing Co.

Vérin, P. 1986. *The History of Civilisation in North Madagascar*. Rotterdam and Boston: A. A. Balkema.

———. 1992. "Etats ou cités etats dans le nord de Madagascar." *Taloha* 11: 65–70.

White, F. 1983. *The Vegetation of Africa*. Paris: UNESCO.

Willis, J. 1993. *Mombasa, the Swahili, and the Making of the Mijikenda*. Oxford: Clarendon Press.

Wilson, T. 1980. "Takwa, an Ancient Swahili Settlement of the Lamu Archipelago." *Kenya Past and Present* 10: 6–16.

———. 1982. "Spatial Analysis and Settlement Patterns on the East African Coast." *Paideuma* 28: 201–219.

Wilson, T., and A. L. Omar. 1996. "Excavation at Pate on the East African Coast." In *Aspects of African Archaeology*, 543–554. Ed. G. Pwiti and R. Soper. Harare: University of Zimbabwe Press.

———. 1997. "Archaeological Investigations at Pate." *Azania* 32: 31–76.

Wright, H. T. 1984. "Early Seafarers of the Comoro Islands: The Dembeni Phase of the IXth–Xth Centuries." *Azania* 19: 13–60.

———. 1993. "Trade and Politics on the Littoral of Africa, A.D. 800–1300." In *The Archaeology of Africa*, 658–672. Ed. T. Shaw, P. J. J. Sinclair, B. Andah, and A. Okpoko. London and New York: Routledge.

Wright, H. T., and J. A. Rakotoarisoa. 1990. "The Archaeology of Complex Societies in Madagascar: Case Studies in Cultural Diversification." In *Urban Origins in Eastern Africa: Proceedings of the 1989 Madagascar Workshop*. Ed. P. J. J. Sinclair and J. A. Rakotoarisoa. Stockholm.

Swartkrans

Swartkrans is a cave in South Africa with deposits dating from 1.7 to 1 million years ago that contain hominid fossils. The first of these fossils was recovered by R. Broom and J. T. Robinson in 1948. Work has continued at the site (most notably by C. K. Brain since 1965), and more than 100 representatives of *Australopithecus robustus* have been identified. This human ancestor is substantially more "robust" than the smaller gracile East African *A. afarensis* and *A. africanus,* although it is younger than them at one million years old. The site has gained additional significance through the discovery of fossils of *Homo erectus* in the same deposits as those of the australopithecines, which indicates that at some time in the early Pleistocene period, both hominids were contemporaneous.

Tim Murray

See also Africa, South, Prehistory
References
Brain, C. K., ed. 1993. *Swartkrans: A Cave's Chronicle of Early Man.* Pretoria: Transvaal Museum.

Sweden

Not only is Sweden's antiquarian/archaeological history closely related to that of the other Scandinavian countries, but the subject has also been influenced by theories from other disciplines as well as by currents of thought in Europe. Sociopolitical changes in Sweden have also contributed to this history. The antiquarian/archaeological discourse thus consists of a multitude of more or less connected assertions that must be understood against this background. A summary of such a multitude is made at the expense of other material, and this article is an attempt to show how the subject successively changed and finally developed. The history is therefore more a question of discontinuities rather than one of continuous development, and the changes can only be understood in relation to earlier ways of thinking.

The 1500s

In the mid-fifteenth century, the first chronicle was written about the history of the Swedish state until the reign of Karl VIII (1448–1457). The author is unknown but was most likely a monk closely connected to the regent. Thus, history was closely tied to power. The chronicle began with the Flood, and Swedish history was

associated with myths about Noah. Scyths and Geats, historically known peoples from around the Black Sea and ancient Thrace, are mentioned. This chronicle was also the first example of the Gothic interpretation of history. The author used older sources, which fueled speculations, and the chronicle's influence on sixteenth-century historians is very apparent.

On 6 June 1523, Gustav I (1496?–1560) was crowned king, and a new era began in Sweden. The country converted to Protestantism, and the entire Swedish society was reformed, including the interpretation of history. One of the more influential reformers was Olaus Petri (1493?–1552), who wrote, at the end of the 1530s, *Svenska krönika* [Swedish Chronicle] as a reaction against the biased nature of the older chronicles. Characterized by a certain freedom from national prejudice, Petri's chronicle was the first original work to be written in the modern Swedish language, and thousands of copies were printed and distributed. According to Petri, the historian should be impartial and seek the truth, but in spite of this claim, the chronicle should be judged in the context of political and religious changes. Petri expressed, for example, doubts about the Goths' migration from Sweden, but he also found fault with Gustav I's church politics and government. Didactic intentions can also be discerned.

Petri believed there was very little knowledge available about Swedish history between the birth of Christ and the introduction of Christianity. Only medieval history was completely clear, because written evidence, such as sealed letters and documents, existed from that time. Petri was also interested in runes, which resulted in a separate work.

If Petri tried to shorten historical perspective, the opposite is true of Johannes Magnus (1488–1544), Sweden's last Catholic bishop. His view of Swedish history in his *Historia de omnibus gothorum sueonumque regibus,* published in 1553 in Rome, was from the perspective of 4,000 years. Although it was supposed to reflect a desire for truth, rather than a desire for eloquence, it hardly succeeded. Instead, the work was characterized by uncritical views of history and pure fabrication. Magnus saw, for example, a connection between the European Goths and the Swedish "Göter," a mythological people, and traced Swedish history back to Japhet's son Magog.

The chronicle was nevertheless a significant work, and the only publications that can compete with it in influence are Petri's reformatory works. Successive Swedish kings and statesmen directly or indirectly obtained their historical knowledge from the chronicle, and Gothicism greatly influenced the sixteenth- and seventeenth-century view of history.

The 1600s

During the 1600s, Sweden became a great power through its victories during the Thirty Years' War, and in that context, antiquarian research went in a direction that had little in common with what had preceded. Sweden's first antiquarian and, moreover, director of national antiquities was JOHAN BURE (1568–1652). In 1599, he devised a system to interpret runes, and in the same year he received a permit from King Karl IX (1550–1611) to travel around Sweden and document rune stones and locate ancient monuments. Bure was a pioneer in rune research, as Petri's documentation had been fairly insignificant.

Although Bure's contributions were limited, his close contact with the kings of Sweden drew their attention to antiquarian research, and as a result, official antiquarian research took shape. On the advice of Bure, King Gustav II Adolf (1594–1632) issued, for example, an "antiquities instruction" whereby he ordered the nation's antiquarians to collect antiquities, and consequently, the Central Board of National Antiquities developed.

Bure's successor, Johan Hadorph (1630–1693) traveled throughout the countryside with draftsmen and scribes and documented about 1,000 runic inscriptions. One of the draftsmen was Elias Brenner (1647–1717), a student of Olof Verelius (1618–1682), who was professor of antiquities at Uppsala. It was, however, from Johannes Schefferus (1621–1679) that Brenner received his first insights into numismatics, which he elevated to a science in the 1690s. Hadorph researched both ancient monuments

and artifacts as well as folk traditions. During the mid-1680s, he also conducted archaeological excavations in the Viking town of Birka. Verelius had also undertaken fieldwork, and so had Olof Rudbeck (1630–1702), who investigated royal Iron Age burial mounds in Old Uppsala.

Place-name research by Petter Dijkman (1647?–1717) developed alongside antiquarian research. Dijkman communicated with Schefferus about his numismatic studies under Brenner, and Dijkman's *Bua Haiti,* one of the first attempts at place-name research, was published in 1711. Dijkman was influenced by Kilian Stobaeus's uncle Anders Stobaeus (1642–1714), a historian, Latin scholar, and poet. One of Dijkman's more important works was published posthumously in 1723. It contained a selection of material from seventeenth-century rune research and was particularly concerned with the Christian faith's influence on the inscriptions. Dijkman made use of previously published material, and of the ninety inscriptions he discussed, some seventy are found in Bure and Verelius.

Hadorph was primarily an organizer and viewed himself as a materialist. In 1666, he was appointed director of national antiquities, and he became powerful within the Antiquities Committee, which was established during the same year. The committee's tasks were to preserve the country's ancient monuments; publish Icelandic sagas and ancient Swedish laws; create a Swedish dictionary; document rune stones, coins, and seals; and carry out archaeological excavations. The committee was first based in Uppsala but was moved in 1690 to Stockholm. Gradually, its organization was tightened, and it was renamed the Antiquities Archive. The chairman had the title of secretary and functioned as the director of national antiquities.

Hadorph also became secretary of the Antiquities Archive but died soon afterward. After the demise of the last secretary in 1777 there was no appointment of a new one, and in 1780, the archive was dissolved. After the reorganization of Queen Lovisa Ulrika's (1720–1782) Literary Academy in 1786, the Academy of Literature, History, and Antiquities took over the duties of the Antiquities Archive, and its secretary became the director of national antiquities.

Legend:
- ▲ Mesolithic site
- ● Neolithic site

Map labels:
- NORWEGIAN SEA
- Kiruna
- ▲ Voullerim
- Lillberget ▲
- Rastklippan ▲
- Luleå
- Bjurselet ●
- Garaselet ▲
- Lundfors ▲
- Tjikkiträsk ●▲
- Strandholm ●
- Stornorrfors
- Umeå
- Nämforsen ●
- NORWAY
- Flatruet ▲●
- Gulf of Bothnia
- FINLAND
- Åloppe ●
- Uppsala
- Östra Vrå ●
- Stockholm
- Lihult ▲
- Ekornavallen, Karleby ●
- Dags mosse ●
- Gothenburg
- Sandarna
- St. Bjärs ●
- Västerbjärs ●
- Gotland
- Köpingsvik ●
- Tingby ▲
- Öland
- BALTIC SEA
- LATVIA
- LITHUANIA
- Gillhög
- Ageröd ▲
- Barum
- Segebro
- Hagestad
- Malmö
- Fosie
- Limhamn
- Skateholm

Scale: 0 — 200 km

Stone Age Archaeological Sites in Sweden

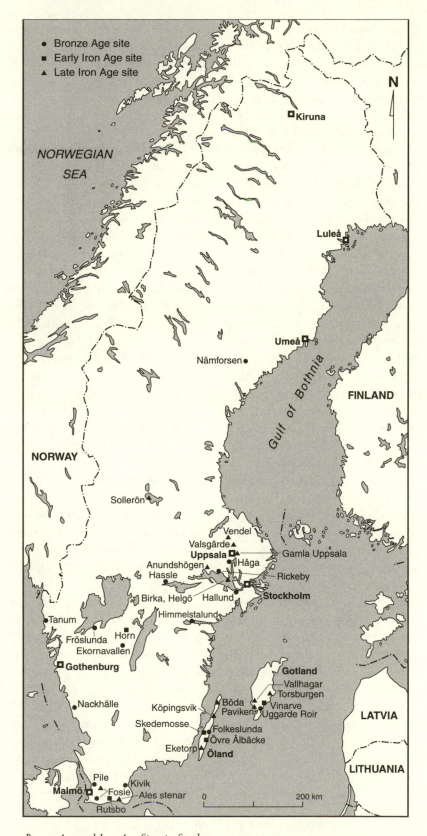

Bronze Age and Iron Age Sites in Sweden

Archaeological excavations were consequently carried out, and Schefferus wrote Sweden's first archaeological dissertation, a work that discussed a bronze sword found in Scania and three gold bracteates. In spite of this work, most of the academy's interests were focused on literary sources and, in particular, on Icelandic ones. During the late seventeenth century, patriotism and Gothicism reached the height of their popularity. Gothicism identified the Goths with the *hyperborés,* an ancient mythological people, a theory that was supported by some evidence from Icelandic material. Olof Rudbeck, in his monumental work *Atlantican* (1679–1702), claimed that Sweden was the lost civilization of Atlantis. Although the work was received with enthusiasm outside of Sweden, it soon lost its standing and was criticized by Schefferus and Hadorph, who had little sympathy for such speculation. Perhaps the most interesting critique of *Atlantican* was by the German philosopher Gottfried Wilhelm von Leibniz (1646–1716), who was one of the forerunners of the scientific revolution. Leibniz's critique was ironic and was an indication that new scientific viewpoints were developing in Europe.

Various bills to protect ancient monuments were issued in 1666 and renewed in 1669, 1676, and 1684, and they laid the groundwork for more organized antiquarian research. Priests and public officials were ordered to participate in field surveys and to send the results of any pillaging of monuments to the Antiquities Committee, and ancient monuments were more closely linked to royal power. During the 1600s, there was still no organized research that focused on the material culture and artifacts associated with ancient monuments. Artifacts were collected and documented but then compared to literary sources. It was unthinkable to view them as something outside the literary historical field.

The 1700s

In 1718, King Karl XII died, and Sweden's period as a great power came to an end. During the following years, known as "the period of liberty," parliamentary power took shape. An unsuccessful war against RUSSIA (1741–1743), bureaucracy, and a disorganized monetary system caused many problems for Sweden during this period. Later, after a successful reorganization of the monetary system, closer ties with England, and the establishment of ties with Russia, the first Swedish law concerning freedom of the press was instigated.

During this period, antiquarian research was still faulty and descriptive, its results were mainly compilations, and any conclusions it drew were speculative and lacked cohesion. Historians continued to interpret Sweden's earliest times. Jacob Wilde (1679–1755) was one of Sweden's first modern historians, and he often dealt with problems with source material. Wilde demolished Johannes Magnus's list of regents and criticized Olof Rudbeck's fantasies. Wilde's work dealt with three historical periods—ancient times, the Middle Ages, and modern times—and his divisions were later accepted by several historiographers. The ancient period was divided into two ages: a "dark age," knowledge of which must be sought among classical authors, and a "mythological age," ca. 120 B.C.–ca. A.D. 1150. Within the latter age, three phases were identified: the cairn age, the cremation age, and the mound age. It was a historical division, based on Icelandic sagas and not on archaeological material. There was no comprehension of a prehistory that demanded an independent chronology. Wilde was followed by Olof von Dalin (1708–1763), Anders af Botin (1724–1790), and Sven Lagerbring (1707–1787).

The doctor and antiquarian Kilian Stobaeus (1690–1742) and the philosopher Andreas Rydelius (1671–1738) taught Dalin in Lund. Stobaeus occupied Lund University's first chair of natural science in 1728 but exchanged it for a professorship in history in 1732. The great philosopher Carolus Linnaeus was one of his many pupils. Stobaeus taught natural science, history, numismatics, and antiquarian research. He donated his significant collection of artifacts and natural objects, known as Museum Stobaeanum, to Lund University in 1735.

Dalin began a state administrative career in Stockholm in 1727 and at the same time, together with Johan Ihre (1707–1780), competed for the position of state historiographer. Although the position was given to Dalin, Ihre was also a significant scholar and university man. His greatest contribution was within the field of comparative linguistics, in the study of ancient Swedish and Icelandic, which resulted in a penetrating study of Snorre's *Edda*. Ihre, too, had a realistic, although not entirely correct, concept of the age of the runic inscriptions, but he did correctly interpret some detailed runic problems.

Dalin was a skillful poet, satirist, and Sweden's first modern author. He introduced the ideas of the Enlightenment to a Swedish audience and, like Petri, he was a national historian who wrote in the modern Swedish language. Beginning in the 1740s, Dalin devoted himself to writing officially commissioned histories. The first volume (1747) dealt with the ancient period, the second (1750) with the Middle Ages, and the third (1760–1761) with King Gustav I and his sons. Dalin was influenced by Wilde and discussed his burial periods; Tacitus and other historical writers are listed among his references. In a historic-moralistic spirit, Dalin thought ancient people splendid, an opinion he derived from the work of the astronomer Anders Celsius (1701–1744) and Isaac Newton's climate theory. As an advocate of modern culture, Dalin was opposed to the philosophy of Frenchman Jean-Jacques Rousseau (1712– 1778), which caused him to describe the flaws of the ancient period. His views of the ancient period were thus somewhat paradoxical.

Dalin based his chronology on the theory of water reduction in accordance with the natural-scientific views of the Enlightenment, which was based on an incorrect interpretation of land elevation and sea changes. Dalin wanted to show that Sweden, during the centuries before Christ, had been an insignificant archipelago, but his interpretation was met by protests from among the clergy and the ultrapatriots. Dalin, like Wilde, also rejected the chronology of the regents, which began with Magog. Dalin also broke with Rudbeck's view of history, although he himself was steered by false etymologies and national prejudice. Dalin's critique was founded on common sense. He sought to be pragmatic, and he avoided writing a chronicle. He sought

the actual causes behind events, and he evaluated them from the viewpoint of society.

Anders af Botin's *Utkast till svenska folkets historia* [History of the Swedish People] (1757–1764) was modeled on the work of the French writer Voltaire in that it paid attention to the economic and cultural questions of history. The work was divided into six epochs, encompassing history from the ancient period to King Gustav I, and was pragmatic in its attempts to determine the causes and effects of events. Each epoch was divided into different subject areas, for example, kings, the populace, and modes of thinking and living. Although Botin was influenced by Dalin, he was also critical of him. Botin believed that Dalin's judgment and knowledge were not sound enough to morally influence the reader. Botin also thought Dalin lacked insight into law and economics and that his chronology, based on the theory of water reduction, was impossible. Dalin's knowledge of literature and sources was faulty, and his source-evaluation was inadequate since he did not distinguish between primary and secondary sources. Botin criticized Dalin harshly, and while some of the criticisms were petty, others were justified.

Botin belonged to "the liberty historians" who, under the influence of the general empirical direction of science, found their way to primary source materials. His pragmatism and nonhistorical evaluation of earlier times after the standards of his own time, and his literary intentions, are examples of the influence of the Enlightenment. He also rationally criticized the Roman Catholic Church, which led him to a rather pessimistic view of the Middle Ages.

Sven Lagerbring studied at Lund University but spent a few years in Stockholm (1736–1741) where he visited the Antiquities Archive, which greatly influenced his main historical work. His stay in Stockholm was also important for the development of his ideas on history, since it coincided with new political changes that resulted from Sweden's period of liberty. Rydelius and Stobaeus were Lagerbring's most important teachers. In 1742, Lagerbring succeeded Stobaeus as professor of history at Lund University.

Lagerbring introduced modern, critical historical research, in the tradition of Dalin, but he had far more impact than Dalin. He contributed to the publication of thirty-six dissertations on Scania's medieval archaeology, and he was also the first to discuss the historical source value of Icelandic literature in a modern way. Lagerbring taught geography, a significant subject for archaeology, and he helped ensure that the eighteenth century was a golden age for recording the details of provinces, towns, and parishes, a descriptive tradition begun by Dijkman and Stobaeus. Lagerbring also made lasting contributions to the organization of the Cabinet of Coins, which was kept for a long time inside his house. He saw truth, founded in historical criticism, as the historian's guiding star. His method of delivery was original in that it was not organized chronologically, as all earlier histories had been. In accordance with Voltaire, and in a manner similar to that of Botin, Lagerbring arranged source materials by subject matter.

Contrary to Dalin, Lagerbring drew a sharp distinction between source and literature, and he made two new demands on the historian: source references and source evaluation. With source references, statements or suppositions could be checked. For source evaluation, the cardinal rule was that the more certain the contemporary nature of the document, the greater its reliability. Agreement among several sources was important as a criterion of truth. But Lagerbring had a didactic and pedagogical delivery, and he viewed history in the light of his contemporary society's political conditions and according to the rational critique of the eighteenth century. He evaluated ancient and medieval religious conditions in the same way as most scholars of the Enlightenment, with little sympathy for medieval people and a belief that monks were frauds.

The 1800s: Period of Transition
The beginning of the nineteenth century was full of change. Sweden surrendered FINLAND to Russia, a new constitution was written in 1809, and foreign policy was changed. The French field-marshal Jean-Baptiste-Jules Bernadotte, one of Napoleon's generals, ascended the Swedish throne as King Karl XIV Johan in 1818, and during the 1830s, liberal political forces grew stronger.

It is this context Nils Henrik Sjöborg (1767–1838) outlined a THREE-AGE SYSTEM in 1797 even though its structure remained unclear. Sjöborg used a comparative ethnographic perspective, inspired by Anders Jahan Retzius (1742–1821), to help formulate his system. Stobaeus had also used ethnographic analogies to confirm that stone artifacts were used as tools before iron artifacts. Retzius, an early natural science student and a pupil of Linnaeus, donated his collection of prehistoric stone tools and natural history to Lund's museum between 1805 and 1811. He also divided the Museum Stobaeanum into separate natural history, art history, and history departments.

Natural-scientific systematization gradually overtook the historical view. Magnus Bruzelius (1786–1855) began as a physical anthropologist but turned to antiquarian research. Modern European geology, which traced nature's successive development, was also a significant influence, contrasting catastrophe theory with biblical chronology, which had dominated historical research since the sixteenth century.

First Half of the 1800s
A new chronological and ethnographical perspective on history took shape during the early nineteenth century. Its founders were CHRISTIAN JÜRGENSEN THOMSEN (1788–1865) from DENMARK and the Swede SVEN NILSSON (1787–1883). Thomsen's three-age system replaced a chronology that was just a step above confusion. The Swede Magnus Bruzelius had formulated a similar system in the 1820s, based on archaeological find-contexts. Thomsen's system was, however, more composite and it schematized find observations. He was also the first to publicize the system, partly in museological form and partly through communication with colleagues (Gräslund 1987, 18). Nilsson later gave this system a culture-historic shape.

As a scientist, Nilsson was a systematizer, but he was also educated in history and philosophy. He made significant contributions not only to archaeology but also to several subjects within the natural sciences. He collaborated with the English geologist SIR CHARLES LYELL, the English archaeologist Sir John Lubbock (LORD AVEBURY), and their compatriot Charles Darwin. Nilsson carried out fieldwork and collected archaeological and ethnographical objects, and through his experiments in flint knapping he was able to confirm the function of knapping stones.

The idea of primitive people had existed since the seventeenth century, and during the nineteenth century, it became the object of classification and development theories within the natural sciences. Nilsson preferred natural science and comparative, ethnographic archaeology, which he formulated on the basis of the French paleontologist and geologist Georges Cuvier's (1769–1832) natural-scientific method, with archaeological methods above historical analogies. Nilsson was the first scholar in Sweden to use the term *prehistory* (Welinder 1991).

This change in the discourse was, among other things, linked to the Enlightenment's division of society into different subject areas, a way of thinking that both Botin and Lagerbring had borrowed from Voltaire. The need to view society from an evolutionary and holistic perspective developed and was related to the popularity of German Romanticism and its advocates Johann Gottfried Herder (1744–1803) and Georg Wilhelm Friedrich Hegel (1770–1831). Thus, Nilsson viewed development as a whole, with everything in nature, including man's culture, evolving from the lowest stages to the highest. Hidden behind the material world was the development of reason. The process was predetermined.

At first (in 1835), he divided the development of mankind into three economic periods: savage, nomad, and agriculturalist. This system and its divisions were completely separate from Thomsen's three-age system, as the two men were not familiar with each other's work at the time. Later, however, they were in close contact. In the late 1830s, Nilsson added a fourth stage: the agriculturalist, with a written language, production, and a division of labor among the members of society (Nilsson 1838–1843).

The three-age system, on the other hand, was not based on an a priori interpretation of cultural development but neither was it socioeconomic. It was chronological, and since it was related to archaeological find-contexts, it had a great impact because it had empirical and scientific proof. It was not an intuitive, practical method of arranging finds but rather the chronological means of assistance for further investigations (Gräslund 1987, 27).

Mid-1800s

It was through Thomsen and Nilsson that antiquarian research became separate from history and modern archaeology took shape. Gradually, comparative ethnography lost its influence because of its alienation from find-contexts. Instead, it became important to improve on Thomsen's three-age system.

The Dane JENS JACOB WORSAAE (1821–1886) laid significant groundwork for archaeology during the mid-nineteenth century. European cave finds of extinct animal species discovered in stratigraphic connection with cultural remains, finds that Lubbock later called Paleolithic, may have been important for Worsaae's initial division of the Stone Age into two periods. Later Worsaae divided the Stone Age into three periods, with cave finds constituting the earliest period, kitchen middens the middle period, and stone chamber graves the youngest period. Today, these periods are called Paleolithic, Mesolithic, and Neolithic.

The division of the Bronze Age into two parts was first expressed in 1854 by the Swede Nils Gustaf Bruzelius (1826–1895). The division was based on stratigraphy and on the fact that cremation burials overlay inhumations. Through various bog finds, Worsaae formulated a division of the Iron Age into two parts, which was successively confirmed by new finds, and the concept of the Iron Age became common in the Scandinavian countries during the 1850s and 1860s.

After a visit to Hallstatt, AUSTRIA, in 1858, Bruzelius asserted that the Iron Age in southern and central Europe must have begun a couple centuries before the birth of Christ. He also noted a sharp border between the Bronze Age and the Iron Age. He did not, however, compare this observation with conditions in Scandinavia. Instead, it was the Dane Emil Vedel (1824–1909) who asserted that the transition between the Bronze and Iron Ages in Scandinavia occurred before the birth of Christ. He drew this conclusion after investigations at Bornholm between 1868 and 1872. Thereafter came a division of the so-called Roman Iron Age (A.D. 0–450) into two parts, formulated mainly by the Danish archaeologist SOPHUS MÜLLER (1846–1934).

Antiquarian/archaeological research changed from being a political and didactic instrument to an empirical, critical science, and archaeology was finally free from the literary historical analogies. It was no longer a matter of writing a country's history; instead, it was important to organize and systematize the country's nonhistorical source material, and the leaders in the change were Thomsen and Nilsson.

Typology
The chief characteristic of the last half of the nineteenth century was the division of the three-age system into subperiods and the formulation of culture-historic guidelines. Find-contexts played an important role. Within Iron Age research, historical analogies were used in the sense that historically datable, Continental material was comparable with Scandinavian conditions. Numismatics also had a high priority in Iron Age research. Around the year 1870, the nature of archaeological discourse changed again, with chronological work directed toward making shorter time divisions while the intensity of research and the amount of source material increased. The increase in material was seen to be connected with the intensification of agriculture, as well as with increased industrialization in general. By this time, researchers and museum scholars both had a specialized university education. It was in this context that a new archaeological discourse on typology was formulated.

The background of typology was empirical. Changes in form had been described by OSCAR MONTELIUS (1843–1921) and HANS HILDEBRAND (1842–1913) as "development" in accordance with the language of the time. The idea that development was continuous and unbroken was thus the basis of typology. This meant that development could also be observed and traced without the support of find-contexts. With the aid of typology, correct chronological conclusions could be drawn entirely on the basis of changes in form, and in this area, statistics were

an important aid. Typology was, however, formulated in a diffuse way and the term consequently has a broad definition.

It was to mark these new methodological directions that Hildebrand formulated the typological method, but typology was of less importance for him than it was for Montelius (Gräslund 1987, 97). Montelius's famous *Tidsbestämning* [Dating in the Bronze Age] (1885, English edition in 1986) was based, to a greater extent, on different find-contexts than on typology. Determining time sequences in the Bronze Age did not require the development of typological analysis. Thus, Montelius worked not only typologically but also, and especially, by empirically combining different find-contexts.

Müller criticized Montelius for neglecting the relationship between the context of artifacts and the typological series and implied that it was impossible to classify artifacts typologically without taking these contexts into account. In other words, Montelius did not differentiate between typology and find-context analysis.

Yet it was Montelius himself who popularized his image as a typologist. After Darwin's works were published in Swedish, Hildebrand and Montelius began to hint at a connection between typology and Darwinism. However, unlike Hildebrand, Montelius never referred to the theory of natural selection, and as a result, the relationship to Darwinism is vague (Gräslund 1987, 104). Typology belonged more to a pre-Darwin theory of development, a way of thinking that had existed during the eighteenth century, a fact that Nilsson emphasized strongly. But typology also belonged to neo-Kantism and to the advance of positivism within historical research. Hildebrand and Montelius never claimed that Darwinism had given rise to typology (Gräslund 1987, 105). Rather, typology was associated with Darwinism only after the relationship became apparent, and it should therefore be viewed as a scientific-political move.

The most decisive "discovery" of the time was, however, Montelius's dating of the Bronze Age and indirectly also providing dating for the Stone and Iron Ages. A more exact dating of the Stone Age had to wait, however, for the scientific methods that first became possible during the 1970s. The Iron Age in Scandinavia acquired the dates of the sixth century B.C. to eleventh century A.D.

In *Tidsbestämning,* Montelius synchronized historically datable comparative finds from the Mediterranean and Middle East with Scandinavian conditions. In so doing, he could set the span of the Bronze Age from 1500 to 500 B.C. In comparison with the eighteenth-century Bible-based datings and the nineteenth-century vague chronological interpretation (Worsaae, for example, maintained in the 1850s that the Bronze Age reached its peak at around the birth of Christ), this was an enormous step forward.

Early 1900s

During the first half of the twentieth century, archaeological source materials increased considerably, new perspectives opened up, and old methods were refined. In general, research was directed toward settlement history and the history of style.

Settlement history had existed during the nineteenth century, but during the first decades of the twentieth, it became more focused and systematic, and better known to a wider circle of researchers. Investigations of regional complexes of settlement remains also began at this time. Oscar Almgren (1869–1945), together with the botanist and Quaternary geologist Rutger Sernander (1866–1944), made early advances in this field. In 1901, they investigated Uppland's settlement history, encouraged by the discovery of the first Middle Neolithic settlement (ca. 2800 B.C.) in central Sweden.

In 1907, Knut Stjerna (1874–1909) initiated extensive archaeological provincial investigations in southern and central Sweden, focusing on the Stone and Bronze Ages. It was hoped that the project would eventually encompass all of Sweden, and the intention was to study the typology and chronology of the artifacts found as well as their topographical distribution. The project resulted in several dissertations and publications, but never encompassed all of Sweden.

Geographical, geological, and ecological factors were all important to an understanding of settlement development. Place-name research and historical and ethnological analogies were applied to the Iron Age. The Royal Place-Name Committee began to publish *Sveriges Ortnamn* [Swedish Place-Names] during the early twentieth century. Within the history of style, typology was more important, visible, for example, in Hanna Rydh's (1891–1964) doctoral dissertation of 1919, the first thesis in archaeology to be written by a woman.

The term *primitive* was used regularly. Within the history of style it was used to characterize the development of different elements of style, and there were also reference to prototypes, manufacturing processes, and industries. These terms coincided with typological and chronological questions. The term *settlement history* was used in debates on ethnicity and race. The basic question to answer was how different Mesolithic cultures developed into Neolithic cultures. A dualistic relationship was sought, which implied either that immigrating people, or people of other races, who had a higher technological and intellectual level had suppressed the first cultural phases or that the Neolithic level had been achieved within the country's boundaries and that more-primitive hunting cultures had been suppressed or assimilated.

In that context, ethnographical and ethnological analogies had some importance. The choice of language revealed uncertainty in the relationship to the "primitive" Mesolithic peoples, which gave rise to theories that implicitly, or occasionally explicitly, expressed a reluctance to accept the idea that such comparative "primitive" cultures had existed in Scandinavia at the same time as the cultures of the Bronze and Iron Ages. On the other hand, the more "developed" and artistically more "talented" cultures of the Bronze and Iron Ages did not have the same problems concerning identification. One could accept and even identify with Neolithic cultures because they depended on agriculture and livestock. The means of distancing oneself from the "primitive" cultures of the Mesolithic was to transfer them into being part of the natural world, and thus to being governed by the laws of nature. In the case of the Bronze and Iron Ages, one could easily identify with the creative powers and great initiatives of these cultures. This pattern has certain parallels with

A prehistoric petroglyph or vase painting from a Bronze Age site in Tanum, Bohuslan, Sweden, depicting three figures standing on the deck of a boat (Hulton Getty)

ideas of the eighteenth century and their erratic views of earliest history.

During the early twentieth century, archaeology lacked composite theories about the composition of and changes in different cultures. This lack does not mean that such questions were ignored—now and then references were made to religious and social conditions—but above all it was a case of diffusionist explanations and an implicit view of man and society. In general, the scientific ideal was empirically inductive with a natural-scientific undertone. Most works were descriptive and pragmatic in character.

Later 1900s

From the end of the 1930s until the 1950s, style-historical research (the use of style in material culture to determine the direction of historical change) in archaeology predominated. During the 1950s, several human geographers took an interest in settlement-history questions, and at the same time, several large field projects were initiated. These resulted in extensive and detailed publications of material. The inductive tendency of these works, as well as the lack of more explicit theories about human society, led to a crisis that developed into a debate on method and theory.

Criticisms burgeoned during the 1950s and 1960s, and especially influential at this time was criticism by Bertil Almgren and MATS MALMER.

Generally speaking, their arguments pointed in two different directions: Almgren took an art-historical, hermeneutics/phenomenological direction while Malmer upheld a rationalistic, positivistic, and scientific ideal or direction. Berta Stjernquist represented a third approach. She worked with traditional typology and also with ecology and ethnicity, and she argued that it was important to give greater emphasis to factors that had influenced the material. This approach demanded theoretical and anthropological knowledge as well as situation studies like those of anthropologist Bronislaw Malinowski (Stjernquist 1955, 2).

The renaissance of settlement historical archaeology during the 1960s is linked to that crisis/debate. Through extensive archaeological excavations, historical maps, and surveys of ancient monuments, an attempt was made to acquire knowledge of the colonization process, settlement structure, and economic conditions during, above all, the Iron Age in Sweden. Attention was given especially to economic variables. Collaboration between archaeologists and human geographers was strengthened, and even place-names and medieval fiscal material were used.

Greater emphasis was placed on local economic factors than on diffusionist factors. Economic aspects were considered to be the basis for man's production possibilities and for living conditions. These could be studied geographically, zoologically, and geologically. Since the beginning of the twentieth century, settlement historical archaeology had been influenced by advances within quantitative methodology. In the area of analysis that has "hardware" as its point of departure, statistics were important along with diagrams and models. These were some of the preconditions for the introduction of the new archeology into Sweden during the 1970s.

As early as 1963, Carl-Axel Moberg (1915–1987) had been in contact with LEWIS R. BINFORD (b. 1929). By the end of the 1960s, Moberg was arguing that a rationalization of archaeology was necessary since the constant increase of material had given rise to a collecting and publishing crisis. In this context, he pointed out the possibilities of processual archaeology as well as the practical revolution that computerized data implied (Moberg 1969, 16–18).

In so doing, Moberg put his finger on the crisis that has been the subject of discussion since the 1960s. He maintained that the cause was a crisis in education, that new directions were needed within archaeology, and that, in the long run, new archaeologists were needed. It was necessary to educate archaeologists in theoretical knowledge and change the goals of archaeology, which implied that an archaeology based on inductive knowledge would be replaced by more objective observations. Technological development would contribute to the globalization of archaeology and the fusing of different archaeologies into one. There were two possible paths: the regional picture could be broadened to include the history of mankind in both time and space; alternatively, world archaeology could be achieved via anthropology. The idea was to determine general laws of human behavior by using deductive methods (Moberg 1969, 21).

Thus, the deductive, scientific ideal was formulated for the first time within Swedish archaeology, and Moberg's future expectations would be realized during the 1970s. At this point, however, we should consider one of the more theoretically knowledgeable and independently active researchers in Sweden during that decade. In Stig Welinder's dissertation on the Scanian Mesolithic (1971), there is no reference to processual archaeology and its aim to trace changes in the environment by conducting natural-historical investigations. In a later work (1975), on the other hand, there are several references to processual archaeology, or "the new archeology." Welinder even eliminated the "a" in the combination "ae" in archaeology and was working explicitly with models and system-theoretical questions. His point of departure was the axiom that the surrounding milieu and technology were society's base. In order to prove this axiom, it was necessary to work system theoretically. Welinder's thinking was similar to that expressed by the English archaeologist DAVID CLARKE's ecological paradigm (Clarke 1972), and Welinder was also interested in Clarke's view of the sociocultural system (Welinder 1975, 22). Economic, ecological,

and demographic aspects composed the foundations of his model. In the long perspective of prehistory, war, trade, religion, social organization, etc. were of secondary importance. Settlement historical conditions could only be understood from an ecological perspective, and societies were interpreted as composite economic/technological complexes (Welinder 1975, 20).

Welinder sometimes doubted the possibility of creating laws for diffusion and social structures, since culture-historical processes and human societies are not repeated in time and space. In his opinion, the model sometimes deviated from the models normally used by the new archeologists (Welinder 1977, 15). Neither could it be used as an explanatory model. Instead, its strength lay in its description of basic structures in the cultural landscape. On a later occasion (Welinder 1979, 24), however, he implied that if it were possible to formulate such laws, then the preconditions could be found within demography. This archaeology could be called "human paleoecology," "ecological archaeology," or "population anthropology" (Welinder 1979, 25). Welinder's thinking has been used as an example of the tendencies of the 1970s, but it should be noted that they are not representative of the subject as a whole. Alongside them there was a traditional, inductive, and typological archaeology. However, Welinder's archaeology, to a certain extent, was representative of a more theoretically oriented archaeology.

Thus, archaeology during the 1970s became more natural-scientific in character. Attempts were made to reduce the preconditions for the formation of society to a single basic norm. The decisive factor was the relationship between man and his surrounding environment, with the latter constituting the basic variable. This line of thinking was linked to the positivistic ideals that were predominant within Swedish society as a whole. Generally speaking, the political model for Swedish society has been characterized by standardization in a positivistic spirit.

Archaeology Since the 1980s
During the 1980s, the reductionist viewpoint was called into question, not only within the

sciences but also within Swedish politics. Multiplicity became the political slogan. But this questioning has not implied, and will not cause, the disappearance of the deductive and inductive ideals. Rather, archaeology's relative homogeneity began to break down, and in the future a broad front of disparate archaeologies will probably develop. On scientific-theoretical grounds, it is difficult to give priority to one archaeology above another. It is therefore no longer clear how Swedish archaeology should be defined.

The possibility, or risk, is that research will be divided up into more and more problem areas. This idea may sound like an exaggeration, but it should be remembered that archaeology has always depended on different auxiliary sciences. In practice, a closer relationship can be established with any subject. We can therefore expect a wide spectrum of archaeologies. The risk is that barriers may be erected among them and each may fight the others' existence. There is the possibility that certain scientific-ethical grounds will be established so that the flood of ideas runs freely and various alternatives develop not only in different directions but also in close relationship with one another. It will be decisive in this context that discourses are not hindered by supposed scientific ideals.

Johan Hegardt; translated by Laura Wrang

References

Clarke, D. L. 1972. "Models and Paradigms in Contemporary Archaeology." In *Models in Archaeology.* Ed. David L. Clarke. London: Methuen.

Gräslund, B. 1987. *The Birth of Prehistoric Chronology: Dating Methods and Dating Systems in 19th-Century Scandinavian Archaeology.* New Studies in Archaeology. Cambridge: Cambridge University Press.

Moberg, C.-A. 1969. "Introduktion." In *Arkeologi: Jämförande och nordisk fornkunskap av professor Carl-Axel Moberg, Med bidrag av professor Holger Arbman.* Stockholm.

Montelius, O. 1986. *Dating in the Bronze Age with Special Reference to Scandinavia.* Introduction by Bo Gräslund. Stockholm: Royal Academy of Letters, History and Antiquities.

Nilsson, S. 1838–1843. *Skandinaviska Nordens Ur-invånare, ett försök i komparativa ethnografien och ett bidrag till menniskoslägtets utvecklings historia.* Vol. 1, *Stenåldern: Innehållande en beskrifning öfver de vilda urfolkens redskap, hus, grifter och lefnadssätt m.m. samt utkast till beskrifning över en i forntiden hit inflyttad kimbrisk koloni.* Lund. 2d ed., 1866.

———. 1868a. *Les habitants primitifs de la Scandinavie: Essai d'ethnographie comparée matériaux pour servir a l'historie du développement de l'homme, première partie l'age de la pierre.* Paris.

———. 1868b. *The Primitive Inhabitants of Scandinavia: An Essay on Comparative Ethnography and a Contribution to the History of the Development of Mankind, Containing a Description of the Implements, Dwellings, Tombs, and Mode of Living of the Savages in the North of Europe during the Stone Age.* 3rd ed., introduction by J. Lubbock. London.

———. 1868c. *Das Steinalter oder die Ureinwohner des Scandinavischen Nordens: Ein Versuch in der comparativen Etnographie und ein Beitrag zur Entwicklungsgeschichte des Menschengeschlechtes.* Hamburg.

Stjernquist, B. 1955. *Simiris: On Cultural Connections of Scania in the Roman Iron Age.* Lund: Akademisk avhandling.

Welinder, S. 1975. *Prehistoric Agriculture in Eastern Middle Sweden.* Acta Archaeologica Lundensia Series in 8∞ Minore, no. 4. Bonn: Habelt; Lund: Gleerup.

———. 1977. *Ekonomiska processer i förhistorisk expansion.* Bonn: Habelt; Lund: Gleerup.

———. 1979. *Prehistoric Demography.* Acta Archaeologica Lundensia Series in 8∞ Minore, no. 8. Bonn: Habelt; Lund: Gleerup.

———. 1991. "The Word *förhistorisk,* "Prehistoric," in Swedish." *Antiquity* 65: 247–295.

Swedish Cyprus Expedition
See Gjerstad, Einar

Switzerland
As long ago as A.D. 1490, excavations financed by the authorities were reported in Switzerland. An early Middle Age cemetery had been fortuitously uncovered during the alterations of Saint Maurice Church in Schotz (Lucerne). The skeletons, seemingly holding their skulls in their hands, were considered to be the martyrs of the Theban legion, put to death with their leader, Saint Maurice, because of their Christian faith.

It is impossible to regard this work as archaeological, as in accordance with the medieval way of thinking, the past was still interpreted through myth and biblical tradition. An excavation could not be of any scientific use because the motivation here was univocal and sacred, that is, to fill the parish reliquary.

With the Renaissance and the rediscovery of Greco-Roman antiquity, looking at the past became more rational. Society and ancient civilizations were questioned through ancient authors, and interest in the sometimes very evident vestiges of local antiquity was a natural consequence, vestiges that were finally interpreted as Gallo-Roman. For the same reason, the authorities of the city of Basel undertook large-scale excavations from 1582 to 1585 on the theater of Augusta Raurica.

For a long time, uncovered vestiges of monuments were not given their own significance and were still considered to be curiosities, at best, illustrations of a past that could be perceived only through history and philology. Unlike Nordic and Anglo-Saxon countries, Switzerland did not experience the romantic exaltation of Celtic antiquity. In Switzerland, the evidence of this remote past in the rural landscape was unreadable to the untrained eye, and calling upon the Celtic past could not answer any ideological need.

No period prior to the Roman occupation could be imagined in Switzerland. The Helvetians, remembered only as the protagonists in historical confrontations with the Romans, were regarded as their approximate contemporaries. So, regardless of the constraining limits of biblical chronology, one was unable, in the absence of Helvetian historians, to even imagine the possibility of any history for this people—just as a past for the primitive peoples of the New World could not be imagined.

Thus, all incomprehensible vestiges of the past were attributed to the Roman period, which flattered local susceptibility and granted certain localities a past regarded as original. Antiquarians and scholars collected and studied the antiquities, but without any systematic order and without seeing in them a possible source of original information. The situation was to change very slowly during the course of the eighteenth century, with some attention paid to written epigraphic and numismatic archaeological documents.

Switzerland waited until well into the nineteenth century to discover its own archaeology and in this respect was far from having a leading role in the development of European archaeology. Switzerland did not participate in the debates about the rediscovery of the Gauls during the French Revolution, nor in the debate around the undermining of biblical chronology through the combined efforts of paleontology and uniformitarian geology. There was nothing in Switzerland that could compare to the confrontations about the existence of primitive man, to the invention of the THREE-AGE SYSTEM by the Scandinavian antiquarians, or to the first differentiation of lithic industries by French archaeologists and paleontologists. On the contrary, the first archaeological work in Switzerland, during the 1830s, was to come from men who had discovered this new discipline while living abroad.

Once inaugurated in Switzerland, however, archaeology developed rapidly. Indeed, having been spared the difficult debate about the origins of man, the Swiss began archaeological research when its doors had already been opened and the necessary conceptual framework had already been established, even if still disputed. Moreover, the very progressive political context in Switzerland at the time enabled much research to be discussed in a dispassionate atmosphere, which scholars in other countries could not hope to experience. Hence, perhaps, the pragmatic nature, rarely explicitly theoretical, of the majority of these archaeological studies.

It was only with some difficulty that the early Swiss archaeologists could be distinguished from the antiquarians of past centuries, but, eventually, they were led by exceptional characters such as FERDINAND KELLER, FREDERIC TROYON, and EDOUARD DESOR, undoubtedly charismatic men who managed to consolidate the specific abilities of each individual. In Switzerland, archaeological research showed an exceptional dynamism, uniting distinguished geologists and naturalists, learned collectors, provincial notables, priests and ministers, schoolteachers, and even farmers with a passion for archaeology. This enthusiasm for national archaeology was unquestionably caused by the discovery of the palaffitic (built on poles) lake dwellings in Obermeilen (Lake Zurich) in 1854. The repercussions of this find were enormous, as much as for scientific as for ideological reasons.

In fact, it would be preferable to speak of the "invention" of the lake dwellings by Keller in 1854. Pile fields on the shores of Lake Bienne had already been discovered by some Bernese antiquarians a few years earlier, but those antiquarians did not advertise their discoveries in the way that Keller did. Above all, Keller gave a the dwellings a global and coherent interpretation. All of the sites discovered on the shores of the Swiss lakes were supposed to be of the same nature, that is, vestiges of prehistoric settlements. According to Keller, they had not been covered by water, as was first thought, but had been built on platforms above the water. Although attributing them at first specifically to the CELTS (a point he preferred to shelve later on), Keller used the durability of this type of dwelling from the Neolithic to the Bronze Age—or even the Iron Age—as proof of continuity between all our Swiss ancestors, in spite of cultural evolution. Keller's interpretation was met with enthusiasm and remained almost unquestioned for about three-quarters of a century, because, apart from the strong authority Keller had over research in Switzerland, his interpretation satisfied certain ideological expectations.

The Switzerland of 1848 was actually a new state, which had at last achieved national unification after a civil war (the Sonderbund War) in 1847. Beyond all religious, ethnic, and linguistic divisions, a new democratic system of government was established. Moreover, Swiss society itself was changing owing to increased industrialization and urbanization. These changes provoked a need to invoke the sources of a common identity from the past. At the same time, historical research developed a critical trend, debunking the fictitious and mythical nature of certain medieval national legends, such as that of William Tell. Thus, patriots turned to prehistory,

which offered liberalism the apparent confirmation of the doctrine of continuous progress, a source of unlimited hope for the future of mankind. Among all prehistoric pasts, the vision of lake dwellers proposed by Keller and his contemporaries was more than welcome.

First was the fact that these remains were of houses and the vestiges of everyday life, which gave these particular ancestors a popularity and a "closeness" that no number of burials or military camps could. Second, modifying the drawing that had inspired him—of the lake dwellers of New Guinea in a travelogue by the explorer Dumont d'Urville—Keller put all the dwellings on one platform shared by the whole village. These small communities thus seemed relatively egalitarian and built upon solidarity, an attribute that patriots wanted to develop in contemporary Switzerland. Moreover, the platforms protected the lake dwellers against outside dangers in the same way that Switzerland wanted to be an island of security in the middle of the disturbances in Europe. Last, the apparent durability, throughout prehistory, of "the lake-dwelling civilization," which stretched the length and breadth of Switzerland, showed evidence of a fundamental antiquity of a community only superficially affected by Roman occupation, and then by its partition into Romano-Burgunds and Alamanni tribes.

Regardless of its scientific value, Keller's theory thus had real mythic value. It was a myth that inspired many painters, poets, and writers and spread very deeply throughout the population thanks to historical processions, popular works, images on calendars, and the like. However, not only did the discovery of the lake dwellers have significance for Swiss history, it also had significance for the history of world archaeological research.

These villages, with their evidences of everyday life and being preserved in an almost perfect state, fulfilled the public's romantic expectations of the past. The villages reduced the humanist scholars, for whom prehistoric vestiges were not meaningful, to silence: a stone axe with its sleeve and handle shows evidence of its function by itself, which actually made the drawing of ethnological parallels easier. Moreover, the villages demonstrated the importance and validity of stratigraphic observations, and, thanks to the excellent state of preservation of botanical and osteological remains, they drew the naturalists' attention to proto-history. Thus, they undoubtedly contributed significantly to the development of prehistoric research, first by reconciling historical, human, and natural sciences in the same subject and then by making this research widely popular. In 1867, during the Universal Exhibition in Paris, the lake-dwelling remains were considered to be the most interesting thing Switzerland had to offer the rest of the world.

Lake-dwelling research developed very swiftly across all the Swiss lakes as well as on dried-out marshes. These studies also extended to neighboring countries, either on Swiss archaeologists' initiative, such as in northern Italy (Aspes 1994), in Savoy, and in AUSTRIA, or more independently, such as in southern Germany.

If the excavations grew in quantity, it was mainly because of the abundance of material and the fact that the assembly of lake-dwelling collections had now become fashionable. The intensive marketing of prehistoric relics resulted in a few unfortunate incidents, such as the case of the fakes of Concise, in 1859, which deceived some famous archaeologists, such as Troyon (Vayson de Pradenne 1932, 62–64). After the first Jura Surface Waters Regulation Scheme (1869–1883), which lowered the water level of Lakes Bienne, Morat, and Neuchâtel by more than two meters, many archaeological sites were exposed and within walking reach. The collectors' frenzy grew so that a general plundering of these archives of the past was feared, and in order to avoid such abuses, the local authorities established legislation that subjected excavations to official permission. The last quarter of the nineteenth century witnessed a decline in the interest for lake-dwelling sites. Contemporaries attribute the decline to "the deposits being worked out," which is clearly at variance with the results of modern excavations.

There is an epistemological problem in the disinterest. Theory having preceded research, research had to confine itself to illustrating and strengthening Keller's interpretation. So, little

by little, one was faced with a lack of real issues. Because their work was essentially centered on the presentation of the objects, the searchers were soon condemned to finding only what they called "doublets." The dogma of the cultural homogeneity of lake-dwelling populations, established by Keller, also hindered attempts at a sharper differentiation, either chronological or typological. With the poverty of stratigraphic observations, which most of the time were limited to discerning "the archaeological layer" from the different sterile ones, each site was individually seen as part of a homogeneous whole. In such circumstances, typological attempts, such as that of V. Gross (1883), were destined to remain purely stylistic. With regard to building methods, the traditional interpretation was so firmly rooted in people's minds that any interest in sharper observations of architectural vestiges could not be imagined. Therefore, because of its success Keller's pattern, which had led to the rapid development of research, turned out to be a strong shackle opposed to any renewal of approach.

Although the lake dwellings were clearly the main subject of archaeological research in the second half of the nineteenth century, work on them was not the only archaeological work being done. Along with many secondary works, both in proto-history and in historical archaeology, two Iron Age sites were discovered: the Tiefenau deposit (Bern) in 1849 and LA TÈNE (Neuchâtel) in 1857. As early as 1865, Desor, comparing the two sites with the ALESIA excavations in FRANCE, organized by the Emperor Napoleon III, compared the first to Iron Age mounds by setting them in a period immediately prior to the Gallic War of about 60 B.C. This observation led him to propose, successfully as we now recognize, the division of the Iron Age into two chronological periods, the earlier Hallstatt and the later LA TÈNE. Moreover, with his French colleague GABRIEL DE MORTILLET, he proved, from excavations at Marzabotta, that the Gauls had invaded northern ITALY by comparing some finds of this site with the remains of Teifenau burials in France and at the La Tène site.

Swiss prehistoric archaeology became more significant during the late nineteenth century, and it was Morlot (in 1859) who brought research developments in Scandinavian countries to the attention of French archaeologists. The first international congress of archaeology, called "paleoethnology" at that time, took place in Neuchâtel, in 1866 under Desor's supervision.

One must also point out the late start of Paleolithic studies in Switzerland, which began later than in other countries. In 1874, a Magdalenian cave at the Kesserlock at Schaffhausen was discovered, providing the first important finds of Paleolithic movable art in central Europe. Merck's excavations there were published in 1875 by the Antiquarian Society of Zurich, but, without the author's knowledge, Keller inserted illustrations of two fake engravings into the publication. These fakes, while accepted by Keller, were not very convincing, and no more was needed to cast doubt and suspicion upon all of the finds, especially a magnificent reindeer engraving (not one of the fakes), a most beautiful piece of Paleolithic movable art. This episode led to violent debates, mainly by German scientists, that actually questioned the very existence of Paleolithic art. The forger was unmasked, and in 1877, the Congress of the German Society of Anthropology gathered in Konstanz to decide on the authenticity of Merck's finds. What they decided was of considerable consequence. The German archaeologist RUDOLF VIRCHOW, president of the society, acknowledged that such observations made the notion of continuous progress more relative. These doubts about the authenticity of material were symptomatic of a more general disillusionment, for an economic crisis at the time was accompanied by a crisis in the liberals' confidence in the doctrine of progress.

At the same time, Theodor Mommsen's study of Roman provincial archaeology in 1854 on the inscriptions of Helvetia, as well as his monumental synthesis of Roman Switzerland published in the same year, established the bases of Gallo-Roman studies. However, it was not until the end of the century that the first large-scale Roman excavations occurred in Switzerland. Several local societies, dedicated to the study and protection of specific sites, such as Aventicum and Vindonissa, were founded at this time, and these societies are a good indication of the "protective" nature of archaeology at the end of the nineteenth century. Excavations were led less for discovery—in all its meanings—than for safeguarding a site.

Disillusion with the doctrine of progress, which had previously sustained the fervor of the prehistorians, was not the only significant problem facing archaeologists in the last two decades of the nineteenth century. The pioneers and architects of the discovery of prehistory were dying out, and it took some time for those who took their place to mature. This new generation of archaeologists at the beginning of the twentieth century differed from the previous one: its members were more serious and more assiduous. Prompted by more sensible ambitions, the new group seemed less dynamic and less enthusiastic. From the beginning, these archaeologists focused their efforts on the systematization and coordination of research. They founded the first national society, the Swiss Society of Prehistory, in 1907 and were concerned with establishing the first large syntheses (Heierli 1901 and others).

At the beginning of the twentieth century, Switzerland passed federal archaeology legislation. In 1912, the federal Civil Code granted the cantons responsibility and power over archaeological affairs. This decision provided for public intervention and finance with a firm legal base, and little by little, archaeological services were created in the cantons. But the decision also led to the geographical fragmentation of research and obvious disparities among the cantons.

The quality and the interest of archaeology was considerably advanced, especially in studies of the La Tène period. Several big cemeteries (Vevey, Munsingen, Saint Sulpice) were conscientiously excavated, and very detailed observations and critical analyses were made, which led, among other things, to Viollier's synthesis (1916). That work gave sharp seriations and combined OSCAR MONTELIUS's "naturalist" typology with the data of horizontal stratigraphy.

With Paul Vouga's excavations in Auvernier on Lake Neuchâtel between 1919 and 1920, lake-dwelling research got off to a new start. Detailed stratigraphic observations enabled the development of a scientific typology for

Artist's rendition of lake dwellings and associated artifacts. In the early twentieth century reinterpretation of the archaeological evidence suggested that the dwellings had been constructed on dry land. (Ann Ronan Picture Library)

"lakeshore Neolithic" (Vouga 1923). Several other lake-dwelling excavations were undertaken in Switzerland at the same time, but it was in Germany that fundamental objections to the basis of the lake-dwelling theory were to originate. In 1926, German archaeologist Hans Reinerth argued that palafittic lake villages, while laid out on platforms, were set back from the water on lakeshores whose levels must have been lower (Reinerth 1926). Later archaeologists went even further and argued that, in fact, lake dwellings had always been situated on dry land.

From then on the debate became impassioned, with Swiss scientists unable to question what had become a sacred national myth. At the same time, because of the Nazi Party's rise to power, Switzerland was trying to protect itself against the designs of *Grossdeutschland* (the view that all German speakers should be in one country) and claims for the incorporation of "Germanic" territories. Swiss archaeologists clung to the image of their country as a cultural unity

from prehistoric times. The background ideological debate assumed even greater importance because Reinerth, beginning in 1932, ran the Prehistory Service of the Nazi Party. In the long term, the debate proved useless, with neither side having the necessary evidence to substantiate a scientific solution. Nonetheless, the impetus to reexamine palafittic building methods was owing to the German archaeologists. Because of the political context, however, these new approaches began to have a further impact only after World War II.

The debate, passionate among archaeologists, made hardly any impact on the rest of the population. Since the end of the nineteenth century, archaeological studies had ceased to engender popular enthusiasm, and archaeologists working during the first part of the twentieth century in Switzerland lacked charisma or any interest in popularizing their research. More importantly, they also lacked direction. Culture-historical archaeology was popular in the rest of contemporary Europe, but in a country like Switzerland, which had a diversity of cultures, ethnic groups, and languages, it was hazardous to take up such a subject. Although Swiss archaeologists could not totally avoid these popular concerns, they remained reserved and uneasy about them. In such a context, it was logical that popular interest in archaeology declined.

The opportunity to reinspire the public unexpectedly arose during the 1930s economic crisis when a coordinated archaeological research program was instigated, with support from the unemployed, as part of a centralized "archaeological work service." Thanks to the considerable amount of manpower available, both Roman and prehistoric sites were excavated, making archaeology widely popular once more—so much so that after the onset of war and general mobilization, it was army personnel who took the place of the disbanded "archaeological work service" at the excavations. Research during the war, however, was confined to praising the richness of the national past.

Since World War II, archaeology has made considerable progress in Switzerland, because of new research methods and a renewal of approaches to the material. With regard to the lake dwellings, there have been numerous excavations, and they have made the issue of building methods more relative and balanced. Data from these excavations, along with analyses based on sedimentology and dendrochronology, revealed that lake villages were often superposed (built on top of other buildings) and that there were sometimes considerable chronological gaps between former occupations and rebuilding. This information completely changed the fundamental knowledge and theories about these prehistoric societies, and it became clear that obsession with one issue could lead to the neglect of others. The unity in question was superficial, for the results of similarly preserved remains across the millennia show that while some lake settlements were built on dry land, some buildings might have been built on platforms, either on the water or on the shore.

Swiss archaeologists did not confine themselves to palafittic studies, and all archaeological research fields took advantage of an increase in funds and in the number of excavations. Very few areas of the Swiss archaeological past remain really unknown. The great new challenge is multidisciplinary, which could lead to an excessive segmentation of research. Improvements in the knowledge of the process of cultural progress have favored an increasing focus on statistical approaches.

The major characteristic of the last decades of the twentieth century was the increasing necessity of large-scale rescue excavations. These first took place during the second Jura Surface Waters Regulation Scheme (1962–1973), but beginning in the 1970s, the building of Switzerland's network of highways caused an increase in the quality and quantity of archaeological research. Most of these efforts were rescue operations, which meant that it was difficult to focus on the real issues. Also, in spite of important federal grants, decisions are always made at the cantonment level. Although both of these factors bring archaeology closer to the public, they also lead to the fragmentation of archaeological research.

Switzerland, unlike most of Europe, with the exception of a few isolated occurrences—such as the 1812 discovery of the city of Petra in JORDAN by Johann Ludwig Burckhardt—has not played an important part in the archaeological exploration of the Mediterranean and Near East. This situation is the result of the country's historic neutrality and its lack of colonialism. Early museum collections did include artifacts collected by diplomats or mercenary officers during their stays abroad. For example, Colonel de Bosset of Neuchâtel brought back vases, which would soon be described as Mycenean in origin, from an excavation in Cephalonia, GREECE, between 1810 and 1814.

Since the beginning of the twentieth century, there have been several notable Swiss archaeological expeditions organized by universities where the discipline has become part of the curriculum. In 1964, a permanent mission for all Swiss university archaeology was established at Eretria, Greece, and it was given the name Swiss School of Archaeology in Greece in 1985. In 1986, the Swiss-Liechtenstein Foundation for Archaeological Research Abroad was founded and granted private funds (Bandi and Egloff 1989) for archaeological research. This is a scientific aid foundation, and it contributes to the preservation of the patrimony of Third World countries, in collaboration with those countries, to promote their cultural identity.

Marc-Antoine Kaeser

See also Lithic Analysis

References

Aspes, A. 1994. "A History of Research on the Lake-dwellings in Northern Italy." *Bulletin of the XIII Congress of the International Union of Prehistoric and Protohistoric Sciences, Forli, Italy, 1996* 2: 75–78.

Bandi, H.-G. 1954. "Hundert jahre Pfahlbauforschung in der Schweiz." *Schweizerische Hochschulzeitung* 27: 185–194.

———. 1983. "Das Pfahlbaubild des 19 Jahrhunderts." *Swissair Gazette* 2: 12–16.

Bandi, H.-G., and M. Egloff. 1989. "Archäologische Entwicklungszusammenarbeit." *Helvetia Archaeologica* 20, no. 80: 138–144.

Capitani, F. de. 1987. "Die Suche nach dem gemeinsamen Nenner, der Beitrag der Geschichtsschreiber." In *Auf dem Weg zu einer schweizerischen Identitat, 1848–1914: Probleme, Errungenschaften, Misserfolge,* 25–38. Ed. F. de Capitani and G. Gerrnann. 8th Kolloquium der Schweizerischen Akademie der Geisteswissenschaften, 1985. Fribourg: Universitatsverlag.

Childe, V. G. 1955. "The Significance of the Lake Dwellings in the History of Prehistory." *Sibrium* 2: 87–91.

Desor, E. 1865. *Les palafittes ou constructions lacustres du Lac de Neuchâtel.* Paris: Reinwald.

Dumont d'Urville, J. 1830–1833. *Voyage de la corvette l'Astrolabe executé par ordre du roi pendant les années 1826, 1827, 1828, 1829: Histoire du voyage.* Paris: Tastu.

Eder, K., and H. Trumpy. 1979. "Wie die Pfahlbauten allgemein bekannt wurden." *Archaologie der Schweiz* 2: 33–39.

Gerhardt, K. 1977. "Der Streit uber die jungpalaolithischen Kunstwerke aus dem Kesslerloch bei Thayngen, Kanton Schaffhausen, und die Deutsche anthropologische Gesellschaft." In *Die Kultur der Eiszeitjager aus dem Kesslerloch, und die Diskussion uber ihre Kunst auf dem anthropologischen Kongress in Konstanz 1877,* 17–48. Ed. S. von Blanckenhagen. Konstanz: Seekreis.

Gross, V. 1883. *Les Protohelvetes ou les premiers colons sur les bords des lacs de Bienne et Neuchâtel.* Berlin: Asher.

Heierli, J. 1901. *Urgeschichte der Schweiz.* Zurich: Muller.

Honeisen, M. 1986. "Kesslerloch und Schweizersbild: Zwei Rentierjager-Stationen in der Nordschwciz." *Archaologie der Schweiz* 9: 28–33.

Jacob-Friesen, G. 1980. "Ein jahrhundert Chronologie der vorromischen Eisenzeit in Mittel und Nordeuropa." *Bonner Jahrbucher* 180: 1–30.

Kaenel, G. 1990. *Recherches sur la période de La Tène en Suisse occidentale: Analyse des sepultures.* Cahiers d'archéologie romande 90. Lausanne: Bibiotheque Historique Vaudoise.

———. 1991. "Troyon, Desor et les 'Helvetiens' vers le milieu du XIXe siècle." *Archaologie der Schweiz* 14: 19–28.

Kaufmann, C. 1979. "Volkerkundliche Anregungen zur Interpretation der Pfahlbaufunde." *Archaologie der Schweiz* 2: 12–19.

Keller, F. 1854. "Die keltischen Pfahlbauten in den Schweizerseen." *Mitteilungen der Antiquarischen Gesellschaft in Zurich* 9: n.p.

Knoepfler, D. 1970. "La provenance des vases myceniens de Neuchâtel." *Museum Helveticum* 27: 107–116.

Largiader, A. 1932. *Hundert jahre antiquarische Gesellschaft in Zurich, 1832–1932.* Zurich: Verlag Antiquarische Gesellschaft.

Marchal, G. P. 1988. "Der erste archäologische Auftrag der Kantonsregierung Luzern 1490 in Schotz." *Archaologie der Schweiz* 11: 106–108.

Merk, K. 1875. "Der Hohlenfund im Kesslerloch bei Thayngen." *Mitteilungen der Antiquarischen Gesellschaft in Zurich* 19: 1–44.

Mommsen, T. 1854a. "Inscriptiones Confoederationis Helveticae Latinae." *Mitteilungen der Antiquarischen Gesellschaft in Zurich* 10: n.p.

———. 1854b. "Die Schweiz in romischer Zeit." *Mitteilungen der Antiquarischen Gesellschaft in Zurich* 9: n.p.

Morlot, A. 1859. "Etudes geologico-archéologiques en Danemark et en Suisse." *Bulletin de la Société vaudoise des sciences naturelles* 6 (1858/60): 259–329.

Mortillet, Gabriel de. 1866. "Compte rendu de la réunion a Neuchâtel (Suisse) du Congres International Paleoethnologique." *Matériaux pour l'histoire primitive et naturelle de l'homme* (September–October): 469–528.

Muller, F. 1990. *Der Massenfund von der Tiefenau bei Bern: Zur Deutung latenezeitlicher Sarnmelfunde mit*

Waffen. Antiqua 20. Basel: Schweizerische Gesellschaft fur Ur- und Fruhgeschichte.

Osterwalder-Maier, C. 1990. "Die Pfahlbauidee: Eine Geschichtsinterpretation macht Geschichte." *Neue Zurcher Zeitung* 21 April, 103–104.

Paret, O. 1942. "Die Pfahlbauten. Ein Nachruf." *Schriften des Vereins fur Geschichte des Bodensees und seiner Umgebung* 68: 75–105.

Reinerth, H. 1926. *Die jungere Steinzeit der Schweiz.* Augsburg: Filser.

Speck, J. 1981. "Pfahlbauten: Dichtung oder Wahrheit? Ein Querschnitt durch 125 Jahre Forschungsgeschichte." *Helvetia Archaeologica* 12 (45/48): 98–138.

Staudacher, W. 1925. "Gab es in vorgeschichtlicher Zeit am Federsee wirklich Pfahlbauten?" *Prahistorische Zeitschrift* 16: 45–58.

Vayson de Pradenne, A. 1932. *Les fraudes en archéologie préhistorique: Avec quelques exemples de comparaison en archéologie générale et sciences naturelles,* 62–64; 149–161. Paris: Nourry.

Viollier, D. 1916. *Les sepultures du second age du fer sur le plateau suisse.* Geneva: Georg.

Von Kaenel, H.-M. 1979. "Fruhe Pfahlbauforschung am Bielersee." *Archaologie der Schweiz* 2: 20–27.

Vouga, P. 1923. "Les stations lacustres du lac de Neuchâtel." *L'Anthropologie* 33: 49–62.

Winiger, J. 1989. *Bestandesaufnahrne der Bielerseestationen als Grundlage demographischer Theoriebildung.* Ufersiedlungen am Bielersee 1. Bern: Staatlicher Lehrmittelverlag.

Wolf, C. 1993. *Die Seeufersiedlung Yverdon, Avenue des Sports (Kanton Waadt): Eine kulturgeschichtliche und chronologische Studie zum Endneolithikurn der Westschweiz und angrenzender Gebiete.* Lausanne: Cahiers d'archéologie romande 59.

Syro-Palestinian and Biblical Archaeology

The history of Syro-Palestinian archaeology, or the archaeology of the southern Levant (ancient Canaan; modern coastal and southern Syria, Lebanon, JORDAN, and ISRAEL), and the history of the specialized branch of this discipline, usually called "biblical archaeology," will be examined.

Roots in the Nineteenth Century: The Exploratory Era

The archaeology of the Holy Land, in the broad sense of the exploration of biblical topography and antiquities, goes back centuries to hundreds of pilgrims' accounts since the Byzantine period. The modern discipline of Palestinian archaeology, however, can be said to have begun with the pioneering visits of the U.S. biblical scholar Edward Robinson to the Holy Land in 1838 and 1852, an account of which was published as *Biblical Researches in Palestine and the Adjacent Regions* (1853). Robinson and his traveling companion Eli Smith correctly identified dozens of long-lost ancient sites. The first modern maps, however, after those made by Napoleon's cartographers, were drawn up by C. R. Conder and H. H. Kitchener for the great *Survey of Western Palestine* (1872–1878; published in six volumes in 1884). This work was sponsored by the British Palestine Exploration Society (1865–), which also undertook the first actual fieldwork, C. W. Wilson and C. Warren's soundings around the Temple Mount in Jerusalem (1867–1870).

In Egypt and MESOPOTAMIA, dramatic archaeological discoveries, which began in the 1840s partly by chance and because of the results of the first deliberate excavations, soon drew attention to Palestine, largely because of its biblical connections. Several foreign societies soon joined the British Palestine Exploration Fund: the German Deutsches Palastina-Vereins (1878–); the French Ecole Biblique et Archéologique in Jerusalem (1892–); and the AMERICAN SCHOOLS OF ORIENTAL RESEARCH (1900–).

Despite mounting interest, however, true excavations did not begin in Palestine until the brief campaign of the legendary English archaeologist SIR WILLIAM MATTHEW FLINDERS PETRIE at Tell el Hesy in the Gaza area (possibly biblical Eglon) in 1890, which was soon followed by American work there under F. J. Bliss in 1893. It was Petrie who laid the foundations of all subsequent fieldwork and research by demonstrating, however briefly and intuitively, the importance of detailed stratigraphy of Palestine's complex multilayered tells, or mounds, and the potential of comparative ceramic typology and chronology.

This first, formative era of archaeological exploration and discovery in Palestine in the nineteenth century was characterized by adventurism, by nationalism and competition among the colonial powers, and by growing expectations that archaeology would shed a unique light upon the biblical world. Yet ancient Syria had scarcely been touched, although some archaeological exploration there had begun as early as the 1860s under French scholars like Ernest Renan.

From the Turn of the Century until World War I: The Formative Period

The first two decades of the twentieth century constituted a sort of "golden age" in Syro-Palestinian archaeology, one that saw the first large-scale, reasonably well-staffed and well-funded field projects. These included the work of the Americans at Samaria (1908–1910); of the British at Tell Gezer (1902–1909); and of the Germans at Taᶜanach (1902–1904), Megiddo (1903–1905), Jericho (1907–1909), and the Galilean synagogues (1905). In Syria, Howard Crosby Butler's splendid surveys of Byzantine Christian sites (1904–1909) for Princeton University deserve mention, but by and large, Syria was ignored as being peripheral to the Holy Land. None of these excavations, however, with the exception of GEORGE A. REISNER's work at Samaria (results of which were not published until 1924), demonstrated more than the rudiments of stratigraphy. Pottery chronology was off by centuries, and the publication volumes, although sometimes lavishly illustrated, are largely useless today. An almost exclusively architectural orientation, and/or biblical biases, marred most of the work.

All of these and other projects were brought to a halt by the onset of World War I, but the foundations of both Syro-Palestinian and biblical archaeology had been laid. Nevertheless, neither an academic discipline nor a profession had yet emerged in this second, formative period.

Between the Great Wars: The Classification Period

Following the corrupt bureaucracy of Ottoman Turkish rule, Palestine became a British mandate in 1918 at the close of World War I. The British government opened a Department of Antiquities, promulgated modern antiquities laws, and undertook the first systematic, comprehensive program of archaeological investigation of the entire area, including Transjordan. During the ensuing period, the foreign schools in Jerusalem flourished, particularly the American School of Oriental Research, which now dominated the field under the direction of WILLIAM F. ALBRIGHT (1920–1929; 1933–1936). Albright, one of the most eminent orientalists of the twentieth century, was then followed by his protégé Nelson Glueck, who was famous for his explorations in Transjordan.

It was Albright who became known as "the father of biblical archaeology" through his unparalleled mastery of the pottery of Palestine, of the broad ancient Near Eastern context in which the results of Palestinian archaeology needed to be placed to illuminate them properly, and of the vast scope of biblical history with which individual discoveries often seemed to correlate. Although Albright himself sometimes used the term *Syro-Palestinian archaeology,* his overriding concern was with the biblical world. Through his genius; his towering status; his own excavations at Tell el-Fûl (1922), Bethel (1934), and especially at Tell Beit Mirsim (1926–1932); and his innumerable disciples, Albright dominated "biblical archaeology" from the early 1920s through the 1960s. One of his protégés, G. Ernest Wright of Harvard, carried on the tradition by coupling "biblical archaeology" more specifically with the "biblical theology" movement that flourished in the 1950s–1970s. A transitional figure, Wright trained most of the older American generation still working in the field today.

Many of the U.S. excavations in Palestine between the two world wars, under Albright's influence, were at biblical sites, staffed by Protestant seminarians and clergymen, and supported by funds from church circles. These included Albright's own excavations and those at Tell en-Nasbeh (1926–1935), Beth-shemesh (1928–1933), and many smaller sites. Nevertheless, there was a parallel, secular U.S. tradition, especially in the large projects of the University of Pennsylvania at Beth-Shan (1926–1933); of the Oriental Institute of the University of Chicago at Megiddo (1925–1939), well funded by the Rockefellers; and of Yale University at Jerash in Transjordan

(1928–1934). These, too, were biblical sites, but the secular stream of U.S. Palestinian archaeology never captured the imagination of the public or succeeded in perpetuating itself as the Albright school did. In retrospect, it seems that, in the United States at least, archaeology in "poor Palestine" was not thought to be able to justify itself without the biblical connection.

British work in Palestine between the two wars combined biblical and nonbiblical interests. The principal excavations were those at Ashkelon (1920–1922); Dor (1923, 1924); Petrie's at Tell Jemmeh (1926, 1927), Tell el Fara (1927–1929), and Tell el Ajjul (1930–1934); the Mt. Carmel prehistoric caves (1925–1934); Petra (1929–1936); Athlit (1930–1933); Samaria (1930–1935); Jericho (1930–1936); Lachish (1932–1940); Kh. Mefjer (1935–1948); and, of course, many projects in Jerusalem.

The French approach between the wars was similar, the major excavations in Palestine being those at Ai (1933–1935), Teleilat al-Ghassul (1929–1938), and several prehistoric sites. The same combination of secular and religious interests characterized the German school, with excavations at Mambre (1926–1928) and Kh. el-Minyeh (1932–1939). However, neither the British, French, German, or any other international school combined Palestinian and biblical archaeology in the deliberate, almost exclusively biblical, and often theological way that much of the American work did.

British advantages during the Mandate period notwithstanding, biblical archaeology in Albright's unique style seemed triumphant on the eve of World War II when all fieldwork came to a halt. Nevertheless, despite differences in approach among the various schools, archaeology in Palestine had made enormous strides in this third era, which may be characterized as "the classification period," when the stratigraphy of the major sites was first worked out and the chronological-cultural history was outlined for the first time from the Paleolithic to the Islamic periods.

The Heyday and the Decline of Biblical Archaeology: 1950–1970

American-style biblical archaeology reached its zenith soon after the resumption of post–World War II fieldwork in Palestine in the early 1950s. Principal excavations were those of Wright at Shechem (1957–1968), J. B. Pritchard at Gibeon (1956–1962), J. A. Callaway at Ai (1964–1969), P. W. Lapp at Teller Rumeith, Tell el Fûl, and Ta'anach (1964–1968), and Pritchard at Tell esSa'aidiyeh (1964–1967). All of those excavations, which were affiliated with the American school in Jerusalem, were at biblical sites; the directors in every case were clergymen and professors of theology or religion; the agenda was often drawn from issues in biblical studies; and funds came largely from religious circles. In addition, the generation of younger American archaeologists who would come to the fore in the 1970s was trained at these sites.

In addition, a series of publications by Albright, Wright, and others attracted international attention to American biblical archaeology and provoked heated controversy in Europe. At issue were both fundamental questions of method in general (biblically biased or not) and certain specific historical questions in biblical studies (the historicity of the patriarchs and the Israelite conquest, Moses and monotheism, Israelite religion and cult, etc.). Neither Albright nor Wright was a fundamentalist (although certainly conservative by more recent standards), yet outside of the United States suspicions prevailed. The misgivings were prescient, for by the early 1970s, biblical archaeology (along with the biblical theology movement, an outgrowth of postwar neo-orthodoxy) was moribund, if not dead.

In retrospect, the demise of biblical archaeology was probably inevitable, for many reasons. First, what may be called the internal weaknesses of the movement were numerous: its reputation for amateurish fieldwork, naive or biased scholarship, and poor publication; its parochial character, related as it was largely to the conservative (if not fundamentalist) character of so much of religious life in the United States; its reactionary nature, locked into dated theological issues, which left its practitioners unable to respond creatively to new developments in or outside the field; its resistance to growing trends toward specialization and professionalism; and, above all, the fact that it failed to achieve its own major objective, i.e., the demonstration of the "historicity" of the Bible (at least as it was seen at the time).

There were also significant, indeed critical, factors that may be regarded as external to biblical archaeology per se, although very much a part of archaeology in general in modern Israel, Jordan, and elsewhere. These included the stratigraphic revolution of the 1950s–1960s led by English archaeologist KATHLEEN KENYON and others, which promised "total retrieval," automatically generating more and more varied data that required analysis by interdisciplinary specialists; the growing complexity and costs of excavation, especially in Israel, which pushed the field inevitably toward professionalization and secular sources of support; field schools and student voluntarism, which not only constituted an intellectual challenge but broke the monopoly of biblical scholars on dig staffs and thus contributed to the secularization of the discipline; the increasing sense that biblical archaeology was indeed parochial and had failed to achieve even its own limited agenda of historical-theological issues; increasing competition among the national schools—especially those now in the Middle East—which highlighted fundamental and legitimate differences in approach and thus called into question any exclusively biblical view of ancient Syria-Palestine; and finally, the advent of "the new archaeology," as it was called, which began in American New World archaeology in the early 1960s and by the end of that decade was beginning to have an impact on archaeological theory and method generally.

The principal aspects of the new archaeology were more anthropological than historical in their orientation, i.e., away from particularization and more toward the study of culture and culture change generally. It was an approach that sought to formulate and test law-like propositions that governed the cultural process (thus the common designation "processualist archaeology") in order to develop a body of theory that would qualify archaeology as not only a discipline but a true science. In addition, it had an ecological thrust, which emphasized techno-environmental factors (rather than simply evolutionary trajectories) in the role of adaptation in culture change. It was a multidisciplinary strategy that involved many of the physical sciences and their statistical and analytical procedures in attempting to reconstruct the ancient landscape, climate, population, economy, sociopolitical structure, and other subsystems (often using the model of general systems theory), and there was an insistence on an overall, up-front "research design" for projects that would integrate all of the above and thus would advance archaeology as a culturally relevant enterprise.

This discussion of biblical and new archaeology in the 1950s and the 1960s, so much of it highly theoretical, does not imply that nothing else was going on during this period, for example, in the area of fieldwork. For one thing, the face of the Middle East was changing rapidly. In particular, the founding of the state of Israel in 1948, the succeeding war between Israel and the Arab states, and the 1967 war—all redrawing international boundaries—had the most profound consequences for the archaeology of ancient Syria-Palestine.

The denouement of the colonial era had an especially significant impact, of course, on the foreign schools that had come to dominate the discipline. Most of the foreign fieldwork in Palestine until 1967 was carried out on the West Bank, the "heartland" of ancient Israel. The American excavations, mostly biblical archaeology, were generally sponsored by the American Schools of Oriental Research, and the results were often published in its periodical, *Bulletin of the American Schools of Oriental Research,* as part of an annual series, and sometimes in the semipopular journal *Biblical Archaeologist.*

British work, which was sponsored chiefly by the British School of Archaeology in Jerusalem, was directed for many years by Professor Kathleen Kenyon and involved in particular her excavations at Jericho (1955–1958) but also those at Qumran (1949–1957), Petra in Transjordan (1958–1968), and Umm el-Biyara and Tawilan (1958–1970). In the late 1960s, the British school in Jerusalem began the publication of its serial *Levant* in addition to the much older journal *Palestine Exploration Quarterly.*

The French École Biblique et Archéologique in Jerusalem excavated at Tell el-Farᶜah (1946–1960), Qumran (1951–1956), Munhata (1962–1967), and Tell Keisan (1971–1976). Preliminary reports appeared in the "Chronique Archéologique" of the *Revue Biblique*. The Dutch, although without an in-country institute, carried out important excavations somewhat later at Tell Deir ᶜAlla in the Jordan Valley (1976–1978).

The 1967 Arab-Israeli war had a considerable impact on archaeology, at least in Palestine if not in Syria. In effect, Palestine was now repartitioned, and the West Bank now fell under Israeli control. The Israelis initiated a surface survey of this area almost immediately as well as launching a large-scale clearance around the Temple Mount in Jerusalem and somewhat later in the restored Jewish Quarter in the Old City. Following the Israeli takeover of the Old City, the British, French, and German schools in Jerusalem maintained a nominal presence, but in practice they transferred their field operations to Jordan, where in time they opened new institutes in Amman. Only the Americans aligned themselves with the Israeli authorities, reconstituting the old American Schools of Oriental Research by changing its name in 1968 to the William Foxwell Albright Institute while at the same time opening a new branch in Amman under the name American Center for Oriental Research.

The result of the shifts was to leave archaeology in "Palestine" after 1967 in the hands of the Israelis, with some American participation; in the occupied territories on the West Bank (now called "Samaria" and "Judea") in the exclusive hands of the Israelis; and in Jordan in the hands of the foreign archaeologists but with growing Jordanian control. In Syria and Lebanon, most foreign work diminished as political instability increased, and at the same time, the nascent national schools found themselves beleaguered.

The Maturation of the Discipline: The 1970s–1980s

In the development of archaeology in Palestine we have noted two parallel streams, as it were, sacred and secular, particularly as the discipline(s) evolved in the United States. Beginning about 1970, however, the new archaeology began to eclipse the old-style biblical archaeology. The latter had always been merely an enterprise, a kind of "applied" archaeology, or what Wright called "armchair archaeology," but it had never evolved into a profession or an academic discipline. Indeed, biblical archaeologists had often resisted specialization, apparently cherishing their amateur status and content for their work to remain an adjunct of biblical studies. By the 1970s, however, both the internal weaknesses of biblical archaeology and the challenge of the new archaeology and other external threats resulted in a separation of the "two archaeologies," gradual at first, but soon virtually complete. And with the ascendancy of Syro-Palestinian archaeology, more in the style of the 1920s and 1930s, biblical archaeology was soon passé. Even the name was largely abandoned, Albright's original term *Syro-Palestinian archaeology* now being generally preferred.

The debate that continued throughout the 1970s was not, as some thought, merely a semantic quarrel. What really happened was the separation of Syro-Palestinian archaeology from its parent, biblical studies, so that the entire enterprise became, for the first time, an independent academic discipline with its own methods and specific aims. This discipline was no longer just a branch of biblical history (much less theology) or even the "handmaiden of history" generally. Syro-Palestinian archaeology now began to be considered as a regional-cultural branch of Near Eastern archaeology, like Anatolian, Egyptian, Mesopotamian, or Iranian archaeology. Its adherents also wished, without denying the natural connections with the history of the ancient Near East, including the biblical period, to ally themselves more with other disciplines. Paramount was anthropology, for its more sophisticated theory and use of cross-cultural comparisons. But the natural sciences were also seen as valuable allies for their analytical methods, even if archaeology, still a discipline within the humanities, could not attain the precision of the so-called hard sciences.

The newer theoretical approaches first began

Excavations under the direction of Kathleen Kenyon of London University on the site of ancient Jericho (Hulton Getty)

to influence fieldwork in Israel, initially in the U.S. excavations at Gezer in 1964–1974, directed by Wright, W. G. Dever, and J. D. Seger, where the staff was multidisciplinary and experimented deliberately with the adaptation of improved stratigraphic and retrieval methods, expanding those pioneered by Kenyon. These methods were then transferred and developed further in the 1970s in other U.S. projects by Gezer-trained excavators, ultimately influencing both Israeli and Jordanian archaeologists. Projects belonging to the Gezer tradition included Tell el Hesy (1970–1979), Galilean synagogue projects (1971–), Lahav (1976–), Tel Miqne/Ekron (1981), and in Jordan, the Hesban/Madeba Plains project (1968–). The new orientation, which had become standard by the 1980s, may seem obvious now, and even inevitable. But there were, and still are, heated controversies, not only on the part of recalcitrant biblicists but also from Israeli archaeologists, many of whom are still more traditional.

Nevertheless, by the 1980s the new look in archaeology was here to stay, and for better or worse, the child had "come of age." The watchwords of the fledgling discipline of Syro-Palestinian archaeology were "secular," "specialized," and "professional." The prospects, if any, for a biblical archaeology are treated separately later.

Dever has argued that all along biblical archaeology of the Albright-Wright style, which fairly or not raised the specter of fundamentalism, was a peculiarly American phenomenon. To be sure, British, French, German, Italian, and other European schools had also seen both sacred and secular approaches to ancient Syria-Palestine, but the theological crisis, or the "faith and history" theme, imported from concerns in biblical scholarship, had never become a principle issue in archaeology in Europe. Nor had clerics and funding from ecclesiastical institutions ever been dominant, except perhaps in Germany. The two archaeologies usually coexisted peacefully. Certainly the debate over biblical versus new archaeology, which raged for a decade or more in the United States, was not replicated in Europe.

The situation in Israel is in many ways unique and thus deserves separate comment. The Israelis claim that they connect with the biblical past not necessarily by means of formal religion and certainly not theologically, since most of the archaeologists are neither personally observant nor academically trained in the Bible and religion, but emotionally and directly. They maintain that the Hebrew Bible is, after all, the virtual constitution of the modern state of Israel and, furthermore, that for Jews displaced for centuries, even secular Jews, digging for their past in the soil of the Holy Land and searching for their roots is a vital matter of identity, an existential quest that no one has the right to deny them. They have a point, although the argument is somewhat disingenuous and can lead to nationalist extremes. In any case, Israeli archaeologists who use the phrase "biblical archaeology" for popular consumption, or for an English-speaking audience, do so with a meaning that differs from typical American usage, and partly to avoid the awkward term "Palestinian." (In Hebrew, the common designation is simply "the archaeology of Eretz Israel," or the state of Israel, exactly parallel to the archaeology of Jordan or Syria.)

National Schools Come to the Fore

The 1970s and 1980s saw not only the maturation of Syro-Palestinian archaeology as an overall discipline but also the ascendancy of national schools in the Middle East, the Israeli school being the prime example. This school, which had its roots in Jewish archaeology in mandatory Palestine in the 1930s, was rooted in the European academic tradition of ancient Near Eastern studies in history, philology, and art but also deeply influenced by Albright and his long years in Palestine. It is grounded in the realia of the landscape, sites, material culture, and long history of the country and is pragmatic in approach, with scant use for theory, including that of the new archaeology. It is characterized less by stratigraphic detail than by large-scale architectural exposure and stress on assemblages of

pottery from living surfaces. It is, and always has been, secular and professional, largely separated from other departments in universities and organized in institutes of archaeology, and often in conflict with the religious establishment rather than allied with it. In recent years, surface surveys and regional projects have become prominent emphases.

The Israeli school really grew out of Yigael Yadin's excavations at Hazor in 1955–1958, where the first generation of Israeli archaeologists was trained. In the 1960s and 1970s, many large projects were carried out, producing another new generation of archaeologists. Archaeological enterprise in Israel is well supported by the Israel Antiquities Authority, institutes of archaeology at four universities, the Israel Exploration Society, many publication series, including the periodicals *Israel Exploration Journal* and *Tel Aviv*, and the national Israel Museum as well as dozens of municipal and regional museums. Not surprisingly, the Israeli school dominates the local scene and has done so almost from the beginning. American field projects (often joint projects) still continue under the auspices of the American school in Jerusalem, but the British, French, German, and other schools transferred most of their operations to Jordan after the founding of the state of Israel in 1948. The latest syntheses by Israeli archaeologists are Amihai Mazar's *Archaeology of the Land of the Bible 10,000–586 B.C.* (1990) and Amnon Ben-Tor's edited volume *The Archaeology of Ancient Israel* (1992).

In the modern Hashemite kingdom of Jordan, which inherited eastern Palestine or Transjordan after the end of the British Mandate, another national school flourishes. There is a vigorous Department of Antiquities, which publishes annually; programs of archaeology at the University of Jordan and Yarmuk University; a large group of professional archaeologists, most with doctorates from European universities; and dozens of field projects. Foreign archaeological work is much more prominent here than in Israel and is sponsored chiefly by American, British, German, and other institutes in Amman. Although the archaeology of Jordan still lags somewhat behind archaeology in Israel, some idea of its rapid progress may be gleaned from such works as the four-volume *Studies in the History and Archaeology of Jordan* (1982–1992). There is no biblical archaeology of any persuasion in Jordan.

Archaeology in Syria has scarcely been covered because Palestine has loomed relatively larger in terms of interest and fieldwork. Yet coastal, central, and southern Syria (plus modern Lebanon) constitute the major part of ancient Canaan, or the southern Levant. The relative neglect is probably because of the area's isolation from Albright's original concept of Syro-Palestinian archaeology because of modern Middle Eastern politics and the instability of the region. Nevertheless, large and important excavations have been carried out in the above areas of Syria and Lebanon since the 1920s. The sites include American work in the Amûq and at Sarafand (the latter in Lebanon); Italian work at Tell Mardikh/Ebla; French work at Ugarit, Byblos (now in Lebanon), Qatna, Qadesh, and many other sites; Danish work at Hama; German work at Kamid el-Lôz and the Bega Valley (in Lebanon); and more recent Syrian-sponsored excavations, especially at Islamic sites. American work has been undertaken recently only on a small scale, principally in connection with the international salvage campaign when the Al-Thawra dam was being built on the Upper Euphrates (1963–1971).

The Syrian Directorate General of Antiquities and Museums continues the traditions of the long French Mandate. There are major museums in Aleppo and Damascus, and important publications include the periodicals *Syria* and *Annales Archéologiques Arabes Syriennes*. Potentially far richer in archaeological remains than Palestine, Syria may well have spectacular prospects in future. In any case, Albright's early intuition that Syria and Palestine were part of the same cultural sphere in antiquity, and should be studied in conjunction, appears to have been well founded, despite the modern political fragmentation of the area. The same may yet be true of Lebanon (part of ancient greater Syria or Canaan), where disruption of the country since the early 1970s has hampered almost all archaeological activities.

Current Status of the Discipline

In the post-biblical archaeology era, the fact that Syro-Palestinian archaeology is no longer a province of biblical studies but a discipline in its own right poses a challenge that must be faced. The only way to relate this new/old discipline and its results to biblical studies is through an interdisciplinary dialogue among professionals. That prospect may seem threatening to some, but there is no acceptable alternative. Certainly the professionalization of Syro-Palestinian archaeology is the only way to guarantee the survival of the field in the United States (as has long since been recognized in the Middle East), and it is also the only means of ensuring healthy growth in all the interrelated disciplines.

What, then, remains of biblical archaeology? What is it, or What can it be? Biblical archaeology, or, to put it more accurately, "the archaeology of Palestine in the biblical period," is not a surrogate for Syro-Palestinian archaeology, or even a discipline at all in the academic sense. It is only a branch of biblical studies, an interdisciplinary pursuit that seeks to utilize the pertinent results of archaeological research to elucidate the historical and cultural setting of the Bible. In short, biblical archaeology is what it always was, except for its brief bid for dominance of Syro-Palestinian archaeology during the Albright-Wright era. The crucial issue for biblical archaeology, properly conceived as a dialogue, has always been (and is even more so now) an understanding and use of archaeology on the one hand, an understanding of the issues in biblical studies that are fitting subjects for archaeological illumination on the other, and the proper relationship between the two.

What are the prospects for the discipline of Syro-Palestinian archaeology now that it has come of age? First, it is obvious that with the colonial era long since past, the various national schools in the Middle East will increasingly dominate the scene. That is already true in Israel, and with the maturation of the national schools in Jordan and Syria it will soon be true in those countries as well. European and North American archaeology will thus inevitably become somewhat peripheral, based less on fieldwork and firsthand materials and becoming more syn-

Ebla, ancient city of northern Syria, discovered in 1968 by the Italian archaeologist Paolo Matthiae at Tell Mardikh. The city dates back to 2500–2200 B.C. (Charles & Josette Lenars/Corbis)

thetic in character. The foreign institutes may become largely research facilities and centers for liaison with in-country archaeologists, who will control most of the fundamental data.

The situation envisaged raises the question of whether Syro-Palestinian archaeology, for all its declarations of independence, will be able to survive as an autonomous academic and professional discipline anywhere outside the Middle East. Full-time positions in European and North American universities and museums are already scarce, and as the older generation retires and academic cutbacks take effect, a severe vocational crisis is likely to arise. The simple fact is that Syro-Palestinian archaeology has enormous popular appeal in the West but that appeal is still based too often on the public's fascination with things biblical. It does not translate into the kind of support that the discipline needs to survive as a scholarly enterprise. Amateur archaeology may be commendable, but it must be matched by a professional field that is adequately supported and able to reproduce itself.

Although the future for the Middle East

schools seems bright, the progress of archaeology throughout the region continues to be threatened by political fragmentation and instability. The severe economic hardships are typical of developing countries everywhere, and modern expansion and industrialization destroy thousands of antiquities sites annually, many of which have never even been mapped. An additional danger is posed by rampant nationalism, which may result in excessive enthusiasm for archaeology, or religious extremism, which may resist any scientific investigation of the past. Both abuses of archaeology are already evident in the Middle East.

Finally, we must again consider theory, which is not merely epiphenomenal or trivial, as some people think. It is a body of theory, whether subconscious or deliberate, that guides fieldwork and research and that ultimately determines results. The theory of the "new" or "processual" archaeology of the 1970s and 1980s is drawn from both anthropology and the philosophy of science, and it emphasizes explaining universal "laws" of the cultural process. By the early

1990s, much of the pretense of science and the positivism of the new archaeology had faltered, although the ecological orientation and interdisciplinary thrust seemed likely to become permanent fixtures. Out of this frustration, came "postprocessual archaeology," which is more particularistic and focuses once again on culture-history. It is also more eclectic and less dogmatic than the previous approaches. Not surprisingly, the historical orientation of postprocessual archaeology is more congenial to Near Eastern archaeologists, who possess a long and textually documented history with which to deal.

Another aspect of the theoretical flux of the early 1990s is a spin-off of postmodernist, poststructuralist critical theory. In this perspective, archaeology should no longer be seen as "antiquarianism" but as a means of applying archaeological reconstructions to current social environmental, socioeconomic, and other problems, an archaeology as "cultural critique" or even political ideology.

Conclusion

Syro-Palestinian archaeology has had a long and checkered history, but it remains a uniquely interesting and significant branch of Near Eastern archaeology. It contributes to our understanding of the Bible by illuminating the context in which it originated, thus giving it tangibility and a certain kind of credibility. Perhaps more important, however, is the contribution that Syro-Palestinian archaeology can make to elucidating the origins of civilization and the long process of social and cultural change along the periphery of the Fertile Crescent between its two principal foci in ancient Mesopotamia and Egypt. The "archaeological revolution" predicted by our forerunners is not over; it has scarcely begun.

William G. Dever

References

Bar-Yosef, O., and A. Mazar. 1982. "Israeli Archaeology." *World Archaeology* 13: 310–325.

Ben-Tor, A., ed. 1992.*The Archaeology of Ancient Israel.* New Haven:Yale University Press.

Dever, W. G. 1985. "Syro-Palestinian and Biblical Archaeology." In *The Hebrew Bible and Its Modern Interpreters,* 31–74. Ed. D. A. Knight and G. M. Tucker. Chico, CA: Scholars Press.

————. 1989. "Archaeology in Israel Today: A Summation and Critique." In *Recent Excavations in Iron Age Archaeology,* 143–152. Ed. S. Gitin and W. G. Dever. Winona Lake, IN: American Schools of Oriental Research.

Dornemann, R. 1983. *The Archaeology of the Transjordan in the Bronze and Iron Ages.* Milwaukee: Milwaukee Public Museum.

Drinkard, J. F., G. L. Mattingly, and J. M. Miller, eds. 1988. *Benchmarks in Time and Culture:An Introduction to Palestinian Archaeology.* Atlanta: Scholars Press.

King, P. J. 1983. *American Archaeology in the Mideast: A History of the American Schools of Oriental Research.* Winona Lake, IN: American Schools of Oriental Research.

Mazar, A. 1990. *Archaeology of the Land of the Bible 10,000–586 B.C.* New York: Doubleday.

Moorey, P. R. S. 1991. *A Century of Biblical Archaeology.* Cambridge: Lutterworth Press.

Perdue, L. G., L. E. Toombs, and G. L. Johnson, eds. 1987. *Archaeology and Biblical Interpretation: Essays in Memory of D. Glen Rose.* Atlanta: Scholars Press.

————. 1982–1992. *Studies in the History and Archaeology of Jordan.* 4 vols. Amman: Jordanian Department of Antiquities.

Ward, W. A. 1994. "Archaeology in Lebanon in the Twentieth Century." *Biblical Archaeologist* 57, no. 2: 66–85.

Weiss, H., ed. 1985. *Ebla to Damascus:Art and Archaeology of Ancient Syria.* Washington, DC: Smithsonian Institution.

T

Tabon Caves

From 1962 through 1966, staff members from the Philippine National Museum led by Robert B. Fox excavated a number of caves located at the limestone formation of Lipuun Point, Quezon, on the southwestern coast of Palawan Island in the PHILIPPINES. Collectively called the Tabon Caves, the excavations and the subsequent analyses of excavated materials revealed a wealth of archaeological data that have extended and detailed the frontiers of Philippine prehistory up until 50,000 years ago.

The findings have profound implications for the Philippine, Southeast Asian, and Pacific region's archaeology because they reveal that "the ancient Filipinos were not only the recipients of cultural complexes from Asia but contributed to the historical developments of neighboring areas" (Fox 1968, 2).

Tabon Cave is the most important cave in the area, revealing a date range from 30,500±1100 B.P. and 9,250±250 B.P., well within the late Paleolithic period in the Philippines. It is large, with the cave mouth measuring sixteen meters wide and eight meters high. Located on higher ground, over thirty meters above the present sea level, the cave is nearly forty-one meters in length. It is bathed by sunlight throughout the day and is generally dry even during the rainy monsoon seasons, making it ideal for extended habitation.

Excavations have established the presence of Pleistocene man in the archipelago and revealed six levels with Paleolithic assemblages. The cave was inhabited continuously during the last glacial period, a time when the sea level was low and the shore, presently just below the cave, was about thirty kilometers away. The presence of a land shelf in this area, as revealed by geological and geomorphological findings, is validated by the total absence of marine shells from all the levels excavated at Tabon Cave.

The habitation levels indicate the ubiquitous presence of chert-flaked tools and waste materials. Attesting to the manufacture and use of stones for tools by the former inhabitants of the cave, thousands of waste flakes and unused cores were recovered in the course of the excavation work at Tabon Cave. One important result of the excavations was the recovery of human fossil bones of at least three individuals. The finds include a large fragment of a frontal bone, including the brow and parts of nasal bones. Although found in a disturbed area of the cave, available comparative data indicate that the fossil finds may be tentatively dated between 22,000 and 24,000 years ago. The late phase at Tabon Cave indicates a jar-burial complex. Archaeological excavations "also yielded jade and stone beads, bracelets, earrings, a few glass beads, and bronze, but no iron" (Fox 1970, 44). Tabon Cave was used for jar burial from about 200 to 500 B.P.

Manunggul Cave was discovered nearly two years after the excavations of Tabon Cave had started. This jar-burial cave was found tucked into the face of a sheer cliff with a majestic view of the South China Sea. It is over 115 meters high from present sea level and has four chambers. The cave has three openings but only two of the chambers, A and B, were used for jar burials. Chamber A contained large jars and covers, smaller decorated and painted vessels, human skulls, and parts of hematite-painted hu-

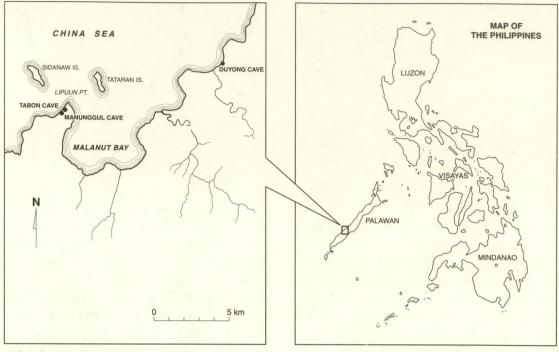

Tabon Caves

man bones on the surface when first seen. Ranging in date from 710 to 890 B.C., this site also contained jade, shell, and stone beads and jade, agate, and shell bracelets.

The most important find in Chamber A was a burial jar, which on its cover bears the motif of a ship-of-the-dead. Now considered a national cultural treasure of the Philippines, the upper portion of the jar has curvilinear incised scroll designs, and it was painted with hematite after firing. There are two human figures on the jar; one is shown paddling the boat and the other has its hands folded over its chest. The figures seem to have bands tied around the crowns of their heads and under their jaws. This band pattern and the manner in which the arms are folded across the chest are still widely practiced in the archipelago as part of funeral rites.

Chamber B has a radiocarbon date of 190 B.C. This part of the cave contains iron in addition to the associated archaeological materials recovered from Chamber A. Shell spoons made from the chambered nautilus were found in Chamber B, and the recovery of two round pebbles with a brilliant sheen on both sides suggests the use of these materials for polishing pottery.

Duyong Cave is located in the Iwaig area about eleven kilometers north of Tabon Cave and is situated near the coast. Excavations here revealed the presence of a flexed male burial with associated cultural materials including a stone adze, four polished shell adzes made from the giant clam *Tridacna gigas,* two ear disks, and a pendant made from the perforated bases of Conus shells. Six lime containers for betel-nut chewing, made from Arca shells, were also recovered. The radiocarbon date for Duyong Cave is 3100 B.C. It is significant that polished shell adzes made from the giant clam *Tridacna gigas* are also found in Micronesia, the Miyako Islands, and the Yaeyama Islands in the southern Ryuku chain as well as on numerous Pacific islands (Asato 1990).

In addition, Duyong Cave contained jade ornaments and a pottery mold for the manufacture of bronze adzes. The jade ornaments include types of ear pendants described as "lingling-o," which are related to ear pendants made of metal and still used by the Ifugao tribe in northern Luzon in the Philippines. Other artifacts made of jade included bracelets, a few beads, and studlike objects. The most unique

Human figures from a burial jar found in Manunggul Cave (Wilfredo P. Ronquillo)

form of ear pendant recovered from Duyong Cave was a double-headed one, probably horse heads, which is a superb example of jade carving in prehistoric times. The designs on the jade earring projections are derived from a stylized bud design, and in many instances a simple point with concave sides also appears in jade bracelets found in the cave.

Archaeological excavations were undertaken in sixteen of the hundreds of caves known to ex-

ist at Lipuun Point, in Quezon, and on Palawan Island, caves used either as habitation or burial sites. The data generated indicate an extensive localized temporal range, a flaked stone tool tradition dating from the late Pleistocene and early post-Pleistocene periods (50,000–9,000 years ago); and a jar-burial complex from the late Neolithic period and continuing into the developed metal age (890 B.C. through to approximately 100 B.C.). In two caves in northern Palawan,

Jade ear pendant found in Duyong Cave (Wilfredo P. Ronquillo)

tradeware ceramics from China dating to the Song and Yuan dynasties (from the tenth through the fourteenth centuries A.D.) were found.

Archaeological work in the Tabon Caves has revealed more than 50,000 years of Philippine prehistory. The excavations of the caves were a boost to archaeology in the area and have contributed significantly to a better understanding of the prehistory of Southeast Asia and the Pacific region.

Wilfredo P. Ronquillo

See also Island Southeast Asia; Philippines

References

Asato, S. 1990. "The Distribution of Shell Adzes in the South Ryuku Island, in the Urasoko Site: A Sketch of the Excavation in Photographs." *Gusukube Town Board of Education* (Okinawa, Japan) March: 1–40.

Fox, R. B. 1966. "First Progress Report to the National Geographic Society on the Explorations and Excavations of Caves Sites of Ancient Man on Palawan Island, Philippines." Unpublished manuscript. National Museum, Manila.

———. 1967. "Excavations in the Tabon Caves and Some Problems in Philippine Chronology." In *Studies in Philippine Archaeology (in Honor of H. Otley Beyer)*. Ed. Mario D. Zamora. Quezon City: Phoenix Press.

———. 1968. "Archaeology and the Philippines." In *Esso Silangan, XIII*, (3). Ed. L. S. Vicente. Manila: Esso Standard Eastern.

———. 1970. *The Tabon Caves*. Monograph no. 1. Manila: National Museum.

Taiwan

See Island Southeast Asia

Tallgren, Aarne Michaël (1885–1945)

Born in Ruovesi, FINLAND, Aarne Tallgren was a professor of archaeology at the University of Tartu (Dorpat), Estonia, from 1920 to 1923, a professor of archaeology at the University of Helsinki from 1923 to 1945, chairman of the Finnish Society of Archaeology (later the Finnish Antiquarian Society) from 1930 to 1942, and a specialist in east European and north Asian prehistory. Tallgren was also the editor of *Eurasia Septentrionalis Antiqua* (published in Helsinki from 1926 to 1938, with a supplementary volume in 1954).

Tallgren can be regarded as the most renowned Finnish archaeologist of the twentieth century. His international fame was largely due to his achievements in the systematization and cultural synthesis of east European and Siberian Bronze Age and early Metal period materials and his involvement in the publication and editing of the journal *Eurasia,* a unique international forum for archaeological discussion in the interwar years.

In 1903 Tallgren enrolled at the University of Helsinki to study history and receive instruction in archaeology, which was not yet an official academic subject. Graduating in 1905, he continued his studies in Stockholm and Uppsala under OSCAR MONTELIUS and O. Almgren. Tallgren's early research concerned the so-called Ural-Altaic Bronze Age as outlined by J. R. Aspelin, the founding figure of Finnish archaeology in the 1870s and 1880s. Aspelin's Bronze Age was in fact ultimately related to the semiromantic quest for the prehistoric homeland of the "Finnish race"—the ancestors of the Finno-Ugrians—which had defined the orientation of early archaeological scholarship and prehistoric research in Finland. Tallgren reformulated the problems set out by Aspelin, pointing out that the assumed Ural-Altaic Bronze Age culture did not exist as a single entity; he stressed that the original ethnic interpretation had to be reconsidered.

Before the October Revolution, Tallgren visited RUSSIA in 1908, 1909, 1915, and 1917. (He would return there in 1924, 1925, 1928, and 1935, as well.) The journeys in 1908 and 1909 were for the purpose of gathering materials on the Bronze Age cultures of East Russia, taking Tallgren first to Saint Petersburg and Moscow and then on to Kazan, Kostroma, and Arkhangelsk. He was able to excavate or inspect a number of sites and worked at Turovskoe (site of the famous Galich treasure) and later at Minusinsk, among other locations. His first expedition to Russia was preceded by a brief period spent at the BRITISH MUSEUM in London and the Musée de Saint-Germain in Paris, where Tallgren studied Asian antiquities and research literature that were not available in Finland. He received grants for this purpose from the Finnish Archaeological Society and support from his old mentor Aspelin. The results of his research appeared in his 1911 thesis, entitled "The Copper and Bronze Ages of North and East Russia." Although the work was criticized for faulty construction, inaccuracies, and errors of reference, Tallgren presented a solid analysis of the East Russian Bronze Age and its chronology. This work finally put to rest the idea that the East Russian Bronze Age was an offshoot of the Siberian Bronze Age, representing the assumed westward migration of the Finno-Ugrian peoples from an Asian homeland. Tallgren's work in Russia also led to a series of works published between 1917 and 1920 that systematized existing collections of East Russian and Siberian antiquities and outlined the Bronze Age Ananyino culture.

In 1920 Tallgren accepted the newly founded chair of archaeology at the University of Tartu (Dorpat) in Estonia. His work in Estonia included the organization of archaeological research on a nationwide basis. Among the many results of Tallgren's professorship in Tartu was the two-volume *Zur Archäologie Eestis I–II* (1922–1925), the first general presentation of the prehistory of Estonia. Although Tallgren enjoyed a unique status in Estonia, he returned to Finland in 1923 to assume the chair of archaeology at the University of Helsinki, serving as a professor until his death in 1945.

Tallgren's efforts in the late 1920s and 1930s were largely focused on the *Eurasia* journal, which he developed as a forum for archaeologists and other scholars from western, central, and eastern Europe alike at a time of mounting ideological and political divisions. It presented materials, results of research and scholarship, and works in progress, as well as items of debate. But it also reflected the liberal views of its editor, calling for free inquiry and the exchange of opinion. Tallgren criticized both Soviet Russian and Nazi German archaeologists for their doctrinaire and ideologically oriented scholarship. In addition to editing the journal, he also published regular and extensive contributions to it, most notably *La Pontide préscythique aprés l'introduction des metaux* (Prescythian Pontus before the introduction of metals; 248 pp., *Eurasia* 2, 1926). His essay *Sur la méthode de l'archéologie prehistorique* (On the method of prehistoric archaeology), published in volume 10 of *Eurasia* in 1936 and in an English translation in ANTIQUITY in 1937, came to be quoted in the 1970s by proponents of the "New Archaeology," who saw it as a fundamental statement of the purpose of archaeological inquiry (see Binford 1972, 79). Tallgren's many publications of the 1930s included *Suomen Muinaisuus* (1931), a general work on the prehistory of Finland.

Aarne Michaël Tallgren was not a field archaeologist, nor was he a meticulous student of detail or a theoretician. He was primarily interested in the terms of cultural history and synthesis, and he displayed a phenomenally broad grasp of the spatial and chronological entities of the archaeological record (an accomplishment that was still possible before World War II when individual specialists could lay claim to whole areas of learning). Tallgren was also extremely productive. His bibliography contains over 700 items published between 1902 and 1944. The years of feverish activity, however, ultimately undermined his health and sapped his energies, leading to his death in Helsinki in 1945 at the age of sixty.

Jyri Kokkonen

See also Latvia; Sweden
References
Binford, L. R. 1972. *An Archaeological Perspective.* New York: Seminar Press.
Kivikoski, Ella. 1954. "A. M. Tallgren." *Eurasia Septentrionalis Antiqua,* supplementary volume.

(This volume contains a comprehensive bibliography of Tallgren's published works.)

———. 1960. *Tehty työ elää. A. M. Tallgren 1885–1945.* Helsinki.

Kokkonen, Jyri. 1985. *Aarne Michaël Tallgren and Eurasia Septentrionalis Antiqua.* Finland: Fennoscandia Archaeologica II.

Tanum

Tanum, an area of northern Bohuslän, southern SWEDEN, has a tremendous wealth of rock art sites, most of them attributed to the Bronze Age, about 3,000 years ago. At that time, the sea level was twenty-five meters higher than at present, and many of the images were carved very close to water. There are thousands of petroglyphs (rock carvings), most of which are figures of warriors (armed men), circles, boats, vehicles, oxen, or plows at Tanum.

Many of the decorated rock surfaces face the sun, and the most visited have now been painted in for easy viewing and photography by the public, a practice that is now frowned on by most specialists—it is possible that they were painted in the Bronze Age, but there is no evidence for this. The so-called Cobbler figure at Backa was the subject of the earliest known rock-art drawing in Europe (seventeenth century B.C.).

Tanum was also the place where Carl Georg Brunius (1792–1869), son of the local parson, made his pioneering drawings of the petroglyphs, a major milestone in rock-art studies that remains almost unknown outside Scandinavia. Today, the best-known and most-visited site is the huge rock of Vitlycke, which has almost 300 figures including the famous "bridal couple."

Paul Bahn

See also Rock Art

Taylor, Joan du Plat

After earlier involvement in archaeology in Great Britain, Joan du Plat Taylor became assistant curator of the Cyprus Museum in 1932, a post she held until the outbreak of World War II, when she served in the Ministry of Information. She was later, for twenty-five years, librarian in the Institute of Archaeology, London University.

She undertook numerous minor excavations in CYPRUS, but her most important work was at two late–Bronze Age sites: Apliki (excavated in 1939) and Myrtou-Pighades (1950–1951).

Apliki, in the northern foothills of the Mount Troodos, remains the only good example of a mining village of the late Cypriot Bronze Age. The excavations at Myrtou-Pighades (a joint project of the ASHMOLEAN MUSEUM, Oxford, and the University of Cyprus) exposed the earliest intramural cult center known in Cyprus within one of the most extensive settlements in the northwestern part of the island.

David Frankel

Taylor, Walter W. (1913–1997)

Walter Willard Taylor was born 17 October 1913 in Chicago, Illinois, and was raised in Greenwich, Connecticut. A Yale University graduate (A.B., 1935), he conducted archaeological fieldwork in Georgia, Arizona, New Mexico, and Coahuila, MEXICO.

Taylor enlisted in the U.S. Marine Corps in 1942 and was sent to Algeria after earning his Ph.D. from Harvard University (1943). He served with distinction in Algeria, Italy, and France (receiving the Bronze Star with citation and the Purple Heart). Captured and interned by the Germans, he taught anthropology and geology in two prisoner of war camps; among the prisoners he taught was an Englishman, Philip J. C. Dark, who, with Taylor's help, earned his Ph.D. in anthropology from Yale in 1954 and became a noted authority on African and Melanesian art.

A furor erupted after the 1948 publication of *A Study of Archeology,* the revised version of Taylor's doctoral dissertation. Most of the reaction centered on Taylor's damning critique of pre–World War II American archaeology in which Taylor specifically criticized the work of six leading archaeologists: ALFRED V. KIDDER, E. W. Haury, F. H. H. Roberts, Jr., W. S. Webb, W. A. Ritchie, and JAMES B. GRIFFIN. In response, Taylor always maintained that his critique was solely theoretical and methodological, but colleagues and students of the six leading archaeologists perceived Taylor's criticisms as prejudicial rather than intellectual. Furthermore, because Taylor had not yet published the supporting materials for his "conjunctive approach" on how archaeology should be carried out, most readers were skeptical of his arguments. In the short term, the book generated far more heat than light.

Consequently, although Taylor received a Guggenheim Fellowship (1950–1951) and recognition as a scholar (made a Fellow of the American Anthropological Association in 1946 and a Fellow of the American Association for the Advancement of Science in 1954), he could not obtain a permanent academic position during the decade following the book's publication. Instead, he held a series of part-time visiting appointments at six institutions, mostly in Mexico.

In 1958, at age forty-five and with the help of his colleague and former Harvard classmate, J. Charles Kelley, Taylor was hired as professor and chair of the newly formed Department of Anthropology at Southern Illinois University–Carbondale (SIU). Over the next five years he developed a strong curriculum and created a highly regarded Ph.D. program at that institution. The death of his wife in 1960 and other personal problems led him to resign the chair in 1963, but he accepted a research professorship, which he held until his retirement from SIU in 1974 as professor emeritus.

Despite his recognized administrative abilities, Taylor was never nominated for an office in any major archaeological or anthropological society. Students found it difficult to work with Taylor, so although he must be considered a "founder" of the new archaeology, there is no cadre of Taylor's students to carry on his work, as there is for LEWIS BINFORD, James Hill, and William Longacre. This fact, combined with a modest publication record (although there are some important papers and *A Study of Archeology* is now in its seventh printing), Taylor's failure to publish the long-awaited Coahuila report, and residual anger on the part of some people (after so many years), has meant that Taylor has been less influential in American archaeology than might otherwise have been expected.

Taylor's last public involvement with archaeology was at the Fiftieth Annual Meeting of the SOCIETY FOR AMERICAN ARCHAEOLOGY, held in Denver, Colorado, in 1985, and his last publication was the mainly descriptive monograph *Contributions to Coahuila Archaeology* (Carbondale: Southern Illinois University Center for Archaeological Investigations, 1988). He resided on the Oregon coast until his death on 14 April 1997.

Jonathan E. Reyman

References
For references, see *Encyclopedia of Archaeology: The Great Archaeologists, Vol. 2,* ed. Tim Murray (Santa Barbara, CA: ABC-CLIO, 1999), pp. 698–700.

Tello, Julio Cesar (1880–1947)

Julio Cesar Tello was born in PERU of INCA background, was educated in Lima, and began his Ph.D. studies in medicine in San Marcos, Peru, where he also worked in the National Library and the Raimondi Museum. In 1909, he won a scholarship to study anthropology at Harvard University in the United States, where he was taught by anthropologist Franz Boas and archaeologists ALES HRDLIKCA and FREDERICK WARD PUTNAM. He finished his M.A. in anthropology in 1911 and traveled to France, England, and Germany, where he studied the conservation and interpretation of archaeological materials at major museums.

He returned to Peru in 1913 as director of the archaeological department of the Museum of Anthropology and Archaeology (formerly the Museum of Natural History). He accompanied U.S. archaeologists, such as Hrdlicka and Alfred Kroeber, into the field, participated in many other expeditions, and was the first Peruvian archaeologist to excavate scientifically. Tello's early fieldwork was in the Peruvian highlands, where he was the first anthropologist to encounter and study the CHAVÍN culture and Chavinoid materials. The site of Chavín in the Peruvian northern highlands comprises a town and temple complex, built and inhabited between 900 and 400 B.C. The Chavín style of art—in sculpture, carvings, textiles, and metallurgy—is distributed across northern, coastal, and central Peru. By the 1930s Tello had worked all over Peru. This diversity in archaeological experience and expertise in the Chavín culture led to his theories about the autochthonous highland origins of Andean civilization, which he published in *Origen y desarrollo de la civilización andina* (Origin and development of the Andean civilization) in 1942. He also wrote newspaper articles on archaeological topics, and these helped to popularize the subject and interest the Peruvian people in it.

Tello became director of the University Museum at San Marcos in 1923, director of the National Archaeological Museum in 1924, and professor of general archaeology at San Marcos in 1923; then at the same institution he became professor of American and Peruvian archaeology in 1928, a position he kept for the rest of his life. He was also briefly professor of anthropology at the Pontifical Catholic University (1931–1933). Through all of this work, Tello influenced and trained a generation of Peruvian archaeologists.

He was drawn into Peruvian politics, which proved ultimately to be to his personal and professional disadvantage, and he was a member of the National Congress from 1917 to 1928. He was honorary curator of archaeology at Harvard University; a fellow of the Royal Anthropological Institute, London; and an executive board member of the Institute of Andean Research.

Tim Murray

See also Moche

References

Tello, J. C. 1967. *Paginas escogidas*. Lima: Universidad Nacional Mayor de San Marcos.

Tenochtitlán

The capital city of the AZTEC empire, Tenochtitlán was founded in A.D. 1325 and fell to the Spaniards under Hernando Cortés on 13 August 1521. In less than 200 years, the island city had a remarkable growth and development, and by the time the Spaniards arrived it was one of the largest cities in the world. Certainly, it was one of the most beautiful: the Spaniards were in awe of it as they gazed upon the city shortly before meeting the Aztec emperor Motecuhzoma (Montezuma). In the words of one eyewitness, the Spanish foot-soldier Bernal Díaz del Castillo:

And in the morning we arrived at a wide causeway and we continued marching toward Izta-

palapa. And from the causeway we saw so many cities and towns in the water, and other great towns on the lakeshore, and that straight and level causeway leading to Mexico [Tenochtitlán] made us marvel, and we said that it was like the enchantments that are written about in the tale of Amadis, on account of the great towers and pyramids and buildings that rise from the water, and all built of stone masonry. And some of our soldiers wondered aloud if the things that we saw were not a dream. (Matthews 307–308)

Aztec descriptions of the city were understandably no less glowing: "The city is spread out in circles of jade, radiating flashes of light like quetzal plumes. Beside it the lords are borne in boats: over them extends a flowery mist," elegized one poet.

According to legend, Tenochtitlán was founded at a nadir in Aztec history. The Aztecs had just been driven out of a city where they had served as mercenaries, having committed atrocities that disgusted their hosts. The Aztecs were forced to flee to a group of low, swampy islands that lay in the western part of Lake Texcoco, the largest of a series of lakes that formed the heart of the basin of MEXICO where Mexico City now stands. It had long been prophesied that they would be given a divine sign by their patron god, Huitzilopochtli, when the time was right to build their city and become ancient Mexico's "chosen people." This sign would be an eagle eating a snake and perched on a prickly-pear cactus, and the Aztec priests saw that sign on those swampy islands in Lake Texcoco.

The Aztecs settled on the islands, driving wooden stakes into the grounds as piles to anchor their building foundations, and gradually their fortunes improved. In A.D. 1428, they attacked and beat the most powerful city in the basin of Mexico, and from that time they were the most powerful nation in the region. The city grew rapidly in both grandeur and size, ultimately reaching a population of 150,000–200,000 people and covering perhaps twenty square miles.

By the time of the Spaniards' arrival, the city was a metropolis of gleaming white houses and temples interspersed by canals and linked to the mainland by a series of causeways. In the center of the city was a sacred precinct, surrounded by a wall and containing the great temples of the city, a ball court, and a "skull-rack"—a structure that contained the skulls of tens of thousands of sacrificial victims skewered on wooden stakes. All buildings were dominated by a huge pyramid topped by twin temples: one was the house of the Aztec rain god, Tlaloc; the other, that of Huitzilopochtli, the war god and patron of the Aztec people.

Outside the precinct wall, but still at the heart of the city, were the palaces of the various Aztec emperors. Beyond these were the houses of the nobles and commoners laid out in a grid with canals serving as streets (many of the Spanish conquerors compared Tenochtitlán most favorably with Venice). The city was divided into quarters, each quarter was divided into smaller units called *calpulli,* and by all accounts, the city was very clean, orderly, and efficiently run. The great market of the Aztecs was in another city, Tlatelolco, immediately to the north of Tenochtitlán. There, some 60,000 people would pour into the market to exchange wares brought in from every corner of the empire.

After conquering the Aztecs, the Spaniards razed the city and began to build their own capital of New Spain—the city now called Mexico City. The Spaniards reduced most of the beautiful Aztec buildings to rubble, reusing many of the stones in their own constructions. Even so, the rubble reached in some parts to a height of three to four meters, which means that in many parts of Mexico City there are preserved remains of Tenochtitlán. Almost any deep excavation in the central part of the city will reveal such remains, and in 1968, excavations to extend Mexico City's subway system uncovered a perfectly preserved Aztec temple. It was kept as the centerpiece of the Pino Suárez subway station.

In 1978, a huge carved stone was found by electrical workers in central Mexico City. The stone was decorated with the relief of an Aztec moon goddess, Coyolxauhqui, sprawled dead and dismembered on the ground. In fact, the Coyolxauhqui stone was at the base of a stairway leading to the temple of Huitzilopochtli and recalled the Aztec myth telling how Huitzilopochtli killed his half-sister Coyolx-

auhqui, dismembered her, and threw her body down from Coatepec (Snake Hill). The Aztec Great Temple of Tenochtitlán, then, was the physical reconstruction of Coatepec, with the broken body of Coyolxauhqui at its base.

Subsequent excavation of the Great Temple has revealed the way in which the structure was enlarged over the years, each construction being larger and more elaborate in direct reflection of the growing fortune of the empire. The Great Temple was the ritual heart of the empire, and it was at the very center of Tenochtitlán.

Peter Mathews

See also Teotichuacán

References

Broda, J. 1987. *The Great Temple of Tenochtitlán: Center and Periphery in the Ancient World.* Berkeley: University of California Press.

Matthews, Peter. 1939. *Historia verdadera de la conquista de la nueva españa* (The conquest of new Spain). 3 vols. Ed. Joaquin Ramires Cabañas. Mexico: Editoria Pedro Robredo.

Teotihuacán

A huge ancient city that dominated central MEXICO for most of the first millennium A.D., Teotihuacán is located in the northeastern part of the basin of Mexico, about forty kilometers northeast of modern Mexico City.

In 1500 B.C., the basin of Mexico was dotted with small agricultural villages. Gradually, some of these villages grew in size and local power, a process that culminated in the dominance of just one city, San Cuicuilco, which today lies underneath Mexico City's southern suburbs. By 300 B.C., San Cuicuilco had an estimated population of more than 10,000 people—perhaps one-third of the basin's entire population. At the time, the vast majority of the population of the basin of Mexico was in the south. The northern half of the basin (which was generally drier and more prone to frosts and which also had saltier lakes than those in the south) was relatively unpopulated, although some small agricultural villages were beginning to farm the Teotihuacán region in the northeast. The pattern was soon to change, however: the villages in the Teotihuacán region grew rapidly (in part perhaps owing to

The main complex at Teotihuacán (Corel)

an influx of population from Tlaxcala, which was to the east of Teotihuacán) and coalesced into a large town that rivaled San Cuicuilco in size by 100 B.C.

The growing rivalry between San Cuicuilco and Teotihuacán was resolved by natural forces. Around the time of Christ, two volcanic eruptions destroyed San Cuicuilco, and the second eruption buried much of the city under several feet of lava. This destruction left Teotihuacán unchallenged in the basin of Mexico, and during the first century A.D., the city grew rapidly. By A.D. 150, the city had a population of about 80,000 people, and probably over 90 percent of the basin's population lived within twenty kilometers of the city at that time. Some of the reason for this rapid growth was probably a result of the volcanic activity in the southern part of the basin, but it is likely that it was largely the result of a forced relocation of almost all the basin's population into the growing metropolis.

By A.D. 300 Teotihuacán had reached its maximum population of between 125,000 and 200,000 people, and the city must have been a source of wonder to all who gazed upon it. It was by far the largest city in MESOAMERICA at the time and one of the largest in the world. The site covered over twenty square kilometers and included

two of the largest temple pyramids ever built in Mesoamerica as well as over 100 smaller ones.

The city was laid out in a strict grid oriented 15°25' east of north. Teotihuacán's central north-south axis (called the Avenue of the Dead by the AZTECS) ran for five kilometers, and most of the city's greatest buildings were alongside it. The massive Pyramid of the Sun, 220 meters to a side and 70 meters high, dominated Teotihuacán. At the northern end of the Avenue of the Dead was the Pyramid of the Moon, and in the center of the city, the huge Citadel faced across the Avenue of the Dead toward the Great Compound. The Citadel was probably where the royalty of Teotihuacán lived, and it is thought that the Great Compound was the marketplace. Inside the Citadel compound was the Pyramid of Quetzalcoatl, with elaborate facade decorations that included images of the Mesoamerican feathered serpent god called Quetzalcoatl by the Aztecs. Flanking this pyramid were two huge palace compounds.

Other elite "palaces" can still be found all along the Avenue of the Dead. The general population was housed in apartment buildings, over 2,000 of which have been mapped (although only a handful have been excavated). These apartment compounds, after about A.D. 200, were highly standardized with regard to outward appearance: each was square with about sixty meters to a side, composed of a single story, and enclosed by an outer wall for privacy. Construction was planned, with drainage and plumbing systems built before the plaster floor was laid. The interior design, however, differed markedly from one apartment compound to another, although all shared certain features. Rooms were arranged around open patios and courtyards, and each compound contained shrines or small temples. Some compounds had large, elegantly decorated rooms and courtyards while others looked more like tenements with tiny, gloomy rooms connected to each other by narrow alleys.

Most of the public architecture had facades of a distinctive style called "talud-tablero." Consequently, each platform of a pyramid had a sloping lower section, on top of which was a vertical, framed panel. In Teotihuacán, these panels were often decorated by stone sculptures or paint.

Teotihuacán gained much of its wealth from trade and tribute, but it was also a major source of goods. Over 600 workshops have been found at the site, 400 of which were obsidian workshops—the volcanic glass, which was the source of everyday tools throughout Mesoamerica, was available from sources all around Teotihuacán. Indeed, much of the city's economic and political power came from the fact that it seems to have controlled many of the obsidian sources in central Mexico. About 200 workshops at Teotihuacán produced ceramics. Many of them were engaged in the production of kitchen wares used in the city; others produced molded figurines in huge numbers. Other workshops specialized in works of shell, ground stone, or lapidary art utilizing semiprecious stones.

Teotihuacán is famous for its art. Perhaps most noteworthy is the mural painting that has been found at the site—many of the elite palaces and apartment compounds have rich ornamentation painted in polychrome on their stuccoed walls. Images range from depictions of birds and animals to images of warriors and deities to more complex scenes, including one that has been interpreted as a depiction of the "paradise of the rain god" with human figures cavorting among trees and flowers, and butterflies.

Burial patterns varied at Teotihuacán. In some cases the dead were buried beneath the rooms and patios of the compounds where they lived; in others, the dead were wrapped in mummy bundles and cremated. Recently, archaeologists have encountered the remains of sacrificial victims at Teotihuacán, and over 100 skeletons have been found in a series of pits beneath the Pyramid of Quetzalcoatl. The skeletons are those of young men, probably warriors, with their hands tied behind their backs. They wore necklaces of shell pieces carved to look like human jaws set with teeth, and they were buried with large projectile points of obsidian. Beneath the center of the pyramid was a large burial pit that contained more skeletons. These included at least one individual of high status, as he was buried with jewelry and other offerings, including a wooden staff carved with the head of a feathered serpent. The sacrificial offerings were probably deposited to dedicate the Pyramid of Quetzalcoatl around A.D. 300.

Although it can be argued that Teotihuacán's decline began early in the sixth century (some trade routes seem to have been severed and little new building was undertaken at Teotihuacán after that time), it wasn't until about A.D. 750 that the site suffered major destruction by fire. Over 600 separate fires were intentionally lit in Teotihuacán, most, but not all, of them in the more elaborate structures adjacent to the Avenue of the Dead. Public buildings were the prime target, and a fury of destruction accompanied the fires. Huge stone balustrades from the stairway of the Pyramid of the Moon were ripped out and dragged hundreds of yards. Other architecture was torn down and smashed. Apartment compounds were not immune to the destruction, although most of the damage involved the temples associated with them. The source of and the reason for the destruction of Teotihuacán are still not clear. The patterns of damage indicate a deliberate ritual destruction, one that probably had a political motive. Whether the destruction was carried out by a disgruntled faction within the city or by outsiders (or both) is not clear, but who-

A restored painting found in Teotihuacán (Gamma)

ever the culprits were, they seemed to have shared Teotihuacán's belief system, for this was not wanton destruction by invading barbarians.

Although Teotihuacán's political power was gone after 750, the city had a sizable population for centuries. For instance, the city still had 40,000 inhabitants in 950. In Aztec times, although the population of Teotihuacán was much reduced, the city was a place of pilgrimage. It was revered by the Aztecs and their contemporaries as the home of the gods, and according to Aztec legend, the current world age was created by the self-sacrifice that the gods made at Teotihuacán. Ironically, that self-sacrifice was done by fire: the gods leaped into a sacred fire to create the sun and other elements of the cosmos.

Despite the tremendous amount that is now known about the great city of Teotihuacán, there is still a great amount that is not known. Even the language that the ancient people of Teotihuacán spoke is not known for certain. Although more is now known about the organization of the city, details of the sociopolitical organization of the city and of the nature of Teotihuacán rulership remain elusive. It is clear,

however, that Teotihuacán was the largest and most powerful city in Mesoamerica until the rise of the Aztec capital TENOCHTITLÁN in the fourteenth and fifteenth centuries A.D.

Peter Mathews

References

Berlo, Janet C., ed. 1992. *Art, Ideology, and the City of Teotihuacán: A Symposium at Dumbarton Oaks 8th and 9th October 1988.* Washington, DC: Dumbarton Oaks Research Library and Collection.

Terracotta Warriors

One of the great archaeological discoveries of the twentieth century was made by accident in the spring of 1974. Peasants from the village of Xiyang in Lintong, Shaanxi Province, in the People's Republic of CHINA, were engaged in digging a well and discovered pottery figures and tiles. The similarity between the tiles discovered in the village well and those unearthed by farmers in the vicinity of the tomb of Qin Shi Huang (China's first emperor) was noted. Excavation of the site by a team from the Shaanxi Provincial Relics Bureau began in July 1974, and within two years, it

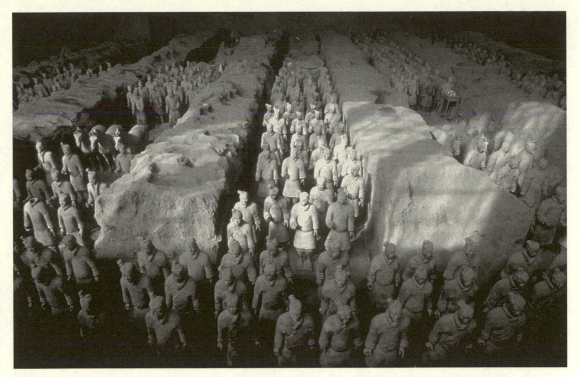

Part of a buried terracotta army related to the mausoleum of China's first emperor, Qin Shi Huang (Gamma)

had become clear that the terracotta warriors (and horses) were indeed part of a buried army related to the mausoleum of Qin Shi Huang.

Excavation at the site has continued ever since, with three major pits being opened, and further explorations in the area surrounding the great mausoleum have revealed new sites. Thus far, over 8,000 warriors and horses have been recovered, along with over 100 wooden war chariots. A major museum has been constructed at the site of Pit 2 displaying many of the weapons found with the warriors, and another housing the incomparable bronze chariot and horses has opened recently.

Tim Murray

References
Wu Xiaocong. 1998. *The Subterranean Army of Emperor Qin Shi Hwang.* Beijing: China Travel and Tourism Press.

Thompson, Sir J. Eric S. (1898–1975)

One of the greatest scholars of the ancient MAYA CIVILIZATION, J. Eric S. Thompson was born and educated in England. He fought in World War I,

and in the early 1920s, he spent some time as a gaucho in Argentina.

In 1926, Thompson traveled to MEXICO to work at CHICHÉN ITZÁ. From 1926 to 1935 he worked for the Chicago Natural History Museum, and in 1935 he joined the staff of the Carnegie Institution, where he spent the rest of his career. Thompson traveled widely in the Maya area and published works covering the archaeology, ethnography, history, mythology, and hieroglyphic writing of the Maya. He was a prolific scholar, writing over 200 books and articles that ranged over a wide array of subjects, from the uses of tobacco among the Maya to legends concerning the moon. Many of Thompson's books were written for the general public, and, along with his great contemporary SYLVANUS MORLEY, he was largely responsible for popularizing the temples and sites of the Maya area. He also published several major scholarly books, one of which, *Maya Hieroglyphic Writing* (1950), was for its time as complete a statement about Maya hieroglyphics and calendars as could be made.

Maya hieroglyphs were Thompson's great love, and it is ironic that Thompson was wrong concerning both of the two most important issues involving Maya writing. The first concerned the content of the thousands of surviving Maya carved stone monuments: Thompson believed that they were carved to commemorate the passage of time and that it would have been sacrilegious for any Maya to glorify individual achievements. This view was dramatically overturned in 1960 when TATIANA PROSKOURIAKOFF showed that the Maya monuments do indeed have historical content; to his credit, Thompson immediately and graciously accepted Proskouriakoff's arguments.

The second issue concerned the nature of the script. Thompson never wavered from his deeply held conviction that Maya hieroglyphic writing was a logographic system (in which signs represent entire words), but it has now been convincingly demonstrated that the script is a "mixed" one, containing both logographs and syllabic signs. Even though Thompson, were he alive today, might not approve of the methods of decipherment, he would be gratified to know that over 90 percent of Maya hieroglyphs have now been deciphered.

Thompson made many great contributions in the advancement of our understanding of the Maya culture. The correlation between Maya and Christian calendars is essentially the one proposed by him in the 1920s, he published a catalog of Maya hieroglyphs that is still widely used today, and one of his last publications was a detailed study of the most famous surviving Maya book, the Dresden Codex.

Peter Mathews

See also Belize; Guatemala; Maya Epigraphy;
  Mesoamerica
References
Thompson, J. Eric S. 1994. *Maya Archaeologist.*
  Norman: University of Oklahoma Press.

Thomsen, Christian Jürgensen (1788–1865)

Born in Copenhagen the son of a wealthy businessman, Christian Jürgensen Thomsen worked in the family business while pursuing his antiquarian interests part-time. He began to collect coins and antiquities and in 1816 was appointed national antiquary and secretary of the Antiquaries Commission. As such, he began to expand and rearrange the collections of the Museum of National Antiquities in Copenhagen. To do this work Thomsen had to devise a chronology or method of explanation for the display of archaeological artifacts and material, and he chose the THREE-AGE SYSTEM of stone, bronze, and iron to organize them and make them coherent. This chronology was put into place in the museum between 1818 and 1825 and appeared in print in the museum's guidebook *(Guide to Northern Antiquities)* eleven years later.

Thomsen was not the first to devise the three-age system, but he was the first archaeologist to formulate, define, and illustrate it with archaeological materials and the first to publish it. Thomsen defined the metal ages primarily on the basis of types of weapons and tools and, as importantly, on their find contexts. Like the great numismatists HANS HILDEBRAND, BROR EMIL HILDEBRAND, and SIR JOHN EVANS, Thomsen found that his numismatic background was of great benefit when investigating the typologies of other material. He was a formidable organizer and administrator, an innovative thinker, and a nationalist—keen to describe and celebrate the origins of DENMARK and the Danish people through the collections in the museum.

Owing to his extensive connections in scientific circles within Scandinavia, Thomsen advised Bror Emil Hildebrand on the arrangement of the collections of Lund University in SWEDEN, which was also based on the three-age system. Hildebrand used the system again in the Stockholm Museum, and it had an impact on the collections in the museum at Christiana (Oslo), Norway, by 1835. By the time it was published the next year, the system had already been widely accepted in archaeological circles across Scandinavia. Consequently, Sandinavian archaeological collections were the first in Europe to be organized both regionally and culturally, and they were homogenous, large, and coherent enough to make the next stage in the development of archaeology—that of scientific analysis, periodization, and more detailed chronology—possible.

In 1839, Thomsen was appointed curator of the Art Museum and Collection of Paintings in

Christian Thomsen (Science Photo)

Copenhagen, where he concentrated on reorganizing and presenting the ethnographic collections along the line of a progression of cultures, from the simplest to the more complex technologically, not dissimilar to the way his three-age system worked. In 1841, he opened the collection to the public and thus became responsible for the first public ethnographic museum. He returned to the Museum of National Antiquities, where he had started thirty years earlier, in 1849 as its director.

Tim Murray

See also Worsaae, Jens Jacob
References
Klindt-Jensen, O. 1975. *A History of Scandinavian Archaeology*. London: Thames and Hudson.

Three-Age System

Rightly regarded as being one of the most significant conceptual advances in prehistoric archaeology, the three-age system had a long gestation that drew on the writings of classical historians and geographers, Enlightenment philosophers, antiquarians in Scandinavia, and the large collections of the Museum of National Antiquities in Copenhagen. Historians of archaeology are fond of demonstrating that the idea of producing a sequence of human history tied to a gradual evolution in the complexity of technology and material culture (from Stone Age to Bronze Age and then to Iron Age) is as old as the ancient Greeks. Certainly, the discovery of contemporary peoples in the Americas (and the Arctic) who used stone tools and who were believed to be in a comparatively uncivilized state provided strong support for such ideas. It is also true, as Swedish archaeologist Bo Gräslund (1987) has argued, that other antiquarians such as the German Freidrich Lisch (1801–1883) were persuaded that the writings of the ancients, the philosophers, and the explorers might provide a valuable key to unlocking the secrets of European prehistory. Nonetheless, it was the Dane CHRISTIAN JÜRGENSEN THOMSEN (1788–1865) who did the most to develop and promote the three-age system.

It is significant that it is easier to discuss the impact of the three-age system through Thomsen's book—*Ledetraad til nordisk Oldkyndighed* (1836), published in a very bad English translation as *Guide to Northern Archaeology* (1848)—than it is to recount the steps Thomsen took to develop the system. Historians of archaeology have stressed that the system was the outcome of Thomsen's desire to rearrange the collections of the Museum of National Antiquities in Copenhagen in a strict chronological form. Gräslund has argued that this process occurred sometime between 1818 and 1825, when the exhibition was completed. He has also noted that this work was achieved at least ten years before the publication of the *Ledetraad* and that the system had been exported to Sweden and Norway by the early 1830s.

Thus, the *Ledetraad* is a museum guidebook that provides an explanation of the objects in the collection within the context of a broader exposition of how archaeologists create information and how artifacts can be dated. In this exposition, Thomsen went well beyond a description of technology to include discussions of a wide range of objects and site types, focusing particularly on the association of artifacts in sites. This more complex understanding of how archaeologists could define chronology in ways that could be directly confirmed by field discoveries was a significant reason for the early and widespread acceptance of the three-age system in Scandinavia and northern Germany. For an understanding of how the system was "exported" from the north to the rest of Europe we need to turn to the advocacy of Thomsen's successor, JENS JACOB WORSAAE, especially the English translation of his book *The Primeval Antiquities of Denmark* (1843), and German scholar LUDWIG LINDENSCHMIDT (1809–1893).

Tim Murray

See also Dating; Denmark
References
Daniel, Glyn. 1943. *The Three Ages*. Cambridge: Cambridge University Press.
Gräslund, Bo. 1987. *The Birth of Prehistoric Chronology*. Cambridge: Cambridge University Press.

Tikal

One of the largest and most important classic Maya sites, Tikal is situated in northern GUATEMALA, and its archaeological sequence spans the years from ca. 800 B.C. to A.D. 900. At its height, during the Maya classic period (A.D. 250–900), Tikal was a massive site, covering some sixty-five square kilometers and containing thousands of structures—the population of Tikal at its height was perhaps 100,000.

Tikal was rediscovered only 150 years ago, and for the second half of the nineteenth century it was visited by a succession of early researchers. It was not until the 1950s, however, that excavations began. From 1955 until 1969,

Mayan ruins at Tikal (Corel)

the Tikal project of the University of Pennsylvania undertook a major excavation program that has contributed enormously to our knowledge of the site. Since 1979, several Guatemalan programs of excavation have also added to our understanding, especially with regard to Tikal's earlier years.

The earliest archaeological evidence for human occupation at Tikal dates from about 800 B.C., with remains of what were perhaps scattered hamlets surrounded by a tropical rainforest. It was not until several centuries later that major developments began taking place at Tikal. By 500 B.C., pyramids were being constructed, and by A.D. 1, there were two major focuses on ritual at the site, adjacent to a residential zone. By A.D. 250, Tikal was a city with a sizable population and imposing public structures.

There is evidence that carved stone monuments began appearing at the site in the late third century (although there undoubtedly were earlier ones that are as yet undiscovered). These monuments provide details of history corresponding to the development of the site that can be discerned from archaeology. From the hieroglyphs it is clear that Tikal had a lengthy dynastic succession of kings (some thirty are referred to), and many of these kings were extremely powerful since for much of its history Tikal was one of the greatest of all Maya kingdoms. But not always: Tikal had a great nemesis—the site of Kalak'mul some 100 kilometers to the north. These sites were the two most powerful kingdoms of the Maya classic period, and most of the other kingdoms of the Maya lowlands were allied with them in complex (and at times shifting) hierarchies of polities.

In the period between A.D. 562 and 679, Tikal suffered a series of devastating defeats in war. Its monuments were smashed, and for almost 100 years no new ones were carved. Finally, a king called Hasaw Chan K'awil came to the throne, and in 695 he defeated the king of Kalak'mul. This victory ushered in a period of splendor at Tikal that lasted for almost 200 years. The latest monument from the site dates to 879, and although the site continued to have a squatter occupation for perhaps another 100 years or so, by the late ninth century it was no longer functioning as the capital city of a great kingdom.

Part of a wooden door lintel from Temple IV, Tikal (Image Select)

Tikal is famous for its lofty pyramid temples and other impressive architecture. The heart of Tikal, the so-called great plaza, is flanked on the east and west side by two great pyramids (Hasaw Chan K'awil was buried in the eastern pyramid); on the north side of the plaza is the ritual heart of the city, and on its south side is the great palace where the kings lived, received tribute, and held court.

Today, Tikal is surrounded by one of Guatemala's national parks, and there is dense tropical forest on all sides. The site has been well developed for tourism, and access to it is very easy—certainly quite different from the several days' ride on muleback that was the only way of access until the 1960s.

Peter Mathews

See also Maya Civilization
References
Harrison, P. 1999. *Tikal.* London: Thames and Hudson

Tindale, Norman (1900–1993)

The professional career of the Australian zoologist, anthropologist, and archaeologist Norman Tindale began in 1917 when he joined the staff of the South Australian Museum in Adelaide. After early zoological work in Cape York and the Gulf of Carpentaria, Tindale moved into anthropological fieldwork in the 1930s, first (1933) in the Mann Ranges of South Australia and subsequently (1935) in the Warburton Ranges of Western Australia.

Tindale is most famous for his work at Devon Downs, a rock shelter on the Murray River in South Australia where the first evidence of cultural change in Australian prehistory was collected. Tindale also gained notoriety for his explanation of these changes as being the product of movements of prehistoric populations.

Tim Murray

See also Australia, Prehistoric

Tiwanaku
See Bolivia

Toltecs

Toltecs is the name given to a group of people who were considered by the AZTECS and most of their contemporaries to have represented "the golden age" in Mesoamerican history. The name "Toltec" means "people of the place of reeds," and Tollan (Tula), "the place of reeds," figures in the origin myths of many Mesoamerican peoples from the Aztecs to the Maya. Descriptions of Tollan as a mountain surrounded by reedy swampland may well have been an evocation of the environment of MESOAMERICA's first civilization, the OLMECS, and their human-made mountains in the swampy lowlands on the southern borders of the Gulf of Mexico.

Because of the widespread origin myths involving Tollan, there are actually many places in MEXICO that have used or incorporated the name (which was corrupted by the Spaniards to Tula). Archaeologically, the Toltecs have been identified specifically with the site of Tula, some seventy kilometers north of Mexico City. This site was first occupied during the eighth century A.D., as the ancient city of TEOTIHUACÁN, which had dominated Mexico for the first millennium A.D., was declining. By A.D. 900, Tula was a major site, and in the following 300 years, it came to dominate central Mexico.

At its height during the eleventh and early twelfth centuries, Tula covered thirteen square kilometers, and had a population of up to 60,000 people. The central part of the site had broad plazas punctuated with temple pyramids, ball courts, and colonnaded palaces. Toltecs who were farther down on the social scale lived in flat-roofed houses with sleeping rooms arranged around open patios where many of the daily activities would be undertaken. Family altars and shrines have been found in the patios of several houses, and the houses themselves were connected by passageways and alleys. There is evidence that much of the city was laid out in a rough grid. Workshops abounded in Tula, especially for work in obsidian and ceramics. Agriculture was carried out with the aid of irrigation (rainfall is low and undependable in the area), and the dozens of small farming hamlets that have been found within fifteen kilometers of the city must have provided much of Tula's food supply. In the Mesoamerican tradition, additional food and other commodities would have flowed into the city as tribute from subject regions.

Ruins of the Toltec city of Tula (Corel)

By the late twelfth century, Tula was in trouble. The central ceremonial part of the site was sacked and burned, and there are signs of destruction in the suburbs as well, for some courtyards and altars were looted. Later historical accounts mention a civil war in the city, but the final collapse of Tula may well have been at the hands of barbarians from the north, the "Chichimeca" peoples.

Despite the devastation of the city, the Toltecs left an important legacy. Tollan was considered to be the metaphor in Mesoamerica for civilized life, and the Toltecs were eulogized as master craftsmen and artists. Later peoples went to great lengths to claim Toltec heritage. For example, the ruling families of the cities in the basin of Mexico all claimed descent from Toltec royal lines, and those groups that didn't have Toltec blood sought to marry into lineages that did: having royal Toltec ancestry was a major prerequisite of legitimacy. The Aztecs were one such group, and their leaders went to great pains to obtain Toltec ancestry through marriage. Once they had achieved that end, the Aztecs reinforced their "Toltec heritage" by looting the site of Tula and incorporating its sculptures and other relics into their own imperial capital's buildings and ritual offerings.

Peter Mathews

References

Davies, N. 1980. *The Toltec Heritage: From the Fall of Tula to the Rise of Tenochtitlan*. Norman: University of Oklahoma Press.

Tomb of Tutankhamun
See Tutankhamun, Tomb of

Troy
See Turkey

Troyon, Frederic (1815–1866)

Frederic Troyon was one of the first and most important Swiss archaeologists of the nineteenth century. In 1838, when archaeology was still in its infancy in SWITZERLAND, Troyon discovered burial places on his family estate of Bel-Air in Cheseaux (in Vaud Canton), which he correctly determined as Burgundian. He soon abandoned theological studies and devoted himself to the new discipline of archaeology. Within three years, he had completely excavated the 162 tombs, and, remarkably, he published the richly illustrated results as early as 1841. That same year, Troyon took the almost revolutionary initiative of trying to make an archaeological map of the canton of Vaud by sending a precise questionnaire about antiquities and monuments observed in the region to all the local authorities, both public and religious.

As a tutor to the royal family of SWEDEN (1843–1846), Troyon passed on his interest in archaeology to the future king Charles XV and helped to create a Swedish institution for the preservation of antiquities. He also took advantage of his stays abroad to acquire a vast archaeological knowledge, and he built up a considerable collection of drawings and watercolors, copies of artifacts in most of the museums of Germany, RUSSIA, and Scandinavia that he visited.

A keen advocate of the THREE-AGE SYSTEM, of which he would be one of the main promoters in Switzerland and FRANCE, Troyon was moreover one of the pioneers of comparative ethnology, using data on "primitive peoples" (as observed in the New World) provided by contemporary travelers. He also made an innovative study of the stylistic typology for Burgundian belt buckles (Troyon 1843).

Appointed curator of the Museum of Antiquities of Lausanne in 1852, Troyon undertook numerous excavations and explorations, including one of the first known underwater excavations in Morges (Vaud) in 1854 with fellow Swiss archaeologists Adolf Morlot and Forel (Ruoff 1990, 29). His interpretations, however, which were often integrated into a mystical and religious network of ideas, are now out of date. He considered the succession of prehistoric ages the result of brutal and successive invasions, and he meant to prove this theory by demonstrating changes in burial ritual: the incinerating CELTS were supposed to have arrived in Switzerland with bronze technology, then to have been supplanted by the mound-builder, iron-working Helvetians.

Nevertheless, Troyon did enjoy the sort of influence he deserved at the time because of his independent nature. Taking a stand against the tutelary figure of Swiss archaeologist FERDINAND KELLER, with whom he fell out, Troyon refused to attribute all lake dwellings to the Celts. Finally, however, as a victim of a fraud, his reputation was besmirched, and some people went so far as to wrongly accuse him of perpetration and collaboration with the fraud's instigators (Vayson de Pradenne 1932). Troyon's work maintains great value today. He had the praiseworthy habit of writing careful and accurate reports and of recording elements that he did not understand, which makes the reinterpretation of his excavations easier.

Marc-Antoine Kaeser

References

Kaenel, G. 1988. "L'archéologie vaudoise a 150 ans. Frederic Troyon et le Musée des antiquités." *Perspectives: Bulletin d'information des departements du canton de Vaud* 2: 24–26.

———. 1990a. "L'archéologie des peuples: Historique des recherches." In *Peuples et archéologie. 6e cours d'initiation a la Préhistoire et a l'Archéologie de la Suisse. Geneve, 3 novembre 1990,* 11–25. Ed. A. Gallay. Geneva: Société Suisse de Préhistoire et d'Archéologie.

———. 1990b. *Recherches sur la période de La Tène en Suisse occidentale: Analyse des sepultures.* Cahiers d'archéologie romande 90. Lausanne: Bibliothèque historique vaudoise.

———. 1991. "Troyon: Desor et les 'Helvetiens' vers le milieu du XIXe siècle." *Archaologie der Schweiz* 14: 19–28.

Rapin, A. 1966. "Un grand archéologue du siècle dernier: Frederic-Louis Troyon (1815–1866)." *Revue historique vaudoise* 141–149. Includes bibliography of Troyon's works.

Ruoff, U. 1990. "Geschichte und Bedeutung der archäologischen Erforschung von Seen und Flussen." In *Die ersten Bauern, Pfahlbaufunde Europas: Forschungsberichte zur Ausstellung im Schweizerischen Landesmuseum und zum Erlebnispark I Ausstellung Pfahlbauland in Zurich.* Vol. 1, *Schweiz,* 29–38. Zurich: Schweizerisches Landesmuseum Zurich.

Troyon, F. 1841. "Description des tombeaux de Bel-Air pres Cheseaux sur Lausanne." *Mitteilungen der Antiquarischen Gesellschaft in Zurich* 1: n.p.

———. 1843. "Bracelets et Agrafes antiques." *Mitteilungen der Antiquarischen Gesellschaft in Zurich* 3: 27–32.

———. 1860. *Habitations lacustres des temps anciens et modernes.* Memoires et documents no. 17. Lausanne: Société d'histoire de la Suisse.

Vayson de Pradenne, A. 1932. *Les fraudes en archéologie préhistorique: Avec quelques exemples de comparaison en archéologie générale et sciences naturelles,* 62–64. Paris: Nourry.

Wahle, F. 1950. "Geschichte der prähistorischen Forschung, Teil I." *Anthropos* 45: 497–538.

Tsountas, Christos (1857–1934)

Archaeologist Christos Tsountas succeeded HEINRICH SCHLIEMANN at Mycenae after the latter decided to return to the excavation of Troy in 1877. Tsountas, who was a far more gifted excavator than Schliemann, excavated the remains of the Bronze Age palace at the summit of the citadel at Mycenae between 1877 and 1902. Although this work was important, Tsountas went on to make significant contributions to our understanding of the Neolithic period in GREECE at the sites of Sesklo and Dimini and through his work *Prehistoric Acropolis of Dimini and Sesklo,* published in 1908. Tsountas then undertook pioneering work in the Cyclades Islands in the Aegean Sea.

Tim Murray

References

Filton, J. L. 1995. *The Discovery of the Greek Bronze Age.* London: British Museum Press.

de Tubières-Grimord, Anne-Claude-Philippe, Comte de Caylus

See Caylus, Comte de

Tunisia

See Mahgreb

Turkey

The most conspicuous geographic feature of Turkey is division, for it is a land of complex terrain partitioned by complicated mountain chains. Anatolia (as the land is known locally) is

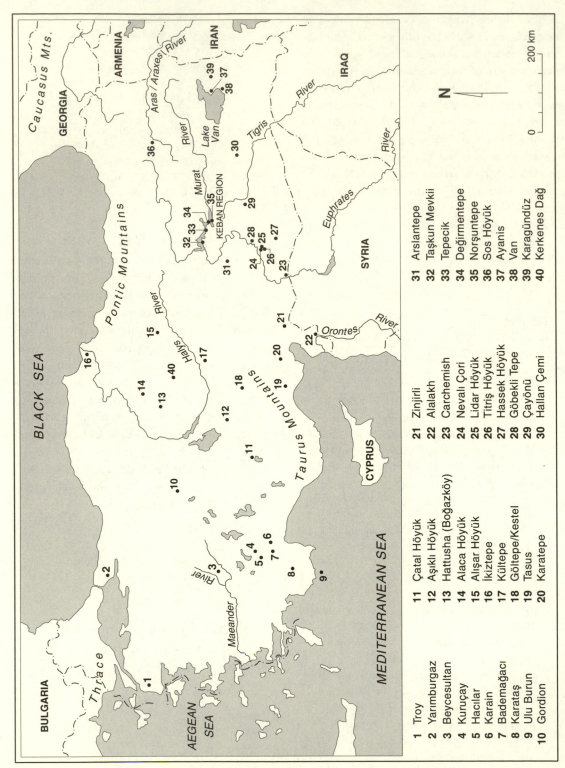

1 Troy	11 Çatal Höyük	21 Zinjirli
2 Yarımburgaz	12 Aşıklı Höyük	22 Alalakh
3 Beycesultan	13 Hattusha (Boğazköy)	23 Carchemish
4 Kuruçay	14 Alaca Höyük	24 Nevalı Çori
5 Hacılar	15 Alişar Höyük	25 Lidar Höyük
6 Karain	16 İkiztepe	26 Titriş Höyük
7 Bademağacı	17 Külfepe	27 Hassek Höyük
8 Karataş	18 Göltepe/Kestel	28 Göbekli Tepe
9 Ulu Burun	19 Tasus	29 Çayönü
10 Gordion	20 Karatepe	30 Hallan Çemi

31 Arslantepe	36 Norşuntepe
32 Taşkun Mevkii	37 Sos Höyük
33 Tepecik	38 Ayanis
34 Değirmentepe	39 Van
35 Norşuntepe	40 Karagündüz
	Kerkenes Dağ

Turkish Archaeological Sites

a mosaic of environmental zones, ranging from coastal fringes through a vast central plateau to the rugged geography of the eastern highlands, offering a range of ecological options for pastoralists (stockbreeders), farmers, and fishing communities alike. In antiquity this broken landscape engendered, for the most part, a spectrum of cultural diversity, which often displayed vigorous local traditions capable of absorbing new cultural stimuli that found their way along the many natural highways that cross the land.

In the nineteenth century an initial interest in Anatolia's past was fueled by the desire to uncover the remnants of civilizations mentioned in the Greco-Roman and biblical historical traditions. Accordingly, the Aegean coast received much attention from early archaeologists, who commenced excavations at EPHESUS, Pergamum, Miletus, and Troy (Hissarlık), perhaps the most celebrated site. Soon after, the Bronze Age cultures on the central plateau, homeland of the Hittites, attracted interest, most especially the extensive site at BOĞAZKÖY (ancient Hattusha). In recent decades the tempo of archaeology in Turkey has increased considerably as dozens of international rescue projects record cultural heritage threatened with destruction by the waters of several dam lakes. Investigations began in the Keban region of east-central Turkey (running from 1964 to 1974), but the focus has shifted to the southeastern regions, where the ongoing development project known by the Turkish acronym GAP has necessitated rescue operations at many sites along the Euphrates and Tigris Rivers and their tributaries (*American Journal of Archaeology* 1955; Tuna and Öztürk 1999).

The Earliest Stages

Although Paleolithic and Mesolithic remains have been found at many sites, especially in the southwestern area, the earliest stages of human occupation of Anatolia are relatively unexplored. We gain a glimpse of the Lower Paleolithic at Yarımburgaz Cave, but the most complete Paleolithic sequence has been attested at Karain Cave near Antalya, noted for its Middle Paleolithic (Mousterian) industry and Upper Paleolithic rock art (Joukowsky 1996). Micro-

lithic stone traditions of the Mesolithic (or Epipaleolithic) at Karain and nearby sites, including Beldibi Cave, bring us to the threshold of the earliest sedentary communities of the Neolithic around 11,000 B.C., when Anatolia experienced a period of climatic amelioration.

The Neolithic

As late as the mid-1950s no archaeologist was prepared to accord Anatolia a Neolithic period, believing that the formative processes that led to the DOMESTICATION OF PLANTS AND ANIMALS, which gradually changed the fundamental basis of subsistence economy in prehistory, took place south of the Taurus Mountains. Then, in 1961, James Mellaart began excavations at Çatal Huyük, which dazzled an unsuspecting discipline with its preservation and rich finds (Matthews 1998; Mellaart 1967). The largest site of its time (late seventh to mid-sixth millennium B.C.), covering 21 hectares, the settlement consisted of blocks of tightly clustered rooms, with rooftop access, and small courtyards. Some of the rooms, called shrines by Mellaart, were decorated with vivid wall paintings, plaster reliefs, and the skulls of horned animals fixed into the walls. Two broad categories of scenes are portrayed on the walls: representational scenes, featuring humans, animals, and birds, and geometric scenes, with patterns that perhaps imitate textile designs. Such exuberance and symbolism, unparalleled in a prehistoric building, likely reflect the community's belief system, which has been a focus of the renewed excavations at the site (Hodder 2000; Matthews 1998). Relatives were buried under the floors of both shrines and houses, and grave goods suggest a modest degree of social differentiation. The funerary gifts, among them Mediterranean shells, metal ores, obsidian, cinnabar, serpentine, and other exotic commodities, do confirm, however, the existence of a significant exchange network.

Today at least four distinct areas attest to intensive Neolithic settlement: the Urfa-Diyarbakır region of the southeast, the Konya-Aksaray region in the center, the Lake District of the southwest, and the Marmara region of the northwest (Özdoğan and Başgelen 1999).

An aerial view of the ancient site of Çatal Huyük in Turkey, ca. 1987 (Yann Arthus-Bertrand/Corbis)

Chronologically the Neolithic was divided into two technological phases: prepottery (or aceramic), which extended from about 11,000 to 6500 B.C., and pottery, which lasted another millennium to 5500 B.C.

The Neolithic also marked the beginnings of village life, and the recent discovery of circular houses dated to the ninth millennium B.C. at Hallan Çemi provided evidence of the earliest permanent settlement known in Anatolia. Yet the inhabitants of this site continued to collect and hunt their food, indicating that sedentarism preceded agriculture and animal husbandry (Özdoğan and Başgelen 1999). Quite different in character is Çayönü, situated in the Upper Tigris region near the Ergani copper mines, a location that facilitated the earliest experimentation with metals in Anatolia—namely, the cold hammering of native copper into pins and beads. Four prepottery occupation subphases have revealed an architectural sequence ranging from oval-shaped dwellings through large buildings with grill-plan basements to promote ventilation to cobble-paved buildings and cell-like structures. Moreover, Çayönü has provided vital

evidence on the transition to food production, from wild cereals, nuts, and animals (phases I to II) to domesticated emmer, peas, sheep, goats, and pigs (phases III to IV). A different settlement pattern is found at Aşıklı Höyük, comprising blocks of tightly packed houses with double walls (Özdoğan and Başgelen 1999; Yakar 1991).

Subsistence matters aside, striking new information on the religious sensibilities of prepottery communities has been unearthed in the Urfa region. At Nevalı Çori one building was paved with stone slabs and centered with a stone stela. Other stelae were found broken, including one, reused within the wall of a building, of a sculpted human face. Stone sculpture formed a striking feature at Göbekli Tepe, where four T-shaped stone pillars, evidently roof supports, were decorated in the upper part with rampant lions in low relief (Özdoğan and Başgelen 1999).

Our best-documented evidence for the ceramic Neolithic comes from the Burdur part of the Lake District, where a number of sites, including Hacılar, Kuruçay, and Bademağacı, have yielded a sophisticated repertoire of pottery that was often painted with bold red patterns on a cream background. Clay figurines found at these sites may have been part of the accoutrements of domestic cult practices. Though hunted animals supplemented the diet, these communities had by that point developed an economy based on agriculture and stock breeding (Özdoğan and Başgelen 1999).

The Chalcolithic

In terms of lifestyle, the transition from the Neolithic to the early stages of the subsequent cultural period, the Chalcolithic, was virtually seamless (Yakar 1985, 1991). But by the end of the Chalcolithic (ca. 3200 B.C.) there was an upsurge in technological innovations and cultural interaction. Although new sites were established in many parts of Anatolia, several large cultural zones can be discerned, largely on the basis of geography and contacts.

The Euphrates Valley and southeastern regions were much influenced by Mesopotamian and Syrian traditions, with the Taurus Mountains, mostly an obstacle to easy communication, determining the degree and nature of interaction with the northern districts (Joukowsky 1996). Although southern interconnections in these districts were pervasive throughout the Chalcolithic and subsequent early Bronze Age, they were more directional than uniform. Initial contact from the south, suggested by the presence of Halaf pottery at several sites, was followed by an expansion into the Middle Euphrates to exploit natural resources, where a late-Ubaid tradition is well documented at Değirmentepe. By the late Chalcolithic period the area below the Taurus Mountains, the northern reaches of MESOPOTAMIA, experienced intensive contact with southern merchant-venturers. Contact between indigenous communities and Uruk Mesopotamia is indicated at several places, especially at Hacınebi, whereas at Hassek Höyük there is evidence of an actual colony of late-Uruk type. Repercussions of this activity were felt north of the mountain range, especially in the Malatya and Elazığ regions, where local cultures adopted Mesopotamian forms of administration. At Ar-

slantepe (Level VIA) centralized economic activity is reflected in a well-preserved complex that contained many bullae (seal impressions) and wheelmade pottery. Emerging connections with different cultural environments farther east, most notably with Transcaucasia, are also clearly indicated by the presence of handmade red-and-black burnished pottery.

West, north, and central Anatolia formed an independent culture province in the Chalcolithic period, with strong links to the Balkans and beyond to the Hungarian plains (Joukowsky 1996). Connections between the Karanova VI and Vinča D traditions of southeastern Europe and Anatolia are best seen at Ilıpinar, Alişar Höyük, Çadır Höyük, and İkiztepe, where curvilinear-decorated and graphite-slipped pottery have been found. In the southwest, Beycsultan and sites in the Elamlı plain demonstrate continuity of late-Neolithic traditions. Architecture varied according to geography and climate. Mud brick was a ubiquitous building medium, though timber and wattle-and-daub houses, usually freestanding, were also common along the wet Pontic zone.

The Bronze Age

In the early Bronze Age (ca. 3200–2000 B.C.) sites displayed distinctive regional traits in every aspect of material culture (Yakar 1985). A unifying thread within this diversity was the impact of innovative metal technologies, especially in the third and final phase of the period, when even pottery imitated metallic vessels through highly burnished surfaces and angular shapes. Anatolian smiths made full use of their land's extensive mineral and polymetallic ore resources. Copper was the metal most widely used at the turn of the third millennium B.C., but attempts to combine it with tin (and in some cases with arsenic) were under way by early Bronze Age II. Despite an ever increasing amount of bronze production, actual sources of tin, perhaps the most highly prized metal at that time, have remained elusive, though crucibles at Göltepe have traces of tin claimed by its excavators to have been mined at Kestel.

Bronze was not the only metal that was worked. Ceremonial artifacts and jewelry of silver, gold, and electrum (an alloy of silver and gold) were already produced by the late fourth millennium B.C. By early Bronze Age III they dramatically increased in number and displayed a high level of craft skills, suggestive of specialization and different metallurgical workshops. Concentrations of wealth such as those found at Troy (the "Treasures of Troy" of Level II) and Alaca Höyük are remarkable and also provide insights into social structures, representing as they do the worldly possessions of elite groups, whose chiefs used these objects to display their importance and prestige. Moreover, the demand for metals had economic implications, fuelling the growing commercial networks that traded both the mineral ores and the finished luxury items.

In western Anatolia, at Troy, Demircihöyük, and Karataş, fortification walls enclosed settlements arranged in either a linear or a circular plan (Joukowsky 1996). Arguably the most celebrated site in Anatolia, Troy (now Hissarlık) was identified as Ilion as early as 1801 by Edward Clarke, a British scientist. Later, during the 1850s and 1860s, Frank Calvert, U.S. consul at the Dardanelles, also convinced of this identification, probed the mound at Hissarlık and encouraged HEINRICH SCHLIEMANN to commence extensive excavations. Schliemann's fervor, personality, and discoveries (from 1871 to 1873 and 1878 to 1879) catapulted ancient Anatolia onto the international scene, leaving an indelible mark on the history of archaeology. These excavations were continued by WILHELM DORPFELD, who discerned nine main periods of occupation at Troy, a sequence that was refined in the 1930s by CARL BLEGEN and his U.S. team. Today the ruins of Troy are being reexamined by a joint German-U.S. expedition, led by Manfred Korfmann, that resumed work in 1988 (Korfmann and Mannsperger 1998). New information on the landscape around Troy over the millennia and the extent of the lower town at the foot of the citadel is forthcoming.

Architectural development is represented at Karataş in early Bronze Age II by a large building of megaron form—a freestanding rectangular structure entered through a porch at one end. Karataş also revealed an extensive ceme-tery outside the settlement that contained many large storage jars buried with the deceased. Similarities in architecture, ceramics, and metalwork between these sites and those on offshore islands and at the coastal settlement of Tarsus, in Cilicia (the easternmost extension of this culture province), are indicative of seafaring.

As in the Chalcolithic, the Turkish Euphrates region in the Bronze Age owed much to both local and foreign influences; it can be divided into two broad cultural zones. The lower reaches of the Euphrates, in the districts of Adıyaman and Urfa, were fully part of the north Syrian early Bronze Age. Tirtriş Höyük, for instance, was the center of a small city-state system that flourished between about 2600 and 2100 B.C. By contrast, at Arslantepe VIB, after the collapse of the VIA administrative complex, and at nearby sites including Norşuntepe, Tepecik, and Taşkun Mevkii, we see an interlude with strong Transcaucasian connections. But the commingling of Syro-Mesopotamian and Transcaucasian connections is most vividly shown in the recent discovery of an early–Bronze Age I elite stone tomb that contained the skeletal remains of four individuals, three of whom had probably been sacrificed, and funerary gifts of metal and ceramics from two cultural worlds. Only late in the third millennium B.C. (early Bronze Age III) did this region experience a resurgence of Syrian connections, when it was probably involved in the commercial network of Ebla.

The impact the Transcaucasians had on eastern Anatolia is well documented at Sos Höyük, near Erzurum and close to the heartlands of Caucasus (Sagona 2000). At Sos their cultural assemblage (known as Kura-Araxes or early Transcaucasian) attests an extraordinary longevity, from about 3300 to 1600 B.C., well into the Middle Bronze Age. Economic data suggest that these people practiced small-scale, mixed farming with varying levels of pastoralism and transhumance, depending on the nature and circumstances of the site. Moreover, the astonishingly swift and widespread dispersal of this distinctive complex, covering eastern Anatolia, Transcaucasia, and northwest IRAN, suggests actual movements of people. In eastern Anatolia these communities lived in villages and built a variety of freestanding houses of rectilinear, subrectangular, or circular plan with mudbrick or wattle-and-daub walls. Typically, each dwelling was single roomed, sometimes with an antechamber, and had an eye-catching circular hearth fixed into the floor, probably the focus of domestic worship. Portable anthropomorphic or zoomorphic potstands, fragments of distinctive black-and-red burnished pottery, and other artifacts were generally strewn on the floors.

In the Pontic region, the inhabitants at İkiztepe also used timber for building constructions, including a palisade around the summit of the town. Noteworthy are the richly furnished shaft burials at Horoztepe and Mahmatlar, which have affinities with similar complexes found elsewhere, including the thirteen "Royal Tombs" discovered farther south at Alaca Höyük and dated to between 2500 and 2200 B.C. (Joukowsky 1996). The practice of covering a shaft or pit grave, as in the case of Alaca, with a mound of earth and stone derives from the steppes north of the Caucasus, where the graves are known as *kurgans*. This connection is supported by the contents of the graves. Funerary gifts included components of wheeled vehicles, a striking feature of Caucasian societies, and animal figures in bronze, inlaid with precious metals, that have broad stylistic similarities with finds from the Maikop burials in the eastern Black Sea region. Indeed, at the end of the third millennium B.C., peoples of different ethnic backgrounds appear to have moved across Anatolia; among them were the Indo-Europeans, speaking a Luwian dialect, who settled in the southwestern region.

In the second millennium B.C. Anatolia, in regions other than the northeast, was composed of city-states with centralized power bases (Joukowsky 1996; van Loon 1985). By the beginning of the Middle Bronze Age (ca. 2000–1600 B.C.) settlement patterns indicate a reduction in the number of villages and a concomitant increase in the size of urban centers that accommodated a larger population. Long-distance trade networks, both overland and maritime, expanded considerably and firmly established commerce as an important component of the economy.

Clear testimony of the scale of these commercial initiatives is afforded by the trading colonies established by Assyrian merchants about 1900 B.C. in central Anatolia. These entrepreneurial newcomers recorded their commercial affairs in Akkadian and introduced cuneiform writing in Anatolia. Their clay tablets, which number over 15,000, are the oldest surviving texts from Anatolia and mark the earliest historical period. The best-documented of these Old Assyrian colonies is the large site of Kültepe, in ancient Kanesh, where over half a century of excavations have revealed an extensive trading area (*karum,* in Akkadian) around a fortified citadel that contained the palace and other buildings. The karum at Kültepe is a circumscribed area some 3 kilometers in diameter. Levels Ib and II correspond to the Old Assyrian period and consist of blocks of multiroom houses separated by pathways. The Assyrian caravanners clearly had no problem acculturating to Anatolian life, for apart from their clay tablets and seals incised with Mesopotamian motifs, they are archaeologically invisible. Acemhöyük, Alişar Höyük, and Boğazköy also had settlements of Assyrian merchants attached to their cities.

Archaeological evidence reveals an abrupt break in the trading patterns between Kültepe and Ashur in the late nineteenth century B.C., which some suggest might represent the conquest of Kanesh by Pitkhanas, a semilegendary figure (as was his son Anitta) whom the Hittites include in their pedigree. Sometime between 1850 and 1750 B.C. the political focus shifted from Kanesh to Hattusha (modern Boğazköy), which went on to become the capital of the Hittite Empire (MacQueen 1996; Seeher 1999). Hittite history is generally divided into two periods, referred to as the Old Kingdom (ca. 1700 to ca. 1500 B.C.) and the Empire (ca. 1400 to ca. 1150 B.C.). Essentially landlocked, the Hittites pursued expansionist policies, effectively using the horse-drawn chariot to become one of the powerbrokers in the second millennium B.C. The Hittites, Indo-Europeans who spoke the Neshite dialect, are known for their governance and civil law codes (*Biblical Archaeologist* 1989). Their society drew heavily on aspects of indigenous (Hattic) and foreign cultures, especially Hurrian and Babylonian, producing its own distinctive blend. Their cities had two sectors surrounded by massive stone fortification walls: a citadel, with two- or three-story buildings (archive, storage and administrative buildings, and residence of the ruler) on stone foundations with a superstructure of mud brick and timber, and a lower, residential area (Seeher 1999). Access into the city was by a gate flanked by towers and protected by guardian creatures or by a postern gate—the best-known example of which at Boğazköy through the Yerkapī rampart, has a corbeled roof and is 71 meters long. Religious worship featured prominently among the Hittites. Boğazköy alone has revealed some thirty temples at this stage, and nearby is the rock sanctuary at Yazılıkaya with its relief panels. The temple complex was situated in a colonnaded courtyard that was surrounded by numerous storage rooms. Other important Hittite sites are Masat, Alaca, Kuşaklı, and Kaman-Kalehöyük.

In the clay tablets found in the archive at Boğazköy, mention is made of the Ahhiyawa, often cited as the Mycenaeans, whose presence is attested along the west coast of Anatolia at about this time. Indeed, the quest to identify Homer's Troy with either Level VI or VIIA, despite the difficulties of disentangling the complicated fabric of that great narrative, has continued unabated. One thing is certain—the internationalism between Anatolia, the Aegean, and Syria-Palestine is evident in the flourishing trading networks vividly reflected by the rich cargo found on board the Uluburun shipwreck.

East-central Anatolian sites in the Malatya-Elazığ region were heavily influenced by trends in the central plateau, as evidenced by the increase in the size of the sites, fortification systems at Arslantepe VB and Korucutepe F, and affinities in ceramic styles. Along the foothills of the southern Taurus Mountains, settlements such as Lidar Höyük (Levels 8–9) have an assemblage indistinguishable from those at sites in the Amuq Plain, including Alalakh VII, which was built by Yarimlim, a vassal of the Yamkhad kingdom based at modern Aleppo.

Still farther east, in the modern provinces of Erzurum, Kars, and Van, the scene in the second millennium B.C. was quite different, and the axis of influence was eastern rather than southern. No city-states were to be found in these highlands. At Sos Höyük there is clear evidence that the earlier Kura-Araxes cultural complex continued to endure in a modified form (Sagona 2000). Dwellings were different, now solidly built and multiroomed, but, significantly, the deceased were buried in deep shaft graves and supplied with grave goods that have marked similarities to the Trialeti kurgan barrow burials of Transcaucasia, which may point to the arrival of newcomers.

The Iron Age

The stable and prosperous late–Bronze Age kingdoms of Anatolia suffered sociopolitical and economic collapse between about 1250 and 1150 B.C., as did many of Anatolia's neighbors in the Aegean and the Near East. The impact of the invasions that brought about the decline in Anatolia had severely shaken the land and radically changed the map of the subsequent Iron Age. New ruling classes emerged in the centuries that followed, often described as a "dark age" because both archaeological and written records are meager, allowing scholars to sketch only the broadest political and social divisions of Anatolia in the Iron Age (Çilingiroğlu and Matthews 1999; Joukowsky 1996).

Eastern Greeks established a number of city-states along the Aegean coast, among them Miletus and Ephesus. Western and central Anatolia was the domain of the Phrygians, the Mushki of the Assyrian records, who had formed a kingdom with centers at Gordion and Midas City by the ninth and eighth centuries B.C. The very few inscriptions in Phrygian, some in beeswax, were written in a new alphabetic script devised by the Phoenicians, which was also adopted by the Greeks, Carians, Lydians, and Lycians. Along the Pontic and in parts of the Hittite homeland, the Kaska, a feared mountainous folk, reigned supreme, whereas the southeast was occupied by the East Luwians, who were ethnically and culturally related to the Hittites. These Luwian-speakers were organized into a number of small neo-Hittite states, including Carchemish, Malatya, Zinjirli, and Karatepe, that extended into northern Syria and were known to the Assyrians as Hatte. Neo-Hittite language was written in the old hieroglyphic script, indicating that there was actually a commingling of Hittites and peoples of the old kingdoms of Kizzuwadna and Arzawa, vassals of the Hittites. But the most powerful of all Anatolian Iron Age kingdoms was Urartu. Emerging from a confederacy of petty principalities centered around and north of Lake Van, it came to control the eastern Anatolian highlands, areas of modern Armenia, and northwest Iran. Urartians revived literacy about 850 B.C. using their own Hurrian language, which they adapted to the cuneiform script.

The archaeological picture for the early Iron Age (ca. 1200–850 B.C.) is not coherent, though it seems the break with the late Bronze Age was not as abrupt as once thought. Then, in the eighth century B.C., there appears to have been a radical change in settlement patterns compared to the second millennium B.C., with the foundation of many hilltop sites and the abandonment of settlements in the plain.

The citadel at Gordion, the Phrygian capital in the eighth century B.C., was defended by a massive mud-brick wall, which enclosed a palace complex that comprised a series of megaron structures facing a courtyard. The largest of these, the Terraced Building, had a wooden gallery along three sides, supported by rows of wooden posts. Timber was extensively used in the construction of buildings, some of which had gabled roofs. Certain smaller buildings, also of a megaron plan, were located behind the complex and had mosaic floors of red, black, and white pebbles arranged in geometric patterns, perhaps to imitate carpet designs. A number of burial mounds outside the settlement, including the great royal tomb (possibly that of the legendary king Midas), contained a rich assemblage of grave goods that attest to outstanding achievements in woodworking, bronzeworking, and weaving. No fewer than six different kinds of wood were used for furniture and other wooden items. Remnants of a variety of textiles—carpets, tapestries, and garments—have survived and show that linen,

hemp, wool, and mohair were woven. Cast-bronze bowls, heavy safety-pin brooches, and great cauldrons on iron stands are testimony to the existence of a mass-production facility.

Neo-Hittite archaeology is dominated by the study of inscribed and relief-decorated orthostats (upright stone roof supports) in basalt and limestone that were incorporated into gateways and important buildings. Chiefly religious in nature, these orthostats reveal at least three different styles—Traditional, Assyrian, and Aramean—each of which displays a high degree of artistic syncretism. Those at Karatepe are famous for bilingual inscriptions in Phoenician and Luwian hieroglyphics, the comparison of which led to the decipherment of the hieroglyphs. Equally important are the finely executed reliefs at Carchemish. Much of our understanding of neo-Hittite cities derives from military architecture, which displays many of the characteristics of earlier cultures. Urban centers generally conformed to the surrounding mountain terrain and were fortified with massive walls. Gates protected by guardian creatures gave access to a palace complex constructed according to a Bit Hilani plan—a rectangular architectural form, often two-storied, that was entered through a pillared gateway leading to a large throne room surrounded by a number of smaller rooms.

In Anatolia the recovery of Urartu's past has focused on the area around Lake Van, where recent investigations at Karagündüz are shedding light on Urartu's obscure origins and work at Ayanis is exposing the unplundered citadel built by Rusa II in about 651 B.C. The majority of known sites are fortified cities strategically positioned on precipitous rocky ridges, each crowned by a citadel and surrounded by a lower town that was protected by an outer wall. The most visually spectacular fort is the citadel of Van, once known as Tushpa, constructed by Saduri I. Masonry was a highlight of Urartian architecture, distinguished by two types: an older semicyclopean style that featured basalt blocks as large as 6 meters long and 75 centimeters high and a later masonry of the ashlar style that used smaller, finely dressed blocks up to 1 meter long. Urartian fortresses contained a

Temple of Apollo in Yeniköy, on the shores of the Bosporus (CFCL)

religious precinct centered by a squarish temple defined at the corners with towers. On entering the courtyard, one's attention would focus on a bronze cauldron on a tripod and ceremonial spears and shields fixed to the walls of the temple. At the center of the temple, the *cella,* stood a bronze statue of the deity, often painted in lapis lazuli blue. Worship was also conducted in open-air shrines within the fortresses. The palatial quarter contained an audience hall with rows of wooden columns set on stone foundations, as well as polychrome wall paintings. That water was an important consideration for the Urartians is shown by the emphasis they placed on irrigation systems and cisterns. Like the Phrygians, Uratians were master bronzesmiths, and their creations were well known in antiquity and in demand as far away as Etruria.

The last chapter of the Iron Age began with the rise of Lydia and its capital at Sardis as a dominant power in western Anatolia. Meanwhile, the Medes, Indo-European-speakers from the Iranian plateau, pursued expansionist policies in the eastern districts and established a massive bastion at ancient Kerkenes Dağ (an-

cient Pteria); it was destroyed by Croesus of Sardis, who, in turn, was defeated by Cyrus, the king of Persia. The Achaemenid Empire that followed lasted from the 540s to the 330s B.C., when Alexander the Great and his invading armies effectively brought an end to the Anatolian Iron Age.

Antonio Sagona

References

American Journal of Archaeology. 1955– . This publication includes a yearly overview of investigations in Turkey, entitled "Archaeology in Anatolia" (formerly "Archaeology in Asia Minor").

Biblical Archaeologist. 1989. "Reflections of a Late Bronze Empire: The Hittites." Entire vol. 52, nos. 2 and 3.

Çilingiroğlu, A., and R. Matthews. 1999. "Anatolian Iron Ages 4: The Proceedings of the Fourth Anatolian Iron Ages Colloquium Held at Mersin, May 19–23, 1997." *Anatolian Studies,* entire vol. 49.

Hodder, I., ed. 2000. *Towards a Reflexive Method in Archaeology: The Example at Çatalhöyük.* Cambridge, UK: McDonald Institute.

Joukowsky, M. S. 1996. *Early Turkey: Anatolian Ar-*

chaeology from Prehistory through the Lydian Period. Dubuque.

Korfmann, M., and D. Mannsperger. 1998. *Troia: Ein Historicher Überblick und Rundgang.* Stuttgart.

MacQueen, J. G. 1986. *The Hittites and Their Contemporaries in Asia Minor.* London: Thames and Hudson.

Matthews, R., ed. 1998. *Ancient Anatolia: Fifty Years' Work by the British Institute of Archaeology at Ankara.* London: British Institute of Archaeology at Ankara.

Mellaart, J. 1967. *Çatal Höyük: A Neolithic Town in Anatolia.* London: Thames and Hudson.

Özdoğan, M., and N. Başgelen. 1999. *Neolithic in Turkey: The Cradle of Civilization—New Discoveries.* Istanbul.

Sagona, A.G. 2000. "Sos Höyük and the Erzurum Region in Late Prehistory: A Provisional Chronology for Northeastern Anatolia." Pp. 329–373 in *Chronologies des pays du Caucase et de l'Euphrate aux IVe–IIIe millenaires.* Ed. C. Marro and H. Hauptmann. Paris: Varia Anatolica XI.

Seeher, J. 1999. *Hattusha-Guide: A Day in the Hittite Capital.* Istanbul.

Tuna, N., and J. Öztürk. 1999. *Salvage Project of the Archaeological Heritage of the Ilisu and Carchemish Dam Reservoirs: Activities in 1998.* Ankara.

van Loon, M. N. 1985. *Anatolia in the Second Millennium B.C.* Leiden: E. J. Brill.

Yakar, J. 1985. *The Later Prehistory of Anatolia: The Late Chalcolithic and Early Bronze Age.* Inter. ser. 268. Oxford: British Archaeological Reports.

———. 1991. *Prehistoric Anatolia: The Neolithic Transition and the Early Chalcolithic Period.* Tel Aviv: Institute of Archaeology, Tel Aviv University. (Supplement no. 1, 1994).

Tutankhamun, Tomb of

The discovery in 1922 of the intact tomb of the eighteenth Dynasty king Tutankhamun (ca. 1333–1323 B.C.) ranks as perhaps the single best-known event in archaeology during the twentieth century. The discovery was the culmination of a methodical search undertaken between 1917 and 1922 by HOWARD CARTER with the patronage of the Earl of Carnarvon. The subsequent excavation of the tomb by Carter, assisted by a team from the Metropolitan Museum of Art in New York, received an unparalleled degree of attention from the international news media; it was the first archaeological project to be the subject of such press coverage. The debate over the fate of the artifacts was responsible for the rescinding of Egypt's until-then liberal antiquities laws, which had formerly permitted equal division of artifacts between the Egyptian Antiquities Service and foreign archaeological projects.

Tutankhamun's tomb is located in the Valley of the Kings, on the west bank of the Nile near the modern town of Luxor (ancient Thebes) in southern Egypt. The Valley of the Kings, a secluded desert wadi five kilometers west of the Nile, was the burial place of nearly all of the pharaohs of the New Kingdom (Dynasties 18–20, ca. 1550–1070 B.C.). The tomb of Tutankhamun was the only one of these to be preserved virtually intact. Most of the others had been plundered by local tomb robbers by the close of the New Kingdom. Although briefly penetrated within a century of the king's burial, the entrance to Tutankhamun's tomb was later obscured and protected by debris created during the construction of the tomb of Ramses VI (Dynasty 20), located just above it.

Tutankhamun's tomb itself is modest in scale, consisting of only four rooms (antechamber, annexe, burial chamber and treasury). Objects that would normally have been deposited in an orderly fashion were piled together. The first two rooms contained an enormous volume of personal possessions including furniture, wooden caskets containing clothing, weapons, chariots, games, jewelry, and ritual couches, as well as containers of food, wine, oil, and other funerary offerings. The king's body was buried in a nested sequence of sarcophagi and shrines that filled most of the burial chamber. The fourth room, the treasury, contained the king's canopic shrine as well as an array of religious and ritual items closely connected to the person of the pharaoh.

Although Tutankhamun's life was comparatively short, his reign falls at the end of one of the most widely discussed periods of ancient Egyptian history: the period of the heretic king Akhenaten. The seventeen-year reign of Tutankhamun's father, Akhenaten (called the Amarna Period), witnessed the abandonment of traditional state religion and the sole veneration

Gold sarcophagus of Tutankhamun (Image Select)

of the sun-disc, the Aten. Court life was centered on a newly constructed royal city, Akhetaten (modern EL AMARNA in Middle Egypt). Tutankhamun, originally named Tutankhaten, was responsible for the restoration of the traditional state religion and the abandonment of the short-lived royal capital at El Amarna. At the time of the discovery, it was hoped that Tutankhamun's tomb would shed light on the history of the Amarna period. The tomb, however, is devoid of written documents. The vast majority of material represents either funerary objects specifically produced for the royal burial or personal possessions of the king. Archaeologically, the tomb represents an unparalleled example of an intact royal burial from the height of Egypt's New Kingdom, but provides little historical information relevant to understanding Tutankhamun's reign.

Despite the meticulous recording by Carter and the Metropolitan Museum team, as well as a series of popular books (Carter and Mace, 1923–1933), the full scholarly publication of the tomb of Tutankhamun was never completed. The records of the excavation, mostly unpublished, are at the ASHMOLEAN MUSEUM, Oxford. Today the body of Tutankhamun remains in his innermost coffin in his tomb in the Valley of the Kings. The artifacts are housed in the Cairo Museum.

Josef Wegner

See also Egypt, Dynastic; Karnak and Luxor
References
Carter, Howard, and A. C. Mace. 1923–1933. *The Tomb of Tutankhamun* I-III. London: Cassell.
Desroches-Noblecourt, C. 1963. *Tutankhamun: Life and Death of a Pharaoh*. New York: New York Graphic Society.
Hoving, Thomas. 1978. *Tutankhamun, The Untold Story*. New York: Simon and Schuster.
Reeves, Nicholas. 1990. *The Complete Tutankhamun*. New York: Thames and Hudson.
Reeves, Nicholas, and Richard Wilkinson. 1996. *The Complete Valley of the Kings*. New York: Thames and Hudson.

Tylor, Sir Edward Burnett (1832–1917)

Born in London, England, the son of a prominent Quaker manufacturer, Edward Burnett Tylor entered the family business at sixteen. Ill health caused him to travel to the United States and Cuba to recuperate, where he befriended HENRY CHRISTY, the banker and archaeologist who supported the research of the French paleontologist ÉDOUARD LARTET. Tylor traveled with Christy for six months through MEXICO visiting the archaeological sites made famous by JOHN LLOYD STEPHENS and FREDERICK CATHERWOOD, all of which was to have a profound impact on the direction of his life and career.

In 1861, he published *Anahuac: Or, Mexico and the Mexicans, Ancient and Modern* based on his observations in Mexico, and his new interest in anthropology is already in evidence in that work. By 1865, his interest had grown into expertise, the outcome of which was the major anthropological work *Researches into the Early History of Mankind*. In that book, Tylor compared languages, myths, customs and beliefs, and the universality of some human behaviors—arguing for both evolutionary and diffusionist explanations of culture. In 1871, his ideas about cultural evolution were further developed in *Primitive Culture*, which led to his being elected to the Royal Society.

Not only is Tylor regarded as the founder of modern anthropology, he also helped to create the acceptance of anthropology as a science. *Primitive Culture* had an enormous impact on the study of anthropology, and his *Anthropology: An Introduction to the Study of Man and Civilization* (1881) was the discipline's first English textbook. Although he was not a university graduate, Tylor commanded great professional respect. Appointed keeper of the University Museum at Oxford in 1883, he became Oxford's first professor of anthropology in 1896. He was twice president of the Royal Anthropological Institute and the first president of the anthropological section of the British Association for the Advancement of Science. He was knighted in 1912.

Tim Murray

References
Stocking, George W. 1987. *Victorian Anthropology.* New York: Free Press.

U

Uhle, Max (1856–1944)

Born in Dresden, Germany, Max Uhle studied languages at the Universities of Göttingen and Leipzig. He worked in the ethnological museums of Leipzig, Dresden, and Berlin, where he became interested in pre-Columbian archaeology.

In 1892, he traveled to South America for the Ethnographic Museum of Berlin to research the INCA and the Indians of BOLIVIA. He excavated in PERU between 1897 and 1899 at Ancon and Pachacamac and between 1899 and 1901 in the MOCHE and Chincha Valleys and at Huamachuco, Ica, and Pisco. Uhle found ceramics from pre-Spanish cultures at all of these sites—CHAVÍN at Ancon and Nazca at Chincha and Ica—and began to interpret the history, cultures, and chronologies of the ancient civilizations that produced them. From 1901 to 1903 he was employed by the University of California, Berkeley, and carried out further excavations of Peruvian coastal cultures and became involved in archaeological research on the shell mounds of California with the American archaeologist NELS C. NELSON.

From 1906 to 1909, Uhle was director of the National Historical Museum in Lima, Peru. Between 1909 and 1933, he excavated in CHILE and ECUADOR, helping to establish an archaeological museum in Santiago, Chile, and working as a professor at the University of Santiago (1912) working at the University of Quito (1919). He returned to Germany, where he was professor at the University of Berlin and worked on Andean archaeology at the Ibero-American Institute until his death during World War II.

Tim Murray

References

Menzel, D. 1977. *The Archaeology of Ancient Peru and the Work of Max Uhle*. Berkeley: R. H. Lowie Museum of Anthropology, University of California.

United Arab Emirates

See Arabian Peninsula

United States of America, Prehistoric Archaeology

There is a tendency to treat the history of archaeology as a single development on the model of the sciences (Daniel 1950, 1963, 1975; Trigger 1988; Willey and Sabloff 1974, 1980). This is inappropriate. As theory-driven disciplines, the "hard sciences" are to a large degree "culture-free," and they do share a more or less politically seamless history. Archaeology, despite wishes and claims to the contrary (Kuznar 1997; Watson, LeBlanc, and Redman 1971), is not science (Dunnell 1982, 1992a). Indeed, if there is a single thread to the history of U.S. archaeology, it has been its aspiration to become scientific for nearly all of its existence (Dunnell 1992a). Such motivation notwithstanding, the lack of scientific theory has permitted the cultural background of individual investigators, common sense, to take over most of the functions of theory (Kuzner 1997). One consequence is that archaeology, unlike science, is heavily influenced by its cultural context. Indeed, the postprocessualists seem to revel in this condition otherwise best construed as our most monstrous failing. Herein lies the fatal er-

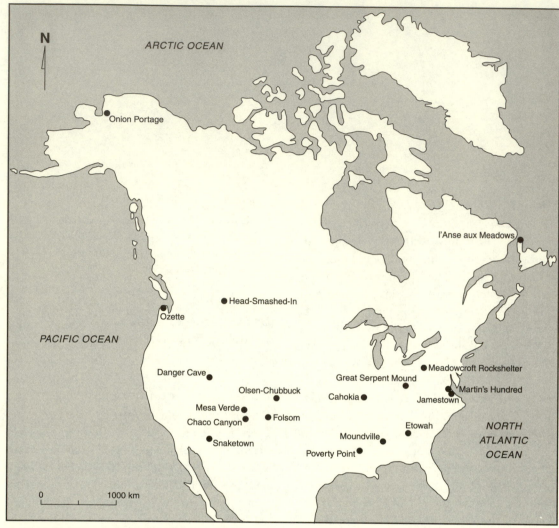

Archaeological Sites in the United States

ror of postprocessualism—assuming that science is a system of understanding comparable to other cultural systems. This premise ignores the epistemological foundations of science, the very features that account for its success and the success of the cultural systems that adopt scientific knowledge as their own.

Whatever other consequences this may entail, it does mean that archaeology has developed along parochial lines (e.g., Fitting 1973). So U.S. archaeology has followed a rather independent course not only because of a different (or so it seemed) archaeological record but also because of contrasting social contexts.

Another consequence of the nonscientific character of archaeology is the lack of the lin-

earity one almost takes for granted in the sciences. Without the epistemological standards that have allowed science to make "progress," archaeology has the embarrassing quality of repeating itself (e.g., Marcus 1983). Furthermore, not only does the historical strand double back on itself, it also periodically frays into multiple strands, or "approaches," that do not succeed one another as less powerful theories give way to more powerful ones; instead, they vie for dominance in a more probabilistic fashion. Not all "kinds" of archaeology are whimsical in the broad sweep of history, however. From a current perspective a persistent partition within archaeology separates work driven by a desire to increase knowledge, of either the past or humanity or both ("academic" archaeology), and that driven by conservation and, of recent, protective legislation, herein termed *cultural resource management* (CRM). Because these kinds of work are differently motivated, they have often developed along divergent lines.

Histories themselves are usually driven by common sense—and that is why, until recently, the word *history* basically meant the history of western culture. One cannot get very far with that tack in examining a discipline that includes common sense as part of its subject. It is not necessary, however, to erect a detailed theoretical structure here. Elucidating but a few concepts will suffice to generate a sufficient framework to analyze American archaeological development. First, since science has played such a role in American developments, it is essential to be crystal clear on what the term *science* denotes. In this context science is an *explanatory system* that uses *theory* to explain phenomena and employs an *empirical epistemological standard,* that is, things don't explain things, events don't explain events, and whether something "works" in physical terms is the arbiter of correctness. All of the commonly cited features of science (i.e., the elements of scientific method) can be traced to these two features (Dunnell 1982).

Second, because of archaeology's particular focus, it is also critical to realize that there are two kinds of structures that meet these general criteria: essentialist (functionalist) science and materialist (historical) science, with the first identifying the ontological position on the significance of variation and the second recognizing different ontological positions on the significance of time. Essentialism sees the variable world as constituted by a finite number of fixed kinds (entities, classes, etc.) between which fixed relations (laws, "generalizations" in the social sciences) obtain. The methodological imperatives that flow from this view can be characterized as ones of "discovery." Explanation in this view takes the form of timeless, spaceless laws that are often characterized as predictive. They are not, of course; they have this appearance and effect only because in this framework time is an elapsed quantity, not an age; thus, there is, strictly speaking, no past or future. Some sciences (e.g., physics, chemistry) operate wholly within this framework or nearly so. Materialism (not to be confused here with the term as used in anthropology) sees the same variable world as in a state of becoming. Because there are no empirical kinds in this view (kinds are analytic tools), there can be no fixed relations or laws, and without laws there is no appearance of prediction. Kinds are created, not discovered, in order to render variability explicable. Explanation takes the form of sets of contingencies interacting with content-free mechanisms to produce a special kind of "history." Realistically, although these two approaches have often been opposed (e.g., Kroeber 1935, 1942; Spaulding 1968), there are no strictly materialistic sciences. Rather, disciplines such as evolutionary biology combine both, using the latter to organize the former so that, though there are no laws of history, all history is a consequence of the operation of laws (Popper 1961).

These aspects of our discipline have been discussed at length in other venues (e.g., Dunnell 1982, 1986a, 1992a), and interested readers can consult those items directly. But such aspects require recitation here because they are integral to an attempt to understand the conceptual development of archaeology in the Americas and its present condition in anything other than the most superficial way.

Coming to Grips with the U.S. Archaeological Record

U.S. archaeology is often taken to have begun with the prescient work of THOMAS JEFFERSON in the excavation and reporting ([1784] 1801) of a small and, as it turned out, rather atypical burial mound at Monticello, Virginia (Heizer 1958; Lehmann-Hartleben 1943). His contribution was by no means isolated. Jefferson's observations and their reporting were certainly unique for the time, but he was in contact both with European scholarship, hardly advanced over his own work in most respects, and with Americans exploring the "west" in North America. For example, Henry Brakenridge, an important explorer of the southeastern (at that time the southwestern) United States, corresponded with Jefferson and shared his understanding of stratification and its significance in the mounds he saw there ([1811] 1848). Indeed, Brakenridge, probably because of his broader field experience, had already come to appreciate that there were different kinds of mounds—some for burial, some for building foundations. He was not alone in noticing this distinction (e.g., Fiske [1815] 1820); such knowledge was clearly predicated on excavations into these structures, though we lack descriptions of those undertakings. Some accounts were entirely secondhand (e.g., Haywood 1823).

Brakenridge also appreciated the authorship of these structures as Indian. Not everyone shared that view, however. CALEB ATWATER (1820), in describing the mounds and earthworks of the "Northwest" (now mostly Ohio) in the early years of the nineteenth century, recognized different kinds of structures as Brakenridge did, but he attributed them to Mound Builders, an extinct, non-Indian race. Others (e.g., Preist 1834) attributed them to known peoples of antiquity (Phoencians, Irish, etc.). However concocted, the Mound Builder as a distinct non-Indian race that created the most impressive American aboriginal monuments is often seen as having played a major role in the development of North American archaeology (e.g., Silverberg 1968; Willey and Sabloff 1974, 1980). The truth is more complex. Popular opinion was, as it still is, the principal repository of the Mound Builder idea. Though such accounts may rank with the alien origins of New World civilizations today (Williams 1991), a variety of evidences could be cited in support of the notion in the nineteenth century. There were certainly political reasons to downplay the accomplishments of Indians (e.g., Schwartz 1967; Silverberg 1968), especially early on when they still constituted a threat in living memory. Political motives, however, explain neither the persistence of the Mound Builder idea nor the broad audience it found. Rather more important was the apparent insufficiency of historically documented Indian population size to account for what seemed to be nearly limitless numbers of mounds (under the common assumption that Indians were recent migrants to the New World) and the denial by Indians themselves that they were the creators of these structures (e.g., Atwater 1820, 220–221; Bartram 1791; Fiske [1815] 1820). Brakenridge was again ahead of his time in clearly stating that depopulation, the cause of which he remained ignorant, had clearly befallen the Indians. He reported Indians *using* mounds as well. The role of epidemic disease in shaping this gross underestimate of aboriginal population at contact and the cultural complexity achieved would not be appreciated until the 1960s and then only very grudgingly (Dobyns 1966; Dunnell 1991; Ramenofsky 1987; contra Fiske [1815] 1820). In short there simply was no compelling evidence in the nineteenth-century public lore that the people who inhabited North America at the time of European contact were the builders of the mounds.

From William Bartram and Jefferson on, educated people—the emerging scientific scholars of the time—never really doubted that, at least in a general way, Indians were responsible for the American archaeological record. Samuel Morton's *Crania Americana* (1839) went well beyond simple plausible assumption and placed the connection on firm anthropometric grounds (again contra Fiske [1815] 1820). Indeed, it seems unlikely that we would talk about a Mound Builder myth today had not Ephraim Squier and E. H. DAVIS adopted this view in *Ancient Monuments of the Mississippi Valley* (1847). That they did so may be attributed to a hazy distinction between professional and amateur in the period—"archaeologists" were lawyers, doctors, and engineers (a doctor and a surveyor, in the case of Bartram and Jefferson) without special credentials in archaeology or even scientific training. But because *Ancient Monuments* appeared as the first of the Smithsonian Contributions to Knowledge, the public view was set back a generation. In the latter nineteenth century numerous often cited but more or less popular accounts of U.S. archaeology (e.g., Foster 1873; Nadaillac 1884) continued the Mound Builders as a distinct non-Indian race concept. It was really against this target that Cyrus Thomas's famous *Report on the Mound Explorations of the Bureau of Ethnology* (1894), as-

The late-nineteenth-century discovery of ruins at Mesa Verde and elsewhere in the Southwest changed archaeological thinking in the United States. (Corel)

signing them an Indian origin, was directed. Scholars had held that view for nearly 100 years already, so his treatise on mounds had little impact on archaeological development per se.

Western exploration, particularly the discovery of spectacularly preserved architectural remains in the American Southwest, eclipsed the fascination with mounds in the later nineteenth century (Rohn 1973; Willey and Sabloff 1980). But unlike the East, the western United States was explored in advance of settlement in many places. Popular and scholarly impressions came through the same filter imposed by explorer reports. Because archaeological development had advanced considerably since the time of the first encounter with the eastern mounds, trained observers played a more important role in formulating a notion of the record of this region. Consequently, although new "mysteries" were embraced (e.g., the disappearance of the Cliff Dwellers), they tended to have a larger kernel of truth and thus to be shared between scholar and nonscholar. Bizarre speculations comparable to

the Mound Builders' notion did not develop to the same degree or enjoy the same currency.

Initial interest in the American archaeological record lay not so much in regard to portable objects—almost universally regarded as Indian—but in upstanding monuments, mounds, walls, and earthworks. Objects were considered important really only insofar as they shed light on the origin of the monuments (e.g., Atwater 1820). But as the frontier moved westward, agriculture and curiosity about the monuments led to more interest in (and collection of) portable antiquities, on a par with that in Europe. Description of both the monuments and the associated artifacts initially relied on English terms and common sense, with the result that the items were understood as part of the contemporary world, as elements of natural rather than cultural history. Portable antiquities were often assigned functional significance (and names) by means of analogy with ethnographic examples, lending strong, if circular, credence to the attribution of such objects to Indians. Indeed, the American example was critically important to European archaeology of the same vintage (e.g., Jensen 1975; Lubbock 1868). Because the initial approach to antiquities generally was functional—an unremarked consequence of common sense—spatial and temporal patterns were obscured, and early accounts were ad hoc (e.g., Haven 1856; Jones 1873; Thruston 1890).

One important feature to note in regard to this initial recognition of the archaeological record is that archaeological data were entirely anecdotal, that is, they were accumulated on a case-by-case basis, largely by accident and without design. Thus, prior to the closing years of the nineteenth century, what sites and monuments were known were largely the product of accidental discovery. Systematic efforts to locate and enumerate sites, almost exclusively mounds and other monuments, initially were spurred on by conservation interests (e.g., Houck 1908; McLean 1879). Archaeological survey organizations, usually organized at the state (or province) level for maintaining such rosters, were creations of the twentieth century (Skinner and Schrabisch 1913). With few exceptions, the organized surveys are of minor research significance, since what they recorded and why remained ad hoc even if the effort to locate sites was not. The twentieth century saw the phenomena deemed worthy of recording expanded to include excavatable (i.e., more or less dense) concentrations of artifacts in the absence of monuments (Smith [1890] 1910) and in recent years the find spots of small numbers of artifacts or even, as some now argue, single objects (Zeidler 1995, appendix 1). These changes have almost always come about through debates on how to define *site* or, to more accurately reflect the spirit of the debates, *what sites are*. The literature illustrates well the absence of theoretical justification for the decisions being made. Although archaeologists certainly have *reasons* for what they do, the argument is made in terms of what is "real," with the result that what parts of the record were recorded, described, managed, or saved has been a matter of historical accident. Whole classes of phenomena (e.g., small burial mounds) have been virtually obliterated, and others (e.g., low-density usages) are on their way to the same fate. Furthermore, the record has often been conceived in ways that preclude explanation (e.g., presence-absence [the site notion] rather than variable density [see Dunnell 1992b, Dunnell and Dancey 1983, and Thomas 1974 for an elaboration of these ideas]).

The range of objects that qualify as artifacts has undergone a similar expansion. Initially, only the most obvious shaped objects were treated as worthy of description and/or preservation. Anything broken, unfinished, or believed to be either was discarded. As whole objects became more rare, broken but "identifiable" objects were included. A few enterprising students (e.g., Wyman 1875) did describe such unshaped objects as shells and bones from middens before the turn of the twentieth century, but by and large such analyses and the systematic collections on which they were based came after the mid-twentieth century. Similarly, although the artificial nature of lithic debitage was recognized long ago, it was as late as the 1970s before its systematic collection and analysis became de rigeur. In some places (e.g., in New Zealand—see Shawcross [1964]) archaeologists moved more quickly in this direction without any fundamental change in methodology simply because of a paucity of shaped objects, but in the United States this shift had to await more fundamental change.

One element of U.S. archaeology, indeed of archaeology everywhere, that emerged early on was the recognition of the importance of conserving the archaeological record. The archaeological record was clearly fragile and being destroyed by vandals, the curious, and simple inattention (Atwater 1833; Schoolcraft 1847; see also Lubbock 1868; Worsaae 1848). As Fiske ([1815] 1820) put it succinctly nearly 200 years ago: The archaeological record is being lost *because* it is being found. This concern was, as just noted, the impetus behind the gradual shift to a systematic recording of monuments. As portable objects became more important, this same concern also led to the development of museums (in contrast to and at the expense of the "curiosity cabinets"). It is therefore not surprising that the museum became the first institution and intellectual seat of archaeology. More important, however, concern for conservation of the archaeological record led to the development of a particular kind of archaeology in the United States—CRM. But in the nineteenth century and indeed up until the 1970s, these concerns were pursued by the same people who were developing academic archaeology. Through lobbying by professional societies such as the American Anthropological Association and Section H of the American Association of the Advancement of Science, an active government role in preservation began with the creation of the CASA GRANDE National Monument in Arizona (1892). Legislation protecting archaeological materials on federal property was adopted shortly thereafter (the Antiquities Act of 1908).

The great amount of time it took for even these modest efforts to be realized can be related, at least in part, to the historical character of archaeology and its lack of scientific standing. The lack of scientific standing meant that archaeology did not enjoy the public support that science as a whole did in the late nineteenth and early twentieth centuries. It remained an esoteric activity without any obvious justification. Archaeology's historical character, however, served to prevent it from being embraced by physical scientists whose essentialist (sometimes obliquely characterized as "generalizing") approach rejected all history as storytelling and seemingly precluded empirical testing. U.S. archaeologists would periodically be consumed by misguided efforts to make their field a generalizing discipline in pursuit of their scientific grail throughout the twentieth century. The same scenario has plagued biology (Mayr and Provine 1980).

The Emergence of Archaeology from Natural History

Although archaeology continues to be pursued as natural history today in the form of the various "amateur"societies of historical sciences, in which data have unique time-space coordinates, retain a role for amateurs long after their contributions to the ahistorical sciences cease. But the late nineteenth and early twentieth centuries saw the emergence of archaeology as a distinct discipline for the first time. Key was the development of a sense of professionalization, first through its incorporation into museums, most notably the SMITHSONIAN INSTITUTION through the National Museum and the Bureau of Ethnology (later the Bureau of American Ethnology, or BAE). Universities, further contributing by training archaeologists, solidified this sense of profession.

These settings saw the first systematic efforts at artifact description. This, in turn, required the development of theory, that is, some principles or rules for how to conceive, tabulate, and discuss archaeological remains independently of common sense. The initial efforts were modeled on the physical sciences and focused on chipped-stone artifacts (e.g., Rau 1876; Wilson 1899; see Dunnell 1986b and references therein). Chipped-stone artifacts in North America meant "arrowheads, spearheads, and knives" (Wilson 1899); that they were tackled first when ceramics have since proved so much more efficacious reveals something of the inner working of the transition from common sense to archaeological theory. Object naming in English is largely functional, based on what the object does. Consequently, it "made sense" to organize only objects that had all their parts. Because sizable collections of whole chipped-stone tools were amassed in advance of more delicate whole ceramic pots, the former were deemed the "logical" starting place. Ceramics, which would come to dominate U.S. analytic efforts for those periods that produced them, followed somewhat later as, on the functional models, pots (and not shards) were deemed the relevant objects of typology (e.g., Holmes 1886a). Charles Rau and Thomas Wilson's efforts based on geometric shape did not bear any intellectual fruit (no temporal or spatial patterns) and thus gained no currency (Dunnell 1986b).

WILLIAM HENRY HOLMES's ceramic analyses (1886a, 1886b) were more successful. His "philosophic approach" (Mason 1886) allowed him to crudely distinguish what today we would call functional and stylistic attributes, a distinction that would later prove critical to method development. Furthermore, he identified most of the parameters now routinely used in ceramic analysis. His most enduring result, the geographic groups of ceramics (Holmes 1903), was largely a fluke, however, being accidental combinations of geography and the chronology of the custom of including vessels in graves. The first lasting accomplishment of U.S. archaeologists, beyond the recognition and accumulation of samples of the record itself, arose at this time as well—the appreciation and understanding of the technology of U.S. artifacts. Here, too, Holmes was a leader, as he "figured out" (via intuitive combinations of engineering, physics, and ethnographic accounts) how virtually all major classes of American artifacts were manufactured (e.g., 1886a, 1886b, 1890, 1897).

The First Paradigm:
Culture History—Science at Last

Archaeology as an ad hoc assemblage of common sense and analogies with ethnographic observation was rather limited in its prospects despite the accumulation of descriptions and objects, even if they were systematic. Although trained as an artist, Holmes was a committed scientist in archaeological matters (Meltzer and Dunnell 1992), and his "philosophical" approach, a step in the right direction, still fell short of qualifying as a general theory. His guiding principles were clearly evolutionary, but, as is so often the case in archaeology, his evolution muddled scientific evolution (e.g., Holmes 1892) and with a more Spenserian evaluation, which was actually influenced by LEWIS HENRY MORGAN et al. (1877) progress-driven framework, little differentiated from Victorian optimism. As crucial as his work has proved to be, Holmes himself lived to see (but never really participated in) archaeology's first and closest approach to becoming science, his lifelong goal.

Three developments proved fundamental to developing a discipline-wide consensus on method, language, and, most important, problem—in short, what Thomas Kuhn (1962) characterized as a paradigm. This consensus has since become known as *culture history*. The first element was the development of a language of observation and an approach to the classification of artifacts. Although critically important, this revolution was confined largely to potsherds, with minor extensions to lithics (stone tools) and bone tools, and it remained restricted to the scale of the portable, discrete object. The second element was adopting a materialist ontology. Like classification, this innovation was far from general in application, being restricted to a narrow methodological role. The final critical ingredient was quantification. Prior to this time, although objects, monuments, and mounds might be enumerated, there was no effort to generate archaeologically meaningful numbers. This new effort entailed wholesale changes in the ways in which archaeologists generated data. What made it all come together as a consensus was that it worked—and for the first time archaeologists could produce conclusions that could be tested empirically like those of other scientists, and they gained a measure of respect that had thus far eluded them.

The so-called stratigraphic revolution (Willey and Sabloff 1980, 84–93) had little to do with stratigraphy per se. It was not an epiphany on the relevance of the geological notion of superposition; U.S. archaeologists from Jefferson on had routinely understood and made stratigraphic observations. Rather, it depended on the coincidence, largely accidental, of the three innovations just named: quantification, materialism, and classification. The success of Europeans using stratigraphy (e.g., de Mortillet 1883; Lubbock 1865; Worsaae 1848) to create archaeological chronologies was not unnoticed by U.S. Archaeologists. They specifically sought out the kinds of deposits that had been key to the European success (especially caves and rock shelters—e.g., Nelson 1917). Even when expanded to include such obviously stratified deposits as shell middens (e.g., Dall 1877; Nelson 1910; Uhle 1907; Wyman 1875), these efforts were unrewarded because they continued to look at the record in qualitative, essentialist terms. European sequences, because of the vastly greater amounts of time involved, yielded coarse chronological kinds or "periods" under such assumptions but not so the much shorter U.S. record. Repeatedly, U.S. archaeologists would observe strata but then conclude they were of no chronological value because there were no differences. Intuitive recognition of differences of a more subtle sort (Uhle 1907) was easily dismissed (e.g., Kroeber 1909). However, once the record was conceived in quantitative terms, as of *varying frequencies,* not *differing kinds,* and combined with *historical types* (or seriation), major changes took place that forever altered the course of U.S. archaeology.

One of these changes was the use of stratigraphy. Now not only could it provide chronology where before it had little to say in the United States, it could also be used to guide excavation and generate chronologically valuable data. This led rather quickly to "metric stratigraphy" and "arbitrary levels," approaches that have been much maligned lately because the early cautions about their use by NELS NELSON (1918) have been ignored.

More important was the development of seriation, the first truly archaeological method and the first serious quantification undertaken by archaeologists. Although SIR W. M. FLINDERS PETRIE is considered the "father of seriation" (e.g., Heizer 1958), his conception of using kind to derive chronology was an extension of the strong European tradition of "kind tells time" begun by JENS J. A. WORSAAE and CHRISTIAN J. THOMSEN and was essentialist in character (Jensen 1975). The U.S. approach, by contrast, relied on quantifying variability. Its origin can be traced to Alfred L. Kroeber and his students and colleagues working the American Southwest (e.g., Kroeber 1916; Nelson 1918; Spier 1917), and it took the form now generally known as "frequency seriation" (Cowgill 1972; Dunnell 1970, 2000). Kroeber (1916) first used the method in its most elemental form to chronologically order otherwise undated and undatable surface ceramic assemblages in the vicinity of Zuni Pueblo. By working backward from modern, recently remembered but abandoned, and completely unknown ruins with varying degrees of preservation, he noticed that the frequencies of different pottery "types" changed in an orderly fashion, with modern types decreasing and types present only anciently increasing with apparent age. Characteristically, he appreciated the significance of sam-

pling and sample size and recognized that superposition could be used to test the order. His student Leslie Spier, working nearby, did just that, introducing most of the modern elements to the method, including normalizing samples with the use of percentages and recognizing the unimodal ("normal") character of frequency distributions (1917). Although further refinements were made, particularly with respect to conditions of application (Ford in Phillips, Ford and Griffin 1951), its use in this form spread throughout the Americas. By the 1950s chronologies nearly everywhere were based on seriation (e.g., Evans and Meggars 1957; Ford 1938, 1949; Mayer-Oakes 1955).

All three of the methodological innovations central to culture-history entered into seriation. First, the types had to be conceived as tools of measurement, not recovered "ideas" in the minds of makers or simply arbitrary conventions for description (Ford 1954, contra Spaulding 1953). Furthermore, as Holmes had dimly envisioned, the attributes used to create types had to be what came to be called "stylistic" or "historical" rather than functional or haphazard confections. Critically, culture-historians employed an empirical test for the historicity of their types—the test of historical significance (Krieger 1944), which required temporal and spatial contiguity. No proposed type could be established unless these conditions were met, and only these kinds of types displayed the unimodal distributions required by the method. Treating types as tools stemmed from seeing the past not as a string of differences but as continuously changing frequencies (materialism). The only way to describe variability (as opposed to difference) was through quantification.

Superposition, an important tool in its own right that was also tied to these three innovations, played a minor role in large-scale culture-history and in seriation. In the latter it was used to determine the direction of time through a seriation (seriation provided only an order, not a direction) to test the results of seriation when some of the seriated assemblages were superimposed and to help select attributes and define types. Correlations (i.e., extension of stratigraphy beyond a single column) also depended upon historical types, and so the two methods were synergistic.

Chronology was not only the product of the application of the new ideas, but also the limit to the application of these new ideas. And only those who actually constructed chronologies (a minority of practitioners, most of whom simply used or tinkered with preexisting chronologies) seem to have participated in or understood this revolution. But being able to relatively date assemblages of objects had important ramifications in almost all archaeological endeavors. Geographic patterns in artifact similarities had been noted since the 1880s (e.g., Holmes 1886b). Broad patterns and the absence of chronology tended to reinforce ethnological interpretations (e.g., Souixan, Algonkin, Iroquoian, Muscogean) of such differences. With the advent of the historical type, independent archaeological connections could be identified, as Frank Setzler (1933) did with "Hopewell" designs over much of the East. So-called whole cultural units also benefited with William McKern's (1939) Midwestern Taxonomic Method, in which ethnic assignments were replaced by phenetic similarity and a hierarchic ranking, a primitive numerical taxonomy well ahead of its time. McKern's approach was strictly phenetic, however, so as chronologies began to become widely available over the next decade, the approach was gradually replaced by nonhierachial units that had distinct temporal connotations, such as GORDON WILLEY and Philip Phillips's (1958) phase. These developments led very quickly to the sine qua non of culture-history—the time-space chart/ culture historical synthesis (e.g., Setzler [1940] in the upper Midwest; Griffin [1946] for the Northeast; Ford and Willey [1941] in the Southeast; Kidder [1924] in the Southwest; and Martin, Quimby, and Collier [1947] for the whole United States and Canada), culminating in Willey's two-volume synthesis entitled *An Introduction to American Archaeology* (1966, 1971) as well as many other less ambitious syntheses.

The crucial thing to notice about this culture-historical success is that it was won not by overt theory construction but by accident, and it was saved only by the use of chronological methods, the results of which were empirically testable. Culture-historians displayed no interest in why the methods worked; their only concern was that they *did* work. Consequently, when pressed, culture-historians had to rely upon arguments of "discovery" and "reality," things that were patently not true when the results were explicitly the product of archaeological creation (compare Rouse 1939 with Rouse 1960). This tendency was reinforced by the success of culture-history. Culture-historical classifications became *the* way to describe the record, even if you were criticizing culture-history (e.g., Spaulding 1960a). Even in matters of chronology, materialism was only skin-deep. To make the archaeological record intelligible in the absence of theory, culture-historians relied on common sense. This meant that they had to describe the record in everyday terms—a warrant for "reconstruction." It also meant that their chronologies, or orders of assemblages, had to be chopped up into groups that could be treated as a kind (essentialism), the archaeological period. Phases were inconceivable without this transformation. The quantitative revolution was just as tenuous. Kroeber (1940), for example, had pointed out that there were quantitative methods for assessing similarity and thus creating units in the Midwestern Taxonomic Method, but these admonitions fell on deaf ears. In short, the chronological methods won by trial and error in the first quarter of the century were applied to create an organization for intuitive, common-sense-driven reconstructions of past lifeways that were no more testable than those of their predecessors, so much so that many preferred to omit the reconstruction in favor of the framework alone. In fact, little of methodological or theoretical significance happened between the first Pecos conference in 1927 and the mid-1900s. To be sure, there were occasional rumblings and grumblings (e.g., Steward and Setzler 1938; Spaulding 1953; Taylor 1948) and alternative models from Europe (Childe 1936; Tallgren 1937) that hindsight shows to have foreshadowed what was to come. By and large, however, this was a period of normal science (Kuhn 1962) during which the goals, methods, and language of observation were unchallenged. Even radiocarbon DATING had little intellectual impact beyond putting absolute dates to archaeological chronologies and improving between-chronology correlation. Almost unnoticed, radiocarbon dating did confirm the accuracy of seriation-based chronology.

Cultural Resource Management

Field methods that could yield the kinds of data required to do culture-history were codified in the late 1930s. The context for codification was provided by an explosion in the number of field archaeologists needed to direct the large-scale excavations that were funded by the federal government to provide work for unskilled laborers during the depression. The ad hoc procedures employed by trained individuals who could be trusted to make the right decisions had to be replaced with a set of rules (in this case, forms) that could be counted on to generate usable data. One rationale for the federal programs lay in conservation (Quimby 1979), even if strategy was determined by political necessity. Still, the locations selected for excavation were usually chosen by professionals—typically to fill in time-space gaps and save spectacular sites—so this federal work contributed directly to the emerging culture-historical syntheses. The program came to an abrupt end with World War II.

Post–World War II conservation archaeology, now nearly synonymous with federal archaeology, restarted with the River Basin Survey program in the Missouri Valley, under the direction of the Smithsonian Institution. New legislation enlarged the federal mandate, especially during the 1960s. The Reservoir Archaeological Salvage and Archaeological and Historic Preservation Acts (1960) put the National Park Service (NPS) in charge of all federal archaeology, a position it maintained until 1974 when the Archaeological Resources Act (or the "Moss-Bennett" act of 1974) gave federal archaeology more stable funding and involved all federal land-managing agencies in archaeological conservation and research.

When the NPS oversaw federal archaeology, CRM was still done by academicians as a part-time activity. A benevolent and informal client-patron relationship between the NPS and university.

sities existed. As the amount of money involved grew and the number of agencies increased, so did the formality of contractual arrangements. This expansion of federal funding and the involvement of less-benevolent agencies than the NPS coincided with a dramatic downturn in academic employment as the first of the bloated crops of Ph.D.'s created by the expansion of university archaeology programs in the 1960s entered the job market. For the first time a separate class of CRM archaeologists emerged, the for-profit contractors. And as luck would have it, this major organizational change took place at the very time that archaeology was in intellectual turmoil. The warranting legislation itself had been framed by culture-historians. That culture-history relied upon common sense was probably an essential ingredient in its passage, but by the time the impact was felt, culture-history was passé and in disrepute but had not yet been replaced by a paradigm of comparable robustness. During the critical years in which archaeologists ought to have been instructing new agencies in why cultural resources were valuable, what archaeology was, and how it was done, no leadership was forthcoming. In such an intellectual vacuum, procedure came to dominate process; compliance—compliance with the law—became the raison d'être. The amount of money spent on archaeology by federal agencies was staggering by previous standards, and soon the bulk of all archaeological fieldwork was CRM.

The Second Paradigm: Processualism—Theory without Practice

One of the distinctive features of U.S. archaeology is that, in spite of its natural history beginnings, it has been in close association with anthropology from the days of the BAE on. Indeed, nonclassical archaeology in the United States is usually called "anthropological archaeology" whenever its intellectual roots are called into question. Why this should have happened in the United States (and in the other places it did) is not obscure. The early linkages were institutional and to some extent political. But the association was lasting and effective in large measure because the methodological problems facing the two disciplines were virtually identical in the U.S. Although Native Americans were still extant in the late nineteenth century, everyone agreed on two things: first, that these people had been greatly changed by contact with Europeans and European culture, and second, that no one cared about studying the extant groups for just that reason. American ethnology was therefore compelled to *reconstruct* an "ethnographic present"—a fictitious, pristine state at the brink of contact. Ethnographers did not study contemporary informants; they used them as a source of information about what the past had been like, the so-called memory culture. But when one elicits a ritual or a recipe for building a canoe or a house at a time when such things were no longer being done, such practices become isolated traits (to say nothing of the other things that happened in this process). Thus, U.S. anthropology came to focus on culture(s) as the static *pattern(s)* of traits. Contemporary archaeologists, once chronologies were constructed, were faced with a similar problem—reconstructing cultures from a set of traits. So U.S. archaeologists and anthropologists not only "studied Indians" but also shared strong methodological similarities, so much so that the distinction between the two fields was often blurred in the works of individuals (e.g., Kroeber 1909, 1916; Spier 1917; Wissler 1916).

Elsewhere, anthropology (notably, that of the British and French schools) was quite different. Ethnologists did not study their own ancestors, as did the archaeologists, but the "primitive" peoples of their empires. Furthermore, unlike the New World, where catastrophic epidemics had destroyed indigenous systems and left only individuals and their memories and musings, the Europeans confronted vibrant, ongoing, and fully functional *systems*. There had been no demographic and cultural bottleneck (Dunnell 1991). From the outset their anthropology was contemporary rather than historical and, above all, *systemic*. Beginning before World War II and continuing dramatically afterward, U.S. anthropology gradually came to be dominated by the British view, a condition exacerbated by the new trend for U.S. anthropologists to study peoples other than American Indians. The net result was that post–World War II archaeologists could, for the first time, be criticized as unanthropological (Taylor 1948), not because they had changed but because U.S. anthropology had. WALTER TAYLOR's *Study of Archaeology* (1948) was an offensive maturation of that realization and is often cited as warranting what came to be called "processualism" (e.g., Watson, LeBlanc, and Redman 1971). As just argued, culture-history was vulnerable on reconstruction issues, and Taylor's critique opened a door to change. Willey and Phillips's famous dictum (1958), Archaeology is anthropology or it is nothing, was undoubtedly a response to this pressure to do anthropology. In point of fact, however, Taylor had little direct theoretical or methodological impact because his "conjunctive" approach had no better scientific warrant that did the ad hoc intuitive tack of the culture-historians.

It was into this context that the larger-than-life LEWIS BINFORD stepped with a series of groundbreaking papers (e.g., 1962, 1964, 1965, 1966, 1968a, 1968b) that seemed to rectify this situation by allowing archaeology to be both anthropological in the new sense *and* scientific at the same time. Although this perception was to prove an illusion, Binford's work and that of his students and colleagues altered the course of archaeology in revolutionary fashion. The central theorem powering the revolution was an argument that runs like this: (1) culture is a system; (2) the value of any one variable in a system is a function of every other variable in a system (this defines the term *system*); and therefore, (3) if one knows some of the values in a system, the other values may be inferred or reconstructed (e.g., Watson, LeBlanc, and Redman 1971). This argument led to the assertion that archaeology's "failures" were inherent not in the nature of the archaeological record but in archaeology's methodology. What was needed was methodological cleverness, and this is precisely what these "New Archaeologists" set about to achieve and what constitutes their main legacy today. This revolution, though more introspective and more given to methodologizing than that of their predecessors, did not begin with first principles or the construction of an explicit general theory. Consequently, the flaws in the warranting argument (point 3 does not follow from points 1 and 2) went largely unnoticed: the argument sounded plausible. The program spread like wildfire at the expense of culture-history in the 1960s and early 1970s, not because it outperformed culture-history (actually, it did not perform at all) but because its appearance coincided with the rapid expansion of the teaching of archaeology and anthropology in North American universities during this period. The dilemma posed by being scientific and being anthropological (in a 1960s' sense) was insoluble because anthropology was not science (Dunnell 1982). Then, as now, anthropology was a matter of interpretation, not empirical testing. The persistence of processualism under these conditions is best characterized by what has been called the "Merlin syndrome" (Dunnell 1989). The key to success lay in asking questions in such a way *that they could not be tested*. This was accomplished by retaining English as the language of observation and common sense and ethnography in the place of theory. The only way questions posed in this fashion can be tested empirically requires a time machine. When common sense does the explaining, the descriptions explained must be common perception.

It was only a matter of time until this flaw was discovered. After all, archaeology was supposed to be a science, and sciences did involve empirical testing. In large measure the life of processualism was prolonged only by the innovative work of Michael Schiffer (1972, 1987), work that came to be known as "formation processes." Schiffer's central insight was to distinguish between what the archaeologist saw (archaeological context) and what the archaeologist wanted to talk about (systemic context) and to recognize that a long series of largely unexplored pattern-inducing processes separated the two. Understanding the variability introduced in archaeological remains by nontarget agents is critical for any effort to understand the archaeological record, giving this research value beyond its role in processualism. In that context, however, this understanding simply seemed to delay the inevitable by obfuscating

the program's logical inconsistencies with a haze of empirical busywork.

The shift to functional questions generated other lasting methodological and technical advances. Perhaps one of the most far-reaching changes, already alluded to, is the expansion of the notion of artifact to include the full range of manufactures, their by-products, and material incidentally modified by the human presence (Spaulding 1960b). Culture-historians, while recognizing the human attributes of a wide range of items, really only worried about manufactures—those that embodied style essential to their goals. This old conception is still embedded in terms such as *diagnostics*. A similar expansion took place at higher levels of organization, so that a greater variety of depositional situations became relevant; even the notion of "site" came under attack on empirical (Thomas 1974) and theoretical (Dunnell 1992b; Dunnell and Dancey 1983) grounds, although in this area CRM procedure has fireproofed the more conservative view.

Whereas these changes can be linked to functionalism, other positive elements of processualism can be linked to CRM, in particular the serious use of sampling. Culture-historians understood the sampling's significance (e.g., Ford 1949; Kroeber 1916), but the character of the paradigm placed little burden on such matters, and they did not avail themselves of the quantitative tools needed. Gary Vescelius (1960) and Binford (1965) made strong theoretical cases for the usefulness of sampling to structure fieldwork, but it was the large amounts of space forced on archaeologists by cultural-resource surveys that finally made sampling part of the package. Although often characterized by its use of quantitative methods, beyond sampling, processualism's quantification was window dressing designed to convince the unwary that archaeology was science. Most of the applications were used to create "kinds" that could be claimed to be natural (read cultural) rather than to describe, analyze, or explain variability (Luedtke 1995).

As argued elsewhere (Dunnell 1986a), what the processualist revolution represented was a shift from asking historical questions to asking functional ones. Partly because radiocarbon dating seemed to have relieved archaeologists of any chronological responsibility beyond the collection of dating samples and partly because archaeological chronologies were seemingly well established in most areas, the functional approach was cast as an alternative to, not a supplement of, culture-history's historicism.

Processualists handled epistemological problems (at least they recognized there were some—not an issue in U.S. archaeology for half a century at that point) by adopting a confirmationist rather than falsification strategy in hypothesis evaluation; analogy (ethnographic and otherwise) effectively replaced empirical testing (Binford 1966; Watson, LeBlanc, and Redman 1971). Deprived of empirical standards for hypothesis evaluation, a pretense of "scientific" rigor could be maintained only by focusing epistemological questions on methods. The correctness of a conclusion was to be judged not by how it worked in the empirical world but by how it was reached, which is a ritualistic view of science (e.g., compare Spaulding 1953 and Ford 1954). The processualist product did not replace culture-historical understandings of the past; those remain strongly in the culture camp (e.g., Fagan 2000; Wenke 1999), albeit with a functionalist-reconstructive overlay but still no better warranted (although infinitely more obscure) than before. In fact, the typical product was either an isolated, never-to-be-used-again demonstration of a method or an exemplary interpretation.

This revolution differed from the culture-historical one in another important respect. Culture-history emerged as a consensus from a natural history context. In fact, the key synthetic pieces (e.g., Ford 1954; Krieger 1944; Willey and Phillips 1958) occurred long after the consensus was in hand. Processualism had to contend with an extant program, and so it was, of necessity (Kuhn 1962), polemical. It had to start with programmatic assertion (Watson, LeBlanc, and Redman 1971). Culture-history was demonized (e.g., Binford 1966, 1968b; Flannery 1967) to make a space for processualism. And, importantly, processualist claims were explicit: science *and* anthropology. As a result, the failure of processualism to achieve its

scientific objectives was equally apparent. With no product to show, the enormous burden—both intellectual (stuff you have to know) and empirical (data quality, quantity, and analytic methods)—imposed by adopting scientific procedure was too much to bear. Processualism was doomed from the outset.

The Modern Ennui: Isms and Schisms—Fatal Division?

One cannot be very analytical about contemporary U.S. archaeology; all analysts have vested interests. The foregoing does, however, provide something of a framework within which a few comments may give perspective. The death of processualism as a paradigm that can be defended in public (it, like culture-history, continues on in practice) is different from the preceding two revolutions. One saw the creation of a paradigm where there had been none; the other saw the replacement of one by the other. Both were rationalized by trying to become scientific and thus like the model of science prepared by the philosopher of science Thomas Kuhn in structure. But with the abandonment of this goal in some quarters, no discipline-wide epistemological basis for constructing a replacement exists. Three strands, some more tightly wound than others, have emerged.

One might be viewed as a continuation of the ideals of processualism but with a new methodology and explicit theory—evolutionary theory (e.g., Dunnell 1978, 1980, 1992c; O'Brien 1996; Teltser 1995). Although there is a growing literature, normal science is still some distance in the future. Use of an explicit theory makes it painfully obvious that facts are created by theories and that one has to start virtually from scratch in generating data that can be explained. After years of no product, this is too much for many who want to get on with the show. Many also have an almost hysterical reaction to the word *evolution;* regrettably, it is the only scientific theory that deals with change. Yet the basis for broad appeal exists. Evolution is undeniably science and can deliver testable hypotheses, allowing us to achieve our historical goal, to say nothing of the benefits that might accrue from knowing why we are the way we are. Evolution also unites in a single framework the historical and functional approaches, the antipathy of which has structured the history of anthropology for a century. Finally, it does, on the model of ecology and evolutionary biology, provide a legitimate vehicle for reuniting anthropology and archaeology.

A second strand in the modern mix also represents a continuing commitment to science but one that is effected not by changing archaeology but by retreating into the other natural sciences. This is the pedology, geology, zoology, botany, and mechanics of archaeological materials. The subject is archaeology, but the theory (and most often the questions being asked of the archaeological materials) derives from the parent science, often the science *in* archaeology rather than the science *of* archaeology.

The variants comprising the third suite of variants are often grouped as "postprocessualist," but they come in as many stripes as those in the second group, if not more. What unites them is the rejection of the science goal and the implied epistemological standards. Although most of the seminal works in this vein are European (e.g., Hodder 1982; Shanks and Tilley 1987), there is homegrown precedent as well (e.g., Leone 1982) in which the historically close ties with anthropology have tended to export the intellectual crisis of anthropology (and the social sciences as a whole) to archaeology. Nonetheless, there are many attractive features of such approaches to archaeology, not the least of which is the lack of any data requirements. Such tacks can be applied to virtually any "data," in contrast to the rather expensive and demanding data requirements of the other two approaches. Further, postprocessualist programs are compatible with just about any other view or interest in the archaeological record (witness the Native American Graves Protection and Repatriation Act). And with much lower costs of doing archaeology, the demand for a product—the bugaboo of all the previous paradigms—is lessened in significance. Whatever else one might want to conclude, one is forced to own up to the realization that unless something happens soon, archaeology is about to run out of time because it will run out of resources.

What we believe about archaeology does make a difference.

Robert C. Dunnell

References

Atwater, Caleb. 1820. "Description of the Antiquities Discovered in the State of Ohio and Other Western States." *Archaeologica Americana* 1: 105–267.

———. 1833. *The Writings of Caleb Atwater.* Columbus: OH: Author, printed by Scott and Wright

Bartram, William. 1791. *Travels through North and South Carolina, Georgia, East and West Florida, the Cherokee Country, the Extensive Territories of the Muscogulges or Creek Confederacy and the County of the Choctaws.* Philadelphia: James and Johnson.

Binford, Lewis R. 1962. "Archaeology as Anthropology." *American Antiquity* 28: 217–225.

———. 1964. "A Consideration of Archaeological Research Design." *American Antiquity* 29: 425–441.

———. 1965. "Archaeological Systematics and Study of Cultural Process." *American Antiquity* 31: 203–210.

———. 1966. "Smudge Pits and Hide Smoking: The Use of Analogy in Archaeological Reasoning." *American Antiquity* 32: 1–13.

———. 1968a. "Archeological Perspectives." In *New Perspectives in Archeology,* 5–33. Ed. S. R. Binford and L. R. Binford. Chicago: Aldine.

———. 1968b. "Some Comments on Historical versus Processual Archaeology." *Southwestern Journal of Anthropology* 24: 267–275.

Brakenridge, Henry M. 1848. "On the Population and Tumuli of the Aborigines of North America (in a letter from H. H. Brakenridge, Esq., to Thomas Jefferson [1811])." *Transactions of the American Philosophical Society* 1: 151–159.

Childe, V. Gordon. 1936. *Man Makes Himself.* London: Watts.

Cowgill, George C. 1972. "Models, Methods and Techniques for Seriation." In *Models in Archaeology,* 381–424. Ed. D. L. Clarke. London: Methuen.

Dall, William H. 1877. "On Succession in the Shell-heaps of the Aleutian Islands." *Contributions to North American Ethnology* 1: 41–91.

Daniel, Glyn E. 1950. *A Hundred Years of Archaeology.* London: Duckworth.

———. 1963. *The Idea of Prehistory.* Cleveland, OH: World Publishing.

———. 1975. *A Hundred and Fifty Years of Archaeology.* Cambridge, MA: Harvard University Press.

de Mortillet, G. 1883. *Le préhistorique*. Paris: Reinwald.

Dobyns, Henry F. 1966. "Estimating Aboriginal American Population: An Appraisal of Technique and a New Hemispheric Estimate." *Current Anthropology* 7: 395–444.

Dunnell, Robert C. 1970. "Seriation Method and Its Evaluation." *American Antiquity* 35: 305–319.

———. 1978. "Style and Function: A Fundamental Dichotomy." *American Antiquity* 43: 192–202.

———. 1980. "Evolutionary Theory and Archaeology." *Advances in Archaeological Method and Theory* 3: 35–99.

———. 1982. "Science, Social Science, and Common Sense: The Agonizing Dilemma of Modern Archaeology." *Journal of Anthropology Research* 38: 1–25.

———. 1986a. "Five Decades of American Archaeology." In *American Archaeology: Past and Future,* 23–49. Ed. D. J. Meltzer, D. Fowler, and J. A. Sabloff. Washington, DC: Smithsonian Institution Press.

———. 1986b. "Methodological Issues in Americanist Artifact Classification." *Advances in Archaeological Method and Theory* 9: 149–207.

———. 1989. "Aspects of the Application of Evolutionary Theory in Archaeology." In *Archaeological Thought in America,* 35–49. Ed. C. C. Lamberg-Karlofsky. Cambridge: Cambridge University Press.

———. 1991. "Methodological Impacts of Catastrophic Depopulation on American Archaeology and Ethnology." In *Columbian Consequences,* 3:561–580. Ed. D. H. Thomas. Washington, DC: Smithsonian Institution Press.

———. 1992a. "Is a Scientific Archaeology Possible?" In *Metaarchaeology,* 75–97. Ed. L. Embree. Boston Studies in the Philosophy of Science, no. 147. Dordrect: Kluwer.

———. 1992b. "The Archaeological Notion 'Sites.'" In *Space, Time and Archaeological Landscapes,* 21–41. Ed. J. Rossignol and L. A. Wandsnider. New York: Plenum.

———. 1992c. "Archaeology and Evolutionary Science." In *Quandries and Quests: Visions of Archaeologys's Future,* 207–222. Ed. L. A. Wandsnider. Carbondale: Southern Illinois University Press.

———. 2000. "Dating: Method and Theory." In *Archaeological Method and Theory: An Encyclopedia,* 141–150. Ed. Linda Ellis. New York: Garland.

Dunnell, Robert C., and William S. Dancey. 1983. "The Siteless Survey: A Regional Scale Data Collection Strategy." *Advances in Archaeological Method and Theory* 6.

Evans, Clifford, and Betty J. Meggers. 1957. *Archaeological Investigations in British Guiana.* Bureau of American Ethnology Bulletin 177. Washington, DC.

Fagan, Brian M. 2000. *Archaeology of North America: The Archaeology of a Continent,* 3d ed. London: Thames and Hudson.

Fiske, Moses. 1820. "Conjectures Respecting the Ancient Inhabitants of North America [1815]." *Archaeologica Americana* 1: 300–307.

Fitting James E. 1973. *The Development of North American Archaeology.* Garden City, NY: Anchor Doubleday.

Flannery, Kent V. 1967. "Culture History versus Culture Process: A Debate in American Archaeology." *Scientific American* 217: 119–122.

Ford, James A. 1938. "A Chronological Method Applicable to the Southeast." *American Antiquity* 3: 260–264.

———. 1949. "Cultural Dating of Prehistoric Sites in the Viru Valley, Peru." *Anthropological Papers of the American Museum of Natural History* 43, 1.

———. 1954. "On the Concept of Types." *American Anthropologist* 56: 42–53.

Ford, James A., and Gordon R. Willey. 1941. "An Interpretation of the Prehistory of the Eastern United States." *American Anthropologist* 43: 325–363.

Foster, J. W. 1873. *Pre-historic Races of the United States of America.* Chicago: S. C. Griggs.

Griffin, James B. 1946. "Cultural Change and Continuity in the Eastern United States." In *R. S. Peabody Foundation for Archaeology Papers.* Ed. F. Johnson, 3: 37–95. Andover, MA: Phillips Academy

Haven, Samuel. 1856. *Archaeology of the United States.* Smithsonian Contributions to Knowledge, vol. 8, art. 2. Washington, DC.

Haywood, John. 1823. *The Natural and Aboriginal History of Tennessee, up to the First Settlements by the White People, in the Year 1768.* Nashville, TN: Printed by George Wilson.

Heizer, Robert F., ed. 1958. *The Archaeologist at Work.* New York: Harper & Row.

Hodder, Ian, ed. 1982. *Symbolic and Structural Archaeology.* Cambridge: Cambridge University Press.

Holmes, William Henry. 1886a. "Pottery of the Ancient Pueblos." *Fourth Annual Report, Bureau of Ethnology, 1882–83,* 257–360. Washington, DC.

———. 1886b. "Ancient Pottery of the Mississippi

Valley." *Fourth Annual Report, Bureau of Ethnology,* 1882–83, 361–436. Washington, DC.

———. 1890. "Excavations in an Ancient Soapstone Quarry in the District of Columbia." American Anthropologist 3: 321–330.

———. 1892. "Evolution of the Aesthetic." *Proceedings, Forty-first Meeting, American Association for Advancement of Science, Rochester 1892,* 239–255.

———. 1897. "Stone Implements of the Potomac-Chesapeake Tidewater Province." *Fifteenth Annual Report of the Bureau of Ethnology,* 1893–94, 13–152. Washington, DC.

———. 1903. "Aboriginal Pottery of the Eastern United States." *Twentieth Annual Report, Bureau of American Ethnology,* 1898–1899, 1–201. Washington, DC.

Houck, Louis B. 1908. *A History of Missouri,* 3 vols. Chicago: R. R. Donnelley & Sons.

Jefferson, Thomas. 1801. *Notes on the State of Virginia,* 3d American ed. New York: Furman and Loudon.

Jensen, Ole Klindt. 1975. *A History of Scandinavian Archaeology.* London: Thames and Hudson.

Jones, Charles C., Jr. 1873. *Antiquities of the Southern Indians, Particularly of the Georgia Tribes.* New York: D. Appleton.

Kidder, Alfred V. 1924. *An Introduction to the Study of Southwestern Archaeology with a Preliminary Analysis of the Excavations at Pecos.* New Haven: Yale University Press.

Krieger, Alex D. 1944. "The Typological Concept." *American Antiquity* 9: 271–288.

Kroeber, Afred L. 1909. "The Archaeology of California." In *The Putnam Anniversary Volume,* 1–42. Ed. F. Boas. New York: G. E. Stechert.

———. 1916. "Zuni Potsherds." *Anthropological Papers of theAmerican Museum of Natural History* 18, 1.

———. 1935. "History and Science in Anthropology." *American Anthropologist* 37: 539–569.

———. 1940. "Statistical Classification." *American Antiquity* 6: 29–44.

———. 1942. "Structure, Function and Pattern in Biology and Anthropology." *Scientific Monthly* 56: 105–113.

Kuhn, Thomas S. 1962. *The Structure of Scientific Revolutions.* Chicago: University of Chicago Press.

Kuznar, Lawrence A. 1997. *Reclaiming a Scientific Anthropology.* Walnut Creek, CA: Altimira Press.

Lehmann-Hartleben, Karl. 1943. "Thomas Jefferson, Archaeologist." *American Journal of Archaeol-*

ogy 37: 161–163.

Leone, Mark P. 1982. "Some Opinions about Recovering Mind." *American Antiquity* 47: 742–760.

Lubbock, Sir John. 1865. *Prehistoric Times.* London: Williams and Norgate.

———. 1868. "[Translator's] Introduction." In S. Nilsson, *The Primitive Inhabitants of Scandinavia.* Trans. Sir John Lubbock. London: Longmans, Green & Co.

Luedtke, Barbara A. 1995. "Review of *Prehistoric Exchange Systems in North America* (Baugh and Ericson)." *Northeast Anthropology* 50: 117–118.

Marcus, Joyce. 1983. "Lowland Mayan Archaeology at the Crossroads." *American Antiquity* 48: 454–488.

Martin, Paul S., George I. Quimby, and Donald Collier. 1947. *Indians before Columbus.* Chicago: University of Chicago Press.

Mason, Otis T. 1886. "Anthropology." *Annual Report of the Bureau of Ethnology for 1885,* 815–870. Washington, DC.

Mayer-Oakes, William J. 1955. *The Prehistory of the Upper Ohio Valley.* Pittsburgh, PA: Carnegie Museum.

Mayr, Ernst, and William C. Provine, eds. 1980. *The Evolutionary Synthesis.* Cambridge, MA: Harvard University Press.

McKern, William C. 1939. "The Midwestern Taxonomic Method as an Aid to Archaeological Culture Study." *American Antiquity* 4: 301–313.

McLean, J. P. 1879. *The Moundbuilders.* Cincinnati, OH: Robert Clarke.

Meltzer, David J., and Robert C. Dunnell. 1992. "Introduction." In *The Archaeology of William Henry Holmes,* VII–1. Ed. D. J. Meltzer and R. C. Dunnell. Washington, DC: Smithsonian Institution Press.

Morgan, Lewis Henry. 1877. *Ancient Society.* New York: World Publishing.

Morton, Samuel George. 1839. *Crania Americana.* Philadelphia: Dobson.

Nadaillac, Marquis de. 1884. *Pre-istoric America.* Trans. N. D'Anvers. New York: Putnam's Sons.

Nelson, Nels C. 1910. "The Ellis Landing Shellmound." *University of California Publications in American Anthropology and Archaeology* 7: 357–426.

———. 1917. *Contributions to the Archaeology of Mammoth Cave and Vicinity, Kentucky.* Anthropological Papers of the American Museum of Natural History 23, 1. New York.

———. 1918. *Chronology in Florida.* Anthropolog-

ical Papers of the American Museum of Natural
History 22, 2. New York.

Noble, Willian S. 1973. "Canada." In *The Development of North American Archaeology,* 49–83. Ed.
J. E. Fitting. Garden City, NY: Anchor Books.

O'Brien, Michael J., ed. 1996. *Evolutionary Archaeology: Theory and Application.* Salt Lake City: University of Utah Press.

Phillips, Philip, James A. Ford, and James B. Griffin. 1951. *Archaeological Survey in the Lower Mississippi Alluvial Valley, 1940–1947.* Papers of the
Peabody Museum of Archaeology and Ethnology no. 25. Cambridge, MA: Harvard University, Cambridge.

Popper, Karl. 1961. *The Poverty of Historicism,*
2d ed. London: Routledge and Kegan Paul.

Priest, Josiah. 1834. *American Antiquities, and Discoveries in the West,* 4th ed. Albany, NY: Hoffman
and White.

Quimby, George I. 1979. "A Brief History of
WPA Archaeology." In *The Uses of Anthropology,*
110–123. Ed. W. Goldschmidt. Washington,
DC: American Anthropological Association.

Ramenofsky, Ann F. 1987. *Vectors of Death: The
Archaeology of European Contact.* Albuquerque:
University of New Mexico Press.

Rau, Charles. 1876. *The Archaeological Collections of
the United States National Museum in Charge of the
Smithsonian.* Smithsonian Contributions to
Knowledge 22, art. 4.

———. 1882. "Aboriginal Trade in North America." In *Articles on Anthropological Subjects Contributed to the Annual Reports of the Smithsonian
Institution from 1863 to 1877 by Charles Rau,*
87–133. Washington, DC: Smithsonian
Institution.

Rohn, Arthur. 1973. "The Southwest and Inter-
montane West." In *The Development of North
American Archaeology,* 185–212. Ed. J. E. Fitting.
Garden City, NY: Anchor Books.

Rouse, Irving B. 1939. *Prehistory in Haiti: A Study in
Method.* Yale University Publications in Anthropology, no. 21. New Haven.

———. 1960. "The Classification of Artifacts in
Archaeology." *American Antiquity* 25: 313–323.

Schiffer, Michael B. 1972. "Archaeological Context
and Systemtic Context." *American Antiquity* 37:
156–165.

———. 1987. *Formation Processes of the Archaeological Record.* Albuquerque: University of New
Mexico Press.

Schoolcraft, Henry R. 1845. "Observations Respecting the Grave Creek Mound in Western

Virginia." *Transactions of the American Ethnological
Society* 1.

———. 1847. *Incentives to the Study of the Ancient
Period of American.* New York: New York Historical Society.

Schwartz, Douglas W. 1967. *Conceptions of Kentucky
Prehistory: A Case Study in the History of Archaeology.* University of Kentucky Studies in Anthropology no. 6. Lexington: University of Kentucky Press.

Setzler, Frank M. 1933. "Hopewell Type Pottery
from Louisiana." *Journal of the Washington Academy of Sciences* 23: 149–153.

———. 1940. *Archeological Perspectives in the
Northern Mississippi Valley.* Smithsonian
Institution Miscellaneous Collections 100:
253–290.

Shanks, M., and Christopher Tilley. 1987. *Reconstructing Archaeology: Theory and Practice.* Cambridge: Cambridge University Press.

Shawcross, Wilfred. 1964. "Stone Flake Industries
in New Zealand." *Journal of the Polynesian Society*
73: 7–25.

Silverberg, Robert. 1968. *Mound Builders of Ancient
America: Tthe Archaeology of a Myth.* Greenwich,
CT: New York Graphic Society.

Skinner, Alanson, and Max G. Schrabisch. 1913.
*Preliminary Report of the Archaeological Survey of
the State of New Jersey.* Trenton, NJ.

Smith, Harlan I. 1910. *The Prehistoric Ethnology of a
Kentucky Site.* Anthropological Papers of the
American Museum of Natural History 10.

Spaulding, Albert C. 1953. "Statistical Techniques
for the Discovery of Artifact Types." *American
Antiquity* 18: 305–313.

———. 1960a. "Statistical Description and Comparison of Artifact Assemblages." In *The Application of Quantitative Methods in Archaeology,*
60–92. Ed. R. F. Heizer and S. F. Cook. Viking
Fund Publication in Anthropology 28. Chicago:
Aldine.

———. 1960b. "The Dimensions of Archaeology."
In *Essays in the Science of Culture,* 437–456. Ed.
G. E. Dole and R. L. Carneiro. New York:
Crowell.

———. 1968. "Explanation in Archeology." In *New
Perspectives in Archeology,* 33–41. Ed. S. R. Binford and L. R. Binford. Chicago: Aldine.

Spier, Leslie. 1917. *An Outline for a Chronology of
Zuni Ruins.* Anthropological Papers of the
American Museum of Natural History 18, 3.

Squier, Ephriam G., and E. H. Davis. 1847. *Ancient
Monuments of the Mississippi Valley.* Smithsonian

Contributions to Knowledge, 1. Washington, DC.

Steward, Julian H., and Frank M. Setzler. 1938. "Function and Configuration in Archaeology." *American Antiquity* 4: 4–10.

Tallgren, A. M. 1937. "The Method of Prehistoric Archaeology." *Antiquity* 11: 152–161.

Taylor, Walter W. 1948. *A Study of Archaeology.* Memoir of the American Anthropological Society no. 69. Menasha, WI.

Teltser, Patrica A., ed. 1995. *Evolutionary Archaeology: Methodological Issues.* Tucson: University of Arizona Press.

Thomas, Cyrus. 1894. "Report on the Mound Explorations of the Bureau of Ethnology." *Twelfth Annual Report of the Bureau of Ethnology, 1890–1891,* 3–742. Washington, DC.

Thomas, David Hurst. 1974. "Nonsite Sampling in Archaeology: Up the Creek without a Site." In *Sampling in Archaeology,* 61–81. Ed. J. W. Mueller. Tucson: University of Arizona Press.

Thruston, Gates P. 1890. *The Antiquities of Tennessee and the Adjacent States.* Cincinnati, OH: Robert Clarke.

Trigger, Bruce G. 1988. *A History of Archaeological Thought.* Cambridge: Cambridge University Press.

Uhle, Max. 1907. *The Emeryville Shellmound.* University of California Publications in American Archaeology 7, 1.

Vescelius, Gary S. 1960. "Archaeological Sampling: A Problem in Statistical Inference." In *Essay in the Science of Culture, in Honor of Leslie A. White,* 457–470. Ed. G. E. Dole and R. L. Carneiro. New York: Crowell.

Watson, Patty Jo, Steven A. LeBlanc, and Charles L. Redman. 1971. *Explanation in Archaeology: An Explicitly Scientific Approach.* New York: Columbia University Press.

Wenke, Robert J. 1999. *Patterns in Prehistory: Humankind's First Three Million Years.* Oxford: Oxford University Press.

Willey, Gordon R. 1966. *An Introduction to American Archaeology.* Vol. 1, *North and Middle America.* Englewood Cliffs, NJ: Prentice-Hall.

———. 1971. *An Introduction to American Archaeology.* Vol. 2, *South America.* Englewood Cliffs, NJ: Prentice-Hall.

Willey, Gordon R., and Philip Phillips. 1958. *Method and Theory in American Archaeology.* Chicago: University of Chicago Press.

Willey, Gordon R., and Jeremy A. Sabloff. 1974. *A History of American Archaeology.* London: Thames and Hudson.

———. 1980. *A History of American Archaeology.* San Francisco: W. H. Freeman.

Williams, Stephen. 1991. *Fantastic Archaeology: The Wild Side of North American Prehistory.* Philadelphia: University of Pennsylvania Press.

Wilson, Thomas. 1899. "Arrowheads, Spearheads and Knives of Prehistoric Times." *United States National Museum, Annual Report (1897),* 811–988.

Wissler, Clark. 1916. "The Application of Statistical Methods to the Data on the Trenton Argillite Culture." *American Anthropologist* 18: 190–197.

Worsaae, Jens J. A. 1848. *Primeval Antiquities of Denmark.* London: Henry Parker.

Wyman, Jefferies. 1875. *Fresh-water Shell Mounds of the St. John's River, Florida.* Memoirs of the Peabody Academy of Science 3: 3–94.

Zeidler, James A. 1995. *Archaeological Inventory and Survey Standards and Cost-Estimation Guidelines for the Department of Defense.* USACERL Special Report 96/40, U.S. Army Corps of Engineers.

University of Pennsylvania Museum of Archaeology and Anthropology

One of the leading institutions of its kind in the world, the University of Pennsylvania Museum (UPM) has played an important role in the development of archaeology for more than a century. It was founded in 1887 and sent its first field expedition to Nippur, in what is now Iraq, in 1889 and recovered a significant number of cuneiform tablets. The first building of the current UPM complex was erected in 1899, and four additional buildings have been added since then, with a fifth addition soon to be constructed (Haller 1999). The UPM has had eight directors—Stewart Culin, George Byron Gordon, Horace H. F. Jayne, George Vaillant, Froelich G. Rainey, Martin Biddle, Robert H. Dyson, Jr., and Jeremy A. Sabloff—and three acting directors—Jane M. McHugh, Marian Angell Godfrey Boyer, and James B. Pritchard—since its founding. The UPM's collections number approximately 1 million objects, the large majority of which were obtained as a result of the museum's field research. The UPM has been an active sponsor of archaeological and ethnographic fieldwork since its inception and at the end of the twentieth century is undertaking research in eighteen different countries around the world (Madeira 1964; Rainey 1992; Winegrad 1993).

Comparable in its history to other important university-based archaeology/anthropology museums in the United States, like Harvard University's PEABODY MUSEUM OF ARCHAEOLOGY AND ETHNOLOGY, the UPM is unique with respect to the size of its staff, collections, research activities, public galleries, and outreach. Although smaller in size than the great natural history museums, such as the American Museum of Natural History, the National Museum of Natural History, and the Field Museum of Natural History, all of which have significant archaeology/anthropology departments, the UPM is closer in its scale of operation to such institutions than it is to its university-based peers.

During the course of its history, the UPM has sponsored research expeditions to all the inhabited continents and has participated in a number of famous projects that have played key roles in the history of world archaeology. Among the latter can be mentioned John Peters, Hermann Hilprecht, and John Haynes's excavation of Nippur; MAX UHLE's early stratigraphic work at Pachacamac; HARRIET BOYD HAWES's pioneering work on Crete; David Randall MacIver and SIR LEONARD WOOLLEY's excavations in NUBIA; Clarence Fisher's excavations at various ancient Egyptian sites; Woolley's renowned work in the royal cemeteries at UR, including the discovery of the famous tomb of Queen Pu-abi; the path-breaking biblical archaeological project at the site of Beth-Shean led by Fisher, Alan Rowe, and Gerald Fitzgerald; the pioneering Alaskan research at Cook Inlet by Frederica de Laguna; Erich Schmidt's key work in IRAN; Edgar Howard's landmark research in New Mexico; Rodney Young's important study of the Phrygian capital of Gordion, TURKEY, including the discovery of the Midas Tomb, work on which continues a half-century later under the leadership of Kenneth Sams, Mary Voigt, and Elizabeth Simpson; Robert Dyson's renowned excavations at Hasanlu; and Edwin Shook and William Coe's trend-setting research at the ancient Maya city of TIKAL.

Not only have these and more recent projects had high public and professional visibility and made significant contributions to scholarly understanding of the ancient world, but in many cases they have also fostered methodological and technical advances in the field of archaeology, especially with regard to the productive use of new scientific techniques in the field and in the laboratory. For example, UPM projects in PERU and what is now Israel helped introduce modern archaeological field techniques, including the use of stratigraphy, in those areas. The museum and its applied science center have also played key roles in the growth or further development of subsurface sensing, radiocarbon DATING, thermoluminescence, analyzing trace residues in ceramics, and computerized survey tools. In addition, under the leadership of George Bass, the UPM helped launch a new subfield of the discipline: underwater, nautical, or maritime archaeology.

Museum-sponsored research also has led to radical alterations in archaeological approaches to particular civilizations or culture areas. One of the best examples of such an impact is the fourteen-year (1956–1970) UPM project at the ancient Maya site of Tikal in Guatemala. Research at the site paved the way for a complete rethinking of the traditional model of MAYA CIVILIZATION. Tikal findings clearly indicated that the older view of a nonurban, peaceful society supported by a maize-based swidden agricultural system was simply not viable. The writings of the Tikal archaeologists rapidly led to the construction of a more complex and variegated model that was more comparable to other early civilizations in both the Old and the New Worlds than was the traditional one. Important research in Thailand, especially at the BAN CHIANG site, initiated by Chester Gorman and now being shepherded to final publication by Joyce White, is another good example regarding the changed understanding of the culture-history of Southeast Asia, especially in relation to the spread of agriculture and the rise of complexity.

Beyond the contributions that the museum has made over many decades to substantive archaeological knowledge, it also has been an integral part of Philadelphia's intellectual and social history in particular (Conn 1998; Kuklick

1996) and of U.S. archaeology in general. Although many of the museum's early expeditions were focused on the gathering of objects for its collections, the overall collections are distinguished by their abundant scholarly documentation. Furthermore, in the 1970s, the UPM was an early and visible proponent of the United Nations Educational, Scientific, and Cultural Organization's convention on looted archaeological materials.

More than a century after the museum's founding by a group of wealthy and civic-minded Philadelphians and enlightened university administrators under the leadership of William Pepper, it is interesting to note that the UPM, with geographically extensive field projects, cutting-edge laboratory research, a successful traveling exhibit program, active conservation and loan programs, an award-winning website, and a highly regarded education department, has retained the same general mission that its founders established in the late nineteenth century. That is to say, through research, care, and study of collections, and dissemination of knowledge to both the scholarly world and the public at large, the museum is still wedded to its original mission of advancing an understanding of the world's cultural heritage.

Jeremy A. Sabloff

See also Mesopotamia

References

Conn, S. 1998. *Museums and American Intellectual Life, 1876–1926.* Chicago: University of Chicago Press.

Haller, D. 1999. "Architectural Archaeology: A Centennial View of the Museum Buildings." *Expedition* 41, no. 1: 31–47.

Kuklick, B. 1996. *Puritans in Babylon: The Ancient Near East and American Intellectual Life, 1880–1930.* Princeton, NJ: Princeton University Press.

Madeira, P., Jr. 1964. *Men in Search of Men: The First Seventy-Five Years of the University Museum of the University of Pennsylvania.* Philadelphia: University of Pennsylvania Press.

Rainey, F. 1992. *Reflections of a Digger.* Philadelphia: University Museum, University of Pennsylvania.

Winegrad, D. 1993. *Through Time, across Continents: A Hundred Years of Archaeology and Anthropology at the University Museum.* Philadelphia: University Museum, University of Pennsylvania.

Ur

A major Sumerian city most closely connected with the excavations of SIR LEONARD WOOLLEY, Ur was first explored in 1854 by J. E. Taylor, a representative of the BRITISH MUSEUM. SIR HENRY RAWLINSON, the prominent nineteenth-century linguist, identified the name of the site from cuneiform cylinder seals that were brought

Ziggurat and ruined walls of the ancient Sumerian city of Ur in Iraq (David Lee/Corbis)

back to the museum. In 1918 and 1919 further explorations and some tests were carried out, but it was not until 1922 that the British Museum (in association with the UNIVERSITY OF PENNSYLVANIA MUSEUM) began serious work in the area, under Woolley's supervision. Between 1922 and 1934 Woolley recovered some of the most magnificent artworks of the ancient world from the cemeteries excavated at the site. Although Ur is justly famous for extraordinary objects made of gold and lapis lazuli, Woolley's excavations also revealed much about the changes in religious architecture and the evolution of the city and its elites.

Tim Murray

References

Woolley, Sir Leonard. 1929. *Ur of the Chaldees: A Record of Seven Years of Excavation.* London: E. Benn.

James Ussher—an engraving by George Vertue after the portrait by Sir Peter Lely (Ann Ronan Picture Library)

Ussher, James (1581–1665)

Born in Dublin, James Ussher was one of the first students of Trinity College, Dublin, which was founded with the help of his family. Ussher studied divinity, Greek, Hebrew, and Latin and became interested in chronology and ecclesiastical antiquarianism. He abandoned the study of law to become a minister in the protestant church of Ireland in 1601. He traveled to England to acquire books for Christ Church College, and while there he met many other Puritan and religious intellectuals and the antiquarians John Camden and Robert Cotton.

Ussher was appointed professor of divinity at Trinity College, Dublin, in 1607, but his title was later changed to professor of theological controversies in recognition of his stance against the Roman Catholic Church and his popularity as a preacher. He was involved in the organization of the Anglican Church in Ireland and came to the notice of King James I, who was impressed by his scholarly vindication of the Protestant and Reformed Church's position in defense against ongoing Roman Catholic attacks.

Ussher was vice-chancellor of the Trinity College, Dublin, and was made a bishop in 1620 and archbishop of Amagh, the primate of Ireland, in 1625. From 1623 to 1626 he lived in London researching his projected work on the antiquities of the British church, which resulted in *A Discourse of the Religion Anciently Professed by the Irish and British* (1623 and 1631), a defense of the independence of the church in England and Ireland based on the history of the ancient Gallic, Celtic, and British churches before their "contamination" by Rome. In the same vein, he published *Britannicarum ecclesiarum antiquitates* in 1639, an account of the spread of Christianity in Britain until the seventh century A.D., when St. Augustine arrived in England.

In the last years of his life, Ussher became interested in establishing a universal chronology for the whole of human history, and in 1650, he published *Annales veteris et Novi Tesamenti* (the English edition, *Annals of the Old and New Testament; Or, The Annals of the World Deduced from the Origin of Time,* was published in 1658). This work involved research in different oriental languages, comparisons of ancient calendars, and the recalibration of different political and national years with astronomical years, and it was built on the work of other Reformation scholars in France and Holland. The work was a triumph of scholarship and it was *the* acknowledged universal chronology for as long as the Bible was regarded as absolutely true—until well into the middle of the nineteenth century. Ussher's findings were so incontestable that his dates were printed in the margins of Bibles for the next few centuries. He is still remembered for precisely dating the flood to 1656 B.C. and the Creation to 6 P.M., Saturday, 22 October 4004 B.C.

Tim Murray

References

Parry, G. 1995. *The Trophies of Time: English Antiquarians of the Seventeenth Century.* Oxford: Oxford University Press.

Uvarov, Count Aleksei Sergeevich (1828–1884)

Born into an aristocratic Russian family as the son of Czar Nicholas I's nationalist ideologue, Aleksei Sergeevich Uvarov promoted archaeological study and helped to organize scholarly associations of archaeologists in the Russian Empire of the nineteenth century. He helped to found the Russian Archaeological Society (in 1864), the first archaeological congress (in 1869), and the Historical Museum in Moscow.

In the 1850s, he excavated burial mounds around Moscow and Vladimir and at the site of the ancient Greek city of Olbia in the Chersonese. In 1877, he excavated the Upper Paleolithic site of Karacharovo on the Oka River. He was regarded as a dilettante by modern scholars of archaeology, but he greatly helped to establish the study of archaeology in Russia.

Tim Murray

See also Russia

V

Valcamonica

Valcamonica is a glaciated valley in the Alpine foothills of Lombardy, ITALY, that contains a rich collection of prehistoric rock art conventionally divided into four chronological phases (Neolithic, Copper Age, Bronze Age, and Iron Age) with subdivisions. Thousands of images were pecked into the glacially smoothed rock surfaces, and they include daggers, chariots, warriors and warfare, sun motifs, hunting and plowing scenes, men and animals, and geometric designs. Certain images are interpreted as huts while some at the site of Bedolina in Valcamonica are usually thought to be maps of settlements.

The known rock art comprises around 300,000 petroglyphs, although hundreds of decorated rocks probably remain buried. The art was first pointed out by a shepherd in 1914, but serious study really began decades later. This was the first rock art in Europe to be named a World Heritage Site by the United Nations Educational, Scientific, and Cultural Organization (UNESCO). The major set of decorated rock surfaces that is arranged for public visitation, with walkways, etc., is that of Naquane (another part of this site).

Paul Bahn

See also Rock Art

Van Giffen, Albert Egges (1884–1973)

Born in Holland, Albert Egges Van Giffen graduated from the University of Groningen, where he studied biology and theology. He became interested in archaeology through his analysis of the faunal remains from prehistoric dwelling mounds or *terps.* He was appointed a keeper in the National Museum of Antiquities in Leiden in 1912, and he began to excavate and publish the results of a number of important sites. He finished his Ph.D. in 1913.

Van Giffen is best known for his skill as an excavator, to which he rigorously applied biological methods. In his early work, structure, periodization, and environmental data took priority over archaeological artifacts. He specialized in coastal geology and archaeozoology and always sought the expertise of paleobotanists, soil scientists, physical anthropologists, and chemists. His multidisciplinary approach to archaeology served widely as a model.

He founded the Biological-Archaeological Institute in 1920 at Groningen University and the Institute of Pre- and Protohistory at Amsterdam University in 1950. In 1947, he became the first head of the State Service for Archaeological Research, and he was responsible for archaeological collections at the Assen (1916– 1955) and Groningen Museums (1917–1955). From 1929 to 1973, he was responsible for the protective governmental acquisition, maintenance, and restoration of megalithic tombs in the NETHERLANDS. The quantity and chronological range of his excavations—from prehistoric *terps,* barrows, and urnfields to provincial Roman *castellum* (forts) and medieval Cistercian abbeys—have ensured that his scientific legacy continues to play a major role in Dutch archaeology.

H. T. Waterbolk

References

For references, see *Encyclopedia of Archaeology: The Great Archaeologists, Vol. 1,* ed. Tim Murray (Santa Barbara, CA: ABC-CLIO, 1999), pp. 352–356.

Vatican Museums

Although the papal museums and galleries were based on the earlier work of Popes Clement IX and Pius VI, it was Pope Gregory XVI who founded the Etruscan Museum in 1837 and the Egytian Museum in 1839. The Vatican used the Etruscan Museum to house material recovered from excavations in southern Etruria, which were begun around 1828. The Egyptian Museum housed not only materials acquired by the Vatican from Egypt but also pieces from its collection of classical (Greek and Roman) artifacts. Since that time, the vast archaeological and ethnographic collections of the Vatican have grown in richness and complexity and are open to the public.

Tim Murray

References
Pietrangeli, C. 1993. *The Vatican Museums: Five Centuries of History.* Rome: Quasar, Biblioteca Apostolica Vaticana.

Ventris, Michael (1922–1956)

Although trained as an architect, Michael Ventris was an accomplished cryptographer who played a significant role in the decipherment of the Linear B script. Ventris published his first paper on the issue at the age of eighteen, but because of war service, he had to wait until 1949 to resume work on the decipherment. In 1952, he announced that he had cracked the secrets of Linear B and had established that it was based on an archaic form of Greek. That same year he was introduced by SIR JOHN L. MYRES to the Cambridge philologist John Chadwick, and together they collected further evidence that Ventris's approach was correct. The 1953 publication of "Evidence for Greek Dialect in the Mycenaean Archives" was a clear and effective statement of their work.

Tim Murray

See also Linear A / Linear B
References
Doblhofer, E. 1973. *Voices in Stone: The Decipherment of Ancient Scripts and Writings.* London: Graxrada.

Vergil, Polydore (ca. 1470–1555)

Polydore Vergil was born in Italy at Urbino about 1470 and studied at the Universities of Bologna and Padua. He became secretary to the duke of Urbino and went on to become chamberlain to Pope Alexander VI. Made famous by two early works, *Proverbiorum libellus* and *De inventoribus rerum,* he was sent by the Pope to England in 1501 as a subcollector of Peter's pence (an annual tribute of a penny paid by each householder in England to the Pope). Vergil so impressed the English king, Henry VII, that in 1505 he was commissioned to write the history of England—the *Anglica Historia,* which was finished by 1512 but not published until 1534. Vergil was made archdeacon of Wells, and on 22 October 1510, he was naturalized as an English subject. Falling out with Cardinal Wolsey in 1514, he was imprisoned in the Tower of London and was not released until the Pope personally intervened.

Polydore Vergil has often been described as the first of the modern historians who placed great store on detailed source criticism and rational argument woven into a continuous narrative. It was Polydore Vergil who first seriously questioned the value of GEOFFREY OF MONMOUTH's legends of the role of the Trojan Brutus in the foundation of England. Vergil left England after the death of King Edward VI in 1553 and returned to Urbino, where he died.

Tim Murray

References
Hay, D. 1952. *Polydore Vergil: Renaissance Historian and Man of Letters.* Oxford: Clarendon Press.

Vilanova y Piera, Juan (1821–1893)

Juan Vilanova y Piera's father was a lawyer, and the son received his primary education in Alcalá de Chisvert in Valencia, SPAIN. Also in Valencia, he read humanities in the Jesuit Real Colegio de San Pablo, and later, he studied medicine, surgery, and sciences. In 1845, he graduated in medicine. In Madrid, he worked toward a doctorate in the Museo de Ciencias Naturales (Museum of Natural Sciences), which is part of the Universidad Central (Central University), and completed the work in 1846. Afterward, he was almost exclusively concerned with the study of the natural sciences and their popularization.

At the suggestion of the director of the museum, Mariano de la Paz Graells, Vilanova y Picra was given a scholarship by the government to study abroad so that, on his return, he could take over the teaching of geology. In 1849, therefore, he studied geology, paleontology, and zoology in Paris at the Museum of Natural Sciences, School of Mines, Botanical Garden, and Sorbonne with Geoffroy de Saint Hilaire, Dufrenoy, Elie de Beaumont, and Cordier. Beginning in 1850, he traveled through FRANCE, BELGIUM, ITALY, SWITZERLAND, AUSTRIA, and Germany and took part in several scientific projects. He gathered and classified an important geological and paleontological collection for the Museum of Natural Sciences in Madrid as well as for the Comisión del Mapa Geológico (Geological Map Commission) and the Cuerpo de Ingenieros del Ejército (Army Engineers), and he started a campaign of international exchanges.

In 1852, Vilanova y Piera was appointed to the chair of geology and paleontology in the Museum of Natural Sciences, and he took up the post in 1853 on his return from abroad. He started teaching in 1854. After the splitting up of the chair in 1873, he chose to go with the paleontology section. Outside the university he also taught in the Ateneo (Athenaeum) of Madrid and in the Enseñanza de Institutrices. As part of his research, he was member of the council of the Geological Map Commission (1849–1858), head of the Sección Geológica del Este de España (Geology Section of Eastern Spain), and a member of the Brigadas Geológicas (Geological Brigades, 1858–1870).

Vilanova y Piera was a full member of the Academia de Medicina (Academy of Medicine); the Academia de Ciencias Exactas, Físicas, y Naturales (Academy of Exact Sciences, Physics, and Natural Sciences); and of the Real Academia de la Historia (Royal Academy of History) as well as being an honorary member of the Real Academia de Ciencias y Artes de Barcelona (Royal Academy of Sciences and Arts of Barcelona). He was a founding member of the Sociedad Española de Historia Natural (Spanish Society of Natural History), the Sociedad Geográfica de Madrid (Geographic Society of Madrid), the Sociedad Antropológica Española (Spanish Anthropological Society), and the Sociedad Prehistórica Española (Spanish Prehistorical Society). He was also a honorary member of the Sociedad Económica de Amigos del País de Valencia (Economic Society of Friends of the Country of Valencia).

Vilanova y Piera's teaching and supervisory activities were very much interrelated, not only in the spheres of geology, paleontology, and prehistory but also in some aspects of medicine and biology, especially after the 1860s. The political situation following the 1868 revolution in Spain favored the vigorous formation of scientific associations and high-class cultural journalism. Vilanova y Piera took part actively in both as the most-qualified spokesman of the "official sciences" because of his conservative political ideas and his adherence to the Catholic cause. His membership in the Spanish academies was of fundamental importance as an indirect means of controlling scientific journalism through the granting of the necessary permits in order for each magazine or journal to achieve state subscription.

Vilanova y Piera's outside activities had three aspects. He took part in the meetings and congresses of the French Geological Society and of the Helvetic Society of Natural Sciences, of which he was a full member, as well as the French Association for the Progress of Science and the International Geology and Anthropology congresses, among others, throughout Europe and in Algiers. Second, he was a member of the French entomological and zoological societies and of the Antiquarians of Copenhagen. Third, in his scientific trips he covered a great deal of Spain and other European countries.

In recognition of his national and international scientific work, Vilanova y Piera received the award of Comendador de Carlos III, the Italian Order of the Iron Crown, and the Danish Donebrog. He is considered to be one of the most outstanding naturalists in the history of Spanish science. With Ezquerra del Bayo and Casiano del Prado, he was most active in the institutionalization of geology in the first half of the nineteenth century. On the international level, he was one of the promoters of international geological congresses.

However, it was in prehistory that Vilanova y Piera's research was its most innovative. He was the first naturalist full member of the Royal Academy of History, through his research activities and his diffusion of prehistory. His interest sprang from discussions with European geologists and through the association of Paleolithic industries with extinct fauna, which was also observed by Casiano del Prado on the banks of the river Manzanares in San Isidro, Madrid (1862). Vilanova y Piera was the author of two unique treaties on the prehistory of the Iberian Peninsula: *Origen, naturaleza, y antigüedad del Hombre* (The Origen, Nature, and Antiquity of Man)(1872) and, with Juan de Dios de la Rada Delgado, *Geología y Protohistoria Ibéricas* (The Geology and Protohistory of Iberia)(1894) in the Historia General de España edited by the Royal Academy of History. He also took part in all the congresses on archaeology and prehistoric anthropology that took place in Europe and in the associations aimed at achieving their institutionalization. By 1869, he was, along with J. F. M. Tubino, the official Spanish representative at the Copenhagen International Archaeology Congress.

In prehistory, Vilanova y Piera is associated with the introduction of a first Copper Age within the Metal Age and with the defense, even at the cost of his scientific credibility, of the authenticity of the ALTAMIRA cave paintings discovered by Marcelino Sanz de Sautuola in 1879.

Throughout his life, Vilanova y Piera endeavored to incorporate European knowledge on the subjects with which he was involved into Spanish science and to present Spanish contributions to this knowledge at the different meetings and congresses that he attended abroad. His task had two main limitations. First, as a naturalist, the very extension of his work involved significant information gaps. Second, his religious attitudes, extreme on certain subjects such as evolution, reduced his objectivity in spite of his attempts to keep within the limits of science.

Isabel Martínez Navarrete

References

Gozalo Gutierrez, Rodolfo. 1993. "Biografía de Juan Vilanova y Piera." In *Homenaje a Juan Vilanova y Piera (Valencia, 25–27 de noviembre de 1993),* 11–83. Valencia: Departamento de Geología Universitat de València, Servicio de Investigación Prehistórica Diputación de Valencia, Sociedad Económica de Amigos del País de Valencia.

Virchow, Rudolf (1821–1902)

Rudolf Virchow was born in Germany and educated at the University of Berlin, where he received his Ph.D. in medicine in 1843 and where he established an archive of anatomy and physiology. In 1849, Virchow became professor of pathological anatomy at the University of Würzburg, and in 1856, he returned to Berlin as professor of pathological anatomy and director of the newly created Pathological Institute, where he included lectures in prehistory in his courses.

Rudolf Virchow (Ann Ronan Picture Library)

He encouraged the development of the discipline of anthropology in Germany by helping to found the National Anthropological Association (1870) at the same time as Germany unified politically and the Berlin Museum für Volkstrachten was founded (1888). He also contibuted to the development of the collections of the Berlin Museum für Volkerkunde (Berlin Museum of Folk Studies) and edited a national journal of ethnology. He excavated in Pomerania and took an interest in the work of HEINRICH SCHLIEMANN, traveling to Hisarlik in TURKEY in 1879 to advise Schliemann on the excavating.

Unlike his student Ernst Haeckel, Virchow was not a Darwinist. He was involved in debates about developments in human paleontology, and he regarded the first Neanderthal discovery at the Feldhofer Cave in the Neander Valley in Germany as a pathological specimen and not a new species of hominid. He also refused to accept Dutch paleontologist EUGENE DUBOIS's discovery of a fossil hominid in Java as evidence of human evolution.

Tim Murray

See also Kossinna, Gustaf

References

Ackerknecht, E. H. 1953. *Rudolf Virchow: Doctor, Statesman, Anthropologist*. Madison: University of Wisconsin Press.

Virú Valley

The small Virú Valley on the coast of PERU was the site of a landmark study in the development of archaeological survey methodology. Research in the valley began in 1946 with the cooperation of U.S. and Peruvian scholars, but it was the innovative work of GORDON WILLEY in the field of settlement archaeology that lifted the program from being yet another site survey. Although Willey (who was much influenced by anthropologist JULIAN STEWARD) was certainly interested in exploring the ecology of 1,500 years of human settlement in the region, he chose to do so against a background of a detailed analysis of the location and distribution of sites within the region. Using both surface and subsurface survey techniques, Willey was able to chart the distribution of sites in the region over time, and he demonstrated the fact that the environmental (both natural and cultural) context of human settlement was also time-dependent and not simply "read off" from surface indications.

Tim Murray

References

Billman, B., and G. Feinman. 1999. *Settlement Pattern Studies in the Americas: Fifty Years since Virú*. Washington, DC: Smithsonian Institution Press.

Willey, Gordon, ed. 1974. *Archaeological Researches in Retrospect*. Cambridge, MA: Winthrop.

W

Waverly Plantation, Mississippi

George Hampton Young founded Waverly Plantation in 1841, and it remained in the Young family until 1963. This National Historic Landmark contains one of the South's finest plantation houses, complete with its own gas plant and swimming pool, built in the 1850s. Young founded the University of Mississippi and was a prominent political figure in Mississippi. He owned 3,420 acres and controlled much more; with 217 slaves, he was a big planter. In 1893, the National Fox Hunters Association was organized at Waverly.

After the American Civil War, a tenant and sharecropping system was established, which lasted until the 1930s. In 1979, archaeological excavations were conducted at six tenant farmer sites, a general store, a brick kiln, and a steam-powered cotton gin and sawmill under the direction of William H. Adams, Timothy B. Riordan, and Steven D. Smith. Historical geographer Howard Adkins researched the documentary history of this tenant-farming community. Folklorists David F. Barton and Betty J. Belanus interviewed eighty-nine informants, forty-three extensively, and their recordings are in the Library of Congress, the Mississippi Department of Archives and History, and the Indiana University Folklore Archives. This study marked the first archaeological investigation of tenant farming in the South. The community approach used to study tenant farmers and planters provided a broader historical context for the material recovered. Adams and Smith compared the purchases recorded in the general-store ledger with the artifacts from those tenant sites to evaluate what kinds of items were not being recovered archaeologically.

William H. Adams

See also United States of America, Prehistoric Archaeology

Wheeler, Sir Eric Mortimer (1890–1976)

After an illustrious career as an archaeologist of the British Iron Age, Eric Mortimer Wheeler was the director-general of the Archaeological Survey of India between 1944 and 1948 and served as the archaeological adviser to the government of Pakistan in the 1950s. His major excavations in the subcontinent as director-general were at Taxila, HARAPPA, Arikamedu, and Brahmagiri and on behalf of the Pakistan Department of Archaeology, at Charsada and Mohenjo Daro. Among his publications on the subcontinent mention should be made of the "Indian" chapters in the autobiographical *Still Digging* (Wheeler 1954) and *Rome beyond the Imperial Frontiers* (Wheeler 1955) and the books *The Indus Civilization* (Wheeler 1968) and *Early India and Pakistan* (Wheeler 1959). His "Indian" writings were published mainly in Ancient India, an official publication of the Archaeological Survey of India, which he himself edited.

His major achievements in the field of South Asian archaeology were the establishment of a training school at Taxila in 1946 to make Indian students familiar with his layer-based method of digging and the basic academic results of his excavations, which included, among other things,

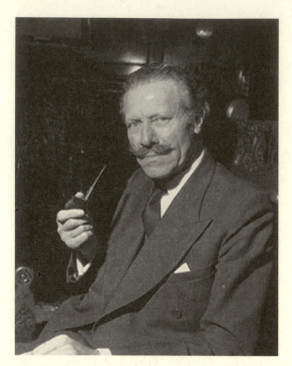

Sir Mortimer Wheeler (Image Select)

the discovery of and a cross-section through the Harappan defenses at Harappa; the identification of a Roman trading station at Arikamedu; and the establishment, on the basis of ceramic correlations with the dated ceramic sequence at Arikamedu, of a chronological sequence for southern Indian archaeology from the Neolithic stage upward. Among other issues, he emphasized the need for prehistoric and proto-historic studies, establishing a separate prehistory branch in the survey, and he underlined the importance of spreading archaeological studies beyond the confines of a government department to the portals of universities in India. Within the short span of time available to him for archaeological researches in the subcontinent, what he achieved and influenced must be considered remarkable.

Barry Cunliffe

See also Indus Civilization; South Asia

References

A longer discussion of Wheeler's life may be found in the *Encyclopedia of Archaeology: The Great Archaeologists,* Vol. 1, ed. Tim Murray (Santa Barbara, CA: ABC-CLIO, 1999), pp. 371–383, and in *Mortimer Wheeler: Adventurer in Archaeology* by Jacquetta Hawkes (London: Weidenfeld and Nicolson, 1982).

Who Owns the Past?

It is a commonplace that archaeological knowledge is not and never has been produced in a cultural and political vacuum. Yet this fact was not formally recognized by archaeologists until the twentieth century. In the 1800s, when the fundamental structures of the discipline were created, the bulk of practitioners (and the general public, which avidly followed their work) firmly believed that archaeologists produced rational, objective, scientific knowledge about the past. Further, the search for knowledge about human history, at least as undertaken by archaeologists, was of sufficient cultural significance to be self-evidently worthwhile. A scientific archaeology was to provide an objective history of humanity, and this history (in the eyes of commentators such as Sir John Lubbock [LORD AVEBURY]) should become the foundation upon which rational societies of the future would be built.

This same search for universal edification (undertaken or controlled by Europeans or, later, North Americans) had been a major factor in fostering the work of collecting expeditions to ITALY, GREECE, and Asia Minor in the eighteenth and nineteenth centuries, which were followed by major expeditions in Egypt and the Middle East. In an important sense the pasts of countries that lay outside the borders of metropolitan Europe were considered to be resources that could be articulated by archaeologists and antiquarians in the search for an understanding of human (read European) history. Thus the great excavations in MESOPOTAMIA, Egypt, Asia Minor, and Greece that began in the nineteenth century and continue to this day were initially launched to explore the roots of Judeo-Christian civilization and to bring back to London, Paris, Berlin, or New York the material representations of that great journey toward civilization.

It is also no coincidence that these explorations outside Europe (especially in Africa, the Americas, and Australia) fulfilled two roles at the same time—providing a reconnaissance of contemporary human diversity and fostering a consideration of the relationship between the histories of such places or people and the history of Europe. The museums of "man" or "natural history" that sprang up all over the western world during this period stored the material culture and frequently the physical remains of subject peoples at the margins of empire, again as scientific and historical resources.

At the turn of the twentieth century few voices questioned the wisdom of such collection practices. But out in the field things were beginning to change. Certainly, after Greece gained its independence from the Ottoman Empire in the nineteenth century, there was a clear policy that the government of Greece should manage the archaeological heritage of the country for the benefit of its citizens. The drafting of a nation's archaeological past as an important element in the definition of the identity of the contemporary population of that country was a phenomenon occurring in other parts of Europe, too, achieving its most notable expression in the nationalist archaeologies propounded by practitioners such as GUSTAF KOSSINNA and JENS JACOB WORSAAE (among many others). One practical consequence of this more overt politicization of archaeology was the potential for conflict between western archaeologists and the governments of the traditional source areas for museum collections, such as Egypt and Mesopotamia. HOWARD CARTER's long-running feud with the Egyptian government over the disposition of the objects recovered from TUTANKHAMUN's tomb is a case in point. But there was also a significant potential for archaeologists to use their work for the edification of the people in whose countries they worked, and notwithstanding continuing debate about the effect of his efforts at site stabilization at KNOSSOS, there is no doubt that SIR ARTHUR EVANS sought to do just that in Crete and Greece.

The gradual recognition that archaeological knowledge was not socially, culturally, or (especially) politically neutral aptly reflected the reality of the situation. Within the boundaries of Europe the perception that archaeology (no matter how scientifically conducted) had political consequences was well understood by the 1880s. This was particularly true in the context of the passage of legislation to protect the "ancient monuments" of countries such as the United Kingdom. In Asia Minor, Egypt, and the Middle East—especially after the collapse of the Ottoman Empire—the activities of archaeologists became subject to increasing regulation. However, little if any recognition of the rights or interests of the indigenous peoples of Africa, the Americas, or Australasia was accorded either by governments or archaeologists in the late nineteenth and early twentieth centuries. In these places excavation and collection continued unfettered.

During the twentieth century much of the innocence (either real or feigned) that characterized the previous century disappeared. In Europe the deeply political nature of archaeology was explicitly revealed by VERE GORDON CHILDE (particularly in his great works *Man Makes Himself* and *What Happened in History*) during the course of his resistance to the distortion of European archaeology by Nazi ideologists prior to World War II. Similarly, the constraints on interpretation placed on Russian archaeologists by Joseph Stalin prompted sharp reactions from scholars such as GRAHAME CLARK. Since 1950, but especially since the 1980s, European archaeologists have continued to explore the cultural, social, and political dimensions of the production (and consumption) of archaeological knowledge. For some this has meant confronting the role of science and objective knowledge in archaeology. For others it has involved a contemplation of the impact of European archaeology on peoples outside Europe. And for all practitioners it has entailed searching for an understanding of the role archaeological information plays in the creation and destruction of nations and ethnic identities within the borders of Europe. Part of this exploration has been devoted to the discussion of the ownership and retention of cultural properties removed to European museums. The most celebrated example of this is, of course, the controversy over LORD ELGIN's marbles, but equally significant have been the requests by indigenous peoples from former European colonies for the repatriation of human skeletal remains for reburial in their home territories. A great deal more work needs to be done on all of these matters, but there is little doubt that most practicing archaeologists in Europe are now well aware that their actions (and those of their predecessors) have consequences for the peoples whose pasts they investigate.

Outside Europe the "loss of innocence" has been even more dramatic since World War II. Indeed, since the 1960s, much of our modern thinking about matters related to the ownership and control of pasts has developed in North America, Australasia, and, more recently, in Africa. In these regions recognition by governments and by archaeologists of the rights and interests of indigenous peoples has completely transformed the archaeological landscape. The practice of archaeology in these places is now highly regulated by legislation (such as the U.S. legislation Native American Graves Protection and Repatriation Act), and former collection and excavation practices have been replaced by models of negotiation and consultation. It is also now far more widely accepted that archaeologists cannot consider the scientific importance of their inquiries to be of such significance as to make their interests automatically more valuable than those of any other group. In Australia, as in some other countries, it is explicitly acknowledged that indigenous people "own" their pasts—an acknowledgment that requires that work can only proceed on the basis of informed consent. Archaeologists now spend a good deal of time developing research projects that produce knowledge of interest and value to indigenous communities, not just to nonindigenous institutions such as museums, universities, or academic disciplines. But again, notwithstanding the great changes that have occurred in the practice of archaeology in these contexts, significant challenges remain.

Against this background of transformation in the social, cultural, and political contexts of archaeological knowledge, at least three matters remain unchanged. Foremost is continued looting of archaeological sites and the theft of cultural properties for sale on the illegal antiquities market. Efforts persist to restrict if not stamp out this trade, but its power to destroy the past remains undiminished. Second, the preservation or conservation of archaeological sites and landscapes requires that all members of society (not just archaeologists) acknowledge the many values of such properties—an acknowledgment that accepts that those values can be diverse and that they must be balanced against other rights and interests existing in society. Third, archaeologists in all countries still need to recognize that interpretation must never be completely free from empirical demonstration and that it is up to them to clearly distinguish between interpretation and demonstration in their writings. It is imperative that archaeologists be honest with their readers—honest about the limits of their interpretations and honest about their biases and presuppositions. Some archaeologists have (wrongly) supposed that if archaeological knowledge is a social and cultural product, then this must mean the end of science as a model for the production of knowledge. Indeed, the history of archaeology aptly demonstrates that no science is or ever has been practiced in a vacuum, but this does not mean (and never has meant) that all opinions about archaeology are equally valid.

Tim Murray

See also Society of Dilettanti

References

Gathercole, P., and D. Lowenthal, eds. 1989. *The Politics of the Past*. London: Unwin Hyman.

McBryde, I., ed. 1985. *Who Owns the Past?* Melbourne: Oxford University Press.

Murray, T. 1993. "Communication and the Importance of Disciplinary Communities: Who Owns the Past?" In *Archaeological Theory: Who Sets the Agenda?* 105–116. Ed. N. Yoffee and A. Sherratt. Cambridge: Cambridge University Press.

———. 1996. "Coming to Terms with the Living: Some Aspects of Repatriation for the Archaeologist." *Antiquity* 70: 217–220.

Willey, Gordon Randolph (1913–)

Gordon Randolph Willey, the foremost Americanist among archaeologists, was born in Chariton, Iowa, and grew up in Long Beach, California. He took his undergraduate and masters degrees at the University of Arizona and pursued doctoral work at Columbia University, completing his dissertation in 1942. A year later, he joined the Bureau of American Ethnology at the SMITHSONIAN INSTITUTION. In 1950, he accepted the Bowditch Professorship in Central

American Archaeology and Ethnology at Harvard University, which he held until 1987. During his productive career, he directed major fieldwork projects in BELIZE, GUATEMALA, Honduras, MEXICO, Nicaragua, PANAMA, and PERU. Within the UNITED STATES, he has worked in Arizona, Georgia, Louisiana, and Florida.

Willey is perhaps best known for creating the subfield of "settlement pattern" archaeology. For him, the distribution of human settlements provided a natural starting point for the functional interpretation of archaeological cultures. Different sites were best understood, not in isolation, but as part of complex economic, social, and political landscapes. Willey devised his settlement pattern approach under the aegis of the VIRÚ VALLEY project, one of the first multidisciplinary research programs in the New World. The widespread popularity of Willey's approach is due to its workable methodology for addressing questions of social structure, demography, and subsistence patterning.

Willey is the preeminent "grand synthesizer" of American archaeology. From 1953 to 1955, in a series of publications with Philip Phillips, he laid out the baseline for the prehistory of the New World. In 1965, he revised this framework in a comprehensive survey of North and Middle American archaeology. Spanning some 40,000 years of prehistory, his book covers the continent from Alaska to Panama. This project was quickly followed by a second volume on South American archaeology. More than any other work by a professional archaeologist, these lavishly illustrated books served to acquaint a popular audience with the broad diversity of past cultures and their rhythms of horizontal integration and regional florescence.

Willey has maintained a strong interest in the professional development of American archaeology. He prepared his first historical essay in commemoration of the one-hundredth anniversary of the PEABODY MUSEUM OF ARCHAEOLOGY AND ETHNOLOGY in 1966, and this essay emphasizes the growing professionalization of the field and its increasing claim to scientific status. In 1973, collaborating with JEREMY SABLOFF, Willey completed his first major book-length history. This volume differs from

Willey's earlier essay by embracing much of the new archaeology, an explicitly scientific approach grounded in positivism. In the third edition, Willey and Sabloff substantially revised their appraisal of the new archaeology and pointed out some of its excesses.

The influence of Gordon Willey on American archaeology is immense. His work on settlement archaeology is regarded as the starting point for all investigations of culture process and social change, his syntheses of New World prehistory and the history of American archaeology are considered classics and are widely used as textbooks, and his writings on functionalism, culture process, and ideology have anticipated many of the recent trends in archaeology since the 1980s. One of Willey's most distinguishing characteristics is his balanced view of archaeological explanation, and throughout his career, he has consistently sought to bridge the tensions between humanist and scientific traditions.

Robert Preucel

References
For references, see *Encyclopedia of Archaeology: The Great Archaeologists,* Vol. 2, ed. Tim Murray (Santa Barbara, CA: ABC-CLIO, 1999), pp. 709–712.

Williamsburg, Colonial

Williamsburg, the eighteenth-century capital of Virginia, earned its place in the annals of archaeology through the pioneering techniques used there to uncover the remains of British colonial buildings and then reconstruct them. In 1928, by excavating and rebuilding the colony's capitol, architects employed by John D. Rockefeller began to turn Williamsburg into a living museum in an ongoing archaeological, architectural, and curatorial process that has continued into the twenty-first century.

The methods developed by the architects and their draftsmen that exposed foundations but ignored stratigraphy and the potential testimony of artifacts were replaced in 1957 after the arrival of British archaeologists who used methods employed in the Old World by the great stratigraphers SIR MORTIMER WHEELER and KATHLEEN KENYON. Emphasis on site cleanliness

Reconstructed dwelling at Colonial Williamsburg (Spectrum Colour Library)

and the introduction of a process that came to be known as artifact cross-mending greatly improved the excavators' ability to interpret the sequential interrelationships between structures and other on-site features. Through the following quarter century, Colonial Williamsburg publications demonstrating the importance of potsherds and a wide range of other artifacts as a means of reading the colonial past had a lasting impact on the birth and growth of the discipline now globally known as historical archaeology.

In 1969, the Colonial Williamsburg Foundation expanded its interpretive interests to include the nearby Carter's Grove plantation, where archaeologists found the remains of the Martin's Hundred settlement (1619–1645), much of which had been destroyed in an Indian uprising in 1622. The settlement's administrative center, Wolstenholme Towne, has been partially reconstructed, and a subterranean museum displays the arms, armor, and other artifacts found there.

Ivor Noël Hume

Wilson, Daniel (1816–1892)

Daniel Wilson was the first person outside Scandinavia to practice the prehistoric archaeology that had been pioneered by CHRISTIAN J. THOMSEN and JENS JACOB WORSAAE. He also elucidated, if he did not invent, the term *prehistory*. Wilson was born in Edinburgh, Scotland, 5 January 1816. Between 1837 and 1852 he worked as an engraver, writer, and shopkeeper. The romanticism of Sir Walter Scott motivated him to use his considerable artistic skills to record old buildings that were being demolished in the course of Edinburgh's urban renewal. *Memorials of Edinburgh in the Olden Times* (1848), which contained many of his more interesting sketches accompanied by a rambling account of the history of the city, consolidated his reputation as a leading Scottish antiquarian.

Wilson was invited to rearrange the collections of the SOCIETY OF ANTIQUARIES OF SCOTLAND according to the THREE-AGE SYSTEM that Thomsen had devised for the National Museum of Antiquities in Copenhagen. His work on this collection and study of prehistoric monuments led him to publish *The Archaeology and Prehistoric Annals of Scotland* (1851), the first comprehensive work of prehistoric archaeology in the English language. It is not clear whether Wilson understood the seriational principles on which Thomsen's work was based or merely copied his sequence. Wilson's major achievements were to distinguish history and prehistory not merely as time periods but as different approaches to the past, and to realize the potential of material objects as a rounded source of information about how human beings lived in the past.

In 1853, Wilson became professor of history and English literature at University College in Toronto, Canada, where in 1857, he began offering a course on ancient and modern ethnology. His encounters with Indians still living in a traditional fashion convinced him that the New World constituted a "laboratory" for studying European prehistory and understanding better the "essential characteristics" of all human beings. In *Prehistoric Man* (1862), Wilson used physical anthropological data to refute claims that American Indians constituted a separate species; interpreted archaeological findings as evidence of parallel, if unequal, cultural development in the Old and New Worlds; and interpreted what had happened to Europeans, Africans, and aboriginal peoples in the Western Hemisphere since 1492 as evidence that all peoples possess the same basic drives and abilities and, hence, could participate in cultural development. Wilson continued to uphold the principles of the eighteenth-century Enlightenment as they had been understood in the Edinburgh of his youth.

Wilson also continued to adhere to a biblical chronology. It was not until the 1870s that he was prepared to admit that human beings might have evolved from other animals, and even then he refused to consider an evolutionary origin for human reason or moral sense. Wilson continued to publish anthropological papers, but the problems he had in coming to terms with Darwinian evolution prevented him from becoming one of the leading anthropologists of the late nineteenth century. In his later years, Wilson continued to publish important works of literary criticism and was increasingly preoccupied with academic administration, which culminated in his becoming president of the University of Toronto in 1887. He died in Toronto 6 August 1892.

Bruce G. Trigger

References
For references, see *Encyclopedia of Archaeology: The Great Archaeologists, Vol. 1,* ed. Tim Murray (Santa Barbara, CA: ABC-CLIO, 1999), pp. 91–92.

Winckelmann, Johann Joachim

Winckelmann was born on 9 December 1717 in Stendal, Germany. He went to the local grammar school and later spent a few months at the Collnisch Gymnasium in Berlin. For two years (1737–1739) he studied theology in Halle and then moved to Jena in 1741, where he enrolled for classes in mathematics and medicine. In 1743 he took a post as associate rector at a school in Seehausen, which he held for five years, a period of intensive study of the classics. He was taken on by Heinrich von Bünau as librarian in Nothnitz near Dresden in 1748; here he did research on the Ottonian emperors for Bünau's *History of the Empire*.

Winckelmann's earliest unpublished writing was notes from a lecture on recent general history in which he brought out the close connections between art and history. He moved to Dresden and published *On the Imitation of the Painting and Sculpture of the Greeks* in 1755, a depiction of classical Greece in which art could develop freely and free citizens could live in a state that was founded on liberty and democracy. Enthusiastic descriptions of the Laocoon group and the Herculanean Vestals form a contrast to the way he conceived his own times. In his theory of imitation he established the need to copy the natural and ideal beauty of Greek sculpture, its "noble simplicity and calm grandeur." He converted to Catholicism and, helped by a stipend from the Saxon court, went to Rome in 1755. He began an inventory of Roman works of art, commenting on them both as iconography and in terms of restoration and described the Belvedere statues in the Vatican. At the same time he was striving for a language that would be appropriate to art and would reflect the essence of the works of art in question. His descriptions had a great influence on German scholarly prose. From his inventory there emerged a new system of historical classification, based on the criteria and the style of na-

Johann Joachim Winckelmann (Ann Ronan Picture Library)

tions, periods, and artists, of the rise, development, flourishing, and decline of the art of different nations, the whole connected with the attempt to classify each individual work of art. He exemplified this theory in his great work, his *History of the Art of Antiquity* in 1764, the work that marked the height of his fame. He described the art of the Egyptians, Phoenicians, Persians, and Parthians; of the Etruscans and Italians; as well as the style of Greek art, which he divided into four separate styles, the more ancient style, the grand, the beautiful, and the style of the imitators. He maintained that, besides nature, climate, and education, it was freedom that had produced the artistic flowering of Greece. In 1757 he became librarian at the Vatican and a year later entered the service of Alessandro Albani. In 1758 he visited Naples, Portici, HERCULANEUM, and POMPEII for the first time and went to the temple at Paestum. In 1762 his *Remarks on the Architecture of the Ancients* appeared and was instrumental in bringing the temple of Paestum to European attention. He saw that Vitruvius had not gone far enough in answering the question of the origins of Greek architecture and that its uniqueness and development could only be made clear through drawings and reproduction. In later writings, *Open Letters from the Discoveries at Herculaneum* (1762) and *News of the Most Recent Herculanean*

Discoveries (1764), he reported on significant finds at Herculaneum and Pompeii. He also described in detail the Roman frescoes and artifacts from daily life and pointed out the artistic and aesthetic aspects of Roman handicrafts. In 1760 he published his *Description of Ancient Gems* by the late Baron de Stosch in Florence, which introduced methodologically significant elements into archaeology as he recognized that many of the themes or images taken from Greek mythology needed to be explained. In 1767 were published two volumes of *Monumenti antichi inediti,* in which he tested out his archaeological-hermeneutic methodology and tried to decipher the mystifying content of classical works, as well as attempting to determine their style and thus their date. In another work, *Attempt at an Allegory, Particularly for Art* (1766) Winckelmann undertook to provide artists with a supply of significant classical themes as a stimulus for their own works. Its impact was to help fertilize the intellectual ground for the rise of Neoclassicism in Europe. On 8 June 1768 he was murdered in Trieste.

Max Kunze; translated by Judith Braid

References

For references, see *Encyclopedia of Archaeology: The Great Archaeologists, Vol. 1,* ed. Tim Murray (Santa Barbara, CA: ABC-CLIO, 1999), pp. 51–63.

Woolley, Sir (Charles) Leonard (1880–1960)

Charles Leonard Woolley was born in London and won a scholarship to New College, Oxford, where he studied humanities and theology. He graduated in 1904 and then traveled to Germany to study modern languages. In 1905, Woolley was appointed assistant to SIR ARTHUR EVANS, keeper of the ASHMOLEAN MUSEUM in Oxford.

Woolley traveled to the Near East in 1907 to excavate in NUBIA with D. Randall-MacIver from the UNIVERSITY OF PENNSYLVANIA MUSEUM. He excavated the Meroitic cemetery at Karanog, unearthing rich finds and receiving an excellent training in field archaeological methods and the management of excavations. In 1912, Woolley was appointed to lead a BRITISH MUSEUM expedition to Carchemish where he discovered Neo-

Sir Leonard Woolley (Image Select)

discovery of the expedition—the royal cemetery of Ur and its wonderful treasures from before 2500 B.C. He also unearthed some of the earliest literature in the world, many remarkable small finds, sculptures, and metal work. He published *The Sumerians* (1928), *The Development of Sumerian Art* (1935), *Abraham* (1936), *The Royal Cemetery* (1934), and *The Ziggurat and Its Surroundings* (1939) on the excavations at Ur. His popular books, such as *Digging Up the Past* (1930), *Ur of the Chaldees* (1929), and *Excavations at Ur: A Record of Twelve Years' Work* (1954), were best-sellers.

Woolley continued to excavate. At Al Mina, an ancient port city near Antioch in Syria, he found ten levels of occupation from between the eighth and third centuries B.C., which shed light on the nature of the trade between Syria and the Aegean. At Tell Atchana, the site of ancient Alakakh in northwestern Syria (1937–1939 and 1946–1949), he discovered seventeen phases of middle and late–Bronze Age occupation, exposing residential, palace, and religious monuments and material culture and archives dating to the fifteenth century B.C.

In 1938, Woolley traveled to India to advise the government on a program of archaeological work for the subcontinent. During World War II, he served as a lieutenant-colonel, and in this capacity he managed to save many of the monuments, art works, museums, archives, and libraries of Europe from invading armies and bombs. He was knighted in 1935, received honorary degrees from the Universities of Dublin and St. Andrews, was awarded the Flinders Petrie Medal in 1957, and unfortunately died just before he received the gold medal of the Royal Society of Antiquaries.

Tim Murray

See also Egypt: Dynastic; Turkey
References
Winstone, H. V. F. 1990. *Woolley of Ur: The Life of Sir Leonard Woolley.* London: Secker & Warburg.

Hittite temples, palaces, and fortifications. He also worked closely with another young archaeologist, T. E. Lawrence, who was to become famous later as "Lawrence of Arabia." Together, after the digging season had finished, they made an archaeological survey of Palestine north of Aqaba toward the southern end of the Dead Sea and managed to observe and note the Turkish government's military strengths and weaknesses in the area at the same time.

The excavation at Carchemish was interrupted by the outbreak of World War I, during which Woolley was an intelligence officer in Egypt and spent two years in a Turkish prison camp after surviving being blown up at sea off the coast of Asia Minor. In 1919, he returned to Carchemish, where completing the excavation was made difficult because of its location between the French and Kurdish armies. Funded by the EGYPT EXPLORATION SOCIETY, Woolley moved to Egypt and excavated the house quarter of EL AMARNA.

In 1922, Woolley began thirteen years of excavation in MESOPOTAMIA at the mound of UR, where he unearthed a long sequence of cities going back to the Ubaid period of the fifth millenium B.C. He unearthed Sumerian temples, palaces, and whole towns, and the most famous

World Archaeological Congress

The World Archaeological Congress (WAC) is an international forum concerned with all aspects of archaeological theory and practice worldwide. It emphasizes academic issues and questions that benefit from a widely oriented and comparative approach. It aims to bridge the disciplinary divisions of the past into chronological periods and to avoid exclusive and particularistic regional concerns. It is explicit in recognizing the historical and social roles and political context of archaeological inquiry and interpretation and acknowledges the need to make archaeological studies relevant to the wider community. Thus, it differs in concept and, as a result, in structure and organization from the UNESCO-linked INTERNATIONAL UNION OF PREHISTORIC AND PROTOHISTORIC SCIENCES (IUPPS), from which it emerged.

Peter Ucko (1987a) has reviewed the precipitating circumstances that arose in the context of the organization of the Eleventh Congress of IUPPS scheduled for September 1986 in Great Britain. The British Executive Committee, of which Ucko was national secretary, planned the meeting with a breadth of international participation, disciplinary discussion, and involvement of interest groups quite unprecedented for IUPPS. When the parent body disowned the congress following the decision of its executive committee to disallow South African (and Namibian) participation in the context of growing anti-apartheid activism during 1985, the intended Eleventh Congress of IUPPS in Southampton and London became the first World Archaeological Congress in Southampton. A plenary session set up a widely representative steering committee of twelve, with a year's brief, to open discussions with IUPPS on a range of issues extending beyond the matter of South Africa to questions of a revised role for the official body of world archaeology (Ucko 1987a, 209, 226–235, 1987b).

All approaches to IUPPS proving unsuccessful, the committee proceeded in September 1987 to the formal establishment of a WAC in fulfillment of its mandate. Its recommendations (Day 1988, 6–11) were the subject of wide discussion within the organization (Day 1989; Draft Statutes 1989) before the adoption of a constitution at the Second World Archaeological Congress in Venezuela in 1990 (WAC 1991).

WAC has a membership, individual and institutional, that is open to anyone with a genuine concern for the study of the past. Positions within the organization are elective. The council, the policymaking body that meets on the occasion of the congresses, which are held every four years, consists of the officers, members of the executive, and one national representative per country selected by the individual members from that country present at a congress.

There are three officers—president, secretary, and treasurer—elected by the council at each congress. The executive, the governing body between meetings of the council, consists of the officers and two representatives from each of (currently) fourteen regional electoral colleges, a senior member (must have more than five years permanent employment in archaeology or a related discipline) and a junior member, elected for eight years by secret ballot of the individual members of each college under procedures designed to favor gender balance. In addition, there are eight representatives of the indigenous (Fourth World) peoples appointed by appropriate organizations for a limited period. Executive members accept the responsibility of promoting WAC in their constituencies.

The organization's major occasions are its four-yearly congresses, of which Southampton in 1986 was the first; the second was held in Barquisimeto, Venezuela, in September 1990; the third met in New Delhi in December 1994; and the fourth in Capetown, South Africa, in 1998. The main, though not exclusive, focus is on themes of universal significance in archaeological practice and research, to which experience in different parts of the world and different disciplines can contribute. True to WAC's wide view of archaeology's role and responsibilities, each congress makes specific provision for basic issues relevant to the archaeological exercise: the interests and concerns of indigenous communities when outsiders study their past; the dissemination of archaeological knowledge through schools, museums, and the electronic media; and archaeology and information technology, in which WAC's attention extends to the provision of the requisite facilities and training at disadvantaged institutions. The languages at the congresses, as generally in WAC transactions, are the official languages of UNESCO plus that of the host country.

Each congress tries to circulate papers ahead of time in order to devote available time in the sessions to discussion and to facilitate the publication of the selected proceedings. Under the title *One World Archaeology,* the twenty volumes from the first congress have inaugurated a "splendid series . . . [that] makes a great gesture in the direction of drawing the squabbling . . . sciences of mankind back together" (Fox 1993, 10). Five volumes from the second congress extend the series, and several have already appeared from the third with another increase in number from the fourth. Publishers' advances and royalties help support the attendance of individuals from poorer countries at executive meetings and congresses, and in various ways (*WAB* 1989, 14, 1991b; Zimmerman 1993), the organization can periodically make volumes available free or at a discount for targeted recipients. There is also an active policy of issuing the volumes in paperback.

In addition to the main congresses, WAC has thus far sponsored, on its own behalf or cooperatively, two smaller intercongresses with a focus on a particular topic: one in Vermillion, South Dakota, in August 1989 on archaeological ethics and the treatment of the dead (*WAB* 1989, 1991a) and the second in Mombasa, Kenya, in January 1993 on the development of urbanism in East Africa in a global perspective.

The inauguration of a biannual newsletter (*WAC NEWS*) in 1992 to keep members abreast of the activities of their organization has allowed the annual *World Archaeological Bulletin,* established in 1987, to concentrate on archaeological subjects of major WAC interest in a thematic format. The first thematic number, volume six (1992), reviews the questions of the collection, study, and display of human remains that are of concern to diverse communities throughout the world (Hubert 1988). WAC's adoption of an ethical position in this matter, the Vermillion Accord on Human Remains (*WAB* 1989, 18; cf. Fforde 1991, 23), has had wide influence (Hubert 1991). WAC has also adopted a code of ethics mediating relationships between its members and indigenous peoples, which has proved equally influential (Fforde 1991, 21–23; cf. Matunga 1991, 52).

Jack Golson

References

Day, M. 1988. "Final Report of the World Archaeological Congress Steering Committee." *World Archaeological Bulletin* 2: 4–11.

———. 1989. "Draft Statutes for the World Archaeological Congress." *World Archaeological Bulletin* 3: 85–90.

Fforde, C. 1991. "WAC Executive and Council Meetings." *World Archaeological Bulletin* 5: 17–23.

Fox, R. 1993. "One World Archaeology: An Appraisal." *Anthropology Today* 9, no. 5: 6–10.

Hubert, J. 1988. "A Proper Place for the Dead: A Critical Review of the 'Reburial' Issue." In *Conflict in the Archaeology of Living Traditions,* 131–166. *One World Archaeology,* vol. 8. Ed. R. Layton. London: Unwin Hyman.

———. 1991. "After the Vermillion Accord: Developments in the 'Reburial' Issue." *World Archaeological Bulletin* 5: 113–118.

Matunga, H. 1991. "The Maori Delegation to WAC 2: Presentation and Reports." *World Archaeological Bulletin* 5: 43–54.

Ucko, P. 1987a. *Academic Freedom and Apartheid: The Story of the World Archaeological Congress.* London: Duckworth.

———. 1987b. "Report of the Steering Committee." *World Archaeological Bulletin* 1: 28–31.

World Archaeological Bulletin (*WAB*). 1989. "WAC First Inter-Congress." *World Archaeological Bulletin* 4: 14–28.

———. 1991a. "Materials Now Available from the 1989 WAC Inter-Congress on 'Archaeological Ethics and the Treatment of the Dead.'" *World Archaeological Bulletin* 5: 109–110.

———. 1991b. "One World Archaeology Series." *World Archaeological Bulletin* 5: 108–109.

World Archaeological Congress. 1989. "Draft Statutes." *World Archaeological Bulletin* 4: 6–13.

———. 1991. "WAC Statutes (adopted September 1990)." *World Archaeological Bulletin* 5: 133–138.

Zimmerman, L. J. 1993. "From the Secretary." *WAC NEWS* (World Archaeological Congress Newsletter) 2, no. 1: 1–2.

World Archaeology

The first edition of the journal *World Archaeology* appeared in June 1969, and the opening issue set out the journal's objectives concisely: "to synthesize the best contemporary thought on matters of common interest to archaeologists the world over. It is the voice, essentially, of a fresh generation of professional archaeologists." With those words, the founders of the journal allied themselves with the methodological revolution that was affecting Anglo-American archaeology during the late 1960s. This stance is particularly clear because they described *World Archaeology* as "designedly a journal of debate" and sought to organize the contents of most issues around a clearly defined theme.

From the start, the journal was run from England, and only occasionally has it drawn on editors outside the British Isles. Until recently, most of the editors have been associated with the Universities of Oxford, Cambridge, or London and have represented the archaeology of those parts of the world in which they have had special interests.

The journal has retained its thematic character, although the nature of the topics selected for particular issues have changed over the years. Early issues tackled broad themes such as subsistence, population, and trade, and sometimes they were concerned with questions that only became really topical some years later, such as archaeology and linguistics. After the first decade, however, the topics became rather more specific, and there was greater emphasis on empirical data and on particular analytical techniques. On the one hand, there were issues concerned with such topics as waste management, ceramics, or archaeology and musical instruments; on the other hand, there were groups of papers on early chemical technology and photogrammetry.

More recent editions of the journal show a subtle change of direction. There is less emphasis on appointing editors to represent particular areas of the world, and some issues have returned to the broader themes first explored in the early years of the journal, such as architectural innovation, craft production, and specialization or concepts of time and the ancient world.

There have also been changes in the authors writing articles for *World Archaeology*. Although contributors who were relative newcomers to archaeology were always encouraged, the early issues contain the names of many people whose careers were already well established. For example, FRANÇOIS BORDES, J. DESMOND CLARK, MARY LEAKEY, Colin Renfrew, JEREMY SABLOFF, and Bruce Trigger all contributed to *World Archaeology* during its first five years. Others were soon to make international reputations for themselves, indeed, the very first issue contained an early article by African prehistoric archaeologist GLYN ISAAC. Relatively few of the contributors to the early editions of *World Archaeology* are still writing for the journal, although there are exceptions such as Charles Higham and Bruce Trigger. More of the articles are submitted by graduate students or by archaeologists who are just beginning their careers.

Last, there have been striking changes in the regions discussed in the journal. Not surprisingly, more articles are concerned with Europe than with other areas (approximately a third), but in the first ten years *World Archaeology* was published, a substantial number of articles also discussed material concerning Africa, MESOAMERICA, and South America. Over the next decade, however, the proportion of articles concerned with the New World declined, probably because other journals had been established dealing with just those areas, and *World Archaeology* carried significantly more articles discussing material from the Near East and Southeast Asia. Throughout its history, the journal has published relatively few articles concerning India, Australia, the UNITED STATES, or the Pacific, although there are signs that the balance may have started to shift. No doubt there will be many more changes over the next quarter century, for the "journal of debate," which was such a radical venture in 1969, still has a role to fulfill.

Richard Bradley

See also *Antiquity;* World Archaeological Congress

Worm, Ole (1588–1654)

Ole Worm was born in DENMARK and educated at the University of Copenhagen. He was successively professor of pedagogy, Greek, physics,

Ole Worm (Ann Ronan Picture Library)

and medicine before becoming personal physician to Christian IV, king of Denmark. Worm was a contemporary and colleague of the Swedish antiquarian JOHAN BURE and had similar interests in rune stones and collecting archaeological and ethnographic artifacts and other antiquities. He corresponded widely with other antiquarians across Europe, learned Old Norse from Icelanders in order to translate runes, and speculated about tumuli with the English antiquarian Sir Henry Spelman. In 1626, he organized a royal circular to be sent to all of the clergy throughout Denmark to submit reports on any rune stones, burial sites, or other historic remains and then sent draftsmen out to record them. The resulting mass of information was the basis of Worm's six volumes on Danish monuments published in 1644, the antiquarian record of Denmark with illustrations and maps.

He also established the Museum Wormianum, a kind of extended cabinet of curiosities, to display his collections and the donations of others. This collection was passed on to King Frederick III after Worm's death. It was installed in the old castle in Copenhagen and then moved in 1680 to a new building in Christiansborg, where it was opened to the public as the Kunstkammer (Royal Collection), which in time became a part of the Danish National Museum of Antiquities.

Tim Murray

References
Schapp, A. 1996. *The Discovery of the Past.* London: British Museum Press.

Wormington, Hannah Marie (1914–1994)

One of the first female archaeologists in North America, Hannah Marie Wormington made significant contributions to Paleo-Indian archaeology. She was born and attended schools in Denver, Colorado, and she would live and work in this city as an adult for over thirty years. Wormington began studying medicine and zoology at the University of Denver, but under the influence of French archaeologist E. B. Renaud, she became interested in the prehistory of the Americas and participated in fieldwork in Colorado and New Mexico.

In 1935 she traveled to Europe, where she met and was greatly impressed by the renowned English archaeologist DOROTHY GARROD. Wormington, whose mother was of French origin, studied in Paris and joined Paleolithic excavations in the Dordogne. She returned to work at the Colorado Museum of Natural History (later the Denver Museum of Nature and Science), where she began studying Paleo-Indian material in the collection. This typological work was the subject of her first paper, presented in 1937 at the International Symposium of Early Man in Philadelphia, Pennsylvania. It was so well received that it established her as a major contributor to the current debate around and study of Paleo-Indians.

Her later publication, *Ancient Man in North America* (1939); was based on this paper and was the first summary and synthesis by an archaeologist of the evidence for Pleistocene and early-Holocene occupations in North America. The book went through four editions (the last in 1957) and is still regarded as a classic in Paleo-Indian studies.

In 1937 Wormington began postgraduate study at Radcliffe College, where she was the first doctoral student in anthropology. She also attended classes at Harvard University and was only the second woman to study in the Department of Anthropology. Over the next seven years Wormington continued to work at the museum, and she undertook fieldwork, studied for her Ph.D., married, and volunteered with the Red Cross during World War II. She excavated sites in Alberta, Canada, for her doctoral fieldwork and received her Ph.D. in 1954.

Four years later Wormington traveled to the USSR, and in 1961 and 1964 she returned there to study Siberian archaeological collections, looking for similarities to and differences from Clovis material in the United States. There were none, and she came to believe that the Clovis people were not the earliest North Americans. Her final fieldwork in the mid-1960s was at the Frazier site near Greeley, Colorado. Many of the next generation of prehistoric archaeologists worked with her at this important Paleo-Indian site, dated to 9500 B.P.

In 1968 Marie Wormington was elected the first female president of the Society for American Archaeology, having served two terms as a vice-president (1950–1951 and 1955–1956). After thirty-one years she left the Denver Museum in 1968 to teach at Arizona State University (1968–1969); she then taught at Colorado College (1969–1970) and the University of Minnesota (1973), and from 1972 to 1986 she was an adjunct professor at Colorado College. In 1983 she became the first female archaeologist to win the SOCIETY FOR AMERICAN ARCHAEOLOGY's Distinguished Service Award.

Tim Murray

See also United States of America, Prehistoric
  Archaeology
References
Stanford, Dennis J., and Jane S. Day, eds. 1992. *Ice Age Hunters of the Rockies.* Denver: Museum of Natural History; Niwot: University Press of Colorado.

Worsaae, Jens Jacob (1821–1886)

As a boy in DENMARK, Jens Jacob Worsaae carried out excavations and published his first archaeological study at the age of seventeen. Worsaae came into contact with CHRISTIAN THOMSEN at the National Museum of Antiquities in Copenhagen and worked as his assistant while studying law.

In 1843, Worsaae wrote and published *The Primeval Antiquities of Denmark* (published in 1849 in English), a result of his work with Thomsen, in which he observed that the THREE-AGE SYSTEM was particularly dependent on the find associations of artifacts (ie. the stratigraphic contexts of the artifacts—where and with what other materials they were found). Unlike Thomsen, Worsaae did not just work in museums—his great strength was that he also worked in the field and was an excavator. In 1844, Worsaae became a full-time antiquarian, and in 1847, he became the inspector of ancient monument preservation in Denmark.

Between 1846 and 1847, Worsaae traveled extensively in Europe, England, and Ireland. He was the first archaeologist to undertake a survey of German archaeological material—which was scattered among dozens of provincial museums, reflecting the fragmentation of Germany's politics. He saw that the preoccupation of English and French archaeologists with Roman monuments had led them to neglect their prehistory and that Thomsen's three-age system could be used across Europe. He understood that as a result of reorganization and their national character, the Scandinavian archaeological collections were unique and provided an opportunity to develop a "scientific" archaeology—and that in this regard they were well ahead of the rest of Europe.

There is no doubt that without Thomsen's and Swedish antiquarian BROR EMIL HILDEBRAND's collections, Worsaae would not have formulated his important chronological advances—his divisions of the Stone Age and the Bronze Age into two periods and the Iron Age into three. On the basis of these collections and his great knowledge of European archaeological material, Worsaae became the first archaeologist to place prehistoric monuments in a wider and comparative context, both socially and historically—as a result, he received the title of "founder of comparative archaeology." In 1854, Worsaae became a professor, and in 1865, he became director of both the Museum of Nordic Antiquities and the Ethnographic Museum in Copenhagen.

In 1848, the Danish Academy of Sciences established a multidisciplinary commission that included the zoologist JAPHETUS STEENSTRUP, the geologist Jörgen G. Forchammer, and Worsaae to study SHELL MIDDENS and geological and sea-level changes. In 1850, they discovered the enormous shell bank at Melgaard in Denmark and excavated numerous implements and bones from it. By the time they had finished the commission, they had studied and recorded over fifty more shell bank habitation sites in Jutland and Zealand in Denmark and in Scania in SWEDEN. It was Worsaae who suggested that the enormous piles of shells represented the remains of meals eaten by Stone Age peoples over a very long period of time and that they were not the result of the action of the sea. In the early 1850s, the three published six volumes of reports on these kitchen middens, demonstrating their human origin and mapping patterns in accumulation. They also proved that the middens were occupied seasonally, and this fact, along with the distributions of hearths and artifacts, provided evidence of human behavior and activities at these sites.

Steenstrup disagreed with Worsaae about the age of the middens, believing that although they were from the Stone Age, they were the same age as the builders and occupants of the Megalithic tombs. Worsaae rightly believed them to be earlier. In his lectures in 1857, Worsaae argued for a chronological division of the Stone Age into two periods, believing the shell bank kitchen middens were from the earlier period and the Megalithic tomb period from the later. He published his observations in greater detail in *A New Division of the Stone and Bronze Ages* (1860), in which the find circumstances were the chronological starting point for observations about differences in types of materials. He argued that the early Stone Age comprised middens and rough implements of flint and bone and the later Stone Age comprised large stone monuments; stone chamber tombs and passage graves; and stone, bone, amber, and clay artifacts.

Meanwhile, the rest of the world caught up, and discoveries of cultural materials in the same stratigraphy (find context) as extinct animal fossils in English and French caves supported Worsaae's hypotheses. He had met French archaeologist JACQUES BOUCHER DE PERTHES in 1847—in fact, it may have been that meeting that caused Worsaae to consider shell middens as earlier phases of the Stone Age. In 1861, Worsaae drew up another chronology for the Stone Age across Europe—with cave finds first and earliest, followed by kitchen middens and then by stone chamber tombs, which later became the accepted designations for the Paleolithic, Mesolithic, and Neolithic periods.

At the same time as his Stone Age work, the examination of numerous archaeological finds in barrows prompted Worsaae to hypothesize that the Bronze Age could be divided into two periods on the basis of burial customs. In a paper published in 1860, he suggested that cremation was used at the end of the Bronze Age because most cremated finds were found at the top of barrows while earlier and uncremated finds or inhumations were always at the bottom of the barrow. Worsaae was not the first to hypothesis about this division in the Bronze Age, but his detailed accounts of find contexts gave the idea scientific credibility. Based on comparisons in stratigraphy and although purely descriptive in nature, Worsaae's divisions nevertheless demonstrated the possibilities of relative chronology, of dating according to the analysis of types of material, which was realized by the next generation of archaeologists. In 1865, in writing about the antiquities of Schleswig and southern Jutland, Worsaae went on to suggest a division of the Iron Age into three periods on the basis of coins (Byzantine and native) found in closed finds (undisturbed archaeological sites).

From 1874 to 1877, Worsaae was minister for Danish cultural affairs. He was also president of the International Archaeological Congresses at Copenhagen in 1869, Bologna in 1871, and Stockholm in 1874.

Tim Murray

See also Kitchenmidden Committee
References
Klindt-Jensen, O. 1975. *A History of Scandinavian Archaeology.* London: Thames and Hudson.

X

Xia Nai (1910–1985)

The British-trained Xia Nai was the premier archaeologist of Communist CHINA. Born in 1910 at Wenzhou (Zhejiang Province), Xia graduated in history from Qinghua University in Beijing in 1934 and subsequently participated in the excavations at anyang. Studying at the University of London from 1935 to 1940, he majored in Egyptology and participated in British excavations in EGYPT and Palestine. He returned to China in 1941, joining the Institute of History and Philology, part of the Academia Sinica, in 1943. In spite of wartime conditions, Xia undertook important excavations at Neolithic sites in Gansu Province in 1944 and 1945. He was awarded a Ph.D. from the University of London in 1946.

In 1950, one year after the Communist takeover of his homeland, Xia was appointed deputy director of the newly founded Institute of Archaeology of the Chinese Academy of Sciences (since 1977 the Chinese Academy of Social Sciences) in Beijing. From the outset, Xia almost single-handedly ran the institute, which he led as its director from 1962 to 1982. A member of the Communist Party since 1959, Xia was criticized and sent to the countryside during the Cultural Revolution (1966–1976) but allowed to resume scholarly activities as early as 1971. From 1982 until his death in 1985, he served as deputy director of the Chinese Academy of Social Sciences.

A brilliant organizer and administrator, Xia established the institute as the paramount archaeological institution in China during a time of tremendous state-sponsored expansion. He was instrumental in creating structures for training, fieldwork, and publication and in framing relevant laws and regulations. During the 1950s Xia launched many major fieldwork projects, personally directing the excavations at Hui Xian (1950) and Changsha (1951), the salvage excavations near the Yellow River dam near Sanmenxia (1956–58), and the 1956 excavation of an imperial Ming tomb near Beijing.

Xia kept abreast of the archaeological discoveries of all periods everywhere in China, editing two syntheses. As the editor of several archaeological journals and a monograph series, he was concerned with divorcing scientific archaeology from antiquarian treasure hunting, and he insisted that excavated evidence should be treated as a separate class of data and scrutinized extensively before being integrated into historical frameworks. Xia's own publications mainly concern the history of technology and Sino-western connections, two areas in which he could capitalize on his knowledge of foreign languages, rare among Chinese archaeologists. Though not completely eschewing a nationalistic agenda or Marxist rhetoric, his work adhered to the highest scholarly standards. In it Xia tried to demonstrate the relevance of archaeology to the scientifically minded Communist elite, as well as strengthen his own position as the representative of Chinese archaeology in the international arena.

Because post–Cultural Revolution Chinese diplomacy used archaeology to generate international goodwill, Xia was frequently sent abroad, where he was showered with academic honors. Although his manner of running Chinese archaeology centrally through the Institute of Archaeology has become impractical since the 1980s, Xia still deserves admiration for the strict professionalism by which he enabled archaeology to flourish during a precarious historical period.

Lothar von Falkenhausen

References

For references, see *Encyclopedia of Archaeology: The Great Archaeologists, Vol. 1,* ed. Tim Murray (Santa Barbara, CA: ABC-CLIO, 1999), pp. 613–614.

Y

Yemen

See Arabian Peninsula

York

York is a prominent city in northeastern England with a long history of invasion, settlement, and trade. Known as Roman Eboracum in the first century A.D., York became the Anglo-Saxon capital of Northumbria in the seventh century and was conquered by the Danes in A.D. 866–867. In both A.D. 700 and 1050 York was the premier settlement in northeast England in political, ecclesiastical, and economic arenas. The archaeological history of York follows the history of archaeology itself. Early studies focused on grave goods; early methods included creating typological series, relative DATING, distribution in settlement patterns, and comparison of artistic motifs. The study of artifacts and environment in York continues at present and detailed studies are published in *The Archaeology of York*.

No direct historical documentation exists on the early history of York, although there are some coinage and runic inscriptions. Heathen Vikings lacked writing, but the neighboring people wrote observations of the Vikings. Most written records are from contemporary Anglo-Saxons and Irish. Other sources include West Saxon writers hostile to the Scandinavians; English monastic writers who include Scandinavian descendants; and the Icelandic sagas that blend fact, fiction, and folklore, but contain detailed records of the twelfth to fourteenth centuries. Recent archaeological evidence now supports the historical sources.

The early fifth century was a period of political, economic, and social change in Britain. At York, the archaeological evidence shows the end of town life after Roman withdrawals, between the fifth and eighth centuries (O'Connor 1990). Long-term excavations show the same at London (Vince 1990) and at Winchester (Biddle 1973). The early Anglo-Saxon settlements that followed were small rural villages. One of the difficulties in York is the problem of the palimpsest factor (approximately all of the site's stratigraphic elements), which creates a confusion of close dates between late Anglian and early Anglo-Scandinavian. The archaeological record does show continuity in land use, agriculture, and animal husbandry practices. Crabtree's work (1982, 1984, 1989a, 1990) and analysis of faunal remains shows continuity in the patterns of raising cattle, sheep, and pigs from the Iron Age to the Anglo-Saxon period.

Viking activity in the British Isles was part of the struggle between Danes and Norwegians for territorial expansion and control of the trade route from the Irish Sea to southwest Norway. The *Anglo-Saxon Chronicle* recorded the first Viking raids in A.D. 793. Archaeological research and place names show that Shetland, the Orkneys, and the Hebrides were colonized by Norwegian pirates by A.D. 800. Danish sailor-raiders known as Vikings attacked churches, farms, towns, and villages. With their shallow-draft boats of fifty men, the Vikings could travel up rivers. They established winter camps at the conquered sites; eventually they settled, converted to Christianity, and brought in family or married into local families. York became a trading center.

The capture of York by the Vikings was quick, almost effortless, and barely noted by historians of the time. Typically Viking raids were planned to coincide with the Christian calendar during feast days. York was invaded November 1, which probably meant a great deal of goods, money, and slaves were taken. A fort was most likely built soon after, probably within or near the wall of the old Roman city. The material record of the Vikings includes stone carving, metal work, weaponry, coinage, houses, temples, and graves.

Archaeological evidence shows the Vikings to be very advanced in the manufacture of arms and jewelry as well as in shipbuilding. The soldier camps they built showed the ability to mobilize resources. Travels in the far north meant coping with and conquering hostile environmental elements. Vikings were skilled in commerce and trade, and brought with them a vernacular literature. Viking sagas tell of family, feuds, the great eleventh and twelfth century kings, and their voyages.

E. T. Leeds laid the groundwork for the study of archaeology with his 1913 publication surveying the holdings of museums across England and explaining the fundamentals of early archaeological method and theory. His work confirmed that some settlements predate the written record, and his observations on museum collections spurred further research and reappraisals. He pioneered excavation methods that brought in evidence beyond grave goods alone.

Excavation in York begun by P. Addyman in 1972 focused on military and defense structures of the Roman period A.D. 71 to 400. Fifth-century Roman occupation evidence comes from the headquarters building and the bath house. Late fourth century severe flooding destroyed many of the harbor facilities. Little archaeological evidence exists for the fifth and sixth centuries, considered a dark age in York. The Anglo-Saxons continued a settlement outside the fortress and eighth- and ninth-century materials found in concentration are domestic. Palliser and Morris suggest the evidence comes from a church complex.

Deposits in the Coppergate area of York are evidence of Viking occupation. Several hundred pottery fragments in early Viking layers suggest continued pottery production. Four gold coins of the 640s suggest a trading center that has not been confirmed. Some areas have not been excavated because they have not been rebuilt since the eighteenth century.

Archaeology of York also includes study of Bronze brooches, pottery, coins, and faunal remains; ongoing research includes Scandinavia and northwest Europe with the British Isles as a whole region. East of the Roman fortress craft finds have been excavated indicating work with leather; cobbling; working of jet, amber, iron, lead, copper alloy, silver, and gold; glassworking; wood lathe; bone and antler work; textile making and dyeing; and trade evidence. By A.D. 900 the pattern of buildings was set. Cultural remains also show the strong influence of the Viking invaders through language, place names, a style of open government used in Iceland, and the jury system. Viking influence ranged from attackers to settlers, storytellers, and craftsmen. In York the Jorvik Viking Center was opened in 1984 to display Danish period artifacts.

Danielle Greene

See also Medieval Archaeology in Europe; Novgorod

References

Crabtree, Pam J., and Kathleen Ryan, eds. 1991. *Animal Use and Culture Change.* Philadelphia: MASCA, University Museum of Archaeology and Anthropology.

Karkov, Catherine E. 1999. *The Archaeology of Anglo-Saxon England: Basic Readings.* New York: Garland.

Leeds, E. Thurlow. 1913. *The Archaeology of the Anglo-Saxon Settlements.* Reprint 1970. Oxford: Oxford University Press.

Smyth, Alfred P. 1977. *Scandinavian Kings in the British Isles 850–880.* Oxford: Oxford University Press.

Smyth, Alfred P. 1975. *Scandinavian York and Dublin: The History and Archaeology of Two Related Viking Kingdoms.* Dublin: Templekieran Press.

Snyder, Christopher A. 1996. *Sub-Roman Britain (AD 400–600): A Gazetteer of Sites.* Oxford: Tempus Reparatum.

Acheulean Lower Paleolithic technology based around the production of bifacially flaked chopping tools. Acheulean industries are found on sites in Africa, Central and Eastern Europe, and in Asia east to India.

actualistic studies Studies undertaken by archaeologists on contemporary materials and processes so that they might gain a clearer understanding of the processes that form the archaeological record.

Age of metal That time succeeding the Stone Age which first saw the introduction of metal artifacts into prehistoric assemblages.

agropastoral Referring to prehistoric agricultural economies.

amino acid racemization An experimental technology used to date bone that can be up to 100,000 years old. It is based on determining the rate of transformation in amino acids from living bone to dead bone.

amphorae Large two-handled jars used to store liquids.

anthropology The discipline that is devoted to the study of human beings (particularly their cultural, physical, and social forms).

antiquarian A person interested in many of the issues and perspectives that coalesced in the mid-nineteenth century as the disciplines of history and archaeology. Antiquarians used documents, oral histories, and artifacts to write about the history of humanity.

applied transformism In Gabriel de Mortillet's terms, the use of archaeology to demonstrate the reality of transformationist ideas in human evolution.

arboriculture The use of fruit and nut trees as part of prehistoric economies.

archaeomagnetic A dating technology based on the fact that hearths or kilns (as heat sources) are sources of paleomagnetism.

archaeometric Relating to ARCHAEOMETRY.

Archaic, early, late, terminal North American sites and contexts that exhibit broad-spectrum foraging, ground stone artifacts, and evidence of increasing sedentism.

assemblage A collection of artifacts that are thought to constitute a single unit of analysis—either by site or by period.

Aterian Group of Upper Paleolithic tool assemblages with little flakes, some blades, and tanged points that was spread throughout northern Africa and the Sahara, dating roughly from 170,000 to around 30,000–20,000 B.P.

Aurignacian An Upper Paleolithic industry that spread from the Levant to Spain and France.

Australopithecine An ancestral genus to *Homo* found in East and South Africa. Skeletal remains (which date from about 3.7 million years ago) are classified into species such as *Australopithecus afarensis* (found in Ethiopia) or *Australopithecus africanus* (found in South Africa).

Austronesian A family of languages found in island southeast Asia, Polynesia, Micronesia, and Melanesia (with the exception of most of Papua New Guinea).

autochthony Referring to something native, indigenous, or "home-grown."

backed blades A stone tool that is a blade shape with one of the longer edges deliberately blunted.

Bandkeramik culture The earliest Neolithic culture of Central Europe (between 4500 B.C. and 3900 B.C.).

Baradostian An Upper Paleolithic stone industry found in Iran.

barrow A mound of earth and stones that in most cases covers a burial or a number of burials.

Bell beaker barrow A burial mound associated

with the Bell beaker, a type of pottery found across Western and Central Europe between 2500 and 1800 B.C.

bifaces Stone tools flaked on two surfaces.

bifacial points Pointed stone tools made by bifacial flaking.

bifacial reduction strategies An approach to stone tool making that results in a single piece of stone being flaked on both sides.

bioturbation A natural process occurring in archaeological sites that leads to the movement of materials in deposits due to the action of root growth or the activities of burrowing animals.

Boasian anthropology Anthropological theory (anti-evolutionary and antidiffusionist) developed by German-American anthropologist Franz Boas.

bovids Cattle.

breccia A rock made up of angular rock fragments cemented together.

burins A blade-shaped stone tool from the European Upper Paleolithic which features a chisel-like working edge. Thought to be used for engraving.

Capsian Group of Epipaleolithic tool assemblages with blades, bladelets, and microliths, as well as the cultures or peoples using them, mainly in Cyrenaica, Tunisia, and eastern or central Algeria, dating roughly from 7500 to 4000 B.C.

causeway camp A Neolithic enclosure, found in England, formed by rings of ditches and earth embankments topped with wooden palisades.

Celtic urnfield Burial complexes found in central Europe in the period between 1200 and 800 B.C. Interments were cremations placed in ceramic urns.

ceramic types and complexes, ceramic seriation Refers to the classification and statistical analysis of ceramics as a class of archaeological data. *See also* **seriation.**

Chalcolithic Copper Age or Eneolithic.

chambered tomb Tombs either cut directly into rock or built of stone and then covered by an earth mound and containing more than one burial.

Chatelperonian The earliest Upper Paleolithic industry found in France, around 36,000 years old.

chorology The local distribution of sites or artifact types.

chronology, relative and absolute The establishment of a sequence of events over time. Relative chronologies are established through the use of

stratigraphy or typology. Absolute chronologies produce specific dates that are established through the application of dating technologies such as radiocarbon to artifacts or contexts.

Clactonian-like A British Lower Paleolithic flaked tool industry which has no bifacially flaked tools.

clasts Archaeological remains as part of natural sedimentary deposits.

closed finds Those located in sealed contexts such as burials that show no signs of alteration or disturbance after deposition.

cordrouletting The use of cord to produce decoration on pottery.

cognitive processual archaeology A branch of processual archaeology that was concerned with exploring the possibilities of reconstructing prehistoric thought patterns.

conjunctive approach Advocated by W. W. Taylor as a means of linking investigations of chronology and the relationships between archaeological sites in a given area with a focus on detailed recording and analysis of artifacts and contexts found within specific sites.

contextualism An approach to the interpretation of archaeological sites and assemblages that stresses the need for archaeologists to also focus on the society and culture of the people who created those assemblages and contexts.

Continental bell barrows Burial mounds in Central Europe where Bell beakers are a significant element in the funerary assemblage.

Continental disc barrows Circular burial mounds found in Europe.

coprolites Feces preserved in archaeological deposits.

crescents Crescent-shaped small stone tools.

culture contact A process brought about by two cultures (usually interpreted as two distinct groups of people) coming into contact.

Cycladic Bronze Age culture of the Cyclades Islands in the Aegean.

Dabban A stone industry from Libya dating to between 40,000 and 14,000 years ago.

Dalton points A class of stone projectile points found in the Midwest and East of North America, spanning the transition period between Paleo-Indian and Archaic cultures.

dates, dating, absolute and relative The physical process of constructing relative and absolute chronologies (*see* **chronology; potassium-argon dating; radiocarbon dating**).

debitage The waste products (usually small chips) of the process of making stone tools, otherwise known as knapping.

decision theory The means by which archaeologists seek to reconstruct processes of decision-making in the past.

deep culture history A goal of many archaeologists who seek to establish the history of a particular culture (or place) by constructing sequences of events. Deep culture histories also have the goal of understanding the norms of specific prehistoric cultures.

dendrochronology A dating technology using tree rings counted from logs found in archaeological contexts.

Dentate-stamped pottery Pottery that has been stamped with a tool that produces toothlike notches in the surface of the fabric.

Developed Oldowan East African stone industry dating from about 1.6 million years ago to about 600,000 years ago, a development of the earliest Oldowan industry first noted at Olduvai Gorge.

diachronic Development (or change) through time.

diffusion, diffusionist A process whereby ideas, artifacts, and other elements of the fabric of prehistoric societies and cultures are thought to have been transferred from one group to another. Diffusion is therefore thought by many culture historians to explain change and transformation in prehistoric cultures.

drift gravels The deposits created by the movement of materials by glacial ice or meltwater.

ecofacts Information about past plants and animals found on archaeological sites.

edaphic Pertaining to the condition of soils on an archaeological site

elongated scalene A small stone tool.

Emiran A Levantine Upper Paleolithic industry.

end scrapers A special class of stone tool made on a flake with thick working edge—in this case on the end of the flake.

Eneolithic Chalcolithic or Copper Age.

eoliths Pieces of chipped stone originally thought to be even older and simpler than the technologies

of the Lower Paleolithic. Now considered to have been created by natural causes.

epigraphy The study of ancient writing wither incised into or painted on stone, ceramic, or other hard surfaces.

Epipaleolithic An intermediate stage between the Paleolithic and the Neolithic.

ethnoarchaeology The study of contemporary societies by archaeologists to gather information about the processes that may have led to the creation of the archaeological record. Ethnoarchaeology is used primarily to build models and to create inferences that can be used to understand prehistoric human behavior.

ethnogenesis The process through which new ethnic groups come into being.

ethnographic distributions The distributions of specific tribes or bands in space and time.

ethnography The study of human beings by observers who participate in the lives of the people they are studying.

facet, faceting Literally meaning one side of a multisided object, a term used by archaeologists to describe the surfaces of stone tools and the processes involved in their manufacture.

facies A part of the stratigraphy of a particular site that can be meaningfully distinguished from the whole.

Fauresmith An early term for late Acheulean assemblages from interior southern Africa.

field school Programs operated by many university departments of archaeology to provide hands-on training in excavation and survey to their students.

find context A detailed description of the specific information related to a particular group of artifacts.

flake A thin slice or fragment of stone that has been removed from a core during the process of stone tool manufacture (knapping). Flakes can either be waste products (*see* **debitage**) or deliberately produced as the basis of tools themselves (after further working or retouching). Archaeologists seek to understand the process of stone tool manufacture by refitting flakes in a way that allows a reconstruction (in reverse order) of the reduction sequence (process of manufacture).

flexed burial An interment where the corpse is buried with its knees bent (usually lying on its side).

foliates Leaf-shaped stone tools.

Folsom points Fluted points found in North America and associated with Paleo-Indian sites occupied by bison hunters from about 11,000 to about 10,200 years ago.

formal systematics Classification of objects on the basis of their form or shape.

formative period, formative type In North America, used to describe the cultural stage associated with the introduction of agriculture and settled village life. In Mesoamerica the formative is synonymous with the preclassic.

French Aurignacian period From about 34,000 B.P. until about 20,000 B.P. in France.

geometric microliths Small geometric-shaped stone tools.

glyph A symbol used in a system of writing.

Hempelian logic A logical form developed by the philosopher Carl Hempel as a means of understanding and describing how scientific statements (theories and hypotheses) should be created and verified.

henge An enclosed space, defined by walls and ditches, frequently circular, and exhibiting one (but sometimes two) entrances. These prehistoric monuments sometimes contained buildings (or, as in the case of Stonehenge, stone circles). They are often interpreted as being places of ritual.

high-level theory That body of archaeological theory most directly concerned with relating the knowledge derived about human beings from archaeological contexts to that which comes from other branches of history and anthropology.

historic contact Indian sites Sites that show archaeological evidence of very early contact between European settlers and indigenous peoples in North America.

Holocene The Quaternary era, comprising two geological stages—the Pleistocene (ca. 1,000,000 to 10,000 B.P.) and the Holocene (from 10.000 B.P. to the present). It should not be confused with the Paleolithic and Neolithic cultural divisions.

Hominids The family of human beings that includes the genus *Homo* and the genus *Australopithecus*.

hominization The process of the evolution of hominid physical and cultural characteristics.

Hopewell mounds Found in southern Ohio and constructed between 100 B.C. and A.D. 500. Hopewell sites are found elsewhere in the Midwest of the United States, and ditches and embankments often enclose associated burial sites.

Hopewell/Havana societies A variant of the general Hopewell culture found in the Lower Illinois Valley.

hydration rind dating A chemical technique used to date obsidian (volcanic glass) artifacts. Based on the fact that water permeates newly broken obsidian edges, dating specialists observe the thickness and penetration of water by measuring the hydration rind.

Iberomaurusian (or Oranian) Group of Epipaleolithic tool assemblages (predominantly featuring bladelets), as well as the cultures or peoples using them, mainly in Algerian coastal regions, Cyrenaica, and Morocco, dating roughly from ca. 20,000 B.C. to ca. 8000 B.C.

Iberomaurusian A stone tool industry found in North Africa and dating from about 22,000 to about 10,000 years ago.

interaction spheres Created by the interaction of adjacent cultural groups, sometimes over large areas. Interactions might be in the form of trade or warfare, or simply be based on the recognition that adjacent groups do not and cannot act as cultural, social, or indeed political isolates.

interlacustrine Between lakes.

jar-burial An inhumation where the body is placed in a jar.

Kulturkreise A German school of diffusionist thought. *See* FRITZ GRAEBNER and FRIEDRICH RATZEL.

La Tène Iron Age site that is used as the type-site for this culture.

lacustrine system Lake system.

Lamarck's transformism An approach to understanding the evolution of life on earth that emphasized the importance of inheritable modifications in the process of adaptation. Some archaeologists have used this notion of inheritable modifications to aid their understanding of the processes that lead to change (transformation) in cultures over time.

Landsat A satellite-based mapping system developed by the U.S. National Aeronautics and Space Administration (NASA) to create the photographic images of the surface of the earth; widely used in a remote sensing role by archaeologists to locate sites and landscape modifications in survey areas.

land-snail shell middens A shell midden composed mostly of the shells of land snails.

Levallois A very widely distributed stone knapping technique based around the preparation of the stone core in such a way as to allow the production of stone flakes of specific size and shape.

limnological analysis Analysis of the sediments found in lake beds.

lithic Stone.

locational analysis An analytical technique focusing on the mapping of the locations of archaeological sites and contexts.

long barrow An elongated variant of the barrow type.

Lusatian culture Late Bronze Age/Early Iron Age culture in Poland and eastern Germany.

Maglemosian The fist Mesolithic culture on the North European Plain.

Master Maximum Method (MMM) A version of the chi square test—a statistical test of the significance of relationships between elements in a classification.

microlith, microlithic Small stone tools most frequently associated in Europe with the Upper Paleolithic and Mesolithic periods. Microliths are thought to have been much used as projectile points or to tip wood or bone implements.

microwear analysis The study of the surfaces and working edges of artifacts to determine their use.

midden A heap of refuse.

middle-range theory That domain of archaeological theories that seeks to link archaeological phenomena with specific human behaviors. It is closely associated with the practice of ethnoarchaeology and experimental archaeology.

Mousterian A middle Paleolithic stone industry distributed from Europe to Asia and Africa, dating from 180,000 to 30,000 years ago. Archaeologists have noted distinct regional traditions within the Mousterian.

multilineal evolution A variant of classical evolutionary theory that recognizes that transformations in prehistoric societies were not the outcome of single causes or the product of simple linear processes of change.

multiseriate explanation A statistical approach to classifying artifacts and using these classifications to establish relative chronologies.

museographic Pertaining to the role of images in museum displays.

Nabatean-Byzantine *See* JORDAN.

natural taxon A natural classificatory unit.

Neanderthal An ancestral form of *Homo sapiens* found in Europe and western Asia, dating between 100,000 and 30,000 years ago. Archaeologists and paleoanthropologists still debate the historical and biological relationship between Neanderthals and modern human beings.

neoevolution A development of classical evolutionary theory particularly associated with the work of North American anthropologists Julian Steward and Leslie White. Neoevolutionism sought to elucidate the impact of ecology, demography, and technology as driving forces in an explanation of transformations in prehistoric societies.

Neolithic The period following the Paleolithic in which people began to use more complex stone tool technologies to cultivate plants and to more actively manage domesticated animals. In some places the Neolithic is also linked to the introduction of pottery, but this is by no means widespread; for example, in Japan pottery occurred in societies still based around foraging subsistence. This change in subsistence patterns is also frequently associated with the development of villages. Dates for the Neolithic vary between 10,000 years ago in the Middle East to about 4,000 years ago in northern Europe, hence primary, middle, and late.

New Archaeology *See* **processual archaeology.**

New World archaeology The archaeology of the Americas.

nomothetic Referring to a law of nature.

nonlinear dynamics An approach to understanding the nature of change that recognizes that the causes of change are both complex and highly variable. Based on what is popularly known as chaos theory, nonlinear dynamics expresses an understanding that small causes can lead to large outcomes and that frequently change can be so complex as to be literally unpredictable.

odeon Roman covered hall, often used for concerts.

Old World archaeology The archaeology of Europe, Asia, Africa, and Australia.

ontology A branch of philosophy that deals with the understanding of the nature and essences of natural and cultural phenomena.

oppidum Fortified town.

orthostats Upright stones supporting the roof of a chamber or passage in a megalithic tomb.

ossuary A place where the bones of many bodies are kept.

ostraca A potsherd onto which ancient Athenians scratched the names of citizens who were to be expelled. Also used in ancient Egypt for sketches and plans.

overburden Soil which lies on top of archaeological deposits.

pa A fortified Maori place. *See* NEW ZEALAND, HISTORICAL ARCHAEOLOGY.

Palaeo-Indian fluted points. *See* **Folsom points.**

paleoenvironment The reconstruction of ancient environments.

palynological Relating to analysis of fallen pollen. *See* PALYNOLOGY.

passage grave A form of chambered tomb in which access to the chamber is via a long passage.

peri-Roman Border of the ancient Roman world.

phalliforme Shaped like a phallus.

phenetic A classification of organisms based on estimates of overall similarity, but not evolutionary relationship.

philology The science of language.

photogrammetry The use of photographs to create maps and scaled drawings of sites and buildings.

phylogeny A classification of organisms believed to reflect evolutionary relationships.

phytoliths Samml silica bodies deposited by plants into soil. These are distinctive for each species and the study of phytoliths assists in the reconstruction of plant communities.

Pithecoid Apelike.

Pitted ware A culture created by groups of foragers occupying northern Scandinavia and the Baltic (Sweden and Finland) between the third and first millennia B.C.

platform mounds Flat-topped earthen structures, found in the Mississippi Valley of North America, that served as bases for both ceremonial buildings and houses.

polygenism The theory that human beings were of multiple origins.

polythetic A set of objects, the members of which do not have to be exactly the same.

positivism A school of philosophy that stresses the importance of the testability or verifiability of statements as being a primary determinant of their scientific adequacy.

postprocessual archaeology, postprocessualism A school of archaeological thought developed in opposition to processual archaeology in the 1980s. Its central focus is on the application of postmodernist forms of social theory to archaeological analysis, an incorporation of colonial theories to critique the relationships between archaeologists and indigenous peoples, and a rejection of evolutionist and positivist frameworks of thought.

potassium-argon dating A dating method based founded on the measurement of the radioactive decay of the isotope ^{40}K (potassium) to the stable isotope ^{40}Ar (argon).

prehistory All of that period in human history during which there are no written records. The duration of prehistory differs across the world—in Australia it ended after the arrival of European explorers and settlers, but in the Middle East it ended with the invention of writing thousands of years previously.

processual archaeology or the "New Archaeology" Processual archaeology, developed during the 1960s with the goal of making archaeology more scientific, embraced neoevolutionism and general systems theory along with positivist approaches to scientific reasoning in order to explore the fundamental assumptions of archaeology. Processual archaeology was in some of its forms also closely associated with a search for general laws thought to underlie human behavior.

proto-history The period that spans the transition between prehistoric societies (those with no written record) and those societies which had the ability to produce written records.

proton-magnetometer A geophysical device that measures the strength of the Earth's magnetic field.

provenance/provenience The precise origin of an artifact.

quadrant method An excavation technique in which a barrow is divided into quadrants and these become the units of recording and analysis.

Quaternary The last major geochronological subdivision of Earth history, covering about the last 2.5 million years.

quern A large grindstone.

racloirs Stone tools shaped like scrapers.

radiocarbon dating An absolute radiometric-dating technique used on organic materials such as wood, shell, charcoal, and bone. The technique is founded on the measurement of the decay of the carbon isotope ^{14}C to nitrogen.

rank-size rules Refers to the correlation between the size of a prehistoric settlement and the complexity of the social hierarchy (social ranks) that governs it.

reduction strategy The process of stone tool manufacture in specific cases (*see* **flake**).

resistivity The mapping of sub-surface features by measuring the differences in electrical resistance as a current is passed through soil.

Rhodesian Wilton An inland Southern African variant of the microlithic later Stone Age industry, first noticed in the Cape Province of South Africa. Although dates vary across these regions, it is thought that the Wilton industry existed between 8,000 and 2,000 years ago.

Riss glaciation A glacial advance in the Swiss Alps beginning around 250,000 years ago and lasting for about 100,000 years.

roof fall Rock fall from the roof of a cave or shelter that is incorporated into an archaeological deposit.

runes Scandinavian writing.

ruprestrian art Rock art.

sarcophagus Coffin.

sequences A succession of occupational or cultural phases in an archaeological site.

seriation, ceramic seriation A technique used to create relative dates in which a temporal sequence is established by ascertaining the relative popularity of ceramic artifacts in an assemblage.

settlement-pattern archaeology An archaeological method involving the recording and analysis of all cultural features in a landscape, then relating these to their topographic settings in order to create a history of human settlement in a particular region.

settlement tiers Refers to the hierarchy of settlement sizes within a particular region.

shell-tempered pottery Pottery with shell incorporated into its fabric.

site catchment analysis The assessment of the potential economic resources of a site and its catchment.

site catchment The total area for which the contents of a site could have been derived.

situla *See* SITULA ART.

slumping A geomorphological process in which deposits collapse.

space-time synthesis An archaeological analysis based on the integration of spatial and temporal data.

spits Units of measurement of depth in the excavation of archaeological sites.

standlines Remnant prehistoric beaches from periods when sea levels were different from those of today.

Stillbay A Middle Stone Age industry from Southern Africa.

stratigraphic pits Pits dug to allow archaeologists to analyze the sedimentary history of a site.

stratigraphy The study of the formation and composition of stratified sediments in archaeological sites.

stylistic variability The capacity of different decorative and technological styles to vary.

sumerologist A person who studies Sumerian civilization.

synchronisms The systematic study of artifacts and contexts and events that occur within the same time period.

tanged Refers to a projection at the base of a stone tool that could be attached to a handle or a shaft.

taphonomy, taphonomic The study of the transformation of materials when they are deposited into the archaeological record. Taphonomy is a central method in reconstructing the processes that formed or created the archaeological record.

Tardenoisian A Mesolithic culture of southwest France.

tells An artificial hill created by the accumulation of mud-brick walls and cultural debris. Tells are particularly common in the Middle East and are a clear indication of human occupation over a long period.

tephrachronology A chronology based on dating layers of volcanic ash.

three-age system A chronological model devised by Christian Thomsen during his tenure at the National Museum of Denmark in Copenhagen. Thomsen organized his displays of artifacts in terms of a temporal sequence from earliest (stone) through middle (bronze) to late (iron), reflecting his perception that human technology had evolved in complexity over successive stages.

time depth A stratigraphic analogy, namely, the deeper the stratigraphy the longer the time recorded.

tradition The continuity of technologies and other cultural forms over long periods of time. It can also mean a sequence of archaeological phases and cultures that share cultural similarities.

Tripolye A major Eneolithic culture of southeastern Europe.

tumuli burials A burial inside a mound of earth and/or stone.

type-concept An approach to artifact classification in which a specific artifact becomes the "ideal example" of that classificatory unit or taxon.

typology, typological seriation The classification of artifacts into types based on the analysis of a range of attributes. Typologies that can be placed in a time series (seriated) are used in the construction of relative chronologies (*see* **chronology**).

Ubaid period The period of the initial agricultural settlement of southern Mesopotamia, generally thought to have begun in the second half of the sixth millennium B.C. and lasted to nearly the end of the fifth millennium B.C.

Urnfield culture A Late Bronze Age/Early Iron Age culture identified with cemeteries of cremation burials in urn. Located in Central Europe between 5200 and 800 B.C.

Visigothic Western Gothic settlements in southern France and Spain around A.D. 800.

Wessex culture An early Bronze Age culture found in the south of England, particularly in Wiltshire.

Wurm glaciation The last glacial advance in the Swiss Alps, dating from about 110,000 years ago until about 10,000 years ago.

zoomorphic Taking the shape of animals.

The Editor and Contributors

Russell Adams, Research Associate, Department of Anthropology, University of California, San Diego, USA

William H. Adams, Department of Archaeology, Flinders University, Adelaide, Australia

William Y. Adams, Department of Anthropology, University of Kentucky, Lexington USA

Sonia Alconini, Department of Anthropology, University of Pittsburgh, USA

Harry Allen, Department of Anthropology, University of Auckland, New Zealand

Jim Allen, Archaeology Program, La Trobe University, Melbourne, Australia

James Ayers, Tucson, Arizona, USA

Paul Bahn, Hull, England

Geoff Bailey, Department of Archaeology, University of Newcastle, England

George Bass, Nautical Archaeology Program, Department of Anthropology, Texas A&M University, College Station, USA

Mary Beaudry, Department of Archaeology, Boston University, USA

Borislav Borislavov, Department of Archaeology, Sofia University St. Kliment Ohridski, Sofia, Bulgaria

Mark Bowden, Archaeology and Survey Department, English Heritage, Swindon, England

Richard Bradley, Department of Archaeology, University of Reading, England

Yvonne Brink, Department of Archaeology, University of Cape Town, South Africa

Stuart Brown, Archaeology Unit, Department of Anthropology, Memorial University of Newfoundland, St. John's, Canada

Olivier Buchsenschutz, ENS, Paris, France

Dilip Chakrabarti, Faculty of Oriental Studies, University of Cambridge, England

Xingcan Chen, Institute of Archaeology, Chinese Academy of Social Sciences, Beijing, China

Nicole Chevalier, Département des Antiquités Orientales, Musée du Louvre, Paris, France

Christopher Chippindale, Museum of Anthropology, University of Cambridge, England

Andrew L. Christenson, Prescott, Arizona, USA

Clark, J. G. D., late of Department of Archaeology, University of Cambridge

Henry Cleere, World Heritage Coordinator, ICOMOS, Paris, France

Norman Clermont, Département d'Anthropologie, Université de Montréal, Canada

Roberto Cobean, Instituto Nacional de Antropología e Historia (INAH), Mexico

Claudine Cohen, École des Hautes Études en Sciences Sociales in Paris, France

Eugen Comša, Institutul de Arheologie ARPR, Bucharest, Romania

Graham Connah, Emeritus Professor of Archaeology, University of New England, Armidale, Australia

Richard Cooke, Archaeology Laboratory, Smithsonian Tropical Research Institute, Panama

John L. Cotter, late of the University of Pennsylvania Museum of Archaeology and Anthropology, Philadelphia, USA

Anick Coudart, Paris, France

Barry Cunliffe, Professor of Archaeology, University of Oxford, England

Janet Davidson, National Museum of New Zealand, Wellington, New Zealand

Hilary Deacon, Department of Archaeology, Stellenbosch University, South Africa

Kathleen Deagan, Department of Anthropology, Florida Museum of Natural History, Gainesville, USA

Bill Dever, Department of Near Eastern Studies, University of Arizona, Tucson, USA

Bojan Djuric, Department of Archaeology, University of Ljubljana, Slovenia

Margaret S. Drower, England

Robert Dunnell, Natchez, Mississippi, USA

Françoise Etienne, École Française d'Athènes, Greece

Roland Etienne, École Française d'Athènes, Greece

Chris Evans, Director, Cambridge Archaeology Unit, University of Cambridge, England.

Rodolfo Fattovich, Dipartimento di Studi e Richerche su Africa e Paesi Arabi, Instituto Universitario Orientale, Naples, Italy

Roland Fletcher, Prehistoric Archaeology, University of Sydney, Australia.

Alba G. Mastache Flores, Instituto Nacional de Antropología e Historia (INAH), Mexico

Bernard L. Fontana, Tucson, Arizona, USA

David Frankel, Archaeology Program, La Trobe University, Melbourne, Australia

Pedro Funari, Departamento de História, Universidade Estadual de Campinas, Brasil

Creighton Gabel, Emeritus Professor, Boston University, USA

Michael Given, Department of Archaeology, University of Glasgow, Scotland

Douglas Givens, Research Associate of the Peabody Museum at Harvard University, Cambridge, USA.

Jack Golson, Australian National University, Canberra, Australia

John Gowlett, Department of Archaeology, University of Liverpool, England

Bo Gräslund, Department of Archaeology at the University of Uppsala, Sweden

Thalia Gray, New York University, USA

Danielle Greene, Santa Barbara, USA

Tatjana Greif, Ljubljana, Slovenia

James Greig, Department of Ancient History and Archaeology, University of Birmingham, England

James B. Griffin, late of the University of Michigan, USA

Nancy de Grummond, Department of Classics, Florida State University, Tallahassee, USA

Norman Hammond, Department of Archaeology, Boston University, USA

Marion Popenhoe de Hatch, Department of Archaeology, University of Del Valle, Guatemala City, Guatemala

Johan Hegardt, Department of Archaeology, University of Uppsala, Sweden

Curtis Hinsley, Department of History, University of Northern Arizona, Flagstaff, USA

Armando Anaya Hernández, Archaeology Program, La Trobe University, Melbourne, Australia

Leonor Herrera, Bogotá, Colombia

Simon Holdaway, Department of Anthropology, University of Auckland, New Zealand

Thomas Holland, Oriental Institute, University of Chicago, USA.

Ivor Noël Hume, Colonial Williamsburg, Virginia, USA

Fumiko Ikawa-Smith, Department of Anthropology, Mc Gill University, Montreal

Siân Jones, Department of Art History and Archaeology, University of Manchester, England

Drasko Josipovic, Kranj, Slovenia

Rosemary Joyce, Department of Anthropology, University of California, Berkeley, USA

Marc-Antione Kaeser, Department of Archaeology, Swiss National Museum, Zurich, Switzerland

Patrick Kirch, Hearst Museum of Anthropology, University of California, Berkeley

Herman O. Kiriama, Department of History, Kenyatta University, Nairobi, Kenya

Fred Kleiner, Department of Art History, Boston University, USA

Jüri Kokkonen, Helsinki, Finland

Roumjana Koleva, Department of Archaeology, Sofia University St. Kliment Ohridski, Sofia, Bulgaria

Leo Klejn, European University, Saint Petersburg, Russia

Kristian Kristiansen, Institute of Archaeology, Gothenborg University, Göteborg, Sweden

Max Kunze, Winckelmann Institute, Berlin, Germany

José Luis Lanata, Department of Anthropology, University of Buenos Aires, Argentina

Josara de Lange, Archaeology Program, La Trobe University, Melbourne, Australia

Fred W. Lange, Managua, Nicaragua

Susan Lawrence, Archaeology Program, La Trobe University, Melbourne, Australia

Irena Lazar, Regional Museum, Celje, Slovenia

Li Liu, Archaeology Program, La Trobe University, Melbourne, Australia

Milan Lovenjak, Department of Archaeology, University of Ljubljana, Slovenia

Ilze Loze, Institute of the History of Latvia, Riga, Latvia

David Lubell, Department of Anthropology, University of Alberta, Canada

Roderick McIntosh, Department of Anthropology, Rice University, Houston, USA

Susan McIntosh, Department of Anthropology, Rice University, Houston, USA

Arkadiusz Marciniak, Institute of Prehistory, University of Poznan, Poland

Jorge Marcos, Servei de Materials Arqueológics, Universitat Autònoma de Barcelona, Spain

Peter Mathews, Archaeology Program, La Trobe University, Melbourne, Australia

Ruth Megaw, Flinders University, South Australia

Vincent Megaw, Flinders University, South Australia

David J. Meltzer Department of Anthropology, Southern Methodist University, Dallas, USA

Martin Millet, Department of Archaeology, University of Southampton, England

Matilde Ivic de Monterroso, Department of Archaeology, University of Del Valle, Guatemala City, Guatemala

Ken Mowbray, American Museum of Natural History

Tim Murray, Archaeology Program, La Trobe University, Melbourne, Australia

Alfred Muzzolini, Lauzerville, France

Harold Mytum, Department of Archaeology, University of York, England

Isabel Navarrete, Consejo Superior de Investigaciones Cientificas, Centro de Estudios Historicos, Madrid, Spain

Jacques Nenquin, Seminaire d'Archéologie de l'Université, Ghent, Belgium

Evžen Neustupný, Institute of Archaeology, Academy of Sciences of the Czech Republic, Prague

Predrag Novakovic, Department of Archaeology, University of Ljubljana, Slovenia

A. Lautaro Nuñez, Departmento de Ciencias Sociales, Universidad del Norte, Antofagasta, Chile

Bernard Nurse, Librarian, Society of Antiquaries of London, England

Laurent Olivier, Museé des Antiquités Nationales, Saint Germain-en-Laye, France

John Olsen, Department of Anthropology, University of Arizona, Tucson, USA.

K. Paddaya, Deccan College, Pune, India.

Yangjin Pak, Department of Archaeology, Chungnam National University, Taejon, Korea

Graham Parry, Department of English, University of York, England.

Dan Potts, Near Eastern Archaeology, University of Sydney, Australia

Tim Potts, Director of the Kimbell Art Museum, Fort Worth, Texas, USA

Robert Preucel, Department of Anthropology, University of Pennsylvania, Philadelphia, USA

Irena Mirnik Prezelj, Department of Archaeology, University of Ljubljana, Slovenia

Chantal Radimilahy, Institut de Civilisations, Musée d'Art et d'Archeologie, Université d'Antananarivo, Madagascar

W. L. Rathje, Stanford Archaeology Center, Stanford University, Stanford, USA

Scott Raymond, Department of Archaeology, University of Calgary, Canada

Jonathan Reyman, Illinois State Museum, Springfield, USA

Nathalie Richard, Centre d'Histoire des Sciences et des Mouvements Intellectuels, University of Paris I (Panthèon-Sorbonne), France

Anna Ritchie, Society of Antiquaries of Scotland, Edinburgh, Scotland

Ted Robinson, Classical Archaeology, University of Sydney, Australia

Wilfredo Ronquillo, Archaeology Division, National Museum, Manila, Philippines

Irving Rouse, Department of Anthropology, Yale University, New Haven, USA

Peter Rowley-Conwy, Department of Archaeology, University of Durham, England

Jeremy Sabloff, Director, University of Pennsylvania Museum of Archaeology and Anthropology, Philadelphia, USA

Antonio Sagona, Centre for Classics and Archaeology, University of Melbourne, Australia

Robert L. Schuyler, Department of Anthropology, University of Pennsylvania Museum of Archaeology and Anthropology, Philadelphia, USA

Niall Sharples, Department of Archaeology, University of Cardiff, Wales

Ian Shaw, Department of Archaeology, University of Liverpool, England

Peter Sheppard, Department of Anthropology, University of Auckland, New Zealand

Paul Sinclair, Department of Archaeology, Uppsala University, Sweden

Anita Smith, Deakin University, Melbourne, Australia

Ian Smith, Department of Anthropology, University of Otago, New Zealand

James Snead, Department of Sociology and Anthropology, George Mason University, Fairfax, USA

Anthony Snodgrass, Museum of Classical Archaeology, University of Cambridge, England

R. P. Soejono, Djkarta, Indonesia

Wilhelm Solheim, Department of Anthropology, University of Hawaii, Honolulu, USA

Marie Louise Sørensen, Department of Archaeology, University of Cambridge, England

Keith Sorrenson, Department of History, University of Auckland, New Zealand

Patricia Spencer, Egypt Exploration Society, London, England

Miriam Stark, Department of Anthropology, University of Hawaii, Honolulu, USA

Nicola Stern, Archaeology Program, La Trobe University, Melbourne, Australia

Judith Storniolo, University of Pennsylvania, USA

Glenn Summerhayes, Australian National University, Canberra, Australia

Eric Taladoire, U.F.R. d'Historie de l'Art et Archéologie, Université de Paris I (Panthéon-Sorbonne), Paris, France

Nikola Theodossiev, Department of Archaeology, Sofia University St. Kliment Ohridski, Sofia, Bulgaria

Eberhard Thomas, Universität Köln, Archäologisches Institut, Köln, Germany

Bruce Trigger, Department of Anthropology, McGill University, Montreal, Canada

Barrie Trinder, School of Technology and Design, University College of Northampton, England

Marion True, J. Paul Getty Museum, Malibu, USA

Peter Turk, National Museum of Slovenia, Ljubljana, Slovenia

Otto Urban, Institut für Ur- und Frügeschichte, Univerity of Vienna, Austria

Phillip van Peer, Institut voor Aardwetenschappen, Leuven, Belgium

Pieter van de Velde, Faculty of Archaeology, University of Leiden, Netherlands

Ruslan Vasilevsky, Institute of Archaeology and Ethnology, Siberian Branch of the Russian Academy of Sciences in Novosibirsk

Ulrich Veit, Institut für Ur- und Frügeschichte und Archäologie des Mittelalters, Tübingen, Germany

Lothar von Falkenhausen, Department of Art History, University of California at Los Angeles, USA

H. T. Waterbolk, formerly at University of Groningen, Netherlands

Patty Jo Watson, Department of Anthropology, Washington University, St. Louis, USA

Josef Wegner, University of Pennsylvania, USA

Fred Wendorf, Department of Anthropology, Southern Methodist University, Dallas, USA

Steve Williams, formerly at Harvard University, Cambridge, USA

Richard Woodbury, formerly at the University of Massachusetts, Amherst, USA

Norman Yoffee, Department of Near Eastern Studies and the University Museum of Anthropology at University of Michigan, Ann Arbor, USA

Gintautas Zabiela, Department of Archaeology, Institute of Lithuanian History, Vilnius, Lithuania

João Zilhão, Instituto Portuguêse de Arqueologica, Lisbon, Portugal

Index

American Anthropological Association
(AAA), 638, 1125, 1172, 1173,
1175, 1177
American Anthropologist (journal), 82,
852, 1172
American Antiquarian Society, 111
American Antiquity (journal), **82–83,**
281, 1125, 1173, 1174, 1175,
1177
American Archaeological Research
Institute, 86
American Association for the
Advancement of Science, 1076
American Association of Physical
Anthropologists, 642
American Center for Oriental
Research (ACOR), 86, 752, 1248
American Civil War, nautical
archaeology, 913, 916
American Ethnological Society, 556
American Exploration Society of
Philadelphia, 615
American Foundation for the Study of
Man expeditions, 89–90, 91
American Institute of Archaeology, 619
American Institute of Iranian Studies,
680
American Journal of Archaeology, **83–84,**
85, 100, 614
American Journal of Physical Anthropology,
642
American Museum of Natural History,
161, 166, 167, 1076
  Canadian archaeology, 252
  Caribbean archaeology, 263
  Davis, Edwin Hamilton, 410
  Ford, James Alfred, 522
  Hrdlicka, Ales, 641
  Marquesas Islands, 1051
American Naturalist, The (journal), 1076
American Oriental Society, 85
American Philosophical Society,
744–745
American School of Architecture at
Rome, 81
American School of Classical Studies at
Athens, **84–85,** 100, 257, 614
American School of Classical Studies at
Rome, 81, 100
American School of Prehistoric
Research, 1008, 1009
American Schools of Oriental Research
(ASOR), 78, **85–86,** 100, 716,
721, 749, 751, 752, 1244, 1245,
1247. *See also* William Foxwell
Albright Institute
American Society for Conservation

Archaeology, 1176
American War of Independence,
nautical archaeology, 912,
915–916, 916–917
Americas, French archaeology,
535–543
Amerikaansche Voyagien (Berkel), 1101
Amerta (journal), 650
Amherst of Hackney, Baron, 279
Ami, Henry, 257
Amiens, 1207
Amiet, P., 877
Amiran, Ruth, 717, 718
Amman, 86, 749, 752, 1248
Amoreira, 483
Ampère, J.-J., 1108
Amphora, Etruscan, 475(photo)
Ampuero, Gonzalo, 311
Amratian culture, 457
Amri, 657, 1190
Amsterdam Kempen Pioneer Project,
930
Amsterdam (ship), 915
Amsterdam University, 1313
Amt Rosenberg. *See* "Rosenberg office"
Amun-Re, 757, 759
Amuq expeditions, 180
Anahuac (Tylor), 1287
Anakara, 836
Analecta Praehistorica Leidensia (journal),
924
Anales de los Chachiqueles, 607
Analytical Archaeology (Clarke), 200,
336
Ananyino culture, 1259
Anasazi
  Chaco Canyon, 295–296
  culture classification, 343
  Pueblo Bonito, 1075–1076
Anatolia. *See* Turkey
Anatolica (journal), 924
Anbarra people, 1156
Anchors, 912
Ancient Bronze Implements (Evans), 211
Ancient Egyptian Materials and Industries
(Lucas), 450
Ancient Egyptian Religion (Frankfort),
534
*The Ancient Egyptians and the Origin of
Civilizations* (Smith), 1170
The Ancient Geography of India
(Cunningham), 386
*Ancient History of North and South
Wiltshire* (Colt Hoare), 369
Ancient India (Wheeler), 1188
Ancient Khotan (Stein), 1209
Ancient Man in North America

(Wormington), 1331
"The Ancient Maya and the Political
Present" (Wilk), 637
Ancient Mesoamerica (journal), 893
Ancient Monuments Conservation Act
(Indonesia), 649–650
Ancient Monuments of the Mississippi Valley
(Squier and Davis), 410, 1170,
1292
Ancient Monuments Preservation Act
(India), 850
Ancient Monuments Protection Act
(Britain), 137, 1035
Ancient Nepal (journal), 1189
Ancient People and Places, 406
Ancient Society (Morgan), 900
Ancient Stone Implements (Evans),
211
Ancient Voyagers in the Pacific (Sharp),
941, 1058
Ancient Wiltshire (Colt Hoare), 204
Ancízar, Manuel, 357
Ancón, 1015, 1289
Anda, 1028
Andaman Islands, 693
Andersen, H. H., 90
Andersen, Johannes, 1057
Anderson, Atholl, 944–945, 946,
947
Anderson, Hamilton, 150–151, 152
Anderson, Joseph, 1182
Anderson, Rowand, 1181
Andersson, Johan Gunnar, **86–87,** 318,
319, 320, 1011
Andrae, Walter, 873
Andreatta, Margarida Davina, 186
Andrews, E. Wyllys, 464, 465, 888
Andrianaivoarivony, Rafolo, 838
Andrian-Werburg, Ferdinand Freiherr
von, 130
Andrieşescu, Ion, 1116
Andronikos, Manolis, 601
Anfray, F., 36
Angel Fernandez, Miguel, 884
Angkor, 241, 242, 244, 245, 246–248,
1098
Angkor, Temple of, 245(photo)
Angkor Borei, 247
Angkor Thom, 248
Angkor Wat, 246, 246(photo),
247(photo), 248
Angles-sur-Anglin, 568
Anglica Historia (Vergil), 1314
Anglo-Saxon Chronicle, 1337
Angulo Valdés, Carlos, 362, 363
Animal, Vegetable and Mineral (television
show), 212–213, 406

Assos, 100

Assunção, M. R., 181

Assyria/Assyrian archaeology, 140,
    871–872, 873, 1281
  Biblical history and, 875
  Dagon (fish god), 952(photo)
  French, 550
  intellectual trends, 875
  Layard, Austen Henry, 807–808
  Louvre Museum, 831
  Nimrud, 951
  Nineveh, 952
  winged bull, 873(photo)
  See also Mesopotamia

Assyrian epigraphy, Oriental Institute
    of Chicago, 970–971

Astor, John Jacob, 556

Åström, Paul, 391

Asturian culture, 484

Asur, 587

Aswan dams, 1, 460, 959–960, 961,
    1093–1094, 1169

Atacama oasis, 308

Atairangikaahu, Dame Te Ariki-nui Te,
    1057

Atajadizo culture, 272

Aten, 1286

Aterian industry, 844

Atgazis, Maris, 800

Athena Nike, Temple of, 596

Athenae Oxoniences (Wood), 113

Athens
  Acropolis, 596–597, 597(photo)
  Agora, 599
  British classical archaeology, 194,
      195, 196
  foreign schools in, 84–85, 123, 258,
      546, 547, 548, 597–598, 731

Athens Archaeological Society in
    Nicosia, 393

Atiquizaya, 464

Atlantican (Rudbeck), 1228

Atlas of African Prehistory (Clark), 336

Atocha (ship), 508, 509(photo)

Atomic Energy Commission, 815

Attempt at an Allegory (Winckelmann),
    1326

Attenbrow, Valerie, 1155

Attic pottery, Beazley, John, 142

Atwater, Caleb, 111–112, 350, 410,
    1292

Aubin, Joseph Marie, 539

Aubrey, John, 95, 112–113, 199, 203,
    287, 432, 814, 1215

Auckland, 936

Audouze, Françoise, 21, 33, 523

Augusta Raurica, 1237

Augustus, 160

Aumassip, Ginette, 843

Aurelian, 1121

Aurignac rock shelter, 792

Aurignacian culture/period, 568
  Breuil, Henri, 193
  in de Mortillet's system, 341, 979
  Maghreb, 23, 28, 46, 840–841
  Peyrony, Denis, 1019
  Potocka Zijalka, 1071

Auroch period, 978

Ausgewählten Problemen der Frühgeschichte,
    133

Austen, R. A. C., 762

Austiracus, Antiquus, 1162

Australasian Journal of Historical
    Archaeology (journal), 114

Australasian Society for Historical
    Archaeology, 114, 1178

Australia
  archaeological sites, 115(map)
  Childe, Vere Gordon, 300
  ethical issues of archaeology, 1322
  Golson, Jack, 589
  historical archaeology, 114–118
  McCarthy, Fred, 860
  Melanesian archaeology, 999
  Mulvaney, John, 905–906
  nautical archaeology, 915
  Nunamira, 124(photo)
  pathway of colonization, 1001
  Philippine archaeology, 1026
  Smith, Grafton, 1169–1170
  Tindale, Norman, 1272
  Wallace line, 1000–1001

Australia, prehistoric archaeology,
    121–126
  Aboriginal Australia, 123–125
  archaeological sites, 122(map)
  contact archaeology, 125–126
  of European civilizations, 122–123
  future of, 126
  Mulvaney, John, 906
  rock art, 1104–1105, 1106, 1113,
      1116
  shell middens, 1155, 1156, 1157

Australian Archaeological Institute at
    Athens, 123

Australian Institute of Aboriginal
    Studies, 860

Australian Institute of Archaeology, 123

Australian Institute of Maritime
    Archaeology, 114

Australian Journal of Historical
    Archaeology (journal), 114, 116

Australian National University, 123,
    125, 589, 1000

Australian Society for Historical
    Archaeology, 114

Australopithecus, 809
  A. afarensis, 789, 811, 1224
  A. africanus, 407, 789, 1224
  A. boisei, 18
  A. robustus, 1224

Austria, 127–134
  archaeological education in, 134
  archaeological research since 1960,
      129
  current state of archaeology in, 134
  Ephesus, 470
  general structure of archaeology in,
      127
  Hallstatt, 288
  prehistoric archaeology, 130–132,
      578
  prescientific period, 127–128
  protection of monuments, 133–134
  proto-historical archaeology,
      132–133
  provincial Roman archaeology,
      128–129
  See also Slovenia

Austrian Anthropological Society, 1163

Austrian Archaeological Institute, 470

Austrian Congress of Anthropology and
    Prehistory, 425

Austronesian languages, 707

Autorité pour la Protection du Site et
    l'Aménagement de la Région
    d'Angkor, 248

Autun-Augustodum, 160

Auvernier, 1240

Auxois, Mont, 292

Avaricum, 159

Avars, 1122

Avebury, Lord (Sir John Lubbock),
    136(photo), 136–137, 199, 201,
    204, 210, 340, 341, 900, 978,
    979, 1034, 1086, 1230

Avebury (site), 112, 113, 135(photo),
    135–136, 287, 369, 1031, 1215

Avebury (Stukeley), 1216

Aveleyra, L., 887

Avendaño y Loyola, Andres de, 605

Aventicum, 1240

Avias, J., 999

Avienus, 285

Avigad, Nahman, 717, 719

Avi-Yonah, Michael, 717, 718

"Awa" peoples, 946

Awash Valley, 38

Awatovi, 626

Awdaghost, 73, 74

Ayacucho, 1018

Aylesford, 211
Aymonier, Etienne, 242, 244
Äyräpää, Aarne, 498–499
Ayub Cave, 1029
Azais, F., 35
Azamit, Jan, 399
Azarnoush, M., 681
Azcapotzalco, 557, 881
Azilian industry/period, 486,
    808–809, 1031
Azraq Basin, 753
The Aztec Image in Western Thought
    (Keen), 635
Aztecs, **137–138,** 871, 969
    calendar stone, 137(photo)
    in El Salvador, 462
    Prescott, William, 1073
    Tenochtitlán, 1262–1263
    Teotihuacán and, 1266
    Toltecs and, 1273, 1274
Azugi, 25

Ba, Hampate, 48
Babadag culture, 1120
BABesch (bulletin), 924
Babuyan Islands, 692
Babylon, 139–140, 871
Babylon and the Monuments of Nineveh
    (Layard), 808
Babylonian civilization, **139–140,** 871,
    872–873, 873–874
    royal stela, 139(photo)
    See also Mesopotamia
"Babylonian Noah," 875
Bacho Kiro cave, 229
Bachué, 360
Backa Brastad, 1100
Bacon, Edward, 631
Bacsonian tradition, 243
The Badarian Civilization (Caton-
    Thompson and Brunton), 283
Badarian culture, 283, 456, 457
Baden-Württemberg, 289
Baekje tombs, 770
Bagdanov, Anatoly, 1139
Bagford, John, 1178
Baghdad, 155
Bagherzadeh, Firouz, 680
Bahamas, 266, 271, 273
Bahawalpur, 657, 659
Bahr, K. K., 794
Bahrain, 90, 92
Bahrami, Mahdi, 679
Baik, Chanlatte, 272
Baikal, Lake, 967
Bailey, G. N., 1156
Bailloud, G., 36

Bairstow, Damaris, 116
Bais Anthropological Project, 703, 1028
Baja California, rock art, 1103, 1110
Baker, Herbert, 53
Baking Pot, 151
al-B'akri, 72, 74, 779
Balbeck, 1006
Baleniunas, Pranas, 827
Bali, 650, 693
Balitung, King, 695
Balkans, 287, 353–354
Ball, Valentine, 521
Ball courts
    Caribbean, 263, 264(photo), 267
    Chichén Itzá, 299, 300
Ballana, 468, 957, 960
Ballard, Robert, 916
Ballivian, Jose, 166
Balloy, Rene de, 676
Balobok Rock Shelter, 700–701,
    1025–1026
Balodis, Francis, 795, 797, 800,
    803–804
Balout, Lionel, 28, 843
Balta archaeologija (magazine), 829
Baltic nationalities, 803
Die Baltischen Provinzen Kurland, Livland,
    Estland (Ebert), 795
Baltzer, Lauritz, 1111
Baluchistan, 1189–1190, 1209
Bamako, 25
Bamps, Anatole, 433
Ban Chiang, **140,** 1308
Banat, 1119, 1120, 1121, 1123
Bancroft, W. L., 1080
Band Pottery culture, 224
Bandel, Ernst von, 580
Bandelier, Adolph, 166, 295, 618, 900
Bandelier National Monument, 618,
    619(photo)
Bandinelli, Ranuccio Bianchi, 731
Bandkeramik culture, 830
Banerji, Rakal Das, **140–141,** 654,
    1188
Bangladesh, 1189, 1193
Bangladesh Archaeology (journal), 1189
Bank of the Republic (Colombia), 363
Banks, Joseph, 938
Banpo, **141,** 322
Banteay Kdei, 248
Banteay Prei Nokor, 245
Banten Lama, 695
Banton, Michael, 1085
Bantry Bay, 1105
Bantu Studies Research Project, 10
Bantu-speaking groups, 10, 60, 67
Bao Caves, 691

Baqt treaty, 957, 958
Bar-Adon, P., 718
Barahona, Amelia, 376
Barata, Frederico, 182
Barbados, 511
Barbosa Rodrigues, J., 181
Barbour, Thomas, 1060, 1061
Barco, Miguel del, 1103, 1104
Bard, K. A., 37
Barghoorn, Elso, 997
Barka, Norman F., 520, 1178
Barley, 428
Baronage of England (Dugdale), 432
Barradas, José Pérez de, 361
Barradas, L., 1220
Barrancas, 274
Barrington, C., 36
Barrio Magsuhot, 703–704
Barrow, John, 60, 1104
Barrow cemeteries, medieval, 863,
    864–865
Barrow robbers, Siberia, 1128
"Barrow-hunting," 1186
Barrows, David P., 158
Barth, Fredrik, 3
Barth, Fritz Eckart, 132, 288
Barth, Heinrich, 43, 1108
Barthelmy, Abbé, 545
Bartholomew, G. A., 983
Bartlett, Alexandra, 997
Bartlett, William, 1036
Bartlow Hills, 218
Barton, David F., 141, 1319
Bartovics, Albert F., 141
Bartram, William, 1292
Bartstra, Gert-Jan, 693, 932
Bary, E. von, 43
Barzitsa treasure, 230
Basarab I, 1123
Basel, 1237
Basketmaker III sites, 296
Basque people, 1202
Basreliefs of Badami (Banerji), 140
Bass, George F., 508, 734, 1308
Bassai frieze, 194
Basse-Yutz, 291–292
Basta, 753
Bastan, Adolf, 776
Bastarns, 1120
Bastet, F. L., 928
Bastian, Adolf, 357
Batan Island, 692
Batanes Islands, 692
Batavia Pacific Science Congress, 646
Batavia (ship), 114, 915
Bataviaasch Genootschap van Kunsten
    en Wetenschappen, 648

Bicknell, Clarence, 1110
Biddle, Martin, 867, 1307
Bielenstein, A., 795, 802
Bienerberg, K. J. Biener von, 396
Biggs, Bruce, 1058
Bilkent University (Turkey), 917
Bin-Bir-Kilisse, 154
Binford, Lewis R., **160–161,** 441,
    1200
  lithic analysis, 818
  Mexican archaeology, 888
  Moberg, Carl-Axel, 1234
  Mousterian debate with Bordes,
    175, 530, 809, 982
  processual archaeology, 627, 1300
  sampling and, 1301
  technological organization concept,
    820–821
  Zhoukoudian, 326
Binford, Sally, 161
Bingham, Hiram, 835, 907
Bio-anthropology, 450
Biodegradation, landfills, 560,
    563–564
Biographies, 634–635
Biologia Centrali-Americana: Archaeology
    (Maudslay), 150
Biological Archaeological Institute
    (Netherlands), 921, 922, 924,
    927, 932
Bir Kiseiba, 49
Bir Sahara, 49
Bir Tarfawi, 49
Bird, Junius B., 107, **161–162,** 306,
    308, 309, 994–995, 1016
Bird, Robert, 994
Birley, A. R., 220
Birley, Eric, 219
Birmingham, Judy, 114, 115, 116
The Birth of Prehistoric Chronology
    (Graslund), 634
Biscayne National Park (U.S.), 508
Bischoff, Henning, 365, 438
Bisheh, Ghazi, 754
Bishop, Ronald L., 373, 382
Bishop Museum. *See* Bernice P. Bishop
    Museum
Bisitun, 675
Biskupin, **162–163,** 162(photo),
    163(photo), 778, 1042(photo),
    1043
Bismark Archipelago, 1001, 1004, 1053
Bison period, 978
Bit Hilani, 1283
Bittmann, B., 313
Black, Davidson, 87, 257, 318, 646,
    1011

Black Athena (Bernal), 637, 1087
Black Country Museum (Britain), 665
"Blackheads building" (Old Town Riga),
    797, 801
Blackiston, A. H., 1061
Blackman, A. M., 447
Blackman, Winifred, 447
Blackmore Museum, 410
Blackwater Draw, 383
Blanc, A. C., 36
Blanco, Aida, 381
Blandford, W. T., 654
Blanton, Richard, 890
Bleed, Peter, 736
Bleek, Dorothea, 66, 1108
Bleek, Wilhelm, 66, 1107–1108
Blegen, Carl William, **163–164,** 594,
    600, 816, 817, 1280
Bliss, F. J., 716, 1244
Bloch, Marc, 187, 527, 530
Bloemers, Johan, 930
"The Blood of the Kings" (exhibition),
    1149
The Blood of the Kings (Miller),
    1149–1150
Blumenbach, Johann Friedrich,
    1086(photo)
Blumentrittt, Ferdinand, 1020
Boas, Franz, 535, 557, 765, 881, 1010,
    1076, 1077, 1110, 1261
Bocoum, H., 32
Bodu, Pierre, 1033
Boeckholtz, F. von, 648, 684
Boerstra, E., 932
Boessneck, J., 1199
Bogdan, 1123
Boggs, Stanley, 462, 463
Boğazköy, **164,** 569, 1277, 1281, 1282
Bogucki, Peter I., 225
Bohemia, 395, 397, 401, 866
Böhm, Jaroslav, 399, 401
Böhner, K., 868
Bohuslän, 1102, 1111
Boian culture, 1118
Boii, 286
Boisselier, Jean, 245
Boisset, Guacolda, 313
Boletin de Arqueologia Medieval (journal),
    869
Bolivia, **164–172**
  archaeology sites, 165(map)
  beginnings of archaeology in,
    166–168
  colonial period, 164
  current archaeology research,
    170–172
  French archaeology, 539

national archaeology, 168–170
republican period, 165–166
rock art, 1101
Bollaert, William, 433
Boman, Eric, 106, 107, 305
Bomansson, K. A., 496, 865
Bómida, Marcelo, 307
Bonampak', **174–175,** 175(photo), 607
Bonaparte, Lucien, 728
Bone Age, 407
Boni, Giacomo, 729
Bonilla, Leidy, 381
Bónis, Éva, 129
Bonk, William, 1051
Bonnel de Mezières, M., 72, 74
Bonsor, George, 1196
Book of the Dead, 918
Boomplaas, 63(photo), 66, 67
Boow, James, 116
Booy, Theodore de, 262
Borbein, Adolf Heinrich, 576
Borchardt, Ludwig, 461, 1093
Borchhardt, Jürgen, 128
Borden, Charles, 253
Border Cave, 65
Bordes, François, **175–176,** 347, 528,
    530, 807, 809, 817–818,
    981–982, 1199
Borger grave, 932
Borgnino, Natcha, 381
Boriskovsky, Pavel, 244
Bormann, Eugen, 129
Borneo, 690–691
Borobudur Temple, 648, 651,
    651(photo), 685, 695
Borovo, 231
Borrell, Pedro, 508
Bosch, F. D., 649, 650, 685
Bosch Gimpera, P., 671, 672
Bosch Gimpera, Pedro, 887
Bosch Gimpera, Pere, 1196, 1197
Boston Museum of Fine Arts, 100,
    615, 960, 1093–1094, 1095
Boston University, 754
Bosumpra rock shelter, 1154
Botany Bay, 1105
Botero, Pedro, 366
Botin, Anders af, 1228, 1229
Botiva, Alvaro, 367
Botta, Carol, 176
Botta, Paul Emile, **176,** 526, 527, 550,
    807, 831, 871, 952
Bottema, S., 987
Botticher, Ernst, 1151
Bouard, Michel de, 867
Bouchard, Jean François, 366
Boucher de Perthes, Jacques, 43,

Dürrnberg-bei-Hallein, 132, 290–291
Dussán, Alicia, 361
Dussaud, René, 552
Dutch East India Company, 60, 114, 118, 915. *See also* Verenigde Oostindische Compagnie
Dutch East Indies, 932. *See also* Indonesia
Dutta, P. C., 693
Duvanli, 231
Duveyrier, Henri, 43, 1108, 1109
Dux Semigallorum Viesthardus, 802
Duxbury, 1036
Duyong Cave, 1026, 1256–1257
    ear pendant from, 1258(photo)
Dying Gaul (statue), 287
The Dynamics of Stylistic Change in Arikara Ceramics (Deetz), 413, 627
Dyson, Robert H., 90, 679, 1307, 1308

The Eagle and the Spade (Ridley), 638
Ear pendants, 1256, 1257, 1258(photo)
Earle, T., 1053
The Early Christian Monuments of Scotland (Allen and Anderson), 1182
"Early History of Agriculture Project" (Britain), 621
Early India and Pakistan (Wheeler), 1319
The Early Iron Age in Norrland (Hildebrand), 622
Early Khartoum (Arkell), 47
Early Man in Britain (Dawkins), 411
Early Man shelter (Australia), 1113
Early Medieval Slavdom (Hensel), 1044
Early Stone Age, 20
Earth Resources Technology Satellites (ERTS), 1098
East Africa
    indigenous archaeologists, 12–14
    Isaac, Glyn, 683
    later archaeology, **5–14**
    Leakey, Louis B., 809–810
    nautical archaeology, 916
    Olduvai Gorge, 968–969
    Olorgesailie, 970
    prehistory, **16, 18–21**
    rock art, 1113–1114
    stone technology, 20–21
    Swahili Coast, 1218–1221
East Carolina University, 917
East Germany, 582
East India Company, 871, 1073
    Falconer, Hugh, 495
    Iranian archaeology, 675
    Rawlinson, Henry, 1092

East Luwians, 1282
East Malaysia, 688, 690–691, 695–698
East Timor, 694
East Turkana Research Project, 683
Easter Island, **433,** 434(photo), 940, 1048, 1050, 1051, 1107
Eastern Cholan, 858
Eastern Europe
    medieval archaeology, 867
    Mesolithic, 485
Eastern Indian School of Medieval Sculpture (Banerji), 140
Eastern Polynesia, 1047
Eberdingen-Hochdorf, 289
Ebert, Max, 795, 804
Ebla, 1252(photo)
Eboracum, 1337
Eburran culture, 8
Échelles, 1220
Eckhel, Johann Josef Hilarius, 127
École Biblique et Archéologique Française (Jerusalem), 552, 751, 752, 1244, 1248
École des Hautes Études en Sciences Sociales, 530, 666
École du Louvre, 547, 1006
École Française d'Athènes, 552
École Française d'extrème Orient, 242, 243, 244, 245
École Française du Caire, 550
École Pratique des Hautes Études, 547
Ecuador, **433, 435–440,** 1289
Edfu, Temple of Horus at, 849(photo)
Edgerton, Harold, 915
Edgren, Torsten, 499
Edinburgh, 1324
Education Nationale (France), 547
Edward VI (king of England), 1314
Edwards, Amelia, 445, 459–460, 1018
Edwards, William, 738, 911
Efate Island, 1005
Efimenko, Petr, 1138, 1139, 1142, 1144
Egami, Namio, 739
Egami, Norio, 679
Eggan, Fred, 3
Egger, Rudolf, 128, 133
Eggers, Hans-Jürgen, 583, 930
Eggert, M., 29
Egloff, Brian, 118
Eglon, 1244
Egypt
    French archaeology, 549–550
    nautical archaeology, 912, 917, 918
    Nubia and, 954, 955–956, 957, 958, 959, 961–962
    popular histories of archaeology, 631

See also Egypt, dynastic; Egypt, predynastic; Nubia
Egypt, dynastic, **440–453**
    Abu Simbel, 1
    Abydos, 2
    antiquarian collecting, 441
    archaeological sites, 452(map)
    Belzoni, Giovanni, 155
    Canadian archaeology, 257, 258
    Carter, Howard, 279–280
    Champollion, Jean-François, 297
    chronological systems, 443
    El Amarna, 461
    Emery, Walter Bryan, 468
    European expeditions, 442, 443–444, 549
    integrating textual and archaeological data, 442–443
    introduction of scientific archaeology, 444–447
    Karnak and Luxor, 757–759
    Lepsius, Karl Richard, 811
    Mariette, Auguste, 444, 849–850
    Naville, Henri Edouard, 918–919
    Nubia and, 955–956
    Petrie, William, 1018–1019
    Pitt Rivers, Augustus, 1035
    proportions of published archaeological fieldwork, 449(table)
    Reisner, George, 1093–1095
    Saqqara, 1148
    scientific analyses, 450–451
    Sema-Tawy tradition, 455–456, 459
    sequence dating, 445–446
    settlement archaeology, 447–449
    theoretical and practical problems facing, 451–453
    Tutankhamun's tomb, 447, 1285–1286
    Woolley, Leonard, 1327
Egypt, predynastic, **455–459**
    Caton-Thompson, Gertrude, 283–284
    chronological systems, 456–457
    cultural areas, 456
    Mesopotamian influence, 459
    Nagada culture, 457–459
    Petrie, William, 1018
    Sema-Tawy tradition, 455–456, 459
    social stratification in, 457–458
Egypt before the Pharaohs (Hoffman), 631
Egypt Exploration Fund (EEF), 257, 279, 445, 460, 918, 1018
Egypt Exploration Society, 223, 257, 441, **459–461,** 468, 534, 639, 918, 960, 1018, 1327

Egyptian Antiquities Organization, 461
Egyptian Antiquities Service, 444, 468, 849, 962
Egyptian Archaeology (journal), 461
Egyptian hieroglyphics, 297
    Champollion, Jean-François, 297
    decipherment, 442
    Lepsius, Karl Richard, 811
Egyptian mummies, scientific analyses, 450
Egyptian Museum of Antiquities, 1093
Egyptian Museum (Vatican), 1314
Ehre des Herzogthums Crain (Valvazor), 1162
Eibner, Clemens, 132
Eichler, Fritz, 128
Eigenbilzen, 143
1859 Hampshire and Isle of Wright Directory (White), 911
1833: Reuvens i Drenthe (Brongers), 638
Einkorn wheat, 428
Einsiedeln Itinerary, 722
Die Eisenzeit Finnlands (Hackman), 498
Die Eisenzeit Finnlands (Kivikoski), 499
Ekade Iktab (Frobenius), 47
Ekholm, G. F., 884, 887
El Adam, 48
El Amarna, 280, 441, 444, 445, 448, 460, **461**, 468, 1018, 1286, 1327
El Caimito culture, 272
El Castillo, 81, 282(photo), 299, 300
El Dorado myth, 357
El Dorado (Zerda), 357
El Gran Grifón (ship), 916
El Hatillo, 992
El Kadada, 49
El Mirador, 852, 853, 887
El Morro, 503
El Oualadgi, 24, 25
El Pilar, 152
El Salvador, **462–466**
El Tajin, 884
Elandsfontein, 64
Electromagnetic energy, 1095–1096
Electron microscopy, 102
Elegies of Illustrious Men of the Indies (Castellanos), 354
Elephanta, 1183
Elephantine, 450
Elephas recki, 19
Elgin, Lord (Thomas Bruce), 194, 195, 223, 467(photo), **467–468**, 595
Elgin Marbles, 223, 467(photo), 467–468, 595, 601, 1321
Elgon, Mount, 7
Elia, Ricardo J., 754

Elizabethan College of Antiquaries, 1178
Elkab, 449
Ellis, William, 1106–1107
Elm decline, 987
Elmenteitan culture, 6, 8, 11
El-Salaam Canal, 461
Elton, Arthur, 662
Emery, Walter Bryan, 460, **468**, 960, 1095
Emmer wheat, 428
Emona, 354, **468–469**, 1163, 1164
Emory, Kenneth P., 940, 1049, 1051, 1058
Emperaire, Joseph, 183
Emphoux, Jean-Pierre, 838
Ename, 147
Encyclopedia of Indian Archaeology, 587
Encyclopedie Berbere, 28
End-Blom, M. J. van den, 650
Eneolithic archaeology, 229
Engaruka ruins, 7
Engel, A., 1196
Engelbach, Reginald, 447
Engelhardt, Conrad, 415
Engels, Friedrich, 141, 400, 616, 900, 1138
Engihoul cave, 1152
Engis cave, 144, 1152
Engis skull, 1064
English Heritage, 663
The English Village (Peake), 1011
Enkomi-Ayios Iakovos, **469–470**
Enlightenment
    attitudes toward classical Greece, 595
    classification systems, 339
    French archaeology, 545, 549
    Guatemalan archaeology, 605
Ensete, 39
Enterprise (ship), 501
Eolithic period, 341
EPA Engrains, 164
Ephesus, **470**, 640, 1282
    Temple of Hadrian, 470(photo)
Epigraphia Indica, 141, 1187
Epigraphy
    Assyrian, 970–971
    Indian, 1186, 1187
    Indonesia, 695
    Roman, 1149
    Sumerian, 970–971
    See also Egyptian hieroglyphics; Maya epigraphy
Epi-Olmec, 970
Epipaleolithic, 485
    Egyptian, 449
    Le Mas d'Azil, 808–809

Épiphylogenèse, 813
Epstein, Claire, 718
Erä-Esko, Aarni, 499
Eranos Vindobonensis, 128
Erech, 873
Erechteum, 596
Erenburg, Ilya, 1135
Erg Thihodaine, 844
Ergani copper mines, 1278
Erickson, Clark, 170–171
Erigaie, 366
Erik Bloodaxe, 418
Eriksen, Thomas H., 1089
Erim, Kenan, 907
Eritrea, 35, 36, 37, 38, 39, 40
Erligang, 322
Erlitou, 322
Erman, Adolf, 1093
Erp, T. van, 685
Erskine, David Steuart, 1181
Erstfeld, 291
Ertebolle culture, 483
Ertebolle (site), 483
Erzepki, Boleslaw, 1040, 1041
Es, W. A. van, 928
Escalante, Javier, 169
Escargotières, 839
Escuela Española de Historia y Arqueología en Roma, 1197, 1198
Escuela Francesa de Arte y Arqueología, 1197
Escuela Internacional de Arqueología y Etnografia Americana (Mexico), 881
Escuela Superior de Diplomatica (Spain), 1196
Escuela Superior Politecnica del Litoral (Ecuador), 439
Españolista, 1202
Espejo, A., 887
Espinoza, Edgar, 376, 377
Essay on the Aboriginal Cultures of the State of Antioquia in Colombia (Posada), 357
Essentialism, 1291
Essentialist classifications, 337
The Establishment of Human Antiquity (Grayson), 634
Estévez, José, 169
Estioko-Griffin, Agnes, 703
Estonia, 1259
Estrada, Emilio, 437–438
Ethiopia, 35, 36–40
Ethiopian Dynasty (Egypt), 956
Ethiopian Institute of Archaeology, 36
Ethiopian-Sabaean culture, 39

"Ethnic becoming," 813
"Ethnic Concepts in German Prehistory" (Veit), 1088
Ethnic Identity in Greek Antiquity (Hall), 1090
Ethnicity, **1085–1090**
    Caribbean archaeology, 267–268
    Celts, 294
Ethnicity and Nationalism (Eriksen), 1089
Ethnoarchaeology, Philippines, 703, 1026
Ethnogeographic Board (U.S.), 1215
Ethnographic Museum of Slovenia, 831, 909
"Ethnographic prehistory," 776
Ethnographical and Archaeological Essay on the Province of Quimbayas (Restrepo), 358
Ethnography. *See* Ethnology
Ethnography of the Slovenes, 832
Ethnologica (journal), 305, 590
Ethnological Institute of Colombia, 362
Ethnological Society of London, 210, 1034
d'Ethnologie (journal), 278
Ethnology
    American, 343, 1300
    archaeological classifications, 348
    British prehistoric archaeology, 209–210
    Cushing, Frank Hamilton, 388
    Gallatin, Albert, 556
    Graebner, Fritz, 590
    Kulturkreislehre concept, 583
    Leroi-Gourhan, André, 812–813
    Mason, Otis, 851–852
    Nilsson, Sven, 951
    Russia, 1137–1138
    Steward, Julian, 1211
Ethnology and Mound Survey (Smithsonian Institution), 1171
Ethnos (journal), 558
Etnología de la Península Iberica (Bosch Gimpera), 1197
Etruria, 197
De Etruria regali libri septem (Dempster), 471
De Etruria regionis (Postel), 471
Etruscan archaeology, **471–477,** 472(map), 724, 725, 726, 728
Etruscan Museum (Vatican), 1314
Etruscans
    Celts and, 285, 286, 290, 292
    nautical archaeology, 917
Etruskische Spiegel (Gerhard), 473, 728

Etrusologia (Pallottino), 476
Études archéologiques (Gagnon), 529, 1080
Eubanks, Thomas H., 766
Eumenes II, 287
Euphrates River, 139
Eurasia Septentrionalis Antiqua (journal), 1258, 1259
Europe
    medieval archaeology, 861–869
    rock art, 1099–1100, 1102–1103, 1110–1111
European Mesolithic, **478–486**
European Symposium for Teachers of Medieval Archaeology, 869
Euting, Julius, 89
Euvreux, Yves d', 180
Evangelista, Alfredo E., 1024
Evans, Sir Arthur, 195, **491–493,** 492(photo), 631, 1321
    archaeology in Greece, 594, 598, 599(photo)
    Ashmolean Museum, 111
    Aylesford cemetery, 211
    Childe, Vere Gordon, 300
    Hawes, Harriet, 614
    Hogarth, David, 640
    Knossos, 598, 599(photo), 767, 768
    Linear B, 816
    Woolley, Leonard, 1326
Evans, Clifford, 183, 184, 188, 266, 308, 363, 437, 438, 1016
Evans, Ivor, 646, 688
Evans, Joan, 631
Evans, Sir John, 211, 491, **493,** 495, 631, 636, 832, 903, 906, 977, 978, 1180
Everyday Archaeology (Gorodcov), 590
"Evidence for Greek Dialect in the Mycenaean Archives" (Ventris), 1314
Evolution et techniques (Leroi-Gourhan), 812
The Evolution of Urban Society (McCormick), 4
Evolutionary artifact classification, 346
Evolutionism
    Russia, 1138
    U.S. prehistoric archaeology, 1302–1303
Evrard, René, 661
Ewert, Ch., 1199
Excavaciones Arqueológicas en España (series), 1199
"The Excavation of a Huron Ossuary" (Kidd), 764
Excavation of Ste Marie I (Kidd), 626, 764

The Existence of Man on Our Soil (Delgado), 1064
Expedient technologies, 822
Expert systems, 370–371
Explorations in Eastern Palestine (Glueck), 750–751
Exteriorization concept, 813
Externalism, 637
The Eye Goddess (Crawford), 386
Eyzies, Les. *See* Les Eyzies

Fabri, Nicolas-Claude de, 544
Fagan, Brian, 631
Fa-Hian, 387, 1186
Fairbanks, Charles H., 502, 504, 505, 507, 511, 626, 628, 734, 766
Fairman, H. W., 449
Fairservis, W. A., 1189
Falabella, F., 313
Falchetti, Ana María, 364
Falconer, Hugh, 177, 223, 409, 411, **495,** 832, 977, 1012
Faldín, Juan, 169
Falkenhausen, Lothar von, 328
False banana, 39
Faras Cathedral, 962
Fardelin, P., 867
Far-Eastern Prehistory Association, 646, 686
Far-Eastern Prehistory Association Newsletter, 647
Far-Eastern Prehistory Congresses, 158, 689, 692
Farmers
    South Africa, 67–68
    See also Agriculture; Plantations
Farnese Bull (statue), 724
Farnese Hercules (statue), 723
The Fasti of Roman Britain (Birley), 220
Fattovich, R., 37
Faure, H., 36
Fauresmith culture, 65
Fausett, Bryan, 203, 863
Fauvel, Louis, 545
Favargettes, 424
Fayum, 456
Fea, Carlo, 727–728
Feathered Serpent, Temple of, 557(photo)
Febvre, Lucien, 527, 530
Feddersen Wierde, 583, 584(map)
Federal Republic of Central America, 605–606
Federal Republic of Germany, 582
Federal University at Pernambuco State (Brazil), 184
Federmesser culture, 147, 486

Frobenius, Ratzel, 306

From Antiquity to Archaeologist (Cunnington), 634–635

From the Abyss of Ages (journal), 777

Fromaget, J., 243, 244

Froslier, Bernard P., 646

Frothingham, Arthur Lincoln, Jr., 83

Frova, A., 228

Fryxell, Roald, 971

Fu Sinian, 319

Fuensalida, Bartolome de, 605

Fuentes y Guzman, Francisco Antonio, 605

Fugitive slave settlements, 187

Fuhao, 324

Fuji, N., 988

Funari, P. P. A., 189

Fundmünzen der römischen Zeit in Österreich (Göbl), 129

"Funnel Beaker Culture," 783

Furtwängler, Adolf, 196, 574

Fusconi, Annesio, 910

FxJj 50 site, 19

Gabel, Creighton, 7, 754

Gabon, 1114

Gabriel, B., 28

Gabrovec, Stane, **555–556,** 910, 1166, 1168, 1211

Gademotta, 21

Gado, B., 30

Gagnan, Emile, 913

Gagnon, A., 1080

Galang, Ricardo E., 1023

Galatia, 551, 552

Galatians, 287

Galich treasure, 1259

Galilee, Sea of, 917

Galilei, Galileo, 725

Galinat, Walton, 994

Galindo, 897

Gallagher, J., 36

Gallatin, Albert, **556,** 744

Gallay, Allan, 31, 32

Galli, 286

Gallia (journal), 533

Gallic languages, 814

Gallieni, 24

Galvez, Mariano, 605

Gamboa, Hector, 380

Gamio, Manuel, **556–558,** 881–882

Ganeshwar culture, 657, 659

Gann, Thomas, 150

Gao, 25, 71, 73, 76. *See also* Kawkaw

Garanger, Jose, 1005

Garbage archaeology, **558–566**

future research areas, 564–566

Garbage Project students and staff, 564

"Parkinson's Law of Garbage," 565–566

rationale for, 560–563

"The Garbage Dilemma" (video), 564

Garbage Project, 559–566

Garbology, **558–566**

Garbsch, Jochen, 129

Garcés, H., 313

Garcia Arévalo, Manuel, 511

Garcia Bellido, Antonio, 1198, 1199

García Elgueta, Manual, 606

García Payón, José, 887, 889

Garda, Lake, 914

Gardin, Jean-Claude, 529, 530

Gardner, Elinor, 283, 284

Garibaldi, Giuseppe, 728–729

Gârla Mare culture, 1119

Garlake, Peter, 1087

Garnier, Francis, 241

Garrard, Andrew, 753

Garrick, H. W., 387, 1186

Garrido, Rafael, 303

Garrod, Sir Archibald, 567

Garrod, Dorothy, 212, 334, **567–568,** 680, 858, 874, 981, 1331

Garstang, John, **569,** 749

Garth, Thomas R., 625

Gateway of the Sun (Tiwanaku), 169(photo)

Gathercole, Peter, 942

Gatún, Lake, 997

Gaudebout, P., 837

Gaudry, Albert, 177, 1207

Gaul, J. H., 228

Gaul Killing Himself and His Wife (statue), 287

Gaul/Gauls, 285

Alesia, 79–80

Belgica, 143

Bibracte, 159–160

See also Celts

Gaumond, Michel, 1080

Gautier, A., 49

Gava culture, 1120

"Gawroniec," 783

Gayton, Anna, 1016

Gaza, Great Pyramid at, 451, 1018

Gebel, Nans Georg, 753

Gebel al-Arak knife, 459

Gebel el-Haridi, 461

Gebel Moya, 959

Geber, Ezion, 751

Geddes, Bill, 1058

Gedi, 1220

Geertman, H., 921, 928

Geiseler, Wilhelm, 1107

Gelada baboons, 970

Gelidonya, Cape, 914

Gelu, 1123

Gemelniţa culture, 1118

Le Gemme antiche figurate (Agostini), 725

Gendrop, P., 541

Generación de 1880, 106, 107

General Directorate of Antiquities and Fine Arts (Italy), 98

General Geography and Historical Compendium of the State of Antioquia (Uribe), 357

General History of the News Kingdom of Granada (Fernández de Piedrahita), 354

"General Views on Archaeology" (Morlot), 630

Genetic prehistory, 782

Gening, Vladimir, 1127, 1143

Gennadeion, 85

Gennadius, Joannes, 85

Genouillac, Abbé Henri de, 551

Genser, Kurt, 128

GEO satellites, 1098

Geoffrey of Monmouth, 207, **569–570,** 1314

Geoffroy Saint-Hilaire, Etienne, 43, 792

Geoglyphs, 1096(photo)

Geographic information systems (GIS), **570–572**

Geographical History in Greek Lands (Myres), 906

Geographical Society Bulletin, 538

Geography, archaeology and, 570

Geología y Prothistoria Ibéricas (Vilanova y Piera), 1316

Geological Conference of Algiers, 48

Geological Evidence of the Antiquity of Man (Lyell), 832

Geological Service of Indochina, 242, 243

Geological Society of London, 177, 493, 495, 832, 1032, 1073

Geological Survey of Canada, 252, 254

Geological Survey of China, 318

Geological Survey of India, 521

"La Géologie du quaternaire au Maroc" (Bourcart), 844

Geologiska Foreningens I Stockholm Forhandlingar (journal), 987

Geology

Lyell, Charles, 832–833

Paleolithic archaeology and, 976

Prestwich, Joseph, 1073

Steno, Nicolas, 1209, 1210(photo)

Geophysical techniques, Egyptian
archaeology, 451
George Heye Foundation, 433
George II (king of England), 223, 1179
George III (king of England), 223, 297,
611, 1179, 1181
Gepids, 1122
Gerasa, 749
Gerhard, Eduard, 424, 473, 574, 728,
1130
Gérin-Lajoie, Albert, 1080
German Archaeological Institute. *See*
Deutsches Archäologisches
Institut
German Archaeological Institute in
Rome, 473
German archaeology, classical,
573–576
Bunsen, Christian von, 236
Curtius, Ernst, 387–388
Deutsches Archäologisches Institut,
424–425
Lepsius, Karl Richard, 811
German archaeology, prehistoric,
576–585
Bersu, Gerhard, 157
development of, 579–582
histories of, 579
Kossinna, Gustaf, 775–776
Ludwig, Lindenschmidt, 816
main contributions of, 582–583,
585
sites and regions, 577(map), 578
terms for, 579
German Democratic Republic, 582
German Empire, 578
German Evangelical Institute, 751
German language, 775–776
German Prehistory (Kossinna), 776
German River Reconnaissance Project,
29
German Scientific Society, 304
German Society for Anthropology,
Ethnology, and Prehistory, 816
Germanic National Museum, 580
Germanisches Nationalmuseum, 580
Germany
archaeological heritage
management, 96, 97
Celts and, 289
Czech archaeology, 399
Danish archaeology, 422
Dutch archaeology, 929
Graebner, Fritz, 590
industrial archaeology, 663
Kossinna, Gustaf, 775–776
Latvian archaeology, 795

medieval archaeology, 864,
865–866, 867
Mesolithic, 481
Mexican archaeology, 880–881
nautical archaeology, 911
Polish archaeology, 1043
pollen analysis, 987, 988, 989
Portuguese archaeology, 1069
Ratzel, Friedrich, 1091
Reinecke, Paul, 1093
Schliemann, Heinrich, 1150–1152
Spanish archaeology, 1196, 1197,
1198, 1199
Swiss archaeology, 1240, 1241
Syro-Palestinian archaeology, 1244,
1246
Uhle, Max, 1289
Virchow, Rudolf, 1316–1317
Winckelmann, Johann Joachim,
1325–1326
See also German archaeology,
classical; German archaeology,
prehistoric; Nazi Germany
Gersike, 800
Gerzean culture, 457
Geschichte der griechischen Kunstler
(Brunn), 574
Geschichte der Kunst des Altertums
(Winckelmann), 573, 726
Geschichte des Herzogthums Krain
(Vodnik), 1162
Geschichtsverein für Kärnten, 127
Le Geste et la Parole (Leroi-Gourhan),
529, 813
Geto-Dacians, 1120–1121
Gets, 1120
Getty Conservation Institute, 586
Getty Museum, **585–586,** 617
Getty Museum Journal, 586
Gezer, 721
Ghaggar Valley, 587
Ghaggar-Hakra drainage system, 654,
659
Ghana, 25, 71, 72, 74, 1153–1154
Ghana, Empire of, 779
Ghana National Museum, 1154
Ghirshman, Roman, 553, 679
Ghosh, Amalananda, **587,** 657
Giant clam shells, 1256
Gibbs, George, 1170
Gibraltar skull, 495, 568
Gibson, Edmund, 113, 814
Gibson-Hill, C. A., 646
Giddy, Lisa, 461
Gi-deok, Hwang, 773
Gieysztor, Aleksander, 1044
Gifford, Edward W., 999, 1050

Gigedo, Conde Revilla, 1103
Gila Pueblo, 1075
Gila Pueblo Archaeological
Foundation, 281, 588
Gilf Kebir, 47
Gilii, Filippo Salvadore, 1103
Gilimanuk, 693
Gille, Bertrand, 531
Gilman, Antonio, 843
Gilmore, Kathleen K., 734
Gimbutas, Marija, 827
Gimbutiene, Marija, 827
Giner de los Rios, Francisco, 1195
Ginters, Voldemars, 795, 797, 803,
804, 805
Gioffredo, Pietro, 1100
Girsu, 873
Givens, Douglas, 638
Giza, 1093, 1094
Gjerstad, Einar, 390, **587**
Glad, 1123
Gladstone, W. E., 195
Gladstone Pottery Museum, 662
Gladwin, Harold Sterling, 281, 344,
346–347, **588**
Gladwin, Winifred, 344, 346–347
Gladwin classification system, 344, 345
Glaize, Maurice, 244
Glanum, 532(photo)
Glasbergen, W. J., 923, 927, 930
Glaser, Eduard, 89
Glaser, Franz, 129
Glassie, Henry, 627
Glauberg, 291
Glazema, W., 928
Glenbow Foundation, 253
Glina culture, 1119
Glob, P. V., 90, 420
Globocnik, A., 1164, 1169
"Globular Amphorae Culture," 783
Gloger, Zygmunt, 1040
Glossography (Lhwyd), 814
Glover, Ian, 636, 694
Glueck, Nelson, 716, 749, 750–751,
1245
Gmelin, I., 1128
Gnecco, Cristóbal, 366
Goats' Hole Cave, 977
Göbekli Tepe, 1278
Gobert, E. G., 841, 842
Göbl, Robert, 129
Godard, André, 553, 678–679, 1012
Godlowski, Kazimierz, 1045
Gods, Graves, and Scholars (Ceram), 631
Godwin, Sir Harry (A. J. H.), 61–62,
65, 66, **588–589,** 987
Godwin, M. E., 987

Gruhn, Ruth, 253
Grunhagen, W., 1199
Grupo de Investigaciones Submarinas, Inc., 508
Grupo Guamá, 504, 506, 509
Grupo para o Estudo do Paleolítico Português, 1068
Gruta da Furninha, 1067
Grygiel, Ryszard, 225
Gsell, Stephane, 547
Gu Jiegang, 317
Gua Sireh, 697
Guanahatabeys, 267, 270
Guanyin cave, 1012
Guaqueros, 437
Guarinello, Norberto Luiz, 188, 189
Guatemala, **604–609**
  French archaeology, 541
  Maya dialects and language groups, 605
  nineteenth century archaeology, 605–606
  Schele, Linda, 1150
  Spanish Conquest and colonial rule, 605
  summary of archaeological projects in, 608
  Tikal, 1270–1272
  twentieth century archaeology, 606–609
Guayabal culture, 272
Gudea, 1217(photo)
Guernsey, S. J., 1008
Guerrero, Blanco and Juan Vicente, 381
Guhl, Ernesto, 362
Guide to Artifacts of Colonial America (Hume), 643
Guide to Northern Archaeology (Thomsen), 204, 1270
Guildhall Museum, 643
Guillemin, P., 541
Guimarães, Carlos Magno, 187
Guinea, 25
Guittierrez Holmes, Calixtla, 887
Gumban cultures, 6, 8
Gumilev, Lev, 1139
Gummel, Hans, 579
Gundestrup Bowl, 415(photo)
Gunhild, Queen, 418
Gunnis, R., 469
Gunthe, Herman, 290
Gunung Piring, 694
Guo Baojun, 319
Guo Moruo, 321, **610**
Gurlitt, Wilhelm, 128
Gurob, 448
Gusinde, Martin, 305

Gustafson, Carl, 971
Gustav I (king of Sweden), 1224
Gustav II Adolf (king of Sweden), 1225
Gustavus Adolphus (king of Sweden), 236, 237
Gustavus VI Adolphus (king of Sweden), 477
Gustin, Mitja, 1169
Gutenwert, 1168
Guthe, Carl E., 82, 688, 1023, 1024, 1172
Gutierrez, Maritza, 381
Guyana, 260, 266, 274. *See also* British Guiana
Guzarishha-yi bastanshinasi (journal), 682
Guzman, Eulalia, 883
Gyarmati, János, 171

Haag, William G., 522
Haagen, J. K. van der, 928
Haaland, R., 1089
Haar, C. ter, 932
Haast, Julius von, 938
Ha'atuatua dunes, 1052
Habbuba Kabbira, 874
Habel, S., 462
Haberland, Wolfgang, 375, 376, 379, 464, 993
Hacinebi, 1279
Hackman, Alfred, 498, 499
Hadaczek, Karol, 1041
Haddon, Alfred C., 939, 1088
Hadhramaut, 89, 90, 284
Hadidi, Adnan, 754
Hadjisavvas, Sophocles, 392
Hadorph, Johan, 1225, 1228
Hadrian, 94, 1121
  temple at Ephesus, 470(photo)
  Villa at Tivoli, 723, 724(photo)
Hadrian's Wall, 197, 218, 219
Hadschra Maktouba (Frobenius and Obermaier), 44
Hafun, 1218
Hagfet et Dabba cave, 858
Haggett, Peter, 570
Haggland, L. F., 912
Haguenauer, C., 646
Haifa University, 720, 917
Hainzmann, Manfred, 129
Haithabu, 583
Haiti, 265, 513
Hajar Bin Humaid, 89
Hájek, Ladislav, 399
Hájek, Václav, 395
Hajj Creiem, 858
Hakra, 657

Hakuseki, Arai, 736
Halbherr, Federico, 731
Halévy, Joseph, 89
Halicarnassus, Mausoleum of, 195
Hall, Jonathan, 623, 1036, 1090
Hall, Martin, 51, 57
Hall, Richard, 591
Hall, Simon, 57–58
Hallan Çemi, 1278
Hällristningar fran Bohuslän (Baltzer), 1111
Hällristningslära (Brunius), 1111
Hallstatt culture/period, 288–290, 785, 1093
  Belgium, 146
  Gabrovec, Stane, 555
  Hildebrand, Hans, 622
  Magdalenska Gora, 839
  Novo Mesto, 953
  Romania, 1119–1120
  situla art, 1159–1160
  Stična, 1211–1212
Hallstatt (site), 130, 131, 132, 291, 578, 580
Hamada, Kosaku, 737
Hamadan, 678
Hamangia culture, 1118
Hamburgian culture, 486
Hamilton, Alexander, 556
Hamilton, Donald, 505, 508, 915
Hamilton, Gavin, 727
Hamilton, John P., 357
Hamilton, R. A. B., 89
Hamilton, Sir William, 142, 194, 196, 467, 473, 611(photo), **611–612,** 727
Hamilton (ship), 916
Hammen, Thomas van der, 363
Hammond, Norman, 755
Hammond, Philip, 751
Hammurabi, 139, 874
Hampl, Franz, 132
Hamy, Ernest, 24
Hamy, Theodore, 1079
Han Chinese, 317, 320, 324, 328
Han dynasty, 94
Han Fei, 1099
Han Fei Zi, 1099
Hanab'-Pakal, 973
Hancarville, Comte d,' 727
Hand-axes, stone, 819
Handbook of Latin American Studies (Rouse), 1125
Handbook of Middle American Indians, 463, 893
Handbook of Northern Arizona Pottery Wares (Colton and Hargrave), 347

Italy, *continued*
   Canadian Academic Centre, 258
   Claustra Alpium Iuliarum, 353–354
   French classical archaeology, 545,
     546, 547, 548
   Herculaneum, 617–618
   medieval archaeology, 869
   Mortillet, Gabriel de, 901
   nationalism, 731
   nautical archaeology, 914
   Valcamonica, 1313
   Vergil, Polydore, 1314
Ithaca, 429
Itinerarium Curiosum (Stukeley), 1215
Itineria (Vodnik), 1163
Itzá people, 299–300
Ivanova, V., 228
Iwajuku, 738
Iwawe archaeological project, 170
Iwo Eleru, 1154
Iximche, 605, 609
Izvestja Muzejskega društva za Kranjsko
   (bulletin), 908

J. C. Harrington Medal, 614, 643,
   733(photo), **733–734,** 764, 1178
J. Paul Getty Museum. *See* Getty
   Museum
Jabr, Manhal, 952
Jack, Ian, 114
Jackal-headed man, 46(photo)
Jackson, Andrew, 112
Jackson, William H., 1075
Jacob-Friesen, Karl-Hermann, 583
Jacobite rebellion, 288
Jacobsen, Thorkild, 3
Jacobsthal, Paul, 291
Jacques, V., 23–24
Jacquot, François Félix, 1108
Jae-won, Kim, 772
Jagiellonian University, 1039, 1041
Jagor, Feodor, 688, 1020
Jahangirnagar University, 1189
Jahn, Otto, 574
Jahrbuch fur Altertumskunde, 469
Jakarta, 650
Jakimowicz, Roman, 782, 1043
Jakobsons, Feliks, 795, 797, 804
Jamaica, 271, 501, 503, 511, 512
James I (king of England), 1310
James Matthews (ship), 118
Jamestown, 625(photo), **734**
   Cotter, John, 383–384, 626
   Harrington, Jean Carl, 613,
     624–625
Jamestown Fort, 643
Jamme, A., 89

Jankuhn, Herbert, 581–582, 867
Janse, Olov R. T., 243, 689, 1023
Janusek, John, 171–172
Japan, **734–741**
   amateur interest in archaeology,
     734, 746
   Angkor archaeology, 248
   archaeological heritage
     management, 96
   archaeology in Iran, 679
   archaeology in Korea, 770–771, 772
   archaeology in Philippines, 704,
     1027
   archaeology in Taiwan, 692
   archaeology sites, 735(map)
   early professional archaeology,
     737–738
   following World War II, 738–739
   Meiji Restoration period, 736–737
   national history and archaeology,
     734–735, 738, 741
   popular interest in archaeology, 734,
     741
   premodern interest in
     archaeological remains, 735–736
   radiocarbon dating, 739–740
   salvage archaeology, 740–741
   settlement archaeology, 740
Japhetic theory, 1132, 1141
Jar burials
   Island Southeast Asia, 687, 692
   Manunggul Cave figures,
     1257(photo)
   Philippines, 1023
   Tabon Caves, 1255–1256
Jarmo, 3, 180, **744,** 874
Jaron, Bronislaw, 163
Jarrige, J., 1189
Jäthenstein, M. Kalina von, 396
Jaussen, A. J., 89
Java, 649, 685, 687, 694, 695, 932
Java Man, 430, 648, 684
Jayne, Horace H. F., 1307
Jazdzewski, Konrad, 224, 1045
Jeans, Denis, 116
Jebel Aruda, 874
Jefferson, Thomas, 556, **744–745,**
   745(photo), 1291–1292
Jeffreys, David, 461
Jehu, King, 875
Jelks, Edward B., 383, 626, 627, 628,
   734
Jenkin, Ian, 638
Jenkins, Thomas, 473
Jenné, 26(photo), **745, 746**
Jenné-jeno, 32, 75, **745–746**
Jenness, Diamond, 253, 1174

Jenning, Humphrey, 662
Jenny, Wilhelm Albert R. von, 133
Jeok-hak, Kim, 772
Jeong-hui, Kim, 770
Jeppesen, K., 90
Jerash, 749
Jericho, 428, 751, 763, 932,
   1249(photo)
Jerôme, P., 227
Jersika, 800
Jerusalem, 719, 751
   American Schools of Oriental
     Research, 86
   foreign schools in, 1245
   Franken, H. J., 932
   Israeli archaeology, 1248
   Kenyon, Kathleen, 763
Jesuit missions, 626, 764
   Brazil, 187
   Canada, 250, 255–256, 764
   See also Mission archaeology
Jesup North Pacific Expedition, 252,
   1076
Jia Lanpo, 326
Jijón y Caamaño, Jacinto, 433, 435, 436
Jilotepeque Viejo, 609
Jiménez Moreno, Wigberto, 887
Jinheung, King, 770
Jinniushan, 325
Jirecek, C., 227
Johansen, Friis, 419
Johanson, D., 36, 37
John Aubrey and the Realm of Learning
   (Hunter), 632
John L. Cotter Award, 1178
Johnny Ward's Ranch, 521, 626,
   746–747, 747(photo)
Johns Hopkins University, 4
Johnson-Sea-Link I (submersible), 916
Jollois, Prosper, 549
Jomon pottery, 737, 738, 739(photo)
Jones, Andrew, 1090
Jones, Inigo, 725, 1162
Jones, Peter, 819
Jones, Rhys, 105
Jones, Siân, 1087, 1090
Jones, Thomas, 333
Jones, William, 1185
Jonsson, S., 37
Jonston, John, 1037
Jordan, **747–754**
   from 1967 to present, 752–754
   American Center of Oriental
     Research, 86
   archaeological sites, 748(map)
   Beidha, 142
   British mandate, 749–751

early phase of exploration, 747–749
foreign schools in, 1248
French classical archaeology, 548
Hashemite kingdom, 751–752
national school of archaeology, 1250–1251
See also Syro-Palestinian archaeology
Jordanian Antiquities Database and Information System, 753
Jorvik Viking Center, 1338
José de Caldas, Francisco, 356
Joshua Judges (Garstang), 569
Josselin de Jong, J. P. B. de, 932
Jouannin, A., 90
Journal de la Société Archéologique de Constantine, 23
Journal El Mexico Antiguo, 883
Journal of Archaeological Sciences, 104
Journal of Cuneiform Studies, 86
Journal of Danish Archaeology, 420
Journal of Egyptian Archaeology, 461
Journal of Field Archaeology, **754–755**
Journal of the Asiatic Society of Bengal, 386, 1073
Journal of the Polynesian Society, 939, 1048, 1056, 1057, 1058
Journal of the Royal Asiatic Society, 1092
Journal of the Society for American Archaeology, 281
Joussaume, R., 36, 37
Jovaisa, Eugenijus, 829
Joyce, R. A., 1062
Joyce, T. A., 150
Judd, Neil M., 620, 907, 1075
Juilius III (pope), 475
Julian Alps, 353
Julius II (pope), 724
Jully, A., 24
Jüngling of Magdalensberg, 127
Junker, Laura, 704, 1028
Junta para la Ampliación de Estudios e Investigaciones Científicas (Spain), 1197
Jura Surface Waters Regulation Scheme (Switzerland), 1239, 1242
Jury, Wilfrid, 253, 256
Jussieu, Adrien, 792
Jussieu, Antoine de, 870
Justeson, John, 970
Jutland, 415, 416, 419, 422, 483
Jydsk Arkaeologisk Selskab, 420

K2 site (South Africa), 67
Kada Hada, 19, 20
Kaduna Valley, 1154
Kafafi, Zeidan, 753
Kafu River, 18

Kafuan industry, 18
Kageran culture, 7
Kahun, 448
Kaipara Harbor pa, 946
Kaiser, Timothy, 755
Kaiser, Werner, 457
Kaiser Friedrich Museum, 1041, 1043
Kakadu National Park, 125
Kakimbon rock shelter, 24
Kalak'mul, 853, 1271
Kalambo Falls, 19, 335, 983
Kalanay Cave, 691
Kalanay Pottery Complex, 691–692, 702
Kalhu. *See* Nimrud
Kalibangan, 657
Kalis, A. J., 987
Kalmar harbor, 912
Kaltwasser, Jorge, 309
Kalumpang, 650, 687
Kamenecky, Igor, 1144
Kaminaljuyu, 462, 464, 607, 609, 765–766
Kamohio rock shelter, 1048
Kamose, 955
Kanaseki, Takeo, 689, 690
Kan-Bahlam II, 973, 974
Kandija (Novo Mesto), 953
Kandler, P., 1164
Kanesh, 1281
Kanheri, 1183
Kano, Tadao, 689, 690, 1023
Kansyore ware, 9
Kao China'ü-hsun, 319
Kaogu (journal), 321, 323
Kaogu xuebao (journal), 321, 323
Kapel, H., 90
Kapilavastu, 1189
Kapitän, Gerhard, 914
Kapthurin, 21
Kaptieljska nijva (Novo Mesto), 953
Karacharovo, 1131, 1311
Karageorghis, Vassos, 392, **757**, 1147
Karagündüz, 1283
Karain Cave, 1277
Karamzin, Nikolay, 1130
Karanovo, 229
Karari Industry, 19
Karataš, 1280
Karatepe, 1283
Karkarichinkat, 31
Karkur Talh, 47
Karl VIII (king of Sweden), 1224
Karl IX (king of Sweden), 1225
Karl XII (king of Sweden), 1228
Karl XIV Johan (king of Sweden), 1230

Karlin, Claudine, 1033
Karnak, 156(photo), 258, **757–759**
Karnitsch, Paul, 129
Kärntner Museumsschriften, 129
Karnups, Adolfs, 795–796, 798, 804
Karskens, Grace, 116–117
Kartoatmojo, Sukarto, 695
Katzev, Michael and Susan, 915
Kashmir, 386
Kashta, 956
Kaska, 1282
Kassites, 139
Kastelic, Jožef, **760,** 909, 1166, 1168, 1211
Katalogi in mongrafije / Dissertationes et monographiae (journal), 908
Kathmandu, 1189
Katsumi, Kuroita, 770
Kattwinkel, Wilhelm, 968
Kaua'i Island, 1049
Kaufman, Terrence, 970
Kaufmann, Angelika, 288
Kauri Point pa, 942, 943(photo)
Kaus, Karl, 134
Kausambi, 1153
Kavousi, 614
Kawharu, Hugh, 1058
Kawkaw, 71, 76. *See also* Gao
Kazanluk tomb, 231(photo)
Kazarow, G., 227
Kazerouni, Serajuddin, 682
Kazichene hoard, 230
Keen, Benjamin, 635
Keeping, Henry, 903
Keil, Josef, 128
Keiller, Alexander, 1031
Keith, Arthur, 407, 411, 1033
Keith, Donald H., 508, 917
Keleia, 284
Keller, Ferdinand, 423, **760–761,** 1237, 1238, 1240, 1275
Kelley, David, 888
Kelley, J. Charles, 1261
Kelley, Jane, 255
Kelly, Isabel, 884, 887
Kelso, William, 643
Die Kelten in Österreich (Dobesch), 132
Kemal-el-Din, Prince, 47
Kemp, Barry, 460
Kempers, Bernet, 932
Kendrick, Sir Thomas Downing, 615, 632, **761–762**
Kennedy, Clyde, 1080
Kenner, Friedrich von, 128
Kenner, Hedwig, 128
Kenniff Cave, 905
K'en-ting, 705–706

Korošec, Josip, 760, **774–775,** 830, 1166, 1167

Korosec, Paola, 775, 830, 1167

Korucutepe, 1282

Kos, Milko, 1166

Kos, P., 1169

Kosaku, Hamada, 770

Kose, Jane, 52

Kosipe, 1001

Koskinen, Yrjö, 496

Kosmas, 395

Kossack, Georg, 579

Kossinna, Gustaf, **775–776**
  "archae-geography," 816
  "archaeological cultures" concept, 583
  ethnic/nationalist archaeology, 300, 583, 816, 979, 1086–1087, 1321
  Kostrzewski, Józef, 777, 1041
  Neolithic chronology, 398
  origins of European cultures, 790
  Reinecke, Paul, 1093
  Spitsyn, Alexander, 1137
  University of Berlin, 579, 581

Kostenki, **777,** 781, 1131, 1207

Kostrzewski, Józef, 163, 616, 777(photo), **777–779,** 782, 1041, 1043, 1045

Kot Diji, 657, 1190

Kota Batu, 691, 698–699

Kotedalen, 484

Kotla Nihang Khan, 654

Koumbi Saleh, 25, 72, 73, 74, **779**

Kourin, **780**

Kovalevskaya, Vera, 1144

Kovrig, Ilona, 129

Kozlowski, Janusz Krzysztof, 273, 1045

Kozłowski, Leon, 780(photo), **780–781,** 1041, 1043

Kozlowski, Stefan Karol, 1045

Krainisch Ständisches Museum (Slovenia), 907

Králové, Hradec, 396

Kramer, Carol, 680

Kramer, Diether, 134

Kramer, Gerhardt, 1213

Kremsmünster Monastery, 127

Krencker, S., 35

Kriama, H. O., 12–13

Krijgsman, J. C., 650

Krinzinger, Fritz, 129

Kroeber, Alfred, 308, 346, 881, 919, 1015, 1214, 1261, 1297, 1298

Krolmus, Václav, 396

Krom, N. J., 649, 685, 932

Kromdraai, **781**

Kromer, Karl, 131, 132

Kronan (ship), 917

Krone, Ricardo, 182

Krukowski, Stefan, **781–782,** 784, 1041, 1043

Kruse, Friedrich, 794

Krzemionki Opatowskie, 781, **782–784,** 783(photo)

Krzemionki Opatowskie (Krukowski), 781

Krzywicki, Ludwik, 826, 1040

Kubitschek, Wilhelm, 128

Kuhn, Thomas, 634, 1296, 1302

Kuipers, E. A., 927–928

Kuk, 589, 1001

Kulikauskas, Pranas, 827

Kulikauskien, Regina, 827, 828

Kültepe, 1281

Kultura prapolska (Kostrzewski), 778

Kulturkreise, 590, 1050, 1091

Kulturkreislehre, 583, 590

Kulturschichten, 590

Kumara, 939

Kuml (journal), 420

Kumma, 460

Kunama, 40

Kunghälla, 866

Kunji Cave, 681

Kunstkammer Museum, 414, 1128, 1331

Kunthistorischen Museum Wien, 127

Kuo Mojo. *See* Guo Moruo

Kupang, 699

Kupe I, 939

Kupe II, 939

Kuper, R., 50

Kura-Araxes culture, 1280, 1282

Kurgens, 1281

Kurjack, Edward B., 700

Kurnatowska, Zofia, 1045

Kus, Suzanne, 29, 1219

Kush, Empire of, 956–957

Kusimba, C., 1219

Kutch, 657, 658

Kuwait, 91

Kuyunjik, 808

Kuzmin, Y. V., 988

Kvass Patriotism, 1130

Kwakiutl, 1110

Kwale, 67

Kwale Matola tradition, 1218

Kyoto University, 737

Kyrenia, 915

Kyrle, George, 131

La Alcudia del Elche, 1196(photo)

La Cotte de Saint Brelade cave, 859

La Isabela, 501, 503, 513

La Madeleine, 333, **785,** 792, 1112

La Majada caves, 1061

La Mouthe cave, 1112

La Mula-Sarigua, 995

La Navidad, 501, 513

La Pasiega, 965

La Plata Island, 435

La Riera, 484

La Roche-à-l'Oiseau, 1102

La Tène culture/period, 290–293
  Bibracte, 159–160
  Bulgaria, 231
  Carniola, Slovenia, 425
  Dezman, Karl, 1163
  Hildebrand, Hans, 622
  Keleia, 284
  Magdalenska Gora, 839
  reconstructed grave, 786(photo)
  Romania, 1120–1121

La Tène (site), 424, **785–787,** 1239

La Trinidad Valencera (ship), 916

La Vega del Sella, count of, 1197

La Venta, **788–789,** 882, 891, 907, 969, 970

La Yeguada, Lake, 995, 997

Laang Spean, 243

Laboratory of Tree-ring Research, 102, 430

Labrousse, H., 37

Lacandon Maya, 174–175

Lachish, 875

Ladd, John, 992

Ladenbauer-Orel, Hertha, 133

"Lady of Elche," 1196(photo)

Laetoli, **789**

Lagar Velho burial, 1068

Lagash, statue of Gudea, 1217(photo)

L'Age de la Pierre au Congo (Stainier), 23

Lagerbring, Sven, 1228, 1229–1230

Lagoa Santa, 181

Lagréd, Doudart de, 241

Laguna, Frederica de, 1174, 1308

Laguna de Bay, 701

Laibacheer Moor. *See* Ljubljansko Barje

Lajonquière, Lunet de, 242, 244, 1113

Lake dwellings
  artifacts, 1241(photo)
  Desor, Edouard, 423–424
  Keller, Ferdinand, 760–761
  Ljubljansko Barje, 830
  Swiss archaeology, 1238–1239, 1240–1241

Lake Lubāna Wetland, 795, 796, 797, 799, 800, 803, 804–805

Laligant, Sophie, 381

Lallo, 702

Lamanai, 152, 153

Lamboglia, Nino, 913

Leite de Vasconcelos, J., 1069
el-Lejjun, 753
Leland, John, 94–95, 863
Lelang tombs, 770
Lelewel, Joachim, 1038
Lembaga Purbakala dan Peninggalan
    Nasional (Indonesia), 651,
    693–694
Lemonnier, Pierre, 531
Lempa River, 463
Lenca, 463
Lengeyl culture, 224
Lenneis, Eva, 131
Leo X (Pope), 94
Leon, Magdalena, 381
Leon, T. B., 1106
Leonardo da Vinci, 724
Leonhardy, Frank C., 1159
Leon-Portilla, Miguel, 1103
Leopold II (king of Belgium), 23
Lepage, C., 36
Lepinski Vir, 485, **811**
Lepkowski, Józef, 1039
Lepontic script, 288
Lepsius, Karl Richard, 43, 443, **811,**
    918, 959
Lerici Foundation, 477
Leroi-Gourhan, André, 21, 33, 523,
    530, 531, 538–539, **812–813,**
    823, 988, 1033–1034, 1114,
    1199
Leroy, J., 36
Les Combarelles cave, 1112
Les Eyzies, 333, 568, 792, 807
Les Mournouards, 813
Lesser Antilles, 266, 269
Lettgallian hillfort, 794, 795
Lettgallians, 800, 803
Levadia, 429
Levallois-type cores, 20–21
Levano, Jorge, 376
Levant
    domestication of plants and animals,
        427–428
    See also Syro-Palestinian archaeology
*Levant and the Palestine Exploration
    Journal,* 721
Levant (series), 1247
Leventis Foundation, 757
Lévesque, Rene, 1080
Levine, Mary Ann, 1213
Levine, Philippa, 199, 636
Lévi-Strauss, Claude, 900
Levkas, 429
Lévy, Paul, 244
Lewis, Meriwether, 744
Lewis and Clark Expedition, 744, 745

Ley de Excavaciones y Antiguedades
    (Spain), 1196
Ley de Patrimonio Historico-Artistico
    (Spain), 1196, 1200
Lhote, Henri, 46, 47, 48
L'Hote, Nestor, 444, 849
Lhuillier, A. Ruz, 543
Lhwyd, Edward, 95, 203, 287, **814**
Li, Kyang-chou, 705, 706
Li Chi, 88, 298, 319, 320, 646, 647,
    692, **815**
Li vessels, 320
Liang Bua, 694
Liang Qichao, 317
Liang Siyong, 319, 321
Liangzhu culture, 327
Libby, Willard Frank, 103, 410, 437,
    451, **815–816,** 1051
Libya, 47, 48, 548, 614, 1108
Libyan Desert, 47
Libyca (journal), 843
Lichtenstein, Henry, 60
Lidar Höyük, 1282
Lielais Ludzas, Lake, 804
Liesegang, G., 1220
Lietuviu etnogeneze, 828
Lietuvos archeologija, 828
Lietuvos gyventoju prekybiniai rysiai, 828
Lietuvos TSR archeologijos atlasas, 828
Light spectrum, 1095–1096
Lighthall, William Douw, 1080
Ligorio, Pirro, 544
Ligurians, 285
Liliuokalani, Queen, 1057
Lima de Toledo, Benedito, 185
Limes, 128, 129, 581
Limpopo Valley, 67
Linares, Olga, 993, 995
Lindbergh, Charles A., 765
Lindenmeier, 383
Lindenschmidt, Ludwig, 580, 583,
    816, 1270
Lindow Man, 988
Lindros, John, 587
Linear A, **816**
Linear B, 601, **816–817,** 906, 1314
Linehan, W., 646
Lines, Jorge, 378
"Lingling-o" ear pendants, 1256
Linguistics
    historical, 789–791
        Marr, Nikolay, 1132, 1141, 1142
        notions of race and, 1086–1087
Linhart, Anton Tomaž, 1162
Link, Edwin and Marion, 505
Linnaeus, Carolus, 95, 339, 975,
    1228

Linné, Carl von. *See* Linnaeus, Carolus
Linné, Sigvald, 360, 881, 883,
    991–992
Linton, Ralph, 1049, 1051
Lion Hill, 6
Lippens, P., 89
Lippert, Andreas, 131
Lisch, Friedrich, 583, 1270
Lishan, 324
Lisimach, 1120
Lista, R., 106
Litherland (ship), 118
Lithic analysis, **817–824**
    dimensions of artifact variability,
        817–820
    foraging strategies and, 821–822
    functionalist approaches, 820–822
    idealist approaches, 822–824
    Leroi-Gourhan, André, 812–813,
        823
    Mortillet, Gabriel de, 902
    Peyrony, Denis, 1019
    Semenov, Sergei Aristarkhovich,
        1152
    style and, 820
    technological organization concept,
        820–821
    See also Stone tools/artifacts
Lithuania, 481, **824–829,** 825(map)
Litovoi, 1123
Little Woodbury, 157, 582
Littmann, E., 35
Liu, Pin-hsiung, 692
Liv hillforts, 795
Liverpool University, 569, 959
Livestock, domestication, 426–428
Living floor excavations, 983
Livlandische Reimschronik, 803
Livonian Order, 802
Livs, 803
Livy, 286
Ljubljana, 354, 760, 831, 1161, 1162,
    1163
    Emona, 468–469
    Lozar, Rajko, 832
    See also Slovenia
Ljubljansko Barje, 425, **830,** 908,
    1163, 1168
Ljubljansko Marsh. *See* Ljubljansko
    Barje
Llagostera, A., 313
Llanos, Héctor, 366
Lleras, Roberto, 366
Lloyd, Lucy, 66
Lloyd, Seton, 614, 631
Locational Analysis in Human Geography
    (Haggett), 570

Maiden Castle, 212(photo)
Maiden Castle (Wheeler), 1180
Maier, F.-G., 999
Mailu Island, 1005
Mainamati, 1189
Maine Maritime Museum, 915
Maine State Museum, 915
Mainland Southeast Asia, 683
Maisieres, 145(photo), 146
Maison des Sciences de l'Homme, 531
Maitre, J.-P., 31
Maiuri, Amadeo, 618, 1060
Maize
    Caribbean peoples, 273
    domestication, 428
    Panama, 994, 995
Majalleh-ye Bastanshinasi va Tarikh
    (journal), 682
Majapahit kingdom, 695
Majewski, Erazm, 780, 781,
    1040–1041
Majid, Zuraina, 696
Majolica, 504–505
Majumdar, N. G., 654, 655, 1188
Makah Indians, 971–972
Makaha Valley Historical Project, 603
Makalia burial site, 6
Makapansgat, 407, 983
Makouria kingdom, 957
Malal, 76
Malan, B. D., 62
Malay Culture Project, 702
Malaysia, East, 688, 690–691,
    695–698
Malcolm, John, 1092
Male, Valdimiro, 307
Maler, Teobert, 606, 1110
Mali, 25, 48, 76
    Jenné and Jenné-jeno, 745–746
    mosque in Jenné, 26(photo)
    Saharan adaptation studies, 30–31
Malian Institut des Sciences Humaines,
    32
Malinalco, 883
Malindi, 1220
Malinowski, Bronislaw, 1234
Malleret, Louis, 242, 243, 245–246
Mallery, Garrick, 1110
Mallon, Alexis, 750
Mallowan, Sir Max, **847–848,**
    848(photo), 951, 952
Malmer, Mats P., **848–849,** 1145, 1234
Malta, 283
Malta Convention, 417, 523, 525
Maluquer de Motes, Juan, 1199
Malwa, 1191
Mamluks, 958

Mammifères fossiles du Maroc
    (Arambourg), 844
Mammoth age, 978, 979
Mammoth tusk, 145(photo)
Man and Environment (journal), 1148
Man and His Past (Crawford), 213, 385
Man Makes Himself (Childe), 301, 876,
    1321
Manatt, J. Irving, 600
Mancheng (China), 324
Manchester University, 411, 500
Manching (Bavaria), 293
Manda, 657, 1219
Manetho, 455
Manhattan Project, 815
Manieles, 511
Manila, 691, 1020, 1024
Manioc, 273
Manitoba, 251
*The Manners and Customs of the Ancient
    Egyptians* (Wilkinson), 443
Man's Discovery of His Past (Heizer), 638
Man's Place in Nature (Huxley), 978
Mansel, A. M., 228
Mansuy, Henri, 242, 243, 244
Mantell, Walter, 938
Manuel, E. Arseno, 647
*Manuel d'archéologie préhistorique, celtique
    et gallo-romain* (Déchelette), 292,
    412
Manuel Larrea, Carlos, 433, 436
Manunggul, 1024, 1255–1256
    burial jar, 1257(photo)
Manus Islands, 1002–1003
Maoism, 324
Maori, 431, 934, 935, 1048
    chronological and demographic
        studies, 946–947
    culture-historical studies, 940–944
    early studies, 938
    economic and ecological
        archaeology, 945–946
    origin studies, 938–940
    Polynesian Society, 1057, 1058
    regional and thematic studies,
        944–945
    Waitangi Tribunal, 947
Maori Purposes Fund Board, 1057
Mapuche, 307, 308
Mapungubwe, 67
Marcelinus, Ammianus, 353
Marchal, Henri, 244
Marche, Alfred, 688, 1020
Marchesetti, Carlo, 902, 1160, 1164
Marconell, J. E., 1110
Marcos, Jorge C., 438
Marcus Aurelius, statue of, 723

Mardokhai-Abi-Sourour, Rabbi,
    1108–1109
Marek, Kurt, 631
Maret, Pierre de, 22, 29
Marguina, Ignacio, 882, 892–893
Mari, 1006
Maria, Hildeberto, 375
Mariano Rothea, Joseph, 1103–1104
Marib, 89
Mariette, Auguste, 444, 549–550, 831,
    849–850, 918, 1148
Marinatos, Spyridon, 594
Marinelli, O., 35
Marinero Siculo, Lucio, 1194
Marion, 586
Maritime archaeology
    Australia, 114, 116, 118
    Caribbean, 505–506, 507,
        508–509, 513–514
    South Africa, 56
    See also Nautical archaeology
Mark Taper Forum, 586
Marker fossils, 46
Marks, A. E., 37
Marliac, A., 29
Marobuduus, 395
Marois, Roger, 1081
Maroon settlements/societies, 187,
    511
Maros, 650
Marquesas Islands, 940, 1049, 1051,
    1052
Marquette, Jacques, 1101
Márquez, Carlos Cuervo, 359
Marquina, I., 888
Marr, Nikolay, 1091, 1132, 1135,
    1137, 1141, 1142
Marret, R. R., 567
Marron societies, 511
Marsden, Barry, 199
Marsden, Peter, 914, 915
Marsh, O. C., 1007
Marshak, Boris, 1144
Marshall, John H., 98, 654, 655,
    850–851, 1187, 1188
Marshall, L. and T. E., 66
Marshall, Yvonne, 944
Martha, Jules, 547
Martin, Colin, 914, 916
Martin, Felix, 250
Martin, Geoffrey T., 460
Martin, V., 31
Martinez, Anibal, 376
Martínez del Río, Pablo, 884, 887
Martinic, Mateo, 311
Martinique, 262
Martin's Hundred (Hume), 643

Medieval archaeology, **861–869**
  Bulgaria, 227–228, 232–233
  early and late traditions in, 861–863
  early descriptions and investigations,
    863
  nineteenth century, 863–866
  Novgorod, 952–953
  recent developments, 868–869
  twentieth century, 866–868
  York, 1337–1338
Medieval Archaeology (journal), 868
Medieval Europe Conference, 869
Medieval Settlement Group (Britain),
    868
Medieval Sweden (Hildebrand), 623
Medieval Village Research Group
    (Britain), 868
Medina, Alberto, 309
Medina, José T., 302–303
Medinet Habu, 446(photo), 850
Mediterranean Archaeology (journal), 123
Medway, Lord, 696
Meehan, Betty, 1156
Meer, 147
Meet the Ancestors (television show), 215
Megalith builders, 405
Megalithic burials/graves
    Netherlands, 926
    Obermaier Grad, Hugo, 966
    See also Cemeteries
Megalithic monuments/stelae
    Aksum, 40(photo)
    Carnac, France, 528(photo)
    Daniel, Glyn, 405
Megalopolis, 196
Megaw, A. H. S., 780
Megaw, Vincent, 116
Meggers, Betty J., 183, 184, 188, 266,
    308, 363, 437, 438, 1174
Mehrgarh, 657–658, 1189–1190
Meijer, D. J. W., 932
Meiji Restoration, 736–737
Meillacan Ostionoid people, 273
Meillacan peoples, 269
Meinander, C. F., 499
Mekong Delta, 245–246
Mekong Exploration Commission, 241
Melanesia, **999–1006**
    Lapita culture, 1003–1004
    origins of Polynesia, 1053
    post-Lapita, 1004–1006
    pre-Lapita, 1000–1003
    shell midden analysis, 1157
Melbourne, 117
Melbourne University, 125
Melgaard middens, 767, 1333
Melka Kontouré, 20, 36, 38

Mellaart, James, 1277
Mellen, Jacob, 1037
Mello, Ulysses Pernambucano de, 186
Meltzer, David, 636
Melville, H. L. Leydie, 649
Mema, 75
Memoir of a Map of Hindoostan
    (Rennell), 1185
*Memoir on Maps of Chinese Turkistan and
    Kansu* (Stein), 1209
Memoirs of Neograndaian Antiques
    (Uricoechea), 357
Memoirs of the American Academy in Rome,
    82
*Memoirs of the Society for American
    Archaeology,* 1174
Memorial de Soloa, 607
Memorial de Tecpan Atitlan, 605
Memorials of Edinburgh in the Olden Times
    (Wilson), 1324
Memory culture, 1300
Memphis (Egypt), 455, 461, 468, 1148
Men Out of Asia (Gladwin), 588
Mena, F., 313
Menchcourt-les-Abbeville, 177
Mendes, 918
Mendes Corrêa, A., 1068
Mendez, Modesto, 606
Mendizábal, Othón de, 886
Mendonça de Souza, Alfredo, 180
Menendez Pidal, Ramon, 1198
Menes, 455, 458(photo), 459
Menghin, Osmund, 131
Menghin, Oswald, 27, 108, 130, 305,
    306, 307–308, 309, 583
Der Mensch der Vorzeit (Obermaier), 966
Menthuhotep II, 919
Menumoruth, 1123
Mercati, Michele, 79, **869–870**
Mercouri, Melina, 601
Mercury Series (Canada), 254
Merhart, Gero von, 131, 555, 582
Merimda Beni-Salama, 456
Mérimée, Prosper, 97
Meroe, 956, 957, 959, 960, 963, 1094
Meroitic civilization, 569, 956
Merrick, Harry, 7
Mertens, Jozef, 146
Merwin, R. E., 150, 1008
Mesa Verde, 572, 1293(photo)
Mesco I, 616, 1044
Mesoamerica, **870–871**
    archaeological sites, 870(map)
    Catherwood, Frederick, 281–283
    Chaco Canyon, 296
    domestication of plants and animals,
        428

French archaeology, 540, 541, 543
Guatemala, 604–609
historical linguistics, 791
La Venta, 788–789
Maya civilization, 852–855
Olmec civilization, 969–970
Palenque, 973–974
satellite and radar imagery, 1098
Stephens, John Lloyd, 1210–1211
Stone, Doris, 1212–1213
Tenochtitlán, 1262–1263
Teotihuacán, 1263–1266
Toltecs, 1273–1274
See also Olmec civilization; Maya
    civilization; Mexico
Mesolithic, 478–486
    archaeology of, 480–481
    chronology of, 480
    Grahame Clark's synthesis of,
        479–480
    continuity with Upper Paleolithic,
        485–486
    defined, 478
    domestication of plants and animals,
        426
    Eastern Europe, 485
    ecological anthropology of,
        481–482
    European prehistory, 478–479
    Iberia, 483–484
    Le Mas d'Azil, 808–809
    microliths, 479, 480, 482, 485–486
    Norway, 484–485
    southern Scandinavia, 482–483
    Turkey, 1277
The Mesolithic Age in Britain (Clark),
    214, 334, 479
*The Mesolithic Settlement in Northern
    Europe* (Clark), 479
Mesopotamia, **871–878**
    Adams, Robert McCormick, 3–5
    archaeological sites, 872(photo)
    Babylonian civilization, 139–140
    Bell, Gertrude, 154–155
    Botta, Paul, 176
    Dutch archaeology, 932
    French archaeology, 550–551
    gold helmet, 878(photo)
    Hassuna, 614
    history of excavation in, 871–874
    Indus civilization and, 656
    intellectual history of archaeology
        in, 874–878
    Layard, Austen, 807–808
    Nimrud, 951
    Nineveh, 952
    Parrot, André, 1006

Mesopotamia, *continued*
  predynastic Egypt and, 459
  Rawlinson, Henry, 1092–1093
  Shanidar, 1152–1153
  Sumerians, 1217
  Woolley, Leonard, 1327
  See also Iraq
Mesopotamian Expeditionary Force,
  155
Messerschmidt, Daniel-Gotlieb, 1102,
  1128
Messiness, 164
Mestne njive (Novo Mesto), 953
Metadata, 370
Metal detectors, 221
Metallotheca Vaticana opus posthumum
  (Mercati), 870
Metalwork, Celtic, 287(photo), 291
Metaponto, 730
Method and Theory in American
  Archaeology (Willey and Phillips),
  1009–1010
Method and Theory in Historical
  Archaeology (Binford), 627
A Method for the Designation of Cultures
  and their Variations (Gladwin and
  Gladwin), 344
A Method for the Designation of
  Southwestern Pottery Types (Gladwin
  and Gladwin), 347
Metropolitan Museum of Art (New
  York), 295, 389, 947, 1285, 1286
Meuse caves, 144
Mexica, 137–138
Mexican Revolution, 881
Mexican Society of Anthropology, 885
Mexico, 535, 537, **878–893**
  Acosta, Jorge, 2–3
  archaeological heritage
    management, 96, 98
  Aztecs, 137–138
  beginnings of archaeology in,
    879–881
  Bernal Garcia, Ignacio, 157
  Bonampak', 174–175
  Chichén Itzá, 299–300
  Christy, Henry, 333
  contemporary archaeology in,
    888–893
  domestication of plants and animals,
    428
  expansion of archaeology in,
    881–885
  French archaeology, 538–540, 541,
    543
  Gamio, Manuel, 556–558
  La Venta, 788–789

Monte Albán, 897–899
  Olmec civilization, 969–970
  Palenque, 973–974
  period of consolidation in
    archaeology, 885–889
  rock art, 1101, 1103, 1110
  Schele, Linda, 1150
  social history of archaeology in,
    635–636
  Stephens, John Lloyd, 1210
  Tenochtitlán, 1262–1263
  Teotihuacán, 1263–1266
  Toltecs, 1273–1274
  Tylor, Edward, 1287
  See also Mesoamerica
Mexico: Panorama histórico y cultural, 893
Mexico City, 1263
Mexico South (Covarrubias), 886
Meydum, 1018
Meyers, Albert, 170
Mezek, 231
Meziéres, Bonnel de, 25, 779
Miaodigou, 321
Michael, Ronald, 1178
Michel, Marcos, 171
Michelangelo, 723, 724
Michelbertas, Mykolas, 829
Michels, J., 36
Michigan Technological University, 665
Microgravimetry, 451
Microliths, 479, 480, 482, 485–486
Microwave radiation, 1096
Midas City, 1282
Midas (king), 1283
Mid-Continental Journal of Archaeology,
  1175
Middle American Research Institute
  (MARI), 462, 1212, 1213
Middle East
  Australian archaeology, 123
  Dutch archaeology, 932
  French archaeology, 550–553
  social histories of archaeology,
    636–637
  See also Biblical archaeology; Israel;
    Jordan; Palestine; Syro-Palestinian
    archaeology
Middle Senegal Valley, 74, 75
Middle Stone Age, 20
Midwestern Taxonomic Model, 344,
  505, 1298
Migrations in Prehistory (Rouse), 1125
The Migrations of Early Culture (Smith),
  1170
Miguel de Barandiaran, Jose, 1197
Mijatev, K., 227
Mika, V., 227

Miklav-ki hrib, 284
Milani, Luigi, 475
Mildensee, Groller von, 128
Miletus, 574, 1282
Military Antiquities of the Romans in
  Northern Britain (Roy), 218
Mill, John Stuart, 1034
Mille, Adrien, 29, 838
Miller, Alexander, 1091, 1140
Miller, Gerhard, 1128, 1134
Miller, Mary, 1149
Millin, Auguste, 526
Millon, Rene, 888, 890
Mills, Anthony J., 962
Milne, John, 736, 737
Milojcic, Vladimir, 583
La Milpa, 152
Miltner, Franz, 129
Milwaukee Public Museum, 376
Mindanao, 702, 1026
Mindeleff, Victor, 1075
Minelli, Laura Laurencich, 379
Ming ceramics, 697
Minias, 1151
Ministère des Affaires Etrangères
  (France), 547
Minoan civilization
  Blegen, Carl, 164
  clay tablet, 817(photo)
  Knossos, 767–768
  Linear B, 816–817
  Schliemann, Heinrich, 1151
Minto, A., 477
Minusinsk, 496, 1259
Mira River, 483
Mirabilia Urbis Romae, 722
Miran, 1208–1209
Mircea cel Bătrân, 1124
Miscellanae eruditae antiquitatis (Spon),
  545
Misra, Rajendra, 647
Mission archaeology, 626
  Caribbean, 504
  Kidd, Kenneth, 764
  See also Jesuit missions
Mission Archéologique et Ethnologique
  Française, 541, 543
Mission de Phoénicie, 551
Mission d'Explorations des
  Monuments Khmers, 241
Mississippi
  Bay Springs Mill, 141
  Waverly Plantation, 1319
Mississippi River, rock art, 1101
Mitchel, Sir Arthur, 1182
Mitchell, C. C., 1107
Mitford, T. B., 999

Mithras, Temple of (London), 220
Mitochondrial DNA, 1054
Mitraand, R. L., 1186
Mitscha-Märheim, Herbert, 133
Mitterrand, François, 523–524
Mittheilungen des historischen Vereins für Krain (bulletin), 908
Mittheilungen des Museal-Vereins für Krain (bulletin), 908
Mixco Viejo, 609
Mixtecs, 883, 899
Mlodsza epoka kamienna (Kozłowski), 780
Mlu Prei, 244
Moa birds, 938, 942, 945, 1048, 1053
Moabone Point Cave, 938
Moai, 433
Moated Sites Research Group (Britain), 868
Moberg, Carl-Axel, 1234–1235
Moche, 642, **896–897,** 1015, 1018, 1159
   Huaca del Sol, 642(photo)
   pottery effigy, 897(photo)
Mochias, tomb of, 1017(photo)
Modderman, P. J. R., 927, 928, 930, 932
Models in Geography (Haggett and Chorley), 570
Modrijan, Walter, 131
Mohammed Ali, Pasha, 176
Mohenjo Daro, 140, 654, 655, 657, 658(photo), 1188
Mohenjodaro and the Indus Civilization (Marshall), 1188
Mohr Chavez, Karen, 170
Moita do Seastião, 483
Molasses Reef, 917
Moldavia, 1117, 1118, 1119, 1120, 1122, 1123, 1124. *See also* Romania
Mole, Vojeslav, 1165, 1166
Molina, Mario, 376
Moluccas Islands, 693
Molyneux, George Edward, 280
Mombasa, 1219, 1220
Mommsen, Theodor, 129, 219, 469, 581, 1162, 1240
Monagrillo culture, 992–993, 993, 995, 997
Monasteries
   Buddhist, 1189
   Kremsmünster, 127
   medieval archaeology, 865
Monasticon (Dugdale), 431, 432
Mongait, A. L., 1127
Mongolians, 1086(photo)

Monitor (ship), 916
Monleon, Julia, 311
Monneret de Villard, Ugo, 960, 961
Monod, Theodore, 25, 46
Monogenesis theory, 978
Monophysite church, 957
Montagu Cave, 64
Montandon, Roberto, 310
Montané, Julio, 308, 311, 313
Montané, Luis, 262
Montano, J., 688, 1020
Montarquía Indiana (Torquemada), 1101
Monte Albán, 2, 157, 883, **897–899,** 898(photo)
Monte Alto, carved head, 606(photo)
Monte Bego, 1110
Montelius, Gustaf Oscar, 211, 409, 527, 621, 622, **899**
   artifacts as cultural markers concept, 979
   diffusionism, 300
   Iron Age and Bronze Age chronologies, 341–342
   Müller, Sophus, 905
   Nilsson, Sven, 951
   seriation, 408
   Tallgren, Aarne, 1258
   typology, 345, 419, 1232
Monteoru culture, 1119
Montet, Pierre, 447
Montezuma. *See* Motecuhzoma
Montfaucon, Bernard de, 95, 526, 545, **899–900**
Montfort, Pierre de, 1100
Monti della Corte, A. A., 35
Monts des Ksour, 43
Montt, Luis, 303
Montu, 759
Montuoro, Paola Zancani, 731, 732(photo)
Monument du Nineve (Botta and Flandin), 176
Monumenta Britannica (Aubrey), 113, 287, 1215
Monumenten Ordonnantie (Indonesia), 649–650
Monumenti antichi inediti (Winckelmann), 573, 1326
Monuments Act (Netherlands), 922, 925
Monuments de Ninive, 550
Monuments in Egypt and Ethiopia (Lepsius), 811
Monzón, Arturo, 888
Moon temple (Hureidha), 284
Moora, Harri, 804
Moore, Andrew, 428

Moore, Clarence, B., 904
Moorehead, Warren K., 1076
Moormann, E., 928
Moosleitner, Fritz, 134
Moqaddam, Mohsen, 679
Moraczewski, Jedrzej, 1038
Morales, Ambrosio de, 1194
Moravia, 395, 397, 426
Moravian Museum in Brno, 402, 403
Moravský Archeologický klub, 403
Morawski, Wojciech, 1038
Mordini, A., 35
More, Jean, 843
Morea, 546
Morel, Léon, 291
Moreno, F. P., 106, 107
Moreno, Jiménez, 885
Moreno, María Cristina, 367
Morešti, 1122
Morga, Antonio de, 1020
Morgan, Lewis Henry, 340, 616, 641, 765, **900,** 951, 1138, 1296
Morges, 1274
Morhana Pahar, 1109
Mori, F., 48
Moriori culture, 939, 940
Morlan, Richard, 254–255
Morley, Sylvanus G., 150, 607, 620, 765, 880, 882, 885, 888, **900–901,** 1008, 1009, 1094, 1267
Morlot, Adolf, 250, 630, 1240, 1274
Mormon Church, 888
Morocco, 23, 1108–1109. *See also* Maghreb
Morris, Craig, 1017
Morris, William, 865, 1180
Morse, Edward Sylvester, 736, 737, 738
Mortelmans, G., 27
Mortensen, P., 90
Mortillet, Gabriel de, 23, 178, 211, 290, 342, 540, 671, **901–902**
   Acheulean industry, 1207
   Anuchin, Dmitry, 1139
   archaeology of Celts, 292
   Carthailac, Emile, 278
   Dawkins, William Boyd, 411
   Delgado, Joaquim, 1067
   French archaeology, 527
   hiatus theory, 479
   Marzabotto, 1239
   Stone Age classification, 340–341, 979
Mortimer Wheeler (Hawkes), 631
Morton, Samuel, 1292
Morton site (Illinois), 603

North of England Open Air Museum, 662

North Vietnam, 246

Northumbria, 1337

Norton, Charles Eliot, 99

Das Norund Östliche Theil von Europa und Asia (Strahlenberg), 1102

Norway, 964
  Heyerdahl, Thor, 1050, 1051
  medieval archaeology, 865, 866
  Mesolithic, 484–485
  nautical archaeology, 911, 912
  See also Scandinavia

Norweb, Albert H., 375

Noten, F. van, 29

Notice sur les Iles du gran océan (Urville), 1047

Notizie degli Scavi (journal), 725

Noua culture, 1119

Les Nouvelles de l'Archéologie (journal), 530, 531, 533

Novaliches, 158, 688–689, 1023

Novgorod, **952–953**
  medieval church, 953(photo)

Novo Mesto, **953–954**

Novorossiysk University, 768

Nowa Huta, 1045

Noyon sur Seine, 763(photo)

Nsongezi shelter, 7

Nubia, **954–963**
  Abu Simbel, 1
  Aswan dams and salvage archaeology, 959–963, 1093
  burial classifications, 350
  cultural history of, 954–958
  Emery, Walter Bryan, 468
  physical description, 954
  Reisner, George, 1093, 1094
  rock art, 1108
  settlement archaeology in, 448
  UNESCO salvage campaign, 449, 460, 468, 961–962
  Woolley, Leonard, 1326

Nubian Salvage Campaign, 449, 460, 468, 961–962

Nueva Cádiz, 271, 503

Numismata Anglo-Saxonica (Hildebrand), 621

Numismatic Chronicle (journal), 493

Numismatics
  Evans, John, 493
  Hildebrand, Bror, 621–622
  Slovenia, 1169
  Sweden, 1225
  Swedish archaeology, 1232
  Thomsen, Christian, 1268
  See also Coins/coinage

Numismatische Kommission der Österreichischen Akademie der Wissenschaften, 129

Nunamira, 124(photo)

Nunamiut people, 820, 821

Núñez, Lautaro, 311, 313

Núñez, Patricio, 311

Nuñez Chinchilla, Jesus, 669

Nusbaum, Jesse, 620

Nušfalău, 1122

Nutall, Zelia, 1076

Nydam bog, 911

Nyerup, Rasmus, **964,** 975

Oakhurst, 62

Oasis theory, 500, 1076

Oaxaca, 883, 897–899

Oberem, Udo, 438

Oberflacht, 864

Obermaier Grad, Hugo, 44, 671, 672, **965–966,** 1140, 1197

Obermeilen, 760–761, 1238

Obrecht, A., 304

Obregon, Alvaro, 557

O'Brien, T. P., 7

O'Bryan, Deric, 1075

Oc Eo, 246

Ocampo, C., 313

Occasional Papers of the Society of Antiquaries of London, 1180

Occasional Papers on Antiquities (Getty Museum), 586

Occupation mounds, Sudan, 75

Oceania, 125–126
  divisions of, 1047
  Golson, Jack, 589
  Graebner, Fritz, 590
  Green, Roger, 602–603
  shell midden analysis, 1157
  See also Melanesia; Polynesia

O'Connor, David, 448

O'Connor, Stanley, 696

Oduber, Daniel, 380

Odyssey (Homer), 586, 914

Offenberger, Hans, 131

Ogawa, H., 1027

Ogo, 75

OH 5. *See Zinjanthropus boisei*

Ohnefalsch-Richter, Max, 389, 1147

Oikonomos, Georgios, 594, 600

Ojibwa Indians, 900

Okiennik Cave, 781

Okinawa, 1029

Okladnikov, Aleksei Pavlovich, **966–968,** 1134

Okulicz, Jerzy, 1045

Olbia, 1311

Old Joseon, 773

Old Persian, 872

Old Routes of Western India (Stein), 1209

The Old Stone Age (Burkitt), 980

Oldawan culture, 809

Oldfield, E., 207–208

Oldishi tradition, 9

Oldowan Industrial Complex, 19, 20

Olduvai Gorge, 18–19, 20, 809, 810, 819, 968(photo), **968–969**
  skulls from, 969(photo)

Olduway. *See* Olduvai Gorge

Olesen, Olaf, 914

Oliver, Douglas, 602

Olmalenge tradition, 9

Olmec civilization, 871, **969–970**
  carved heads, 788(photo), 789(photo)
  in El Salvador, 465
  La Venta, 788–789
  Mexican archaeology, 882–883, 885–886, 888, 891
  writing system, 970

Olomouc, 402

Olorgesailie, 19, 20, 683, 809, 810, **970,** 983

Olschevien, 1071

Oltenia, 1117, 1118, 1119, 1120, 1121, 1123

Oltome tradition, 9

O-luan-pi, 705

Olympia, 85, 574, 599–600
  Curtius, Ernst, 387–388
  Dorpfeld, Wilhelm, 429
  French classical archaeology, 546

Oman, 91, 93, 658

Omar, A. L., 1219

Omar, Matussin, 699

el-Omari, 456

Omo Valley, 36, 37, 38, 93, 94

Omori shellmound, 736, 738

"On Cultural Influences on the Prehistoric Soils of Russia" (Anuchin), 1140

"On Some of the Bearings of Ethnology upon Archaeological Science" (Davis), 209

"On the Decorated Iron Lanceheads as Attribute of Ancient Germans" (Kossinna), 1137

"On the History of the Systematic Classification of Primeval Relics" (Rhind), 209

On the Imitation of the Painting and Sculpture of the Greeks (Winckelmann), 1325

On the Origin of the Species (Darwin), 832, 978

Propylaea, 596

Proskouriakoff, Tatiana, 607, 766, 857, 882, 888, **1074–1075**, 1268

Protic, A., 227

Protohistoric archaeology, 412, 615

Proto-Indo-European language, 790

Proton-induced X-ray emission and proton-induced gamma ray emission (PIXE-PIGME), 102

Prous, André, 180, 187

Proverbium libellus (Vergil), 1314

Provincial Museum of Carniola, 425

Proyecto Arqueológico El Cajón (Honduras), 670

Proyecto Arqueológico Sula (Honduras), 670

Proyecto Santa María, 995, 997

Prümers, Heiko, 171

Prunner, Johann Dominikus, 127

Prussia, 236

Pryahkihn, V. F., 1127

Prygl, August, 1161–1162

Przeglad Archeologiczny (journal), 777, 1043

Przezdziecki, Aleksander, 1039

Przyborowski, Józef, 1040

Przybyslawski, Wladyslaw, 1040

Przyjaciel Ludu (magazine), 1038

Pteria, 1284

Ptolemy Keraunos, 286

Ptuj, 1164–1165

Public archaeology, 98

Pucará de Tilcara, 108(photo)

Puccioni, N., 36

Pueblo Bonito, 907, **1075–1076**

Pueblo culture, 343. *See also* Anasazi

Puerta, Maruicio, 364

Puerto Hormiga, 361

Puerto Real, 501, 513

Puerto Rico, 260, 262, 265, 269, 270, 273, 274, 275, 503
    ball and dance courts, 263, 264(photo), 267

Puglisi, S. M., 35, 731

Puichard, P., 1201

Puig, Francisco Prat, 504

Pulltrouser Swamp, 152

"Pulvials," 18

Pumpelly, Raphael, 500, 765, **1076**

Punt, 37, 39

Pusat Penelitian Arkeologi Nasional (Indonesia), 651, 693–694

Pusat Penelitian Purbakala dan Peninggalan Nasional (Indonesia), 651

Pusilhà, 150

Putnam, Frederic Ward, 641, 765, 900, 1007, 1008, **1076–1077**, 1261

Pu'u Ali'i, 1052

Puuk, 299

Puzinas, Jonas, 826, 827

Pygmy hippopotamus, 78

Pylos, 164, 817

Pyongyang, 773, 774

Pyramid of the Moon (Teotihuacán), 1264

Pyramid of the Quetzalcoatl (Teotihuacán), 1264, 1265

Pyramid of the Sun (Teotihuacán), 3, 1264

Qaboos, Sultan, 91

Qalat al-Bahrain, 90

Qana, 90

Qaryat al-Fau, 92

Qasr Ibrim, 460, 963

Qau, 283

Qedem (journal), 719

Qianshanyang, 323

Qijia culture, 320

Qin dynasty, 324

Qin Shi Huang, tomb of, 1266–1267

Qinshihuangdi, 324

Quagliati, Q., 730–731

Quaternary geology, 950–951

Quatrefages, Jean Louis Armand de, 539, 902, 903, 904, **1079**

Quebec, 250, **1079–1083**, 1102

Queensland, 1106

Quelepa, 462, 464, 465

Querimba archipelago, 1220

Quetzalcoatl, 1101, 1264, 1265

Quetzalpopalotl, Palace of, 3

Quevedo, S. Lafone, 107, 308, 311

Quibell, James, 1018

Quiche Maya, 605, 609

Quick Time Virtual Reality (QTVR), 371

Quilombo, 187

Quilter, Jeffrey, 381

Quimbaya Treasure, 358, 359(photo)

Quimby, George I., 522, 626, 734

Quintanilla, Ifigenia, 381

Qujaling, 323

Qumran, 718, 751, 752

Qustul, 960

Quxi leixing, 327–328

Quyunjik, 176, 550, 847

Rabeder, Gernot, 131

Rabel Cave, 1026

Race, **1085–1090**

British prehistoric archaeology, 209–210

concepts of racial heritage, 1086–1087

culture-history and, 1087–1088

German prehistoric archaeology, 581

Indian archaeology, 1192–1193

nineteenth century concepts and classifications, 1085–1086

North American archaeology, 636

recent approaches and debates, 1088–1090

twentieth century politics, 1087

Race (Hannaford), 1085

"Races, Peoples and Cultures in Prehistoric Europe" (Childe), 1088

Racial classifications, 1085–1086

Rada Delgado, Juan de Dios de la, 1316

Radar, 1096

Radar imagery, 1097–1099

Radarsat systems, 1098

Radcliffe College, 1331

Radcliffe-Brown, A. R., 900

Raddatz, Klaus, 787, 1199

Radics, P., 1164

Radimilahy, Chantal, 838

Radin, Lars, 377

Radiocarbon dating, 103, 105, 409–410

British prehistoric archaeology, 214–215

Caribbean archaeology, 266–267

Chinese archaeology, 323

Clark, Grahame, 334

Ecuador, 437

Egyptian archaeology, 451

Griffin, James, 604

Japanese archaeology, 739–740

Libby, Willard, 815–816

medieval archaeology, 868

Netherlands, 922

Polynesia, 1051

shell middens, 1156

U.S. prehistoric archaeology, 1299

Radiography, analysis of Egyptian mummies, 450

Radnóti, Aladar, 129

Raedwald, 1217

Rafalski, Julian Witold, 163

Raffles, Stamford, 685

Raffray, A., 35

Rafn, C. A., 417

Rahr Civic Center and Public Museum, 831

Raimondi, Antonio, 1013, 1015

Raimondi Stone, 1015

Research Laboratory for Archaeology
and History of Art (Great
Britain), 101, 104
*Research Reports of the Society of
Antiquaries of London,* 1180
Research Unit for the Archaeology of
Cape Town, 57
Researches in the Early History of Mankind
(Tylor), 210, 1287
Reservoir Archaeological Salvage Act
(U.S.), 1299
Resistivity surveys, 451
Restrepo, Vicente, 358
Restrepo Tirado, Ernesto, 358
Retoka Island, 1005
Retzius, Anders Jahan, 1230
Retzius, Gustaf, 622
Reuvens, Caspar J. C., 921, 923,
925–926, 930, 933
Revett, Nicholas, 194, 546, 595, 1182
Revista Colombiana de Antropología
(journal), 362
Revista de Arqueología (journal), 184
Revista de Pré-História (journal), 184
*Revista do Museu de Arqueologia e
Etnologia* (journal), 184
Revista do Museu Paulista (journal), 184
*Revista Mexicana de Estudios
Antropologicos* (Acosta), 3
Revoil, G., 35
Revolutionary War (U.S.). *See*
American War of Independence
Revue Biblique (journal), 721
Revues d'Anthropologie (journal), 278
Rex Semigalliae Nameisis, 802, 803
Rey, Paul, 688, 1020
Reyes, Francisco, 309
Reygasse, Maurice, 840–841, 843, 844
Reyman, Jonathan, 638
Reyman, Tadeusz, 1041
Reyna Barrios, José Maria, 606
Reza Shah Pahlavi, 675, 678
Rhapta, 1218
Rhind, A. H., 208–209, 1182
Rhind Lectures, 1182
Rhinoceros age, 978, 979
Rhodesia, 591. *See also* Zimbabwe
Rhodes-Livingstone Memorial
Museum, 334
Ribeiro, Carlos, 1064, 1065
Ribeiro, Oliveira, 185
Ribes, Rene, 1080, 1081
Ricci, L., 36
Rice cultivation
Ban Chiang, 140
China, 326
origins, 428

Philippines, 1027
Taiwan, 705–706
Rich, Claudius, 871
Richborough, 219
Richmond, Ian, 219
Rick, John, 256
Ricketson, Oliver and Edith, 1062
Ridley, Ronald, 638
Rift Valley, 36, 37, 38, 809, 968
Riga, 802
Riga, Old Town, 797, 801, 805
Rigat, Dominique, 377
Rijeka, 354
Rijksdienst voor Oudheidkundig
Bodemonderzoek, 922, 927, 928
Rijksmuseum van Oudheden, 460,
921, 922, 923, 924, 925, 926,
927
Rimantien, Rimut, 828
Ringkloster, 483
Riordan, Timothy B., 141, 1159, 1319
Ritchie, Neville, 935
Ritchie, W. A., 1260
River basin surveys
Smithsonian Institution, 1171, 1299
Society for American Archaeology,
1175–1176
Rivera, Mario, 311, 313
Rivera Sundt, Oswaldo, 169, 170
Rivers, W. H. A., 900
Riverview Estates, 64
Rivet, A. L. F., 220
Rivet, Paul, 183, 361, 436, 646
Riviale, Pascal, 536
Rivière, Emile, 1110
Rix, Michael, 661, 665
Rizal, José P., 688, 1020, 1022
Rizal-Bulacan Archaeological Survey,
1023
Robbins, Larry, 7
Robbins, R. W., 1036
Robenhausian period, 341
Robert, Serge, 779
Roberts, Daniel G., 384
Roberts, F. H. H., Jr., 1260
Roberts, Henry, 991
Roberts, Mark, 178
Robertshaw, P., 8, 9
Robertson, Martin, 196
Robinson, Edward, 715–716, 749,
1244
Robinson, George Augustus, 1106
Robinson, J. T., 1224
Roca dels Moros, 1113
Roche, Jean, 843, 1068
Rock art, **1099–1116**
Altamira, 80–81

classifications, 350
earliest references, 1099–1100
eighteenth-century discoveries and
descriptions, 1102–1105
Lascaux, 793, 793(photo)
Leakey, Mary, 811
New World, 1100–1102,
1103–1104
nineteenth century descriptions and
discoveries, 1105–1112
Saharan, 43, 44–45, 46–47, 48–49
South African, 60, 66–67, 69
Tanum, 1260
twentieth-century discoveries and
interpretations, 1112–1116
Valcamonica, 1313
Vaufrey, Raymond, 842
Rockefeller, John D., 599, 624, 970,
1323
Rockefeller Foundation, 609
Rockefeller Museum (Israel), 718
Rodeffer, Stephanie H., 1178
Roder, Joseph, 687
Rodríguez, Camilo, 367
Roe, Derek, 199, 859
Rogawski, Karol, 1039
Roger, Ph., 37
Roghi, Gianni, 913
Rogozen, 231
Rojas, Myrna, 381
Rollefson, Gary, 753
Rolt, L. T. C., 662–663
Roma (film), 728
Roman archaeology
Austria, 128–129
Bulgaria, 227, 231–232
Celeia, 284–285
Celts, 286
Claustra Alpium Iuliarum, 353–354
Emona, 468–469
epigraphy, 1149
Forum of Rome, 725(photo), 727,
729, 730(photo)
German archaeology, 576
Glanum, 532(photo)
Herculaneum, 617–618
Klemenc, Josip, 767
nautical, 910, 911–912, 913
Paphos, 998–999
Pompeii, 1058–1060
Portugal, 1069
Romania, 1121–1122
Switzerland, 1240
See also Britain, Roman archaeology;
Rome
Roman Britain and the English Settlements
(Collingwood), 220

Santa Ana Sites, 1024
Santa Barbara Museum of Natural
    History, 588
Santa Cruz Islands, 603
Santa Gertrudis, Juan de, 354
Santa Isabel Ixtapan, 887
Santa Leticia, 465
Santa Lucia. *See* Most na Soči
Santa Maria La Antigua del Darién, 360
Santa María Project, 995, 997
Santa Rita, 150
Sântana-Cerneahov culture, 1121
Santiago, 303, 305
Santiago, R. A., 1026, 1029
Santiago Ahuizotla, 881
Santo Antonio de Tanna (ship), 916
Santo Domingo, 504, 513
Santubong, 691, 696
Sanxingdui, 327
Sanz de Sautuola, Marcelino, 80, 81,
    1112, 1197, 1316
"Sao" habitation mounds, 27
São Paulo, 181–182
São Paulo State Heritage, 185
São Paulo State University, 182, 183,
    184, 189
Sapir, Edward, 252
Sapir, Linares de, 31
Sapper, Karl, 375, 462, 606
Saqia, 956
Saqqara, 444, 460–461, 468, 831, 849,
    850, **1148**
    step pyramid, 1148(photo)
Sarakole pottery, 32
Sǎrata Monteoru, 1119, 1122
Sarauw, Georg, 415, 419
Sarawak, 688, 690–691, 695–697
Sarawak Museum, 696, 697
Sardis, 1284
Sarfaraz, Ali Akbar, 681
Sargon II, 176, 550, 871
Saria, Balduin, 767, 909, 1165
Sarian, Haiganuch, 188, 189
Sarmathians, 1121
Sarmento, Martins, 1069
Sarmisegetusa, 1121
Sarnate, 481, 802
Sarzec, Ernest de, 551, 873
SAS Research Notes (journal), 105
Šašel, Ana, 1149
Šašel, Jaroslav, 469, **1148–1149,** 1169
Saskatchewan, 253
Saskatoon Archaeological Society, 253
Satellite imagery, 1097–1099
Satterthwaite, Linton, 151, 1074
Saud Emir Feisal, 155
Saudi Arabia, 91–92, 93

Sauer, Carl, 997
Sauer, J., 90
Saulcy, Félicien de, 551, 716
Saurin, Edmond, 243, 244
Savages and Scientists (Hinsley), 636
Savanna Pastoral Neolithic, 8–9, 11
Save the Past for the Future project,
    1177
Savignac, R., 89
Saville, Marshall, 433, 435, 436, 1076
Sawankhalok pottery, 697
Sawicki, Ludwik, 1041
Scandinavia
    development of culture
        classifications, 340
    Malmer, Mats, 848–849
    medieval archaeology, 863–864,
        865, 866–867, 868
    Mesolithic, 482–483
    origins of scientific archaeology and,
        339
    rock art, 1100, 1102, 1111–1112
    shell middens, 767
    Thomsen, Christian, 1268–1269
    three-age system, 1268
    See also Denmark; Norway; Sweden
Scandurra, Enrico, 914
Schabel (Jesuit missionary), 1103
Schaedel, Richard, 308
Schaeffer, Claude, 469, 552
Schaeffer, Enrico, 185
Schávelzon, Daniel, 1062
Scheans, Daniel, 703
Schefferus, Johannes, 1225, 1228
Schele, Linda, 892, **1149–1150**
Scheurleer, Lunsingh, 922, 925
Schiappacasse, Virgilioi, 311
Schiffer, Michael, 441, 635, 1301
Schild, Romuald, 1045
Schinkel, Karl-Frederich, 97
Schliemann, Heinrich, 195, 387, 574,
    1150(photo), **1150–1152,**
    1151(photo), 1280
    archaeology in Greece, 594, 596,
        597, 599
    Dorpfeld, Wilhelm, 429
    Evans, Arthur, 491
    field archaeology, 583
    Knossos, 767
    Layard, Austen Henry, 808
    Mycenae, 597
    Society of Antiquaries of London,
        1180
    Virchow, Rudolf, 1317
Schlunk, Helmut, 1197, 1199
Schmerling, Philippe Charles, 144,
    977, **1152**

Schmid, Walter, 909, 1163–1164
Schmidt, Erich F., 679, 1012, 1308
Schmidt, Hubert, 1197
Schmidt, Matt, 946
Schmidt, Peter, 10, 375, 376
Schmidt, R., 780
Schmidt, Wilhelm, 33, 130, 583, 1091
Schnapp, Alain, 284
Schneider, H., 932
Schneider, R., 36
Schneider, Robert von, 128
Schober, Arnold, 128–129
Schoenwetter, J., 989
Schönleben, Janez Ludvik, 1162
School of American Archaeology, 100,
    619–620
School of American Research, 100,
    619–620
School of Oriental and African Studies
    (Britain), 284
Schoolcraft, Henry Rowe, 1110
Schörgendorfer, August, 129
Schottelius, Justus W., 361
Schránil, Josef, 399, 401
Schrimpff, Marianne Cardale, 365,
    366
Schrire, Carmel, 55
Schubart, H., 1069, 1199
Schuchhardt, Carl, 583, 790, 865, 866,
    926
Schuhmacher, K., 866
Schule, W., 1199
Schulten, Adolph, 1197
Schumacher, Johannes, 1104
Schvindt, Theodor, 498
Schwab, Friedrich, 785
Schwab, Hanni, 787
Schwartz, Douglas, 633
Schwed, P., 1111
Schweich Lectures, 679
Science Based Archaeology Committee
    (Britain), 215
Science in Archaeology (Higgs and
    Brothwell), 621
The Science of Civilization (Majewski),
    1040
Scientism, 1144
Scientific archaeology, origins,
    339–340
Scientific Archaeology (Hildebrand), 622
Scientific Committee of the Council of
    Europe, 673
Scientific Society of Chile, 304
Scoglio del Tonno, 730–731
Scordisci Celts, 1120
"Scorpion Macehead," 459
Scotland, 288, 814, 1324–1325

national school of archaeology,
1250–1251

Woolley, Leonard, 1327

See also Mesopotamia; Syro-
Palestinian archaeology

Syria (journal), 1251

Syro-Palestinian archaeology,
1244–1253

Beidha, 142

current status and future of,
1251–1253

height and decline of biblical
archaeology, 1246–1248

national schools, 1250–1251

nineteenth century, 1244–1245

twentieth century, 1245–1250

"System of nature" classifications, 339

Systems of Consanguinity and Affinity
(Morgan), 900

Szmit, Zygmunt, 784

Szombathy, Josef, 131, 902, 1160

Szubert, Jozef, 163

Szukiewicz, Wandalin, 825

Szumowski, George, 25

Taavitsainen, Jussi-Pekka, 499

Tabaczynski, Stanislaw, 1045

*A Table of Indian Languages in the United
States* (Gallatin), 556

*Tableau géographique de l'Ouest Africain
au Moyen Age* (Mauny), 25, 73

Tablet of the Cross, 974

Tabon Caves, 700, 1024, **1255–1258,**
1256(map)

Tabula Imperii Romani, 1149

Tache, Joseph-Charles, 250, 1080

Tacitus, 1229

Tadahiro, Aizawa, 738

Tadashi, Sekino, 770

Tadjikistan, 967

Tadmekka, 25

Taft Commission (U.S.), 1022

Tagalagal, 48

Taieb, M., 36

Taillez, Philippe, 913

Taimur, Sultan, 91

Taino Indians, 260, 265, 267, 275

chiefdoms, 271–272

cultural-historical archaeology,
269–270

religious studies, 274

three-pointed zemi, 269(photo)

Tairona, 359, 364, 365

Tairua, 602

Taiwan, 692, 705–707

Chang, Kwang-chi, 298

colonial archaeology, 689–690

Li Chi, 815

See also Island Southeast Asia

Taj Mahal, 1186

Takedda, 25

Takiroa rock shelter, 1106

Taklamakan Desert, 1208, 1209

Takrur, 74, 75–76

Takwa, 1219

Talamanco, Juan de, 260

Talaud Islands, 693

Talikod rock shelter, 702, 1026

Tallgren, Aarne Michaël, 497, 498,
1258–1259

Talman, John, 1178

Taloha (journal), 837

Talud-tablero, 898, 1265

Tamadjert paintings, 47

Tamanaco Indians, 1103

Tamar Hat, 94

Tamaulipas, 888

Tamtama Cave, 681

Tanaka, K., 1027

Tango Maare Jaabel, 75

Tanis, 460, 1018

Tanjon Batu, 699

Tanjong Kubor pottery complex, 699

Tano ruins, 346

Tansley, A. G., 588

Tanum, **1260**

vase painting from, 1234(photo)

Tanzania

Laetoli, 789

Olduvai Gorge, 968–969

rock art, 1114

Swahili civilization, 1219

See also East Africa

Tapadong Cave, 697

Taphonomy, 407

Taplin, Oliver, 586

Taracena, Blas, 1198

Taranaki Museum, 935

Taranaki wars, 935

Taranto, 730

Taranto Museum, 731

Tarasenka, Petras, 826

Tarco archaeological project, 170

Tardenoisian epoch, 341, 479, 480,
1117

Taro, 1002, 1003

Tarquinia, 473, 477, 728

Tarsatica, 354

Tartars, 1123

Tasmania, 1106

Tassili, 47, 48, 1108

Tate, George, 1111

Taung skull, 407

Taurisci tribe, 284, 469

Tautavicius, Adolfas, 828

Taxila, 851, 1187, 1188, 1319

Taxonomy, 338

cultural, 268–271

Midwestern Taxonomic Model, 344,
505, 1298

See also Classification

Tayacian phase, 341

Taylor, Clyde, 1057

Taylor, J. E., 1309

Taylor, Joan du Plat, **1260**

Taylor, Meadows, 1186

Taylor, Timothy, 88

Taylor, Walter W., 633, 885, 1010,
1139, **1260–1261,** 1300

Taylor, William E., Jr., 254

Tayma, 89

Tazumal, 463

Tchernia, André, 914

"Te Maori" (exhibition), 947

Tebessa assemblages, 840

Techniques et culture (journal), 531

Technological organization concept,
820–821

Technology studies, 531

Teeple, John Edward, 901

Tegdaoust, 25, 73, 74, 75

Teghaza, 25

Tehran, 678

Tehuacán Valley, 888, 889

Tei culture, 1119

Teilhard de Chardin, Pierre, 35, 36,
318, 1011

Tejeda, Antonio, 607

Tel Aviv Institute of Archaeology, 720

Tel Aviv (journal), 718, 1250

Tel Aviv University, 718

Telco Block Site (New York),
629(photo)

Teleilat el-Ghassul, 749–750

Television, British archaeological
programs, 212–213, 215, 406

Telizzharen, 1108

Tell, Safwan, 754

Tell Atchana, 1327

Tell Beit Mirsim, 78

Tell Brak, 848

Tell el Amarna. *See* El Amarna

Tell el Hesy, 445–446, 446, 1018, 1244

Tell el-Balatah, 751

Tell el-Dab'a, 450

Tell el-Farah, 751

Tell el-Fûl, 78

Tell el-Hesi, 716, 721

Tell el-Kheleifeh, 751

Tell el-Maskhuta, 460, 918

Tell en-Nasbeh, 78

Willems, W. J. A., 686, 927, 930, 932
Willendorf, 578
    Venus figurine, 578(photo)
Willey, Gordon Randolph, 375,
    633–634, 884, **1322–1323**
    aerial photography, 1097
    Belize Valley, 151, 888
    Chang, Kwang-chi, 298
    chronology of American
        archaeology, 1298
    Ecuadorian archaeology, 433,
        435–436
    Ford, James, 522
    Green, Roger, 602
    History of American Archaeology, 535,
        633–634
    *Method and Theory in American
        Archaeology,* 1009–1010
    New World chronology, 344–345
    Panama, 992, 993, 995
    Peru, 1016, 1017
    Steward, Julian, 1211
    Strong, William, 1214
    Virú Valley, 3, 680, 1317
William Foxwell Albright Institute,
    1248
William I (king of Belgium), 143
William Salthouse (ship), 118
William Stukeley (Piggott), 632–633,
    634
Williams, Stephen, 1212–1213
Williams, W. F., 676
Williamsburg, Colonial, 624, 643,
    1323–1324
Williamson, Andrews, 91
Williamson, J., 411
Willvonseder, Kurt, 131
Wilmsen, Edwin N., 83
Wilson, C. W., 716, 1244
Wilson, Daniel, 208, 210, 250, 251,
    1324–1325
Wilson, Sir Erasmus, 460
Wilson, Franzella, 376
Wilson, John, 631
Wilson, Thomas, 1219, 1220, 1295
Wilton Neolithic cultures, 7
Winchester, 615, 867, 1337
Winckelmann, Johann Joachim, 195,
    573, 595, 726, 727, 1137,
    1325–1326, 1326(photo)
Winckler, Hugo, 164
Windmill Hill, 135
Windward Islands, 266, 271
Wing, Elizabeth, 506, 510, 994
Winged bull, Assyrian, 873(photo)
Winkler, Hans A., 47
Winlock, Herbert, 1095

Winnett, F., 751
Winslow, Edward, 1036
Winstedt, Richard, 646
Winstone, H. V. F., 631
Wintemberg, William J., 252–253, 1080
Winter, I., 878
Winter, William John, 734
Winterbourne, 114, 115
"Winton Domesday," 1179
Wiseman, James R., 754
Wislanski, Tadeusz, 1045
Wissewalduc, 800
Wissmann, H. von, 89
Witsen, Nicolaas, 1100
Wittfogel, Karl, 888
Woldring, H., 987
Wolf, Eric, 888
Wolf, J. W., 865
Wolff, Reiner van der, 924
Wolfman, D., 32
Wolstenholme Town, 643
Wolter, Eduar, 825
Woman's Share in Primitive Culture
    (Mason), 852
Women
    French archaeology, 533
    Society for American Archaeology,
        1174
Women in Archaeology (Joyce), 1062
Wonderwerk, 64
Wonoboyo Hoard, 695
Won-yong, Kim, 772
Wood, Anthony, 113, 432
Wood, John, 470
Woodbury, Nathalie F. S., 1174
Woodbury, Richard B., 634, 1171
Woodward, Arthur Smith, 624, 626,
    734, 1032
Wookey Hole, 411
Woolley, Sir Leonard, 87, 223, 640,
    847, 874, 1188, 1308, 1309,
    1326–1327, 1327(photo)
Woolley of Ur (Winstone), 631
Wooly mammoth age, 978, 979
Works Progress Administration
    (WPA), 502, 1175
World Archaeological Congress, 215,
    589, 672, **1327–1329**
World Archaeology Bulletin, 1329
World Archaeology (journal), 215,
    522–523, 636, **1330**
World Heritage Sites
    Khirokitia-Vouni, 764
    Valcamonica, 1313
The World of the Past (Hawkes), 631
World Wide First, Inc., 1029
Worm, Ole, 95, 863, 1100,

    1330–1331, 1331(photo)
Wormington, Hannah Marie, 1174,
    1331–1332
Wormius, Olaus. *See* Worm, Ole
Worsaae, Jens Jacob, 206, **1332–1333**
    archaeological heritage management
        in Denmark, 97
    Aspelin, Johannes, 497
    contributions to prehistoric
        archaeology, 975
    Danish archaeology, 414, 415, 416,
        417–418, 419, 422
    Denmark's Olden Times, 205
    division of Stone Age, 1231
    Kitchenmidden Committee, 1208
    Melgaard middens, 767
    Müller, Sophus, 905
    nationalist archaeology, 1321
    rock art, 1111
    seriation, 408, 958, 1297
    shell midden analysis, 1155
    three-age system, 204, 340, 1270
Wortham, John, 444
Wostenholme Towne, 1324
Wotschitzky, Alfons, 128
WRAP Resource Manual, 564
Wright, Basil, 662
Wright, E. V., 912
Wright, G. Ernest, 78, 721, 751,
    1245, 1246, 1249
Wright, Henry, 29, 838
Wright, James V., 254, 1082
Wright, Thomas, 204, 218
The Writings of Caleb Atwater (Atwater),
    112
Wroxeter, 219, 615
Wu Jinding, 319
Wuding (Chinese king), 324
Wyckoff, Lydia, 376
Wydra, Feliks, 163
Wylie, Alison, 255
Wyman, Jeffries, 1007–1008, 1076

Xanantunich, 151(photo)
Xanthos, 195, 552
Xenophon, 286, 675
Xerxes I, 1012
    carvings from palace, 1013(photo)
Xia dynasty, 322
Xia Nai, 319, 320–321, 815, 1217,
    1335–1336
Xianrendong, 326
Xiaotun, 316, 317
Xia-Shang-Zhou Chronology Project,
    329
Xibun Valley, 152
Ximenez, Francisco, 605

SOUTH ORANGE PUBLIC LIBRARY

3 9507 00112288 5

WITHDRAWN